The WILEY *advantage*

Dear Valued Customer,

We realize you're a busy professional with deadlines to hit. Whether your goal is to learn a new technology or solve a critical problem, we want to be there to lend you a hand. Our primary objective is to provide you with the insight and knowledge you need to stay atop the highly competitive and ever-changing technology industry.

Wiley Publishing, Inc., offers books on a wide variety of technical categories, including security, data warehousing, software development tools, and networking — everything you need to reach your peak. Regardless of your level of expertise, the Wiley family of books has you covered.

- For Dummies – The *fun* and *easy* way to learn
- The Weekend Crash Course –The *fastest* way to learn a new tool or technology
- Visual – For those who prefer to learn a new topic *visually*
- The Bible – The *100% comprehensive* tutorial and reference
- The Wiley Professional list – *Practical* and *reliable* resources for IT professionals

The book you hold now, *C# Bible,* is your 100% comprehensive guide to building next-generation applications for the .NET Platform. If you are new to programming, or are a veteran developer, *C# Bible* is everything you need to build Windows or web-based applications with this exciting new language. Starting with C# language basics, our expert authors guide you through object-oriented concepts, building Windows Forms and Web Forms-based applications, ASP.NET and even Web Services. Not just a C# language tutorial, *C# Bible* is your source for practical application development with the .NET Framework.

Our commitment to you does not end at the last page of this book. We'd want to open a dialog with you to see what other solutions we can provide. Please be sure to visit us at www.wiley.com/compbooks to review our complete title list and explore the other resources we offer. If you have a comment, suggestion, or any other inquiry, please locate the "contact us" link at www.wiley.com.

Finally, we encourage you to review the following page for a list of Wiley titles on related topics. Thank you for your support and we look forward to hearing from you and serving your needs again in the future.

Sincerely,

Richard K Swadley

Richard K. Swadley
Vice President & Executive Group Publisher
Wiley Technology Publishing

Independent Thinkers

15 HOUR WEEKEND CRASH COURSE

Visual

Bible

DUMMIES

*more information
on related titles*

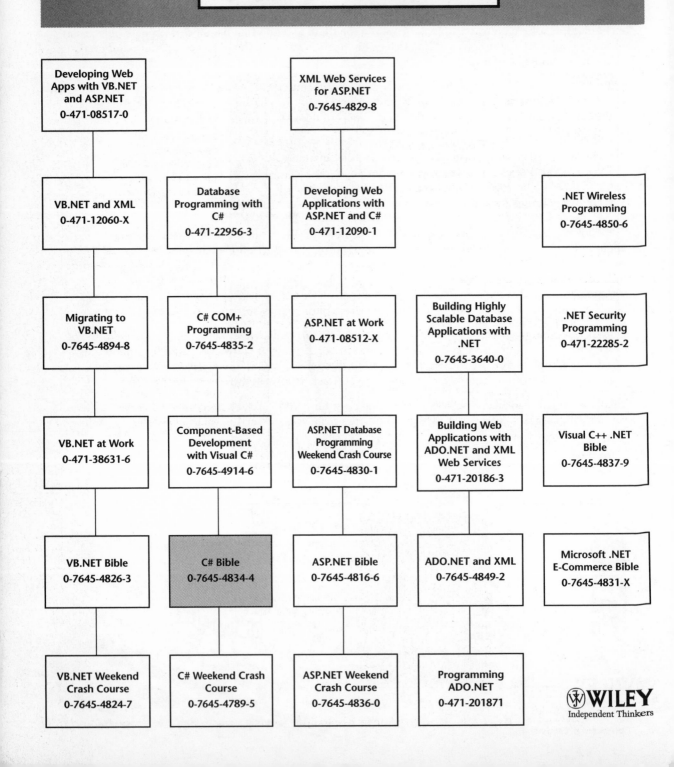

WILEY PUBLISHING .NET Books

Developing Web Apps with VB.NET and ASP.NET 0-471-08517-0		**XML Web Services for ASP.NET** 0-7645-4829-8	
VB.NET and XML 0-471-12060-X	**Database Programming with C#** 0-471-22956-3	**Developing Web Applications with ASP.NET and C#** 0-471-12090-1	**.NET Wireless Programming** 0-7645-4850-6
Migrating to VB.NET 0-7645-4894-8	**C# COM+ Programming** 0-7645-4835-2	**ASP.NET at Work** 0-471-08512-X	**Building Highly Scalable Database Applications with .NET** 0-7645-3640-0	**.NET Security Programming** 0-471-22285-2
VB.NET at Work 0-471-38631-6	**Component-Based Development with Visual C#** 0-7645-4914-6	**ASP.NET Database Programming Weekend Crash Course** 0-7645-4830-1	**Building Web Applications with ADO.NET and XML Web Services** 0-471-20186-3	**Visual C++ .NET Bible** 0-7645-4837-9
VB.NET Bible 0-7645-4826-3	**C# Bible** 0-7645-4834-4	**ASP.NET Bible** 0-7645-4816-6	**ADO.NET and XML** 0-7645-4849-2	**Microsoft .NET E-Commerce Bible** 0-7645-4831-X
VB.NET Weekend Crash Course 0-7645-4824-7	**C# Weekend Crash Course** 0-7645-4789-5	**ASP.NET Weekend Crash Course** 0-7645-4836-0	**Programming ADO.NET** 0-471-201871	

WILEY Independent Thinkers

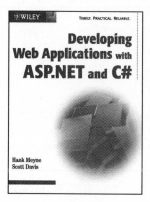

C# Bible

C# Bible

**Jeff Ferguson, Brian Patterson, Jason Beres,
Pierre Boutquin, and Meeta Gupta**

Wiley Publishing, Inc.

C# Bible

Published by
Wiley Publishing, Inc.
10475 Crosspoint Boulevard
Indianapolis, IN 46256
www.wiley.com

Copyright © 2002 by Wiley Publishing, Inc., Indianapolis, Indiana

Published simultaneously in Canada

Library of Congress Control Number: 2001092884

ISBN: 0-7645-4834-4

Manufactured in the United States of America

10 9 8 7 6 5 4 3 2 1

1B/ST/QX/QS/IN

About the Authors

Jeff Ferguson is a senior consultant with Magenic Technologies, a software consulting company dedicated to solving business problems exclusively using Microsoft tools and technologies. He has been a professional software developer since 1989 and has developed software using C, C++, and C# for Unix, DOS, and Windows systems. Send e-mail to Jeff at JeffF@magenic.com (remember to include all three "F"s in the name portion of the address).

Brian Patterson currently works for Affina, Inc., as a Technical Team Leader, where he is generally working with C++ on HP-UX or Windows development with any number of the Visual Studio languages. Brian has been writing for various Visual Basic publications since 1994 and has co-written several .NET-related books, including *Migrating to Visual Basic .NET* and *.NET Enterprise Development with VB.NET*. You can generally find him posting in the MSDN newsgroups or you can reach him by e-mail at BrianDPatterson@msn.com.

Jason Beres has been a software developer for 10 years. He is currently a consultant in south Florida and works exclusively with Microsoft technologies. Jason holds the MCT, MCSD, and MCDBA certifications from Microsoft. When he is not teaching, consulting, or writing, he is formatting his hard drive, installing the latest beta products from Microsoft, and keeping up with the latest episodes of "Star Trek."

Pierre Boutquin is a senior software architect in the treasury of a major Canadian bank, where he helps develop leading-edge market risk management software. He has more than a decade of experience implementing PC-based computer systems, with in-depth knowledge of distributed systems design, data warehousing, Visual Basic, Visual C++, and SQL. He has co-written many programming books and has contributed material on VB, COM+, XML, and SQL to other books. Koshka and Sasha, his two adorable Burmese cats, own most of Pierre's spare time. While petting them, he often thinks how nice it would be to find more time and get back into chess or keep up with news from Belgium, his native country. You can reach him at boutquin@hotmail.com.

Meeta Gupta has a master's degree in computer engineering. Networking is her first love. She is presently working at NIIT Ltd., where she designs, develops, and authors books on a varied range of subjects. She has co-written books on TCP/IP, A+ Certification, ASP.NET, and PHP. She also has an extensive experience in designing and developing ILTs. Besides writing, Meeta has conducted courses on C++, Sybase, Windows NT, Unix, and HTML for a diverse audience, from students to corporate clients.

NIIT is a global IT solutions company that creates customized multimedia training products and has more than 2,000 training centers worldwide. NIIT has more than 4,000 employees in 37 countries and has strategic partnerships with a number of major corporations, including Microsoft and AT&T.

About the Series Editor

Michael Lane Thomas is an active development community and computer industry analyst who presently spends a great deal of time spreading the gospel of Microsoft .NET in his current role as a .NET technology evangelist for Microsoft. In working with over a half-dozen publishing companies, Michael has written numerous technical articles and written or contributed to almost 20 books on numerous technical topics, including Visual Basic, Visual C++, and .NET technologies. He is a prolific supporter of the Microsoft certification programs, having earned his MCSD, MCSE+I, MCT, MCP+SB, and MCDBA.

In addition to technical writing, Michael can also be heard over the airwaves from time to time, including two weekly radio programs on Entercom (http://www.entercom.com/) stations, including most often in Kansas City on News Radio 980KMBZ (http://www.kmbz.com/). He can also occasionally be caught on the Internet doing an MSDN Webcast (http://www.microsoft.com/usa/webcasts/) discussing .NET, the next generation of Web application technologies.

Michael started his journey through the technical ranks back in college at the University of Kansas, where he earned his stripes and a couple of degrees. After a brief stint as a technical and business consultant to Tokyo-based Global Online Japan, he returned to the States to climb the corporate ladder. He has held assorted roles, including those of IT manager, field engineer, trainer, independent consultant, and even a brief stint as Interim CTO of a successful dot-com, although he believes his current role as .NET evangelist for Microsoft is the best of the lot. He can be reached via e-mail at mlthomas@microsoft.com.

Credits

Senior Acquisitions Editor
Sharon Cox

Project Editor
Eric Newman

Development Editor
Sydney Jones

Copy Editor
Luann Rouff

Technical Editor
Sundar Rajan

Editorial Manager
Mary Beth Wakefield

Vice President & Executive Group Publisher
Richard Swadley

Vice President and Publisher
Joseph B. Wikert

Project Coordinator
Ryan T. Steffen

Graphics and Production Specialists
Beth Brooks, Melanie DesJardins,
Joyce Haughey, Barry Offringa,
Laurie Petrone, Betty Schulte,
Jeremey Unger

Quality Control Technicians
Laura Albert, Susan Moritz

Proofreading and Indexing
TECHBOOKS Production Services

For my family and my friends.

Jeff Ferguson

This book is dedicated to my uncle, Brian Weston, who didn't seem to mind when I came to visit and spent all day with his TRS-80 Model II.

Brian Patterson

To Nitin, who was the driving force.

Meeta Gupta

Preface

Microsoft's .NET Framework represents the most significant change in software development methodology for a Microsoft operating system since the introduction of Windows. It is built using an architecture that allows software languages to work together, sharing resources and code, to provide developers with the advanced tools necessary to build the next generation of desktop and Internet-enabled applications. Microsoft's Visual Studio .NET product includes new versions of their Visual Basic and C++ compiler products that target .NET development, as well as a brand new language called C# (pronounced "C-sharp").

C# Bible will show you how to write code using this brand new language. Language constructs such as statements, variables, control loops, and classes are all covered. In addition, the book will show you how to apply C# to programming tasks that developers often face in the real world. The final portions of the book will show you how to use C# to develop Web sites, access databases, work with legacy COM and COM+ objects, develop Windows desktop applications, work with various .NET Framework concepts, and more.

The primary focus of this book is .NET development using C# as the implementation language and the .NET Framework's C# command-line compiler as the primary development tool. C# development using the Visual Studio .NET tool is not covered in this book, although the task of using Visual Studio .NET to develop C# applications can be easily mastered once the fundamentals of .NET development using C# are well understood.

Who Should Read This Book

This book was written with both the novice and experienced developer in mind. If you know nothing at all about the basics of software development, this book will get you started with the fundamentals, teaching you how variables, control loops, and classes work. The book will also speak to developers of any skill level, showing you the .NET tools available for C# development and providing you with tips to make your own C# applications work seamlessly within the .NET Framework development guidelines.

If you already have delved into the world of creating .NET applications, you will find this book a useful resource, because it covers almost every aspect of .NET development in depth. The first three parts of the book serve as an illustrative reference to using features of the C# language. By contrast, the final two portions of the book are dedicated to showcasing C# as an application development platform, illustrating the role of C# in desktop-, Web-, database-, and component-based applications.

This book assumes that you are seeing C# for the very first time and aims to provide an understanding of the language without requiring any previous language expertise. The book does assume, however, that you are familiar with the application environments used in conjunction with your C# applications. The final portions of this book cover the use of C# with desktop, Web, database and component applications, but does not explain those platforms in detail. Rather, the book assumes that you have a working knowledge of those application platforms.

How This Book Is Organized

This book is organized into five parts, plus an appendix.

Part I: C# Language Fundamentals

This first part of the book provides a brief overview of the C family of programming languages and moves to discuss basic syntax issues with C#. Variables, statements, flow control loops, and method calls are all discussed. First-time developers will also find a discussion of the usage of these syntax elements and will be able to understand how to build code using these constructs.

Part II: Object-Oriented Programming with C#

The chapters in Part II cover the notion of a class in C#. The class is the fundamental unit of code in a C# application, and understanding classes is key to the construction of a working C# application. Part II covers topics such as class design, base classes, derived classes, and operator overloading.

Part III: Advanced C#

The third part of the book focuses on specific language features employed by more advanced C# applications. Topics such as exception handling, interface implementation, namespaces, attributes, and unsafe code are all covered. The final chapter in Part III is devoted to presenting some tough programming problems and solutions implemented using C#.

Part IV: Developing .NET Solutions Using C#

Part IV shows how to use C# in applications that make use of various parts of the .NET Framework. This part of the book is a departure from the other sections, which are devoted to presenting the language features of C#. Part IV uses C# to build applications using a variety of .NET application platforms, from Windows forms to Web Forms to ASP.NET applications and database access. We will also take a look at working with some advanced .NET technologies using C#, including threading, assemblies, and reflection.

Part V: C# and the .NET Framework

The final part of the book describes how C# can be used to work with the .NET Framework itself. Framework concepts such as assemblies, reflection, threading, and COM/COM+ component interoperability are explained. Each chapter explains the appropriate Framework concept and also shows how to take advantage of the technology using C# as the implementation language.

Appendix

The final section of the book is devoted to an appendix, "XML Primer," which provides an overview of the eXtensible Markup Language (XML). It provides an overview of the history of XML and how developers can take advantage of XML to describe data in a standardized way. Many .NET projects make use of XML in one form or another, and several .NET configuration files are based on the XML infrastructure.

Companion Web site

This book provides a companion Web site from which you can download the code from various chapters. All the code listings reside in a single WinZip file that you can download by going to www.wiley.com/extras and selecting the *C# Bible* link. After you download the file, and if you have WinZip already on your system, you can open it and extract the contents by double-clicking. If you don't currently have WinZip, you can download an evaluation version from www.winzip.com.

How to Approach This Book

Readers who are completely new to software development (readers coming from a Webmaster background, perhaps) will get the most benefit from this book by first reading Parts I and II to get a good handle on how the mechanics of a software application work. It will be important for new developers to understand the basics of software development and how all of the pieces fit together to construct a complete C# application.

Readers approaching C# with a background in C++ will find C# very familiar. C# was built with C and C++ in mind, and the syntax resembles that of these older languages. These readers might wish to skim through Parts I and II to get a feel for the variance in syntax, and then might want to dive right in to Part III to understand the advanced features of the language. Many of the topics in Part III delve into concepts that distinguish C# from its predecessors.

Developers already familiar with C# will also find useful material. Parts IV and V showcase the use of C# in a variety of .NET platform applications and present several examples that illustrate C# code that can be used to perform a variety of tasks. These final two parts move the book from a theoretical language level to a practical level and are ideal for developers of any level wishing to understand how C# can be used to implement a variety of applications.

Conventions Used in This Book

Each chapter in this book begins with a heads-up of the topics covered in the chapter and ends with a summary of what you should have learned by reading the chapter.

Throughout this book, you will find icons in the margins that highlight special or important information. Keep an eye out for the following icons:

 A Caution icon indicates a procedure that could potentially cause difficulty or even data loss; pay careful attention to Caution icons to avoid common and not-so-common programming pitfalls.

 Cross-Reference icons point to additional information about a topic, which you can find in other sections of the book.

 A Note icon highlights interesting or supplementary information and often contains extra bits of technical information about a subject.

 Tip icons draw attention to handy suggestions, helpful hints, and useful pieces of advice.

In addition to the icons listed previously, the following typographical conventions are used throughout the book:

- ✦ Code examples appear in a `fixed width font`.
- ✦ Other code elements, such as data structures and variable names, appear in `fixed width`.
- ✦ File names and World Wide Web addresses (URLs) also appear in `fixed width`.

✦ The first occurrence of an important term in a chapter is highlighted with *italic* text. *Italic* is also used for placeholders — for example, ICON *<icon file name>*, where *<icon file name>* represents the name of a bitmap file.

✦ Menu commands are indicated in hierarchical order, with each menu command separated by an arrow. For example, File ➪ Open means to click the File command on the menu bar, and then select Open.

✦ Keyboard shortcuts are indicated with the following syntax: Ctrl+C.

What Is a Sidebar?

Topics in sidebars provide additional information. Sidebar text contains discussion that is related to the main text of a chapter, but not vital to understanding the main text.

Acknowledgments

Jeff Ferguson: Few books of this size and scope are ever the work of a single individual, and this one is no exception. I owe a debt of gratitude to many people for their help and encouragement in writing this book.

First, I must thank my parents for the upbringing that I received. Without their parental guidance, I would not have turned out to be the person I am today and would not have been able to complete tasks of any size. I am always grateful not only to you but also to the entire family for the love and support I always receive.

I would like to thank everyone at Wiley for their leadership in the production of this material. Thank you, Andrea Boucher, Sharon Cox, Eric Newman, and Chris Webb, for leading me through the daunting world of technical book publishing. Thanks also go to Rolf Crozier, who initially discussed this project with me in the early days. I owe a special thank you to my colleague Bob Knutson, who reviewed drafts of the material in this book.

Thanks go to Greg Frankenfield and Paul Fridman for creating a top-notch Microsoft-based consulting organization that allows me to work on client projects as well as my own. The technical growth I have experienced throughout my time at Magenic has been immeasurable. Here's to Magenic's continued success.

Thanks to everyone on the DOTNET mailing lists and newsgroups on the Internet. I am learning a tremendous amount about the .NET Framework and C# simply by reading your posts. The banter sent back and forth has given me a better understanding of how all of these new pieces fit together.

Brian Patterson: I'd like to thank my wife, Aimee, for allowing me the many hours hidden away in the computer so I could complete my work on this book. A special thanks to Steve Cisco for the hard work he put into this book, which led the way for the rest of us; to Sharon Cox, the acquisitions editor, who constantly kept me on track; to the project editor, Eric Newman, for keeping all my ducks in a row; and to the series editor, Michael Lane Thomas, who reviewed each and every chapter, making some very good suggestions and providing some valuable insight into Microsoft and the .NET framework.

Pierre Boutquin: Much hard work goes into the creation of a book, and not just from the people mentioned on the cover. I must especially thank the Wiley team for their tremendous dedication to produce a quality book. The reviewers deserve a lot of credit for making me look like an accomplished writer.

Finally, this effort would not have been possible without the support from my family and friends: Sandra, Andrea, Jennifer and Paul, Tindy and Doel, Marcel and Diana Ban, Margaret Fekete, and John and Nadine Marshall.

Meeta Gupta: I thank Anita for giving me the opportunity. However, my biggest thanks go to Nitin for, well, everything.

Contents at a Glance

Contents

PART II: Object-Oriented Programming with C#   145

C# Language Fundamentals

An Introduction to C#

✦   ✦   ✦   ✦

In This Chapter

Introducing the .NET
Framework

Understanding the
basics of Web
development with
.NET

Understanding the
basics of application
programming with
.NET

Tracing the evolution
of C, C++, and C#

Introducing the C#
language

✦   ✦   ✦   ✦

For the past 20 years, C and C++ have been the languages of choice for commercial and critical business applications. These languages provided a severe degree of control to the developer by letting them use pointers and many low-level system functions. However, when you compare languages. such as Microsoft Visual Basic to C/C++, you come to realize that while C and C++ are much more powerful languages, it takes a great deal longer to develop applications. Many C/C++ programmers have dreaded the notion of switching to languages such as Visual Basic because they would lose much of the low level control they are used to.

What the developer community needed was a language that fell somewhere in between these two. A language that would help with rapid application development but would also allow for a great deal of control and a language that would integrate well with Web-application development, XML, and many of the emerging technologies.

Easing the transition for existing C/C++ programmers, while also providing an easy-to-learn language for inexperienced programmers are only two of the benefits to the new language on the block, C#. Microsoft introduced C# to the public at the Professional Developer's Conference in Orlando, Florida, in the summer of 2000. C# combines the best ideas from languages such as C, C++, and Java with the productivity enhancements found in the Microsoft .NET Framework and provides a very productive coding experience for both new and seasoned developers.

This chapter dives into the four components that make up the .NET platform as well as explores the support for emerging Web technologies. It then briefly discusses many of the features found in the C# language and how it compares to other popular languages.

The .NET Framework

Microsoft designed C# from the ground up to take advantage of its new .NET Framework. Because C# is a player in this new .NET world, you should have a good understanding of what the .NET Framework provides and how it increases your productivity.

The .NET Framework is made up of four parts, as shown in Figure 1-1: the Common Language Runtime, a set of class libraries, a set of programming languages, and the ASP.NET environment. The .NET Framework was designed with three goals in mind. First, it was intended to make Windows applications much more reliable, while also providing an application with a greater degree of security. Second, it was intended to simplify the development of Web applications and services that not only work in the traditional sense, but on mobile devices as well. Lastly, the framework was designed to provide a single set of libraries that would work with multiple languages. The following sections examine each of the .NET Framework components.

| Common Language Runtime |
| Class Libraries |
| Programming Languages
(C#, VC++, BV.NET, JScript.NET) |
| ASP.NET |

Figure 1-1: The four components of the .NET Framework

Web development

The .NET Framework was designed with one thing in mind: to fuel Internet development. This new fuel to add to Internet development is called *Web Services*. You can think of Web Services as a Web site that interacts with programs, rather than people. Instead of delivering Web pages, a Web Service takes a request formatted as XML, performs a particular function, and then returns a response to the requester as an XML message.

 Note   XML or eXtensible Markup Language is a self describing language much like that of HTML. XML on the other hand has no predefined tags thus allowing it great flexibility in representing a wide variety of objects.

A typical application for a Web Service would be to sit as a layer on top of a corporate billing system. When a user surfing the Web purchases products from your Internet site, the purchase information is then sent to the Web Services, which totals all the products, adds a record to the accounts receivable database, and then returns a response with an order confirmation number. Not only can this Web Service interact with Web pages, it can interact with other Web Services, such as a corporate accounts payable system.

In order for the Web Service model to survive the natural evolution of programming languages, it must include much more than a simple interface to the Web. The Web service model also includes protocols that enable applications to find Web Services available across a LAN or the Internet. This protocol also enables the application to explore the Web Service and determine how to communicate with it, as well as how to exchange information. To enable Web Service discovery, the Universal Discovery, Description and Integration (UDDI) was established. This allows Web Services to be registered and searched, based on key information such as company name, type of service, and geographic location.

Application development

Aside from Web development, you can still build traditional Windows applications with the .NET Framework. Windows applications created with the .NET Framework are based upon *Windows Forms*. These Windows Forms are somewhat of a cross-breed between Visual Basic 6 forms and the forms of Visual C++. Though forms look the same as their predecessors, they are completely object-oriented and class-based, much like form objects in the Microsoft Foundation Class.

These new Windows Forms now support many classic controls found in Visual Studio, such as the `Button`, `TextBox`, and `Label`, as well as ActiveX controls. Aside from the traditional controls, new components such as `PrintPreview`, `LinkLabel`, `ColorDialog`, and `OpenFileDialog` are also supported.

Building applications with .NET also provides you with many enhancements not found in other languages, such as security. These security measures can determine whether an application can write or read a disk file. They also enable you to embed digital signatures into the application to ensure that the application was written by a trusted source. The .NET Framework also enables you to embed component information, and version information, within the actual code. This makes it possible for software to install on demand, automatically, or with no user intervention at all. Together, all of these features greatly reduce support costs within the enterprise.

Common Language Runtime

Programming languages usually consist of both a compiler and a runtime environment. The compiler turns the code that you write into executable code that can be run by users. The runtime environment provides a set of operating system services to your executable code. These services are built into a runtime layer so that your code does not need to worry about the low-level details of working with the operating system. Operations such as memory management and file I/O are good examples of services that might be provided by a runtime environment.

Before .NET came along, each language shipped with its own runtime environment. Visual Basic shipped with a runtime called MSVBVM60.DLL. Visual C++ shipped with a DLL called MSVCRT.DLL. Each of these runtime modules provided a set of low-level services to code that developers wrote. Developers would write code and then build that code with the appropriate runtime in mind. The executable code would ship with the runtime, which would be installed on a user's machine if it weren't already present.

The main problem with these runtime environments is that they were designed for use with a single language. The Visual Basic runtime provided nice features for operations like working with memory and launching COM objects, but these features were only available to Visual Basic users. Developers using Visual C++ could not use the features of the Visual Basic runtime. Visual C++ users had their own runtime, with its own long list of features, but those features were unavailable to Visual Basic users. This "separate runtime" approach prevented languages from working together seamlessly. It's not possible, for example, to grab some memory in a piece of Visual Basic code and then hand it off to a piece of Visual C++ code, which frees the memory. The different runtimes implement their own feature set in their own way. The feature sets of the various runtimes are inconsistent. Even features that are found in more than one runtime are implemented in different ways, making it impossible for two pieces of code written in different languages to work together.

One of the design goals of the .NET Framework was to unify the runtime engines so that all developers could work with a single set of runtime services. The .NET Framework's solution is called the *Common Language Runtime (CLR)*. The CLR provides capabilities such as memory management, security, and robust error-handling to any language that works with the .NET Framework. Thanks to the CLR, all .NET languages can use a variety of runtime services without developers worrying about whether their particular language supports a runtime feature.

The CLR also enables languages to interoperate with one another. Memory can be allocated by code written in one language — Visual Basic .NET, for instance — and can be freed by code written in another language, say, C#. Similarly, errors can be raised in one language and processed in another language.

.NET class libraries

Developers like to work with code that has already been tested and shown to work, such as the Win32 API and the MFC Class libraries. Code re-use has long been the goal of the software development community. However, the practicality of code re-use has not lived up to expectations.

Many languages have had access to bodies of pre-tested, ready-to-run code. Visual C++ has benefited from class libraries such as the Microsoft Foundation Classes (MFC), which enabled C++ developers to build Windows applications quickly, and the Active Template Library (ATL), which provided support for building COM objects. However, the language-specific nature of these libraries has made them unavailable for use in other languages. Visual Basic developers are locked out of using ATL when building their COM objects.

The .NET Framework provides many classes that help developers re-use code. The .NET class libraries contain code for programming topics such as threading, file I/O, database support, XML parsing, and data structures, such as stacks and queues. Best of all, this entire class library is available to any programming language that supports the .NET Framework. Thanks to the CLR, any .NET language can use any class in the .NET class library. Because all languages now support the same runtime, they can re-use any class that works with the .NET Framework. This means that any functionality available to one language will also be available to any other .NET language.

The class library re-use picture painted by the .NET Framework gets even better when you realize that re-use extends to your code, not just code that Microsoft ships with .NET. The code that Microsoft ships in the .NET class library code base is architecturally no different from the code you write. The Microsoft code is simply code that was written using a language supported by .NET and built using a .NET development tool. This means that Microsoft is using the same tools that you will use to write your code. You can write code that can be used in other .NET languages, just as Microsoft has with its class library. The .NET Framework enables you to write code in C#, for example, and hand it off to Visual Basic .NET developers, who can use your compiled code in their applications. Figure 1-2 contains a high level overview of the .NET Class Libraries.

.NET programming languages

The .NET Framework provides a set of tools that help you build code that works with the .NET Framework. Microsoft provides a set of languages that are already ".NET-compatible". C# is one of those languages. New versions of Visual Basic and Visual C++ have also been created to take advantage of the .NET Framework, with a version of Jscript.NET on the way.

The development of .NET-compatible languages is not restricted to Microsoft. The .NET group at Microsoft has published documentation showing how language vendors can make their languages work with .NET, and vendors are making languages such as COBOL and Perl compatible with the .NET Framework. There are currently 20 or more languages in the works from third party vendors and institutions that plug into the .NET Framework.

ASP.NET environment

The Internet was originally intended to deliver static content to Web browsers. These Web pages never changed and were the same for every user that surfed to their location. Active Server Pages were released by Microsoft to enable the creation of dynamic pages based on user input and interaction with a Web site. This was accomplished by scripting behind the Web page, typically in VB Script. When users visited a Web site, they could be prompted for verifying information (either manually or from a cookie), and then the scripting would generate a resulting Web page to return to the user.

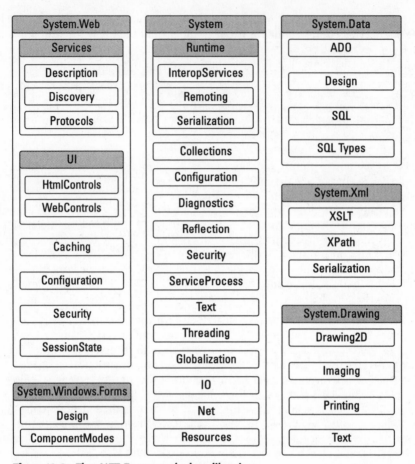

Figure 1-2: The .NET Framework class libraries

ASP.NET improves upon the original ASP by providing *code-behind*. In ASP, the HTML and script were mixed within one document. With ASP.NET and code-behind, the code and HTML can be separated. Now, when the logic of a Web site needs to change, it is not necessary to sift through hundreds or thousands of lines of HTML to locate the Script that needs to be changed.

Much like Windows Forms, ASP.NET supports Web Forms. Web Forms enable you to drag and drop controls onto your forms, and code-behind them as you would in any typical Windows application.

Because ASP.NET uses the .NET Framework, it also uses the just-in-time (JIT) compiler. Traditional ASP pages ran very slow because the code was interpreted. ASP.NET compiles the code when it is installed on the server or the first time that it is requested, which greatly increases the speed.

A History of C, C++, and C#

The C# programming language was created in the spirit of the C and C++ programming languages. This accounts for its powerful features and easy learning curve. The same can't be said for C and C++, but because C# was created from the ground up, Microsoft took the liberty of removing some of the more burdensome features — such as pointers. This section takes a look at the C and C++ languages, tracing their evolution into C#.

The C programming language was originally designed for use on the UNIX operating system. C was used to create many UNIX applications, including a C compiler, and was eventually used to write UNIX itself. Its widespread acceptance in the academic arena expanded to include the commercial world, and software vendors such as Microsoft and Borland released C compilers for personal computers. The original Windows API was designed to work with Windows code written in C, and the latest set of the core Windows operating system APIs remain compatible with C to this day.

From a design standpoint, C lacked a detail that other languages such as Smalltalk had already embraced: the concept of an object. You'll learn more about objects in Chapter 8, " Writing Object-Oriented Code." For now, think of an object as a collection of data and a set of operations that can be performed on that data. Object-style coding could be accomplished using C, but the notion of an object was not enforced by the language. If you wanted to structure your code to resemble an object, fine. If you didn't, fine. C really didn't care. Objects weren't an inherent part of the language, so many people didn't pay much attention to this programming paradigm.

After the notion of object-oriented development began to gain acceptance, it became clear that C needed to be refined to embrace this new way of thinking about code. C++ was created to embody this refinement. It was designed to be backwardly compatible with C (such that all C programs would also be C++ programs and could be compiled with a C++ compiler). The major addition to the C++ language was support for this new object concept. The C++ language added support for classes (which are "templates" of objects), and enabled an entire generation of C programmers to think in terms of objects and their behavior.

The C++ language is an improvement over C, but it still has some disadvantages. C and C++ can be hard to get a handle on. Unlike easy-to-use languages like Visual Basic, C and C++ are very "low level" and require you to do a lot of coding to make your application run well. You have to write your own code to handle issues such as memory management and error checking. C and C++ can result in very powerful applications, but you need to ensure that your code works well. One bug can make the entire application crash or behave unexpectedly. Because of the C++ design goal of retaining backward compatibility with C, C++ was unable to break away from the low level nature of C.

Microsoft designed C# to retain much of the syntax of C and C++. Developers who are familiar with those languages can pick up C# code and begin coding relatively quickly. The big advantage to C#, however, is that its designers chose *not* to make it backwardly compatible with C and C++. While this may seem like a bad deal, it's actually good news. C# eliminates the things that makes C and C++ difficult to work with. Because all C code is also C++ code, C++ had to retain all of the original quirks and deficiencies found in C. C# is starting with a clean slate and without any compatibility requirements, so it can retain the strengths of its predecessors and discard the weaknesses that made life hard for C and C++ programmers.

Introducing C#

C#, the new language introduced in the .NET Framework, is derived from C++. However, C# is a modern, objected-oriented (from the ground up) type-safe language.

Language features

The following sections take a quick look at some of the features of the C# language. If some of these concepts don't sound familiar to you, don't worry. All of them are covered in detail in later chapters.

Classes

All code and data in C# must be enclosed in a class. You can't define a variable outside of a class, and you can't write any code that's not in a class. Classes can have *constructors,* which execute when an object of the class is created, and a *destructor,* which executes when an object of the class is destroyed. Classes support single inheritance, and all classes ultimately derive from a base class called *object*. C# supports versioning techniques to help your classes evolve over time while maintaining compatibility with code that uses earlier versions of your classes.

As an example, take a look at a class called Family. This class contains the two static fields that hold the first and last name of a family member as well as a method that returns the full name of the family member.

```
class Class1
{
    public string FirstName;
    public string LastName;
    public string FullName()
    {
        return FirstName + LastName;
    }
}
```

Note   Single inheritance means that a C# class can inherit from only one base class.

C# enables you to group your classes into a collection of classes called a *namespace*. Namespaces have names, and can help organize collections of classes into logical groupings. As you begin to learn C#, it becomes apparent that all namespaces relevant to the .NET Framework begin with `System`. Microsoft has also chosen to include some classes that aid in backwards compatibility and API access. These classes are contained within the `Microsoft` namespace.

Data types

C# lets you work with two types of data: value types and reference types. *Value types* hold actual values. *Reference types* hold references to values stored elsewhere in memory. Primitive types such as `char`, `int` and `float`, as well as enumerated values and structures, are value types. Reference types hold variables that deal with objects and arrays. C# comes with predefined reference types (`object` and `string`), as well as predefined value types (`sbyte`, `short`, `int`, `long`, `byte`, `ushort`, `uint`, `ulong`, `float`, `double`, `bool`, `char`, and `decimal`). You can also define your own value and reference types in your code. All value and reference types ultimately derive from a base type called `object`.

C# allows you to convert a value of one type into a value of another type. You can work with both *implicit* conversions and *explicit* conversions. Implicit conversions always succeed and don't lose any information (for example, you can convert an `int` to a `long` without losing any data because a `long` is larger than an `int`). Explicit conversions may cause you to lose data (for example, converting a `long` into an `int` may result in a loss of data because a `long` can hold larger values than an `int`). You must write a cast operator into your code to make an explicit conversion happen.

Cross-Reference   Refer to Chapter 3, "Working with Variables," for more information about implicit and explicit conversions.

You can work with both one-dimensional and multidimensional arrays in C#. Multidimensional arrays can be `rectangular`, in which each of the arrays has the same dimensions, or `jagged`, in which each of the arrays has different dimensions.

Classes and structures can have data members called *properties* and *fields*. *Fields* are variables that are associated with the enclosing class or structure. You may define a structure called Employee, for example, that has a field called Name. If you define a variable of type Employee called `CurrentEmployee`, you can retrieve the employee's name by writing `CurrentEmployee.Name`. *Properties* are like fields, but enable you to write code to specify what should happen when code accesses the value. If the employee's name must be read from a database, for example, you can write code that says, "when someone asks for the value of the `Name` property, read the name from the database and return the name as a string."

Functions

A function is a callable piece of code that may or may not return a value to the code that originally called it. An example of a function would be the FullName function shown earlier, in this chapter, in the Family class. A *function* is generally associated to pieces of code that return information whereas a *method* generally does not return information. For our purposes however, we generalize and refer to them both as functions.

Functions can have four kinds of parameters:

✦ Input parameters have values that are sent into the function, but the function cannot change those values.

✦ Output parameters have no value when they are sent into the function, but the function can give them a value and send the value back to the caller.

✦ Reference parameters pass in a reference to another value. They have a value coming in to the function, and that value can be changed inside the function.

✦ Params parameters define a variable number of arguments in a list.

C# and the CLR work together to provide automatic memory management. You don't need to write code that says "allocate enough memory for an integer" or "free the memory that this object was using." The CLR monitors your memory usage and automatically retrieves more when you need it. It also frees memory automatically when it detects that it is no longer being used (this is also known as Garbage Collection).

C# provides a variety of operators that enable you to write mathematical and bitwise expressions. Many (but not all) of these operators can be redefined, enabling you to change how the operators work.

C# supports a long list of statements that enable you to define various execution paths within your code. Flow control statements that use keywords such as if, switch, while, for, break and continue enable your code to branch off into different paths, depending on the values of your variables.

Classes can contain code and data. Each class member has something called an *accessibility scope,* which defines the member's visibility to other objects. C# supports public, protected, internal, protected internal, and private accessibility scopes.

Variables

Variables can be defined as constants. *Constants* have values that cannot change during the execution of your code. The value of pi, for instance, is a good example of a constant, because its value won't be changing as your code runs. *Enum type declarations* specify a type name for a related group of constants. For example, you could define an enum of Planets with values of Mercury, Venus, Earth, Mars, Jupiter, Saturn, Uranus, Neptune and Pluto, and use those names in your code. Using the enum names in code makes code more readable than if you used a number to represent each planet.

C# provides a built-in mechanism for defining and handling events. If you write a class that performs a lengthy operation, you may want to invoke an event when the operation is completed. Clients can subscribe to that event and catch the event in their code, which enables them to be notified when you have completed your lengthy operation. The event handling mechanism in C# uses *delegates*, which are variables that reference a function.

Note An event handler is a procedure in your code that determines the actions to be performed when an event occurs, such as the user clicking a button.

If your class holds a set of values, clients may want to access the values as if your class were an array. You can write a piece of code called an *indexer* to enable your class to be accessed as if it were an array. Suppose you write a class called Rainbow, for example, that contains a set of the colors in the rainbow. Callers may want to write MyRainbow[0] to retrieve the first color in the rainbow. You can write an indexer into your Rainbow class to define what should be returned when the caller accesses your class, as if it were an array of values.

Interfaces

C# supports *interfaces*, which are groups of properties, methods, and events that specify a set of functionality. C# classes can implement interfaces, which tells users that the class supports the set of functionality documented by the interface. You can develop implementations of interfaces without interfering with any existing code, which minimizes compatibility problems. Once an interface has been published, it cannot be changed, but it can evolve through inheritance. C# classes can implement many interfaces, although the classes can only inherit from a single base class.

Let's look at a real-world example that would benefit from interfaces to illustrate its extremely positive role in C#. Many applications available today support add-ins. Assume that you have created a code editor for writing applications. This code editor, when executed, has the capability to load add-ins. To do this, the add-in must follow a few rules. The DLL add-in must export a function called CEEntry, and the name of the DLL must begin with CEd. When we run our code editor, it scans its working directory for all DLLs that begin with CEd. When it finds one, it is loaded; and then it uses the GetProcAddress to locate the CEEntry function within the DLL, thus verifying that you followed all the rules necessary to create an add-in. This method of creating and loading add-ins is very burdensome because it burdens the code editor with more verification duties than necessary. If an interface were used in this instance, your add-in DLL could have implemented an interface, thus guaranteeing that all necessary methods, properties, and events were present with the DLL itself, and functioning as documentation specified.

Attributes

Attributes declare additional information about your class to the CLR. In the past, if you wanted to make your class self-describing, you had to take a disconnected approach in which the documentation was stored in external files such as IDL or even HTML files. Attributes solve this problem by enabling you, the developer, to bind information to classes — any kind of information. For example, you can use an attribute to embed documentation information into a class. Attributes can also be used to bind runtime information to a class, defining how it should act when used. The possibilities are endless, which is why Microsoft includes many predefined attributes within the .NET Framework.

Compiling C#

Running your C# code through the C# compiler produces two important pieces of information: code and metadata. The following sections describe these two items and then finish up by examining the binary building block of .NET code: the assembly.

Microsoft Intermediate Language (MSIL)

The code that is output by the C# compiler is written in a language called Microsoft Intermediate Language, or MSIL. MSIL is made up of a specific set of instructions that specify how your code should be executed. It contains instructions for operations such as variable initialization, calling object methods, and error handling, just to name a few. C# is not the only language in which source code changes into MSIL during the compilation process. All .NET-compatible languages, including Visual Basic .NET and Managed C++, produce MSIL when their source code is compiled. Because all of the .NET languages compile to the same MSIL instruction set, and because all of the .NET languages use the same runtime, code from different languages and different compilers can work together easily.

MSIL is not a specific instruction set for a physical CPU. It knows nothing about the CPU in your machine, and your machine knows nothing about MSIL. How, then, does your .NET code run at all, if your CPU can't read MSIL? The answer is that the MSIL code is turned into CPU-specific code when the code is run for the first time. This process is called "just-in-time" compilation, or JIT. The job of a JIT compiler is to translate your generic MSIL code into machine code that can be executed by your CPU.

You may be wondering about what seems like an extra step in the process. Why generate MSIL when a compiler could generate CPU-specific code directly? After all, compilers have always done this in the past. There are a couple of reasons for this. First, MSIL enables your compiled code to be easily moved to different hardware. Suppose you've written some C# code and you'd like it to run on both your desktop and a handheld device. It's very likely that those two devices have different types of CPUs. If you only had a C# compiler that targeted a specific CPU, then you'd need two C# compilers: one that targeted your desktop CPU and another that targeted your handheld CPU. You'd have to compile your code twice, ensuring that you put the right code on the right device. With MSIL, you compile once. Installing the .NET Framework on your desktop machine includes a JIT compiler that translates your MSIL into CPU-specific code for your desktop. Installing the .NET Framework on your handheld includes a JIT compiler that translates that same MSIL into CPU-specific code for your handheld. You now have a single MSIL code base that can run on any device that has a .NET JIT compiler. The JIT compiler on that device takes care of making your code run on the device.

Another reason for the compiler's use of MSIL is that the instruction set can be easily read by a verification process. Part of the job of the JIT compiler is to verify your code to ensure that it is as clean as possible. The verification process ensures that your code is accessing memory properly and that it is using the correct variable types when calling methods that expect a specific type. These checks ensure that your code doesn't execute any instructions that could make the code crash. The MSIL instruction set was designed to make this verification process relatively straightforward. CPU-specific instruction sets are optimized for quick execution of the code, but they produce code that can be hard to read and, therefore, hard to verify. Having a C# compiler that directly outputs CPU-specific code can make code verification difficult or even impossible. Allowing the .NET Framework JIT compiler to verify your code ensures that your code accesses memory in a bug-free way and that variable types are properly used.

Metadata

The compilation process also outputs metadata, which is an important piece of the .NET code-sharing story. Whether you use C# to build an end-user application or you use C# to build a class library to be used by someone else's application, you're going to want to make use of some already-compiled .NET code. That code may be supplied by Microsoft as a part of the .NET Framework, or it may be supplied by a user over the Internet. The key to using this external code is letting the C# compiler know what classes and variables are in the other code base so that it can match up the source code you write with the code found in the precompiled code base that you're working with.

Think of metadata as a "table of contents" for your compiled code. The C# compiler places metadata in the compiled code along with the generated MSIL. This metadata accurately describes all the classes you wrote and how they are structured. All of the classes' methods and variable information is fully described in the metadata, ready to be read by other applications. Visual Basic .NET, for example, may read the metadata for a .NET library to provide the IntelliSense capability of listing all of the methods available for a particular class.

If you've ever worked with COM (Component Object Model), you may be familiar with *type libraries.* Type libraries aimed to provide similar "table of contents" functionality for COM objects. However, type libraries suffered from some limitations, not the least of which was the fact that not all of the data relevant to the object was put into the type library. Metadata in .NET does not have this shortcoming. All of the information needed to describe a class in code is placed into the metadata. You can think of metadata as having all of the benefits of COM type libraries without the limitations.

Assemblies

Sometimes, you will use C# to build an end-user application. These applications are packaged as executable files with an extension of .EXE. Windows has always worked with .EXE files as application programs, and C# fully supports building .EXE files.

However, there may be times when you don't want to build an entire application. Instead, you may want to build a code library that can be used by others. You may also want to build some utility classes in C#, for example, and then hand the code off to a Visual Basic .NET developer, who will use your classes in a Visual Basic .NET application. In cases like this, you won't be building an application. Instead, you'll be building an *assembly*.

An assembly is a package of code and metadata. When you deploy a set of classes in an assembly, you are deploying the classes as a unit; and those classes share the same level of version control, security information, and activation requirements. Think of an assembly as a "logical DLL." If you're familiar with Microsoft Transaction Server or COM+, you can think of an assembly as the .NET equivalent of a package.

There are two types of assemblies: *private assemblies* and *global assemblies*. When you build your assembly, you don't need to specify whether you want to build a private or a global assembly. The difference is apparent when you deploy your assembly. With a private assembly, you make your code available to a single application. Your assembly is packaged as a DLL, and is installed into the same directory as the application using it. With a deployment of a private assembly, the only application that can use your code is the executable that lives in the same directory as your assembly.

If you want to share your code among many applications, you might want to consider deploying your code as a global assembly. Global assemblies can be used by any .NET application on the system, regardless of the directory in which it is installed. Microsoft ships assemblies as a part of the .NET Framework, and each of the Microsoft assemblies is installed as a global assembly. The .NET Framework contains a list of global assemblies in a facility called the *global assembly cache,* and the .NET Microsoft Framework SDK includes utilities to both install and remove assemblies from the global assembly cache.

Summary

In this chapter, you learned the basics of the .NET Framework. After tracing the evolution from C to C++ to C#, you examined the high points of the C# feature list. You also investigated the output of the C# compiler, MSIL code, and metadata, and reviewed the use of assemblies as the building blocks of compiled .NET code.

✦   ✦   ✦

Writing Your First C# Program

In This Chapter

Writing Hello World! to the console

Compiling your applications with the C# compiler

Using the Main() function as your application's starting point

Adding comments to your source code

◆　◆　◆　◆

his chapter walks you through the development of a simple C# application. You also learn about how simple C# applications are structured and how to invoke the C# compiler to turn your source code into code that can be executed by the .NET Framework. Finally, you learn how to document your code using source code comments and how you can automatically turn your comments into an XML document.

Choosing an Editor

You have many options when it comes to writing code for the .NET Framework in C#. The most logical choice is to use Visual Studio .NET. By using Visual Studio, you get the benefit of IntelliSense, syntax highlighting, and many other productivity-enhancing tools.

Many third-party editors try to envelop the productivity tools that are contained within Visual Studio. Several of these tools can be downloaded as shareware, and others are freeware. The examples provided in this chapter simply use Windows Notepad. By using Notepad, not only do you learn that any text editor can be used to write C# applications, but you also learn the basics necessary to compile applications. Also by using Notepad, you learn that you don't need to rely on wizards to generate code for you. You can simply concentrate on the language itself, without having to learn the ins and outs of an IDE. Keep in mind though that for larger applications, you may prefer to use an editor that displays line numbers, which can help when you are tracking down faulty code.

Writing Hello World!

The code shown in Listing 2-1 is a complete C# application. It runs from within a console window and prints the message

`Hello World!` to the screen. The sections that follow walk through this code one line at a time.

> ### Listing 2-1: **Writing to the Console**
>
> ```
> class HelloWorld
> {
>     public static void Main()
>     {
>           System.Console.WriteLine("Hello World!");
>     }
> }
> ```

Building a class

The first line in our C# program defines a class. A class is a container for all the code that is contained within the application. Unlike in C/C++, all your code must be contained within a class, with few exceptions. The exceptions to this rule are the `using` statement, structure declarations, and a `namespace` declaration. Any attempt to write code that is not contained within a class results in a compiler error.

The first line in your Hello World application starts with the `class` keyword and then the word `HelloWorld`. `HelloWorld` is the name of the class that the code is creating. All classes must be assigned a unique name so you can reference them later.

Immediately following the class declaration, you must have an opening brace. The opening brace is used to open your class's body of code. All the code that you write in your class must be placed after this opening brace. In addition to an opening brace, there must also be a closing brace, as seen in the last line of the HelloWorld application. Ensure that all of your programming is placed between these two braces.

Beginning with the Main() method

Every application in C# must have a method called `Main()`. A method is a set of instructions that perform an action. This method can return information to the section of code that called it but under certain circumstances it doesn't necessarily have to.

Note

> The terms *method* and *function* are generally used interchangeably, but there is a distinction. A *method* is a function contained within a class. A *function* is generally a group of instructions not contained within a class and generally in a language, such as C or C++. Because you cannot add code outside of a class in C#, you should never have a function.

The `public` keyword in your declaration of the `Main()` method also contains the word `public`, which informs the compiler that your `Main()` method should be publicly accessible. Not only is the Main() method available from within your application by other methods, but also externally from other applications. By declaring your Main() method as public, you are creating an entry point for Windows to start the application when a user wants to run it.

When a user double-clicks the HelloWorld application icon, Windows searches the executable for an entry point by that name. If it finds no entry, the application is unable to run.

The word Static in the method declaration means that the compiler should allow only one copy of the method to exist in memory at any given time. Because the Main() method is the entry point into your application, it would be catastrophic to allow the entry point to be loaded more than once; this would generate more than one copy of the application in memory and undoubtedly some severe errors.

Just before the word Main, you see the word Void. Void is what your main function returns when it has completed running. Void means that your application returns no value after it has completed. This sample application isn't very advanced, so no return value is needed; under normal circumstances, however, the Main() function would typically return an integer value by replacing the word void with int. Valid return values are any simple data type defined within the .NET Framework.

Much like a class declaration, any methods you define must also contain an opening and closing brace within which all code for the method is placed. You can see the opening and closing brace for the Main() method on lines 4 and 6 in Listing 2-1.

Writing to the console

Line 5 of Listing 2-1 contains a call to the WriteLine method. This method is contained within the .NET Framework and writes a string to the console. If run from within a console window, the text would be shown on the screen. If you run this command from within the Visual Studio environment, any output it produces shows up in the output window.

You already learned that all functions in C# must be defined inside of a class. The functions found in the .NET Framework are no exception. The WriteLine() function is found in a class called Console. The Console keyword, used just before the WriteLine() function call, tells the compiler that the WriteLine() function can be found in a class called Console. The Console class is one of the many classes in the .NET Framework, and the WriteLine() function is a member of the Console class. A period separates the name of the class from the name of the function being called.

The name System appears immediately before the Console class name. Classes in the .NET Framework are organized into groups called *namespaces*. Namespaces are covered in more detail within Chapter 12. For now, you can think of a namespace as a collection of classes. The Console class is found in a .NET Framework namespace called System, and you must write this namespace name into your code. The C# compiler needs to find the code for WriteLine() so that your application runs properly, and you must give the compiler enough information about namespaces and classes before it can find the code for `WriteLine()`.

The text inside the `WriteLine()` parentheses is a string. A *string* in C# is a collection of characters enclosed in double quotes and kept together as a unit. Putting the string inside the parentheses tells the compiler that you intend to pass the string as a parameter to the `WriteLine()` function. The `WriteLine()` function writes a string to the console, and the parameter to the function tells `WriteLine()` which string should be written out.

There's a lot of information on line 5, which you can read as follows: "C# compiler, I want to call the `WriteLine()` with a string parameter of 'Hello World!' The `WriteLine()` function can be found in a class called `Console`, and the `Console` class can be found in a namespace called `System`."

Line 5 ends with a semicolon. All C# statements must end with a semicolon. The semicolon separates one statement from another in C#.

Compiling and Running the Program

Now that you've reviewed the code in Listing 2-1, it's time to make it run. Type the code from Listing 2-1 into your favorite text editor and save it as a file called Listing2-1.cs. The `cs` extension is the extension for all files that contain C# code.

Note   Before compiling the C# example, you must ensure that the C# compiler is within your `Path`. The csc.exe application is typically in the `c:\windows\Microsoft. NET\Framework\v1.0.xxxx` (replace `V1.0.Xxxx` with the version of your .NET Framework) folder, which you can verify by searching for it within Windows. To add entries to your path, search your Windows Help file for the keyword `Path`.

Now open up a command-prompt window and navigate to the folder in which you saved your `HelloWorld.cs` file. Once there, you can type the following command:

```
csc HelloWorld.cs
```

The `csc` command invokes the .NET Framework's C# compiler. Running this command produces an executable called `HelloWorld.exe`, which you can run just as you would any Windows application. Running this executable writes text to the console window as shown in Figure 2-1.

Congratulations! You have just written your first C# application.

Figure 2-1: The command-prompt window shows the Hello World application in action.

Understanding keywords and identifiers

The C# application in Listing 2-1 contains many words, separated by spaces. It uses two types of names: keywords and identifiers. This section describes the differences between these two types of names.

Keywords are words that have special meaning in the C# language. These words have been set aside in C# and are referred to as *reserved* words. The words class, static, and void are the reserved words in Listing 2-1. Each keyword has been defined by the C# language as having a special meaning. The following list contains all of the keywords defined by C#.

abstract	continue	finally	is
as	decimal	fixed	lock
base	default	float	long
bool	delegate	for	namespace
break	do	foreach	new
byte	double	goto	null
case	else	if	object
catch	enum	implicit	operator
char	event	in	out
checked	explicit	int	override
class	extern	interface	params
const	false	internal	private

protected	short	this	unchecked
public	sizeof	throw	unsafe
readonly	stackalloc	true	ushort
ref	static	try	using
return	string	typeof	virtual
sbyte	struct	uint	void
sealed	switch	ulong	while

Identifiers are names that you use in your applications. C# does not reserve identifier names. Identifiers are words that name items in your C# code. Your class needed a name, and you used the name HelloWorld for your class. This makes the name HelloWorld an identifier. Your method also needed a name, and you used the name Main for your function. This makes the name Main an identifier.

The C# compiler does not ordinarily allow you to use any of the reserved keywords as an identifier name. You'll get an error if, for example, you try to name a class static. If you really need to use a keyword name as an identifier, however, you can precede the identifier with the @ symbol. This overrides the compiler error and enables you to use a keyword as an identifier. Listing 2-2 shows how this is done. It is a modification to the code in Listing 2-1 and defines the word virtual as the name of the class.

Listing 2-2: **Using the virtual Keyword as a Class Identifier**

```
class @virtual
{
    static void Main()
    {
        System.Console.WriteLine("Hello World!");
    }
}
```

Without the leading @ symbol, you get an error from the compiler, as shown in Figure 2-2.

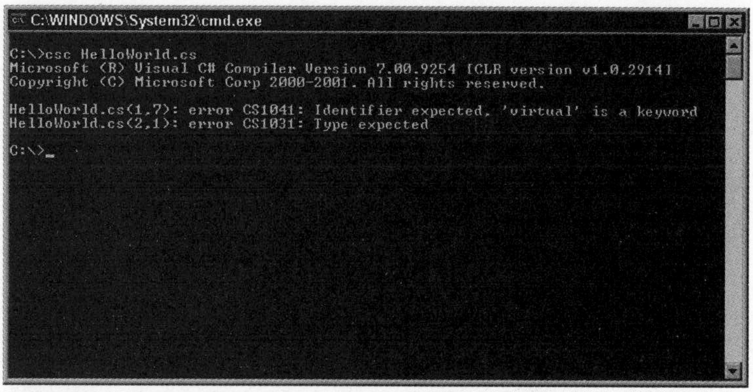

Figure 2-2: Forgetting @ generates compiler errors.

Using whitespace

The text of C# applications can include spaces, tabs, and carriage returns. These characters are called *whitespace* characters. Whitespace characters, which can be placed anywhere except in the middle of a keyword or identifier, help improve the readability of your code.

The C# compiler ignores the placement of whitespace when compiling a program. This means that you can place any whitespace character anywhere that the compiler accepts a whitespace character. The compiler remains indifferent to your use of carriage returns, tabs, and spaces, and you are free to use any combination of whitespace characters in your code.

The listings in this book reflect personal styles of whitespace layout: carriage returns are placed before and after opening and closing braces, and code is indented from the braces. However, this layout is *not* required by the C# application. Listing 2-3 shows an alternative layout of the code, using different whitespace characters. Feel free to experiment with the style that works best for you.

Listing 2-3: **An Alternative Whitespace Layout**

```
Class
HelloWorld
{
    static void Main()
    {System.Console.WriteLine("Hello World!");}
}
```

If you compile and run Listing 2-3, you see that it behaves just as the code in Listing 2-1 does: it outputs the string Hello World! The new whitespace layout style has no effect on the compiler's ability to compile the code; nor does it have any effect on the behavior of the code executing at runtime.

Starting Programs with the Main() Function

The application shown in Listing 2-1 defines a class with a function called Main(). The Main() function is an important part of C# applications, as the Main() function is where execution of your program begins.

Every C# application that you write must have one class with a function called Main(). The Main() function is referred to as your application's entry point, and the execution of your C# applications begin with the code in Main(). If your code contains more than one class, only one class can have a function called Main(). If you forget to define a Main() function, you will receive several errors from the compiler, as shown in Figure 2-3.

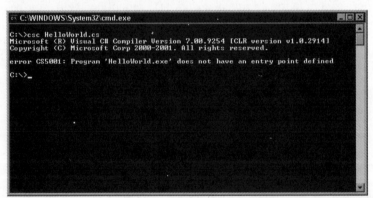

Figure 2-3: The absence of a Main() function generates compiler errors.

The Main() function defined in Listing 2-1 returns nothing (hence the void keyword), and takes no arguments (hence the empty parentheses). The C# compiler does, in fact, accept any of four possible constructs for the Main() function:

- ✦ public static void Main()
- ✦ public static void Main(string[] Arguments)
- ✦ public static int Main()
- ✦ public static int Main(string [] Arguments)

The first form, `public static void Main()`, is the form that used in Listing 2-1.

The second form, `public static void Main(string[] Arguments)`, does not return a value to the caller. It does, however, take in an array of strings. Each string in the array corresponds to a command-line argument supplied when the program executes. For example, suppose that you modify the code in Listing 2-1 so that the `Main()` method accepts a string array as its argument. Moreover, suppose that you run that code and supply some command-line arguments:

```
Listing2-1.exe Param1 Param2 Param3
```

In this case, the string array passed into the `Main()` function holds the following contents:

```
Arguments[0]: Param1
Arguments[1]: Param2
Arguments[2]: Param3
```

The third form, `public static int Main()`, returns an integer value to the caller. The integer return value is specified by the `int` keyword found in the declaration. Integer return values from `Main()` are used as program termination codes. For example, you may want to design your applications to return one value (0, perhaps) if its operation were successful, and another value (1, perhaps) if its operation were not successful. If you launch your .NET application from within an environment that can read this program termination code, you have enough information to determine whether your program ran successfully.

The last form of the `Main()` function, `public static int Main(string []
Arguments)`, specifies a function that supplies command-line arguments in a string array and allows the function to return a program termination code.

Keep a few things in mind when working with the `Main()` function:

✦ The `void` return forms of the `Main()` function always have a program termination code of 0.

✦ The `static` keyword is required in all forms of the `Main()` function.

When a C# application runs, the user always supplies command-line arguments. However, if the C# application is written with one of the forms of the `Main()` function that does not take any arguments, the application is unable to read the arguments. It is legal for a user to specify arguments to a C# application that was not written to support them (although that would not be very useful).

Commenting Your Code

Commenting your code lets you add notes to your C# source files. These notes can help you document the design and flow of your application. Comments can appear anywhere in your C# source code where whitespace is legal.

Using one-line comments

One-line comments begin with two slashes and remain in effect for the rest of the line:

```
{ // this is an opening brace
System.Console.WriteLine("C#"); // call WriteLine()
} // this is a closing brace
```

Using regular comments

Regular comments begin with a slash followed by an asterisk and remain in effect until an asterisk followed by a slash is found. Regular comments can span multiple lines:

```
/*
This is a regular comment in C#.
It contains multiple lines of text,
Separated by NewLine characters.
*/
```

The C# compiler does not let you embed one regular comment within another:

```
/*
outer comment
  /*
  inner comment
  */
more outer comment text
*/
```

You can't embed one regular comment in another because the compiler finds the first */ characters and assumes that it has reached the end of the multiline comment. It then assumes that the text following the */ characters is C# source code and tries to interpret it as such.

You can, however, embed a single-line comment within a regular comment:

```
/*
outer comment
  // inner comment
more outer comment text
*/
```

Generating XML documentation from comments

An interesting feature of the C# compiler is that it can read specially formatted comments and generate XML documentation from the comments. You can then display this XML on the Web to provide an extra level of documentation to developers who need to understand the structure of your applications.

To use this feature, you must do two things:

✦ Use three slashes for comments. The C# compiler does not generate any XML documentation for any comments that do not begin with three slashes. Nor does the C# compiler generate any XML documentation for regular, multiline, comments.

✦ Use the /doc option of the C# compiler to specify the name of the file that should contain the generated XML documentation.

Listing 2-4 shows the Hello World! application with XML documentation comments.

Listing 2-4: **The Hello World! Application with XML Comments**

```
/// The HelloWorld class is the one and only class in the
/// "HelloWorld" class. The class implements the application's
/// Main() function. The class does not contain any other
/// functions.

class HelloWorld
{
  /// This is the Main() function for the Listing2_4 class.
  /// It does not return a value and does not take any
  /// arguments. It prints the text "Hello from C#!" to the
  /// console and then exits.

    static void Main()
    {
        System.Console.WriteLine("Hello World!");
    }
}
```

You can compile this application with the /doc option to generate XML documentation for the source code:

```
csc /doc:HelloWorld.xml HelloWorld.cs
```

The compiler produces HelloWorld.exe as expected and also outputs a file called HelloWorld.xml. This file contains an XML document with your XML documentation comments embedded within it. Listing 2-5 shows the XML document that is generated when the code in Listing 2-4 is compiled with the /doc option.

Listing 2-5: **Generated XML Document for Code in Listing 2-4**

```
<?xml version="1.0"?>
<doc>
    <assembly>
        <name>HelloWorld</name>
    </assembly>
    <members>
        <member name="T:HelloWorld">
            The HelloWorld class is the one and only class in the
            "HelloWorld" class. The class implements the applications
            Main() function. The class does not contain any other
            functions.
        </member>
        <member name="M:HelloWorld.Main">
            This is the Main() function for the HelloWorld class.
            It does not return a value and does not take any
            arguments. It prints the text "Hello World!" to the
            console and then exits.
        </member>
    </members>
</doc>
```

You can then write a style sheet for this XML document and display it in a Web page, providing others with an up-to-date set of documentation for your code.

The main portion of the XML document is found in the <members> element. This element contains one <member> tag for each documented item in the source code. The <member> tag contains one attribute, name, which names the member being documented. The value of the name attribute starts with a one-letter prefix describing the type of information being described. Table 2-1 describes the options for the first letter of the name attribute's value and its meaning.

Table 2-1
<member> "name=" Attribute Prefixes

Prefix	Meaning
E	The element is providing documentation for an event.
F	The element is providing documentation for a field.
M	The element is providing documentation for a method.
N	The element is providing documentation for a namespace.
P	The element is providing documentation for a property.

Prefix	Meaning
T	The element is providing documentation for a user-defined type. This could be a class, an interface, a structure, an enum, or a delegate.
!	The C# compiler encountered an error and could not determine the correct prefix for this member.

A colon and the name of the member follow the prefix. The `name=` attribute lists the name of the class for type members. For method members, the `name=` attribute lists the name of the class containing the method, followed by a period, followed by the name of the method.

Your XML documentation comments can embed any valid XML element to assist in your documentation efforts. The .NET Framework documentation recommends a set of XML elements that you may want to use in your documentation. The remainder of this section examines each of these elements. Remember that you must encode valid XML into your comments, which means that every element must contain a matching end element somewhere in your comments.

 Note The term *tag* refers to any descriptive item contained within XML. Tags are always enclosed with the symbols < and >.

<c>

You can use the `<c>` tag to indicate that a small part of your comment should be treated as code. Style sheets may use this element to display the code portion of your comment in a fixed-width font, such as Courier:

```
/// This is the <c>Main()</c> function for the
/// HelloWorld class.
```

<code>

You can use the `<code>` tag to indicate that multiple lines of text in your comments should be treated as code:

```
/// Calling this application with three arguments will
/// cause the string array supplied to Main() to
/// contain three elements:
/// <code>
/// Argument[0]: command line argument 1
/// Argument[1]: command line argument 2
/// Argument[2]: command line argument 3
/// </code>
```

\<example\>

You can use the \<example\> tag to provide an example of how other developers can use the classes that you develop. Examples usually include a code sample, and you may want to use the \<example\> and \<code\> tags together:

```
/// <example>Here is an example of a client calling
/// this code:
/// <code>
/// code sample here
/// </code>
/// </example>
```

\<exception\>

You can use the \<exception\> tag to document any exceptions that may be raised from the member's code. The \<exception\> tag must contain an attribute called cref whose value specifies the type of exception being documented. The cref attribute value must be enclosed in quotes. The text of the element describes the conditions under which the exception is thrown:

```
/// <exception cref="System.Exception">
/// Raised if the input is less than 0.
/// </exception>
```

The C# compiler ensures that the cref attribute value is a legal data type. If it is not, the compiler issues a warning. Documenting a Main() function as follows:

```
/// <exception cref="junk">testing</exception>
```

causes the C# compiler to issue a warning like the following:

```
warning CS1574: XML comment on 'Main()' has cref attribute
'junk' that could not be found
```

In this case, the C# compiler still writes the \<exception\> tag to the XML file, but prefixes the cref attribute with an exclamation point:

```
<member name="M:MyClass.Main">
<exception cref="!:junk">testing</exception>
</member>
```

Cross-Reference   Exceptions are covered in Chapter 16.

\<list\>

You can use the \<list\> tag to describe a list of items in your documentation. You can describe a bulleted list, a numbered list, or a table. The \<list\> tag uses an attribute called type to describe the list's type. Table 2-2 lists the possible values for the type attribute and describes their meaning.

Table 2-2
<list> "type" Attribute Values

Value	Meaning
bullet	The list is a bulleted list.
number	The list is a numbered list.
table	The list is a table.

The bullet and number styles should also include one or more <item> tags within the <list> tag. Each <item> tag corresponds to one item in the list. Each <item> tag should contain a <description> tag, whose text defines the list item's text:

```
/// <list type="bullet">
/// <item>
/// <description>This is item 1.</description>
/// </item>
/// <item>
/// <description>This is item 2.</description>
/// </item>
/// </list>
```

The table list type should also include a <listheader> tag. The <listheader> tag contains one or more <term> tags that describe the table's headings:

```
/// <list type="table">
/// <listheader>
/// <term>Table Item</term>
/// </listheader>
/// <item>
/// <description>This is item 1.</description>
/// </item>
/// </list>
```

<param>

Use the <param> tag to document a parameter to a function. The <param> tag uses one attribute, name, whose value names the parameter being documented. The text of the <param> tag provides a description of the parameter:

```
/// <param name="Flag">
/// Value should be 0 for off, or 1 for on.
/// </param>
```

The C# compiler ensures that the value of the name attribute actually specifies the name of a parameter. If it doesn't, the compiler issues two warnings. For example, source code like this:

```
/// <param name="junk">This is junk.</param>

public static void Main(string [] strArguments)
{
}
```

produces warnings like the following:

```
warning CS1572: XML comment on 'Main(string[])' has a param tag
for 'junk', but there is no parameter by that name

warning CS1573: Parameter 'strArguments' has no matching param
tag in XML comment (but other parameters do)
```

The first warning says that a `<param>` tag was found with a `name` attribute whose value does not match any of the function's parameters. The second warning says that one of the parameters is missing a `<param>` tag.

The `<param>` tag is placed in the XML documentation file, even if the `name` attribute is incorrect:

```
<member name="M:Class1.Main(System.String[])">
<param name="junk">This is junk.</param>
</member>
```

`<paramref>`

You can use the `<paramref>` tag to reference a parameter from within a description. The tag must not have any text; however, it does carry an attribute called `name`. The value of the `name` attribute must list the name of the parameter being referenced:

```
/// The <paramref name="Arguments" /> array contains
/// parameters specified on the command line.
```

`<permission>`

Use the `<permission>` tag to document the permissions available on a given function or variable. Access to a class's code and data can mean access to all of the code or it can be restricted to a certain subset of code. You can use the `<permission>` tag to document the availability of your code and data.

The `<permission>` tag makes use of one attribute: `cref`. The value of the `cref` element must name the function or variable whose permissions are being documented:

```
/// <permission name="Main()">
/// Everyone can access Main().
/// </permission>
```

<remarks>

Use the <remarks> tag to add information about an item. The <remarks> element is great for providing an overview of a method or variable and its usage. The <remarks> tag carries no attributes and its text contains the remarks:

```
/// <remarks>
/// The Main() function is the entry point into the
/// application. The CLR will call Main() to start
/// the application after the application loads.
/// </remarks>
```

<returns>

Use the <returns> tag to describe a return value from a function. The <returns> tag carries no attributes and its text contains the return value information:

```
/// <returns>
/// The Main() function will return 0 if the application
/// processed the data successfully, and will return 1
/// if the data was not processed successfully.
/// </returns>
```

<see>

Use the <see> tag to add a reference to a function or variable found elsewhere in the file. The <see> element uses an attribute called cref whose value specifies the name of the method or variable being referenced. The <see> tag should not contain any text:

```
/// <see cref="Class1.Main" />
```

The C# compiler ensures that the value of the cref attribute actually specifies the name of a method or variable. If it doesn't, the compiler issues a warning. Therefore, source code like this:

```
/// <see cref="junk" />

public static void Main(string [] strArguments)
{
}
```

produces a warning like the following:

```
warning CS1574: XML comment on 'Class1.Main(string[])' has cref
attribute 'junk' that could not be found
```

The <see> tag is placed in the XML documentation file, even if the cref attribute is incorrect:

```
<member name="M:Class1.Main(System.String[])">
    <see cref="!:junk"/>
</member>
```

<seealso>

Like <see>, you can use the <seealso> tag to add a reference to a function or variable found elsewhere in the file. You may need to generate documentation that contains a section of <see> references as well as a section of See Also references, and the C# compiler enables you to make that distinction by supporting both <see> and <seealso> tags. The <seealso> tag uses an attribute called cref whose value specifies the name of the method or variable being referenced. The <seealso> tag should not contain any text:

```
/// <seealso cref="Class1.Main" />
```

The C# compiler ensures that the value of the cref attribute actually specifies the name of a method or variable. If it doesn't, the compiler issues a warning. Again, source code like this:

```
/// <seealso cref="junk" />

public static void Main(string [] strArguments)
{
}
```

produces a warning like the following:

```
warning CS1574: XML comment on 'Class1.Main(string[])' has cref
attribute 'junk' that could not be found
```

The <seealso> tag is placed in the XML documentation file, even if the cref attribute is incorrect:

```
<member name="M:Class1.Main(System.String[])">
    <seealso cref="!:junk"/>
</member>
```

<summary>

Use the <summary> tag to provide a summary description for a piece of code. This tag does not support any attributes. Its text should describe the summary information:

```
/// <summary>
/// The Main() function is the entry point into
/// this application.
/// </summary>
```

The `<summary>` tag is like the `<remarks>` tag. Generally, you should use the `<summary>` tag to provide information about a method or variable, and you should use the `<remarks>` tag to provide information about the item's type.

<value>

Use the `<value>` tag to describe a property of your class. The `<value>` tag does not carry any attributes. Its text should document the property:

```
/// <value>
/// The MyValue property returns the number of records
/// read from the database.
/// </value>

public int MyValue
{
    // ... property code goes here ...
}
```

Summary

This chapter teaches you how C# applications can be created with simple text editors, such as Notepad. You also examined several alternatives to Visual Studio for writing code.

You built your very first C# application. C# applications, regardless of their size, must contain a class with a function called `Main()`. The `Main()` function is the starting point of your C# application.

You also learned how you can add comments to your C# source code. You can add comments to your code to help other developers understand how your source code is structured. You can also format your comments in such a way that the C# compiler can turn the comments into an XML document; and by adding special keywords, you can make the XML document very rich and informative.

✦   ✦   ✦

Working with Variables

Your C# code often works with values that aren't known when you write your code. You may need to work with a value read from a database at runtime, or you may need to store the result of a calculation. When you need to store a value at runtime, use a variable. *Variables* are placeholders for values that you work with in your code.

Naming Your Variables

Each variable that you use in your C# code must have a name. Variable names are interpreted as *identifiers* by the C# compiler and must follow the naming conventions for an identifier:

✦ The first character in an identifier must start with an uppercase or lowercase letter or an underscore character.

✦ The characters following the first character can be any of the following:

- An uppercase or lowercase letter
- A digit
- An underscore

Note C# supports source code written using Unicode characters. If you are writing your C# source code using a Unicode character set, you can use any characters from Unicode character classes Lu, Ll, Lt, Lm, Lo, Nl, Mn, Mc, Nd, Pc, and Cf as characters in your identifier. See section 4.5 of the Unicode specification for more information about Unicode character classes.

You can also use a C# keyword as a variable name, but only if you precede the name with the @ character. This isn't recommended, however, as it can make your code hard to read, but it is legal and the C# compiler allows it.

Assigning a Type to a Variable

Variables in C# are assigned a *type,* which is a description of the kind of data that the variable will be holding. You may want to work with whole numbers, floating-point numbers, characters, strings, or even a type that you define in your code. When you define your variable in your C# code, you must give the variable a type. Table 3-1 describes some of the basic C# variable types.

	Table 3-1

Common C# Data Types

Type	Description
sbyte	Variables with an sbyte type can hold 8-bit signed integers. The *s* in sbyte stands for signed, meaning that the variable's value can be either positive or negative. The smallest possible value for an sbyte variable is -128; the largest possible value is 127.
byte	Variables with a byte type can hold 8-bit unsigned integers. Unlike sbyte variables, byte variables are not signed and can only hold positive numbers. The smallest possible value for a byte variable is 0; the largest possible value is 255.
short	Variables with a short type can hold 16-bit signed integers. The smallest possible value for a short variable is -32,768; the largest possible value is 32,767.
ushort	Variables with a ushort type can hold 16-bit unsigned integers. The *u* in ushort stands for unsigned. The smallest possible value of a ushort variable is 0; the largest possible value is 65,535.
int	Variables with an int type can hold 32-bit signed integers. The smallest possible value of an int variable is -2,147,483,648; the largest possible value is 2,147,483,647.
uint	Variables with a uint type can hold 32-bit unsigned integers. The *u* in uint stands for unsigned. The smallest possible value of a uint variable is 0; the largest possible value is 4,294,967,295.
long	Variables with a long type can hold 64-bit signed integers. The smallest possible value of a long variable is 9,223,372,036,854,775,808; the largest possible value is 9,223,372,036,854,775,807.
ulong	Variables with a ulong type can hold 64-bit unsigned integers. The *u* in ulong stands for unsigned. The smallest possible value of a ulong variable is 0; the largest possible value is 18,446,744,073,709,551,615.
char	Variables with a char type can hold 16-bit Unicode characters. The smallest possible value of a char variable is the Unicode character whose value is 0; the largest possible value is the Unicode character whose value is 65,535.

Type	Description
float	Variables with a float type can hold a 32-bit signed floating-point value. The smallest possible value of a float type is approximately 1.5 times 10 to the 45th; the largest possible value is approximately 3.4 times 10 to the 38th.
double	Variables with a double type can hold a 64-bit signed floating-point value. The smallest possible value of a double is approximately 5 times 10 to the 324th; the largest possible value is approximately 1.7 times 10 to the 308th.
decimal	Variables with a decimal type can hold a 128-bit signed floating-point value. Variables of type decimal are good for financial calculations. The smallest possible value of a decimal type is approximately 1 times 10 to the 28th; the largest possible value is approximately 7.9 times 10 to the 28th.
bool	Variables with a bool type can hold one of two possible values: true or false. The use of the bool type is one of the areas in which C# breaks from its C and C++ heritage. In C and C++, the integer value 0 was synonymous with false, and any nonzero value was synonymous with true. In C#, however, the types are not synonymous. You cannot convert an integer variable into an equivalent bool value. If you want to work with a variable that needs to represent a true or false condition, use a bool variable and not an int variable.

Declaring Your Variables

Before you can use your variable, you must declare it in your code. *Declaring* a variable tells the C# compiler about your variable's name and type. You declare a variable by writing its type, following the type with some whitespace, and following that with the name of your variable. End the declaration with a semicolon. Examples of variable declarations include the following:

Sizing Your Variables

You may be wondering why C# supports all of these different variables. Smaller values can be placed into variables of larger types, so why have the smaller types? If a short can hold values from -32,768 to 32,767, and a long can hold values from -9,223,372,036,854,775,808 to 9,223,372,036,854,775,807, then it's clear that all possible short values can be stored in a long variable. Why, then, have short at all? Why not just use a long for everything?

One answer is memory usage. A long variable can hold larger values than a short variable can, but it also takes up more memory. A short uses 16 bits (two bytes) of memory, whereas a long uses 32 bits (four bytes) of memory. If you'll be working with values that won't exceed the limit of a short variable, use a short. It's good practice to use all the memory you need, but not to use more than you need.

```
byte MyByteVariable;
int _Value123;
ulong AVeryLargeNumber;
```

Note   *Whitespace* is defined as any number of spaces required for readability.

You must declare your variables within a class or within a function. The following code is legal:

```
class MyClass
{
    int MyIntegerVariable;

    static void Main()
    {
        float AnotherVariable;

        System.Console.WriteLine("Hello!");
    }
}
```

Note   Where you declare your variable is up to you, but keep this in mind: If you declare it in a function, as shown in the AnotherVariable variable in the preceding example, only the code in that function can work with the variable. If you declare it within the class, as with the MyIntegerVariable variable (also shown in the preceding example), any code in that class can work with the variable. If you take the code in the example and add another function to the class, the code in that new function can work with the MyIntegerVariable variable but cannot work with the AnotherVariable variable. If that new function tries to access the AnotherVariable variable declared in the Main() function, you get the following error message from the C# compiler:

```
error CS0103: The name 'AnotherVariable' does not exist
in the class or namespace 'MyClass'
```

Using Default Values for Variables

In other programming languages, it is legal to work with a variable without first giving it a value. This loophole is a source of bugs, as the following code demonstrates:

```
class MyClass
{
    static void Main()
```

```
    {
        int MyVariable;

        // What is the value of "MyVariable" here?
    }
}
```

What is the value of `MyVariable` when `Main()` executes? Its value is unknown, because the code does not assign a value to the variable.

The designers of C# were aware of the errors that can pop up as a result of using variables that have not been explicitly given a value. The C# compiler looks for conditions like this and issues an error message. If the `MyVariable` variable shown in the preceding code is referenced in `Main()` without a value assignment, the C# compiler presents the following error message:

```
error CS0165: Use of unassigned local variable 'MyVariable'
```

C# makes a distinction between *assigned* and *unassigned* variables. Assigned variables are given a value at some point in the code, and unassigned variables are not given a value in the code. Working with unassigned variables is forbidden in C#, because their values are not known and using the variables can lead to errors in your code.

In some cases, C# gives default values to variables. A variable declared at the class level is one such case. Class variables are given default values if you do not assign a value to them in your code. Modify the preceding code by moving the `MyVariable` variable from a variable declared at the function level to a variable declared at the class level:

```
class MyClass
{
static int MyVariable;

static void Main()
    {
        // MyVariable is assigned a default
        // value and can be used here
    }
}
```

This action moves the variable's declaration into the class variable, and the variable is now accessible to all code in the class, rather than just the `Main()` function. C# assigns default values to class-level variables, and the C# compiler enables you to work with the `MyVariable` variable without giving it an initial value.

Table 3-2 lists the default values given to class-level variables.

Table 3-2
Default Values for Variables

Variable Type	Default Value
sbyte	0
byte	0
short	0
ushort	0
int	0
uint	0
long	0
ulong	0
char	Unicode character with value of 0
float	0.0
double	0.0
decimal	0.0
bool	false

Assigning Values to Variables

At some point in your code, you want to give your variables a value. Assigning a value to a variable is simple: You write the variable name, an equals sign, the value, and then end the statement with a semicolon:

```
MyVariable = 123;
```

You can also assign a value to a variable when you declare the variable:

```
int MyVariable = 123;
```

You learn other ways to assign values to variables in the sections "Initializing Array Element Values" and "Understanding Value Types and Reference Types" later in this chapter.

Using Variable Arrays

Arrays are simply contiguous bytes of memory that store data elements that are accessed using an index into the array. This section examines single arrays, multi-dimensional arrays, and jagged arrays.

Declaring single-dimensional arrays

Suppose that you are writing a C# application that teachers can use to input test scores from each of the students in their class. You want to declare variables to hold each student's test score. Because test scores fall between 0 and 100, you may decide to use byte types. If your program supports 25 students in a class, your first thought may be to declare 25 separate variables:

```
Byte      TestScoreForStudent1;
Byte      TestScoreForStudent2;
Byte      TestScoreForStudent3;
// ... more ...
byte      TestScoreForStudent25;
```

That's going to be a lot of typing, and your code is going to be hard to read and maintain with all of those variables. What you need is a way to say, "I want to hold a collection of 25 variables." This calls for an array.

An *array* is a collection of variables, each of which has the same variable type. Arrays have a size, which specifies how many items the array can hold. An array declaration looks like the following:

```
byte [] TestScoresForStudents;
```

The byte declaration specifies that all of the items in the array are values of type, byte. The square brackets tell the C# compiler that you want to create an array of variables, rather than a single variable, and the TestScoresForStudents identifier is the name of the array.

The one item missing from this declaration is the size of the array. How many items can this array hold? You specify the array's size by using the C# new operator. The new operator tells the C# compiler that you want to set aside enough memory for a new variable—in this case, an array of 25 byte variables:

```
byte [] TestScoresForStudents;

TestScoresForStudents = new byte[25];
```

The `byte` keyword tells the compiler that you want to create a new array of byte variables, and `[25]` tells the compiler that you want to set aside enough storage for 25 byte variables. Each variable in the array is called an *element* of the array, and the array that you just created holds 25 elements.

You must remember to specify the array type when you use the `new` keyword, even though you already specified the array's type when you declared it. If you forget the type when you use `new`, you get an error message from the compiler. The code

```
byte [] TestScoresForStudents;

TestScoresForStudents = new [25];
```

causes the C# compiler to issue an error:

```
error CS1031: Type expected
```

This error pops up because the code does not have a variable type between the `new` keyword and the array size.

You must also remember to use the same type that you used when you declared the array. If you use a different type, you get a different error message, as demonstrated by the following code:

```
byte [] TestScoresForStudents;

TestScoresForStudents = new long[25];
```

This code causes the C# compiler to issue an error:

```
error CS0029: Cannot implicitly convert type 'long[]' to
'byte[]'
```

The error occurs because the type in the declaration (`byte`) does not match the type used in the `new` statement (`long`).

Arrays like this are called *single-dimensional arrays*. Single-dimensional arrays have one factor that determines their size. In this case, the single factor that determines the size of the array is the number of students in the class.

The initial value of the items in the array is set according to the default values of the array's type. Each element in the array is initialized with a default value according to Table 3-2. Because this array contains byte elements, each element in the array has a default value of 0.

Working with values in single-dimensional arrays

You just created an array with 25 byte elements. Each element in the array has a number. The first element in the array starts at index zero, and the last element in the array is one less than the number of elements in the array (in this case, the last element is element 24). C# arrays are called *zero-based arrays* because their element numbers start with zero.

Working with an individual element in the array is simple. To get a value from an array, access it with the array name and the variable number in brackets, as shown in the following code:

```
byte      FirstTestScore;

FirstTestScore = TestScoresForStudents[0];
```

This code accesses the first element of the TestScoresForStudents array and assigns its value to the FirstTestScore variable.

To put a value into the array, simply access the element using the same syntax, but move the array name and element number to the leftside of the equals sign:

```
TestScoresForStudents[9] = 100;
```

This code stores the value 100 in the tenth element in the TestScoresForStudents array.

C# won't let you access an element that cannot be found in an array. Because the array you defined holds 25 elements, legal element numbers are 0 through 24, inclusive. If you use an element number less than 0 or greater than 24, you'll get a run-time error, as shown in the following code:

```
TestScoresForStudents[1000] = 123;
```

This code compiles without any errors, but running the application fails because there is no such element as element 1000 in your array of 25 elements. When this statement is reached, the Common Language Runtime (CLR) halts the program and issues an exception message:

```
Exception occurred: System.IndexOutOfRangeException:
An exception of type System.IndexOutOfRangeException
was thrown.
```

The IndexOutOfRangeException means that the application tried to access an element with an element number that doesn't make sense to the array.

Exceptions are covered in Chapter 16.

Initializing array element values

Suppose that you want to create an array of five integers, and you want the value of each element to be something other than its default. You can write individual statements to initialize the values in the array:

```
int []    MyArray;

MyArray = new int [5];
MyArray[0] = 0;
MyArray[1] = 1;
MyArray[2] = 2;
MyArray[3] = 3;
MyArray[4] = 4;
```

If you know the values that you want to initialize the array with when you are writing your code, you can specify the values in a comma-separated list surrounded by curly braces. The list is placed on the same line as the array declaration. You can put all the preceding code on one line by writing the following:

```
int [] MyArray = { 0, 1, 2, 3, 4};
```

Using this syntax, you do not specify the new operator or the size of the array. The C# compiler looks at your list of values and figures out the size of the array.

Declaring multidimensional arrays

You can think of a simple array as a line. It extends in one direction. A multidimensional array with two dimensions can be thought of as a piece of graph paper. Its dimensions extend not only out but down as well. This section covers the most common types of arrays.

Using rectangular arrays

Continue with the test scores example. The single-dimensional array defined in the previous section holds a set of test scores for 25 students. Each student has an element in the array to store a test score. But what happens if you want to store multiple test scores for multiple students? Now you have an array with two factors affecting its size: number of students and number of tests. Suppose that your 25 students will be taking ten tests over the course of a year. That means the teacher needs to grade 250 tests throughout the year. You could declare a single-dimensional array to hold all 250 test scores:

```
byte []    TestScoresForStudents;

TestScoresForStudents = new byte[250];
```

But that can get confusing. How is that array used? Do all test scores for a single student come first, or do the test scores for all students from the first test come first?

A better way to declare the array is to specify each dimension separately. Declaring a multidimensional array is as easy as putting commas inside the brackets. Place one less comma than the number of dimensions you need in your multidimensional array, as shown in the following declaration:

```
byte [,] TestScoresForStudents;
```

This declaration defines a multidimensional array with two dimensions.

Using the new operator to create a new array of this type is as easy as specifying the individual dimensions, separated by commas, in the square brackets, as shown in the following code:

```
byte [,] TestScoresForStudents;

TestScoresForStudents = new byte [10, 25];
```

This tells the C# compiler that you want to create an array with one dimension of 10 and another dimension of 25. You can think of a two-dimensional array as a Microsoft Excel spreadsheet with 10 rows and 25 columns. Table 3-3 shows how this array might look if its data were in a table.

Table 3-3
Table Representation of a Two-Dimensional Array

Test	Student 1	Student 2	Student 3...	Student 25
Test 1	90	80	85	75
Test 2	95	85	90	80
...	...	...	...	
Test 10	100	100	100	100

To access elements in a two-dimensional array, you use the same element numbering rules as you do with a single-dimensional array. (Element numbers run from 0 to one less than the dimension's size.) You also use the same comma syntax that you used when you used the new operator. Writing code to store a score of 75 for the 25th student's first test would look like the following:

```
TestScoresForStudents[0, 24] = 75;
```

Reading the score for the 16th student's fifth test would look like this:

```
byte FifthScoreForStudent16;

FifthScoreForStudent16 = TestScoresForStudents[4, 15];
```

In other words, when working with a two-dimensional array and thinking of the array as a table, consider the first dimension as the table's row number, and the second number as the table's column number.

You can initialize the elements of a multidimensional array when you declare the array variable. To do this, place each set of values for a single dimension in a comma-delimited list surrounded by curly braces. The set of curly braces is itself comma-delimited, and the entire list is surrounded by another set of curly braces:

```
int [,] MyArray = {{0, 1, 2}, {3, 4, 5}};
```

This statement declares a two-dimensional array with two rows and three columns. The integer values 0, 1, and 2 are in the first row; and the values 3, 4, and 5 are in the second row.

Two-dimensional arrays with a structure like this are called *rectangular arrays*. Rectangular arrays are shaped like a table; each row in the table has the same number of columns.

C# allows you to define arrays with more than two dimensions. Simply use more commas in the array declaration. You can define a four-dimensional array of longs, for example, with the following definition:

```
long [,,,] ArrayWithFourDimensions;
```

Be sure to define all the dimensions when you use the new operator:

```
ArrayWithFourDimensions = new long [5, 10, 15, 20];
```

You access elements in the array in the same manner. Don't forget to specify all the array elements:

```
ArrayWithFourDimensions[0, 0, 0, 0] = 32768436;
```

Defining jagged arrays

C# allows you to define *jagged arrays,* in which each row can have a different number of columns. Return to the student test scores example for an explanation. Suppose that the 25 students in the class take a different number of tests. Suppose also that there is a maximum of ten tests, but some students are excused from taking later tests if they do well on earlier tests. You are free to create a rectangular array for your storage needs, but you may end up with unused elements in the rectangular array. If some students don't take all the tests, you end up with unused array elements in your rectangular array. Unused elements equate to wasted memory, which you want to avoid.

A better approach is to define an array in which each element in the array is itself an array. Figure 3-1 illustrates this concept. It shows student 1 with space for three test scores, student 2 with space for five test scores, student 3 with space for two test scores, and student 25 with space for all ten test scores (the other students are not shown in the figure).

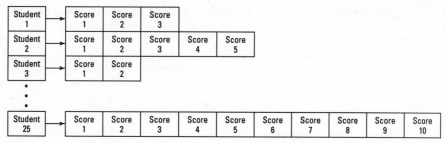

Figure 3-1: Jagged arrays let you define one array holding other arrays, each having a different number of elements.

These jagged arrays are two-dimensional, like rectangular arrays, but each row can have a different number of elements (which gives the arrays their jagged shape).

You define jagged arrays by using two empty sets of square brackets immediately following the array's type name. When you call new, you specify a size for the first dimension (the student array in our example), but not the second. After the first array is defined, call new again to define the other arrays (the score arrays in this example):

```
byte [][]          ArraysOfTestScores;

ArraysOfTestScores = new byte [25][];
ArraysOfTestScores[0] = new byte[3];
ArraysOfTestScores[1] = new byte[5];
ArraysOfTestScores[2] = new byte[2];
ArraysOfTestScores[24] = new byte[10];
```

After the jagged array is built, you can access its elements just as you would with a rectangular array.

Understanding Value Types and Reference Types

Recall from our discussion of arrays that you must use the new keyword to create the array. This requirement differs from the types that have been discussed so far. When you work with code that uses int or long variables, for instance, you can use the variable without calling new:

```
int IntegerVariable;

IntegerVariable = 12345;
```

Why are the arrays different? Why is new required when creating an array? The answer lies in the difference between value types and reference types.

With a value type, the variable holds the value of the variable. With a reference type, the variable holds a reference to a value stored elsewhere in memory. You can think of a reference as a variable that points to another piece of memory. Figure 3-2 shows the difference.

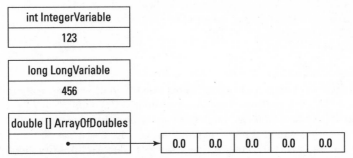

Figure 3-2: Value types hold data. Reference types hold references to data placed elsewhere in memory.

Each of the types discussed until this point is a value type. The variables provide enough storage for the values that they can hold, and you don't call new to create space for their values. Arrays of value types and objects are reference types. Their values are held elsewhere in memory, and you need to use the new keyword to create enough space for their data.

Although you need to use the new keyword to create memory space for a reference type, you don't need to write any code to delete the memory when you are finished using the variable. The CLR contains a mechanism called a *garbage collector,* which performs the task of releasing unused memory. The CLR runs the garbage collector while your C# application runs. The garbage collector searches through your program looking for memory that is no longer being used by any of your variables. It is the job of the garbage collector to free the unused memory automatically.

Converting Variable Types

You may run into a situation in which you have a variable of one type, but you need to work with a piece of code that needs another type. If, for example, you are working with a variable of type int, and need to pass the value to a function that needs a variable of type long, then you need to perform a conversion from the int variable to the long variable.

C# supports two kinds of conversions: implicit conversions and explicit conversions. The following sections describe each of these types of conversions.

Understanding implicit conversions

Implicit conversions are performed automatically by the C# compiler. Consider the following code:

```
int       IntegerVariable;
long      LongVariable;

IntegerVariable = 123;
LongVariable = IntegerVariable;
```

In this code, an integer variable is assigned a value of 123, and a `long` variable is assigned the value assigned to the integer variable. When this code executes, the value of `LongVariable` is 123.

The C# compiler converts the integer's value to a `long` value because the conversion from an `int` value to a `long` value is one of the implicit conversions allowed by C#. Table 3-4 lists the implicit conversions that C# allows. The first column lists the variable's original type, and the columns across the top list the data types to which you can convert it. An X in a cell means that you can implicitly convert from the type at the left to the type at the top.

Table 3-4
Implicit Value Type Conversions

----	sbyte	byte	short	ushort	int	uint	long	char	float	ulong	decimal	double
sbyte	X	-	X	-	X	-	X	-	X	-	X	-
byte	-	X	X	X	X	X	X	-	X	X	X	-
short	-	-	X	-	X	-	X	-	X	-	X	X
ushort	-	-	-	X	X	X	X	-	X	X	X	X
int	-	-	-	-	X	-	X	-	X	-	X	X
uint	-	-	-	-	-	X	X	-	X	X	X	X
long	-	-	-	-	-	-	X	-	X	-	X	X
char	-	-	-	X	X	X	X	X	X	X	X	X
float	-	-	-	-	-	-	-	-	X	-	-	X
ulong	-	-	-	-	-	-	-	-	X	X	X	X

Note You can't convert any type to a `char` type (except through the `char` variable, which isn't really a conversion). Also, you cannot convert between the `floating-point` types and the `decimal` types.

Understanding explicit conversions

If you write code that tries to convert a value using types that are not supported by an implicit conversion, the C# compiler raises an error, as shown by the following code:

```
char    CharacterVariable;
int     IntegerVariable;

IntegerVariable = 9;
CharacterVariable = IntegerVariable;
```

The C# compiler raises the following error:

```
error CS0029: Cannot implicitly convert type 'int' to 'char'
```

This error results because a conversion from a `int` variable to a `char` variable is not a supported implicit conversion.

If you really need to make this conversion, you have to perform an explicit conversion. Explicit conversions are written in your source code and tell the compiler to "make this conversion happen even though it can't be performed implicitly." Writing an explicit conversion in your C# code requires you to place the type you are converting to in parentheses. The parentheses are placed just before the variable that you are using as the source of the conversion. Following is the code shown previously if an explicit conversion is used:

```
char    CharacterVariable;
int     IntegerVariable;

IntegerVariable = 9;
CharacterVariable = (char)IntegerVariable;
```

This technique is referred to as *casting* the integer variable to a character variable.

Some types cannot be converted, even when you write an explicit cast operation into your code. Table 3-5 lists the explicit conversions that C# supports. The first column lists the variable's original type, and the columns across the top list the data types to which you can convert it. An X in a cell means that you can explicitly convert from the type on the left to the type at the top using the casting operation.

Table 3-5
Explicit Value Type Conversions

----	sbyte	byte	short	ushort	int	uint	long	char	float	ulong	decimal	double
sbyte	X	X	-	X	X	-	X	X	-	-	-	-
byte	X	X	-	-	-	-	-	X	-	-	-	-
short	X	X	X	X	-	X	X	X	-	-	-	-
ushort	X	X	X	X	-	-	-	X	-	-	-	-
int	X	X	X	X	X	X	-	X	-	X	-	-
uint	X	X	X	X	X	X	-	X	-	X	-	-
long	X	X	X	X	X	X	X	X	-	X	-	-
char	X	X	X	-	-	-	-	X	-	-	-	-
float	X	X	X	X	X	X	X	X	X	X	X	-
ulong	X	X	X	X	X	X	X	-	X	-	-
double	X	X	X	X	X	X	X	X	X	X	X	X
decimal	X	X	X	X	X	X	X	X	X	X	X	X

You can also perform explicit conversions on value types by casting the value to the appropriate type, as shown in the next example.

C# enables you to use a casting operator even with implicit conversions, if you want:

```
int    IntegerVariable;
long   LongVariable;

IntegerVariable = 123;
LongVariable = (long)IntegerVariable;
```

This syntax is not required, because C# allows implicit conversions from int variables to long variables, but you can write it if you want.

Working with Strings

C# supports a reference type called string. The string data type represents a string of Unicode characters.

Note Unicode is a world-wide standard for character encoding. Unicode characters are 16 bits, which allows for 65,536 possible characters. The ANSII characters are 8 bits, and allow for 256 possible characters.

Use the following to create and initialize a string in C#:

```
string MyString;

MyString = "Hello from C#!";
```

As with all variables, you can initialize a string on the same line as its declaration:

```
string MyString = "Hello from C#!";
```

Using special characters in strings

C# enables you to use a special syntax to embed special characters in your string. These special characters are listed in Table 3-6.

<table>
<tr><td colspan="2" align="center">Table 3-6
C# Special Characters</td></tr>
<tr><td>*Characters*</td><td>*Purpose*</td></tr>
<tr><td>\t</td><td>The special characters \t embed a tab into the string. A string defined as hello\tthere is stored in memory with a tab character between the words *hello* and *there*.</td></tr>
<tr><td>\r</td><td>The special characters \r embed a carriage return into the string. A string defined as hello\rthere is stored in memory with a carriage return character between the words *hello* and *there*. The carriage return character returns the cursor to the beginning of the line but does not move the cursor down a line.</td></tr>
<tr><td>\v</td><td>The special characters \v insert a vertical tab into the string. A string defined as hello\vthere is stored in memory with a vertical tab character between the words *hello* and *there*.</td></tr>
<tr><td>\f</td><td>The special characters \f insert a form-feed character into the string. A string defined as hello\fthere is stored in memory with a form-feed character between the words *hello* and *there*. Printers usually interpret a form-feed character as a signal to advance to a new page.</td></tr>
</table>

Characters	Purpose
\n	The special characters \n insert a newline into the string. A string defined as hello\nthere is stored in memory with a newline character between the words *hello* and *there*. The software development community has long debated the interpretation of the newline character. It has always meant, "move the next output position down one line." The question is whether the operation also includes moving the next position to the first character on the previous line. The .NET Framework interprets the newline character as both moving down a line and returning the next character position to the beginning of the next line. If you are unsure, you can always write the special characters \n and \r together.
\x	The special characters \x enable you to specify an ASCII character using two hexadecimal digits. The two hexadecimal digits must immediately follow the \x characters and must be the hexadecimal value of the ASCII character that you want to output. For example, the ASCII space character has an ASCII character code of decimal 32. The decimal value 32 is equivalent to the hexadecimal value 20. Therefore, a string defined as hello\x20there is stored in memory with a space character between the words *hello* and *there*.
\u	The special characters \u enable you to specify a Unicode character using exactly four hexadecimal digits. The four hexadecimal digits must immediately follow the \u characters and must be the hexadecimal value of the Unicode character that you want to output. For example, the Unicode space character has a Unicode character code of decimal 32. The decimal value 32 is equivalent to the hexadecimal value 20. Therefore, a string defined as hello\u0020there is stored in memory with a space character between the words *hello* and *there*. Be sure to use exactly four digits after the \u characters. If the value is less than four digits, use leading zeros to pad your value to four digits.
\\	The special characters \\ enable you to specify a backslash character at the current position. A string defined as hello\\there is stored in memory with a backslash character between the words *hello* and *there*. The reasoning behind having two backslashes is simple: Using a single backslash might cause the C# compiler to mistake it as the start of another special character. For example, suppose that you forget the second backslash and write hello\there in your code. The C# compiler sees the backslash and the *t* in the word *there* and mistakes it for a tab character. This string would then be stored in memory with a tab character between the words *hello* and *here*. (Remember that the *t* in *there* would be interpreted as the tab character and would not be a part of the actual word.)

Turning off special characters in strings

You can instruct the C# compiler to ignore special characters in a string by prefixing the string with the @ sign:

```
string MyString = @"hello\there";
```

This code sets the value of the MyString variable to the text hello\there. Because the string is prefixed with the @ sign, the default behavior of interpreting the \t characters as a tab marker is turned off.

This syntax also enables you to write directory names in C# filename strings without using the double backslash syntax. By default, you always need to use the double backslashes:

```
string MyFilename = "C:\\Folder1\\Folder2\\Folder3\\file.txt";
```

However, with the @ prefix, you can get away with a single backslash:

```
string MyFilename = @"C:\Folder1\Folder2\Folder3\file.txt";
```

Accessing individual characters in the string

You can access characters in the string as if the string were an array. Conceptually, you can think of a string as an array of characters. You can use the array element square bracket syntax to access any of the characters in the string:

```
char MyCharacter;
string MyString = "Hello from C#!";

MyCharacter = MyString[9];
```

This code places the value m in the MyCharacter variable. The character m is at element 9 in the string, if you think of the string as an array of characters. Also, keep in mind that this array of characters is zero-based. The first character in the string is actually located at element 0. The tenth character in this string, as you have learned, is located at element 9.

Declaring Enumerations

Unlike the variables discussed thus far, an enumeration is not a type in itself but a special form of a value type. An enumeration is derived from System.Enum and supplies names for values. The underlying type that an enumeration represents must be a `byte`, `short`, `int`, or `long`. Each field within an enumeration is static and represents a constant.

To declare an enumeration, you must provide the keyword `enum` followed by the name of the enumeration. Then you must provide an opening bracket followed by a list of the enumeration strings, and end with a closing bracket, as shown in the following example:

```
public enum Pizza
{
   Supreme,
   MeatLovers,
   CheeseLovers,
   Vegetable,
}
```

This code creates an enumeration called `Pizza`. The pizza enumeration contains four different name/value pairs describing different kinds of pizza, but no values are defined. When you declare an enumeration, the first name you declare takes on the value of 1. The second name listed takes on the value of 1, and so on. You can override this functionality by assigning a value to each name, as shown here:

```
public enum Pizza
{
   Supreme       = 2,
   MeatLovers    = 3,
   CheeseLovers  = 4,
   Vegetable     = 5,
}
```

The value of each enumeration field has been incremented by 1. Not all of this code is necessary, though. By assigning `Supreme` a value of 2, the following fields follow in sequence. Therefore, you can remove the assignments to `MeatLovers`, `CheeseLovers`, and `Vegetable`.

Enumerators can be referenced in one of two ways. You can program around their field names or you can program around their values. As an example, you can assign the field name to a string variable with the following code:

```
string MyString = Pizza.Supreme;
```

You might also want to reference the value of a field. You can accomplish this by explicit typecasting. For example, you can retrieve the value of the `Supreme` field with the following code:

```
int MyInteger = (int)Pizza.Supreme;
```

Summary

This chapter looks at variables and their types. There are many different kinds of value types and each has its own characteristics and memory requirements. Some types can be implicitly converted to other types, while some types must be explicitly converted using the casting syntax.

Arrays contain collections of variables of the same type. Arrays are useful when you need to maintain a set of like variables. C# supports single-dimensional and multidimensional arrays. C# arrays are zero-based: that is, the first element number in an array is element 0.

Strings help you work with pieces of text in your code. They are collections of Unicode characters. C# enables you to embed special characters in your strings, but provides the @ prefix to specify cases for which you do not need special characters to be processed. Characters in a string can be accessed as if they were arrays of characters.

✦   ✦   ✦

Expressions

Expressions are the most basic and fundamental piece of any programming language. Through the use of operators, expressions allow an application to perform simple comparisons, assignments and even very complex operations that would take people millions of years to accomplish.

This chapter covers the use of operators to perform mathematical functions, assign values to variables, and perform comparisons. After you have these basic elements down you look at some advanced expressions that use operators very specific to the C# language that give it an advantage over most other programming languages. To finish this chapter up, you look at expressions that use operators to manipulate the tiny parts of a byte — the bit.

Using Operators

Expressions can be written using variables; hard-coded values, called *literal values* (refer to the section "Using literals," later in the chapter); and symbols called *operators*. C# supports a variety of operators, each performing a different action. The variables or literal values that appear in an expression are called *operands*. Operators are applied to operands, and the result of the operation is another value.

C# categorizes operators into one of three types:

✦ **Unary operators** work with a single operand. An expression with an operand and an operator produces a single value.

✦ **Binary operators** work with two operands. An expression with two operands and an operator produces a single value.

✦ **Ternary operators** work with three operands. C# supports only one ternary operand.

Using Primary Expressions

Primary expressions are the basic building blocks of your C# code. C# defines several different types of primary expressions:

- ✦ Literals
- ✦ Identifiers
- ✦ Parenthesized expressions
- ✦ Member access
- ✦ Invocation expressions
- ✦ Element access
- ✦ The this keyword
- ✦ Base access
- ✦ Postfix increment and decrement operators
- ✦ The new operator
- ✦ The typeof operator
- ✦ The checked and unchecked operators

Primary expressions enable you to define the order of operations within an expression, define new literal (for example, hard-coded values) as well as declare new variables for use in your application. In the next few sections you explore what these primary expressions are, and just how to use them.

Using literals

Literals are hard-coded values that you can write directly in your C# source code. There are many different types of literals. To demonstrate a literal, lets examine the following line of C# code that uses the literal value of Brian.

```
if (FirstName == "Brian")
```

Here we have hard coded in a value of Brian for use in a comparison. Rather than hard-coding in a value, it is preferable to store string within variables so if the value ever needs to change, you can change them in one place and not have to search through every line in your application for an occurrence. The following lines would be the preferred method for storing and using a string for comparison purposes:

```
string MyFirstName = "Brian;
if (FirstName == MyFirstName)
```

As you can see, this is a much cleaner approach to using a literal value.

Understanding Boolean literals

C# defines two Boolean literal values—the keywords True and False:

```
bool MyTrueVariable = true;
bool MyFalseVariable = false;
```

Both values have a value type of bool. The keyword True is the integer equivalent of negative one (-1), whereas the equivalent of False is zero.

Using integer literals in decimal and hexadecimal notations

You can write integer literals using a decimal notation or a hexadecimal notation. Much like the literals previously discussed, using literals is a way to clean up your code. Literal values can be placed at the top of your code listing. If these values ever need to change it is a very simple task to change the one occurrence of the value.

Decimal integer literals are written as a series of one or more digits using the characters 0, 1, 2, 3, 4, 5, 6, 7, 8, and 9:

```
int MyVariable = 125;
```

Decimal literals can also contain a one-character suffix that specifies the literal's type. If the literal is suffixed with an uppercase or lowercase U, the decimal literal is considered to be an unsigned type:

```
uint MyVariable = 125U;
```

The term *unsigned type* means that the number is not specifically a positive or negative number. Therefore, if you convert a value of negative 100 (-100) to an unsigned value, your result would simply be one hundred (100).

If the value is small enough to fit into a uint type, the C# compiler sees the literal as a uint type. If the value of the integer literal is too large for a uint type, the C# compiler sees the literal as a ulong type. The different types represent the size of the information that you are storing. A uint type can contain a number ranging from 0 to 4,294,967,295; whereas a ulong value can contain a value ranging from 0 to 18,446,744,073,709,551,615.

If the literal is suffixed with an uppercase or lowercase L, the decimal literal is considered a long type:

```
long MyVariable = 125L;
```

If the value is within the range of a long type, the C# compiler sees the literal as a long type. If the value is not within the range of a long type, the C# compiler sees the literal as a ulong type.

Note Although the C# compiler accepts either a lowercase l or an uppercase L as a suffix, you will probably want to use the uppercase L. The lowercase l looks a lot like the number 1, and other developers reading your code might mistake the l for a 1.

If the literal is suffixed with both an L and a U, the decimal literal is considered to be an unsigned long type:

```
ulong MyVariable = 125LU;
```

The C# compiler accepts both a suffix in which the L comes before the U as well as a suffix in which the U comes before the L. In addition, the C# compiler accepts a mix of uppercase and lowercase letters. The suffixes LU, Lu, lU, lu, UL, Ul, uL, and ul all denote the ulong suffix.

Writing integer literals in hexadecimal format enables you to write a literal using the letters A through F as well as the digits 0 through 9. Hexadecimal literals must be prefixed with the characters 0X or 0x:

```
int MyVariable = 0x7D;   // 7D hex = 125 decimal
```

You can use uppercase or lowercase letters in your hexadecimal notation. You can also use the same character suffixes that are available for decimal literals:

```
long MyVariable = 0x7DL;
```

The choice to use a hexadecimal value is strictly up to the discretion of the programmer. Using hexadecimal over another type of literal yields no differences to any other type of number. It is, however, a good idea to use hexadecimal values when you are building an application that has specifications in hexadecimal format. For example, you might be writing an interface to the modem card in your computer. The programmer's reference for your modem might specify values of certain operations in hexadecimal format. Rather than reading through the programmer's reference and converting all the numbers to decimal, you would generally just code these hexadecimal numbers directly into your application thus avoiding any conversion errors.

Using real literals for floating-point values

Real literals enable you to write floating-point values into your C# code. Real literals may include a decimal point as well as an exponent.

Decimal points can appear in real literals, and digits can appear before and after the decimal point. It is also legal for a real literal to begin with a decimal point, which is useful when you want to write a value greater than zero but less than one. Values such as *2.5* and *.75* are examples of real literals. C# does not impose any limit on the number of digits that can appear before or after the decimal point, as long as the value of the literal fits within the range of the intended type.

You can also specify an exponent in your real literals. Exponents are written with an uppercase or lowercase E immediately following the decimal portion of the number. One or more decimal digits follow the E, signifying the exponent's value. This means that you can write the value 750 as a real literal of 7.5e2. A plus or minus sign can also appear between the E and the exponent value. A plus sign signifies a positive exponent value; a minus sign signifies a negative exponent value. The real literal 7.5e+2 defines a value of 750, and the real literal 7.5e-2 defines a value of .075. If you don't use either sign, the C# compiler assumes that your exponent value is positive.

Like decimal literals, real literals can also be followed by a one-character suffix that specifies the literal's type. If you do not use a suffix on your real literal, the C# compiler assumes that your literal has a type of double.

If the real literal is suffixed with an uppercase or lowercase F, the decimal literal is considered to be a float type:

```
float MyVariable = 7.5F;
```

If the real literal is suffixed with an uppercase or lowercase D, the decimal literal is considered to be a double type:

```
double MyVariable = 7.5D;
```

If the real literal is suffixed with an uppercase or lowercase M, the decimal literal is considered to be a decimal type:

```
decimal MyVariable = 7.5M;
```

Using character literals to assign character values

Character literals enable you to write character values into your C# code. Usually, character literals appear between single quotes:

```
char MyVariable = 'a';
```

You can also use the escape sequences discussed in Chapter 3, (in the section that covers strings) to write character literals into your C# code. These character literals must be enclosed in single quotes:

```
char MyVariable = '\t';  // tab character
```

Note If you want to write a single quote character as a character literal, you need to precede it with a backslash. Writing ''' confuses the C# compiler. Write '\'' instead.

You can define hexadecimal values as character literals by using the \x escape sequence and following it with one, two, or three hexadecimal characters:

```
char MyVariable = '\x5C';
```

Using string literals to embed strings

String literals enable you to embed strings in your C# code. You write string literal as discussed in Chapter 3, by enclosing the string in double quotes:

```
string MyVariable = "Hello from C#!";
```

The C# compiler reuses multiple string literals with the same contents, which conserves space in your final executable, as shown in the following code:

```
string String1 = "Hello";
string String2 = "Hello";
```

When this code is compiled, the executable contains one copy of the string literal Hello. Both string variables read their value from the single copy stored in the executable. This optimization enables the C# compiler to conserve your code's memory usage, as storing only one copy of the literal takes up less memory than storing two copies of the same literal.

Using null literals

The null literal is a C# keyword that enables you to set an object to a null, or unused, state:

```
object MyObject = null;
```

Cross-Reference   The null literal is covered in more detail in Chapter 8.

Using identifiers

The identifiers that you write in your C# code are examples of simple expressions. Identifiers have a type, and the type is specified when you declare the identifier, as shown in the following code:

```
int MyVariable = 123;
```

The identifier MyVariable is considered an expression, and it has a type of int. Identifiers can be defined in any code block that is enclosed by curly braces, but their type cannot change:

```
public static void Main()
{
    int MyVariable = 123;

    MyVariable = 1; // "MyVariable" is still an "int"
    MyVariable = 2; // "MyVariable" is still an "int"
}
```

If you try to redefine the type of an identifier within the same code block, the C# compiler issues an error message, as demonstrated by the following code:

```
public static void Main()
{
    int MyVariable = 123;
    float MyVariable = 1.25;
}
```

The C# compiler issues an error message at the line that tries to redefine MyVariable as a *float* value:

```
error CS0128: A local variable named 'MyVariable' is already
defined in this scope
```

You can, however, reuse the identifier if it appears in a separate code block:

```
public static void Main()
{
    int MyVariable = 123;
}

public void AnotherFunction()
{
    float MyVariable = 1.25;
}
```

Understanding parenthesized expressions

As their name suggests, parenthesized expressions are expressions enclosed in parentheses. The C# compiler evaluates the expression inside the parentheses, and the value of the parenthesized expression is the result of the evaluation. For example, the value of the parenthesized expression (3+2) is 5.

Calling methods with member access expressions

When you need to call a method in an object, you write the object name, followed by a period, followed by the name of the method. When the CLR calls your Main() method to begin running your application, it creates an object from your class and calls the Main() function on that object. If you were to write this code in C#, you might write something like the following:

```
MyClass MyObject;

MyObject = new MyClass();
MyObject.Main();
```

Objects are covered in detail in Chapters 8 and 9. The important item to note now is that the statement that calls Main() contains a *member access expression*, which contains an object, a period, and a function call.

In later chapters, you see that objects can have data as well as code. You can access the data by using the same member access expression syntax.

Calling methods with invocation expressions

You use invocation expressions to make a call to a method in an object. The code used in the member access case also shows an invocation expression. The code calls a method — Main(), in this case — which causes the code to invoke the Main() method on the object.

If you call a method from another method on the same object, you can use the name of the method in the call. You do not need to specify an object or class name, and the member access syntax is not necessary, as shown in Listing 4-1.

Listing 4-1: **Invocation Expression**

```
class MyClass
{
    public static void Main()
    {

        MyClass myclass = new MyClass();
myclass.DoWork();
    }

    void DoWork()
    {
        // do work here
    }
}
```

In this example, the Main() method calls a DoWork() method. However, first you need to create a reference to myClass and then invoke the DoWork() method.

The type of an invocation expression is the type returned by the function being called. If, for example, your C# code calls a function that returns an int type, the invocation expression that calls that method has a type of int.

Specifying array elements with element access expressions

Element access expressions enable you to specify array elements. You write the array element number within square brackets:

```
int [] MyArray;

MyArray = new int [5];
MyArray[0] = 123;
```

In this example, element zero of the array named MyArray is assigned a value of 123.

C# allows any expression resulting in type int, uint, long, or ulong to be used as the element expression. C# also allows the use of any expression whose result is of a type that can be implicitly converted into an int, uint, long, or ulong type. In the preceding code, an integer literal is used as the element expression. You could just as easily write a different kind of expression to specify the element, as shown in Listing 4-2.

Listing 4-2: **Element Access**

```
class MyClass
{
    public static void Main()
    {
        int [] MyArray;
        MyClass myclass = new MyClass();
        MyArray = new int [5];
        MyArray[myclass.GetArrayIndex()] = 123;
    }

    int GetArrayIndex()
    {
        return 0;
    }
}
```

This code works because the GetArrayIndex() method returns an int, and the result of the method invocation expression is an int. Because any expression whose value is an int can be used as an array element expression, C# allows this code to execute.

The result of the element access expression itself is the type of the element being accessed, as shown in the following code:

```
int [] MyArray;

MyArray = new int [5];
MyArray[0] = 123;
```

The MyArray[0] element access expression is of type int because the element being accessed in the expression is of type int.

Accessing objects with the this keyword

C# defines a this keyword that you can use to specify an object to a piece of code that needs access to that object. The this keyword is covered in more detail in the section that takes a look at classes. Listing 4-3 uses the this keyword.

Listing 4-3: Keyword Access

```
class MyClass
{
    public static void Main()
    {
      // call DoWork() on this object
      MyClass myclass = new MyClass();
      myclass.DoWork();
    }

    void DoWork()
    {
      MyClass myclass = new MyClass();
      this.DoWork2();
      // do work here
    }

    void DoWork2()
    {
    }
}
```

In this example, the this access expression has a type of MyClass because the MyClass class contains the code that contains the this access expression.

Accessing objects with the base keyword

C# also defines the `base` keyword for use with objects. In Chapter 8, you learn that you can use classes as a starting point to construct new classes. The original classes are called *base classes,* and the classes constructed from them are called *derived classes.*

To instruct your C# code in derived classes to access data in base classes, use the `base` keyword. The type for expressions using the `base` is the base class of the class containing the `base` keyword.

Using postfix increment and decrement operators

C# enables you to increment or decrement numeric values using special symbols. The ++ operator increments the value, and the – operator decrements the value. You can apply these operators to expressions of type `sbyte`, `byte`, `short`, `ushort`, `int`, `uint`, `long`, and `ulong`. Listing 4-4 illustrates the `increment` and `decrement` operators in use.

Listing 4-4: **Increment and Decrement Operators**

```
class MyClass
{
    public static void Main()
    {
        int MyInteger;

        MyInteger = 125;
        MyInteger++; // value is now 126
        MyInteger--; // value is now back to 125
    }
}
```

The type of an expression using the postfix increment and decrement operators matches the type whose value is being incremented or decremented. In Listing 4-4, the increment and decrement operators have a type of `int`.

Creating new reference types with the new operator

You use the `new` operator to create new instances of reference types. So far, the `new` operator has been used to create new arrays, and when you look at objects, you learn how the `new` operator is used to create new objects.

The new operator is considered an expression, and the type of the expression matches the type of variable being created with the new keyword.

Returning type information with the typeof operator

The typeof operator is a C# keyword that returns information about a type of a variable. You use it as if it were a function, using the typeof keyword and following it with an expression:

```
class MyClass
{
    public static void Main()
    {
        System.Console.WriteLine(typeof(int));
    }
}
```

The typeof keyword returns an object called System.Type describing the variable's type. The type of a typeof expression is the System.Type class.

Using the checked and unchecked operators

With the checked and unchecked operators, you can enable or disable runtime checking of your mathematical operations. If you include a mathematical operation in a checked operator, an error is reported if the operation doesn't make sense. If you include a mathematical operation in an unchecked operator, an error is reported even if the operation doesn't make sense.

Listing 4-5 demonstrates a mathematical overflow problem. It declares two integers, Int1 and Int2, and a third, Int1PlusInt2, whose value stores the sum of the other two. The two integers are added together and the result of the addition is stored in the third integer variable. The value of the third variable is then printed to the console.

Listing 4-5: **Overflow in Mathematical Operations**

```
class Listing4_5
{
    public static void Main()
    {
        int Int1;
        int Int2;
        int Int1PlusInt2;

        Int1 = 2000000000;
```

```
        Int2 = 2000000000;
        Int1PlusInt2 = Int1 + Int2;
        System.Console.WriteLine(Int1PlusInt2);
    }
}
```

The `Int1` and `Int2` integers each are assigned a value of two billion. This is not a problem because integer variables can store values just above 2.1 billion. However, adding these two integers together and storing the result in another integer is going to be a problem. The sum will be four billion, which is larger than the maximum integer value of just over 2.1 billion.

Compile the preceding code with the standard command line:

```
csc Listing4-1.cs
```

When you run Listing 4-1.exe, you get a large negative number, as shown in Figure 4-1.

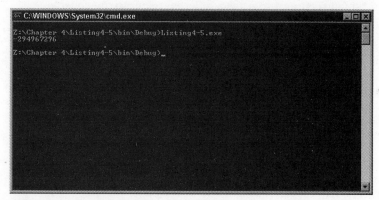

Figure 4-1: Overflows yield unpredictable results.

You get a negative number because of the way in which C# handles values that are too big to fit in the variables meant to hold them. C# couldn't represent the entire value in an integer, so it took the intended value, four billion, and subtracted the maximum value of a 32-bit value (4,294,967,296) from it, out putting the result to the console.

Obviously, your code has generated a result other than what you intended. If you're unaware of this sort of mathematical error, your code could behave unpredictably. To insert a measure of safety into code like this, you can use the `checked` operator, as shown in Listing 4-6.

**Listing 4-6: Checking for Overflow
                in Mathematical Operations**

```
class Listing4_6
{
  public static void Main()
  {
      int Int1;
      int Int2;
      int Int1PlusInt2;

      Int1 = 2000000000;
      Int2 = 2000000000;
      Int1PlusInt2 = checked(Int1 + Int2);
      System.Console.WriteLine(Int1PlusInt2);
  }
}
```

Compiling and running Listing 4-6 writes a different result to the console:

```
Exception occurred: System.OverflowException: An exception of
type System.OverflowException was thrown.
        at Listing4_1.Main()
```

Rather than writing a nonsensical mathematical value to the console, an overflow exception message lets you know that the value of the addition was checked for legality, and that the check failed the test. An exception is reported and the application terminates.

The unchecked() expression is the default case. Expressions marked with unchecked() are not checked for legal values, and the application continues running using the unchecked, nonsensical values.

The default behavior is not to check any operations. However, if you want to have all your operations checked for legal values without using the checked() operator in your code, you can use the /checked+ option to the compiler. Compile Listing 4-1 with the following command line:

```
csc /checked+ Listing4-1.cs
```

When you run the executable for Listing 4-1, you get the same exception message as you did with Listing 4-2, because the /checked+ option causes all mathematical operations to be checked for valid values.

Understanding Unary Expressions

Unary expressions operate on a single operand. C# supports the following unary expressions:

✦ Unary plus operator

✦ Unary minus operator

✦ Logical negation operator

✦ Bitwise complement operator

✦ Indirection operator

✦ Address operator

✦ Prefix increment and decrement operators

✦ Cast expressions

The following sections discuss these unary expressions in detail.

Returning operand values with the unary plus operator

The unary plus operator (+) returns the value of the operand. You can think of it as the *mathematical positive* operator. C# defines the unary plus operator for operands of type `int`, `uint`, `long`, `ulong`, `float`, `double`, and `decimal`.

Returning operand values with the unary minus operator

The unary minus operator (-) returns the value of the operand. You can think of it as the *mathematical negative* operator. The value of an operand with a unary minus operator is the operand's mathematical negative counterpart. C# defines the unary minus operator for operands of type `int`, `long`, `float`, `double`, and `decimal`.

Negating Boolean expressions with the logical negation operator

The logical negation operator negates the value of a Boolean expression. The operator changes `True` values to `False`, and changes `False` values to `True`.

Use the exclamation point to write a logical negation operator in your C# code. Place the operator before the Boolean expression you want to negate, as shown in Listing 4-7.

Listing 4-7: Logical Negation Operator

```
class MyClass
{
    public static void Main()
    {
        bool MyBoolean;

        MyBoolean = true;
        MyBoolean = !MyBoolean; // "MyBoolean" now false
    }
}
```

Understanding bitwise complement operator

C# enables you to apply a bitwise complement operation to `int`, `uint`, `long`, and `ulong` expressions. Bitwise complement operations view your value as if they are a binary, and flip all of the bits. Bits that had a value of 1 become 0, and bits that had a value of 0 become 1.

You specify bitwise complement operators by placing the tilde character (~) before the expression that should be bitwise complemented, as shown in Listing 4-8.

Listing 4-8: Bitwise Complement Operator

```
class MyClass
{
  public static void Main()
  {
      int Int1;

      Int1 = 123;
      Int1 = ~Int1;
  }
}
```

Prefixing increment and decrement operators

The postfix operators ++ and – operators can be used in one of two ways. You've already looked at the postfix versions of the operators, which appear after the expression. The prefix versions appear before the expression, as shown in Listing 4-9.

Listing 4-9: **Prefix Increment and Decrement Operators**

```
class MyClass
{
    public static void Main()
    {
        int MyInteger;

        MyInteger = 125;
        ++MyInteger; // value is now 126
        --MyInteger; // value is now back to 125
    }
}
```

The type of an expression using the prefix increment and decrement operators matches the type whose value is being incremented or decremented.

Note the subtle difference between these prefix operators and the postfix operators discussed previously: With the prefix operators, the value is changed before the expression is evaluated. With the postfix operators, the value is changed after the expression is evaluated. Listing 4-10 illustrates this difference.

Listing 4-10: **Differences Between Postfix and Prefix Operators**

```
class Listing4_10
{
    public static void Main()
    {
        int Int1;

        Int1 = 123;
        System.Console.WriteLine(Int1++);
            System.Console.WriteLine(++Int1);
    }
}
```

Compile and run Listing 4-3. The output from this application is shown in Figure 4-2.

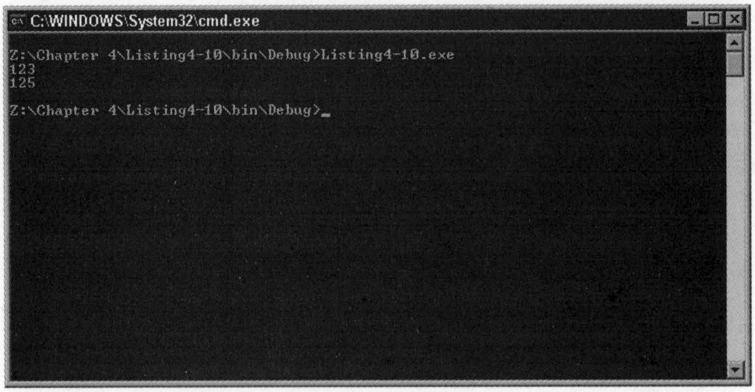

Figure 4-2: Postfix and prefix operator usage

The first statement in Listing 4-10 uses the postfix increment operator, which means that the value increments after the statement executes. The application writes the current value, 123, to the console and then increments the value to 124. The second statement uses the prefix increment operator, which means that the value is incremented before the statement executes. The application first increments the current value to 125 and then writes the current value to the console.

Understanding Arithmetic Operators

Arithmetic operators enable you to perform arithmetic in your C# code. Expressions that use arithmetic operators are binary expressions because two operands are required to perform a mathematical operation.

Assigning new values with the assignment operator

The assignment operator assigns a new value to a variable. The equals sign is used as the assignment operator:

```
MyInteger = 3;
```

The value of MyInteger is set to 3, and the previous value of MyVariable is lost.

Compound assignment operators enable you to use the assignment operator more than once in a statement:

```
MyInteger = MyOtherInteger = 3;
```

The value of the rightmost expression is used as the new value for the variables. In this example, both `MyInteger` and `MyOtherInteger` are given a new value of 3.

Using the multiplication operator

The value of an expression using the `multiplication` operator is the product of the values of the two operators. The asterisk character is used as the `multiplication` operator, as shown in Listing 4-11.

Listing 4-11: **Multiplication Operator**

```
class MyClass
{
    public static void Main()
    {
        int MyInteger;

        MyInteger = 3 * 6; // MyInteger will be 18
    }
}
```

If you are multiplying a value to a variable and placing the result in the same variable, you can write a shortcut statement to perform the multiplication. Writing an asterisk followed by an equals sign multiplies a value to a variable, and updates the variable's value with the result:

```
MyInteger *= 3;
```

This statement is shorthand for the following:

```
MyInteger = MyInteger * 3;
```

Using the division operator

The value of an expression using the `division` operator is the product of the values of the two operators. The forward slash character is used as the `division` operator, as shown in Listing 4-12.

Listing 4-12: **Division Operator (Example 1)**

```
class MyClass
{
    public static void Main()
    {
        int MyInteger;

        MyInteger = 6 / 3; // MyInteger will be 2
    }
}
```

If the division operation results in a remainder, only the quotient itself is the result of the operation (see Listing 4-13).

Listing 4-13: **Division Operator (Example 2)**

```
class MyClass
{
    public static void Main()
    {
        int MyInteger;

        MyInteger = 7 / 3;
    }
}
```

When this code is executed, the MyInteger variable has a value of 2, because dividing 7 by 3 results in a quotient of 2 and a remainder of 1.

If you are dividing a value into a variable and placing the result in the same variable, you can write a shortcut statement to perform the division. Writing a forward slash character followed by an equals sign divides a value into a variable, and updates the variable's value with the result:

```
MyInteger /= 3;
```

The preceding statement is shorthand for the following:

```
MyInteger = MyInteger / 3;
```

Using the remainder operator

The value of an expression using the `remainder` operator is the remainder of a division operation. The percent character is used as the `division` operator (see Listing 4-14).

Listing 4-14: **Remainder Operator**

```
class MyClass
{
    public static void Main()
    {
        int MyInteger;

        MyInteger = 7 % 3;
    }
}
```

When this code is executed, the `MyInteger` variable has value of 1, because dividing 7 by 3 results in a quotient of 2 and a remainder of 1.

If you are calculating a remainder using a variable and placing the result in the same variable, you can write a shortcut statement to perform the remainder operation. Writing a percent sign followed by an equals sign calculates the remainder from a variable and updates the variable's value with the result:

```
MyInteger %= 3;
```

The preceding statement is shorthand for the following:

```
MyInteger = MyInteger % 3;
```

Using the addition operator

The value of an expression using the `addition` operator is the sum of the values of the two operators. The plus character is used as the `multiplication` operator (see Listing 4-15).

Listing 4-15: **Addition Operator**

```
class MyClass
{
    public static void Main()
```

Continued

Listing 4-15 *(continued)*

```
    {
        int MyInteger;

        MyInteger = 3 + 6; // MyInteger will be 9
    }
}
```

If you are adding a value to a variable and placing the result in the same variable, you can write a shortcut statement to perform the addition. Writing a plus sign followed by an equals sign adds a value to a variable and updates the variable's value with the result:

```
MyInteger += 3;
```

The preceding statement is shorthand for the following:

```
MyInteger = MyInteger + 3;
```

The `addition` operator has special meaning when the two operands are strings. Adding two strings together concatenates the first string with the second string:

```
string CombinedString = "Hello from " + "C#";
```

The value of `CombinedString` is `Hello from C#` when this code is executed.

Using the subtraction operator

The value of an expression using the `subtraction` operator is the difference of the values of the two operators. The hyphen character is used as the `subtraction` operator (see Listing 4-16).

Listing 4-16: Subtraction Operator

```
class MyClass
{
    public static void Main()
    {
        int MyInteger;

        MyInteger = 7 - 3; // MyInteger will be 4
    }
}
```

If you are subtracting a value from a variable and placing the result in the same variable, you can write a shortcut statement to perform the subtraction. Writing a minus sign followed by an equals sign subtracts a value from a variable and updates the variable's value with the result:

```
MyInteger -= 3;
```

The preceding statement is shorthand for the following:

```
MyInteger = MyInteger - 3;
```

Understanding Shift Operators

Shift operators enable you to move bits around in a value in your C# code. Expressions that use shift operators are binary expressions because two operands are required to perform a shift operation.

Moving bits with the shift-left operator

The value of an expression using the `shift-left` operator moves bits left by a specific amount. Two less-than characters (<<) are used as the `shift-left` operator (see Listing 4-17).

Listing 4-17: **Shift-Left Operator**

```
class MyClass
{
    public static void Main()
    {
        int MyInteger;

        MyInteger = 6 << 3;
    }
}
```

When this code executes, the `MyInteger` variable has a value of 48, because the original value, 6, is viewed as a binary number with a binary value of 00000110. Each bit in the original value is shifted three places, which is the value shown after the shift left operator, and zeros are placed in the low bits. Shifting each bit three places gives a binary value of 00110000, or 48 decimal.

Expressions of type `int`, `uint`, `long`, and `ulong` can have left shifts applied to their values. Other expressions that can be converted to one of those types can be left shifted as well. Expressions of type `int` and `uint` can be shifted up to 32 bits at a time. Expressions of type `long` and `ulong` can be shifted up to 64 bits at a time.

If you are calculating a left-shift operation on a value and a variable and placing the result in the same variable, you can write a shortcut statement to perform the left-shift operation. Writing two less-than signs followed by an equals sign calculates the left-shift operation on a variable and a value and updates the variable's value with the result:

```
MyInteger <<= 3;
```

The preceding statement is shorthand for the following:

```
MyInteger = MyInteger << 3;
```

Moving bits with the shift-right operator

The value of an expression using the shift-right operator moves bits right by a specific amount. Two greater-than characters (>>) are used as the shift-right operator (see Listing 4-18).

Listing 4-18: **Shift-Right Operator**

```
class MyClass
{
    public static void Main()
    {
        int MyInteger;

        MyInteger = 48 >> 3;
    }
}
```

When this code executes, the MyInteger variable has a value of 6 because the original value, 48, is viewed as a binary number with a binary value of 00110000. Each bit in the original value is shifted three places, which is the value shown after the shift right operator, and zeros are placed in the high bits. Shifting each bit three places gives a binary value of 00000110, or 6 decimal.

Expressions of type int, uint, long, and ulong can have right shifts applied to their values. Other expressions that can be converted to one of those types can be right shifted as well. Expressions of type int and uint can be shifted up to 32 bits at a time. Expressions of type long and ulong can be shifted up to 64 bits at a time.

If you are calculating a right-shift operation on a value and a variable and placing the result in the same variable, you can write a shortcut statement to perform the right-shift operation. Writing two greater-than signs followed by an equals sign calculates the right shift operation on a variable and a value and updates the variable's value with the result:

```
MyInteger >>= 3;
```

The preceding statement is shorthand for the following:

```
MyInteger = MyInteger >> 3;
```

Comparing expressions with relational operators

Relational operators enable you to compare two expressions and obtain a Boolean value that specifies the relation between the two expressions. Expressions that use relational operators are binary expressions because two operands are required to perform a relational operation.

Testing for equality with the equality operator

The equality operator is used to test the values of two expressions for equality. If the expressions have the same value, the equality operator evaluates to True; if they are unequal, the equality operator evaluates to False. Two equals signs are used as the equality operator:

```
MyInteger == 123;
```

If the value of the MyInteger variable is 123, the equality operator evaluates to True. If it has any other value, the equality operator evaluates to False.

The equality operator has special meaning when the two operands are strings. Comparing two strings compares the string's contents. Two strings are considered equal if they have identical lengths and identical characters in each position of the string.

Testing for inequality with the inequality operator

The inequality operator is used to test the values of two expressions for inequality. If the expressions have different values, the inequality operator evaluates to True. If they are equal, the inequality operator evaluates to False. An exclamation point followed by an equals sign is used as the inequality operator:

```
MyInteger != 123;
```

If the value of the MyInteger variable is 123, the inequality operator evaluates to False. If it has any other value, the inequality operator evaluates to True.

The inequality operator has special meaning when the two operands are strings. Comparing two strings compares the string's contents. Two strings are considered unequal if they have different lengths or if they have different characters in at least one position of the string.

Testing values with the less-than operator

The less-than operator is used to test the values of two expressions to see if one value is less than the other value. If the first expression has a value less than the value of the second expression, the less-than operator evaluates to True. If the first expression has a value greater than or equal to the value of the second expression, the less-than operator evaluates to False. A less-than sign (<) is used as the less-than operator:

```
MyInteger < 123;
```

If the value of the MyInteger variable is less than 123, the less-than operator evaluates to True. If it has a value greater than or equal to 123, the less-than operator evaluates to False.

Testing values with the greater-than operator

The greater-than operator is used to test the values of two expressions to see whether one value is greater than the other value. If the first expression has a value greater than the second expression's value, the greater-than operator evaluates to True. If the first expression has a value less than or equal to the second expression's value, the greater-than operator evaluates to False. A greater-than sign (>) is used as the greater-than operator:

```
MyInteger > 123;
```

If the value of the MyInteger variable is greater than 123, the greater-than operator evaluates to True. If it has a value less than or equal to 123, the greater-than operator evaluates to False.

Testing values with the less-than-or-equal-to operator

The less-than-or-equal-to operator is used to test the values of two expressions to see whether one value is less than or equal to the other value. If the first expression has a value less than or equal to the value of the second expression, the less-than-or-equal-to operator evaluates to True. If the first expression has a value greater than the value of the second expression, the less-than-or-equal-to operator evaluates to False. A less-than sign followed by an equals sign is used as the less-than-or-equal-to operator:

```
MyInteger <= 123;
```

If the value of the MyInteger variable is less than or equal to 123, the less-than-or-equal-to operator evaluates to True. If it has a value greater than 123, the less-than-or-equal-to operator evaluates to False.

Testing values with the greater-than-or-equal-to operator

The `greater-than-or-equal-to` operator is used to test the values of two expressions to see if one value is greater than or equal to the other value. If the first expression has a value greater than or equal to the value of the second expression, the `greater-than-or-equal-to` operator evaluates to `True`. If the first expression has a value less than the value of the second expression, the `greater-than-or-equal-to` operator evaluates to `False`. A greater-than sign followed by an equals sign is used as the `greater-than-or-equal-to` operator:

```
MyInteger >= 123;
```

If the value of the `MyInteger` variable is greater than or equal to 123, the `greater-than-or-equal-to` operator evaluates to `True`. If it has a value less than 123, the `greater-than-or-equal-to` operator evaluates to `False`.

Understanding Integer Logical Operators

Integer logical operators enable you to perform Boolean arithmetic on two numeric values. Expressions that use integer logical operators are binary expressions because two operands are required to perform a logical operation.

Computing Boolean values with the AND operator

The `AND` operator is used to compute the Boolean `AND` value of two expressions. The ampersand sign (&) is used as the `AND` operator:

```
MyInteger = 6 & 3;
```

The value of `MyInteger` is 2. Recall that a bit in an `AND` operation is 1 only if the two operand bits in the same position are 1. The value of 6 in binary is 110, and the value of 3 in binary is 011. Performing a Boolean `AND` of 110 and 011 results in a Boolean value of 010, or 2 in decimal.

If you are calculating an `AND` operation on a value and a variable and placing the result in the same variable, you can write a shortcut statement to perform the `AND` operation. Writing an ampersand character followed by an equals sign calculates the `AND` operation on a variable and a value, and updates the variable's value with the result:

```
MyInteger &= 3;
```

The preceding statement is shorthand for the following:

```
MyInteger = MyInteger & 3;
```

Computing Boolean values with the exclusive OR operator

The exclusive OR operator is used to compute the Boolean exclusive OR value of two expressions. The caret sign (^) is used as the exclusive OR operator:

```
MyInteger = 6 ^ 3;
```

The value of MyInteger is 5. Recall that a bit in an exclusive OR operation is 1 only if one of the two operand bits in the same position is 1. The value of 6 in binary is 110, and the value of 3 in binary is 011. Performing a Boolean exclusive OR of 110 and 011 results in a Boolean value of 101, or 5 in decimal.

If you are calculating an exclusive OR operation on a value and a variable and placing the result in the same variable, you can write a shortcut statement to perform the exclusive OR operation. Writing a caret sign followed by an equals sign calculates the exclusive OR operation on a variable and a value, and updates the variable's value with the result:

```
MyInteger ^= 3;
```

The preceding statement is shorthand for the following:

```
MyInteger = MyInteger ^ 3;
```

Computing Boolean values with the OR operator

The OR operator is used to compute the Boolean OR value of two expressions. The pipe character (|) is used as the OR operator:

```
MyInteger = 6 | 3;
```

The value of MyInteger is 7. Recall that a bit in an OR operation is 1 only if one or both of the two operand bits in the same position are 1. The value of 6 in binary is 110, and the value of 3 in binary is 011. Performing a Boolean OR of 110 and 011 results in a Boolean value of 111, or 7 in decimal.

If you are calculating an OR operation on a value and a variable and placing the result in the same variable, you can write a shortcut statement to perform the OR operation. Writing an ampersand character followed by an equals sign calculates the OR operation on a variable and a value, and updates the variable's value with the result:

```
MyInteger |= 3;
```

The preceding statement is shorthand for the following:

```
MyInteger = MyInteger | 3;
```

Understanding Conditional Logic Operators

Conditional logic operators are the conditional counterparts of the integer logical operators. Expressions that use conditional logical operators are binary expressions because two operands are required to perform a conditional logic operation.

Comparing Boolean values with the conditional AND operator

The `conditional AND` operator is used to compare two Boolean expressions. The result of the operation is `True` if both of the operands evaluate to `True`, and `False` if one or both of the operands evaluate to `False`. Two ampersand signs are used as the `conditional AND` operator:

```
MyBoolean = true && false;
```

The value of `MyBoolean` is `False` because one of the operands evaluates to `False`.

Comparing Boolean values with the conditional OR operator

The `conditional OR` operator is used to compare two Boolean expressions. The result of the operation is `True` if one or both of the operands evaluate to `True`, and `False` if both of the operands evaluate to `False`. Two pipe characters are used as the `conditional OR` operator:

```
MyBoolean = true || false;
```

The value of `MyBoolean` is `True` because one of the operands evaluates to `True`.

Comparing Boolean values with the conditional logic operator

The `conditional logic` operator evaluates a Boolean expression. The result of the expression has one value if the input expression evaluates to `True` and another if the input expression evaluates to `False`. Expressions that use conditional operators are tertiary expressions because three operands are required to perform a conditional logic operation. The conditional operator is the only tertiary expression supported in the C# language.

Writing a conditional operator involves writing the input expression, followed by a question mark. The `True` value comes next, followed by a colon, followed by the `False` value:

```
MyInteger = (MyVariable == 123) ? 3: 5;
```

You can read this statement as "Compare the value of `MyVariable` with 123. If that expression evaluates to `True`, set the value of `MyInteger` to 3. If that expression evaluates to `False`, set the value of `MyInteger` to 5."

Understanding the Order of Operations

C# enables you to place multiple operators in a single statement:

```
MyVariable = 3 * 2 + 1;
```

What is the value of `MyVariable` here? If C# applies the multiplication first, it reads the statement as "multiply 3 and 2 and then add 1," which results in a value of 7. If C# applies the addition first, it reads the statement as "add 2 and 1, and then multiply by 3," which results in a value of 9.

C# combines operators into groups and applies an order of precedence to each group. This order of precedence specifies which operators are evaluated before the others. The C# order of precedence list is as follows, listed in order from highest precedence to lowest precedence:

- ✦ Primary expressions
- ✦ Unary operators + - ! ~ ++ –
- ✦ Multiplicative operators * / %
- ✦ Additive operators + -
- ✦ Shift operators << >>
- ✦ Relational operators < > <= >=
- ✦ Equality operators == !=
- ✦ Logical AND
- ✦ Logical exclusive OR
- ✦ Logical OR
- ✦ Conditional AND
- ✦ Conditional OR
- ✦ Conditional tertiary
- ✦ Assignment operators

Take another look at the following statement:

```
MyVariable = 3 * 2 + 1
```

C# gives `MyVariable` a value of 7 because the `multiplication` operator has a higher precedence than the `addition` operator. This means that the `multiplication` operator is evaluated first, and the `addition` operator second.

You can override the order of precedence with parentheses. Expressions in parentheses are evaluated before the operator precedence rules are applied:

```
MyVariable = 3 * (2 + 1)
```

In this case, C# gives `MyVariable` a value of 9, because the addition expression is enclosed in parentheses, forcing it to be evaluated before the multiplication operation is evaluated.

Summary

C# defines many operators to help you evaluate your expressions and calculate new values from those operations. The language enables you to write expressions that perform mathematical functions and Boolean operations, and compare two expressions and obtain a Boolean result from the comparison.

In this chapter, you were introduced to the C# operators and you learned how to use those operators in expressions with literals and variables. You also reviewed operator expressions and the precedence of using these operators in expressions. When you examine classes in Chapter 8, you will find that your classes can redefine some of these operators. This is called *operator overloading,* and it enables you to redefine how the operators calculate their results.

✦   ✦   ✦

Controlling the Flow of Your Code

The behavior of your C# code often depends on conditions that are determined at runtime. You may want to
write an application that greets its users with a message of
"Good morning" if the current time is before 12:00 P.M., for
example; or "Good afternoon" if the current time is between
12:00 P.M. and 6:00 P.M.

Behavior like this requires that your C# code examine values
at runtime and take an action based on the values. C# supports a variety of code constructs that enable you to examine
variables and perform one or many actions based upon those
variables. This chapter looks at the C# flow control statements
that will act as the brains for the applications you write.

Statements in C#

A *statement* is a valid C# expression that defines an action
taken by your code. Statements can examine variable values,
set new values into a variable, call methods, perform an operation, create objects, or take some other action.

The shortest possible statement in C# is the *empty statement*.
The empty statement consists of only the semicolon:

```
;
```

You can use the empty statement to say, "Do nothing here."
This may not seem too useful, but it does have its place.

Note   All statements in C# end with a semicolon.

Statements are grouped into *statement lists*. Statement lists consist of one or more statements written in sequence:

```
int MyVariable;

MyVariable = 123;
MyVariable += 234;
```

Usually, statements are written on their own line. However, C# does not require this layout. C# ignores any whitespace between statements and accepts any layout as long as each statement is separated by a semicolon:

```
int MyVariable;

MyVariable = 123; MyVariable += 234;
```

Statement lists are enclosed in curly brackets. A statement list enclosed in curly brackets is called a *statement block*. You use statement blocks most often when you write code for a function. The entire statement list for the function is enclosed in a statement block. It is perfectly legal to use only one statement in a statement block:

```
public static void Main()
{
    System.Console.WriteLine("Hello!");
}
```

C# does not impose any limit on the number of statements that you can place in a statement block.

Using statements to delcare local variables

Declaration statements declare local variables in your code. You've seen many examples of this kind of statement already. Declaration statements specify a type and a name for a local variable:

```
int MyVariable;
```

You can also initialize the variable when you declare it by using an equals sign and assigning a value to the variable:

```
int MyVariable = 123;
```

C# allows you to list multiple variables in the same statement. Use commas to separate the variable names:

```
int MyFirstVariable, MySecondVariable;
```

Each variable in the statement has the specified type. In the preceding example, both the MyFirstVariable and MySecondVariable are of type int.

Constant declarations define a variable whose value cannot change during the execution of the code. Constant declarations use the C# keyword `const` and must assign a value to the variable when the variable is declared:

```
const int MyVariable = 123;
```

The benefits of constant declarations include readability and code management. You may have constant values in your code, and assigning them names makes your code more readable than if their value were used. In addition, using values throughout your code poses a tedious task should these values need to be changed. When a constant is used, you need to change only one line of code. For example, suppose you're writing code for an application that performs geometric measurements. One of the values that you'll want to work with is pi, the ratio of a circle's circumference to its diameter. Without a constant declaration, you may be writing code like the following:

```
Area = 3.14159 * Radius * Radius;
```

Using a constant expression makes the code a bit easier to understand:

```
const double Pi = 3.14159;

Area = Pi * Radius * Radius;
```

This is especially useful if you're using the value of pi many times in your code.

Using selection statements to select your code's path

Selection statements select one of several possible code paths for execution. The selected code path is based on the value of an expression.

The if statement

The `if` statement works with an expression that evaluates to a Boolean value. If the Boolean expression evaluates to `true`, the statement embedded in the `if` statement is executed. If the Boolean expression evaluates to `false`, the statement embedded in the `if` statement is not executed:

```
if(MyVariable == 123)
    System.Console.WriteLine("MyVariable's value is 123.");
```

The Boolean expression is enclosed in parentheses. The embedded statement follows the parentheses. A semicolon is used to close the embedded statement, but not the Boolean expression.

Note

When you use the `if` statement to check for equality, you must always use two equals signs. Two equals signs check for equality, whereas one equals sign performs an assignment. If you accidentally use one equals sign within an `if` statement, the `if` statement will always return a `true` condition.

In the preceding example, the value of MyVariable is compared to the literal value 123. If the value is equal to 123, the expression evaluates to true and the message MyVariable's value is 123. is written to the console. If the value is not equal to 123, the expression evaluates to false and nothing is printed to the console.

The if statement can be followed by an else clause. The else keyword is followed by an embedded statement that is executed if the Boolean expression used in the if clause evaluates to false:

```
if(MyVariable == 123)
    System.Console.WriteLine("MyVariable's value is 123.");
else
    System.Console.WriteLine("MyVariable's value is not 123.");
```

In the preceding example, the value of MyVariable is compared to the literal value 123. If the value is equal to 123, the expression evaluates to true and the message MyVariable's value is 123. is written to the console. If the value is not equal to 123, the expression evaluates to false and the message MyVariable's value is not 123. is written to the console.

The else clause can be followed by an if clause of its own:

```
if(MyVariable == 123)
    System.Console.WriteLine("MyVariable's value is 123.");
else if(MyVariable == 124)
    System.Console.WriteLine("MyVariable's value is 124.");
else
    System.Console.WriteLine("MyVariable's value is not 123.");
```

The if and else clauses enable you to associate a statement with the clause. Ordinarily, C# enables you to associate only a single statement with the clause, as shown in the following code:

```
if(MyVariable == 123)
    System.Console.WriteLine("MyVariable's value is 123.");
System.Console.WriteLine("This always prints.");
```

The statement that writes This always prints. to the console always executes. It does not belong to the if clause and executes regardless of whether the value of MyVariable is 123. The only statement that is dependent on the comparison of MyVariable to 123 is the statement that writes MyVariable's value is 123. to the console. If you want to associate multiple statements with an if clause, use a statement block:

```
if(MyVariable == 123)
{
    System.Console.WriteLine("MyVariable's value is 123.");
    System.Console.WriteLine("This prints if MyVariable ==
123.");
}
```

You can also use statement blocks in `else` clauses:

```
if(MyVariable == 123)
{
    System.Console.WriteLine("MyVariable's value is 123.");
    System.Console.WriteLine("This prints if MyVariable ==
123.");
}
else
{
    System.Console.WriteLine("MyVariable's value is not 123.");
    System.Console.WriteLine("This prints if MyVariable !=
123.");
}
```

Because statement blocks can enclose a single statement, the following code is also legal:

```
if(MyVariable == 123)
{
    System.Console.WriteLine("MyVariable's value is 123.");
}
```

The switch statement

The `switch` statement evaluates an expression and compares the expression's value to a variety of cases. Each case is associated with a statement list, called a *switch section*. C# executes the statement list associated with the switch section matching the expression's value.

The expression used as the driver for the `switch` statement is enclosed in parentheses that follow the `switch` keyword. Curly brackets follow the expression, and the switch sections are enclosed in the curly brackets:

```
switch(MyVariable)
{
    // switch sections are placed here
}
```

The expression used in the `switch` statement must evaluate to one of the following types:

  ✦ `sbyte`

  ✦ `byte`

  ✦ `short`

  ✦ `ushort`

  ✦ `int`

  ✦ `uint`

✦ long

✦ ulong

✦ char

✦ string

You can also use an expression whose value can be implicitly converted to one of the types in the preceding list.

Switch sections start with the C# keyword case, which is followed by a constant expression. A colon follows the constant expression, and the statement list follows the colon:

```
switch(MyVariable)
{
    case 123:
        System.Console.WriteLine("MyVariable == 123");
        break;
}
```

The break keyword signals the end of your statement block.

C# evaluates the expression in the switch statement and then looks for a switch block whose constant expression matches the expression's value. If C# can find a matching value in one of the switch sections, the statement list for the switch section executes.

A switch statement can include many switch sections, each having a different case:

```
switch(MyVariable)
{
    case 123:
        System.Console.WriteLine("MyVariable == 123");
        break;
    case 124:
        System.Console.WriteLine("MyVariable == 124");
        break;
    case 125:
        System.Console.WriteLine("MyVariable == 125");
        break;
}
```

C# enables you to group multiple case labels together. If you have more than one case that needs to execute the same statement list, you can combine the case labels:

```
switch(MyVariable)
{
    case 123:
    case 124:
```

```
            System.Console.WriteLine("MyVariable == 123 or 124");
            break;
        case 125:
            System.Console.WriteLine("MyVariable == 125");
            break;
    }
```

One of the case labels can be the C# keyword `default`. The `default` label can include its own statement list:

```
    switch(MyVariable)
    {
        case 123:
            System.Console.WriteLine("MyVariable == 123");
            break;
        default:
            System.Console.WriteLine("MyVariable != 123");
            break;
    }
```

The `default` statement list executes when none of the other switch sections define constants that match the `switch` expression. The `default` statement list is the catchall that says, "If you can't find a matching switch block, execute this default code." Using the `default` keyword is optional in your `switch` statements.

Using iteration statements to execute embedded statements

Iteration statements execute embedded statements multiple times. The expression associated with the iteration statements controls the number of times that an embedded statement executes.

The while statement

The `while` statement executes an embedded statement list as long as the `while` expression evaluates to `true`. The Boolean expression that controls the `while` statement is enclosed in parentheses that follow the `while` keyword. The statements to be executed while the Boolean expression evaluates to `true` follow the parentheses:

```
    int MyVariable = 0;

    while(MyVariable < 10)
    {
        System.Console.WriteLine(MyVariable);
        MyVariable++;
    }
```

This code prints the following to the console:

```
0
1
2
3
4
5
6
7
8
9
```

The code embedded in the while statement continues to be executed as long as the value of MyVariable is less than 10. The embedded statements print the value of MyVariable to the console and then increment its value. When the value of MyVariable reaches 10, the Boolean expression MyVariable < 10 evaluates to false and the statement list embedded in the while statement no longer executes. The statement following the while statement is executed as soon as the while statement's Boolean expression evaluates to false.

The do statement

The while statement executes its embedded statements zero or more times. If the Boolean expression used in the while statement evaluates to false, none of the embedded statements execute:

```
int MyVariable = 100;

while(MyVariable < 10)
{
    System.Console.WriteLine(MyVariable);
    MyVariable++;
}
```

This code does not print anything to the console because the Boolean expression used in the while statement, MyVariable < 10, evaluates to false the first time it executes. Because the Boolean expression evaluates to false right away, the embedded statements are never executed.

If you want to ensure that the embedded statements are executed at least once, you can use a do statement. The do statement is followed by embedded statements, which are followed by a while keyword. The Boolean expression that controls the number of times that the loop executes follows the while keyword:

```
int MyVariable = 0;

do
{
    System.Console.WriteLine(MyVariable);
    MyVariable++;
```

```
}
while(MyVariable < 10);
```

This code prints the following to the console:

```
0
1
2
3
4
5
6
7
8
9
```

The embedded statements always execute at least once, because the Boolean expression is evaluated after the embedded statements execute, as shown in the following code:

```
int MyVariable = 100;

do
{
    System.Console.WriteLine(MyVariable);
    MyVariable++;
}
while(MyVariable < 10);
```

This code prints the following to the console:

```
100
```

The for statement

The for statement is the most powerful of the iteration statements. The control code in a for statement is in three parts:

✦ An *initializer*, which sets the starting conditions of the for statement loop

✦ A *condition*, which specifies the Boolean expression that keeps the for statement executing

✦ An *iterator*, which specifies statements that are executed at the end of every pass through the embedded statements

The for statement begins with the for keyword, followed by parentheses. The parentheses contain the initializer, the condition, and the iterator statements, all separated by semicolons. The embedded statements follow the parentheses.

Take a look at the following simple `for` loop:

```
int MyVariable;

for(MyVariable = 0; MyVariable < 10; MyVariable++)
{
    System.Console.WriteLine(MyVariable);
}
```

The initializer in this `for` loop is the statement `MyVariable = 0`. The initializer executes only once in a `for` loop and executes before the embedded statements execute for the first time.

The condition in this `for` loop is the statement `MyVariable < 10`. The condition in a `for` loop must be a Boolean expression. The embedded statements in a `for` loop are executed as long as this Boolean expression evaluates to `true`. When the expression evaluates to `false`, the embedded statements no longer execute.

The iterator in this `for` loop is the statement `MyVariable++`. The iterator executes after each pass through the embedded statements in the `for` loop.

When you put all this information together, you can read the `for` statement as follows: "Set `MyVariable` equal to zero. As long as the value of `MyVariable` is less than 10, write the value to the console and then increment the value of `MyVariable`". These instructions print the following to the console:

```
0
1
2
3
4
5
6
7
8
9
```

The initializer, the condition, and the iterator in a `for` loop are all optional. If you choose not to use one of the parts, just write a semicolon without specifying the statement. The following code is logically equivalent to the preceding code:

```
int MyVariable = 0;

for(; MyVariable < 10; MyVariable++)
{
    System.Console.WriteLine(MyVariable);
}
```

This code is also equivalent to the original code:

```
int MyVariable;

for(MyVariable = 0; MyVariable < 10; )
{
    System.Console.WriteLine(MyVariable);
MyVariable++;
}
```

Use caution when omitting the condition section of the `for` loop. The following code illustrates the problems that can arise from leaving out conditions:

```
int MyVariable;

for(MyVariable = 0; ; MyVariable++)
{
    System.Console.WriteLine(MyVariable);
}
```

This code runs until `MyVariable` eventually causes an error because it contains a number too large to store. This occurs because no condition in the `for` loop eventually evaluates to `false`, which allows the variable to increment until it exceeds its limitations. Missing conditions evaluate to `true` in a `for` loop. Because the condition in the preceding code example is always `true`, it never evaluates to `false` and the `for` statement never stops executing its embedded statement.

The initializer, condition, and iterator expressions can contain multiple statements, separated by commas. The following code is legal:

```
int MyFirstVariable;
int MySecondVariable;

for(MyFirstVariable = 0, MySecondVariable = 0;
    MyFirstVariable < 10;
    MyFirstVariable++, MySecondVariable++)
{
    System.Console.WriteLine(MyFirstVariable);
    System.Console.WriteLine(MySecondVariable);
}
```

The foreach statement

You can use the `foreach` statement to iterate over the elements in a collection. Arrays in C# support the `foreach` statement, and you can use the `foreach` statement to work easily with each element in the array.

Use the `foreach` statement by typing the `foreach` keyword, followed by parentheses. The parentheses must contain the following information:

✦ The type of the element in the collection

✦ An identifier name for an element in the collection

✦ The keyword `in`

✦ The identifier of the collection

Embedded statements follow the parentheses.

Listing 5-1 shows the `foreach` statement in action. It creates a five-element integer array and then uses the `foreach` statement to visit each element in the array and write its value to the console.

Listing 5-1: Using the foreach Statement

```
class Listing5_1
{
  public static void Main()
  {
        int [] MyArray;

        MyArray = new int [5];
        MyArray[0] = 0;
        MyArray[1] = 1;
        MyArray[2] = 2;
        MyArray[3] = 3;
        MyArray[4] = 4;

        foreach(int ArrayElement in MyArray)
            System.Console.WriteLine(ArrayElement);
  }
}
```

The `ArrayElement` identifier is a variable defined in the `foreach` loop. It contains the value of an element in the array. The `foreach` loop visits every element in the array, which is handy when you need to work with each element in an array without having to know the size of the array.

Using jump statements to move around in your code

Jump statements jump to a specific piece of code. Jump statements always execute and are not controlled by any Boolean expressions.

The break statement

You saw the `break` statement in the section about `switch` statements. C# also enables you to use the `break` statement to break out of the current block of statements. Usually, the `break` statement is used to break out of an iteration statement block:

```
int MyVariable = 0;

while(MyVariable < 10)
{
    System.Console.WriteLine(MyVariable);
    if(MyVariable == 5)
        break;
    MyVariable++;
}
System.Console.WriteLine("Out of the loop.");
```

The preceding code prints the following to the console:

```
0
1
2
3
4
Out of the loop.
```

The code reads: "If the value of MyVariable is 5, break out of the while loop."
When the break statement executes, C# transfers control to the statement following an iteration statement's embedded statements. The break statement is usually
used in switch, while, do, for, and foreach statement blocks.

The continue statement

The continue statement returns control to the Boolean expression that controls an
iteration statement, as shown in the following code:

```
int MyVariable;

for(MyVariable = 0; MyVariable < 10; MyVariable++)
{
    if(MyVariable == 5)
        continue;
    System.Console.WriteLine(MyVariable);
}
```

The preceding code prints the following to the console:

```
0
1
2
3
4
6
7
8
9
```

This code reads: "If the value of `MyVariable` is 5, continue to the next iteration of the `for` loop without executing any other embedded statements." This is why 5 is missing from the output. When the value of `MyVariable` is 5, control returns to the top of the `for` loop and the call to `WriteLine()` is never made for that iteration of the `for` loop.

Like the `break` statement, the `continue` statement is usually used in `switch`, `while`, `do`, `for`, and `foreach` statement blocks.

The goto statement

The `goto` statement unconditionally transfers control to a labeled statement. You can label any statement in C#. Statement labels are identifiers that precede a statement. A colon follows a statement label. A label identifier follows the `goto` keyword, and the `goto` statement transfers control to the statement named by the label identifier, as shown in the following code:

```
int MyVariable = 0;

while(MyVariable < 10)
{
    System.Console.WriteLine(MyVariable);
    if(MyVariable == 5)
        goto Done;
    MyVariable++;
}
Done: System.Console.WriteLine("Out of the loop.");
```

The preceding code prints the following to the console:

```
0
1
2
3
4
Out of the loop.
```

When the value of `MyVariable` is 5, the `goto` statement executes and control transfers to the statement with a label of `Done`. The `goto` statement always executes, regardless of any iteration statements that may be executing.

You can also use the `goto` keyword in conjunction with the case labels in a `switch` statement, instead of the `break` statement:

```
switch(MyVariable)
{
    case 123:
        System.Console.WriteLine("MyVariable == 123");
        goto case 124;
```

```
    case 124:
        System.Console.WriteLine("MyVariable == 124");
        break;
}
```

Note   Using the `goto` statement in a lot of places can make for confusing, unreadable code. The best practice is to avoid using a `goto` statement if at all possible. Try to restructure your code so that you don't need to use any `goto` statements.

Using statements to perform mathematical calculations safely

You've already seen how the `checked` and `unchecked` keywords can control the behavior of error conditions in your mathematical expressions. You can also use these keywords as statements that control the safety of mathematical operations. Use the keywords before a block of statements that should be affected by the `checked` or `unchecked` keywords, as in the following code:

```
checked
{
    Int1 = 2000000000;
    Int2 = 2000000000;
    Int1PlusInt2 = Int1 + Int2;
    System.Console.WriteLine(Int1PlusInt2);
}
```

Summary

C# provides several ways to control the execution of your code, giving you options to execute a block of code more than once, or sometimes not at all, based on the result of a Boolean expression.

The `if` statement executes code once, but only if the accompanying Boolean expression evaluates to `true`. The `if` statement can include an `else` clause, which executes a code block if the Boolean expression evaluates to `false`.

The `switch` statement executes one of many possible code blocks. Each code block is prefixed by a case statement list. C# evaluates the expression in the `switch` statement and then looks for a case statement list whose value matches the expression evaluated in the `switch` statement.

The `while`, `do`, and `for` statements continue to execute code as long as a specified Boolean expression is `true`. When the Boolean expression evaluates to `false`, the embedded statements are no longer executed. The `while` and `for` statements can be set up so that their Boolean expressions immediately evaluate to false, meaning that their embedded statements never actually execute. The do statement, however, always executes its embedded statements at least once.

The foreach statement provides a nice way to iterate through elements in an array quickly. You can instruct a foreach loop to iterate through the elements in an array without knowing the size of the array or how its elements were populated. The foreach statement sets up a special identifier that is populated with the value of an array element during each iteration of the foreach loop.

The break, continue, and goto statements disrupt the normal flow of an iteration statement, such as while or foreach. The break statement breaks out of the iteration loop, even if the Boolean expression that controls the loop's execution still evaluates to true. The continue statement returns control to the top of the iteration loop without executing any of the embedded statements that follow it. The goto statement always transfers control to a labeled statement.

You can surround mathematical operations in checked or unchecked statements to specify how you want to handle mathematical errors in your C# code.

✦   ✦   ✦

Working with Methods

Methods are blocks of statements that when executed return some type of value. They can be called by name, and calling a method causes the statements in the method to be executed.

You've already seen one method: the Main() method. Although C# enables you to put all of your code in the Main() method, you will probably want to design your classes to define more than one method. Using methods keeps your code readable because your statements are placed in smaller blocks, rather than in one big code block. Methods also enable you to take statements that may be executed multiple times and place them in a code block that can be called as often as needed.

In this chapter, you learn to create functions that do and do not return data. You learn how to pass parameters into methods, and you learn how best to structure a method to make your applications modularized.

Understanding Method Structure

At a minimum, a method is made up of the following parts:

+ Return type
+ Method name
+ Parameter list
+ Method body

Note   All methods are enclosed in a class. A method cannot exist outside of a class.

Methods have other optional parts, such as attribute lists and scope modifiers. The following sections focus on the basics of a method.

Return type

A method starts out by defining the type of data that it will return when it is called. For example, suppose you want to write a method that adds two integers and returns the result. In that case, you write its return type as int.

C# permits you to write a method that doesn't return anything. For example, you may write a method that simply writes some text to the console, but doesn't calculate any data worth returning to the code that called the method. In that case, you can use the keyword void to tell the C# compiler that the method does not return any data.

If you want to return a value from your method, you use the return keyword to specify the value that should be returned. The return keyword is followed by an expression that evaluates to the type of value to be returned. This expression can be a literal value, a variable, or a more complicated expression.

Expressions are covered in more detail in Chapter 4.

Method name

All methods must have a name. A method name is an identifier, and method names must follow the naming rules of any identifier. Remember that identifiers must begin with an uppercase or lowercase letter or an underscore character. The characters following the first character can be an uppercase or lowercase letter, a digit, or an underscore.

Parameter list

Methods may be called with parameters that are used to pass data to the method. In the preceding example, in which a method adds two numbers together, you would need to send the method the values of the two integers to be added. This list of variables is called the method's *parameter list*.

The method's parameter list is enclosed in parentheses and follows the method name. Each parameter in the parameter list is separated by a comma, and includes the parameter's type followed by its name.

You can also prefix parameters in the parameter list with modifiers that specify how their values are used within the method. You'll look at those modifiers later in this chapter.

You can define a method that doesn't take any parameters. If you want to write a method that doesn't take any parameters, simply write the parentheses with nothing inside them. You've already seen this in the `Main()` methods you've written. You can also place the keyword `void` inside the parentheses to specify that the method does not accept any parameters.

Method body

The method body is the block of statements that make up the method's code. The method body is enclosed in curly braces. The opening curly brace follows the method's parameter list, and the closing curly brace follows the last statement in the method body.

Calling a Method

To call a method, write its name in the place where the method's code should be executed in your code. Follow the method name with a pair of parentheses, as shown in Listing 6-1. As with all statements in C#, the method call statement must end with a semicolon.

Listing 6-1: **Calling a Simple Method**

```
class Listing6_1
{
  public static void Main()
  {
      Listing6_1 MyObject;

      MyObject = new Listing6_1();
      MyObject.CallMethod();
  }

  void CallMethod()
  {
      System.Console.WriteLine("Hello from CallMethod()!");
  }
}
```

Note   You need the statements in `Main()` that create a new `Listing6_1` object before you can call the object's methods. Chapter 9 discusses C#'s class and object concepts.

If the method is defined with a parameter list, the parameter values must be specified when you call the method. You must specify the parameters in the same order as they are specified in the method's parameter list, as shown in Listing 6-2.

Listing 6-2: **Calling a Method with a Parameter**

```
class Listing6_2
{
  public static void Main()
  {
      int        MyInteger;
      Listing6_2 MyObject;

      MyObject = new Listing6_2();
      MyObject.CallMethod(2);
      MyInteger = 3;
      MyObject.CallMethod(MyInteger);
  }

  void CallMethod(int Integer)
  {
      System.Console.WriteLine(Integer);
  }
}
```

When you compile and run Listing 6-2, you see output similar to that of Figure 6-1.

Figure 6-1: A simple call to a method results in the output shown here.

This is because the Main() method calls the CallMethod() twice: once with a value of 2 and once with a value of 3. The method body of the CallMethod() method writes the supplied value to the console.

When you supply a value for a method parameter, you can use a literal value, as in the 2 in Listing 6-2, or you can supply a variable whose value is used, as in the MyInteger variable in Listing 6-2.

When a method is called, C# takes the values specified and assigns those values to the parameters used in the method. During the first call to CallMethod() in Listing 6-2, the literal 2 is used as the parameter to the method, and the method's Integer parameter is given the value of 2. During the second call to CallMethod() in Listing 6-2, the variable MyInteger is used as the parameter to the method, and the method's Integer parameter is given the value of the MyInteger variable's value: 3.

The parameters that you specify when calling a method must match the types specified in the parameter list. If a parameter in a method's parameter list specifies an int, for example, the parameters you pass into it must be of type int, or a type that can be converted to an int. Any other type produces an error when your code is compiled. C# is a type-safe language, which means that variable types are checked for legality when you compile your C# code. Where methods are concerned, this means that you must specify the correct types when specifying parameters. Listing 6-3 shows the correct types during parameter specification.

Listing 6-3: **Type Safety in Method Parameter Lists**

```
class Listing6_3
{
  public static void Main()
  {
      Listing6_3 MyObject;

      MyObject = new Listing6_3();
      MyObject.CallMethod("a string");
  }

  void CallMethod(int Integer)
  {
      System.Console.WriteLine(Integer);
  }
}
```

This code does not compile, as you can see in Figure 6-2.

Figure 6-2: Calling a method with an invalid data type generates compiler errors.

The C# compiler issues these errors because the `CallMethod()` method is being executed with a string parameter, and the `CallMethod()` parameter list specifies that an integer must be used as its parameter. Strings are not integers, and cannot be converted into integers, and this mismatch causes the C# compiler to issue the errors.

If the method returns a value, you should declare a variable to hold the returned value. The variable used to hold the return value from the function is placed before the method name, and an equal sign separates the variable's identifier from the method name, as shown in Listing 6-4.

Listing 6-4: **Returning a Value from a Method**

```
class Listing6_4
{
  public static void Main()
  {
      Listing6_4 MyObject;
        int        ReturnValue;

      MyObject = new Listing6_4();
      ReturnValue = MyObject.AddIntegers(3, 5);
      System.Console.WriteLine(ReturnValue);
  }

  int AddIntegers(int Integer1, int Integer2)
  {
      int Sum;

      Sum = Integer1 + Integer2;
      return Sum;
  }
}
```

Several things are happening in this code:

✦ A method called `AddIntegers()` is declared. The method has two parameters in its parameter list: an integer called `Integer1` and an integer called `Integer2`.

✦ The method body of the `AddIntegers()` method adds the two parameter values together and assigns the result to a local variable called `Sum`. The value of `Sum` is returned.

✦ The `Main()` method calls the `AddIntegers()` method with values of 3 and 5. The return value of the `AddIntegers()` method is placed in a local variable called `ReturnValue`.

✦ The value of `ReturnValue` is printed out to the console.

Figure 6-3 contains the results of the program shown in Listing 6-4.

Figure 6-3: Data is returned from a method and shown in the console window.

Understanding Parameter Types

C# allows four types of parameters in a parameter list:

✦ Input parameters

✦ Output parameters

✦ Reference parameters

✦ Parameter arrays

Input parameters

Input parameters are parameters whose value are sent into the method. All the parameters used up to this point have been input parameters. The values of input parameters are sent into the function, but the method's body cannot permanently change their values.

Listing 6-4, shown in the previous example, defines a method with two input parameters: Integer1 and Integer2. The values for these parameters are input to the method, which reads their values and does its work.

Input parameters are passed *by value* into methods. The method basically sees a copy of the parameter's value, but is not allowed to change the value supplied by the caller. See Listing 6-5 for an example.

Listing 6-5: **Modifying Copies of Input Parameters**

```
class Listing6_5
{
   public static void Main()
   {
       int         MyInteger;
       Listing6_5 MyObject;

       MyObject = new Listing6_5();
       MyInteger = 3;
       MyObject.CallMethod(MyInteger);
       System.Console.WriteLine(MyInteger);
   }

   void CallMethod(int Integer1)
   {
       Integer1 = 6;
       System.Console.WriteLine(Integer1);
   }
}
```

In Listing 6-5, the Main() method sets up an integer variable called MyInteger and assigns it a value of 3. It then calls MyMethod() with MyInteger as a parameter. The CallMethod() method sets the value of the parameter to 6 and then prints out its value to the console. When the CallMethod() method returns, the Main() method continues, and prints the value of MyInteger.

When you run this code, the output should resemble that of Figure 6-4.

Figure 6-4: Demonstrate input parameters with the CallMethod() function.

This output occurs because the CallMethod() method modifies its copy of the input parameter, but that modification does not affect the value of the original method supplied by Main(). The value of MyInteger is still 3 after the CallMethod() method returns, because CallMethod() cannot change the value of the caller's input parameter. It can only change the value of its copy of the value.

Output parameters

Output parameters are parameters whose values are not set when the method is called. Instead, the method sets the values and returns the values to the caller through the output parameter.

Suppose, for example, that you want to write a method to count the number of records in a database table. Suppose that you'd also like to specify whether or not the operation was successful. (The operation may be unsuccessful, for instance, if the database table is not available.) You now have two pieces of information that need to be returned by the method:

✦ A record count

✦ An operational success flag

C# allows methods to return only one value. What should you do when you want two pieces of information to return?

The answer lies in the output parameter concept. You can have your method return the operational success flag as a Boolean value, and specify the record count as an output parameter. The method stores the record count in an output variable, whose value is picked up by the caller.

Output parameters are specified in parameter lists with the keyword out. The out keyword must precede the parameter's type in the parameter list. When you call a method with an output parameter, you must declare a variable to hold the output parameter's value, as shown in Listing 6-6.

Listing 6-6: Working with Output Parameters

```
class Listing6_6
{
  public static void Main()
  {
      int        MyInteger;
      Listing6_6 MyObject;

      MyObject = new Listing6_6();
      MyObject.CallMethod(out MyInteger);
      System.Console.WriteLine(MyInteger);
  }

  void CallMethod(out int Integer1)
  {
      Integer1 = 7;
  }
}
```

Listing 6-6 defines a method called CallMethod(), which defines an output parameter integer called Integer1. The method's body sets the value of the output parameter to 7. The Main() method declares an integer called MyInteger and uses it as the output parameter to the CallMethod() method. When CallMethod() returns, the value of MyInteger is written to the console. Figure 6-5 contains the result of these output parameter test applications.

Figure 6-5: An output parameter returns the appropriate value.

You must use the keyword out twice for each parameter: once when you declare the parameter in the parameter list, and once when you specify the output parameter when you call the method. If you forget the out keyword when you call a method with an output parameter, you get the following errors from the C# compiler:

```
Listing6-6.cs(9,6): error CS1502: The best overloaded method
match for 'Listing6_6.CallMethod(out int)' has some invalid
arguments
Listing6-6.cs(9,26): error CS1503: Argument '1': cannot convert
from 'int' to 'out int'
```

Any value assigned to variables used as output parameters before the method is called are lost. The original values are overwritten with the values assigned to them by the method.

Reference parameters

Reference parameters supply values by reference: In other words, the method receives a reference to the variable specified when the method is called. Think of a reference parameter as both an input and an output variable: The method can read the variable's original value and also modify the original value as if it were an output parameter.

Reference parameters are specified in parameter lists with the keyword ref. The ref keyword must precede the parameter's type in the parameter list. When you call a method with a reference parameter, you must declare a variable to hold the reference parameter's value, as shown in Listing 6-7.

Listing 6-7: **Working with Reference Parameters**

```
class Listing6_7
{
  public static void Main()
  {
      int        MyInteger;
      Listing6_7 MyObject;

      MyObject = new Listing6_7();
      MyInteger = 3;
      System.Console.WriteLine(MyInteger);
      MyObject.CallMethod(ref MyInteger);
      System.Console.WriteLine(MyInteger);
  }

  void CallMethod(ref int Integer1)
  {
      Integer1 = 4;
  }
}
```

The `CallMethod()` method in Listing 6-7 uses a reference parameter called `Integer1`. The method body sets the value of the reference parameter to 4.

The `Main()` method declares an integer variable called `MyInteger` and assigns it a value of 3. It prints the value of `MyInteger` to the console, and then uses it as the parameter to the `CallMethod()` method. When the `CallMethod()` returns, the value of `MyInteger` is printed to the console a second time.

Running the code in Listing 6-7 should result in the values shown in Figure 6-6.

Figure 6-6: A reference parameter changes your variable directly.

The second line reads 4 because the reference parameter syntax allows the method to change the value of the original variable. This is a change from the input parameter example in Listing 6-5.

You must use the keyword `ref` twice for each parameter: once when you declare the parameter in the parameter list, and once when you specify the reference parameter when you call the method.

Parameter arrays

Methods are often written to take a specific number of parameters. A method with a parameter list with three parameters always expects to be called with exactly three parameters—no more and no less. However, sometimes a method may not know how many parameters it should accept when it is designed. You may be writing a method that accepts a list of strings specifying the names of files to be deleted from the disk. How many strings should the method allow? To be flexible, the method should be designed so that the caller can specify as many or as few strings as needed. This makes calling the method a bit more flexible because the caller can decide how many strings should be passed to the method. How do you write the method's parameter list, however, when the method won't know how many parameters will be passed into it?

Parameter arrays solve this design dilemma. *Parameter arrays* enable you to specify that your method accept a variable number of arguments. You specify the parameter array in your parameter list by using the C# keyword params, followed by the type of variable that should be supplied by the caller. The type specification is followed by square brackets, which are followed by the identifier of the parameter array, as shown in Listing 6-8.

Listing 6-8: **Working with Parameter Arrays**

```
class Listing6_8
{
  public static void Main()
  {
      Listing6_8 MyObject;

      MyObject = new Listing6_8();
      MyObject.CallMethod(1);
      MyObject.CallMethod(1, 2);
      MyObject.CallMethod(1, 2, 3);
  }

  void CallMethod(params int[] ParamArray)
  {
      System.Console.WriteLine("------------");
      System.Console.WriteLine("CallMethod()");
      System.Console.WriteLine("------------");
      foreach(int ParamArrayElement in ParamArray)
          System.Console.WriteLine(ParamArrayElement);
  }
}
```

In Listing 6-8, the CallMethod() method is written to accept a variable number of integers. The method receives the parameters as an array of integers. The method body uses the foreach statement to iterate through the parameter array, and prints each element out to the console.

The Main() method calls the CallMethod() method three times, each with a different number of arguments. This is legal only because CallMethod() is declared with a parameter array.

Figure 6-7 indicates that all of the parameters were passed to the method intact.

Figure 6-7: The params keyword allows for any number of parameters.

You can use one parameter array in your method's parameter list. You can combine a parameter array with other parameters in your method's parameter list. If you use a parameter array in a method parameter list, however, it must be specified as the last parameter in the list. You cannot use the out or ref keywords on a parameter array.

Overloading Methods

C# enables you to define multiple methods with the same name in the same class, as long as those methods have different parameter lists. This is referred to as *overloading* the method name. See Listing 6-9 for an example.

Listing 6-9: **Working with Overloaded Methods**

```csharp
class Listing6_9
{
  public static void Main()
  {
      Listing6_9 MyObject;

      MyObject = new Listing6_9();
      MyObject.Add(3, 4);
      MyObject.Add(3.5, 4.75);
  }

    void Add(int Integer1, int Integer2)
    {
        int Sum;
```

```
        System.Console.WriteLine("adding two integers");
        Sum = Integer1 + Integer2;
        System.Console.WriteLine(Sum);
    }

    void Add(double Double1, double Double2)
    {
        double Sum;

        System.Console.WriteLine("adding two doubles");
        Sum = Double1 + Double2;
        System.Console.WriteLine(Sum);
    }
}
```

Listing 6-9 implements two Add() methods. One of the Add() method takes two integers as input parameters, and the other takes two doubles as input parameters. Because the two implementations have different parameter lists, C# allows the two Add() methods to coexist in the same class. The Main() method calls the Add() method twice: once with two integer parameter values and once with two floating-point values.

As you can see in Figure 6-8, both methods run successfully, processing the correct data.

Figure 6-8: The overloaded method adds integers and doubles.

When the C# compiler encounters a call to a method that has more than one implementation, it looks at the parameters used in the call and calls the method with the parameter list that best matches the parameters used in the call. Two integers are used in the first call to Add(). The C# compiler then matches this call up with the implementation of Add() that takes the two integer input parameters because the parameters in the call match the parameter list with the integers. Two doubles are used in the second call to Add(). The C# compiler then matches this call up with the implementation of Add() that takes the two double input parameters because the parameters in the call match the parameter list with the doubles.

Not all overloaded methods need to use the same number of parameters in their parameter lists, nor do all the parameters in the parameter list need to be of the same type. The only requirement that C# imposes is that the functions have different parameter lists. One version of an overloaded function can have one integer in its parameter list, and another version of the overloaded function can have a string, a long, and a character in its parameter list.

Virtual Methods

To follow the discussion of virtual methods, you have to understand inheritance. *Inheritance* bases one class on an existing class, adding and removing functionality as needed. In the following sections, you examine how virtual methods are created and used.

Overriding methods

To begin in this section, you build a sample class called Books. This class contains two methods named Title and Rating. The Title method returns the name of a book, and the Rating method returns a string indicating the number of stars that the particular book rated. The code in Listing 6-10 is the complete source for your application. Type it into your favorite editor and compile it as you have done before.

Listing 6-10: Displaying a Book Title and Rating Information with the Following Classes

```csharp
using System;

namespace BookOverride
{
  class Book
  {
      public string Title()
      {
          return "Programming Book";
      }
      public string Rating()
      {
```

```
            return "5 Stars";
        }
    }

    class Class1
    {
        static void Main(string[] args)
        {
            Book bc = new Book();
            Console.WriteLine(bc.Title());
            Console.WriteLine(bc.Rating());
        }
    }
}
```

Before you run this program, take a quick look at it. As you can see, one class contains your Main() method. This method is where you instantiate an instance of your BookOverride class, which contains the Title and Rating methods. After you instantiate an instance of the class, you call the Title and Rating methods and write the output to the console. The result can be seen in Figure 6-9.

Figure 6-9: The title and rating of your book returns as expected.

Next, you override the Title method by creating a class based on the Book class. To create a class based upon another class (thereby enabling you to override methods), simply declare a class as normal and follow the class name with a colon and the name of the class that you want to base it on. Add the following code shown in Listing 6-11 to the application you just created.

Listing 6-11: **Overriding Methods by Inheriting the Book Class**

```
class Wiley : Book
{
  new public string Title()
  {
        return "C# Bible";
  }
}
```

This code creates a Wiley class that inherits the Book class. Now you are free to create a new public method called Title. Because you have given this method the same name as the one defined in your Book class, you override the Title method while still having access to all the other members within the Book class.

 Note   The term *member* refers to methods, properties, and events that are defined within a class. It is a general term that refers to all items within the class.

Now that you have overridden the Title method, you must change the Main() method to use your new class. Change your Main() method as shown in Listing 6-12.

Listing 6-12: **Altering the Main() Method to Override a Class**

```
static void Main(string[] args)
{
    Wiley bc = new Wiley();
    Console.WriteLine(bc.Title());
    Console.WriteLine(bc.Rating());
}
```

In your Main() method, you change your bc variable to instantiate from the new Wiley class. As you may have guessed, when you call the Title method, the title of the book changes from Programming Book to C# Bible. Note that you still have access to the Rating method that was originally defined in the Book class.

Overriding methods within a base class in an excellent way to change specific functionality without reinventing the wheel.

Summary

C# enables you to write methods in your C# classes. Methods can help you partition your code into easy-to-understand pieces and can give you a single place to store code that may be called multiple times.

Functions can receive parameters. Input parameters have values passed into the methods, but their values cannot change. Output parameters have values assigned to them by a method, and the assigned value is visible to the caller. Reference parameters have values that can be supplied into the function, and they can also have their value changed by the method. Parameter arrays enable you to write methods that take a variable number of arguments.

C# also enables you to overload methods. Overloaded methods have the same name but different parameter lists. C# uses the parameters supplied in a call to determine which method to invoke when the code executes.

✦   ✦   ✦

Grouping Data Using Structures

C# enables you to group variables into structures. By defining a structure for your data, the entire group can be managed under a single structure name, regardless of the number of variables that the structure contains. The entire set of variables can be easily manipulated by working with a single structure, rather than having to keep track of each individual variable separately. A structure can contain fields, methods, constants, constructors, properties, indexers, operators, and other structures.

Structures in C# are value types, not reference types. This means that structure variables contain the structure's values directly, rather than maintaining a reference to a structure found elsewhere in memory.

Some of the variables that you declare in your C# code may have a logical relationship to other variables that you have declared. Suppose, for example, that you want to write code that works with a point on the screen. You may declare two variables to describe the point:

```
int XCoordinateOfPoint;
int YCoordinateOfPoint;
```

The point has two values — its x coordinate and its y coordinate — that work together to describe the point.

Although you can write your C# code in this way, it gets cumbersome. Both values must be used together in any code that wants to work with the point. If you want a method to work with the point, you'll have to pass the values individually:

```
void WorkWithPoint(int XCoordinate, int
YCoordinate);
void SetNewPoint(out int XCoordinate, out int
YCoordinate);
```

The situation gets even more complicated when several variables work together to describe a single entity. An employee in a human resources database, for example, may have variables representing a first name, a last name, an address, phone numbers, and a current salary. Managing those as separate variables and ensuring that they are all used as a group can get messy.

Declaring a Structure

You declare a structure's contents by using the `struct` keyword. You must name a structure with an identifier that follows the `struct` keyword. The list of variables that make up the structure are enclosed in curly braces that follow the structure identifier. The structure member declarations should usually be prefixed with the keyword `public` to tell the C# compiler that their values should be publicly accessible to all of the code in the class. Each member declaration ends with a semicolon.

Declaring a structure that defines a point may look like the following:

```
struct Point
{
    public int X;
    public int Y;
}
```

In the preceding example, the members of the structure, X and Y, have the same type. This is not a requirement, however. Structures may also be made up of variables of different types. The employee example previously discussed may look like the following:

```
struct Employee
{
    public string   FirstName;
    public string   LastName;
    public string   Address;
    public string   City;
    public string   State;
    public ushort   ZIPCode;
    public decimal  Salary;
}
```

As with all statements in C#, you can declare a structure only from within a class.

Note　　C# does not allow any statements to appear outside of a class declaration.

The initial values of structure members follow the rules of value initialization described in Table 3-1 of Chapter 3, "Working with Variables." Values are initialized to some representation of zero, and strings are emptied. C# does not allow you to initialize structure members when they are declared. Take a look at the error in the following code:

```
struct Point
{
    public int X = 100;
    public int Y = 200;
}
```

This declaration produces errors from the compiler:

```
error CS0573: 'MyClass.Point.X': cannot have instance field
initializers in structs
error CS0573: 'MyClass.Point.Y': cannot have instance field
initializers in structs
```

You can use a special method called a *constructor* to initialize structure members to nonzero values. You'll examine constructors later in this chapter.

Using Structures in Your Code

After you have defined your structure, you can use its identifier as a variable type, just as you would an `int` or a `long` type. Supply the identifier of the structure, followed by some whitespace, followed by the identifier of the structure variable:

```
Point MyPoint;
```

 Cross-Reference Identifiers can be found in Chapter 3, "Working with Variables."

This statement declares a variable called `MyPoint` whose type is the `Point` structure. You can use this variable just as you would any variable, including within expressions and as a parameter to a method.

Accessing the individual members of the structure is as easy as writing the name of the structure variable identifier, a period, and then the structure member. Listing 7-1 shows how a structure may be used in code.

Listing 7-1: **Accessing Structure Members**

```
class Listing7_1
{
    struct Point
    {
        public int X;
        public int Y;
    }

    public static void Main()
```

Continued

Listing 7-1 *(continued)*

```
    {
        Point MyPoint;

        MyPoint.X = 100;
        MyPoint.Y = 200;
        System.Console.WriteLine(MyPoint.X);
        System.Console.WriteLine(MyPoint.Y);
    }
}
```

The output for the example show would be as follows:

```
100
200
```

You can assign one structure variable to another, as long as the structures are of the same type. When you assign one structure variable to another, C# sets the values of the structure variable shown before the equal sign to the values of the corresponding values found in the structure shown after the equal sign, as shown in Listing 7-2.

Listing 7-2: Assigning One Structure Variable to Another

```
class Listing7_2
{
    struct Point
    {
        public int X;
        public int Y;
    }

    public static void Main()
    {
        Point MyFirstPoint;
        Point MySecondPoint;

        MyFirstPoint.X = 100;
        MyFirstPoint.Y = 100;
        MySecondPoint.X = 200;
        MySecondPoint.Y = 200;

        System.Console.WriteLine(MyFirstPoint.X);
        System.Console.WriteLine(MyFirstPoint.Y);

        MyFirstPoint = MySecondPoint;
```

```
        System.Console.WriteLine(MyFirstPoint.X);
        System.Console.WriteLine(MyFirstPoint.Y);
    }
}
```

The preceding code sets the MyFirstPoint members to 100 and the MySecondPoint members to 200. The MyFirstPoint values are written to the console, and then the values in the MyFirstPoint variable is copied into the values found in the MySecondPoint variable. After the assignment, the MyFirstPoint values are again written to the console. When this code is compiled and executed, the output should be that of Figure 7-1.

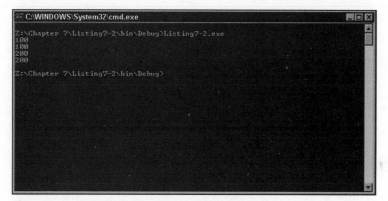

Figure 7-1: Assigning one structure to another

Any values in a structure are overwritten in an assignment with the values from the structure variable listed after the equal sign.

Defining Methods in Structures

You can include methods in structures as well as variables. If you need to write code that works with the contents of a structure, you might consider writing the method inside of the structure itself.

Using constructor methods

A structure may include a special method called a *constructor*. A constructor method executes when a variable declaration using the structure type is executed at runtime.

Structures may have zero or more constructors. Structure constructor declarations are much like class method declarations, with the following exceptions:

✦ Constructors do not return any values. Do not use a return type keyword when writing a structure constructor — not even `void`.

✦ Constructor identifiers have the same name as the structure itself.

✦ Constructors must have at least one parameter. C# does not allow you to define a constructor with no parameters. C# always defines a default constructor with no parameters for you. This is the constructor that initializes all of the structure members to zero, or their equivalent.

A structure may define more than one constructor, as long as the constructors have different parameter lists. Listing 7-3 shows a `Point` structure with two constructors.

Listing 7-3: **Structure Constructors**

```
class Listing7_3
{
    struct Point
    {
        public int X;
        public int Y;

        public Point(int InitialX)
        {
            X = InitialX;
            Y = 1000;
        }

        public Point(int InitialX, int InitialY)
        {
            X = InitialX;
            Y = InitialY;
        }
    }

    public static void Main()
    {
        Point MyFirstPoint = new Point();
        Point MySecondPoint = new Point(100);
        Point MyThirdPoint = new Point(250, 475);

        System.Console.WriteLine(MyFirstPoint.X);
        System.Console.WriteLine(MyFirstPoint.Y);

        System.Console.WriteLine(MySecondPoint.X);
        System.Console.WriteLine(MySecondPoint.Y);
```

```
        System.Console.WriteLine(MyThirdPoint.X);
        System.Console.WriteLine(MyThirdPoint.Y);
    }
}
```

Figure 7-2 shows what appears on the console if you compile and run the code in Listing 7-3.

Figure 7-2: The structures reveal predefined values as expected.

Note several interesting concepts in Listing 7-3:

✦ The `Point` structure declares two constructors. One takes a single integer as an argument and the other takes two integers as an argument. Both are pre-fixed with the keyword `public` so that their code is publicly accessible to the rest of the code in the class.

✦ The constructor with one integer parameter sets the structure's X member to the value of the integer argument, and sets the structure's Y member to 1,000.

✦ The constructor with two integer parameters sets the structure's X member to the value of the first integer argument, and sets the structure's Y member to the value of the second integer argument.

✦ The code declares three variables of type `Point`. They each call one of the `Point` constructors. The declaration of `MyFirstPoint` calls the constructor with zero arguments. This is the default constructor that C# defines for every structure. The declaration of `MySecondPoint` calls the constructor with one argument, and the declaration of `MyThirdPoint` calls the constructor with two arguments.

Pay close attention to the syntax in Listing 7-3 that invokes a structure constructor. If you want to invoke a constructor on a structure, you must use the new keyword, followed by the name of the structure, followed by the constructor parameters in parentheses. The value of that expression is assigned to the variable you are declaring. Take a look at the following statement:

```
Point MyThirdPoint = new Point(250, 475);
```

This statement says: "Create a new Point structure using the constructor with two integers. Assign its value to the MyThirdPoint variable. Because of the rules of structure assignment previously described, the MyThirdPoint variable has its members set to the values of the members of the new structure. You do not need to do anything else with the new structure created when new was called. The Common Language Runtime (CLR) detects that the structure is no longer in use and disposes of it through its garbage collection mechanism.

The parameterless constructor syntax is also shown in Listing 7-3:

```
Point MyFirstPoint = new Point();
```

This tells the C# compiler that you want to initialize the structure using its default behavior. You must assign values to all of the members of a structure before you use a structure, either by invoking its parameterless constructor or by explicitly setting all of its fields to a value. Take a look at Listing 7-4.

Listing 7-4: **Using a Structure Before Initialization Results in Compiler Errors**

```
class Listing7_4
{
    struct Point
    {
        public int X;
        public int Y;
    }

    public static void Main()
    {
        Point MyPoint;

        System.Console.WriteLine(MyPoint.X);
        System.Console.WriteLine(MyPoint.Y);
    }
}
```

The preceding code is in error, and compiling it produces the following error messages from the C# compiler:

```
error CS0170: Use of possibly unassigned field 'X'
error CS0170: Use of possibly unassigned field 'Y'
warning CS0649: Field 'Listing7_4.Point.X' is never assigned
to, and will always have its default value 0
warning CS0649: Field 'Listing7_4.Point.Y' is never assigned
to, and will always have its default value 0
```

The error messages are telling you that the calls to `WriteLine()` use data members in the structure, but that those data members have not yet been given a value. The `MyPoint` variable has not been initialized with a call to a parameterless constructor, nor have its members been explicitly set to any values. C# does not invoke the parameterless constructor unless you write the call in your code.

This is another example of the C# compiler protecting your code from unpredictable behavior. All variables must be initialized before they are used.

Calling methods from structures

You may also write methods in your structures. These methods follow the same rules as class methods: They must specify a return type (or `void`), and have an identifier and an argument list, which may be empty. Calling a method in a structure uses the same `dot` notation syntax that is used when you access a class method. Take a look at Listing 7-5.

Listing 7-5: **Calling Structure Methods**

```
class Listing7_5
{
    struct Point
    {
        public int X;
        public int Y;

        public Point(int InitialX, int InitialY)
        {
            X = InitialX;
            Y = InitialY;
        }

        public bool IsAtOrigin()
        {
            if((X == 0) && (Y == 0))
                return true;
            else
                return false;
        }
```

Continued

Listing 7-5 *(continued)*

```
    }

    public static void Main()
    {
        Point MyFirstPoint = new Point(100, 200);
        Point MySecondPoint = new Point();

        if(MyFirstPoint.IsAtOrigin() == true)
            System.Console.WriteLine("MyFirstPoint is at the origin.");
        else
            System.Console.WriteLine("MyFirstPoint is not at the origin.");

        if(MySecondPoint.IsAtOrigin() == true)
            System.Console.WriteLine("MySecondPoint is at the origin.");
        else
            System.Console.WriteLine("MySecondPoint is not at the origin.");
    }
}
```

The Point structure in Listing 7-5 declares a method called IsAtOrigin. The code in that method checks the values of the structure methods, returning true if the coordinates of the point are (0, 0) and false otherwise.

The Main() method declares two variables of type Point: the MyFirstPoint variable is set to coordinates of (100, 200) using the explicit constructor, and the MySecondPoint variable is set to coordinates of (0, 0) using the default parameterless constructor. The Main() method then calls the IsAtOrigin method on both points and prints out a message based on the method's return value.

If you compile and run the code in Listing 7-5, you see the following output on the console:

```
MyFirstPoint is not at the origin.
MySecondPoint is at the origin.
```

Be sure to prefix your methods with the keyword public if you want them to be publicly accessible to the rest of the code in the class.

Defining Properties in Structures

Properties within a structure enable you to read, write, and compute values with the use of accessors. Unlike fields, properties are not considered variables; therefore, they do not designate storage space. Because a property does not allocate storage space, it cannot be passed as a ref or out parameter.

Cross-Reference Properties is discussed in detail in Chapter 9., "C# Classes."

Listing 7-6 includes a property within the Point structure.

Listing 7-6: **Defining a Property Within a Structure**

```
class Listing7_6
{
  struct Point
  {
        private int x;
        public int X
        {
                get
                {
                        return x;
                }
                set
                {
                        x = value;
                }
        }
  }

  public static void Main()
  {
        int RetValue;
        Point MyPoint = new Point();

        MyPoint.X = 10;
        RetValue = MyPoint.X;
        System.Console.WriteLine(RetValue);
  }
}
```

This code assigns a value to the X member of the Point structure and then retrieves this value into the RetValue variable. The output from Listing 7-6 is shown in Figure 7-3.

Using properties is an excellent means to read, write, and calculate data within a structure. You don't need to include bulky methods that perform the calculations for you, and you can define how and when the get and set accessors are allowed to operate.

Figure 7-3: Defining a property within a structure

Defining Indexers in Structures

Indexers are objects that enable a structure to be indexed in very much the same way that arrays do. With an indexer, you can declare several structures at the same time and refer to each structure using an index number. This is demonstrated in Listing 7-7, which declares a structure called MyStruct containing a string and an index.

Listing 7-7: Including an Indexer Within a Structure

```
class Listing7_7
{

    struct MyStruct
    {
        public string []data ;
        public string this [int index]
        {
            get
            {
                return data[index];
            }
            set
            {
                data[index] = value;
            }
        }
    }
    public static void Main()
```

```
        {
            int x;
            MyStruct ms = new MyStruct();
            ms.data = new string[5];
            ms[0] = "Brian D Patterson";
            ms[1] = "Aimee J Patterson";
            ms[2] = "Breanna C Mounts";
            ms[3] = "Haileigh E Mounts";
            ms[4] = "Brian W Patterson";
            for (x=0;x<5;x++)
                System.Console.WriteLine(ms[x]);
        }
    }
```

As you can see, this example has created a new MyStruct object and then set its data member to 5, indicating that five copies of this structure are used. You reference each copy of this structure using an index number (0 through 5) and store names within this structure. To ensure that all of your data remains intact, you do a simple loop through the possible index numbers and write the output to the console.

You can see the output for Listing 7-7 in Figure 7-4.

Figure 7-4: Include an indexer within a structure for easy retrieval of data.

An indexer within a structure can come in very handy when you are dealing with large amounts of the same data. For example, if you were to read in address information from a database, this would be an excellent place to store it. You maintain all the fields while providing a mechanism to easily access each piece of data within the records.

Defining Interfaces in Structures

Interfaces are a way of ensuring that someone using your class has abided by all the rules you set forth to do so. This can include implementing certain methods, properties, and events. When you expose an interface, users of your interface must inherit that interface; and in doing so, they are bound to create certain methods and so forth. This ensures that your class and/or structure is used as it was intended.

You can include an interface within a structure as well. Listing 7-8 shows you how to properly implement an interface.

Listing 7-8: Implementing an Interface Within a Structure

```
class Listing7_8
{

    interface IInterface
    {
        void Method();
    }
    struct MyStruct : IInterface
    {
        public void Method()
        {
            System.Console.WriteLine("Structure Method");
        }
    }

    public static void Main()
    {
        MyStruct DemoStructure = new MyStruct();
        DemoStructure.Method();
    }
}
```

This code creates an interface called IInterface. This interface contains the definition for one method called Method. You create your structure and end the structure name with a colon followed by the name of the interface from which you wish to inherit. Within your structure, you include the method, which simply writes a line of text out to the console. You can see the output for this program in Figure 7-5.

To demonstrate how important the interface is, comment out the four lines that make up the Method method within the MyStruct structure. Now recompile the program, and you should see the following error message:

```
Class1.cs(8,9): error CS0535: 'Listing7_8.MyStruct' does not
implement interface member 'Listing7_8.IInterface.Method()'
```

Figure 7-5: Implementing an interface within a structure

The C# compiler determined that you did not implement all the methods set forth by the interface. Because the correct method was not implemented, the program could not be compiled, thereby ensuring that you follow all the rules.

Using C# Simple Types as Structures

The primitive types described in Chapter 3 — int, uint, long, and the like — are actually implemented as structures in the .NET CLR. Table 7-1 lists the C# value variable keywords and the names of the .NET structures that actually implement them.

Table 7-1
.NET Structure Names for Value Types

C# Keyword	.NET Structure Name
sbyte	System.SByte
byte	System.Byte
short	System.Int16
ushort	System.Uint16
int	System.Int32
uint	System.Uint32

Continued

Table 7-1 *(continued)*	
C# Keyword	*.NET Structure Name*
`long`	`System.Int64`
`ulong`	`System.Uint64`
`char`	`System.Char`
`float`	`System.Single`
`double`	`System.Double`
`bool`	`System.Boolean`
`decimal`	`System.Decimal`

This design is a part of what makes your C# code portable to other .NET languages. The C# values map to .NET structures that can be used by any .NET language, because any .NET structure can be used by the CLR. Mapping C# keywords to .NET structures also enables the structures to use techniques such as operator overloading to define the value's behavior when the type is used in an expression with an operator. You'll examine operator overloading when you learn about C# classes.

If you feel so inclined, you can use the actual .NET structure names in place of the C# keywords. Listing 7-9 shows how the code in Listing 7-5 would look if it were written using the .NET structure names.

Listing 7-9: **Using .NET Structure Type Names**

```
class Listing7_9
{
    struct Point
    {
        public System.Int32 X;
        public System.Int32 Y;

        public Point(System.Int32 InitialX, System.Int32 InitialY)
        {
            X = InitialX;
            Y = InitialY;
        }

        public System.Boolean IsAtOrigin()
        {
            if((X == 0) && (Y == 0))
                return true;
            else
                return false;
```

```
        }
    }

    public static void Main()
    {
        Point MyFirstPoint = new Point(100, 200);
        Point MySecondPoint = new Point();

        if(MyFirstPoint.IsAtOrigin() == true)
            System.Console.WriteLine("MyFirstPoint is at the origin.");
        else
            System.Console.WriteLine("MyFirstPoint is not at the origin.");

        if(MySecondPoint.IsAtOrigin() == true)
            System.Console.WriteLine("MySecondPoint is at the origin.");
        else
            System.Console.WriteLine("MySecondPoint is not at the origin.");
    }

}
```

Summary

Structures enable you to group a set of variables under a single name. Variables can be declared using the structure identifier.

Structures are declared using the C# keyword `struct`. All C# structures have a name and a list of data members. C# does not place any limit on the number of data members that a structure can hold.

Structure members are accessed using the `StructName.MemberName` notation. You can use the members anywhere that their data type is allowed, including expressions and as parameters to methods.

Structures may implement methods as well as variables. Structure members are invoked using the `StructName.MethodName` notation and are used just as class method names are used. Structures may also implement special methods, called *constructors*, which initialize the structure to a known state before the structure is used.

The C# value types are actually mapped to structures defined by the .NET CLR. This is what enables your data to be used by other .NET code—all of your variables are compatible with the .NET CLR because your variables are defined using structures compatible with the CLR.

✦   ✦   ✦

Object-Oriented Programming with C#

Writing Object-Oriented Code

CHAPTER

8

◆ ◆ ◆ ◆

In This Chapter

Understanding abstraction

Using abstract data types

Understanding encapsulation

Understanding inheritance

Understanding polymorphism

◆ ◆ ◆ ◆

Software programming languages have always been designed around two fundamental concepts: data and the code that acts on the data. Languages have evolved over time to change the way these two concepts interact. Originally, languages such as Pascal and C invited developers to write software that dealt with code and data as two separate, disconnected entities. This approach gives developers the freedom, but also the burden, to choose how their code handles the data. Furthermore, this approach forces a developer to translate the real world that needs to be modeled using software into a computer-specific model using data and code.

Languages like Pascal and C were built around the concept of a *procedure*. A procedure is a named block of code, just as a C# method is built today. The style of software developed using these kinds of languages is called *procedural programming*. In procedural programming, the developer writes one or more procedures and works with a set of independent variables defined in the program. All procedures are visible from any piece of code in the application, and all variables can be manipulated from any piece of code.

In the 1990s, procedural programming gave way to languages such as Smalltalk and Simula, which introduced the concept of objects. The inventors of these languages realized that human beings don't express ideas in terms of blocks of code that act on a set of variables; instead, they express ideas in terms of objects. *Objects* are entities that have a defined set of values (the object's *state*) and a set of operations that can be executed on that object (the object's *behaviors*). Take the space shuttle, for example. A space shuttle has state, such as the amount of fuel on board and the number of passengers, as well as behaviors, such as "launch" and "land." Furthermore, objects belong to *classes*. Objects of the same class have similar state and the same set of behaviors. An object is a concrete instance of a class. Space shuttle is a class, whereas the space shuttle named Discovery is an object, a concrete instance of the space shuttle class.

Note

> Actually, even in procedural programming, not all procedure and variables are visible. Just as in C#, procedural languages have *scoping rules*, which govern the visibility of the code and the data. Procedures and variables, which in this chapter are referred to as *items,* typically could be made visible at the procedure, source file, application, or external level. The name of each scope is self-explanatory. An item visible at the procedure level is accessible only within the procedure in which it is defined. Not all languages allow you to create procedures within procedures. An item visible at the source-file level is visible within the file in which the item is defined. At the application level, the item is visible from any piece of code in the *same* application. At the external level, the item is visible from any piece of code in *any* application.
>
> The main point is that, in procedural programming, the interaction of data and code is governed by implementation details, such as the source file in which a variable is defined. Once you decide to make a variable visible outside your own procedures, you get no help in protecting access to this variable. In large applications with several thousands of variables, this lack of protection frequently leads to hard-to-find bugs.

Object-oriented software development has two distinct advantages over procedural software development. The first advantage is that you can now specify what the software should do and how it will do it by using a vocabulary that is familiar to nontechnical users. You structure your software using objects. These objects belong to classes that are familiar to the business user for whom the software is intended. For example, during the design of ATM software, you use class names such as BankAccount, Customer, Display, and so on. This reduces the work that needs to be done to translate a real-world situation into a software model, and makes it easier to communicate with the nonsoftware people that have a stake in the final product. This easier method of designing software has led to the emergence of a standard for describing the design of object-oriented software. This language is called Unified Modeling Language, or UML.

The second advantage of object-oriented software development comes into play during implementation. Because you can now have class-level scope, you can hide variables within a class definition. Each object will have its own set of variables, and these variables will typically only be accessible through the operations defined by the class. For example, the variables holding a BankAccount object's state will only be accessible by calling the Withdraw() or Deposit() operation associated with this object. A BankAccount object (or any other object for that matter) does not have access to another BankAccount object's private state, such as the balance. This principle is called *encapsulation*. More about this follows in the section called Encapsulation.

Object-oriented software development grew more popular over time as developers embraced this new way of designing software. C# is an object-oriented language, and its design ensures that C# developers follow good object-oriented programming concepts.

Note SmallTalk, Java, and C# are *pure* object-oriented languages because you cannot write a program without using objects. Other languages, such as C and Pascal, are called procedural or non-object oriented languages because they have no built-in support that enables you to create objects. A third type of language, such as C++, are hybrid languages in which you can choose whether you use objects. Bjarne Stroustrup, the inventor of C++, chose not to force C++ programmers to use objects because C++ was also a better version of the C programming language. Compatibility with existing C code helped C++ become a major language.

In this chapter you learn about the concepts that make up an object-oriented language, starting with the building stone (classes and objects), then progressing in the more advanced terms (abstraction, abstract data types, encapsulation, inheritance and polymorphism). The discussion centers around the concepts and tries to avoid discussing specifics about how these concepts are implemented in C#. These specifics follow in the following chapters.

Classes and Objects

First, this section revisits the difference between an object and a class. This book uses both terms quite a bit, and it's important to distinguish between the two.

A *class* is a collection of code and variables. Classes manage state, in the form of the variables that they contain, and behaviors, in the form of the methods that they contain. A class is just a template, however. You never create a class in your code. Instead, you create objects. For example, BankAccount is a class with a variable that contains the account balance and Withdraw(), Deposit(), and ShowBalance() methods.

Objects are concrete instances of a class. Objects are constructed using a class as a template. When an object is created, it manages its own state. The state in one object can be different from the state of another object of the same class. Consider a class that defines a person. A person class is going to have state — a string representing the person's first name, perhaps — and behavior, through methods such as GoToWork(), Eat(), and GoToSleep(). You may create two objects of the person class, each of which may have different state, as shown in Figure 8-1. Figure 8-1 shows the person class and two person objects: one with a first name of "Alice" and another with a first name of "Bob." The state of each object is stored in a different set of variables. Re-read the previous sentence. It contains an essential point for understanding how object-oriented programming works. A language has support for objects when you don't have to do any special coding to have a different set of variables each time you create a different object.

 Note If a language has support for automatic state management within objects but is lacking some of the other features discussed in this section, then it is frequently called an *object-based language*. Visual Basic 6 supports objects but has no support for implementation inheritance; therefore, it is not considered a true object-oriented language. Examples of true object oriented languages are SmallTalk, Java and C#.

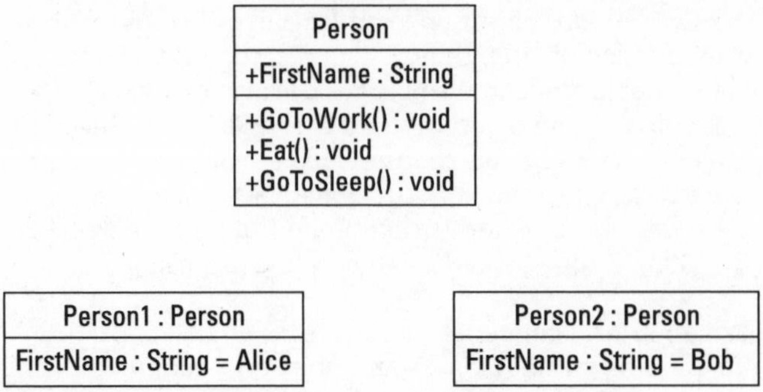

```
┌─────────────────────────┐
│         Person          │
├─────────────────────────┤
│ +FirstName : String     │
├─────────────────────────┤
│ +GoToWork() : void      │
│ +Eat() : void           │
│ +GoToSleep() : void     │
└─────────────────────────┘
```

```
┌──────────────────────────────┐    ┌──────────────────────────────┐
│       Person1 : Person       │    │       Person2 : Person       │
├──────────────────────────────┤    ├──────────────────────────────┤
│  FirstName : String = Alice  │    │  FirstName : String = Bob    │
└──────────────────────────────┘    └──────────────────────────────┘
```

Figure 8-1: This person class has two person objects.

The Terminology of Object-Oriented Software Design

You run across many terms when you read literature describing object-oriented software development, and you will most likely run across many of these terms while working on C# code. A few of the most frequently used terms include the following:

✦ Abstraction

✦ Abstract data types

✦ Encapsulation

✦ Inheritance

✦ Polymorphism

The following sections define each of these terms in detail.

Abstraction

It's important to realize that programming is *not* about replicating every single real-world aspect about a given concept. When you program a Person class, for example, you are not trying to model everything known about a person. Instead, you work within the context of a specific application. You model only those elements that are needed for this application. Certain characteristics of a person, such as nationality, may exist in the real world, but are omitted if they are not required for your particular application. A person in a banking application will be interested in different aspects than, say, a person in a first-person shooter game. This concept is called *abstraction* and is a necessary technique for handling the unlimited complexity of real-world concepts. Therefore, when you ask yourself questions about objects and classes, always keep in mind that you should ask most of these questions in the context of a specific application.

Abstract data types

Abstract data types were the first attempt at fixing the way data is used in programming. Abstract data types were introduced because in the real world data does not consist of a set of independent variables. The real world is comprised of sets of related data. A person's state for a particular application may, for example, consist of first name, last name, and age. When you want to create a person in a program, you want to create a set of these variables. An abstract data type enables you to package three variables (two strings and an integer) as a whole, and conveniently work with this package to hold the state of a person as shown in the following example:

```
struct Person
{
    public String FirstName;
    public String LastName;
    public int Age;
}
```

When you assign a data type to a variable in your code, you can use a *primitive* data type or an *abstract* data type. Primitive data types are types that the C# language supports as soon as it is installed. Types such as `int`, `long`, `char`, and `string` are primitive data types in the C# language.

Abstract data types are types that the C# language does not support upon installation. You must declare an abstract data type in your code before you can use it. Abstract data types are defined in your code, rather than by the C# compiler.

Consider your `Person` structure (or class), for instance. If you write C# code that uses a `Person` structure (or class) without writing code to tell the C# compiler what a `Person` structure (or class) looks like and how it behaves, you'll get an error from the compiler. Take a look at the following code:

```
class MyClass
{
  static void Main()
  {
      Person MyPerson;

      Person.FirstName = "Malgoska";
  }
}
```

Compiling this code produces the following error from the C# compiler:

```
error CS0234: The type or namespace name 'Person' does not
exist in the class or namespace 'MyClass'
```

The problem with this code is that the data type Person is not a primitive data type and is not defined by the C# language. Because it is not a primitive type, the C# compiler assumes that the type is an abstract data type and searches the code looking for the declaration of the Person data type. The C# compiler cannot find any information about the Person abstract data type, however, and raises an error.

After you define an abstract data type, you can use it in your C# code just as you would a primitive data type. Structures and classes in C# are examples of abstract data types. Once you have defined a structure (or class), you can use variables of that type inside another structure (or class). The following LearningUnit structure contains two Person variables, for example:

```
struct LearningUnit
{
    public Person Tutor;
    public Person Student;
}
```

Encapsulation

With encapsulation, data is tucked away, or *encapsulated,* inside of a class, and the class implements a design that enables other pieces of code to get at that data in an efficient way. Think of encapsulation as a protective wrapper around the data of your C# classes.

For an example of encapsulation, take another look at the Point structure that you worked with in Chapter 7.

```
struct Point
{
    public int X;
    public int Y;
}
```

The data members of this structure are marked as public, which enables any piece of code that accesses the structure access to the data members. Because any piece of code can access the data members, the code can set the values of the data members to any value that can be represented in an int value.

There may be a problem with allowing clients to set the values of data members directly, however. Suppose you're using the Point structure to represent a computer screen with a resolution of 800 × 600. If that's the case, it only makes sense to allow code to set X to values between 0 and 800, and to set Y to values between 0 and 600. With public access to the data members, however, there's really nothing to prevent the code from setting X to 32,000 and Y to 38,000. The C# compiler allows that because those values fit in an integer. The problem is that it doesn't make logical sense to allow values that large.

Encapsulation solves this problem. Basically, the solution is to mark the data members as private, so that code cannot access the data members directly. You may then write methods on a point class like SetX() and SetY(). The SetX() and SetY() methods could set the values, and could also contain code that raises an error if the caller tries to call SetX() or SetY() with parameters whose values are too large. Figure 8-2 illustrates how a Point class may look.

Point
-X : int
-Y : int
+SetX() : bool
+SetY() : bool
+GetX() : int
+GetY() : int

Figure 8-2: The member variables in the Point class are encapsulated.

Note   The minus sign in front of the data members is a UML notation stating that the members have private visibility. The plus sign in front of the methods is a UML notation stating that the methods have public visibility.

Marking the data members as private solves the problem of code setting its values directly. With the data members marked as private, only the class itself can see the data members, and any other code that tries to access the data members gets an error from the compiler.

Instead of accessing the data members directly, the class declares public methods called SetX() and SetY(). These methods are called by code that wants to set the values of the point's X and Y values. These methods can accept the coordinate's new value and a parameter, but can also check the new values to ensure that the new value falls within the appropriate range. If the new value is out of range, the method returns an error. If the new value is within range, the method can proceed to set the new value. The following pseudo-code illustrates how the SetX() method may be implemented:

```
bool SetX(int NewXValue)
{
    if(NewXValue is out of range)
        return false;
    X = NewXValue;
    return true;
}
```

This code has encapsulated the X coordinate data member, and allows callers to set its value while preventing callers from setting the X coordinate to an illegal value.

Because the X and Y coordinate values are now private in this design, other pieces of code cannot examine their current values. Private accessibility in object-oriented design prevents callers from both reading the current value and storing a new value. To expose these private variables, you can implement methods such as GetX() and GetY() to return the current value of the coordinates to the caller.

In this design, the class encapsulates the X and Y values while still allowing other pieces of code to read and write their values. The encapsulation provides an additional benefit, in that the accessor methods prevent the X and Y data members from being set to nonsensical values.

Inheritance

Some classes, like the Point class, are designed from the ground up. The class's state and behaviors are defined in the class. Other classes, however, borrow their definition from another class. Rather than writing another class from scratch, you can borrow state and behaviors from another class and use them as a starting point for the new class. The act of defining one class using another class as a starting point is called *inheritance*.

Single inheritance

Suppose you're writing code using the Point class and you realize that you need to work with three-dimensional points in the same code. The Point class that you've already defined models a two-dimensional point, and you can't use it to describe a three-dimensional point. You decide that you need to write a new class called Point3D. You can design the class in one of two ways:

✦ You can write the Point3D class from scratch, defining data members called X, Y, and Z and writing methods to get and set the data members.

✦ You can inherit from the Point class, which already implements support for the X and Y members. Inheriting from the Point class gives you everything you need to work with for the X and Y members, so all you need to do in your Point3D class is implement support for the Z member. Figure 8-3 illustrates how this might look in UML.

Note   The pound sign in front of the data members is a UML notation stating that the members have protected visibility. Protected means that the visibility is public for derived classes, private for all other classes.

Figure 8-3 illustrates *single inheritance*. Single inheritance allows a class to derive from a single base class. Using inheritance in this manner is also known as deriving one class from another. Some of the state and behavior of the Point3D class is derived from the Point class. In this inheritance situation, the class used as the starting point is known as the *base class*, and the new class is called the *derived class*. In Figure 8-3, Point is the base class and Point3D is the derived class.

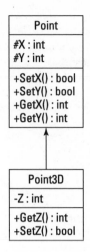

Figure 8-3: The Point3D class inherits the methods and variables from the Point class.

Deriving a class from another class automatically enables the public (and protected) data members and public (and protected) methods of the base class to be available in the derived class. Because the GetX(), GetY(), SetX(), and SetY() methods are marked as public in the base class, they are automatically available to derived classes. This means that the Point3D class has public methods called GetX(), GetY(), SetX(), and SetY() available to it, as they were derived from the Point base class. A piece of code can create an object of type Point3D and call the GetX(), GetY(), SetX(), and SetY() methods, although the methods were not explicitly implemented in that class. They were inherited from the Point base class and can be used in the Point3D derived class.

Multiple inheritance

Some object-oriented languages also allow *multiple inheritance,* which enables a class to derive from more than one base class. C# allows only single inheritance. C# classes can derive from only a single base class. This restriction is due to the fact that the .NET CLR does not support classes with multiple base classes, mostly because other .NET languages, such as Visual Basic, do not have any language support for multiple inheritance. Languages that support multiple inheritance, such as C++, have also demonstrated the difficulty of correctly using multiple inheritance.

Note   If you come across a situation in which you want to use multiple inheritance (for example wanting to have a ClockRadio class inherit from both AlarmClock and Radio), you can get most of the desired behavior by using *containment.* Containment embeds a member variable of the class you want to derive from. Here this technique calls for adding both an AlarmClock and a Radio variable to the ClockRadio class and delegating the wanted functionality to the appropriate private member variable. This technique also works for single inheritance, but it is the only workaround you have to mimic multiple inheritance in .NET—unless Microsoft surprises everyone by adding multiple inheritance in a subsequent version.

Polymorphism

Inheritance allows a derived class to redefine behavior specified by a base class. Suppose you create a base class `Animal`. You make this base class abstract, because you want to code generic animals where possible, but create specific animals, such as a cat and a dog. You read more about this in Chapter 11 where inheritance is covered in detail. The following snippet shows how to declare the class with its abstract method.

```
abstract class Animal
{
        public abstract void MakeNoise();
}
```

Now you can derive specific animals, such as `Cat` and `Dog`, from the abstract `Animal` base class:

```
class Cat : Animal
{
        public override void MakeNoise()
        {
                Console.WriteLine("Meow!");
        }
}

class Dog : Animal
{
        public override void MakeNoise()
        {
                Console.WriteLine("Woof!");
        }
}
```

Notice how each class has its own implementation of the `MakeNoise()` method. The stage is now set for polymorphism. As shown in Figure 8-4, you have a base class with a method that is overridden in two (or more) derived classes. *Polymorphism* is the capability of an object-oriented language to correctly call the overridden method based on which derived class is issuing the method call. This usually happens when a collection of derived objects is stored.

The following code snippet creates a collection of animals, appropriately called a zoo. It then adds a dog and two cats to this zoo.

```
        ArrayList Zoo;
        Zoo = new ArrayList(3);

        Cat Sasha, Koshka;
        Sasha = new Cat();
```

```
Koshka = new Cat();

Dog Milou;
Milou = new Dog();
```

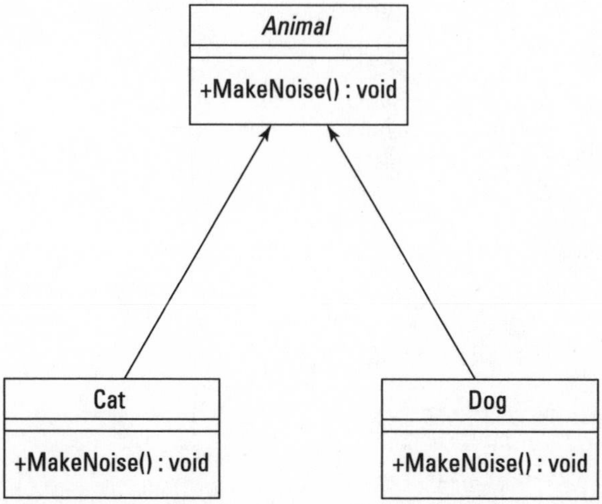

```
            Animal

    +MakeNoise() : void
```

```
       Cat                    Dog

+MakeNoise() : void    +MakeNoise() : void
```

Figure 8-4: This example of inheritance shows one base class and two derived classes.

The zoo collection is a polymorphic collection, because all of its classes are derived from the abstract `Animal` class. You can now iterate through the collection and have each animal make the proper noise:

```
foreach (Animal a in Zoo)
{
        a.MakeNoise();
}
```

Running the preceding code will result in the following output:

```
Woof!
Meow!
Meow!
```

What is going on here? Because C# supports polymorphism, at runtime the program is smart enough to call the dog version of `MakeNoise` when a dog is retrieved from the zoo, and the cat version of `MakeNoise` when a cat is retrieved from the zoo.

Listing 8-1 shows the full C# code illustrating polymorphism.

Listing 8-1: **The Cat and Dog Classes Demonstrate Polymorphism**

```
using System;
using System.Collections;

namespace PolyMorphism
{
  abstract class Animal
  {
        public abstract void MakeNoise();
  }

  class Cat : Animal
  {
        public override void MakeNoise()
        {
            Console.WriteLine("Meow!");
        }
  }

  class Dog : Animal
  {
        public override void MakeNoise()
        {
            Console.WriteLine("Woof!");
        }
  }

  class PolyMorphism
  {
        static int Main(string[] args)
        {
            ArrayList Zoo;
            Zoo = new ArrayList(3);

            Cat Sasha, Koshka;
            Sasha = new Cat();
            Koshka = new Cat();

            Dog Milou;
            Milou = new Dog();

            Zoo.Add(Milou);
            Zoo.Add(Koshka);
            Zoo.Add(Sasha);

            foreach (Animal a in Zoo)
            {
                a.MakeNoise();
            }
```

```
                    // wait for user to acknowledge the results
                    Console.WriteLine("Hit Enter to terminate...");
                    Console.Read();
                    return 0;
                }
            }
        }
```

Summary

C# is an object-oriented language, and the concepts used in object-oriented languages apply to C#.

Abstract data types are data types that you define in your own code. Abstract data types are not built into the C# language, unlike primitive data types. You can use abstract types in your code just as you use primitive data types, but only after you define the abstract data type in your code.

Encapsulation is the act of designing classes that provide a full set of functionality to your class's data without exposing the data directly. Oftentimes, you will want to write code that protects your class from illegal values supplied by other pieces of code. Encapsulation enables you to "hide" your data members by making them private, while making methods that get and set the data member's values public. Other pieces of code can call the methods, which can check the values and issue an error if the values are not appropriate.

Inheritance enables you to define one class in terms of another. Derived classes inherit from the base class. Derived classes automatically inherit the state and the behaviors of the base class. You can use inheritance to add new functionality to existing classes without rewriting a new class completely from scratch. Some object-oriented languages support both single inheritance and multiple inheritance, although C# allows only single inheritance.

Polymorphism enables you to treat a collection of classes derived from a single base class in a uniform way. You retrieve the derived classes as a base class, and C# automatically calls the correct method in the derived class.

This chapter discusses object-oriented concepts in a general sense, without examining how the concepts are used in C# code. The rest of the chapters in this part of the book illustrate how these concepts are implemented in C#.

✦　　✦　　✦

C# Classes

The design of C# is heavily influenced by the concepts of object-oriented software development. Because the class is the foundation of object-oriented software, it should come as no surprise that classes are the single most important idea in C#.

Classes in the object-oriented software development world contain code and data. In C#, data is implemented using data members, and code is implemented using methods. *Data members* are any item for which you can pass data in and out of a class. The two main types of data members are fields and properties. You can write as many data members and methods as you'd like in your C# code, but all of them must be enclosed in one or more classes. The C# compiler issues an error if you try to define any variables or implement any method outside of a class definition.

This chapter discusses the basics of building classes. You learn how to build constructors and destructors, add methods and members as well as using classes after they have been created.

Declaring a Class

Declaring a class is much like declaring a structure. The main difference is that the declaration begins with the C# keyword `class`, rather than `struct`. You've already seen a class definition in previous chapters, but let's review the layout of a class declaration:

- ✦ Optional class modifiers
- ✦ The keyword `class`
- ✦ An identifier used to name the class
- ✦ Optional base class information
- ✦ The class body
- ✦ An optional semicolon

The minimal class declaration in C# looks like the following:

```
class MyClass
{
}
```

The curly brackets surround the body of the class. Class variables and methods are placed within the curly brackets.

Understanding the Main Method

Every C# application must contain a method called `Main`. This is the entry point for the application to run. You can place this method within any class in your project because the compiler is smart enough to look for it when the time arrives.

The `Main` method has two special requirements that must be met before an application can work correctly. First, the method must be declared as `public`. This ensures that the method is accessible. Second, the method must be declared as `static`. The `static` keyword ensures that only one copy of the method can be loaded at any given time.

With those rules in mind, look at the following code:

```
class Class1
{
   public static void Main()
   {
   }
}
```

As you see, this example has one class called `Class1`. This class contains the `Main` method into the application. This `Main` method is where you place all the code to run your application. Although it is OK to put this method in the same class and file as the rest of the code in your application, it's generally a good idea to create a separate class and file for the `Main` method. This helps other developers who may need to deal with your code.

Using command-line arguments

Many applications built for the Windows platform accept command-line parameters. To accept command-line parameters within your C# application, you must declare a string array as the only parameter to the `Main` method, as shown in the following code:

```
class Class1
{
    public static void Main(string[] args)
    {
```

```
            foreach (string arg in args)
                System.Console.WriteLine(arg);
        }
    }
```

Here, a typical class contains the `Main` method. Note that the `Main` method has one parameter defined, a string array that is to be stored in the `args` variable. It uses the `foreach` command to iterate through all the strings that are stored within the `args` array, and then you write those strings out to the console.

 Note   If you are using Visual Studio .NET for your C# development, the string array is automatically added for you when you create a console application.

If you were to run the preceding application with no parameters, nothing would happen. If you were to run the application like this:

```
Sampleap.exe parameter1 parameter2
```

the output from the application would look like the following:

```
parameter1
parameter2
```

Command-line arguments are an excellent way to provide switches to your application; for example, to turn on a log file while your application executes.

Returning values

When you create an application, it often proves useful to return a value to the application that launched it. This value is an indicator to the calling program or batch script that your program succeeded or failed. You can accomplish this simply by giving your `Main` method a return value of `int`, rather than `void`. When your `Main` method is ready to end, you must use the `return` keyword and a value to return, as shown in the following example:

```
class Class1
{
    public static int Main(string[] args)
    {
        if (args[0] == "fail")
            return 1;
        return 0;
    }
}
```

This application accepts a parameter of `fail` or any other word — perhaps `success`. If the word `fail` is passed as a parameter to this application, the program returns a value of 1, indicating a failure of the program. Otherwise, the program returns 0, indicating that the program exited normally. You could test this program using a simple batch file to run the application and then take certain actions depending on the return code. The following code is a simple batch file that performs this function for you:

```
@echo off
retval.exe success

goto answer%errorlevel%

:answer0
echo Program had return code 0 (Success)
goto end

:answer1
echo Program had return code 1 (Failure)
goto end

:end
echo Done!
```

In the preceding code, you can see that the program is called with a parameter of `success`. When you run this batch program, you should see the following message:

```
Program had return code 0 (Success)
```

If you edit this batch program to pass the word `fail` as a parameter, you then see a message confirming that your program terminated with an exit code of 1.

Understanding the Class Body

The class body can include statements whose function falls into one of the following categories:

- ✦ Constants
- ✦ Fields
- ✦ Methods
- ✦ Properties
- ✦ Events
- ✦ Indexers
- ✦ Operators
- ✦ Constructors
- ✦ Destructors
- ✦ Types

Using constants

Class *constants* are variables whose value does not change. Using constants in your code makes the code more readable because constants can include identifiers that describe the meaning of the value to people reading your code. You can write code like the following:

```
if(Ratio == 3.14159)
    System.Console.WriteLine("Shape is a circle");
```

 Cross-Reference Constants are covered in Chapter 4, "Expressions."

The C# compiler happily accepts this code, but it may be a bit hard to read, especially for someone reading the code for the first time and wondering what the floating-point value is. Giving a name to the constant — pi, for example — let's you write code like the following:

```
if(Ratio == Pi)
    System.Console.WriteLine("Shape is a circle");
```

There are other benefits to using constants in your code:

✦ You give constants a value when they are declared, and their name, rather than their value, is used in the code. If for some reason you need to change the value of the constant, you only need to change it in one place: where the constant is declared. If you hardcode the actual value in your C# statements, a change in value means that you need to go through all of your code and change the hardcoded value.

✦ Constants specifically tell the C# compiler that, unlike normal variables, the value of the constant cannot change. The C# compiler issues an error against any code that attempts to change the value of a constant.

The structure of a constant statement is as follows:

✦ The keyword const
✦ A data type for the constant
✦ An identifier
✦ An equals sign
✦ The value of the constant

Defining a constant for pi may look like the following:

```
class MyClass
{
    public const double Pi = 3.1415926535897932384626433832795;
```

```
public static void Main()
{
}
}
```

Cross-Reference This chapter uses the keyword public to describe class body elements as being publicly available to the rest of the code in an application. Chapter 11, "Class Inheritance," looks at alternatives to the public keyword that you can use when you inherit one class from another.

C# enables you to place multiple constant definitions on the same line, provided that all of the constants share the same type. You can separate your class constant definitions with a comma, as follows:

```
class MyClass
{
    public const int One = 1, Two = 2, Three = 3;

    public static void Main()
    {
    }
}
```

Using fields

Fields are data members of a class. They are variables contained within a class and, in object-oriented terms, manage the class's state. Fields defined in a class can be accessed by any method defined in the same class.

You can define a field just as any variable is defined. Fields have a type and an identifier. You may also define a field without an initial value:

```
class MyClass
{
    public int Field1;

    public static void Main()
    {
    }
}
```

You can also define fields with an initial value:

```
class MyClass
{
    public int Field1 = 123;

    public static void Main()
    {
    }
}
```

To mark fields as read-only, prefix the declaration with the `readonly` keyword. If you use the `readonly` keyword, it should appear just before the field's type:

```
class MyClass
{
    public readonly int Field1;

    public static void Main()
    {
    }
}
```

The value of a read-only field may be set when the field is declared or in the constructor of the class. Its value cannot be set at any other time. Any attempt to change the value of a read-only field is caught by the C# compiler and appears as an error:

```
error CS0191: A readonly field cannot be assigned to (except in
a constructor or a variable initializer)
```

Read-only fields behave much like constants in that they are both initialized when an object of the class is created. The main difference between a constant and a read-only field is that the value of constants must be set at compile time — in other words, you must give them a value when you write your code. Read-only fields enable you to determine a value for the field at runtime. Because you can set the value of a read-only field in a class constructor, you can determine its value at runtime and set it when the code is running.

Suppose, for example, that you are writing a C# class that manages a group of records read from a database. You may want to have the class publish a value that specifies the number of records maintained by the class. A constant is not the right choice for this value because the value of a constant must be set when you write the code, and you won't know how many records the class holds until the code runs. You may decide to put this data in a field whose value can be set after the class starts to execute and the number of records can be determined. Because the number of records don't change during the lifetime of your class, you may want to mark the field as read-only so that other pieces of code cannot change its value.

Using methods

Methods are named blocks of code in a class. You can learn more about methods in Chapter 6. They provide the behaviors of your class. Methods can be executed by any other piece of code in the class and, as you learn in Chapter 11, other classes can execute them as well.

Using properties

Chapter 7 discusses a `Point` structure that can describe a point on a screen with a resolution of 640 × 480 pixels. One way to implement this structure is to define it with public data members that describe the coordinates of the point:

```
struct Point
{
    public int X;
    public int Y;
}
```

Using a structure like this, clients can use the structurename.field syntax to work with one of the fields in the structure:

```
Point MyPoint = new Point();

MyPoint.X = 100;
```

This code is easy for clients to write. Clients can access the field directly and use its value in an expression.

The problem with this approach is that clients may set a field to a value allowed by C#, but not logically appropriate for the code. For example, if you're managing a `Point` structure that is used to describe a point on a screen that is 640 × 480 pixels, the largest logical value for X should be 639 (assuming that legal values for X are between 0 and 639). However, because the X coordinate is specified in the structure as an `int`, clients can set the value to any legal value in the range of integers:

```
MyPoint.X = -500;

MyPoint.X = 9000;
```

This code is accepted by the C# compiler because the values assigned to X are within the legal range of integer values.

One solution to this problem is to make the values private, which makes them inaccessible to other pieces of code, and then add a `public` method to the structure that sets the value of X:

```
struct Point
{
    private int X;
    private int Y;

    public bool SetX(int NewXValue)
    {
        if((NewXValue < 0) || (NewXValue > 639))
            return false;
        X = NewXValue;
```

```
                    return true;
            }
      }
```

The advantage of this approach is that it forces clients who want to set the value of X to call a method to get the job done:

```
Point MyPoint = new Point();

MyPoint.SetX(100);
```

The advantage of the method is that you can write code to validate the new value before it is actually stored in the field, and the code in the method can reject the new value if it is not logically appropriate. Clients would then call the method to set a new value.

While this approach works, calling a method to set a value takes a bit more typing than simply setting a value directly. It is more natural for code to assign a value to a field than to call a method to set it.

Ideally, you'd like the best of both worlds: You would like clients to be able to read and write field values directly using simple assignment statements, but you'd also like code to step in beforehand and do any work that is necessary to either get the latest value of a field or validate the new value before it is set. Fortunately, C# provides this feature with a class concept called *properties*.

Properties are named members that provide access to an object's state. Properties have a type and an identifier, and have one or two pieces of code associated with them: a `get` code base and a `set` code base. These code bases are called *accessors*. When a client accesses a property, the `get` accessor of the property is executed. When a client sets a new value for a property, the `set` accessor of the property is executed.

To illustrate how properties work, Listing 9-1 uses a `Point` class that exposes its X and Y values as properties.

Listing 9-1: **Point Values as Class Properties**

```
class Point
{
    private int XCoordinate;
    private int YCoordinate;

    public int X
    {
        get
        {
```

Continued

Listing 9-1 *(continued)*

```
            return XCoordinate;
        }
        set
        {
            if((value >= 0) && (value < 640))
                XCoordinate = value;
        }
    }

    public int Y
    {
        get
        {
            return YCoordinate;
        }
        set
        {
            if((value >= 0) && (value < 480))
                YCoordinate = value;
        }
    }

    public static void Main()
    {
        Point MyPoint = new Point();

        MyPoint.X = 100;
        MyPoint.Y = 200;
        System.Console.WriteLine(MyPoint.X);
        System.Console.WriteLine(MyPoint.Y);
        MyPoint.X = 600;
        MyPoint.Y = 600;
        System.Console.WriteLine(MyPoint.X);
        System.Console.WriteLine(MyPoint.Y);
    }
}
```

The objective of this code is to declare a `Point` class with the X and Y values as properties of the class. The `Main()` method creates a new object of the `Point` class and accesses the class's properties.

The `Point` class defines two private fields that hold the point's coordinate values. Because these fields are private, their values cannot be accessed by code outside of the `Point` class. The class also defines two public properties that enable other pieces of code to work with the point's coordinate values. The properties are public, and other pieces of code can use them. The X property is the public property that manages the value of the private `XCoordinate` field, and the Y property is the public property that manages the value of the private `YCoordinate` field. Both properties both have a `get` and a `set` accessor. The output from Listing 9-1 is shown in Figure 9-1.

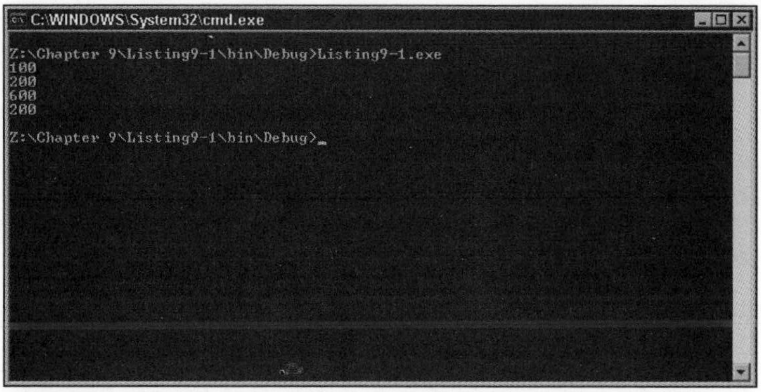

Figure 9-1: Class properties help to store your point values.

Get accessors

The `get` accessors simply return the current value of the corresponding field: the `get` accessor for property `X` returns the current value of `Xcoordinate`, and the `get` accessor for property `Y` returns the current value of `YCoordinate`.

Each `get` accessor must eventually return a value that either matches or can be implicitly converted to the type of the property. If you forget to return a value from a `get` accessor, the C# compiler issues the following error message:

```
error CS0161: 'MyClass.Property.get': not all code paths return
a value
```

Set accessors

The `set` accessors in the example are a bit more complicated because they need to validate the new value before it is actually assigned to the associated field.

Note that the `set` accessors use a keyword called `value`. The value of this identifier is the value of the expression found after the equals sign when the `set` accessor is called. For example, examine the following statement from Listing 9-1:

```
MyPoint.X = 100;
```

The C# compiler determines that the statement is setting a new value to the `Point` object's `X` property. It executes the class's `set` accessor for the `Point` class to satisfy the assignment. Because the property is being set to a value of 100, the value of the `value` keyword in the `set` accessor will be 100.

The set accessors in Listing 9-1 set the corresponding field, but only if the value is within a legal range. In C#, returning values from set accessors are not allowed.

Note   Because C# does not allow set accessors to return a value, you cannot return a value that specifies whether or not the assignment was successful. However, you can use exceptions to report any errors. Chapter 16, "Handling Exceptions," covers exceptions.

Read-only and write-only properties

The properties in Listing 9-1 can be read from using its get accessor and written to using its set accessor. These properties are referred to as *read/write properties*. When you design your C# classes, you may have a need to implement a read-only or a write-only property. This is easy to do in C#.

If you need to implement a read-only property, specify a property with a get accessor but no set accessor:

```
public int X
{
    get
    {
        return XCoordinate;
    }
}
```

If you need to implement a write-only property, specify a property with a set accessor, but no get accessor:

```
public int X
{
    set
    {
        if((value >= 0) && (value < 640))
            XCoordinate = value;
    }
}
```

Using events

C# allows classes to notify other pieces of code when an action occurs in the class. This capability is called the *event mechanism*, and it enables callers to be notified when an event occurs in a C# class. You can design C# classes to notify other pieces of code when certain events take place in the class. The class can send an event notification back to the original piece of code.

You may want to use an event, for example, to inform other pieces of code when a lengthy operation completes. Suppose, for example, that you're designing a C# class that reads from a database. If the database activity is going to take a long time, it may be better for another piece of code to do other things while the database is being read. When the read is complete, the C# class can fire an event that says "the read has completed." Other pieces of code can be notified when this event is sent out, and the code can take appropriate action when the event is received from the C# class.

Cross-Reference The event-handling mechanism in C# works in conjunction with another C# concept called a *delegate*. You take closer look at delegates and events in Chapter 15, "Events and Delegates."

Using indexers

Some classes that you design may actually act as containers for other values. Suppose, for example, that you write a C# class called `Rainbow` that enables clients to access string values naming the colors of the rainbow in order. You want callers to be able to retrieve the string values, so you use some public methods that allow callers to access the values. Listing 9-2 illustrates what your C# code might look like.

Listing 9-2: A Class with a Set of String Values

```
class Rainbow
{
    public int GetNumberOfColors()
    {
        return 7;
    }

    public bool GetColor(int ColorIndex, out string ColorName)
    {
        bool ReturnValue;

        ReturnValue = true;
        switch(ColorIndex)
        {
            case 0:
                ColorName = "Red";
                break;
            case 1:
                ColorName = "Orange";
                break;
            case 2:
                ColorName = "Yellow";
                break;
            case 3:
                ColorName = "Green";
                break;
            case 4:
                ColorName = "Blue";
```

Continued

Listing 9-2 *(continued)*

```
                    break;
                case 5:
                    ColorName = "Indigo";
                    break;
                case 6:
                    ColorName = "Violet";
                    break;
                default:
                    ColorName = "";
                    ReturnValue = false;
                    break;
            }
            return ReturnValue;
        }

    public static void Main()
    {
        int     ColorCount;
        int     ColorIndex;
        Rainbow MyRainbow = new Rainbow();

        ColorCount = MyRainbow.GetNumberOfColors();

string ColorName;
        bool    Success;

        for(ColorIndex = 0; ColorIndex < ColorCount;
ColorIndex++)
        {
            Success = MyRainbow.GetColor(ColorIndex, out
ColorName);
            if(Success == true)
                System.Console.WriteLine(ColorName);
        }
    }
}
```

The Rainbow class in Listing 9-2 has two public methods:

✦ GetColorCount(), which returns the number of colors in the class

✦ GetColor(), which returns the name of one of the colors in the class, based on a color number

The Main() method creates a new object of class Rainbow and asks the object for the number of colors that it maintains. It then sits in a for loop, requesting the name of each color. The color name is written to the console. The output of this application is shown in Figure 9-2.

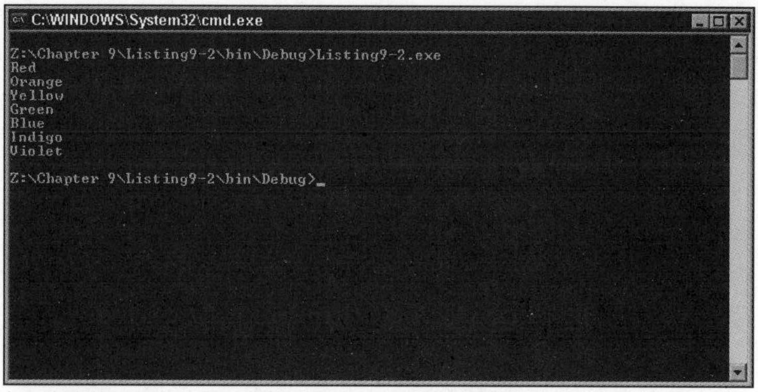

Figure 9-2: Indexers are to retrieve color names.

You might recognize that the class is maintaining a collection of values of the same value type, which sounds a lot like an array. In fact, this `Rainbow` class could also be implemented as an array, and the caller could use the array element accessor square bracket syntax to retrieve an individual color name:

```
ColorName = Rainbow[ColorIndex];
```

The C# concept of indexers enables you to let your class be accessed as if it were an array. You write a piece of code called an *indexer accessor* to specify what should be returned when callers use the square bracket syntax to access an element in your class.

Knowing this, you can rewrite the `Rainbow` class to allow callers to access color names using the square bracket syntax. Remove the `GetColor()` method and replace it with an indexer. Replace the `GetColorCount()` method with a read-only property called `Count`, as shown in Listing 9-3.

Listing 9-3: **The Rainbow Class with an Indexer**

```
class Rainbow
{
    public int Count
    {
        get
        {
            return 7;
        }
    }

    public string this[int ColorIndex]
    {
```

Continued

Listing 9-3 *(continued)*

```
        get
        {
            switch(ColorIndex)
            {
                case 0:
                    return "Red";
                case 1:
                    return "Orange";
                case 2:
                    return "Yellow";
                case 3:
                    return "Green";
                case 4:
                    return "Blue";
                case 5:
                    return "Indigo";
                case 6:
                    return "Violet";
                default:
                    return "";
            }
        }
    }

    public static void Main()
    {
        int     ColorIndex;
        Rainbow MyRainbow = new Rainbow();

string ColorName;

        for(ColorIndex = 0; ColorIndex < MyRainbow.Count;
ColorIndex++)
        {
            ColorName = MyRainbow[ColorIndex];
            System.Console.WriteLine(ColorName);
        }
    }
}
```

Indexers are much like properties in that they have get and set accessors. Either accessor may be left off, if necessary. The indexer in Listing 9-3 does not have a set accessor, which means that the class can have its collection read from but not written to.

Indexers are structured with the following items:

✦ A type denoting the type of data being returned from the accessor

✦ The keyword this

✦ An opening square bracket

✦ A parameter list, structured just as parameter lists in methods are structured

✦ A closing square bracket

✦ A body of code, enclosed by curly braces

The indexer in Listing 9-4 takes an integer argument and returns a string, much like the GetColor() method in Listing 9-2.

Listing 9-4: **An Integer Argument Returning a String**

```
string ColorName;

for(ColorIndex = 0; ColorIndex < MyRainbow.Count; ColorIndex++)
{

ColorName = MyRainbow[ColorIndex];
System.Console.WriteLine(ColorName);
}
```

The new code is using the array element square bracket syntax to get a color name from the MyRainbow object. This causes the C# compiler to call the class's indexer code, which passes the value of ColorIndex in as a parameter. A string is returned from the indexer, and the string is written out to the console.

A class can implement more than one indexer, as long as the indexers have different parameter lists. Parameter lists in indexers can have more than one parameter, and they can be of any type that you can use in your code. Indexers do not have to use integers as indexers. For the Rainbow class, you could have just as easily implemented an indexer that accepts a double value:

```
public string this[double ColorIndex]
```

Note   Like properties, C# does not allow set accessors in indexers to return a value. However, you can use exceptions to report any errors. Chapter 16 covers exceptions.

Using operators

An operator enables you to define how your class behaves when it is used in an expression with a unary or binary operator. This means that you can extend the behavior of predefined operators to suit the needs of your class. The Point class, for example, could implement code specifying that two Point objects can be added together with the + operator. The result of the addition would be a third Point object whose state is the result of adding two other points together.

 Cross-Reference Chapter 10, Overloading Operators," looks at operators.

Using constructors

Structure *constructors* are special methods that are executed when a variable of the structure type is created. Constructors are usually used to initialize a structure to a known state.

You can use constructors in your C# classes just as you can in your C# structures. You can define as many constructors as you want, as long as each constructor has a different parameter list. You can write a Point class with constructors just as you did with the Point structure, as shown in Listing 9-5.

Listing 9-5: A Point Class with Two Constructors

```
class Point
{
    public int X;
    public int Y;

    public Point()
    {
        X = 0;
        Y = 0;
    }

    public Point(int InitialX, int InitialY)
    {
        X = InitialX;
        Y = InitialY;
    }


    public static void Main()
    {
        Point MyFirstPoint = new Point(100, 200);
        Point MySecondPoint = new Point();
    }
}
```

The Point class in Listing 9-5 has two public fields: X and Y. It also implements two constructors. One of the constructors doesn't use any parameters, and the other constructor uses two parameters.

Constructors in C# classes are much like constructors in C# structures. Class constructors do not return values and their name must match the name of the class. The main difference between structure constructors and class constructors is that class constructors can implement a constructor with no parameters, whereas a structure constructor cannot.

If you define a class without any constructors, C# supplies a default constructor for you. The default constructor simply sets all the fields in the class to their default values.

If you initialize any of the fields in a class with the equals sign syntax, they are initialized before the constructor is executed:

```
class Point
{
    public int X = 100;
    public int Y;

    public Point(int InitialY)
    {
        Y = InitialY + X;
    }
}
```

In this Point class, an assignment statement initializes the X field, and the constructor initializes the Y field. When this code is compiled, the C# compiler ensures that the X field is initialized first.

Using destructors

Classes in C# can define a destructor, which is a special method that executes when objects of the class are destroyed by the CLR (Common Language Runtime). You can think of destructors as the opposite of constructors: constructors execute when objects are created, and destructors execute when the objects are destroyed by the built in Garbage Collection facility. This process occurs behind the scenes with no consequence to the developer.

Destructors are optional. It is certainly legal to write a C# class without a destructor (and, up to this point, the examples have been doing just that). If you do write a destructor, you can only write one.

Note   Unlike constructors, you cannot have more than one destructor defined for a class.

Destructors have the following layout:

◆ The tilde character (~)

◆ The destructor identifier, which must match the name of the class

◆ A set of parentheses

Listing 9-6 updates the Point class in Listing 9-5 with a destructor.

Listing 9-6: **A Point Class with a Destructor**

```
class Point
{
    public int X;
    public int Y;

    public Point()
    {
        X = 0;
        Y = 0;
    }

    public Point(int InitialX, int InitialY)
    {
        X = InitialX;
        Y = InitialY;
    }

    ~Point()
    {
        X = 0;
        Y = 0;
    }

    public static void Main()
    {
        Point MyFirstPoint = new Point(100, 200);
        Point MySecondPoint = new Point();
    }
}
```

Destructors cannot return any values; nor can they accept any parameters. You cannot call a destructor in code. If you try to call a destructor, the C# compiler issues an error.

In many object-oriented programming languages, class destructors are called when the variable can no longer be used. Suppose, for example, that you write a method and declare a Point object as a local variable in the method. When the method is called, the Point object is created, and the method can work with the Point object. When the method reaches the end of its code block, the Point object can no longer be used, and it is destroyed. In languages such as C++, this causes the class's constructor to be called when the method exits.

This is not necessarily true with C#. In fact, a class destructor may not be called at all. Remember that the CLR implements a feature called garbage collection, which destroys objects that are no longer used in code. This garbage collection may happen long after an object is inaccessible. Take a look at the Main() method in Listing 9-7:

Listing 9-7: **Using Point Structure to Demonstrate Garbage Collection**

```
public static void Main()
{
    Point MyFirstPoint = new Point(100, 200);
    Point MySecondPoint = new Point();
}
```

The Main() method creates two local Point objects. After the Main() method finishes executing, the local Point objects can no longer be used and will be noted by the CLR as objects that can be destroyed when the garbage collector executes. However, the garbage collector won't necessarily kick in right away, which means that the object's destructor won't necessarily be called right away.

Note   Destructors in C# classes are called when an object is destroyed, not when its variable is no longer accessible. Be sure to keep this in mind when you are designing your C# classes.

As an example, suppose that you want to write a C# class that manages a file on disk. You might write a class called File with a constructor that opens the file, and a destructor that closes the file:

```
class File
{
    File(string Name)
    {
        // open file
    }
    ~File()
```

```
        {
            // close file
        }
    }
```

You may want to use this class to work with a file in a method:

```
public static void Main()
{
    File MyFile = new File("myfile.txt");
}
```

The destructor for the `File` class closes the file, but the destructor is actually executed until the CLR garbage collector kicks in. This means that the file may still be open long after the `MyFile` variable becomes inaccessible. If you want to ensure that the file is closed as soon as possible, consider adding to the `File` class a `Close()` method, which closes the file when called.

Note   You can ask the CLR to execute the garbage collection algorithm on demand, which increases the chance (but still does not guarantee) that the garbage collector collects your object and call its destructor. See Chapter 20, "Brainteasers,," for more information.

Using class types

Classes can use one of the types built in to C#—for example, `int`, `long`, and `char`—and they can define their own types. Classes can include declarations of other items, such as structures or even other classes.

Cross-Reference   Take another look at Listing 7-6 in Chapter 7, "Grouping Data Using Structures." The listing defines a class called `Listing7_6`. The class contains the definition of a structure called `Point`. This `Point` structure is defined within the `Listing7_6` class, and it can be used as a type, just as the class uses any of the types built in to C#.

Using the this Keyword as an Identifier

With C#, you can use the `this` keyword to identify an object whose code is being executed, which in turn enables you to reference the current object.

You can use the `this` keyword in a variety of ways. You've already seen how it is used in an indexer. You can also use it as a prefix to a variable identifier to tell the C# compiler that an expression should reference a class field.

For example, consider the `Point` class in Listing 9-8.

Listing 9-8: **Fields and Parameters with the Same Name**

```
class Point
{
    public int X;
    public int Y;

    Point(int X, int Y)
    {
        X = X;
        Y = Y;
    }

    public static void Main()
    {
    }
}
```

This code won't behave as expected because the X and Y identifiers are used twice: once as class field identifiers and once in the constructor's parameter list. The code needs to distinguish the field identifier X from the parameter list identifier X. With ambiguous code like this, the C# compiler assumes that the references to X and Y in the constructor statements refer to the parameters, and the code just sets the parameters to the value that they already contain.

You can use the this keyword to differentiate the field identifier from the parameter identifier. Listing 9-9 shows the corrected code with the this keyword used as the prefix for the field name.

Listing 9-9: **Using this with Fields**

```
class Point
{
    public int X;
    public int Y;

    Point(int X, int Y)
    {
        this.X = X;
        this.Y = Y;
    }

    public static void Main()
    {
    }
}
```

Understanding the Static Modifier

When you define a field or a method on a class, each object of that class created by code has its own copy of field values and methods. By using the static keyword, you can override this behavior, which enables multiple objects of the same class to share field values and methods.

Using static fields

As an example, let's return to our Point class. A Point class may have two fields for the point's x and y coordinates. Every object created from the Point class has copies of those fields, but each object can have its own values for the x and y coordinates. Setting the x and y coordinates of one object does not affect the settings of another object:

```
Point MyFirstPoint = new Point(100, 200);
Point MySecondPoint = new Point(150, 250);
```

In this example, two objects of class Point are created. The first object sets its copy of the x and y coordinates to 100 and 200, respectively, while the second object sets its copy of the x and y coordinates to 150 and 250, respectively. Each object is keeping its own copy of x and y coordinates.

Placing the static modifier before a field definition indicates that all objects of the same class will be sharing the same value. If one object sets a static value, all other objects of that same class will share that same value. Take a look at Listing 9-10.

Listing 9-10: **Static Fields**

```
class Point
{
    public static int XCoordinate;
    public static int YCoordinate;

    public int X
    {
        get
        {
            return XCoordinate;
        }
    }

    public int Y
    {
        get
        {
            return YCoordinate;
```

```
        }
    }

    public static void Main()
    {
        Point MyPoint = new Point();

        System.Console.WriteLine("Before");
        System.Console.WriteLine("======");
        System.Console.WriteLine(MyPoint.X);
        System.Console.WriteLine(MyPoint.Y);

        Point.XCoordinate = 100;
        Point.YCoordinate = 200;

        System.Console.WriteLine("After");
        System.Console.WriteLine("=====");
        System.Console.WriteLine(MyPoint.X);
        System.Console.WriteLine(MyPoint.Y);
    }
}
```

The `Point` class in Listing 9-10 maintains two static integer fields called `XCoordinate` and `YCoordinate`. It also maintains two read-only properties, called `X` and `Y`, that return the values of the static variables.

The Main() method creates a new `Point` object and outputs its coordinates to the console. It then changes the values of the static fields and outputs the coordinates of the `Point` object a second time. The results are shown in Figure 9-3.

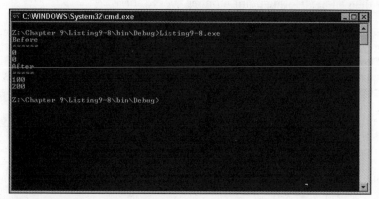

Figure 9-3: The usage of static fields simplifies coding.

Note that the values of the `Point` object coordinates have changed, although the values in the object itself were not changed. This is because the `Point` object shares static fields with all other `Point` objects, and when the `Point` class's static fields change, all the objects in that class reflect the change.

Also note the syntax for working with static fields. Static fields used in expressions are prefixed not with an object identifier, but with the name of the class that holds the static fields. The following statement is in error because `MyPoint` refers to an object, and `XCoordinate` refers to a static field:

```
MyPoint.XCoordinate = 100;
```

Writing code like this causes an error to be raised from the C# compiler:

```
error CS0176: Static member 'Point.XCoordinate' cannot be
accessed with an instance reference; use typename instead
```

The static field must be prefixed with the name of the class:

```
Point.XCoordinate = 100;
```

Using static constants

Constants work just as fields do unless they are prefixed by the `static` keyword; if so, each object of the class maintains its own copy of the constant. However, making each object in a class maintain its own copy of a constant is a waste of memory.

Suppose you're writing a class called `Circle`, which manages a circle. Because you're working with a circle, you'll probably be using the value `pi` quite a bit. You wisely decide to make `pi` a constant, so you can refer to it in your code with a name, rather than a long floating-point number every time.

Now, what happens if you create one thousand circle objects? By default, they each get their own copy of the `pi` constant. You'll have one thousand copies of `pi` sitting in memory. This is a waste of memory, especially because `pi` is a constant and its value never changes. It makes more sense for every object in your `Circle` class to use a single copy of the `pi` constant.

This is where the `static` keyword comes in. Using the `static` keyword with a constant ensures that each object of a class works with a single in-memory copy of the constant's value:

```
const double Pi = 3.1415926535897932384626433832795;
```

In general, try to make all of your constants *static* constants so that only one copy of the constant's value is in memory at any one time.

Using static methods

When you first took a look at the Main() method, recall that it needed to be defined with the static keyword. Methods that are defined with the static keyword are called *static methods*. Methods that are not defined with the static keyword are called *instance methods*.

Static methods are listed in a class but do not belong to a specific object. Like static fields and static constants, all objects of a class share one copy of a static method. Static methods cannot refer to any part of an object that is not also marked as static, as shown in Listing 9-11.

Listing 9-11: **Static Methods Calling Class Instance Methods**

```
class Listing9_9
{
    public static void Main()
    {
        CallMethod();
    }

    void CallMethod()
    {
        System.Console.WriteLine("Hello from CallMethod()");
    }
}
```

The preceding code doesn't compile, and the C# compiler issues the following error:

```
error CS0120: An object reference is required for the nonstatic
field, method, or property 'Listing9_9.CallMethod()'
```

The problem with the code in Listing 9-11 is that a static method, Main(), is trying to call an instance method, CallMethod(). This is forbidden because instance methods are part of an object instance, and static methods are not.

To correct this code, the static Main() method must create another object of the class and call the instance method from the new object, as shown in Listing 9-12.

Listing 9-12: **Static Methods Calling Object Instance Methods**

```
class Listing9_10
{
    public static void Main()
    {
        Listing9_10 MyObject = new Listing9_10();

        MyObject.CallMethod();
    }

    void CallMethod()
    {
        System.Console.WriteLine("Hello from CallMethod()");
    }
}
```

The output from Listing 9-12 is shown in Figure 9-4.

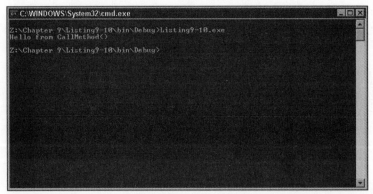

Figure 9-4: Demonstrating a static method call from within the same class

Like all static class items, static methods appear only once in memory, which is why you must mark the Main() method as static. When .NET code is loaded into memory, the CLR starts by executing the Main() method. Remember that only one Main() method can be in memory at any one time. If a class had multiple Main() methods, the CLR would not know which Main() method to execute when the code needs to run. Using the static keyword on the Main() method ensures that only one copy of the Main() method is available in memory.

Note   By using command-line parameters with the C# compiler, it is possible to include more than one Main() method within your application. This can be very handy when you want to try more than one method for debugging purposes.

Summary

C# is an object-oriented language, and the concepts that are used in object-oriented languages apply to C#. C# classes can make use of several types of class members:

✦ *Constants* give a name to a value that doesn't change throughout the code. Using constants makes your code more readable because you can use the names of the constants in place of hardcoded literal values in your code.

✦ *Fields* maintain the state of your classes. Fields are variables that are associated with an object.

✦ *Methods* maintain the behavior of your classes. Methods are named pieces of code that perform a particular action for your class.

✦ *Properties* enable you to expose your class's state to callers. Callers access properties with the same object.identifier syntax used to access fields. The advantage of properties over fields is that you can write code that is executed when property values are retrieved or set. This enables you to write validation code against new values assigned to properties, or to dynamically calculate the value of a property being retrieved. You can implement read-write properties, read-only properties, or write-only properties.

✦ *Events* enable your class to notify callers when certain actions take place within it. Callers can subscribe to class events and can receive notifications when the events actually occur.

✦ *Indexers* enable your class to be accessed as if it were an array. Callers can use the square bracket array element syntax to execute your class's indexer accessor code. Use indexers when your class contains a collection of values and it makes sense to think of your class as an array of items.

✦ Your class can redefine operators, as you see in Chapter 10. The operators can help determine how the class behaves when it is used in an expression with an operator.

✦ *Constructors* are special methods that execute when objects of the class are created. You may define more than one constructor, each with a different parameter list. You can also define a class without a constructor. In this case, the C# compiler generates a default constructor that simply initializes all the fields in the object to a zero value.

✦ *Destructors* are special methods that execute when objects of the class are destroyed. A class can have only one destructor. Because of the interaction with .NET code and the CLR, destructors execute when an object is garbage collected, not simply when the object's identifier is no longer accessible by code.

✦ Classes can define types of their own, and these types can contain structure definitions and even definitions of other classes. After these types are defined, the class can use them just as it would use the types built into C#.

The this keyword refers to the current instance of an object. It is used as a prefix to differentiate a field identifier from a parameter identifier with the same name.

The static keyword tells the C# compiler that only one copy of a field or method is shared by all objects of the class. By default, each field and method in a C# class maintains its own copy of field values. Class items that do not use the static keyword are called *instance methods*. Class items that do use the static keyword are called *static methods*.

✦   ✦   ✦

Overloading Operators

Chapter 4 looked at the variety of operators available for use with expressions in C#. The C# language defines the behavior of these operators when used in an expression with the C# built-in data types. For example, C# defines the behavior of the addition operator as adding the values of two operands and providing the sum as the value of the expression.

With C#, you can define the behavior of many of the standard operators for use with your own structures and classes. You write special methods that define the behavior of your class when it appears in an expression using a C# operator. This enables your classes to be used in expressions that seem natural for other pieces of code to write. Suppose, for example, that you're writing a class that manages a set of records read from a database. If another piece of code has two objects of your class, it may want to write an expression that joins the records together into a third object. This sounds like an addition operation, and it seems natural for other pieces of code to write code like the following:

```
Records Records1;
Records Records2;
Records Records3;

Records3 = Records1 + Records2;
```

Your `Records` class would include a method that specifies how objects of the class would behave when used in an expression with the addition operator.

These methods are called *user-defined operator implementations*, and the object-oriented terminology for defining operator behavior in a class is called *operator overloading*. The word "overloading" is used because your body of code overloads the meaning of the same operator and makes it behave differently, depending on the context in which the operator is used.

All operator overloading methods must be declared with both the `static` and `public` keywords.

Overloadable Unary Operators

C# enables you to overload the behavior of the following unary operators in your classes and structures:

✦ Unary plus

✦ Unary minus

✦ Logical negation

✦ Bitwise complement operator

✦ Prefix increment

✦ Prefix decrement

✦ The `true` keyword

✦ The `false` keyword

Overloading unary plus

If you need to overload the unary plus, unary minus, negation, or bitwise complement operators in your class or structure, define a method with the following characteristics:

✦ A return type of your choice

✦ The keyword `operator`

✦ The operator being overloaded

✦ A parameter list specifying a single parameter of the type of class or structure containing the overloaded operator method

As an example, revisit the `Point` class from Chapter 9. Suppose that you want to add a unary plus operator to the class that, when used, ensures that the coordinates of the point are both positive. This is implemented in Listing 10-1.

Listing 10-1: **Overloading the Unary Plus Operator**

```
class Point
{
    public int X;
    public int Y;

    public static Point operator + (Point RValue)
    {
        Point NewPoint = new Point();

        if(RValue.X < 0)
```

```
            NewPoint.X = -(RValue.X);
        else
            NewPoint.X = RValue.X;

        if(RValue.Y < 0)
            NewPoint.Y = -(RValue.Y);
        else
            NewPoint.Y = RValue.Y;

        return NewPoint;
    }

    public static void Main()
    {
        Point MyPoint = new Point();

        MyPoint.X = -100;
        MyPoint.Y = 200;
        System.Console.WriteLine(MyPoint.X);
        System.Console.WriteLine(MyPoint.Y);

        MyPoint = +MyPoint;
        System.Console.WriteLine(MyPoint.X);
        System.Console.WriteLine(MyPoint.Y);
    }
}
```

The Main() method creates an object of type Point and sets its initial coordinates to (100, 200). It then applies the unary plus operator to the object and reassigns the result to the same point. It prints out the *x* and *y* coordinates to the console.

The output of Listing 10-1 is shown in Figure 10-1.

Figure 10-1: Overloading the unary operator

The coordinates of the point have changed from (-100, 200) to (100, 200). The overloaded operator code is executed when the following statement is reached:

```
MyPoint = +MyPoint;
```

When this statement is reached, the unary plus operator overload for the Point class is executed. The expression on the right side of the equal sign is supplied as the parameter to the method.

Note   The expression on the right-hand side of an assignment operator is often referred to as an rvalue, which is short for "right value." The expression on the left-hand side of an assignment operator is often referred to an lvalue, which is short for "left value." Naming the parameter in the operator overload method RValue makes it clear that the rvalue of the assignment is being passed in. This is just a naming convention and not a requirement. You are free to name your parameters using any legal identifier allowed by C#.

This method creates a new Point object and then examines the coordinates of the supplied rvalue. If either of the parameters is negative, their values are negated, thereby turning them to positive values; and the now-positive values are assigned to the new point. Values that are not negative are assigned to the new point without any conversion. The new point is then returned from the method. The return value from the operator is used as the lvalue for the original statement.

The return type of operator overloads for the unary plus, unary minus, negation, or bitwise complement operators does not have to be the same type as the rvalue. It can be any C# type that makes the most sense for the operator.

Overloading unary minus

Much like the unary plus, you can perform the unary minus override in the very same fashion. Listing 10-2 overrides the minus operator to handle the Point class.

Listing 10-2: **Overloading Unary Minus**

```
class Point
{
  public int X;
  public int Y;

  public static Point operator - (Point RValue)
  {
        Point NewPoint = new Point();

        if (RValue.X > 0)
                NewPoint.X = -(RValue.X);
        else
```

```
                NewPoint.X = RValue.X;

        if (RValue.Y > 0)
                NewPoint.Y = -(RValue.Y);
        else
                NewPoint.Y = RValue.Y;

        return NewPoint;
    }
    public static void Main()
    {
        Point MyPoint = new Point();
        MyPoint.X = -100;
        MyPoint.Y = 200;
        System.Console.WriteLine(MyPoint.X);
        System.Console.WriteLine(MyPoint.Y);

        MyPoint = -MyPoint;
        System.Console.WriteLine(MyPoint.X);
        System.Console.WriteLine(MyPoint.Y);
    }
}
```

After you define your new `Point` operator, you simply define the action it should take when presented with a variable of type `Point`. Listing 10-2 declares the *x* coordinate as -100 and the *y* coordinate as 200. You print these values out to the console for visual verification and then use your overloaded operator.

After your sample application has subtracted from the `Point` class, the resulting values are printed to the console window to indicate that it behaved as expected. Figure 10-2 is the output from Listing 10-2.

Figure 10-2: Overloading unary minus

So far, this chapter has covered unary minus and unary plus. These operators perform operations given one value—hence, the "unary." Other basic mathematical operators that can be used on one value are overloaded in the same fashion.

The next section describes an operator of a different kind—the bitwise complement operator.

Overloading bitwise complement

The bitwise complement operator only has definitions for int, uint, long, and ulong. Listing 10-3 overloads it to work with the point class.

Listing 10-3: **Overloading the Bitwise Complement Operator**

```
class Point
{
  public int X;
  public int Y;

  public static Point operator ~ (Point RValue)
  {
    Point NewPoint = new Point();
    NewPoint.X = ~RValue.X;
    NewPoint.Y = ~RValue.Y;

    return NewPoint;
  }

  public static void Main()
  {
    Point MyPoint = new Point();

    MyPoint.X = 5;
    MyPoint.Y = 6;
    System.Console.WriteLine(MyPoint.X);
    System.Console.WriteLine(MyPoint.Y);
    MyPoint = ~MyPoint;
    System.Console.WriteLine(MyPoint.X);
    System.Console.WriteLine(MyPoint.Y);
  }
}
```

The output of a bitwise complement operation doesn't become apparent until you view the hex results of the operation. Listing 10-3 generates the complement of the integer values 5 and 6. The output of this operation (shown in Figure 10-3) is -6 and -7, respectively. When you view the hex values of the input and output values, you soon realize what is actually happening.

Figure 10-3: Overloading the bitwise complement

Table 10-1 Input and Output Values for a Bitwise Complement Operation	
Input	*Output*
0x0000000000000005	0xfffffffffffffffA
0x0000000000000006	0xfffffffffffffff9

Before you overload an operator, it is imperative that you fully understand how it works. Otherwise, you may end up with some unexpected results.

Overloading the prefix increment

If you need to overload the prefix increment or prefix decrement operators in your class or structure, define a method with the following characteristics:

✦ A return type specifying the type of class or structure containing the overloaded operator method

✦ The keyword `operator`

✦ The operator being overloaded

✦ A parameter list specifying a single parameter of the type of class or structure containing the overloaded operator method

For an example, look at Listing 10-4. This class modifies the `Point` class to overload the prefix increment operator. The operator is overloaded to increment the *x* and *y* coordinates by one unit.

Listing 10-4: Overloading the Prefix Increment

```
class Point
{
    public int X;
    public int Y;

    public static Point operator ++ (Point RValue)
    {
        Point NewPoint = new Point();

        NewPoint.X = RValue.X + 1;
        NewPoint.Y = RValue.Y + 1;
        return NewPoint;
    }

    public static void Main()
    {
        Point MyPoint = new Point();

        MyPoint.X = 100;
        MyPoint.Y = 200;
        System.Console.WriteLine(MyPoint.X);
        System.Console.WriteLine(MyPoint.Y);

        MyPoint = ++MyPoint;
        System.Console.WriteLine(MyPoint.X);
        System.Console.WriteLine(MyPoint.Y);

    }
}
```

Compiling and running the code in Listing 10-4 writes the following to the console:

```
100
200
101
201
```

Overloading the prefix decrement

Now you'll examine how to overload the decrement operator to handle the Point class. Listing 10-5 contains the complete code listing to overload the operator much like that of the prefix increment operator just covered.

Figure 10-4: Output from compiling and running the code in Listing 10-4

Listing 10-5: **Overloading the Prefix Decrement Operator**

```
class Point
{
    public int X;
    public int Y;

    public static Point operator -- (Point RValue)
    {
        Point NewPoint = new Point();

        NewPoint.X = RValue.X - 1;
        NewPoint.Y = RValue.Y - 1;
        return NewPoint;
    }

    public static void Main()
    {
        Point MyPoint = new Point();

        MyPoint.X = 100;
        MyPoint.Y = 200;
        System.Console.WriteLine(MyPoint.X);
        System.Console.WriteLine(MyPoint.Y);

        MyPoint = --MyPoint;
        System.Console.WriteLine(MyPoint.X);
        System.Console.WriteLine(MyPoint.Y);
    }
}
```

Again, you pass in an *x* coordinate of 100 and a *y* coordinate of 200. Figure 10-5 contains the output of this program after your overload decrement operator has subtracted from both *x* and *y*.

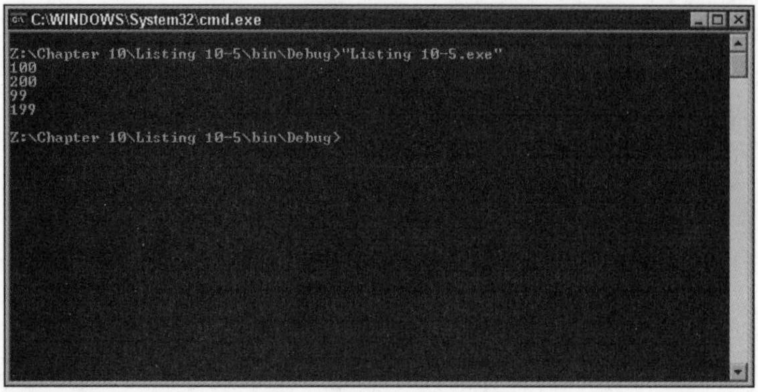

Figure 10-5: Overloading the prefix decrement operator

Always assume the worst when overloading operators. It is always possible that the data being passed in may be bad, and you'll find that your overloaded function isn't equipped to handle the data. The previous examples don't bother to catch exceptions that may be thrown when bad or unexpected values are passed in. It's a good idea to play around with the functions and attempt to beef up the error trapping a bit.

Overloading the true and false operators

If you need to overload the `true` or `false` operators in your class or structure, define a method with the following characteristics:

✦ A return type of `bool`

✦ The keyword `operator`

✦ The operator being overloaded

✦ A parameter list specifying a single parameter of the type of class or structure containing the overloaded operator method

For an example, look at Listing 10-6. It modifies the `point` class to evaluate to `true` whether the point is on the origin and to evaluate to `false` otherwise.

Listing 10-6: **Overloading the True and False Operators**

```
class Point
{
    public int X;
    public int Y;

    public static bool operator true (Point RValue)
    {
        if((RValue.X == 0) && (RValue.Y == 0))
            return true;
        return false;
    }

    public static bool operator false (Point RValue)
    {
        if((RValue.X == 0) && (RValue.Y == 0))
            return false;
        return true;
    }

    public static void Main()
    {
        Point MyPoint = new Point();

        MyPoint.X = 100;
        MyPoint.Y = 200;

        if(MyPoint)
            System.Console.WriteLine("The point is at the origin.");
        else
            System.Console.WriteLine("The point is not at the origin.");
    }
}
```

Overloading the true and false operators allows objects of the `Point` class to be used as Boolean expressions, as in the `if` statement. Because the `MyPoint` object is not at the origin, the object evaluates to `false`, as shown in Figure 10-6.

If either the true or false operators are overloaded for a class or structure, they both must be overloaded. If you overload one but not the other, the C# compiler issues an error message like the following:

```
error CS0216: The operator 'Point.operator true(Point)'
requires a matching operator 'false' to also be defined
```

Figure 10-6: Overloading the true and false operators

Overloadable Binary Operators

Following is a list of the binary operators that can be overloaded:

✦ Addition

✦ Subtraction

✦ Multiplication

✦ Division

✦ Remainder

✦ AND

✦ OR

✦ Exclusive OR

✦ Shift left

✦ Shift right

✦ Equality

✦ Inequality

✦ Greater than

✦ Less than

✦ Greater than or equal to

✦ Less than or equal to

If you need to overload any of the binary operators in your class or structure, define a method with the following characteristics:

✦ A return type of your choice

✦ The keyword `operator`

✦ The operator being overloaded

✦ A parameter list specifying two parameters, at least one of which must be of the type of class or structure containing the overloaded operator method

Overloading binary operators enables you to be very flexible. You can use different parameters for the two parameters in the parameter list, which means that you can apply the operator to two values of different types if you wish. You can also use any available type as the return value from the overloaded operator. If you need to add together an object and a floating-point value and get a Boolean result, you can write an overloaded method as follows:

```
static public bool operator + (Point MyPoint, float FloatValue)
```

You can define multiple overloads of the same operator if you want, but only if the parameter lists use different types:

```
static public bool operator + (Point MyPoint, float FloatValue)
static public bool operator + (Point MyPoint, int IntValue)
static public bool operator + (Point MyPoint, uint UIntValue)
```

Listing 10-7 provides an example. It adds overloaded equality and inequality operators to the `Point` class. The operators return Boolean results that evaluate to `true` if two `Point` objects have the same coordinates; otherwise, the results evaluate to `false`.

Listing 10-7: **Overloading the Equality and Inequality Operators**

```
class Point
{
    public int X;
    public int Y;

    public static bool operator == (Point Point1, Point Point2)
    {
        if(Point1.X != Point2.X)
            return false;
        if(Point1.Y != Point2.Y)
            return false;
        return true;
    }

public override bool Equals(object o)
    {
        return true;
```

Continued

Listing 10-7 *(continued)*

```
  }

  public override int GetHashCode()
  {
    return 0;
  }

  public static bool operator != (Point Point1, Point Point2)
  {
      if(Point1.X != Point2.X)
          return true;
      if(Point2.Y != Point2.Y)
          return true;
      return false;
  }

  public static void Main()
  {
      Point MyFirstPoint = new Point();
      Point MySecondPoint = new Point();
      Point MyThirdPoint = new Point();

      MyFirstPoint.X = 100;
      MyFirstPoint.Y = 200;

      MySecondPoint.X = 500;
      MySecondPoint.Y = 750;

      MyThirdPoint.X = 100;
      MyThirdPoint.Y = 200;

      if(MyFirstPoint == MySecondPoint)
          System.Console.WriteLine("MyFirstPoint and MySecondPoint are at the
same coordinates.");
      else
          System.Console.WriteLine("MyFirstPoint and MySecondPoint are not at
the same coordinates.");

      if(MyFirstPoint == MyThirdPoint)
          System.Console.WriteLine("MyFirstPoint and MyThirdPoint are at the
same coordinates.");
      else
          System.Console.WriteLine("MyFirstPoint and MyThirdPoint are not at
the same coordinates.");
  }
}
```

The `Main()` method defines three points:

- ✦ `MyFirstPoint`, with coordinates of (100, 200)
- ✦ `MySecondPoint`, with coordinates of (500, 750)
- ✦ `MyThirdPoint`, with coordinates of (100, 200)

The method then uses the equality operator to determine whether the `MyFirstPoint` point and the `MySecondPoint` refer to the same coordinates. It then uses the equality operator to determine whether the `MyFirstPoint` point and the `MyThirdPoint` refer to the same coordinates.

Compiling and executing the code in Listing 10-7 results in the output shown in Figure 10-7.

Figure 10-7: Overloading the equality and inequality operators

The following pairs of operators must be overloaded together:

- ✦ Equality and inequality
- ✦ Less than and greater than
- ✦ Less than or equal to and greater than or equal to

If you overload one of these pairs but not the other, the C# compiler issues an error message like the following:

```
error CS0216: The operator 'Point.operator ==(Point, Point)'
requires a matching operator '!=' to also be defined
```

Overloadable Conversion Operators

You can also write operator overload methods that convert one type into another type. Your overload method can also define whether the C# compiler should treat the conversion as an implicit or explicit conversion.

If you need to define a new conversion operator in your class or structure, define a method with the following characteristics:

✦ The keyword implicit if the conversion is to be treated as an implicit conversion, or the keyword explicit if the conversion is to be treated as an explicit conversion

✦ The keyword operator

✦ A type specifying the target type of the conversion

✦ A parameter list specifying the source type of the conversion

Listing 10-8 defines an implicit conversion from a Point class object to a double. The double specifies the distance from the origin to the point, using the Pythagorean theorem.

Listing 10-8: Defining an Implicit Conversion

```
class Point
{
    public int X;
    public int Y;

    public static implicit operator double(Point RValue)
    {
        double Distance;
        double Sum;

        Sum = (RValue.X * RValue.X) + (RValue.Y * RValue.Y);
        Distance = System.Math.Sqrt(Sum);
        return Distance;
    }

    public static void Main()
    {
        double Distance;
        Point MyPoint = new Point();

        MyPoint.X = 100;
```

```
        MyPoint.Y = 200;
        Distance = MyPoint;
        System.Console.WriteLine(Distance);
    }
  }
```

Note The `System.Math.Sqrt()` method is defined by the .NET Framework and calculates the square root of the supplied parameter. The method is static, so you can call it without having an object of the `System.Math` type to call it on.

The `Main()` method declares an object of type `Point` and sets its coordinates to (100, 200). It then assigns the object to a variable of type `double`, which is legal because the `Point` class defines a conversion operator that converts a `Point` object to a double. Because the conversion operator is defined as an implicit conversion, no casting is required. The `Main()` method then prints the value of the converted double to the console.

Figure 10-8 shows the output of Listing 10-8.

Figure 10-8: Defining an implicit conversion

Operators That Cannot Be Overloaded

C# does not enable you to redefine the behavior of the operators in the following list. This is mainly for simplicity's sake. The designers of the C# language wanted these operators kept simple, and to always perform their intended function; therefore, no overloading is allowed.

✦ Assignment

✦ Conditional AND

✦ Conditional OR

✦ Conditional

✦ The `new`, `typeof`, `sizeof`, and `is` keywords

Summary

C# enables you to tailor the behavior of several of the built-in operators to your own needs. Classes and structures can include methods called *operator overload methods* that define the behavior of an operator when it appears in an expression with your class or structure.

To overload the unary plus, unary minus, negation, or bitwise complement operators in your class or structure, you define a method with a return type of your choice, the operator being overloaded, and a single parameter of the type of class or structure containing the overloaded operator method.

To overload the prefix increment or prefix decrement operators in your class or structure, you define a method with a return type specifying the type of class or structure containing the overloaded operator method. You also need to define the operator being overloaded and a single parameter of the type of class or structure containing the overloaded operator method.

To overload the true or false operators in your class or structure, you define a method with a Boolean return type, the operator being overloaded, and a single parameter of the type of class or structure containing the overloaded operator method.

To overload any of the binary operators in your class or structure, you define a method with a return type, the operator being overloaded, and two parameters. At least one of the two parameters must be of the type of class or structure containing the overloaded operator method.

You can also define new conversions for your classes or structures. You specify whether the conversion is to be treated as an implicit operator or an explicit operator. The conversion operator method specifies both the type of the variable being converted as well as the type to which the variable should be converted.

✦   ✦   ✦

Class Inheritance

CHAPTER

11

Simple C# projects may use one or two classes. However, you will most likely write many classes in your larger C# projects. Many of these classes may have similar fields or methods, and it may make sense to share common code among a set of classes.

C# embraces the object-oriented concept of *inheritance*, which allows one class to inherit code from another class. C# classes can inherit code from parent classes, and the inherited constructs can be used in your own classes.

Inheritance is used in object-oriented software development to re-use common code. Take, for example, the single-selection and multiple-selection list boxes found in Windows. The two list boxes have different functionality—one allows multiple items to be selected and the other doesn't—but they also have many similarities. They both look the same, they both behave the same when the user scrolls through the list, and the color used for a selected item is the same. If you were to write these two list boxes as C# classes, you could write them separately, with each one having no knowledge of the other. However, that would be a waste. Much of the code would be identical. It would make more sense to write a class to contain the common code and have classes that derive from the common code class that implement the different functionality. You can write a C# class called `ListBox` to hold the common code, for example, and you can then write a C# class called `SingleSelectionListBox` that inherits from ListBox and supplies the code unique to the single-selection list box. You may also write a C# class called `MultipleSelectionListBox` that also inherits from `ListBox` but supplies the code unique to the multiple-selection list box.

Another advantage in this scenario relates to maintaining your code. If you find a bug in your list box, you can trace it back to a bug in the common code. If you can fix the bug in the common code, recompiling your project will fix the bug in both the single-selection and multiple-selection list box classes. One bug fix fixes the problem in two classes.

In object-oriented terminology, inheritance is discussed in terms of a base class and a derived class. The class being inherited from is called the *base class,* and the class inheriting from the base class is called the *derived class*. In the list box scenario, the ListBox class is the base class and the SingleSelectionListBox and the MultipleSelectionListBox classes are the derived classes.

Compiling with Multiple Classes

Working with inheritance in C# means that you'll be working with more than one C# class. C# is not picky about how those classes are arranged relative to your source files. You can put all of your classes in a single source file, or you can put each class in a separate source file.

Obviously, in all but the smallest of projects, implementing all the classes in a single file is a poor way of organizing your code. One reason this is a poor idea is that all classes are recompiled every time you make a change anywhere in the program. To compile a project using separate source files from the command line, you simply list each file after the compiler name as follows:

```
csc file1.cs file2.cs file3.cs
```

The C# compiler names the output executable after the first source filename by default. The previous compiler command line produces an executable called file1.exe. If you don't like this default, you can use the /out argument to change the output file's name:

```
csc /out:myapp.exe file1.cs file2.cs file3.cs
```

This compiler command line produces an executable called myapp.exe.

Note   Remember that one, and only one, of your classes must specify a static Main() method.

Specifying a Base Class in C#

Let's return to our Point class example for a look at how inheritance works in C#. Suppose you've designed a class called Point2D, which describes a point in 2D space with X and Y coordinates:

```
class Point2D
{
    public int X;
```

```
    public int Y;
    // more code
}
```

Now suppose that you'd like to add support for points in 3D space while still keeping the `Point2D` class. Inheritance enables you to design a new class that keeps all of the code written for the `Point2D` class and adds a Z coordinate.

Naming the base class in C# is done by following your derived class name with a colon and the name of the base class. Deriving the `Point3D` class from the `Point2D` class looks like the following:

```
class Point3D : Point2D
{
    public int Z;
    // code for Point3D class
}
```

Depending on the base class's scoping rules, which are covered in the "Scope" section of this chapter, all the fields and properties in the base class (`Point2D`) are available for use in the derived class (`Point3D`). For example, when a class is derived from a base class, the code in the derived class has access to the fields and properties in the base class, depending on the scope.

You can list only a single base class when inheriting one class from another. Some object-oriented languages, such as C++, allow you to specify more than one base class for a derived class. This concept is called *multiple inheritance*. C# supports single inheritance but not multiple inheritance. In the section discussing containment. you see a technique to simulate multiple inheritance in C#.

Listing 11-1 shows how the `Point3D` class and the `Point2D` class can be used together.

Listing 11-1: **Deriving Point3D from Point2D**

```
class Point2D
{
    public int X;
    public int Y;
}

class Point3D : Point2D
{
    public int Z;
}

class MyMainClass
```

Continued

Listing 11-1 *(continued)*

```
{
    public static void Main()
    {
        Point2D My2DPoint = new Point2D();
        Point3D My3DPoint = new Point3D();

        My2DPoint.X = 100;
        My2DPoint.Y = 200;

        My3DPoint.X = 150;
        My3DPoint.Y = 250;
        My3DPoint.Z = 350;
    }
}
```

Note that the `Main()` method creates a `Point2D` object and a `Point3D` object.
The `Point3D` object has fields for X, Y, and Z coordinates, although the declaration
of `Point3D` only declares a field called `Z`. The `X` and `Y` fields are inherited from
the `Point2D` base class and can be used just as if they were declared directly
in the `Point3D` class.

Scope

When you design your class inheritance architecture, you may decide that members in your base class should not be visible to derived classes or to the outside
world. For example, you may write a method in a base class that helps calculate a
value. If that calculation is not useful in a derived class, you may want to prevent
the derived class from even calling the method.

In programming terminology, the visibility of a variable or method is referred to as
its *scope*. Some variables or methods may be publicly scoped, others may be pri-
vately scoped, and still others may be somewhere in between.

C# defines five keywords that enable you to define the scope of any member (either
variable or method) in a class. A member's scope affects its visibility to derived
classes and code that creates instances of the class. These keywords, outlined in
the following list, are placed before any other keywords in a member declaration.

✦ Members marked `public` are visible to derived a class and to code that creates objects of the class. We've been using `public` up to this point.

✦ Members marked `private` are visible only to the class in which they are
defined. Private members are not accessible from derived classes, nor are
they accessible from code that creates objects of the class.

✦ Members marked `protected` are visible only to the class in which they are defined or from classes derived from the class. Protected members are not accessible from code that creates objects of the class.

✦ Members marked `internal` are visible to any code in the same binary file, but are not visible to any code in other binary files. Remember that the .NET Framework embraces the concept of assemblies, which are libraries of pre-compiled code that can be used by external applications. If you write a class in C# and compile the class into an assembly, internal class members can be accessed by any piece of code in the assembly. However, if another piece of code uses your assembly, it has no access to the member, even if it derives a class from your assembly class.

✦ Members marked `protected internal` are visible to any code in the same binary file and to external classes that derive from the class. If you write a class in C# and compile the class into an assembly, internal class members can be accessed by any piece of code in the assembly. If another piece of external code uses your assembly, and derives a class from the class in the assembly, the protected `internal` member is accessible to the derived class. The member is not, however, accessible to code that works with objects of the base class.

C# enables you to specify a class member without specifying any scope keywords. If you declare a class member without specifying any scope keywords, the member is given private accessibility by default. Members declared without any scope keywords can be used in other parts of the class, but cannot be used by derived classes or by code that uses objects of the class.

Re-using Member Identifiers in Derived Classes

C# enables you to re-use base class identifiers in derived classes, but the C# compiler issues a warning when this is detected. Consider the code shown in Listing 11-2.

Listing 11-2: **Re-using Base Class Identifiers**

```
class Point2D
{
    public int X;
    public int Y;
}

class Point3D : Point2D
{
```

Continued

Listing 11-2 *(continued)*

```
    public int X;
    public int Y;
    public int Z;
}

class MyMainClass
{
    public static void Main()
    {
        Point2D My2DPoint = new Point2D();
        Point3D My3DPoint = new Point3D();

        My2DPoint.X = 100;
        My2DPoint.Y = 200;

        My3DPoint.X = 150;
        My3DPoint.Y = 250;
        My3DPoint.Z = 350;
    }
}
```

The derived `Point3D` class defines X and Y fields that clash with the identifiers used in the `Point2D` base class. The C# compiler issues warnings when this code is compiled:

```
warning CS0108: The keyword new is required on 'Point3D.X'
because it hides inherited member 'Point2D.X'
warning CS0108: The keyword new is required on 'Point3D.Y'
because it hides inherited member 'Point2D.Y'
```

The C# compiler issues the warnings because the identifiers in the derived class hide the definitions using the same identifier in the base class. If you want to re-use the names and want to instruct the C# compiler not to issue the warnings, use the `new` operator when re-using the identifiers in the derived class. The code shown in Listing 11-3 compiles with no warnings.

Listing 11-3: **Using new to Re-use Base Class Identifiers**

```
class Point2D
{
    public int X;
    public int Y;
}

class Point3D : Point2D
```

```
    {
        new public int X;
        new public int Y;
        public int Z;
    }

    class MyMainClass
    {
        public static void Main()
        {
            Point2D My2DPoint = new Point2D();
            Point3D My3DPoint = new Point3D();

            My2DPoint.X = 100;
            My2DPoint.Y = 200;

            My3DPoint.X = 150;
            My3DPoint.Y = 250;
            My3DPoint.Z = 350;
        }
    }
```

Working with Inherited Methods

C# enables methods in base and derived classes to interact in a variety of ways. The language allows for the following method constructs:

- ✦ Virtual and override methods
- ✦ Abstract methods

Virtual and override methods

You may want a derived class to change the implementation of a method in a base class while keeping the method name the same. Suppose, for example, that our Point2D class implements a method called PrintToConsole(), which prints the point's X and Y coordinates out to the console. You may also want the derived Point3D class to provide its own implementation of PrintToConsole(). It cannot use the PrintToConsole() method provided in the Point2D class, however, because that implementation only works with X and Y coordinates, and the Point3D class has a Z coordinate as well. The Point3D class must provide its own implementation of the same PrintToConsole() method.

Method names can be re-used in derived classes if the base class method allows the method to be re-implemented. Re-implementing a base class method in a derived class is called *overriding* the base class method. You need to be aware of two requirements when overriding a base class method in C#:

✦ The base class method must be declared with the keyword `virtual`.

✦ The derived class method must be declared with the keyword `override`.

Base class methods using the `virtual` keyword are called *virtual methods*, and derived class methods using the `override` keyword are called *override methods*.

Listing 11-4 shows how the `PrintToConsole()` method can be implemented for both the `Point2D` and the `Point3D` classes.

Listing 11-4: **Overriding Virtual Methods**

```
class Point2D
{
    public int X;
    public int Y;

    public virtual void PrintToConsole()
    {
        System.Console.WriteLine("({0}, {1})", X, Y);
    }
}

class Point3D : Point2D
{
    public int Z;

    public override void PrintToConsole()
    {
        System.Console.WriteLine("({0}, {1}, {2})", X, Y, Z);
    }
}

class MyMainClass
{
    public static void Main()
    {
        Point2D My2DPoint = new Point2D();
        Point3D My3DPoint = new Point3D();

        My2DPoint.X = 100;
        My2DPoint.Y = 200;

        My3DPoint.X = 150;
        My3DPoint.Y = 250;
        My3DPoint.Z = 350;

        My2DPoint.PrintToConsole();
```

```
            My3DPoint.PrintToConsole();
        }
    }
```

Note The syntax of the WriteLine() calls made in Listing 11-4 is different than the syntax used previously in this book. The numbers in curly brackets in the string are placeholders. The values of the other parameters are written to the console instead of the placeholder. The {0} placeholder is replaced with the value of the first parameter after the string parameter, the {1} placeholder is replaced with the value of the second parameter after the string parameter, and so on.

Listing 11-4 prints the following to the console:

```
(100, 200)
(150, 250, 350)
```

You cannot override a base class method unless the base class method uses the virtual keyword. If you try to do this, the C# compiler issues an error:

```
error CS0506: 'Point3D.PrintToConsole()' : cannot override
inherited member 'Point2D.PrintToConsole()' because it is not
marked virtual, abstract, or override
```

You can, however, override an override method. If, for some odd reason, you decide to implement a Point4D class and derive it from Point3D, you can override the Point3D's PrintToConsole() method.

Polymorphism

The concept of overriding methods leads to the concept of *polymorphism*. When you override a method, you want the correct method called from any methods that call this overridden method.

Listing 11-5 shows this concept in action. You have added a UsePrintToConsole() method to Point2D that calls the virtual method PrintToConsole(). Point3D inherits this method from Point2D. When PrintToConsole() is called in this function, you want to call the version that belongs to the appropriate class. In other words, in the UsePrintToConsole() method that belongs to the Point2D class, you want to call the PrintToConsole() method that belongs to the Point2D class. In the UsePrintToConsole() method that belongs to the Point3D class, you want to call the overridden PrintToConsole() method that belongs to the Point3D class. Because the PrintToConsole() method was declared as a virtual method, this detecting of which version to run happens automatically.

This is exactly what happens, as Listing 11-5 prints the following to the console:

```
(100, 200)
(150, 250, 350)
```

Listing 11-5: **Polymorphism**

```csharp
class Point2D
{
    public int X;
    public int Y;

    public virtual void PrintToConsole()
    {
        System.Console.WriteLine("({0}, {1})", X, Y);
    }

    public void UsePrintToConsole()
    {
        PrintToConsole();
    }
}

class Point3D : Point2D
{
    public int Z;

    public override void PrintToConsole()
    {
        System.Console.WriteLine("({0}, {1}, {2})", X, Y, Z);
    }
}

class MyMainClass
{
    public static void Main()
    {
        Point2D My2DPoint = new Point2D();
        Point3D My3DPoint = new Point3D();

        My2DPoint.X = 100;
        My2DPoint.Y = 200;

        My3DPoint.X = 150;
        My3DPoint.Y = 250;
        My3DPoint.Z = 350;

        My2DPoint.UsePrintToConsole();
        My3DPoint.UsePrintToConsole();
    }
}
```

Abstract methods

Some base classes may not be able to provide an implementation of a method but you may still want to require that derived classes provide an implementation. Suppose, for example, that you're writing a geometry application in C# and write classes called Square and Circle. You decide upon some common functionality that every shape will use in your application, so you implement a base class called Shape and derive the Square and Circle classes from Shape:

```
Class Shape
{
}

class Circle : Shape
{
}

class Square : Shape
{
}
```

Now suppose that you decide that all shapes should be able to calculate their area, so you write a method called GetArea(). The problem with writing that code in the Shape base class is that the base class does not have enough information to calculate an area. Each shape calculates its area using a different formula.

What you can do is define an abstract method in the Shape base class. Abstract methods do not provide an implementation of their own, but provide a method signature that derived classes must implement. Abstract methods say, "I don't know how to implement this method, but my derived classes will, so make sure that they implement it with the parameters and the return code that I specify." The following snippet shows how you can declare an abstract method in the Shape class.

```
abstract class Shape
{
    public abstract double GetArea();
}
```

Note   Abstract classes use the abstract keyword. They do not have a method body; a semicolon follows the parameter list instead.

Abstract classes are also, by definition, virtual methods, and must be overridden by derived classes using the override keyword:

```
class Square : Shape
{
    public override double GetArea()
```

```
    {
        // implement area calculation
    }
}
```

Classes containing at least one abstract method are called abstract classes, and must include the abstract keyword before the class keyword. If you forget the abstract keyword when defining the class, you get an error from the C# compiler:

```
error CS0513: 'Shape.GetArea ()' is abstract but it is
contained in nonabstract class 'Shape'
```

The C# compiler doesn't allow you to create objects from abstract classes. If you try to create an object from an abstract class, the C# compiler issues an error:

```
error CS0144: Cannot create an instance of the abstract class
or interface 'Shape'
```

Abstract classes are used most often to create a common base class to a set of classes. This enables you to use polymorphism when storing derived classes in a collection of some sort. You saw this in action in Chapter 8, " Writing Object-Oriented Code," with the Zoo example.

Base Classes: Working with Inherited Properties and Indexers

With C#, you can mark properties and indexers in base and derived classes as virtual, override, and abstract, just like methods.

Note   Indexers are roughly equivalent to the overloaded [] operator and are declared using the this[] syntax. You use them where you want to access a class property in an array-like manner.

Virtual and override properties and indexers work just like virtual and override properties. Properties and indexers may be marked as virtual in a base class and overridden in a derived class.

Base classes may define abstract properties and indexers, which do not have an implementation of their own. Base classes containing at least one abstract property or indexer must be marked as an abstract class. Abstract properties and indexers must be overridden in a base class.

Using the base keyword

The C# language provides the base keyword so that derived classes can access functionality in their base class. You can use the keyword base to call a base class constructor when an object of a derived class is created. To call a base class constructor, follow the derived class constructor with a colon, the base keyword, and then the parameters to be passed to the base class.

Listing 11-6 shows how this works. It adds constructors for the Point2D and Point3D classes, and the Point3D constructor calls the constructor of its base class.

Listing 11-6: **Calling Base Class Constructors**

```
class Point2D
{
    public int X;
    public int Y;

    public Point2D(int X, int Y)
    {
        this.X = X;
        this.Y = Y;
    }

    public virtual void PrintToConsole()
    {
        System.Console.WriteLine("({0}, {1})", X, Y);
    }
}

class Point3D : Point2D
{
    public int Z;

    public Point3D(int X, int Y, int Z) : base(X, Y)
    {
        this.Z = Z;
    }

    public override void PrintToConsole()
    {
        System.Console.WriteLine("({0}, {1}, {2})", X, Y, Z);
    }
}

class MyMainClass
{
    public static void Main()
    {
        Point2D My2DPoint = new Point2D(100, 200);
        Point3D My3DPoint = new Point3D(150, 250, 350);
```

Continued

Listing 11-6 *(continued)*

```
        My2DPoint.PrintToConsole();
        My3DPoint.PrintToConsole();
    }
}
```

The constructor for the `Point2D` class sets the class's X and Y fields using the two integers passed to the constructor. The constructor for the `Point3D` class accepts three parameters. The first two parameters are passed to the base class's constructor using the `base` keyword, and the third is used to set the derived class's Z field.

Accessing base class fields with the base keyword

You can also use the `base` keyword to access members in the base class. In your derived class, you can work with a base class member by prefixing the member's name with the keyword `base` and a period. You can access base class fields using the following syntax:

```
base.X = 100;
```

You can also invoke base class methods using this syntax:

```
base.PrintToConsole();
```

Sealed Classes

If you do not want code to derive from your class, you can mark your class with the `sealed` keyword. You cannot derive a class from a sealed class.

You can specify a sealed class by placing the keyword `sealed` before the `class` keyword as follows:

```
sealed class MySealedClass
```

If you try to derive a class from a sealed class, the C# compiler issues an error:

```
error CS0509: 'Point3D' : cannot inherit from sealed class
'Point2D'
```

Containment and Delegation

Whereas inheritance is an IS-A relationship, *containment* is a HAS-A relationship. A Burmese IS A cat (so you might want to inherit your Burmese class from your generic Cat class); whereas a Car HAS 4 tires (so your Car class may contain 4 Tire objects). The interesting aspect of containment is that you can use it as a surrogate for inheritance. The main drawback to using containment instead of inheritance is that you lose the benefits of polymorphism. However, you get all the advantages of code re-use.

In C#, there are two common instances in which you have little choice but to use containment instead of inheritance: when dealing with multiple inheritance and when dealing with sealed classes. An example follows illustrating how this technique works. In addition, you will see polymorphism in action.

Suppose you have an `AlarmClock` class and a `Radio` class as shown in the following snippet, and you want to create a `ClockRadio` class combining these two classes. If C# supported multiple inheritance, you could have `ClockRadio` inherit from both the `AlarmClock` class and the `Radio` class. You could then add a `radioAlarm` Boolean variable to determine whether the buzzer or the radio goes off and override `SoundAlarm()` to use this variable. Alas, C# does not support multiple inheritance. Not to worry; you can use containment instead of inheritance and still get all the benefits of code re-use. Note how this works, step by step:

```
class Radio
{
    protected bool on_off;

    public void On()
    {
        if (!on_off) Console.WriteLine("Radio is now
on!");
        on_off = true;
    }

    public void Off()
    {
        if (on_off) Console.WriteLine("Radio is now
off!");
        on_off = false;
    }
}

class AlarmClock
{
    private int currentTime;
```

```
        private int alarmTime;

        private void SoundAlarm()
        {
                Console.WriteLine("Buzz!");
        }

        public void Run()
        {
                for (int currTime = 0; currTime < 43200;
currTime++)
                {
                SetCurrentTime(currTime);
                if (GetCurrentTime() == GetAlarmTime())
                    {
                    Console.WriteLine("Current Time = {0}!",
                            currentTime);
                        SoundAlarm();
                  break;
                  }
              }
        }

        public int GetCurrentTime()
        {
            return currentTime;
        }

        public void SetCurrentTime(int aTime)
        {
            currentTime =    aTime;
        }

        public int GetAlarmTime()
        {
            return alarmTime;
        }

        public void SetAlarmTime(int aTime)
        {
            alarmTime =      aTime;
        }
    }
```

Because you want to override the SoundAlarm() method in AlarmClock, it is best to select to inherit ClockRadio from AlarmClock. As you will see later, this requires a minor change in the AlarmClock implementation. However, as a reward, you will nicely get the benefit of polymorphism. Now that you have selected a base class, you cannot inherit from Radio. Instead of inheriting, you will create a private Radio member variable inside the ClockRadio class. You create the private member in the ClockRadio constructor and delegate the work for the RadioOn() and RadioOff() methods to this private member. You have some extra work to do, but you get all the benefits of code re-use. Whenever the implementation of the Radio class changes (for example, because of bug fixes), your `AlarmClock` class will automatically incorporate these changes. One inconvenience of the containment/ delegation approach is that new functionality in the contained class (e.g., adding new methods to set the volume) requires changes to the containing class in order to delegate this new functionality to the private member.

```
class ClockRadio : AlarmClock
{
    private Radio radio;
    // Declare other member variables...

    public ClockRadio()
    {
        radio = new Radio();
        // Set other member variables...
    }

    //---------- Delegate to Radio ----------
    public void RadioOn()
    {
        radio.On();
    }

    public void RadioOff()
    {
        radio.Off();
    }
}
```

You have now implemented full radio functionality using the containment/delegation pattern. It's time to add the `AlarmClock` functionality. First, quickly add a `radioAlarm` private variable to determine whether the radio should start blaring or the buzzer should sound when the alarm goes off:

```
class ClockRadio : AlarmClock
{
    private bool radioAlarm;
            // Declare other member variables...
    public ClockRadio()
    {
        radioAlarm = false;
        // Set other member variables...
    }

    //---------- New ClockRadio functionality ----------
    public void SetRadioAlarm(bool useRadio)
    {
        radioAlarm = useRadio;
    }
}
```

Because you want to override the SoundAlarm() function in AlarmClock, you need to change the SoundAlarm() method declaration to be protected. Furthermore, because you will want polymorphic behavior in the Run() function, you need to make this method virtual:

```
class AlarmClock
{
        private int currentTime;
        private int alarmTime;

        protected virtual void SoundAlarm()
        {
                Console.WriteLine("Buzz!");
        }

        // Other Methods...
}
```

Overriding SoundAlarm() in AlarmClock is straightforward. Depending on the radioAlarm setting, you either turn the radio on or call the SoundAlarm() method in the base class to sound the buzzer, as follows:

```
class ClockRadio : AlarmClock
{
        private Radio radio;
        private bool radioAlarm;

        //---------- Overridde AlarmClock ----------
        protected override void SoundAlarm()
        {
                if (radioAlarm)
                {
                        RadioOn();
                }
                else
                {
                        base.SoundAlarm();
                }
        }

        // Other Methods...
}
```

That's basically it! Something very interesting is happening inside the Run() method of the AlarmClock class (shown in the following code snippet): the polymorphic behavior alluded to previously. The ClockRadio class inherits this method from its base class and does not override it. This Run() method can therefore be executed from either an AlarmClock object or a RadioClock object. Because we declared the SoundAlarm() to be virtual, C# is smart enough to call the appropriate SoundAlarm() depending on which class is invoking the Run() method.

```
class AlarmClock
{
      private int currentTime;
      private int alarmTime;

      public void Run()
      {
            for (int currTime = 0; currTime < 43200;
currTime++)
            {
                  SetCurrentTime(currTime);
                  if (GetCurrentTime() == GetAlarmTime())
                  {
                  Console.WriteLine("Current Time = {0}!",
                              currentTime);
                        SoundAlarm();
                        break;
                  }
            }
      }

      // Other Methods...
}
```

This example clearly highlights one of the major strengths of inheritance: polymorphism. In addition, when you add new public (or protected) methods to the base class, they become automatically available in the derived class. Listing 11-7 is the full listing with a sample `main()` method so you can experiment with this sample.

Listing 11-7: Multiple Inheritance Can Be Simulated Using Containment

```
using System;

namespace Containment
{
  class Radio
  {
      protected bool on_off;

      public void On()
      {
            if (!on_off) Console.WriteLine("Radio is now
on!");
            on_off = true;
      }

      public void Off()
```

Continued

Listing 11-7 *(continued)*

```
        {
                if (on_off) Console.WriteLine("Radio is now
off!");
                on_off = false;
        }
    }

  class AlarmClock
  {
        private int currentTime;
        private int alarmTime;

        protected virtual void SoundAlarm()
        {
                Console.WriteLine("Buzz!");
        }

        public void Run()
        {
                for (int currTime = 0; currTime < 43200;
currTime++)
                {
                        SetCurrentTime(currTime);
                        if (GetCurrentTime() == GetAlarmTime())
                        {
                                Console.WriteLine("Current Time =
{0}!",
currentTime);

                                SoundAlarm();
                            break;
                        }
                }
        }

        public int GetCurrentTime()
        {
                return currentTime;
        }

        public void SetCurrentTime(int aTime)
        {
                currentTime =  aTime;
        }

        public int GetAlarmTime()
        {
                return alarmTime;
        }

        public void SetAlarmTime(int aTime)
        {
```

```
              alarmTime =      aTime;
        }
}

class ClockRadio : AlarmClock
{
      private Radio radio;
      private bool radioAlarm;

      public ClockRadio()
      {
            radio = new Radio();
            radioAlarm = false;
      }

      //---------- Delegate to Radio ----------
      public void RadioOn()
      {
            radio.On();
      }

      public void RadioOff()
      {
            radio.Off();
      }

      //---------- Overridde AlarmClock ----------
      protected override void SoundAlarm()
      {
            if (radioAlarm)
            {
                RadioOn();
            }
            else
            {
                  base.SoundAlarm();
            }
      }

      //---------- New ClockRadio functionality ----------
      public void SetRadioAlarm(bool useRadio)
      {
            radioAlarm = useRadio;
      }
}

class ContInh
{
      static int Main(string[] args)
      {

            ClockRadio clockRadio;
```

Continued

Listing 11-7 *(continued)*

```
        clockRadio = new ClockRadio();

        clockRadio.SetRadioAlarm(true);
        clockRadio.SetAlarmTime(100);
        clockRadio.Run();

        // wait for user to acknowledge the results
        Console.WriteLine("Hit Enter to terminate...");
        Console.Read();
        return 0;
    }
  }
}
```

The .NET Object Class

All the classes in C# end up deriving from a class built into the .NET Framework called object. If you write a class in C# and do not define a base class for it, the C# compiler silently derives it from object. Suppose that you write a C# class declaration without a class declaration, as follows:

```
class Point2D
```

This is equivalent to deriving your class from the .NET base class System.Object:

```
class Point2D : System.Object
```

The C# keyword object can be used as an alias for the System.Object identifier:

```
class Point2D : object
```

If you do derive from a base class, just remember that your base class either inherits from object or inherits from another base class that inherits from object. Eventually, your class inheritance hierarchy will include the .NET object class.

Thanks to the rules of inheritance in C#, the functionality of the .NET object class is available to all classes in C#. The .NET object class carries the following methods:

✦ public virtual bool Equals(object obj): Compares one object to another object and returns true if the objects are equal and false otherwise.

This method is marked as virtual, which means that you can override it in your C# classes. You may want to override this method to compare the state of two objects of your class. If the objects have the same values for the fields, you can return `true`; you can return `false` if the values differ.

✦ `public virtual int GetHashCode()`: Calculates a hash code for the object. This method is marked as virtual, which means that you can override it in your C# classes. Collection classes in .NET may call this method to generate a hash code to aid in searching and sorting, and your classes can override this method to generate a hash code that makes sense for the class.

Note   Hash code is a unique key for the specified object.

✦ `public Type GetType()`: Returns an object of a .NET class called `Type` that provides information about the current class. This method is not marked as virtual, which means that you cannot override it in your C# classes.

✦ `public virtual string ToString()`: Returns a string representation of your object. This method is marked as virtual, which means that you can override it in your C# classes. An object's `ToString()` method is called when .NET methods such as `System.Console.WriteLine()` need to convert a variable into a string. You can override this method to return a string more appropriate for representing your class's state. You may for example want to add the proper currency sign in front of the string representation of your Money class.

✦ `protected virtual void Finalize()`: May (or may not) becalled when the Common Language Runtime's garbage collector destroys the object. This method is marked as virtual, which means that you can override it in your C# classes. This method is also marked as protected, which means that it can only be called from within the class or a derived class, and cannot be called from outside the class hierarchy. The .NET `object` implementation of `Finalize()` does nothing, but you can implement it if you wish. You can also write a destructor for your class, which achieves the same effect (but be careful using this). In fact, the C# compiler translates your destructor code into an overridden `Finalize()` method.

✦ `protected object MemberwiseClone()`: Creates a clone of the object, populates the clone with the same state as the current object, and returns the cloned object. This method is not marked as virtual, which means that you cannot override it in your C# classes. This method is also marked as protected, which means that it can only be called from within the class or a derived class, and cannot be called from outside the class hierarchy.

Structures in C# cannot have explicitly defined base classes, but they do implicitly inherit from the `object` base class. All the behavior of the `object` class is available to structures in C# as well as classes.

Using Boxing and Unboxing to Convert to and from the Object Type

Because all classes and structures ultimately derive from the .NET `object` type, it is used quite often in parameter lists when the method needs to be flexible regarding the data it receives.

For example, consider the `System.Consle.WriteLine()` method used throughout this book. This same method has been used to write strings, integers, and doubles to the console without using any casting operators. In Listing 11-4, it prints a string with placeholders, and the placeholders are replaced with the values of the parameters supplied to it. How does this actually work? How does `System.Console.WriteLine()` know what types you'll be passing into it?

The answer is that it can't know. Microsoft built the `System.Console.WriteLine()` method long before you worked on Listing 11-4, so they couldn't possibly know what types of data you would pass into it. Microsoft implemented a `System.Console.WriteLine()` method with the following signature:

```
public static void WriteLine(string format, params object[]
arg);
```

The first parameter is the string to be output, and the second parameter is a parameter array holding a number of items calculated when the code is compiled. But what is the type of the parameter array? The parameter array is of type `object`. Consider this call to `WriteLine()`:

```
System.Console.WriteLine("({0}, {1})", X, Y);
```

The C# compiler turns the X and Y parameters into a parameter array for us and calls `WriteLine()`. The X and Y parameters are of type integer, which, as you've already seen, is an alias for a structure called `System.Int32`. Because C# structures inherit from the .NET `object` type, these variables inherit from the `object` type and can be used in the parameter array.

Literals, which are discussed in Chapter 4, are a trickier issue. Instead of using objects, you can just as easily write the following code:

```
System.Console.WriteLine("({0}, {1})", 100, 200);
```

This code also works as expected. How does C# know how to convert a literal value into an object so that it can be used in a method call that needs an object? The answer lies in a technique called *boxing*.

Boxing allows any value type, including a literal, to be converted to an object. When the C# compiler encounters a value type for which a reference type is needed, it creates a temporary object variable and populates it with the value from the value type. This technique "boxes" up the value into an object. Take another look at the previous WriteLine() call:

```
System.Console.WriteLine("({0}, {1})", 100, 200);
```

The C# compiler encounters the literals and boxes them both into objects. The objects are supplied to the method call in the parameter array, and then the temporary objects are disposed of. Take a look at the following statements:

```
int MyValue = 123;
object MyObject = MyValue;
```

C# boxes the value of MyValue into the MyObject object.

C# also allows unboxing, which is simply the reverse process of boxing. Unboxing converts reference types back into value types.

Ultimately, every type is an object. Boxing and unboxing help us conceptualize this idea. Because everything is an object, everything — including literals — can be treated as objects and can have methods from the class object called on them. Thanks to boxing by the C# compiler, the following code can actually work:

```
string MyString;

MyString = 123.ToString();
```

The C# compiler simply boxes the literal value 123 into an object and calls the ToString() method on that object.

Summary

In object-oriented software development terminology, inheritance is used to describe a class that inherits members from a base class. C# supports single inheritance, in which a class can be derived from a single base class. C# does not support multiple inheritance, which is supported by some object-oriented languages to enable a class to be derived from more than one base class.

Base classes in C# are specified when a class is declared. The base class identifier follows the name of the derived class when the derived class is declared.

C# enables class members to be associated with a scoping attribute. The scope of a member determines its accessibility to both derived classes and pieces of code that work with objects of the class. Class members marked public are visible to derived classes and to code that creates objects of the class. Class members marked private are visible only to the class in which they are defined. Class members marked protected are visible only to the class in which they are defined, or from classes derived from the class. Class members marked internal are visible to any code in the same binary file, but are not visible to any code outside the binary files. Class members marked `protected internal` are visible to any code in the same binary file and to external classes that derive from the class. Class members lacking any specific scoping keyword are private by default.

Methods and properties in base classes can be re-implemented in derived classes to provide new implementations. Virtual methods and properties, which are marked with the C# keyword `virtual`, can be re-implemented in derived classes, as long as the new implementation retains the same identifier, return type, and parameter list. New implementations of virtual methods and properties are called *overridden*, and must be marked with the C# keyword `override`.

Abstract methods are methods in base classes that cannot be implemented. Abstract methods are usually not implemented in base classes because the base class does not have enough information to provide a complete implementation. Classes containing at least one abstract method are called *abstract classes* and must use the `abstract` keyword in the class declaration.

C# provides the `base` keyword to enable derived classes to access members of a base class. Member identifiers can be prefixed with the `base` keyword, and you can use the `base` keyword to call a base class's constructor from a derived class constructor.

By default, you can use any C# class as a base class, and any class can derive from any other class. You can prevent this behavior by marking a C# class with the keyword `sealed`. Sealed classes cannot be used as a base class, and the C# compiler doesn't allow classes to derive from sealed classes.

All classes in C# and, in fact, any class implemented in a .NET language, ultimately derive from the .NET class `System.Object`. The C# keyword `object` is an alias for the `System.Object` class identifier. The `System.Object` class contains some methods that derived classes can use, and many of the methods can be overridden. The `System.Object` class provides functionality for defining object equality, hash code calculation, string representations, finalization code, and object cloning. The `object` type can be used as a method or variable type name and any C# variable can be used as an `object` object. C# automatically converts between value types, such as value types and numeric literals, and objects of type `object` using the concepts of boxing and unboxing. Boxing packages a value into an object, and unboxing unpackages an object value back into a value type.

✦   ✦   ✦

Advanced C#

Working with Namespaces

The C# classes that you design will be used by code that you write and possibly by code that other people write. Your C# classes may be used by a VB.NET application or from within an ASP.NET page. Moreover, your classes may very well be used alongside other classes designed by other .NET developers.

Code written in a .NET language references classes by their names, and all of these classes used together suggests an obvious dilemma: What happens if a developer wants to use two classes that have the same name?

Suppose you write a C# class that reads records from a database and you name the class Recordset. Code that wants to use your class may create objects as follows:

```
Recordset MyRecordset = new Recordset();
```

Now suppose that you package your classes into a .NET assembly and distribute your assembly for use by other applications. Furthermore, suppose that someone obtains your assembly and integrates it into his or her application. What happens if that same application also makes use of another assembly written by someone else, which also contains a class called Recordset? When the application code creates a new Recordset object, which class is used to create the object: yours or the class in the other assembly?

This problem can be solved through the C# concept of *namespaces*. Namespaces organize classes under a named group, and the namespace name can be used to help distinguish between two classes with the same name. Your C# code should use namespaces to help further identify your classes under a common grouping, especially if you are planning to build an assembly for use by other developers. Namespaces may even come in handy in C# applications that you build, because your C# applications may use an external assembly that uses class names which mirror yours.

Declaring a Namespace

You declare a namespace with the C# namespace keyword. A namespace identifier and curly brackets follow the namespace keyword. Classes to be included in the namespace must be declared within the namespace's curly brackets, as the shown in the following code:

```
namespace MyClasses
{
    class MyFirstClass
    {
    }
}
```

This piece of code declares a class called MyFirstClass in a namespace called MyClasses. Another developer may also write a class called MyFirstClass, but as long as the other developer uses a different namespace name, the C# compiler finds the correct class to be used for a particular statement.

You can declare a namespace within a namespace, if you wish. Simply enclose another namespace declaration from within the first declaration:

```
namespace MyClasses
{
    namespace MyInnerNamespace
    {
        class MyFirstClass
        {
        }
    }
}
```

Tip

It's generally a good idea to nest namespaces when you plan to offer more than one distinct product in the form of classes. For example, Widget Corporation offers a compression product and some terminal emulation routines. These namespaces would then become Widget.Compression and Widget.Emulation, which group the products by company but also keep them separated under the Widget namespace.

If you don't want to nest namespaces in this manner, you can achieve the same effect by declaring both namespace declarations on the same statement and separating them with a period, as follows:

```
namespace MyClasses.MyInnerNamespace
{
    class MyFirstClass
    {
    }
}
```

The following types of declarations can appear in a namespace:

✦ Classes

✦ Structures

✦ Interfaces (see Chapter 13 for more information)

✦ Enumerations (see Chapter 14 for more information)

✦ Delegates (see Chapter 15 for more information)

Any type declaration not in this list results in compiler errors when you attempt to build your application.

Declaring a Namespace in Multiple Source Files

The C# compiler enables you to use the same namespace name in multiple source files. It then builds a binary file that combines all the classes into the same namespace.

Suppose, for example, that you want to build an assembly whose classes reside in a namespace called MyAssembly. You want to write two classes for inclusion in that assembly and you want to define the classes in separate files. You can simply re-use the namespace name in both source files. The first source file can contain the declaration of the first class, as follows:

```
namespace MyAssembly
{
    class MyFirstClass
    {
    }
}
```

The second source file can contain the declaration of the second class and can use the same namespace name:

```
namespace MyAssembly
{
    class MySecondClass
    {
    }
}
```

When the two source files are built into a single assembly, the C# compiler builds an assembly with a single namespace, MyAssembly, with two classes in the namespace.

This provides a benefit to you, the developer, should you want to separate certain functionality into separate files or simply want to keep the length of each source file to a minimum.

Using Classes in a Namespace

If you want to refer to a class in a specific namespace, you prefix the class name with the name of its namespace:

```
MyClasses.MyFirstClass MyObject = new MyClasses.MyFirstClass();
```

Using this syntax helps you distinguish between classes in different code bases with the same name. The C# compiler now has enough information to find the right class, because it also knows what namespace to interrogate in order to find the class you are looking for.

If you are working with classes declared in nested namespaces, all namespace names must appear when you refer to the class:

```
Namespace1.Namespace2.MyClass MyObject = new
Namespace1.Namespace2.MyClass();
```

Listing 12-1 illustrates the namespace concept.

Listing 12-1: Classes in Different Namespaces

```
namespace Namespace1
{
    class TestClass
    {
        public TestClass()
        {
            System.Console.WriteLine("Hello from
Namespace1.TestClass!");
        }
    }
}

namespace Namespace2
{
    class TestClass
    {
        public TestClass()
        {
            System.Console.WriteLine("Hello from
Namespace2.TestClass!");
```

```
        }
    }
}
class MainClass
{
    public static void Main()
    {
        Namespace1.TestClass Object1 = new
Namespace1.TestClass();
        Namespace2.TestClass Object2 = new
Namespace2.TestClass();
    }
}
```

The code in Listing 12-1 declares two classes called `TestClass`. The two class declarations are in different namespaces, and the constructor for each class prints a message to the console. The messages differ slightly so that you are able to tell which message came from which class.

The `Main()` method in Listing 12-1 creates two objects: one of type `Namespace1.TestClass` and one of type `Namespace.TestClass`. Because the constructors for the classes write messages out to the console, running the code in Listing 12-1 results in the output shown in Figure 12-1.

Figure 12-1: Referencing classes within namespaces

Note that the `MainClass` class in Listing 12-1 is not enclosed in a namespace declaration. This is legal in C#. You do not have to enclose classes in namespace declarations. However, classes that are not enclosed in namespaces cannot use the same name in another class defines without a namespace.

If you need to use a class that is declared in a namespace, you must use its namespace name when you use the class name. If you forget to do this, you get an error message from the C# compiler. Suppose, for example, that the `Main()` method in Listing 12-1 tries to create an object of class `TestClass`:

```
TestClass Object1 = new TestClass ();
```

The C# compiler cannot find a class called `TestClass` defined outside of a namespace, and it issues the following error:

```
error CS0234: The type or namespace name 'TestClass' does not
exist in the class or namespace 'MainClass'
```

If you review the examples from previous chapters, you'll find that you've been using this syntax all along in your calls to `WriteLine()`, as shown in the following example:

```
System.Console.WriteLine("Hello from C#!");
```

The `WriteLine()` method is in a class called `Console`, and the `Console` class is defined in a .NET namespace called `System`.

Namespace Assistance with the using Keyword

You can use the C# keyword `using` in a variety of ways to make working with namespaces easier, and save yourself a great deal of typing. At first sight, the `using` keyword resembles the typical C/C++ directive `#include`. Don't let it fool you; the benefits are much more empowering. The following sections describe some of these benefits.

Aliasing class names with the using keyword

Writing out fully qualified class names that include namespace identifiers can get a bit tedious, especially if the names are long. You can use the `using` keyword to provide an aliased name for the fully qualified class identifier, and you can use the alias name instead of the fully qualified class identifier once the alias is established.

You can alias a name with a statement having the following structure:

  ✦ The `using` keyword
  ✦ The alias name

✦ An equals sign

✦ The fully qualified class name with the namespace identifier

✦ A statement terminating semicolon

Listing 12-2 adds to Listing 12-1 by aliasing the class names to shorter equivalents. The shorter names are then used by the Main() method to work with objects of the classes.

Listing 12-2: **Aliasing Class Names**

```
using Class1 = Namespace1.TestClass;
using Class2 = Namespace2.TestClass;

namespace Namespace1
{
    class TestClass
    {
        public TestClass()
        {
            System.Console.WriteLine("Hello from
Namespace1.TestClass!");
        }
    }
}

namespace Namespace2
{
    class TestClass
    {
        public TestClass()
        {
            System.Console.WriteLine("Hello from
Namespace2.TestClass!");
        }
    }
}

class MainClass
{
    public static void Main()
    {
        Class1 Object1 = new Class1();
        Class2 Object2 = new Class2();
    }
}
```

As with the previous example, Listing 12-2 outputs the same messages you have previously seen. You can see these results in Figure 12-2.

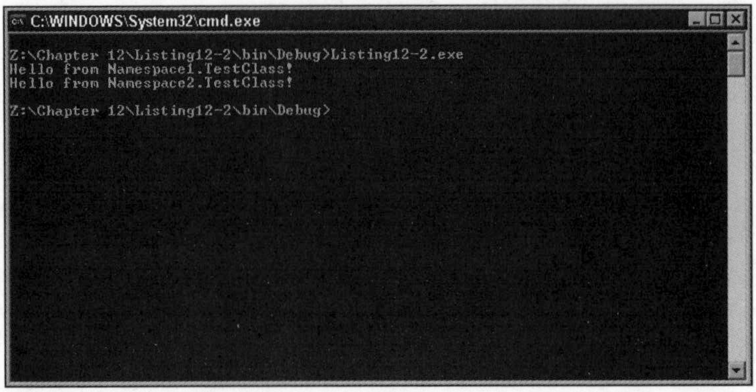

Figure 12-2: Aliasing class names

The `using` statements must appear in the source code before the namespaces themselves are declared. If the `using` statements appear after namespace declarations, you receive the following error message from the C# compiler:

```
error CS1529: A using clause must precede all other namespace
elements
```

In Chapter 7, you see that the C# keywords defining variable types are actually structures defined by the .NET Framework. Take another look at Table 7-1 and notice the following:

✦ The value type structures reside in the .NET `System` namespace.

✦ The `using` keyword is used to alias the .NET structure names to the equivalent C# keywords. You may imagine Table 7-1 being implemented within the .NET Framework using C# statements such as the following:

```
using sbyte = System.SByte;
using byte = System.Byte;
using short = System.Int16;
// ... more declarations ...
```

You can alias namespace names as well as classes, as shown in Listing 12-3.

Listing 12-3: Aliasing Namespace Names

```
using N1 = Namespace1;
using N2 = Namespace2;

namespace Namespace1
{
    class TestClass
    {
        public TestClass()
        {
            System.Console.WriteLine("Hello from
Namespace1.TestClass!");
        }
    }
}

namespace Namespace2
{
    class TestClass
    {
        public TestClass()
        {
            System.Console.WriteLine("Hello from
Namespace2.TestClass!");
        }
    }
}

class MainClass
{
    public static void Main()
    {
        N1.TestClass Object1 = new N1.TestClass();
        N2.TestClass Object2 = new N2.TestClass();
    }
}
```

Declaring namespace directives with the using keyword

If you use a class declared in a namespace, you must prefix the class name with the namespace name, even if you aren't working with any other namespaces that may have a class with the same name. This is why the examples used until now have always called WriteLine() with the System namespace qualifier:

```
System.Console.WriteLine("Hello from C#!");
```

By default, forgetting to use the namespace name causes the C# compiler to issue an error:

```
error CS0234: The type or namespace name 'Console' does not
exist in the class or namespace 'Namespace1'
```

Prefixing every class name with namespace names like System gets tedious, especially if you need to do it many times. Fortunately, you can use the using keyword to help reduce your coding time.

Using the using keyword with a namespace name tells the C# compiler that you want to refer to classes in the named namespace without prefixing the class names with the namespace name. For example, take a look at the following statement:

```
using System;
```

This is called a *namespace directive*. Namespace directives tell the C# compiler that the code will be using classes from the namespace and that the classes won't be prefixed with the namespace name. The C# compiler does the work of finding the definition of each class in one of the namespaces referenced in a namespace directive.

Listing 12-4 is a modification of Listing 12-2; it includes a using statement that references the .NET System namespace.

Listing 12-4: **Using a Namespace Directive**

```
using System;

using Class1 = Namespace1.TestClass;
using Class2 = Namespace2.TestClass;

namespace Namespace1
{
    class TestClass
    {
        public TestClass()
        {
            Console.WriteLine("Hello from
Namespace1.TestClass!");
        }
    }
}

namespace Namespace2
{
    class TestClass
```

```
      {
          public TestClass()
          {
              Console.WriteLine("Hello from
Namespace2.TestClass!");
          }
      }
  }

  class MainClass
  {
      public static void Main()
      {
          Class1 Object1 = new Class1();
          Class2 Object2 = new Class2();
      }
  }
```

The System namespace directive in Listing 12-4 enables the code to reference the Console class without prefixing it with the System namespace.

A Quick Tour of the .NET Namespaces

The .NET Framework contains classes in a variety of predefined namespaces that you can use in your C# code. The following list describes a few of them:

✦ The System namespace contains classes that implement basic functionality, such as data type conversions, mathematical operations, program invocation, and process environment management. The System namespace is the largest one provided with .NET. The .NET Framework also contains a Microsoft namespace that provides backward compatibility functionality as well as some other generally useful purposes.

✦ The System.CodeDOM namespace contains classes that represent the elements of a source code document.

✦ The System.Collections namespace contains classes that implement collections of objects, such as lists, queues, arrays, hash tables, and dictionaries.

✦ The System.ComponentModel namespace contains classes that are used to create runtime and design-time components and controls. This namespace provides interfaces and classes for creating attributes, binding to various data sources, building licensing components, as well as for type converters.

✦ The `System.Data` namespace contains classes that make up the ADO.NET data access architecture. The ADO.NET architecture enables you to build components that can manage data from multiple data sources in either disconnected or connected mode.

✦ The `System.Diagnostics` namespace contains classes that help you debug .NET applications and enable you to trace the execution of your code. The `System.Diagnostics` namespace also contains classes that enable you to monitor performance of your application using performance counters and read and write to event logs. Though the functionality is not really considered diagnostic, this namespace also enables you to start and stop processes.

✦ The `System.Drawing` namespace contains classes that implement Graphics Device Interface (GDI) drawing functionality. This namespace is not available by default; you must add a reference to it from the Project menu.

✦ The `System.IO` namespace contains classes that can read from and write to data streams and disk files. The classes contained within this namespace can manage both synchronous and asynchronous input/output.

✦ The `System.Messaging` namespace contains classes that work with message queues. This namespace is not available by default; you must add a reference to it from the Project menu.

✦ The `System.Net` namespace contains classes that provide a class wrapper around the many network protocols available today. This namespace provides classes to handle DNS requests, HTTP, and FTP requests. Aside from general network access classes, a large number of network security classes are also available for dealing with security issues, ranging from accessing a Web site to socket-level access.

✦ The `System.Reflection` namespace contains classes that provide a view of the types, methods, and fields available to a .NET application. You can even dynamically create and invoke types at runtime using the classes in the `System.Reflection` namespace.

✦ The `System.Resources` namespace provides classes that enable developers to create, store, and manage culture-specific resources for use within an application.

✦ The `System.Runtime` namespace in itself is not very useful. It does, however, provide dozens of classes that provide a wealth of functionality. For example, `System.Runtime.InteropServices` allows access to COM objects and native APIs from .NET.

✦ The `System.Security` namespace contains classes that enable you to access the security structure underlying the .NET Framework. The security name-space is the starting point for other more advanced namespaces for many cryptographic services. These services include encryption and decryption of data, hash generation, and random number generation.

✦ The `System.Text` namespace contains classes that enable you to work with ASCII, Unicode, UTF-7, and UTF-8 character encodings.

✦ The `System.Threading` namespace contains classes that enable you to implement multiple operating system threads in your .NET applications, thereby creating a true multi-threaded application.

✦ The `System.Timers` namespace contains classes that enable you to fire an event on a timed interval or on a more complex time schedule. These timers are server-based timers. A server-based timer has the capability to move among threads in order to raise the elapsed event, which provides greater flexibility over the typical Windows timer.

✦ The `System.Web` namespace contains classes that implement the Hypertext Transfer Protocol (HTTP) used by Web browsers to access pages through the World Wide Web. This namespace is not available by default; you must add a reference to it from the Project menu.

✦ The `System.Windows.Forms` namespace contains classes that you can use to build full-featured Windows applications. Classes in the `System.Windows. Forms` namespace provide a .NET class framework around familiar Windows controls such as dialog boxes, menus, and buttons. This namespace is not available by default; you must add a reference to it from the Project menu.

✦ The `System.Xml` namespace contains classes that can process XML data. The namespace includes support for XML 1.0, XML namespaces, XML schemas, XPath, XSL and XSLT, DOM Level 2, and SOAP 1.1.

This is by no means a complete list, but it should give you a feel for the vast amount of code in namespaces already implemented by the .NET Framework. Check the .NET Framework SDK documentation for a complete list of namespaces and classes.

Summary

The classes and structures that you develop can be wrapped in a named grouping called a *namespace*. Namespaces help distinguish your classes and structures from other classes and structures that have the same name.

A fully qualified class or structure name includes the name of the namespace that houses the class or structure. When you refer to a class or a structure in a namespace, you must qualify the name by prefixing it with the name of the namespace and a period.

You can use the C# `using` keyword to help you work with namespace names in your C# code. The `using` keyword can be used to provide a shortened, aliased name for a particular class in a particular namespace. It can also be used as a namespace directive, which tells the C# compiler that your code will be referencing classes in a specific namespace and that the code will *not* be prefixing the classes in that namespace with the namespace identifier.

You can build your own namespaces, and you can use code in namespaces developed by others using the techniques outlined in this chapter. The .NET Framework ships with a variety of class-populated namespaces, helping you code everything from Windows applications to XML processors and security programs. Namespaces in the .NET Framework also provide classes that you can use to build C# code using advanced techniques, such as multithreaded software and reflection.

✦   ✦   ✦

Understanding Interfaces

An interface in C# is a set of method, property, event, or indexer signatures grouped under a common name. Interfaces serve as sets of defined functionality that can be implemented by a C# class or structure. Classes or structures that implement an interface provide implementations for all of the methods defined in the interface.

Suppose, for example, that you want the classes in your C# project to support saving their field values to a database and retrieving them from the database later. In implementing this requirement, you might decide that all of your classes should implement a method called Load() and another method called Save(). You might also decide to define the methods in an interface called IPersistToDisk (interface names traditionally start with the letter *I*, although this is not a requirement of C#) and require that your classes implement this interface.

C# code can interrogate an object to determine whether it supports an interface. Interrogating an object for an interface is basically asking the question, "Do you support this interface?" The object either says, "Yes, I do" or "No, I don't." If the object says, "Yes, I do," you can call the methods on the interface. The methods called on an interface always have the same parameter lists and return values, although their implementations may differ.

Think of an interface as a contract — a promise that a class will implement a specific set of functionality. If an object says, "Yes, I support the interface you are asking for," it is guaranteeing that it provides an implementation for each of the methods defined on the interface.

Interfaces do not provide method implementations of their own. They only provide method identifiers, parameter lists, and return codes. It is the responsibility of the classes that implement the interface to provide an implementation for an interface. Two classes that implement the same interface may implement the interface methods in vastly different ways. This is fine, as long as the classes maintain the method signatures defined in the interface definition.

Let's use the `IPersistToDisk` interface as an example. You might have objects in your application that need to load their state from disk and save their state back to disk. You might decide to implement the `IPersistToDisk` interface on these objects. For each of the objects that implement `IPersistToDisk`, you need to write code for the interface's `Load()` and `Save()` methods. Some of your objects might have simple state storage needs, so those objects can implement the `Save()` and `Load()` methods using simple disk I/O code. Other objects might be more complicated and might need to support transactional I/O, in which the entire persistence operation must succeed or fail as a whole. For those objects, you might want to implement, the `Load()` and `Save()` methods using more robust transactional code. The point is that the code that uses these objects does not need to know whether the object uses simple or transactional code in its implementation. It simply asks each object, "Do you support the `IPersistToDisk` method?" For the objects that say "yes", then the code that uses the objects can call `Load()` or `Save()` without needing to know how the methods are actually implemented.

Conceptually, interfaces are much like abstract base classes: Both provide a list of methods that must be implemented by other pieces of code. However, there is one important difference — interfaces can be implemented without regard to the implementation class' place in a class hierarchy. Using abstract base classes, all of the classes that want to implement the functionality must derive directly or indirectly from the abstract base class. This is not the case with interfaces: Interfaces can be implemented on any class, regardless of its base class. Classes do not need to derive from any specific base class before they can implement an interface.

The concept of an interface as a software design pattern has been around for a while; however, Microsoft's Component Object Model (COM) popularized the concept. COM brought the idea of interfaces — specific sets of functionality implemented by an object — to the forefront of Windows-based software development. C# takes the concept further, embracing the concept as a language feature at the source-code level. Although COM interfaces were built with earlier versions of C++ or Visual Basic, these languages did not support the concept as a language feature. The C# `interface` keyword provides source-code support for the interface programming concept and makes it available to code even if the code doesn't use COM.

This chapter shows you how to work with interfaces using C#. You see how to define an interface using the `interface` keyword. You also learn how to define and implement methods, properties, indexers, and events on an interface and how to access an interface implemented by an object.

Defining an Interface

The first step in working with interfaces in C# is to define the methods that make up the interface. Interfaces are defined in C# with the following syntax:

✦ The `interface` **keyword**

✦ An interface identifier

✦ Optional base interfaces

✦ An opening curly brace

✦ One or more interface member declarations

✦ A closing curly brace

Interfaces can define methods, properties, indexers, and events. These language constructs work on interfaces just as they work with classes in C#. Interface methods define named blocks of code; properties define variables that can validated with accessor code, and events define actions that can occur within code.

Defining interface methods

Adding a method to an interface means that any object that wishes to implement the interface must provide an implementation of the interface method. It provides a guarantee to code that objects that implement the interface, including an implementation of the method and that the implementation, can be called by code. To define a method in an interface, provide a method declaration that supplies the method's return type, identifier, and parameter list. Defining the `IPersistToDisk` interface mentioned in the chapter introduction in C# might look like the following:

```
interface IPersistToDisk
{
    bool Load(string FileName);
    bool Save(string FileName);
}
```

The interface defines two methods, but does not provide any implementation for the methods. The method declarations end with a semicolon. C# classes that implement the `IPersistToDisk` interface are promising that they will provide an implementation of the `Load()` and `Save()` methods just as they are defined in the interface.

Defining interface properties

Properties define variables that can be defined by an interface. Like class properties, interface properties are associated with accessor functions that define code that should be executed when the property value is read or written. To define a property in an interface, provide the property type, the identifier, and the accessor keywords followed by semicolons. The accessor keywords are enclosed in curly brackets. The class or structure implementing the interface is responsible for providing the implementation of the property accessors.

To define a read/write property in an interface, use both the `get` and `set` accessor keywords:

```
interface Interface1
{
    int RecordCount { get; set; }
}
```

To define a read-only property in an interface, include only the `get` accessor keyword:

```
interface Interface1
{
    int RecordCount { get; }
}
```

To define a write-only property in an interface, include only the `set` accessor keyword:

```
interface Interface1
{
    int RecordCount { set; }
}
```

Defining interface indexers

Indexers are special properties that allow code to access data as if it were stored in an array. Indexers can be defined in an interface just as they can be defined in a class. To define an indexer in an interface, provide the indexer type, the keyword `this`, the indexer's parameter list in square brackets, and the accessor keywords followed by semicolons. The accessor keywords are enclosed in curly brackets. The class or structure implementing the interface is responsible for providing the implementation of the indexer accessors.

To define a read/write indexer in an interface, use both the `get` and `set` accessor keywords:

```
interface Interface1
{
    int this [int Index] { get; set; }
}
```

To define a read-only indexer in an interface, include only the `get` accessor keyword:

```
interface Interface1
{
    int this [int Index] { get; }
}
```

To define a write-only indexer in an interface, include only the `set` accessor keyword:

```
interface Interface1
{
    int this [int Index] { set; }
}
```

Defining interface events

Events can be defined on an interface, just as they can be defined on a class. You might want to add an event on the `IPersistToDisk` interface mentioned in the chapter introduction, for example, to be raised when the implementations of `Save()` and `Load()` actually start working with the disk to load or save the object's data, To define an event in an interface, use the keyword `event`, a type for the event, and an event identifier:

```
interface Interface1
{
    event EventHandler ClickEvent;
}
```

 Cross-Reference   Chapter 15 takes an in-depth look at events.

Deriving from Base Interfaces

Interfaces can derive from base interfaces, just as classes derive from base classes. Base interfaces are listed after the colon that follows the derived interface name. Unlike base classes, interfaces can derive from more than one base interface. Multiple base interface names are separated by commas, as shown in the following example:

```
interface Interface1
{
    void Method1();
}

interface Interface2
{
    void Method2();
}

interface Interface3 : Interface1, Interface2
{
}
```

Deriving from a base interface is useful when an interface contains a set of method, property, and event signatures that need to be added to after an interface is designed. The .NET Framework, for example, defines several interfaces that can be implemented and used in C#. Because the interfaces are already a part of the .NET Framework, the list of methods, properties, indexers, and events that they support has been solidified and cannot change. If you would like to use a defined interface and you need to add additional signatures onto the interface for your own use, then you might consider deriving from the already defined interface and adding your new signatures in your derived interface.

Classes that implement a derived interface must provide implementations for all methods the base interfaces define. When a class implements an interface, it must provide code bodies for each of the methods defined in the interface. If a class implements Interface3, using the previous example, the class must provide method implementations for both Method1() and Method2().

You cannot derive an interface from itself. Take a look at the following interface definition:

```
interface Interface1 : Interface1
{
    void Method1();
}
```

This error causes the C# compiler to issue the following error message:

```
error CS0529: Inherited interface 'Interface1' causes a cycle
in the interface hierarchy of 'Interface1'
```

This error message states that the code is trying to derive an interface from itself, which is not allowed in C#. Interfaces can only be derived from other interfaces.

Using the new Keyword to Reuse Identifiers

You can use the new keyword to redefine an identifier used in a base class. Suppose you are working with an interface that defines a property called ID:

```
interface BaseInterface
{
    int ID { get; }
}
```

Now suppose that you'd like to derive from that interface, but you'd like to use the ID identifier as the name of a method:

```
interface DerivedInterface : BaseInterface
{
    int ID();
}
```

This construct causes the C# compiler to issue a warning relating to the reuse of the identifier ID:

```
warning CS0108: The keyword new is required on
'DerivedInterface.ID()' because it hides inherited member
'BaseInterface.ID'
```

The compiler is warning that the identifier ID is used twice: once in the base interface as a property identifier, and once in the derived interface as a method name. This name reuse will most likely be confusing to users of the interface. The compiler warning means that the use of the ID keyword in the derived interface takes precedence over the use of the ID keyword in the base interface. If a piece of code obtains an implementation of the DerivedInterface interface, the code is unable to call the ID() method but cannot access the ID property in the base interface. The reuse of the ID identifier in the derived interface hides the ID identifier in the base class, and clients cannot access the base interface's property.

To work around this issue, you can use the keyword new when the identifier is reused. This use of the new keyword, shown in the following example, tells the C# compiler that you intend to provide a new usage for the reused symbol:

```
interface DerivedInterface : BaseInterface
{
    new int ID();
}
```

Implementing Interfaces in Classes and Structures

After an interface is defined, you can implement the interface in your C# classes and structures. Implementing an interface on a class or structure tells users of the class or structure that it provides implementations for the constructs defined in the interface. For example, implementing the IPersistToDisk interface mentioned during the introduction on a class informs users that the class that it provides implementations of the interface's Save() and Load() methods and that the methods can be called. You name the interfaces that you are implementing just as you would base classes — with a list of names following a colon that follows the class or structure identifier:

```
interface Interface1
{
    void Method1();
}
```

```
class MyClass : Interface1
{
    void Method1()
    {
    }
}
```

This code defines an interface called Interface1. The Interface1 method declares one method: a method called Method1(). The code also declares a class called MyClass, which implements the Interface1 interface. The MyClass class includes an implementation for the Method1() method defined by the Interface1 interface.

Although your class can derive from only one base class, your class can implement as many interfaces as you want. Simply list the interfaces after the class identifier and separate each interface name with a colon as follows:

```
class MyClass : Interface1, Interface2, Interface3
```

Multiple interface implementation is used throughout the .NET Framework. For example, the System.String class implements four interfaces defined by the .NET Framework:

- ✦ IComparable, which compares the values of two objects of the same type
- ✦ ICloneable, which makes a new object having the same state as another object
- ✦ IConvertible, which converts the value of a type to a value of another type
- ✦ IEnumerable, which allows code to iterate over a collection

Because the System.String class implements these four interfaces, the functionality each of the interfaces provides is supported by the System.String class. This means that strings can be compared to other strings, can be cloned, can be converted into other types and can have the characters in the string iterated over as a collection. This multiple interface implementation concept is also available to you as a C# developer.

C# also enables you to derive your class from a base class and implement interfaces at the same time:

```
class MyDerivedClass : CMyBaseClass, Interface1, Interface2
```

Classes must implement any method, property, indexer, or event declaration found in an interface that it implements. If you forget to do this, you get an error back from the C# compiler. The following code fails because the MyClass class implements Interface1 but does not provide an implementation of the Method1() method defined in Interface1:

```
interface Interface1
{.
    void Method1();
```

```
    }

class MyClass : Interface1
{
    public static void Main()
    {
    }
}
```

The C# compiler issues the following error message when the code is compiled:

```
error CS0535: 'MyClass' does not implement interface member
'Interface1.Method1()'
```

The class must provide an implementation for the Method1() interface defined by Interface1, since the class implements Interface1. The following example corrects the error:

```
interface Interface1
{
    void Method1();
}

class MyClass : Interface1
{
    public static void Main()
    {
    }

    public void Method1()
    {
    }
}
```

Implementing Interface Methods with the Same Name

Because it is possible for a method name to appear in more than one interface, and because it is possible for a C# class to implement more than one interface, a C# class might be required to provide multiple implementations of methods from different interfaces that have the same name. Take a look at the DoWork() method in the following code:

```
interface Interface1
{
    void DoWork();
}

interface Interface2
```

```
{
    void DoWork();
}

class MyClass : Interface1, Interface2
{
    void DoWork()
    {
    }
}
```

This code does not compile. The C# compiler displays the following scoping syntax in error messages that it produces:

```
error CS0536: 'MyClass' does not implement interface member
'Interface1.DoWork()'. 'MyClass.DoWork()' is either static, not
public, or has the wrong return type.
error CS0536: 'MyClass' does not implement interface member
'Interface2.DoWork()'. 'MyClass.DoWork()' is either static, not
public, or has the wrong return type.
```

The interface/method name syntax is displayed in the error messages, offering a reminder of the syntax needed in the class implementations.

The problem is that the MyClass class needs to provide implementation code for the DoWork() method defined by Interface1 as well as the DoWork() method defined by Interface2, and both interfaces reuse the method name DoWork(). A C# class cannot include two methods with the same name, so how can you define both of the interface methods?

The solution is to prefix the method implementation with the interface name and a period separating the interface name from the implementation name, as follows:

```
class MyClass : Interface1, Interface2
{
    void Interface1.DoWork()
    {
    }

    void Interface2.DoWork()
    {
    }
}
```

This class compiles, as it contains two DoWork() implementations, one for each defined interface. Because the method names are qualified with the interface names, the C# compiler can distinguish one from the other and can verify that both interfaces have been implemented in the class.

Accessing Interface Members

Working with classes that implement interfaces is straightforward in C#. You usually perform three operations when working with objects whose classes implement interfaces:

✦ Query an object to see whether it supports a specific interface

✦ Access an interface on an object

✦ Access an object's class member originally defined in an interface

The following sections take a look at these operations.

Querying an object for an interface

Because you design and implement your own code, you already know which classes are used in your application and which interfaces they support. However, when you're writing code that can be used in other .NET applications, and other code passes objects to you, you can't really be sure which interfaces are supported on those objects. If you're writing an assembly, for example, and you write code that accepts a generic object type, you can't know whether the objects support a given interface.

You can use the C# keyword `is` to see whether an object supports an interface. The `is` keyword is used as a part of a Boolean expression constructed as follows:

✦ An object identifier

✦ The keyword `is`

✦ An interface identifier

The expression evaluates to `True` if the object supports the named interface and `False` otherwise. Listing 13-1 shows how the `is` keyword works:

Listing 13-1: Using the is Keyword to Work with an Interface

```
using System;

public interface IPrintMessage
{
    void Print();
};

class Class1
```

Continued

Listing 13-1 *(continued)*

```
{
    public void Print()
    {
        Console.WriteLine("Hello from Class1!");
    }
}

class Class2 : IPrintMessage
{
    public void Print()
    {
        Console.WriteLine("Hello from Class2!");
    }
}

class MainClass
{
    public static void Main()
    {
        PrintClass    PrintObject = new PrintClass();

        PrintObject.PrintMessages();
    }
}

class PrintClass
{
    public void PrintMessages()
    {
        Class1       Object1 = new Class1();
        Class2       Object2 = new Class2();

        PrintMessageFromObject(Object1);
        PrintMessageFromObject(Object2);
    }

    private void PrintMessageFromObject(object obj)
    {
        if(obj is IPrintMessage)
        {
            IPrintMessage PrintMessage;

            PrintMessage = (IPrintMessage)obj;
            PrintMessage.Print();
        }
    }
}
```

Listing 13-1 defines an interface called `IPrintMessage`. The `IPrintMessage` interface defines one method, called `Print`. As with all interface members in C#, the `IPrintMessage` interface defines members but does not implement them.

The listing then implements two test classes, called `Class1` and `Class2`. The `Class1` class implements one method called `Print()`. Because `Class1` does not inherit from the `IPrintMessage` interface, the `Print()` method implemented by the class has nothing to do with the `Print()` method defined by the `IPrintMessage` interface. The `Class2` class implements one method called `Print()`. Because `Class2` inherits from the `IPrintMessage` interface, the `Print()` method implemented by the class is considered by the C# compiler to be an implementation of the `Print()` method defined by the `IPrintMessage` interface.

Listing 13-1 then goes on to define a class called `MainClass`, which implements the application's `Main()` method, and another class called `PrintClass`. The `Main()` method in Listing 13-1 creates an object of the `PrintClass` class and calls its public method to do the real work.

Listing 13-1 finishes up by declaring a class called `PrintClass`. The `PrintClass` class implements a public method called `PrintMessages()` and a private helper method called `PrintMessageFromObject()`. The `PrintMessages()` method is the method called by the `Main()` method. Because the `PrintMessageFromObject()` is marked as private, it can only be called from other pieces of code in the `PrintClass` object and cannot be called from code in other classes.

The `PrintMessages()` method creates an object of class `Class1` and an object from `Class2` and passes each object to the private `PrintMessageFromObject()` method. The private `PrintMessageFromObject()` method accepts a parameter of type `object` as a parameter.

Note
Using a parameter of type `object` is legal because all variable types supported by the CLR ultimately derive from `System.Object`, and the C# keyword `object` is an alias for the `System.Object` type. Any variable type that can be represented in C# can be used as a parameter to a method that expects an object type, because all types are ultimately `System.Object` objects.

In the following line from Listing 13-1, the `PrintMessageFromObject()` method starts out by examining the object to see whether it implements the `IPrintMessage` interface:

```
if(obj is IPrintMessage)
```

If the object implements the interface, the Boolean expression `obj is IPrintMessage` evaluates to `True`, and the code beneath the `if` test executes. If the object does not implement the interface, the Boolean expression `obj is IPrintMessage` evaluates to `False`, and the code beneath the `if` test does not execute.

If the object supports the interface, the object's implementation of the interface can be accessed. You can access an object's interface implementation by declaring a variable of the interface type and then casting the object to the interface type as follows:

```
IPrintMessage PrintMessage;
PrintMessage = (IPrintMessage)obj;
```

After you initialize a variable of the interface type, you can access the interface's members using the familiar period notation:

```
PrintMessage.Print();
```

In Listing 13-2, Object1 is passed into the PrintMessageFromObject() method, and nothing is printed to the console, because the Object1 object is of class Class1, and Class1 does not implement the IPrintMessage interface. When Object1 is passed into the PrintMessageFromObject() method, the following text is written out to the console:

```
Hello from Class2!
```

This message appears because the Object2 object is of class Class2, and Class2 implements the IPrintMessage interface. The call to the object's implementation of the interface's Print method prints the message to the console.

Accessing an interface on an object

Using the is operator to work with an interface requires your code to access an object twice:

✦ Once to query the object to see whether it implements an interface

✦ Once to access the object's interface implementation using the casting operator

You can combine these two accesses by using the as operator. The as operator performs both activities in a single statement. Listing 13-2 is a modified version of Listing 13-1 that uses the as statement instead of the is statement:

Listing 13-2: **Using the as Keyword to Work with an Interface**

```
using System;

public interface IPrintMessage
{
    void Print();
};

class Class1
{
```

```
    public void Print()
    {
        Console.WriteLine("Hello from Class1!");
    }
}

class Class2 : IPrintMessage
{
    public void Print()
    {
        Console.WriteLine("Hello from Class2!");
    }
}

class MainClass
{
    public static void Main()
    {
        PrintClass    PrintObject = new PrintClass();

        PrintObject.PrintMessages();
    }
}

class PrintClass
{
    public void PrintMessages()
    {
        Class1      Object1 = new Class1();
        Class2      Object2 = new Class2();

        PrintMessageFromObject(Object1);
        PrintMessageFromObject(Object2);
    }

    private void PrintMessageFromObject(object obj)
    {
        IPrintMessage PrintMessage;

        PrintMessage = obj as IPrintMessage;
        if(PrintMessage != null)
            PrintMessage.Print();
    }
}
```

The as operator is used as a part of an expression constructed as follows:

✦ An object identifier

✦ The keyword as

✦ An interface identifier

If the object named in the expression implements the interface named in the expression, the object's implementation of the interface is returned as the result of the expression. If the object named in the expression does not implement the interface named in the expression, the result of the expression is assigned an empty value represented by the C# keyword `null`.

The new implementation of the private `PrintMessageFromObject()` method uses the `as` operator. It declares a local variable of the `IPrintMessage` interface type and uses the `as` operator to access the object's implementation of the method.

After the `as` operation completes, the interface implementation variable is checked to see whether it has the value `null`. If the variable is not equal to `null`, the supplied object is known to implement the interface, and the interface's method can be called.

Listing 13-2 is functionally equivalent to Listing 13-1, and Listing 13-2 writes the following text out to the console:

```
Hello from Class2!
```

Understanding interface declarations and scoping keywords

When you design an interface, you can mark the interface as `public`, `protected`, `internal`, or `private`. If you decide to use one of these keywords to provide a scoping level for the interface, it must appear immediately before the `interface` keyword.

✦ Interfaces marked `public` are visible to any piece of code that has access to the code in which the interface definition can be resolved at runtime. If you develop an assembly and implement a public interface in that assembly, any .NET application that accesses the assembly can work with the interface.

✦ Interfaces marked `private` are visible only to the class in which they are defined. Only interfaces whose definitions are nested in classes can be marked as `private`.

✦ Interfaces marked `protected` are visible only to the class in which they are defined, or from classes derived from the class. Only interfaces whose definitions are nested in classes can be marked as `protected`.

✦ Interfaces marked `internal` are visible to any code in the same binary file, but are not visible to any code in other binary files. If you define an interface in C# and compile the class into an assembly, `internal` interfaces can be accessed by any piece of code in the assembly. However, if another piece of code uses your assembly, it has no access to the interface.

C# enables you to specify an interface without specifying any scope keywords. If you declare an interface without specifying any scope keywords, the interface is given public accessibility by default.

Implementing Interfaces Defined by the .NET Framework

The .NET Framework defines several interfaces that you can implement in your classes. Earlier this chapter mentioned that the .NET Framework defines interfaces, such as ICloneable, IEnumerable, ICompareable, and IConvertible interfaces that are implemented by the System.String class. Implementing interfaces defined by the .NET Framework can help your classes integrate with the .NET Framework and the Common Language Runtime (the CLR, for short). Let's look at an example.

Supporting foreach with IEnumerable and IEnumerator

Listing 9-3 in Chapter 9, implements a class called Rainbow, which includes an indexer that allows the class' contents — strings naming the colors of the rainbow — as elements of an array, as shown in the following example:

```
Rainbow MyRainbow = new Rainbow();

for(ColorIndex = 0; ColorIndex < MyRainbow.Count; ColorIndex++)
{
    string ColorName;

    ColorName = MyRainbow[ColorIndex];
    System.Console.WriteLine(ColorName);
}
```

You can reduce this code even further by using the foreach keyword with the class, as shown in the following code snippet:

```
Rainbow MyRainbow = new Rainbow();

foreach(string Color in MyRainbow)
    Console.WriteLine(ColorName);
```

By default, classes cannot support the foreach keyword, and using the keyword to access class elements causes the C# compiler to issue the following error message:

```
error CS1579: foreach statement cannot operate on variables of
type 'Rainbow' because 'Rainbow' does not contain a definition
for 'GetEnumerator', or it is inaccessible
```

You can use foreach with your classes, however, if the class implements a .NET Framework interface called IEnumerable. The IEnumerable interface contains methods that the .NET Framework uses to extract elements from your objects. If your class contains a collection of elements, and you want other pieces of code to use the foreach keyword to iterate over each of the elements in the collection, you should implement the IEnumerable interface on your class.

The IEnumerable interface contains a single method definition:

```
IEnumerator GetEnumerator();
```

The GetEnumerator() method must be implemented in your class, and it must return an object that implements another .NET Framework interface called IEnumerator. The IEnumerator interface is responsible for implementing the code that returns individual class elements.

The IEnumerator interface defines a property and two methods as follows:

- ✦ object Current {get;}
- ✦ bool MoveNext();
- ✦ void Reset();

The Current property returns a reference to the current element in the collection. The MoveNext() method moves to the next element in the collection, and returns True if there is a next element or False if the end of the collection has been reached and there is no next element. The Reset() method resets the integrator back to the beginning of the collection.

When you access a class's data with the foreach construct, the .NET Framework accesses your class' IEnumerable and IEnumerator interfaces with code like the following pseudo-code:

```
IEnumerable IEnumerableImplementation;
IEnumerator IEnumeratorImplementation;

IEnumerableImplementation = YourClass as IEnumerable;
if(IEnumerableImplementation != null)
{
    IEnumeratorImplementation =
IEnumerableImplementation.GetEnumerator();
    If(IEnumeratorImplementation != null)
    {
        while(IEnumeratorImplementation.GetNext() == true)
            CurrentValue = IEnumeratorImplementation.Current;
    }
}
```

Both the IEnumerable and IEnumerator interfaces are defined in a .NET Framework namespace called System.Collections, and that namespace must be referenced when you work with these interfaces. You can reference the namespaces explicitly:

```
class MyClass :
    System.Collections.IEnumerable,
    System.Collections.IEnumerator
```

If you want, you can use the `using` keyword to reference the namespaces instead:

```
using System.Collections;

class MyClass :
    IEnumerable,
    IEnumerator
```

Listing 13-3 reworks Listing 9-3 and uses the `Rainbow` class to implement `IEnumerable` and `IEnumerator` interfaces; it also uses the `foreach` construct in the `Main()` method to iterate over the elements in the class.

Listing 13-3: **Supporting foreach with IEnumerable and IEnumerator**

```
using System;
using System.Collections;

class Rainbow : IEnumerable, IEnumerator
{
    private short IteratorIndex = -1;

    public IEnumerator GetEnumerator()
    {
        return this;
    }

    public object Current
    {
        get
        {
            switch(IteratorIndex)
            {
                case 0:
                    return "Red";
                case 1:
                    return "Orange";
                case 2:
                    return "Yellow";
                case 3:
                    return "Green";
                case 4:
```

Continued

Listing 13-3 *(continued)*

```
                        return "Blue";
                case 5:
                        return "Indigo";
                case 6:
                        return "Violet";
                default:
                        return "*** ERROR ***";
            }
        }
    }

    public bool MoveNext()
    {
        IteratorIndex++;
        if(IteratorIndex == 7)
            return false;
        return true;
    }

    public void Reset()
    {
        IteratorIndex = -1;
    }

    public static void Main()
    {
        Rainbow MyRainbow = new Rainbow();

        foreach(string ColorName in MyRainbow)
            Console.WriteLine(ColorName);
    }
}
```

Executing the code in Listing 13-3 writes the following out to the console:

```
Red
Orange
Yellow
Green
Blue
Indigo
Violet
```

The Rainbow class implements both the IEnumerable and IEnumerator interfaces. The class maintains a private field called IteratorIndex, which is used to

keep track of the next element to be returned in the foreach loop. It is initialized to -1; you'll see why when you look at the implementation of MoveNext() in the following pages.

The class' implementation of IEnumerable.GetEnumerator() returns a reference to the object being called with the following statement:

```
return this;
```

Remember that the method must return a reference to a class that implements the IEnumerator interface. Because the object used to call IEnumerable.GetEnumerator() also implements the IEnumerator class, you can return the object being called. You can use the this keyword as a return value. In this context, the this keyword refers to the current object whose code is executing.

Because the C# compiler can determine at runtime that the current object implements IEnumerable, the code does not need to cast the this keyword to a variable of type IEnumerator. You could have written code like the following:

```
return this as IEnumerator;
```

However, this is redundant, because the C# compiler can already see that the this object — the object currently executing — implements the IEnumerator interface. If you use this code to return an IEnumerator reference, you get the following warning from the C# compiler:

```
warning CS0183: The given expression is always of the provided
('System.Collections.IEnumerator') type
```

The remainder of the Rainbow class implements members of the IEnumerator interface. The first member provides the implementation for the IEnumerator.Current property. It examines the value of the class' private IteratorIndex property and returns a string that represents the rainbow color at the index referenced by the value of the IteratorIndex property. The Current property returns a variable of type object, but because strings are objects just like all other data types, the CLR accepts the string-based return values.

The implementation of the IEnumerator.MoveNext() method increments the value of the private IteratorIndex property. Because the rainbow has seven colors, the MoveNext() implementation assumes that legal values of IteratorIndex range from 0 to 6. If the value is incremented to 7, the implementation of MoveNext() assumes that the iterator has reached its limit and will return False. Otherwise, the implementation returns True. The statement that increments the value of IteratorIndex requires that the initial value of IteratorIndex be set to -1. When MoveNext() is called the first time, the increment statement increments the value of IteratorIndex from -1 to 0, giving a legal value for IteratorIndex on the first iteration of the loop.

The implementation of the IEnumerator.Reset() method simply resets the value of the private IteratorIndex to -1. This method is called if more than one foreach construct is called on the object and the .NET Framework needs to reset the object's enumeration state back to its initial value.

All of this implementation makes the Main() method very straightforward. The method can create an object of class Rainbow and use foreach to iterate through each color name in the class.

Supporting cleanup with IDisposable

The CLR contains a mechanism for automatic cleanup of objects called *garbage collection*. It is important to understand how this system works, how it differs from other systems and how your C# code can be as compatible as possible with this algorithm for the disposal of created objects.

In C++, an object is created with the new keyword, and the operation returns a pointer to the object as it is created on the application's memory heap. It is the responsibility of the C++ developer to explicitly release this memory by calling delete on that same pointer when the object is no longer needed. Calling delete releases the memory used by the object and calls the class' destructor so that the class could perform any class-specific cleanup operations. Forgetting to call delete on an object pointer returned by new causes a memory leak.

In certain runtimes, such as Visual Basic and COM, objects are reference counted. The runtimes keep a count of threads of code that attach to an object and automatically release the object when its reference count reaches zero. This frees the developer from remembering to call a destruction statement like delete and helps eliminate a whole class of bugs relating to memory leak issues.

The CLR uses a memory reclamation scheme called garbage collection. Objects are not destroyed when their last reference is released, as is the case with reference-counted systems such as COM and COM+. Rather, objects are destroyed sometime later when the CLR garbage collector executes and destroys objects ready to be deleted. Destructors on C# objects are executed not when the last reference is released on the object, but when the garbage collector frees the internal CLR data structures used to keep track of the object.

It is important to keep this garbage collection design in mind when you design C# classes. Classes that manage resources that need to be explicitly closed when the object is destroyed, such as file handles or database connections, should be closed as soon as the object is no longer used. Putting cleanup code in the class' destructor means that the resources will not be released until the garbage collector destroys the object, which may be much later than when the last reference on the object is released.

The .NET Framework supports an interface called IDisposable that classes can implement to support cleanup of class resources. The IDisposable interface is found in the .NET Framework's System namespace. It supports a single method called Dispose(), which takes no parameters and returns nothing, as shown in the following example:

```
using System;

public class MyClass : IDisposable
{
    public MyClass()
    {
    }

    ~MyClass()
    {
    }

    public void Dispose()
    {
    }
}
```

This class supports a constructor, which is called when objects of the class are created; a destructor, which is called when objects of the class are destroyed by the garbage collector; and Dispose(), which can be called when client code disposes of the object.

Client code can query objects for support of the IDisposable interface and can call its Dispose() method to free class resources before the garbage collector destroys the object. The C# language makes this querying easy through a special syntax involving the using keyword. The using keyword can be used in a parenthetical expression that includes the creation of a new object:

```
using(MyClass MyObject = new MyClass())
{
    // use "MyObject" here
}
```

In this example, the using keyword is used to create a new object called MyObject. The new object is of class MyObject. The object can be used in any statements included within the braces following the using keyword. The object is automatically destroyed when the code path reaches the closing brace of the using block. If the class of the object created in the using statement supports IDisposable, then the class' Dispose() method is automatically called without any effort on the client side. Listing 13-4 shows a class called MyClass, which implements the IDisposable interface.

Listing 13-4: **IDisposable and the using Keyword**

```csharp
using System;

public class MyClass : IDisposable
{
    public MyClass()
    {
        Console.WriteLine("constructor");
    }

    ~MyClass()
    {
        Console.WriteLine("destructor");
    }

    public void Dispose()
    {
        Console.WriteLine("implementation of
IDisposable.Dispose()");
    }
}

public class MainClass
{
    static void Main()
    {
        using(MyClass MyObject = new MyClass())
        {
        }
    }
}
```

This console application implements the MyClass class shown in Listing 13-4 and contains statements in its constructor, destructor, and Dispose() implementation that write messages out to the console. Listing 13-4 also includes a using statement in its Main() method that creates an object of type MyClass. Executing Listing 13-4 results in the following messages being written out to the console:

```
constructor
implementation of IDisposable.Dispose()
destructor
```

Note that the Dispose() implementation of the IDisposable interface is called automatically without any intervention on the part of the Main() method.

Keep in mind that you should implement the IDisposable interface only for classes that maintain resources that must be explicitly freed, such as database connections or window handles. If your class maintains only references to objects managed by the CLR, then you do not need to implement IDisposable. Implementing IDisposable means that the CLR needs to perform extra work to destroy your objects, and this extra work can slow down the garbage collection process. Implement IDisposable when necessary, but do not implement it unless you have to.

Summary

Think of an interface as a promise that a class will implement the methods, properties, indexers, and events defined in the interface. Interfaces provide definitions of members but do not provide any implementation. A class that implements an interface is required to provide an implementation of each of the members of the interface. A class can implement multiple interfaces, although it can inherit from only one base class. Interfaces can inherit from other interfaces, just as classes can inherit from base classes.

The C# keywords is and as can be used to work with objects that implement interfaces. The is keyword is used in a Boolean expression that evaluates to True if an object implements an interface, and False otherwise. The as keyword converts an object variable to a variable of an interface type. Expressions that use the as keyword return null if the object does not implement the named interface.

In this chapter, you examined an example of implementing an interface defined by the .NET Framework. The .NET Framework implements many interfaces, and you should go through the documentation and research them all. The interfaces in the .NET Framework begin with the letter *I*. Take a look at each one. You can use the .NET Framework interfaces to implement everything from custom console formatting to serialization to garbage collection object disposal semantics.

✦   ✦   ✦

Enumerations

Some of the variables that you define in your code might be used to hold a value taken from a set of possible values. For example, you might need to keep track of the status of a file. You might choose to define a variable that can describe whether a file is open, closed, or not found. One way to accomplish this would be to set aside some constants to define the various options and an integer to contain the actual value, as in the following code:

```
const int FileOpen = 1;
const int FileClosed = 2;
const int FileNotFound = 3;

int FileStatus;

FileStatus = FileClosed;
```

This code is valid C# code and will compile. However, a developer can legally set the variable to a value not available in the set of defined constants. The data type of `FileStatus` above is an integer, and the C# compiler happily accepts any code that sets the variable to any legal integer value, even though the intent is to restrict the set of legal values to the set defined by the constants. Ideally, setting the value of `FileStatus` to a value not defined by the constants should be illegal, because the original intent is to restrict the set of possible values to the set defined for that variable.

The ideal development situation in cases like this is that you should be able to define a variable and associate the value with a set of legal possible values. In addition, the C# compiler should be able to prevent developers from setting the variable to a value not defined in the set of possible values. As it turns out, C# supports a construct called an enumeration that handles this very case.

Enumerations are a group of constants defined under a common name. The name of the enumeration can be used as a variable type after the enumeration is defined. When a variable defined as an enumeration type is used, the C# compiler ensures that values assigned to variables of the enumeration type match one of the values in the set of constants defined in the enumeration definition.

Enumerations are ideal for use in situations in which a variable should be associated with a specific set of values. Suppose, for example, that you're writing a C# class that controls an electronic door. You decide to add a property to your class called DoorState, which opens or closes the door:

```
public int DoorState
{
    set
    {
        InternalDoorState = value;
    }
}
```

You might also decide to define some constants that the code can use to make the code a bit more readable:

```
public const int DoorStateOpen = 1;
public const int DoorStateClosed = 2;
```

The property and the constants enable code that works with objects of your class to write readable code like the following:

```
DoorStateObject = new DoorClass();

DoorObject.DoorState = DoorClass.DoorStateOpen;
DoorObject.DoorState = DoorClass.DoorStateClosed;
```

The preceding code compiles and executes without any problems. However, the DoorState property is defined as an int, and there is nothing to stop callers from using nonsense values and assigning them to the DoorState property:

```
DoorObject.DoorState = 12345;
```

This code is legal as well, because the literal 12345 falls within the legal range of a C# integer, and the DoorState property is defined as having an int type. Although this code is legal from the C# compilation point of view, it doesn't make logical sense at the class level, because the door state should actually only be open or closed.

You could build some error-checking into the DoorState property to accept only legal values, but it would be even nicer to have the C# compiler enforce the constraint for you when the code is built.

Enumerations provide the compile-time mechanism that you're looking for. They enable you to group related constants, such as the DoorStateOpen and DoorStateClosed constants, under a group name, and use that group name as a value type. You might group the DoorStateOpen and DoorStateClosed constants under an enumeration called LegalDoorStates, for example; and you could redefine the `DoorState` property to work with a type of `LegalDoorStates`, rather than an `int`. The C# compiler would then ensure that the values assigned to the property are members of the enumeration, and it would produce an error if the value does not exist in the enumeration.

Declaring an enumeration

You can declare an enumeration in C# by using the following syntax:

✦ The keyword `enum`

✦ An enumeration identifier

✦ An optional base type

✦ Comma-separated enumeration value identifiers enclosed in curly brackets

The `LegalDoorStates` enumeration discussed in the previous section might be defined as follows:

```
enum LegalDoorStates
{
    DoorStateOpen,
    DoorStateClosed
}
```

The members of the enumerations each have an associated numeric value. By default, the numeric value of the first value is zero; and the value of every other member is one greater than the value of the previous enumeration. Using these rules and the enumeration defined previously, the default value of `DoorStateOpen` is 0, and the value of `DoorStateClosed` is 1. If you want, you can override these values by assigning values to the members when they are defined using the assignment operator:

```
enum LegalDoorStates
{
    DoorStateOpen = 100,
    DoorStateClosed = 150
}
```

You can assign the members to a literal value or to the result of a constant expression:

```
enum LegalDoorStates
{
    DoorStateOpen = (75 + 25),
    DoorStateClosed = 150
}
```

If you do not assign a value to a particular enumeration member, the default value assignment rules apply. Consider the following enumeration:

```
enum LegalDoorStates
{
    DoorStateOpen = 100,
    DoorStateClosed
}
```

Using this enumeration and the default value assignment rules, the value of `DoorStateOpen` is 100, and the value of `DoorStateClosed` is 101.

C# also enables you to use one enumeration identifier to assign a value to another identifier:

```
enum LegalDoorStates
{
    DoorStateOpen = 100,
    DoorStateClosed,
    LastState = DoorStateClosed
}
```

In this example, the value of the `LastState` enumeration is equal to the value of the `DoorStateClosed` enumeration, which is equal to 101 in this case. This shows that two identifiers in an enumeration can have the same value.

Enumerations correspond to a particular value type. This corresponding type is called the enumeration's *underlying type*. Enumerations can be explicitly converted to their underlying type. By default, the underlying type of all enumerations is `int`. If you want to use a different underlying type, specify the underlying type after a colon that follows the enumeration identifier:

```
enum LegalDoorStates : short
{
    DoorStateOpen = 100,
    DoorStateClosed
}
```

Any explicit value assignments that you specify must use values that fall in the legal range of the enumeration's underlying type. Look at the error in the following enumeration:

```
enum Weather : uint
{
    Sunny = -1,
    Cloudy = -2,
    Rain = -3,
    Snow = -4
}
```

This enumeration declaration is in error because the underlying type is `uint` and the assignments use negative values that are outside of the range of a `uint`. Compiling the preceding enumeration produces errors from the C# compiler:

```
error CS0031: Constant value '-1' cannot be converted to a 'uint'
error CS0031: Constant value '-2' cannot be converted to a 'uint'
error CS0031: Constant value '-3' cannot be converted to a 'uint'
error CS0031: Constant value '-4' cannot be converted to a 'uint'
```

Using an enumeration

After the enumeration is defined, you can use the enumeration identifier as a variable type. Listing 14-1 shows how the DoorController class might use an enumeration.

Listing 14-1: Using the LegalDoorStates Enumeration

```csharp
public enum LegalDoorStates
{
    DoorStateOpen,
    DoorStateClosed
}

class DoorController
{
    private LegalDoorStates CurrentState;

    public LegalDoorStates State
    {
        get
        {
            return CurrentState;
        }

        set
        {
            CurrentState = value;
        }
    }
}

class MainClass
{
    public static void Main()
    {
        DoorController Door;

        Door = new DoorController();

        Door.State = LegalDoorStates.DoorStateOpen;
    }
}
```

The `LegalDoorStates` enumeration is defined outside of a class declaration. This is legal in C#, and doing so makes the enumeration visible to all classes in the source file. As an alternative, you can define enumerations inside of a class declaration, using one of the scoping keywords (`public`, `protected`, `internal`, or `private`) to specify how the enumeration is visible to other classes.

After you define the `LegalDoorStates` enumeration, you can use its name as a variable type. It is used as the type for the private `CurrentState` field in the `DoorController` class, as well as the type for the public `State` property of the same class.

You refer to an enumeration in code using both the name of the enumeration and one of the identifiers in the enumeration. These identifiers are separated by a period, as shown in the following statement:

```
Door.State = LegalDoorStates.DoorStateOpen;
```

The `LegalDoorStates.DoorStateOpen` expression has a value equal to the value of the `DoorStateOpen` identifier in the `LegalDoorStates` enumeration. This value is assigned to the `State` property.

The advantage of this enumeration-based design is that the compiler can now identify places where code tries to set the `State` property to a value other than a value that comes from the enumeration. Examine the error in the following statement:

```
Door.State = 12345;
```

The preceding code is in error because the `State` property is defined as taking a value of type `LegalDoorStates`, and an integer is being assigned instead. The code in the previous example produces the following error from the C# compiler:

```
error CS0029: Cannot implicitly convert type 'int' to
'LegalDoorStates'
```

Using operators on enumeration values

Because enumerated values have an underlying type and a value, it makes sense that you can write code that deals with the underlying values. You can use several C# operators with enumerated values:

✦ equality

✦ inequality

✦ less than

✦ greater than

✦ less than or equal to

✦ greater than or equal to

✦ addition

✦ subtraction

✦ AND

✦ exclusive OR

✦ inclusive OR

✦ bitwise complement

✦ increment

✦ decrement

For example, look at Listing 14-2.

Listing 14-2: **Using Operators with Enumerations**

```
using System;

public enum FileAttributes
{
    AttrNone = 0,
    AttrReadOnly = 1,
    AttrHidden = 2,
    AttrReadyForArchive = 4
}

class MainClass
{
    public static void Main()
    {
        FileAttributes FileAttr;

        FileAttr = FileAttributes.AttrReadOnly |
FileAttributes.AttrHidden;
        Console.WriteLine(FileAttr);
    }
}
```

The code in Listing 14-2 defines a set of enumerated values that specify attributes for a file on disk. A file can have no special attributes (FileAttributes.AttrNone), read-only attributes (FileAttributes.AttrReadOnly), hidden attributes (FileAttributes.Hidden), or ready-for-archival attributes (FileAttributes. AttrReadyForArchive).

The code in the `Main()` method specifies a local variable called `FileAttr`, which is of type `FileAttributes`. The code sets the value to specify a hidden, read-only file by performing an `OR` operation on the `FileAttributes.AttrReadOnly` and `FileAttributes.Hidden` attributes. The value of the local variable is then written to the console.

Compiling and executing Listing 14-2 produces the following console output:

```
3
```

Listing 14-2 outputs the value 3 because the value of the `FileAttributes.AttrReadOnly` enumeration, 1, was joined in an `OR` operation with the value of the `FileAttributes.Hidden` enumeration, 2. Performing a Boolean `OR` operation on values of 1 and 2 produces a result of 3.

You can also cast an enumerated value to a value having a type of the enumeration's underlying type:

```csharp
enum IntEnum
{
    EnumOne = 1,
    EnumTwo,
    EnumThree
}

IntEnum IntEnumValue;
int IntValue;

IntEnumValue = EnumTwo;
IntValue = (int) IntEnumValue; // value is 2
```

This code converts the value in the enumeration variable `IntEnumValue` to its integer equivalent and assigns the integer `IntValue` to that value. Because the `IntValue` variable is a standard integer, it can be set to any legal value for an integer. It is not bound by the value set defined by the enumeration, even though it is assigned a value that came from an enumerated variable.

Using the .NET System.Enum Class

The `enum` type in C# is actually an alias for the `System.Enum` class defined in the .NET Framework. You can use any of the members of the .NET `System.Enum` class on the enumerations that you define.

Retrieving enumeration names

Listing 14-3 illustrates how your code can work with enumerations as `System.Enum` objects. It is an enhancement of Listing 14-1 that retrieves the current door state and prints the state's name to the console.

Listing 14-3: **Retrieving an Enumeration Name with GetName()**

```
using System;

public enum LegalDoorStates
{
    DoorStateOpen,
    DoorStateClosed
}

class DoorController
{
    private LegalDoorStates CurrentState;

    public LegalDoorStates State
    {
        get
        {
            return CurrentState;
        }

        set
        {
            CurrentState = value;
        }
    }
}

class MainClass
{
    public static void Main()
    {
        DoorController  Door;
        string          EnumName;

        Door = new DoorController();

        Door.State = LegalDoorStates.DoorStateOpen;
        EnumName = LegalDoorStates.GetName(typeof(LegalDoorStates), Door.State);
        Console.WriteLine(EnumName);
    }
}
```

The Main() method in Listing 14-3 uses the GetName() method of the System. Enum class to obtain a string that represents an enumeration value. The first parameter is a Type object that specifies the enumeration being queried. The expression typeof(LegalDoorStates) returns a .NET Type object for the specified type—in this case, the `LegalDoorStates` enumeration. The second parameter is the actual enumeration value whose string representation should be returned. The following statement shows how the `GetName()` method can be used to obtain the name of an enumerated value:

```
EnumName = LegalDoorStates.GetName(typeof(LegalDoorStates),
Door.State);
```

This statement reads as follows: "Return a string that represents the name of the value in the `Door.State` property. This value is a part of the `LegalDoorStates` enumeration."

Running and executing Listing 14-3 prints the following to the console:

```
DoorStateOpen
```

You can also use the `Format()` method to retrieve the name of an enumeration value, given its numeric value. The `GetName()` call in Listing 14-3 could have been replaced with the following call to `Format()`:

```
EnumName = LegalDoorStates.Format(typeof(LegalDoorStates), 0, "g");
```

The first parameter to `Format()` is the same as the first parameter to `GetNames()`, which is the enumeration type to be used in the call. The second parameter to `Format()` is the numeric value whose enumeration name is to be returned from the call. The last parameter to `Format()` is a string that specifies the contents of the string to be returned by the call. The format string can be one of the following:

✦ g, which specifies that the enumeration value with the numerical value matching the value of the second parameter is to be returned

✦ x, which specifies that the value of the second parameter to be returned as a string representing the value in hexadecimal notation

✦ d[P1], which specifies that the value of the second parameter to be returned as a string representing the value in hexadecimal notation

✦ f, which specifies that the value is to be treated as a set of combined enumerated values and that the method should return a comma-delimited value list as a string

The f format value is designed for use with enumerations that represent bit values. Consider the following enumeration:

```
public enum BitsToSet
{
    Bit0Set = 1,
    Bit1Set = 2,
    Bit2Set = 4,
    Bit3Set = 8,
    Bit4Set = 16,
```

```
        Bit5Set = 32,
        Bit6Set = 64,
        Bit7Set = 128
}
```

The preceding enumeration represents a set of bits that could be set in a byte. Various bits can be set in a variable using the Boolean OR operator, as in the following example:

```
BitsToSet Byte;
Byte = BitsToSet.Bit1Set | BitsToSet.Bit3Set | BitsToSet.Bit6Set;
```

Calling the Format() method on the Byte variable with the f format parameter returns a string representing the names of the enumerated values whose values are found in the variable:

```
  Bit1Set, Bit3Set, Bit6Set
```

Comparing enumeration values

The CompareTo() method of the System.Enum class can compare one enumeration value to another and returns an integer describing the relationship between the two values. Take a look at Listing 14-4, which compares the value of an enumerated variable to a named value from the same enumeration:

Listing 14-4: **Comparing Enumeration Values with CompareTo()**

```
using System;

public class MainClass
{
    public enum Color
    {
        Red = 0,
        Orange,
        Yellow,
        Green,
        Blue,
        Indigo,
        Violet
    }

    static void Main()
    {
        Color MyColor;

        MyColor = Color.Green;
```

Continued

Listing 14-4 *(continued)*

```
        Console.WriteLine("{0}", MyColor.CompareTo(Color.Red));
        Console.WriteLine("{0}", MyColor.CompareTo(Color.Green));
        Console.WriteLine("{0}", MyColor.CompareTo(Color.Violet));
    }
}
```

Listing 14-4 declares a class with a public enumeration called `Color`. Its values range from 0 to 6. The `Main()` method declares a variable of type `Color` called `MyColor` and assigns a value of `Green` to the variable. It then calls `CompareTo()` to compare the variable's value to other values in the enumeration. The `CompareTo()` method returns one of three values:

- ✦ `-1` if the value passed in as the argument to `CompareTo()` has a higher value than the enumerated value used to call the method

- ✦ `1` if the value passed in as the argument to `CompareTo()` has a lower value than the enumerated value used to call the method

- ✦ `0` if the two values are equal

In Listing 14-4, the `CompareTo()` method is called three times. In the first call, the `MyColor` variable is compared to the value of `Red`. Because `Green`, which has a value of 3, has a higher value than `Red`, which has a value of 0, `CompareTo()` returns 1. In the second call, the `MyColor` variable is compared to the value of `Green`. Because the values are equal, `CompareTo()` returns 0. In the final call, the `MyColor` variable is compared to the value of `Violet`. Because `Green`, which has a value of 3, has a lower value than `Violet`, which has a value of 6, `CompareTo()` returns `-1`.

The argument used in the call to `CompareTo()` must be of the same type as the enumeration used to call the method. Using any other type, including the underlying type of the enumeration, produces an error at runtime.

Discovering the underlying type at runtime

Discovering the underlying type of an enumeration at runtime is easy with the `GetUnderlyingType()` method. This method, which is called on the enumeration type, rather than a variable of the type, takes in a `Type` parameter representing the enumeration type and returns another `Type` object representing the enumeration's underlying type. The `ToString()` method can be called on the returned `Type` object to obtain a readable name for the type, as shown in the following code:

```
string    FormatString;
Type      UnderlyingType;

UnderlyingType = BitsToSet.GetUnderlyingType(typeof(BitsToSet));
Console.WriteLine(UnderlyingType.ToString());
```

This code retrieves the underlying type for an enumeration called BitsToSet and prints the type's name out to the console, which produces a string such as the following:

```
System.Int32
```

Retrieving all enumeration values

The GetValues() method returns an array of all enumeration values sorted in ascending order by their numeric value, as shown in the following code:

```
Array ValueArray;

ValueArray = Color.GetValues(typeof(Color));
foreach(Color ColorItem in ValueArray)
    Console.WriteLine(ColorItem.ToString());
```

This code calls GetValues() on the Color enumeration defined previously. The GetValues() method returns an array, and the items in the array are visited one at a time using the foreach keyword. The name of each item in the array is printed out to the console, as follows:

```
Red
Orange
Yellow
Green
Blue
Indigo
Violet
```

Parsing strings to retrieve enumeration values

The Enum class contains a string parsing method called Parse(), which accepts a string as input and returns the enumeration value whose name matches the supplied string, as shown in the following example:

```
Color.Parse(typeof(Color), "Blue");
```

This call returns an object representing the enumerated value named Blue in an enumeration called Color. Like many other enumeration methods, the Parse() method is called on the type, rather than a variable of the type. The Parse() method returns an object, which needs to be casted to a value of the appropriate type. The following example shows how the Parse() method might be used as one of several ways to represent an enumerated value:

```
Color ColorValue;
object ParsedObject;

ParsedObject = Color.Parse(typeof(Color), "Blue");
Console.WriteLine(ParsedObject.GetType().ToString());
ColorValue = (Color)ParsedObject;
```

```
Console.WriteLine(ColorValue.ToString());
Console.WriteLine(Color.Format(typeof(Color), ColorValue, "d"));
```

In this code, Parse() is called on the Color enumeration type and is given an input string of Blue. This call returns an object, and the code writes the object's type to the console. The object is then casted to a variable of type Color, and the enumeration value's name and decimal value is written to the console. This code produces the following output:

```
MainClass+Color
Blue
4
```

This output shows that the object returned by the Parse() method is of type Color. The casted variable, which is a Color variable, has a string name of Blue and a decimal value of 4.

Summary

Enumerations are used to group a set of related constants. By giving your enumerations a name, you can use that name as a variable type in your code once you have defined the enumeration. Enumerations, by default, are based on a set of int constants. You may override this default by specifying an underlying type for the enumeration. You can use many of the C# numeric types as an underlying type for an enumeration. You should use enumerations when you want the C# compiler to ensure that the constants you work with in your code come from a set of legal values.

By default, the C# compiler assigns numeric values to the identifiers in enumerations. The first identifier has a value of zero, and the other enumerations increase in value from there. If you want to, you can use the assignment operator to set a value for an enumeration identifier when you define the enumeration.

You specify a value in an enumeration by writing the name of the enumeration, a period, and the name of the enumeration identifiers. Enumeration identifiers can be implicitly converted to the enumeration's underlying type. This implicit conversion also enables you to use several of the operators in C# to work with the enumeration values.

All enumerations in C# derive from a .NET base class called System.Enum. The System.Enum class contains several helpful methods that help you get the most out of your enumerations. This chapter examined most of those methods.

✦　　✦　　✦

Events and Delegates

In the general flow of a typical object-oriented piece of software, a piece of code creates an object of a class and calls methods on the object. In this scenario, the caller is the active code because it is the code calling methods. The object is passive, in that it waits around and performs an action only when one of its methods is called.

However, the reverse scenario is also possible. An object can perform work and notify the caller when something happens during the process. This *something* is called an *event*, and the object's publication of that event is called *raising an event*.

Event-driven processing, in which pieces of code inform other pieces of code when interesting events occur, is not new to .NET. The Windows user interface layer has always used a form of events to inform Windows applications when users work with the mouse, press a key on the keyboard, or move a window. ActiveX controls raise events to ActiveX control containers when the user takes an action that affects the control.

The C# language contains special keywords that make it easy for you to fire, publish and subscribe to events in your C# code. You can use these keywords to allow your C# classes to fire and process events with a minimum of effort.

Defining Delegates

When you design the events that your C# classes raise, you need to decide how other pieces of code receive the event. Other pieces of code need to write a method that receives and processes the events you publish. Suppose, for example, that your class implements a Web server and wants to fire an event whenever a request for a page comes in from the

Internet. Other pieces of code may want to perform some action when your class fires this `new request` event, and that code should include a method that is executed when the event is fired.

The method that the users of your class implement to receive and process your events is defined by a C# concept called a *delegate*. A delegate is a sort of "function stencil" that describes what your user's event handler must look like. A delegate is also a class that has a signature and holds references to methods. It's like a function pointer, but it can hold references to static and instance methods. For instance methods, the delegate stores a reference to the function's entry point, as well as to the object. A delegate defines what the user's event handler should return, and what its parameter list should be.

To define a delegate in C#, use the following syntax:

- ✦ The C# keyword `delegate`
- ✦ The event handler's return type
- ✦ The delegate identifier
- ✦ The event handler's parameter list, enclosed in parentheses

If you declare delegates in the class that fires the event, you can prefix them with the `public`, `protected`, `internal`, or `private` keywords as seem here in a sample `delegate` definition.

```
public delegate void EvenNumberHandler(int Number);
```

In this example, you create a `public delegate` called `EvenNumberHandler` that return nothing. This delegate defines only one parameter to be passed in, of type `int`. The delegate identifier, `EvenNumberHandler`, can be any name you choose as long as you don't give it the name of a C# keyword.

Defining Events

To clarify what an event actually is, start with an example. You are driving down the road in your car and the low fuel light appears on your dash. What has actually happened is that a sensor in your gas tank signaled the computer that your fuel is low. The computer then fires an event that in turn, illuminates the dash light so you know to purchase more fuel. In simplest terms, an event is a means by which a computer alerts you to a condition.

You use the C# keyword `event` to define an event that your class fires. In their simplest form, C# event declarations use the following syntax:

✦ The C# keyword `event`

✦ The event type

✦ The event identifier

The event type matches a delegate identifier, as shown in the following Web server example:

```
public delegate void NewRequestHandler(string URL);

public class WebServer
{
    public event NewRequestHandler NewRequestEvent;
    // ...
}
```

This example declares a delegate called `NewRequestHandler`. The `NewRequestHandler` defines a delegate that serves as a method template for methods processing the `new request` event. Any methods that need to process the `new request` event must follow the calling conventions of the delegate: They must not return any data and must have a single string as their parameter list. The event handler implementations can have any method name as long as their return type and parameter list match the delegate stencil.

The `WebServer` class defines an event called `NewRequestEvent`. This event has a type of `NewRequestHandler`. This means that only event handlers written to match the delegate's calling conventions can be used to process the `NewRequestEvent` event.

Installing Events

After you write your event handler, you must create a new instance of it and install it into the class that fires the event. You create a new event handler instance by creating a new variable of the delegate type, passing in the name of your event handler method as an argument. Using the Web browser example, the creation of a new event handler instance may look like the following:

```
public void MyNewRequestHandler(string URL)
{
}

NewRequestHandler HandlerInstance;

HandlerInstance = new NewRequestHandler(MyNewRequestHandler);
```

After you create the new event handler instance, use the += operator to add it to the event variable:

```
NewRequestEvent += HandlerInstance;
```

This statement hooks the HandlerInstance delegate instance, which supports the MyNewRequestMethod method, to the NewRequestEvent event. Using the += operator, you can hook as many delegate instances as you like to an event.

Similarly, you can use the -= operator to remove a delegate instance from an event:

```
NewRequestEvent -= HandlerInstance;
```

This statement unhooks the HandlerInstance delegate instance from the NewRequestEvent event.

Firing Events

You can fire an event from a class by using the event identifier (such as the name of the event) as if it were a method. Calling an event as a method fires the event. Firing the new request event in your Web browser example may look something like the following:

```
NewRequestEvent(strURLOfNewRequest);
```

The parameters used in the event firing call must match the parameter list of the event's delegate. The delegate of the NewRequestEvent event was defined as accepting a string parameter; therefore, a string must be supplied when the event is fired from the Web browser class.

Tying It All Together

Listing 15-1 shows delegates and events in action. The code implements a class that counts from 0 to 100 and fires an event when an even number is found during the counting process.

Listing 15-1: Retrieving Even-Numbered Events

```
using System;

public delegate void EvenNumberHandler(int Number);

class Counter
{
```

```
    public event EvenNumberHandler OnEvenNumber;

    public Counter()
    {
        OnEvenNumber = null;
    }

    public void CountTo100()
    {
        int CurrentNumber;

        for(CurrentNumber = 0; CurrentNumber <= 100; CurrentNumber++)
        {
            if(CurrentNumber % 2 == 0)
            {
                if(OnEvenNumber != null)
                {
                    OnEvenNumber(CurrentNumber);
                }
            }
        }
    }
}

class EvenNumberHandlerClass
{
    public void EvenNumberFound(int EvenNumber)
    {
        Console.WriteLine(EvenNumber);
    }
}

class MainClass
{
    public static void Main()
    {
        Counter MyCounter = new Counter();
        EvenNumberHandlerClass MyEvenNumberHandlerClass = new
EvenNumberHandlerClass();
        MyCounter.OnEvenNumber += new
EvenNumberHandler(MyEvenNumberHandlerClass.EvenNumberFound);
        MyCounter.CountTo100();
    }
}
```

To compile this application, create a new console application in Visual Studio and
paste the source code in or you can simple use Notepad to save the file and then use:

```
csc <filename>
```

Listing 15-1 implements three classes:

✦ The Counter class is the class that performs the counting. It implements a public method called CountTo100() and a public event called OnEvenNumber. The OnEvenNumber event is of delegate type EvenNumberHandler.

✦ The EvenNumberHandlerClass class contains a public method called EvenNumberFound. This method serves as the event handler for the Counter class's OnEvenNumber event. It prints out to the console the integer supplied as a parameter.

✦ The MainClass class contains the application's Main() method.

The Main() method creates an object of class Counter and names the object MyCounter. It also creates a new object of class EvenNumberHandlerClass and calls the object MyEvenNumberHandlerClass.

The Main() method calls the CountTo100() method of the MyCounter object, but not before installing a delegate instance into the Counter class. The code creates a new delegate instance managing the EvenNumberFound method of the MyEventNumberHandlerClass object and adds it to the MyCounter object's OnEvenNumber event using the += operator.

The implementation of the CountTo100 method uses a local variable to count from 0 to 100. Each time through the counting loop, the code checks to see if the number is even by seeing whether the number has no remainder when divided by two. If the number is indeed even, the code fires the OnEvenNumber event, supplying the even number as the argument to match the parameter list of the event's delegate.

Because the EvenNumberFound method of the MyEvenNumberHandlerClass was installed as an event handler, and because that method prints the supplied parameter to the console, compiling and running the code in Listing 15-1 causes all even numbers between 0 and 100 to be printed out to the console.

Standardizing an Event Design

Although C# happily accepts any delegate design that compiles, the .NET Framework encourages you to adopt a standard design for delegates. The preferred delegate design uses two arguments; for example, the SystemEventhandler:

✦ A reference to the object that raised the event

✦ An object that contains data related to the event

The second parameter, which contains all of the event data, should be an object of a class that derives from a .NET class called System.EventArgs.

Listing 15-2 reworks Listing 15-1 using this preferred design.

Listing 15-2: Retrieving Even-Numbered Events with the .NET Delegate Convention

```csharp
using System;

public delegate void EvenNumberHandler(object Originator, OnEvenNumberEventArgs
EvenNumberEventArgs);

class Counter
{
    public event EvenNumberHandler OnEvenNumber;

    public Counter()
    {
        OnEvenNumber = null;
    }

    public void CountTo100()
    {
        int CurrentNumber;

        for(CurrentNumber = 0; CurrentNumber <= 100; CurrentNumber++)
        {
            if(CurrentNumber % 2 == 0)
            {
                if(OnEvenNumber != null)
                {
                    OnEvenNumberEventArgs EventArguments;

                    EventArguments = new OnEvenNumberEventArgs(CurrentNumber);
                    OnEvenNumber(this, EventArguments);
                }
            }
        }
    }
}

public class OnEvenNumberEventArgs : EventArgs
{
    private int EvenNumber;

    public OnEvenNumberEventArgs(int EvenNumber)
    {
        this.EvenNumber = EvenNumber;
    }

    public int Number
    {
        get
        {
```

Continued

Listing 15-2 *(continued)*

```
            return EvenNumber;
        }
    }
}

class EvenNumberHandlerClass
{
    public void EvenNumberFound(object Originator, OnEvenNumberEventArgs
EvenNumberEventArgs)
    {
        Console.WriteLine(EvenNumberEventArgs.Number);
    }
}

class MainClass
{
    public static void Main()
    {
        Counter MyCounter = new Counter();
        EvenNumberHandlerClass MyEvenNumberHandlerClass = new
EvenNumberHandlerClass();
        MyCounter.OnEvenNumber += new
EvenNumberHandler(MyEvenNumberHandlerClass.EvenNumberFound);
        MyCounter.CountTo100();
    }
}
```

Listing 15-2 adds a new class called OnEvenNumberEventArgs that derives from the .NET EventArgs class. It implements a constructor that takes an integer and stores it in a private variable. It also exposes a read-only property called Number, which returns the value of the private variable.

The delegate's signature has also changed to conform to the new convention. It accepts two input parameters: a reference to the object firing the event and an object of type OnEvenNumberEventArgs.

When the Counter class prepares to fire the event, it first creates a new object of type OnEvenNumberEventArgs and initializes it with the even number. It then passes this object as the second parameter to the event.

The new implementation of the EvenNumberFound method examines the second parameter, an object of class OnEvenNumberEventArgs, and writes the value of the object's Number property out to the console.

Using Event Accessors

In the general implementation of events, you must have one event field defined in your class for each possible event that your class can fire. In examples like Listing 15-2, in which the class fires only one event, defining one event field per event is not a big deal. However, that procedure becomes unwieldy when your class can fire one of several events.

Take, for example, a C# class that manages a Windows user interface component. Typical Windows user interface components can receive one of many possible messages from the operating system, and you might want to design your class so that the messages that your user interface component receives from the operating system are reported to users of the class through a C# event. Defining an event field in your class for each possible Windows message would force your class to store a lot of fields, making your class object sizes huge.

C# supports an alternative whereby events can be defined as properties, rather than fields. Event properties work just like standard class properties, which are implemented with code, rather than a data field. Unlike a standard property, an event property uses the C# keywords add and remove to define blocks of code:

```
public event EvenNumberHandler OnEvenNumber
{
    add
    {
    }
    remove
    {
    }
}
```

The code in the add code block is called when a user adds a new event handler to the event using the += operator. The code in the remove code block is called when a user adds a new event handler to the event using the -= operator.

The advantage to using event accessors is that you have total freedom regarding how you store event handlers. Rather than defining separate fields for each event, you can store a single linked list or array of handlers. You could implement the add event accessor to add an event handler to the array or list, and you could implement the remove event accessor to remove an event handler from the array or list.

Like standard properties, you can use the C# keyword value to reference the event handler being added or removed, as shown in the following statement:

```
MyCounter.OnEvenNumber += new
EvenNumberHandler(MyEvenNumberHandlerClass.EvenNumberFound);
```

In this statement, a new `EvenNumberHandler` object is being added to the `OnEvenNumber` event. If the event were implemented as a property, the add code block could use the `value` keyword to reference the new `EvenNumberHandler` object:

```
public event EvenNumberHandler OnEvenNumber
{
    add
    {
        AddToList(value);
    }
    remove
    {
        RemoveFromList(value);
    }
}
```

When used in event accessors, the `value` keyword is a variable of type `Delegate`.

Using Event Modifiers

You can prefix an event declaration with one of the following modifiers:

✦ Static

✦ Virtual

✦ Override

✦ Abstract

Static events

Events modified with the `static` keyword behave much like static fields, in that while each copy of a class contains separate copies of all fields, there can only be one copy of a static member at any given time. All objects of the class share static events. When they are referenced, they must be referenced by the class name and not the object name, as shown in the following:

```
public class Counter
{
    public static event EvenNumberHandler OnEvenNumber;
    // ...
}

Counter.OnEvenNumber += new
EvenNumberHandler(MyEvenNumberHandlerClass.EvenNumberFound);
```

As you can see, you must reference the static event `OnEvenNumber` by specifying the class name and the object name.

Virtual events

Events modified with the `virtual` keyword mark any `add` or `remove` event accessors as virtual. Virtual event accessors can be overridden in derived classes.

Override events

Events modified with the `override` keyword mark any `add` or `remove` event accessors as overriding `add` or `remove` events with the same name in a base class.

Abstract events

Events modified with the `abstract` keyword mark any `add` or `remove` event accessors as abstract. Abstract event accessors do not provide an implementation of their own; instead, an implementation is provided by an overridden event found in a derived class.

Summary

Your classes can fire events when a design calls for clients to be notified of actions taken by the class. Without events, users call a method to perform an operation, but they really don't have any idea of the progress of the operation. Consider, for instance, a method that retrieves a Web page from a Web site. That operation consists of several steps:

✦ Connect to the Web server

✦ Request the Web page

✦ Retrieve the returned Web page

✦ Disconnect from the Web server

You can design a class like this with events that fire when each of these actions begins. Firing events at critical steps in your processing give users of your class some idea of where your code is in its processing.

Callers respond to events by registering methods called *event handlers*. Event handlers are called when the class fires events. These methods match the parameter list and return a value of a special method stencil called a *delegate*. A delegate describes the design of an event handler, dictating which parameters it must support and what its return code must be.

Event handlers are installed using the += operator. Events are usually declared as public fields in a class, and callers add their event handlers to the class by creating a new object of the delegate class and assigning the object to the event using the += operator. C# allows you to specify multiple event handlers for a single event, and it also allows you to use the -= operator to remove an event handler from an event.

C# does not force you to use a single design pattern for your delegates, but the .NET Framework does recommend a design. Using the recommended design provides a standard that, when followed, can give your delegates a method parameter list that is consistent with delegates designed by other developers. The .NET Framework recommends that all delegates be designed with two items in the parameter list: an object specifying the object that fired the event, and an object of a class derived from the .NET System.EventArgs class, which contains the arguments to the event.

C# makes it very easy for you to implement events in your classes. At the simplest level, each event is declared as a public field, and you can manage as many events as you wish. If your class will be managing many events, and the number of public fields within this class seems like an excessive amount of coding, you can write event accessors that enable you to control how the event handlers are managed by your class. Instead of defining public fields for your events, event accessors enable you to define your events as properties with add and remove blocks of code. The add code block is called when an event handler is added to your event, and the remove code block is called when an event handler is added to your event. You can implement these blocks of code by storing the event handler in an array or a list for use later.

The C# concept of events and delegates is a new feature to the C family of languages. Events could be fired using C and C++ using some other mechanisms, but these languages don't define keywords to make events work. In C#, events and delegates are fully defined items in their own right, and full support for event handling has been built into the language and the compiler.

Another benefit of using events in C# is that they are supported by the CLR, which means that you can set up an event mechanism in C# and can fire events that are handled by another .NET language. Because the CLR supports events at the runtime level, you can fire an event in C# and have it handled and processed by another language, such as Visual Basic .NET.

✦   ✦   ✦

Handling Exceptions

Checking for errors and handling them appropriately is a fundamental principle of correctly designed software. Ideally, you would write your code and every line would work as advertised and every resource that you use would always be available. However, this simply isn't the case in the real world. Other programmers (not you, of course) can make mistakes, network connections can be broken, database servers can be shut down, and disk files may not have the contents that applications expect them to have. In short, the code that you write has to be able to detect errors like these and respond appropriately.

The mechanisms for reporting errors are as diverse as the errors themselves. Some methods may be designed to return a Boolean value indicating the success or failure of a method. Other methods might write errors to a log file or database of some sort. The diversity of error reporting models means that the code you write to monitor errors must be relatively robust. Every method you use might report an error in a different way, which means that your application would be littered with extensive code needed to detect different kinds of errors from different method calls.

The .NET Framework provides a standard mechanism, called *structured exception handling (SEH)*, for error reporting. This mechanism relies on exceptions to indicate failures. Exceptions are classes that describe an error. They are used by the .NET Framework to report errors, and they can be used by the code that you write. You can write code to watch for exceptions generated by any piece of code, whether it comes from the CLR or from your own code, and you can deal with the generated exception appropriately. Using SEH, you only need to create one error handling design in your code.

This unified approach to error processing is also crucial to enable multilingual .NET programming. When you design all of your code using SEH, you can safely and easily mix and match code (for example, C#, C++, or VB.NET). As a reward for following the rules for SEH, the .NET Framework ensures that all errors are properly propagated and handled across the different languages.

Detecting and handling exceptions in your C# code is straightforward. You need to identify three blocks of code when working with exceptions:

✦ The block of code that should use exception processing

✦ A block of code that executes if an exception is found when processing the first block of code

✦ An optional block of code that executes after the exception is processed

In C#, the generation of an exception is referred to as *throwing* an exception. Being notified of a thrown exception is referred to as *catching* an exception. The piece of code that is executed after the exception has been processed is the `finally` block. In this chapter, you see how these constructs are used in C#. You also learn the members of the exception hierarchy.

Note

A recurring and long-standing debate in the object-oriented community is whether exceptions should be used for all errors (including errors that you can expect to occur with some frequency) or for the catastrophic errors only (the so-called exceptional errors, which only occur when a resource unexpectedly fails). The crux of this debate is the relatively significant overhead needed to throw and catch exceptions, overhead that you can avoid through the use of another error handling approach such as return codes. The .NET Framework's answer to this dilemma is to use structured exception handling for all errors because it enables you to ensure that all resources are properly released when an error occurs. This corresponds to the current consensus on this contentious debate. In-depth research (mainly by the C++ community) has concluded that avoiding resource leaks without exceptions is practically impossible. Of course, C# avoids memory leaks through garbage collection, but you still need a mechanism to avoid resource leaks of the various types of operation system handles.

Like all design guidelines, blindly using exceptions for every single error is overkill. When the error is local to a block of code, error return codes may be appropriate. You frequently see such an approach when implementing form validation. This is an acceptable trade-off because validation errors are typically localized to the form that gathers the input. In other words, when a validation error occurs, you display an error message and request that the user re-enter the required information correctly. Because both the error and the handling code are localized, handling resource leaks is straightforward. Another example is handling an end-of-file condition when reading a file. This condition can be nicely handled without paying the overhead required of exceptions. Again, the error condition is fully handled within the block of code where the error occurs. When you see calls made to code outside of the block of code where the error occurs, you should strongly lean toward handling errors using SEH.

Specifying Exception Processing

The C# keyword `try` specifies that you have a block of code that should watch for any exceptions thrown while the code is executing. Working with the `try` keyword is simple. Use the `try` keyword, followed by an opening brace, followed by the statements that should be watched for exceptions thrown while the statements execute, followed by a closing brace:

```
try
{
    // place statements here
}
```

If an exception is thrown while any of the statements in the `try` block are executing, you can catch the exception in your code and deal with it appropriately.

Catching Exceptions

If you use the `try` keyword to specify that you'd like to be notified about exceptions thrown, you need to write code that catches the exception and deals with the error reported from your code.

The C# keyword `catch` following a `try` block is used to specify what code should be executed when an exception is caught. The `catch` keyword works much like the `try` keyword.

Using the try keyword

The simplest form of the `catch` code block catches any exceptions thrown by code in the preceding `try` block. The `catch` block is structured like the `try` block, as shown in the following example:

```
try
{
    // place statements here
}
catch
{
    // place statements here
}
```

The statements in the `catch` block are executed if an exception is thrown from the `try` block. If none of the statements in the `try` block throw an exception, then none of the code in the `catch` block executes.

Catching specific classes of exceptions

You can also write a catch block that handles a specific class of exception thrown by one of the statements in the try block. You learn more about the type of class exceptions in the section, "Introducing the Exceptions Defined by the .NET Framework," later in this chapter. This form of the catch code block uses the following syntax:

✦ The catch keyword

✦ An opening parenthesis

✦ The class of exception that you want to handle

✦ A variable identifier for the exception

✦ A closing parenthesis

✦ An opening curly brace

✦ The statements that should be executed when an exception of the specified type is thrown from the preceding try block

✦ A closing curly brace

Consider the following code:

```
try
{
    // place statements here
}
catch(Exception thrownException)
{
    // place statements here
}
```

The catch block in this example catches exceptions of type Exception that are thrown by the preceding try block. It defines a variable of the Exception type called ThrownException. The ThrownException variable can be used in the code in the catch block to get more information about the exception that was thrown.

The code in the try block may throw different classes of exceptions, and you want to handle each different class. C# lets you specify multiple catch blocks, each of which handles a specific class of error:

```
try
{
    // place statements here
}
catch(Exception ThrownException)
{
    // Catch Block 1
```

```
}
catch(Exception ThrownException2)
{
    // Catch Block 2
}
```

In this example, the code in the `try` block is checked for thrown exceptions. If the CLR finds that the code in the `try` block throws an exception, it examines the exception class and executes the appropriate catch block. If the thrown exception is an object of class `Exception`, the code in `Catch Block 1` is executed. If the thrown exception is an object of class `Exception2`, the code in `Catch Block 2` is executed. If the thrown exception is an object of some other class, neither `catch` block is executed.

You can also add a generic `catch` block to your list of `catch` code blocks, as shown in the following example:

```
try
{
    // place statements here
}
catch(Exception ThrownException)
{
    // Catch Block 1
}
catch
{
    // Catch Block 2
}
```

Here, the code in the `try` block is checked for exceptions. If the thrown exception is an object of class `Exception`, the code in `Catch Block 1` is executed. If the thrown exception is an object of some other class, the code in the generic `catch` block — `Catch Block 2` — is executed.

Cleaning up after an exception

A block of code may follow your `catch` blocks. This block of code is executed both after an exception is processed *and* when no exception occurs. If you want to execute such code, you can write a `finally` block. The C# keyword `finally` specifies that you have a block of code that should execute after a `try` code block executes. A `finally` code block is formatted just as `try` blocks are formatted:

```
finally
{
    // place statements here
}
```

The `finally` code block is a great place to release resources that were allocated earlier in your method. Suppose, for example, that you're writing a method that opens three files. If you surround your file access code in a `try` block, you'll be able to catch exceptions related to opening, reading from, or writing to the files. At the end of the code, however, you'll want to close the three files, even if an exception is thrown. You will most likely want to put the file close statements in a `finally` block, and you may structure your code as follows:

```
try
{
    // open files
    // read files
}
catch
{
    // catch exceptions
}
finally
{
    // close files
}
```

The C# compiler enables you to define a `finally` block without any `catch` blocks. You can write a `finally` code block just after your `try` block.

Understanding the Exception Class

All exceptions thrown by the .NET Framework are classes derived from the `System.Exception` class. Table 16-1 describes some useful members of this class.

Table 16-1 Members of the System.Exception Class	
HelpLink	A link to the help file that provides more information about the exception
Message	The text that was supplied, usually as part of the exception constructor, to describe the error condition
Source	The name of the application or object that caused the exception
StackTrace	A list of the method calls on the stack
TargetSite	The name of the method that threw the exception

Introducing the Exceptions Defined by the .NET Framework

The .NET Framework defines a variety of exceptions that can be thrown when certain errors are found in your C# code or in methods that you call. All of these exceptions are standard .NET exceptions and can be caught using a C# catch block.

Each of the .NET exceptions is defined in the .NET System namespace. The following sections describe some of the common exceptions. These exceptions represent only a very small fraction of those defined in the base class library of the .NET framework.

OutOfMemoryException

The CLR throws the OutOfMemoryException exception when it runs out of memory. If your code attempts to create an object using the new operator and the CLR does not have enough memory to fulfill the request, the CLR throws the OutOfMemoryException exception, shown in Listing 16-1.

Listing 16-1: **OutOfMemoryException Exception**

```
using System;

class MainClass
{
    public static void Main()
    {
        int [] LargeArray;

        try
        {
            LargeArray = new int [2000000000];
        }
        catch(OutOfMemoryException)
        {
            Console.WriteLine("The CLR is out of memory.");
        }
    }
}
```

The code in Listing 16-1 tries to allocate an array of two billion integers. Because one integer takes four bytes of memory, eight billion bytes are needed to hold an array of this size. Chances are good that this amount of memory is not available on your machine, and the allocation will fail. The code surrounds the allocation in a try block and also defines a catch clock to handle any OutOfMemoryException exceptions thrown by the CLR.

Note   The code in Listing 16-1 does not list an identifier for the exception in the catch block. This syntax — in which you specify the class of an exception but do not give it a name — is legal. It works well when you want to catch a class of exceptions but do not need any information from the specific exception object itself.

StackOverflowException

The CLR throws the StackOverflowException exception when it runs out of stack space. The CLR manages a data structure called a *stack*, which keeps track of the methods that were called and the order in which they were called. The CLR has a finite amount of stack space available, and if it gets full, the exception is thrown Listing 16-2 shows the StackOverflowException exception.

Listing 16-2: **StackOverflowException Exception**

```
using System;

class MainClass
{
    public static void Main()
    {
        try
        {
            Recursive();
        }
        catch(StackOverflowException)
        {
            Console.WriteLine("The CLR is out of stack space.");
        }
    }

    public static void Recursive()
    {
        Recursive();
    }

}
```

The code in Listing 16-2 implements a method called Recursive(), which calls itself before returning. This method is called by the Main() method and eventually causes the CLR to run out of stack space because the Recursive() method never returns. The `Main()` method calls `Recursive()`, which in turn calls `Recursive()`, which again calls `Recursive()`, and so on. Eventually, the CLR runs out of stack space and throws the `StackOverflowException` exception.

NullReferenceException

In this example, the compiler catches an attempt to dereference a null object. Listing 16-3 shows the `NullReferenceException` exception.

Listing 16-3: **NullReferenceException Exception**

```
using System;

class MyClass
{
    public int Value;
}

class MainClass
{
    public static void Main()
    {
        try
        {
            MyObject = new MyClass();
            MyObject = null;

            MyObject.Value = 123;

            // wait for user to acknowledge the results
            Console.WriteLine("Hit Enter to terminate...");
            Console.Read();
        }
        catch(NullReferenceException)
        {
            Console.WriteLine("Cannot reference a null object.");

            // wait for user to acknowledge the results
            Console.Read();
        }
    }

}
```

The code in Listing 16-3 declares an object variable of type `MyClass` and sets the variable to `null`. (If you do not use the new statement, but just declares an object variable of type `MyClass`, the compiler will issue the following error when compiled, "Use of unassigned local variable `MyObject`.") It then tries to work with the object's public `Value` field, which is illegal because `null` objects cannot be referenced. The CLR catches this error and throws the `NullReferenceException` exception.

TypeInitializationException

The CLR throws the `TypeInitializationException` exception when a class defines a static constructor and the constructor throws an exception. If there are no `catch` blocks in the constructor to catch the exception, the CLR throws a `TypeInitializationException` exception.

InvalidCastExpression

The CLR throws the `InvalidCastExpression` exception if an explicit conversion fails. This situation can occur in interface situations. Listing 16-4 shows an `InvalidCastExpression` exception.

Listing 16-4: **InvalidCastException Exception**

```
using System;

class MainClass
{
    public static void Main()
    {
        try
        {
            MainClass       MyObject = new MainClass();
            IFormattable    Formattable;

            Formattable = (IFormattable)MyObject;

            // wait for user to acknowledge the results
            Console.WriteLine("Hit Enter to terminate...");
            Console.Read();
        }
        catch(InvalidCastException)
        {
            Console.WriteLine("MyObject does not implement the IFormattable
interface.");

            // wait for user to acknowledge the results
            Console.Read();
        }
    }

    }
```

The code in Listing 16-4 uses a cast operator to try to obtain a reference to a .NET interface called IFormattable. Because the MainClass class does not implement the IFormattable interface, the cast operation fails and the CLR throws the InvalidCastException exception.

ArrayTypeMismatchException

The CLR throws the ArrayTypeMismatchException exception when the code attempts to store an element in an array whose type does not match the type of the array.

IndexOutOfRangeException

The CLR throws the IndexOutOfRangeException exception when the code attempts to store an element in an array using an element index that is out of the bounds of the array. Listing 16-5 illustrates the IndexOutOfRangeException exception.

Listing 16-5: IndexOutOfRangeException Exception

```
using System;

class MainClass
{
    public static void Main()
    {
        try
        {
            int [] IntegerArray = new int [5];

            IntegerArray[10] = 123;

            // wait for user to acknowledge the results
            Console.WriteLine("Hit Enter to terminate...");
            Console.Read();
        }
        catch(IndexOutOfRangeException)
        {
            Console.WriteLine("An invalid element index access was attempted.");

            // wait for user to acknowledge the results
            Console.Read();
        }
    }

}
```

The code in Listing 16-5 creates an array with five elements and then tries to set a value in array element 10. Because an index of 10 is out of bounds for the integer array, the CLR throws the IndexOutOfRangeException exception.

DivideByZeroException

The CLR throws the DivideByZeroException exception when the code attempts to execute a mathematical operation that results in a division by zero.

OverflowException

The CLR throws the OverflowException exception when a mathematical operation guarded by the C# checked operator results in an overflow. Listing 16-6 shows the OverflowException exception.

Listing 16-6: OverflowException Exception

```
using System;

class MainClass
{
    public static void Main()
    {
        try
        {
            checked
            {
                int Integer1;
                int Integer2;
                int Sum;

                Integer1 = 2000000000;
                Integer2 = 2000000000;
                Sum = Integer1 + Integer2;
            }

            // wait for user to acknowledge the results
            Console.WriteLine("Hit Enter to terminate...");
            Console.Read();
        }
        catch(OverflowException)
        {
            Console.WriteLine("A mathematical operation caused an overflow.");
```

```
            // wait for user to acknowledge the results
            Console.Read();
        }
    }
}
```

The code in Listing 16-6 adds two integers, each having a value of two billion. The result, four billion, is assigned to a third integer. The problem is that the result of the addition is larger than the largest possible value that can be assigned to a C# integer, and a mathematical overflow exception is thrown.

Working with Your Own Exceptions

You can define your own exceptions and use them in your code just as you would an exception defined by the .NET Framework. This design consistency enables you to write `catch` blocks that work with any exception that can be thrown from any piece of code, whether that code is in the .NET Framework, in one of your own classes, or in an assembly that you execute at runtime.

Defining your own exceptions

The .NET Framework declares a class called `System.Exception`, which serves as the base class for all exceptions in the .NET Framework. The pre-defined common language runtime classes are derived from `System.SystemException`, which itself derives from `System.Exception`. The exceptions to this rule are the `DivideByZeroException`, `NotFiniteNumberException`, and `OverflowException` exceptions, which derive from a class called `System.ArithmeticException`, which itself derives from `System.SystemException`. Any exception classes that you define must derive from `System.ApplicationException`, which also derives from `System.Exception`.

The `System.Exception` class contains four read-only properties that the code in `catch` blocks can use to get more information about the exception that was thrown:

 ✦ The `Message` property contains a description of the reason for the exception.

 ✦ The `InnerException` property contains the exception that caused the current exception to be thrown. This property may be `null`, which indicates that no inner exception is available. If the `InnerException` is not `null`, it refers to an exception object that was thrown, which caused the current exception to be thrown. It is possible for a `catch` block to catch one exception and throw a different one. In this case, the `InnerException` property would contain a reference to the original exception object caught by the `catch` block.

✦ The `StackTrace` property contains a string that displays the stack of method calls that were underway when the exception was thrown. Eventually, this stack trace will trace all the way back to the CLR's original call to the application's `Main()` method.

✦ The `TargetSite` property contains the method that has thrown the exception.

Some of these properties can be specified in one of the constructors for the `System.Exception` class:

```
public Exception(string message);
public Exception(string message, Exception innerException);
```

The exceptions that you define can call the base class's constructor in your constructor so that the properties can be set, as shown in the following code:

```
using System;

class MyException : ApplicationException
{
    public MyException() : base("This is my exception message.")
    {
    }

}
```

This code defines a class called `MyException`, which derives from the `ApplicationException` class. Its constructor uses the `base` keyword to call the base class's constructor. The base class's `Message` property is set to `This is my exception message`.

Throwing your exceptions

You can throw your own exceptions using the C# `throw` keyword. The `throw` keyword must be followed by an expression that evaluates to an object of class `System.Exception` or a class derived from `System.Exception`.

Consider the code shown in Listing 16-7.

Listing 16-7: **Throwing Your Own Exceptions**

```
using System;

class MyException : ApplicationException
{
    public MyException() : base("This is my exception message.")
    {
    }
}

class MainClass
{
    public static void Main()
    {
        try
        {
            MainClass MyObject = new MainClass();

            MyObject.ThrowException();

            // wait for user to acknowledge the results
            Console.WriteLine("Hit Enter to terminate...");
            Console.Read();
        }
        catch(MyException CaughtException)
        {
            Console.WriteLine(CaughtException.Message);

            // wait for user to acknowledge the results
            Console.Read();
        }
    }

    public void ThrowException()
    {
        throw new MyException();
    }

}
```

The code in Listing 16-7 declares a new class called MyException, which derives from the base class ApplicationException as defined by the .NET Framework.

The `MainClass` class contains a method called `ThrowException`, which throws a new object of type `MyException`. The method is called by the `Main()` method, which surrounds the call in a `try` block. The `Main()` method also contains a `catch` block, whose implementation outputs the exception's message to the console. Because the message was set when the `MyException` class object was constructed, it is available and can be printed. Compiling and running Listing 16-7 prints the following to the console:

```
This is my exception message.
```

Using exceptions in constructors and properties

A few constructs in C# contain code that can execute but can't return a value to indicate the success or failure of the code being executed. Class constructors and `set` property accessors are a prime example. Throwing exceptions is a great way to report errors from blocks of code like these.

In Chapter 9, you examined a class that implemented a point on a computer screen. The class had properties that represented the point's x and y coordinates, and the `set` accessors for the properties ensured that the value was in a valid range before it was actually stored. The problem with the code in Listing 9-1 is that there is no error reporting for situations in which the supplied value is out of range.

Listing 16-8 is an improvement over Listing 9-1 because it adds exception handling to report on coordinates that are out of range.

Listing 16-8: **Throwing Exceptions from Property Accessors**

```
using System;

public class CoordinateOutOfRangeException : ApplicationException
{
    public CoordinateOutOfRangeException()
        : base("The supplied coordinate is out of range.")
    {
    }
}

public class Point
{
    private int XCoordinate;
    private int YCoordinate;

    public int X
    {
        get
        {
```

```
            return XCoordinate;
        }
        set
        {
            if((value >= 0) && (value < 640))
                XCoordinate = value;
            else
                throw new CoordinateOutOfRangeException();
        }
    }

    public int Y
    {
        get
        {
            return YCoordinate;
        }
        set
        {
            if((value >= 0) && (value < 480))
                YCoordinate = value;
            else
                throw new CoordinateOutOfRangeException();
        }
    }

    public static void Main()
    {
        Point MyPoint = new Point();

        try
        {
            MyPoint.X = 100;
            MyPoint.Y = 200;
            Console.WriteLine("({0}, {1})", MyPoint.X, MyPoint.Y);
            MyPoint.X = 1500;
            MyPoint.Y = 600;
            Console.WriteLine("({0}, {1})", MyPoint.X, MyPoint.Y);

            // wait for user to acknowledge the results
            Console.WriteLine("Hit Enter to terminate...");
            Console.Read();
        }
        catch(CoordinateOutOfRangeException CaughtException)
        {
            Console.WriteLine(CaughtException.Message);

            // wait for user to acknowledge the results
            Console.Read();
        }
```

Continued

Listing 16-8 *(continued)*

```
    catch
    {
        Console.WriteLine("An unexpected exception was caught.");

        // wait for user to acknowledge the results
        Console.Read();
    }
  }

}
```

The code in Listing 16-8 checks the value in the set property accessors to ensure that the supplied value is in a valid range. If it is not, an exception is thrown. The first point assignment is successful, as the values are both in the allowable range. The second point assignment, however, is not successful, as the *x* coordinate is out of range. This out-of-range value causes an object of class CoordinateOutOfRangeException to be thrown.

Compiling and running Listing 16-8 writes the following out to the console:

```
(100, 200)
The supplied coordinate is out of range.
```

Summary

The .NET Framework uses exceptions to report a variety of errors to .NET applications. The C# language fully supports exception processing and enables you to define your own exceptions in addition to working with the exceptions defined by the .NET Framework. Exceptions can be thrown and caught by C# code. C# code can also catch exceptions thrown by the .NET Framework.

The advantage to using exceptions is that you don't need to check every single method call for an error. You can enclose a group of method calls in a try block, and you can write your code as if every method call in the block were successful. This makes the code in your try block much cleaner, because it does not need any inline error checking. Any exceptions thrown from code in your try block are dealt with in a catch block.

✦   ✦   ✦

Working with Attributes

Previous chapters looked at keywords that define the behavior of a class and its members. The `public`, `private`, `protected`, and `internal` keywords, for example, define the accessibility of the declaration to other classes in your code. These modifiers are implemented by predefined keywords whose meanings are built into the C# language and cannot be changed.

C# also enables you to improve your class and class member declarations with information that is interpreted by other C# classes at runtime. This information is specified using a construct called an *attribute*. Attributes enable you to include directives in your class and its members. The behavior of the attribute is defined by either code that you write or code that is provided by the .NET Framework. Attributes enable you to extend the C# language by writing attribute classes that enhance the behavior of other classes when the code executes, although you write your attribute implementation class before other users apply the attribute to their own classes.

When you compile your applications, the attribute information that you added is emitted to the metadata of the assembly, enabling other applications or tools to view the attribute usage. Using the IL Disassembler (ILDASM) or the classes in the `System.Reflection` namespace, you can easily see which attributes have been added to sections of code, and you can determine whether they are useful. In C#, two types of attributes can be used: those that are built into the language, and custom attributes that you create. In the first section of this chapter, you learn how to use attributes and examine some of the built-in attributes that C# offers. In the second section, you learn how to write custom attributes and how your application or other applications can take advantage of those attributes.

Introducing Attributes

C# allows attributes to appear as a prefix on the following C# language constructs:

✦ Classes

✦ Class members, including constants, fields, methods, properties, events, indexers, operator overloads, constructors, destructors

✦ Structures

✦ Interfaces

✦ Interface members, including methods, properties, events, and indexers

✦ Enumerations and enumeration members

✦ Delegates

You specify an attribute in your code by using its name and placing it in square brackets. The attribute specification must appear before the declaration to which the attribute should apply. Simple attributes may look like the following:

```
[MyAttribute]
```

A good example of a simple attribute is the threading model applied when you create a console application in C#. In the following snippet, notice the `[STAThread]` attribute applied to the `Main()` function. This attribute tells the compiler that the `Main()` function must enter a COM Single Threaded Apartment (STA) before any COM based code is executed.

```
/// <summary>
/// The main entry point for the application.
/// </summary>
[STAThread]
static void Main(string[] args)
  {
    //
    // TODO: Add code to start application here
    //
  }
```

You can also prefix an attribute with a modifier that defines the C# element to which the attribute applies. The attribute modifier appears before the attribute name and is followed by a colon. This is called *binding* an attribute. Table 17-1 lists the types of declarations and their targets for the specific attributes. The targets for attribute classes are predefined; for example, if a .NET class contains an attribute class that is targeted for enumerations only, then the attribute can only be used for enumerations and cannot be applied to other C# code constructs, such as classes and structures. Later in this chapter, you learn how to specify attribute targets for your custom attribute classes.

Table 17-1
Attribute Targets Enumeration

Declaration	Target
Assembly	Assembly
Module	Module
Class	Type
Struct	Type
Interface	Type
Enum	Type
Delegate	Type (default) or Return Value
Method	Method (default) or Return Value
Parameter	Param
Field	Field
Property – Indexer	Property
Property – Get Accessor	Method (default) or Return Value
Property – Set Accessor	Method (default), Param or Return Value
Event – Field	Event (default), Field or Method
Event – Property	Event (default), Property
Event – Add	Method (default) or Param
Event – Remove	Method (default) or Param

To explicitly bind an attribute to a method, for example, you write something like the following:

```
[method:MyAttribute]
int MyMethod()
{
}
```

Attribute modifiers are useful for situations in which their binding might be ambiguous, as shown in the following example:

```
[MyAttribute]
int MyMethod()
{
}
```

This example doesn't really make the binding clear. Does the `MyAttribute` attribute apply to the method or its return type? Explicitly specifying the binding, as shown in the preceding example, makes it clear to the C# compiler that the attribute applies to the entire method. In the example of the `[STAThread]` attribute applied to the `Main()` function when creating a console application, you can modify it to the following to make the binding more obvious:

```
/// <summary>
/// The main entry point for the application.
/// </summary>
[method: STAThread]
static void Main(string[] args)
  {
    //
    // TODO: Add code to start application here
    //
  }
```

Some attributes are built to accept parameters. Attribute parameters follow the attribute name and are enclosed in parentheses. The parentheses are themselves enclosed in the square brackets. An attribute with a parameter may look like this:

```
[MyAttribute(Parameter)]
```

Now that you have a basic understanding of the syntax of attributes, you can examine the built-in attribute classes that .NET offers. Note that the attribute classes work across languages, so although you are writing attributes on types in C#, the attribute information can be used by Visual Basic .NET, JScript .NET, and all languages targeted to the Common Language Runtime (CLR). The goal of using attributes is to extend the functionality of the language.

Working with .NET Framework Attributes

The .NET Framework provides hundreds of predefined, built-in attributes. They are not obvious at first sight, as the SDK does not provide a list of each attribute in alphabetical order. Depending on which classes you are using, attributes are derived from the `System.Attribute` class, and these attributes can be used with specific objects. For example, when working with the .NET Framework's ability to allow .NET code to interoperate with legacy COM code (known as COM Interop), over 20 attribute classes can be used on modifiers, ranging from the `ComAliasName` attribute to the `TypeLibType` attribute. The following code illustrates the `DllImportAttribute` attribute, which gives you an idea of how to call external methods in Win32 DLL's from C#:

```
namespace System.Runtime.InteropServices
{
    [AttributeUsage(AttributeTargets.Method)]
    public class DllImportAttribute: System.Attribute
    {
        public DllImportAttribute(string dllName) {...}
        public CallingConvention CallingConvention;
        public CharSet CharSet;
        public string EntryPoint;
        public bool ExactSpelling;
        public bool PreserveSig;
        public bool SetLastError;
        public string Value { get {...} }
    }
}
```

Without attributes, you would have no way to effectively tell the C# compiler how you intend to use a specific method in an external DLL; and if the C# language included this functionality in the base language, it would not be generic enough to run on other platforms. With the capability to call Win32 components through the language by using attributes, you have control over what properties to use, if any, when calling external methods.

 Note Chapter 34 describes the DLLImportAttribute **class in detail.**

Because there are so many attribute classes in the .NET Framework, it is impossible to describe each of them in a single chapter. Moreover, because attribute classes are specific to the classes in which they are defined, they are useful only within the context of those classes. As you code your applications and become more familiar with the .NET Framework namespaces for which you are coding, the attribute classes associated with the namespaces will become more obvious.

Several reserved attribute classes can stand on their own and directly affect the C# language itself. The System.ObsoleteAttribute class, System. SerializableAttribute class, and System.ConditionalAttribute class are attribute classes that can be used on their own and which directly affect the outcome of your code.

 Note In the .NET Framework, attribute classes have aliases, so when using attribute classes, you often see the name of the attribute class without the "Attribute" suffix. The suffix is assumed, so the short form does not cause an error. For example, ObsoleteAttribute **can be used as** Obsolete, **as the attributes are enclosed in brackets, making it obvious that they are attributes and not some other modifier type.**

Let's take a look at a few of the many attribute classes available in the .NET Framework. In doing so, you'll get a feel for how these classes work and how attributes can be applied to your C# code.

System.Diagnostics.ConditionalAttribute

The `Conditional` attribute is the alias for the `System.Diagnostics.ConditionalAttribute`, which you can apply only to class method declarations. It specifies that the method should be included as a part of the class only if the C# compiler defines the symbol that appears as the attribute's parameter.

Listing 17-1 illustrates how the `Conditional` attribute works.

Listing 17-1: **Working with the Conditional Attribute**

```
using System;
using System.Diagnostics;

public class TestClass
{
    public void Method1()
    {
        Console.WriteLine("Hello from Method1!");
    }

    [Conditional("DEBUG")]
    public void Method2()
    {
        Console.WriteLine("Hello from Method2!");
    }

    public void Method3()
    {
        Console.WriteLine("Hello from Method3!");
    }

}

class MainClass
{
    public static void Main()
    {
        TestClass MyTestClass = new TestClass();

        MyTestClass.Method1();
        MyTestClass.Method2();
        MyTestClass.Method3();
    }
}
```

Note Remember to reference the `System.Diagnostics` namepsace in your code so that you do not have to use the fully qualified namspace when using the `Conditional` attribute class and the C# compiler can find the class's implementation.

Listing 17-1 declares two classes: `TestClass` and `MainClass`. The `TestClass` class contains three methods: `Method1()`, `Method2()`, and `Method3()`. The `Method1()` and `Method3()` classes are implemented without any attributes, but `Method2()` uses the `Conditional` attribute with a parameter named DEBUG. This means that the `Method2()` method is a part of the class only when the C# compiler builds the code with a symbol called DEBUG defined. If the C# compiler builds the class with the DEBUG symbol not defined, the method is not included as a part of the class and any calls to the method are ignored.

The `MainClass` class implements the application's `Main()` method, which creates an object of type `TestClass` and calls all three methods on the class.

The output of Listing 17-1 varies depending on how the code is compiled. First, try compiling Listing 17-1 with the DEBUG symbol defined. You can use the C# compiler's /D command-line argument to define symbols for the compiler:

```
csc /D:DEBUG Listing17-1.cs
```

When the code in Listing 17-1 is compiled while the DEBUG symbol is defined, the `Method2()` method in the `TestClass` class is included in the build, and running the application writes the following to the console:

```
Hello from Method1!
Hello from Method2!
Hello from Method3!
```

Now try compiling Listing 17-1 without the DEBUG symbol defined:

```
csc Listing17-1.cs
```

When the code in Listing 17-1 is compiled while the DEBUG symbol is not defined, the `Method2()` method in the `TestClass` class is not included in the build, and the call to the `Method2()` method made in the `Main()` method is ignored. Building the code in Listing 17-1 without the DEBUG symbol defined produces code that writes the following out to the console when it is executed:

```
Hello from Method1!
Hello from Method3!
```

As you can see, the `Conditional` attribute is powerful and useful. Before you start using this class, note the following rules that apply:

✦ The method marked with the `Conditional` attribute must be a method in a class.

✦ The method marked with the `Conditional` attribute must not be an `override` method.

✦ The method marked with the `Conditional` attribute must have a return type of `void`.

✦ Although the method marked with the `Conditional` attribute must not be marked with the override modifier, it can be marked with the `virtual` modifier. Overrides of such methods are implicitly conditional, and must not be explicitly marked with a `Conditional` attribute.

✦ The method marked with the `Conditional` attribute must not be an implementation of an interface method; otherwise, a compile-time error will occur.

System.SerializableAttribute class

The `Serializable` attribute is the alias for the `System.SerializableAttribute` class, which can be applied to classes. It signals to the .NET Framework that the class's members can be serialized to and from a storage medium, such as a hard disk. Using this attribute makes it superfluous to add the capability for the state in your classes to be saved to disk and restored later. When serializing types, all of the data in the class marked as `Serializable` is saved in the state that it is in when the data is persisted. If there are types within a class that you do not want to be persisted, you can mark them with the `NonSerialized` attribute, which is the alias for the `System.NonSerializableAttribute` class. In the following code snippet, the data in the password string marked as `NonSerialized` is not persisted to the file or stream to which the class data is being written:

```
[Serializable()]
public class Users{

    public string username;
    public string emailaddress;
    public string phonenumber;

    // Add a field that will not be persisted

    [NonSerialized()] public string password;

    public FillData() {

        username = "admin";
        password = "password";
        emailaddress = "billg@microsoft.com";
        phonenumber = "555-1212";
    }
}
```

To illustrate a complete serialization sample, Listing 17-2 takes another look at the Point2D class you worked with in previous chapters. The class is marked with the Serializable attribute, signifying that it can be saved to and read from a data stream.

Listing 17-2: **Working with the Serializable Attribute**

```
using System;
using System.IO;
using System.Runtime.Serialization.Formatters.Binary;

[Serializable]
class Point2D
{
    public int X;
    public int Y;
}

class MyMainClass
{
    public static void Main()
    {
        Point2D My2DPoint = new Point2D();

        My2DPoint.X = 100;
        My2DPoint.Y = 200;

        Stream WriteStream = File.Create("Point2D.bin");
        BinaryFormatter BinaryWrite = new BinaryFormatter();
        BinaryWrite.Serialize(WriteStream, My2DPoint);
        WriteStream.Close();

        Point2D ANewPoint = new Point2D();

        Console.WriteLine("New Point Before Deserialization: ({0}, {1})",
ANewPoint.X, ANewPoint.Y);
        Stream ReadStream = File.OpenRead("Point2D.bin");
        BinaryFormatter BinaryRead = new BinaryFormatter();
        ANewPoint = (Point2D)BinaryRead.Deserialize(ReadStream);
        ReadStream.Close();
        Console.WriteLine("New Point After Deserialization: ({0}, {1})",
ANewPoint.X, ANewPoint.Y);
    }

}
```

The code in Listing 17-2 creates a new Point2D object and populates it with coordinates of (100, 200). It then serializes the class to a file called Point2D.bin. The code then creates a new point and deserializes the contents of the Point2D.bin file to the new Point2D object. The deserialization process reads the Point2D.bin file and sets the values of the object to the values found in the binary file. Executing the code in Listing 17-2 outputs the following to the console:

```
New Point Before Deserialization: (0, 0)
New Point After Deserialization: (100, 200)
```

When the new Point2D object is created, its members are initialized to their default values of 0. The values are changed by the deserialization process, which sets the values according to the data stored in the Point2D.bin file.

Listing 17-2 makes use of two .NET Framework classes in its serialization process. The Stream class is found in the System.IO namespace and manages access to data streams, including disk files. The BinaryFormatter is found in the System.Runtime.Serialization.Formatters.Binary namespace and handles the serialization of data into a binary representation. The .NET Framework includes other formatters that you can use to represent serialized data in other formats. The SoapFormatter class, for example, formats serialized data into a format suitable for an XML SOAP call.

Note   The BinaryFormatter class is proprietary to the .NET Framework. If you plan to target other systems that may not be able to understand the binary format, consider using the SoapFormatter class to persist data in an XML format that can be understood by other systems.

System.ObsoleteAttribute class

The Obsolete attribute can be applied to any type in C# with the exception of assemblies, modules, parameters, and return values. The Obsolete attribute enables you to define portions of code that are being replaced or are no longer valid. The Message and IsError properties of the Obsolete class give you control over how the compiler handles types marked with the Obsolete attribute. By setting the IsError property to True, the compiler produces an error, with the error message being the string property set on the Message property. The default value for the IsError property is False, which causes a warning to occur when your code is compiled. In the following code, the HelloWorld method is marked as Obsolete.

```csharp
using System;
public class RunThis
{
  public static void Main()
  {
    // This generates a compile-time warning.
```

```
      Console.WriteLine(HelloWorld());
      Console.ReadLine();
    }

  // Mark HelloWord as Obsolete
  [Obsolete("Next version uses Hello Universe")]
  public static string HelloWorld()
  {
    return ("HelloWorld");
  }
}
```

Figure 17-1 shows the task list for the compiler warnings that result from compiling the preceding code.

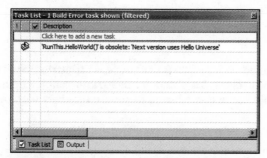

Figure 17-1: Warning output from using the Obsolete attribute

If you want to ensure that an error occurs and not just a warning message, you can modify the marked code with the true value for the IsError property and the class will not compile. If you modify the Obsolete attribute in the previous code to the following, an error occurs:

```
[Obsolete("Next version uses Hello Universe", true)]
```

As you can see, using the Obsolete attribute enables you to preserve existing code while ensuring that developers are not using out-of-date types.

Writing Your Own Attribute Classes

The .NET Framework ships with a significant number of attribute classes that you can use for a variety of purposes. You might need an attribute, however, that covers functionality not included in the .NET Framework. For example, you might like to have a code review attribute that labels a class with a date specifying the last time that code for a class was reviewed by your peers. In cases such as these, you will need to define your own attributes and have them operate just like any of the attributes that ship with the .NET Framework. As it turns out, the .NET Framework fully supports the construction of new attribute classes. In this section, you see how new attribute classes are developed and used by .NET code.

You can write your own attribute classes and use them in your code just as you would use an attribute from the .NET Framework. Custom attribute classes act like regular classes; they have properties and methods that enable the user of the attribute to set and retrieve data.

Attributes are implemented with attribute classes. Attribute classes derive from a class in the .NET System namespace called Attribute. By convention, attribute classes are suffixed with the word Attribute:

```
public class CodeAuthorAttribute : Attribute
{
}
```

This class defines an attribute called CodeAuthorAttribute. This attribute name can be used as an attribute after the class is defined. If the attribute name ends with the Attribute suffix, the attribute name can be used in square brackets with or without the suffix:

```
[CodeAuthorAttribute]
[CodeAuthor]
```

Both of these attributes refer to the CodeAuthorAttribute class. After you define an attribute class, you use it like any other .NET attribute class.

Restricting attribute usage

Attribute classes can themselves use attributes. The most common example is an attribute called AttributeUsage. The AttributeUsage attribute contains a parameter that specifies where the attribute can be used. Some attributes might not make sense on all valid C# constructs. For example, the Obsolete attribute discussed previously only makes sense on methods. It doesn't make sense to mark a single variable as obsolete, so the Obsolete attribute should apply only to methods and not to other C# constructs. The AttributeUsage attribute class contains a public enumeration called AttributeTargets, whose members appear in Table 17-1.

These AttributeTargets members can appear together in an OR expression and be used as a parameter to the AtrributeUsage attribute to specify that the attribute class defines an attribute that can only be used in certain contexts, as shown in the following example:

```
[AttributeUsage(AttributeTargets.Class |
AttributeTargets.Struct)]
public class CodeAuthorAttribute : Attribute
{
}
```

This construct declares a class called `CodeAuthorAttribute` and specifies that the attribute can be used only with classes and structures.

The C# compiler enforces your usage of the attribute to make sure that it is used in accordance with the `AttributeTargets` enumeration values specified in the `AttributeUsage` attribute. If you use an attribute on an expression that is not allowed by the definition of the attribute, you get an error from the compiler.

Suppose, for example, that you write an attribute called `Name` and use only the `AttributeTargets.Class` enumeration as the parameter to the `AttributeUsage` attribute:

```
[AttributeUsage(AttributeTargets.Class)]
public class NameAttribute : Attribute
{
}
```

If you then try to apply the `Name` attribute to anything other than a class, you get an error message from the compiler that looks something like the following:

```
error CS0592: Attribute 'Name' is not valid on this declaration
type. It is valid on 'class' declarations only.
```

Allowing multiple attribute values

You can also use the `AttributeUsage` attribute to specify whether your class allows multiple instances of an attribute to be used on a particular piece of C# code. This is specified through an attribute parameter called `AllowMultiple`. If the value of `AllowMultiple` is set to `True`, you can use multiple instances of the attribute on a particular C# element. If `AllowMultiple` is set to `False`, you can use only a single instance on any particular C# element (although you are still allowed to apply the attribute to more than one C# construct):

```
[AttributeUsage(AttributeTargets.class, AllowMultiple = true)]
public class NameAttribute : Attribute
{
    public NameAttribute(string Name)
    {
    }
}
```

Using multiple attributes enables you to assign multiple values to a C# construct using a single attribute. The following construct marks the Name attribute as a multi-use attribute and enables developers to use the attribute more than once on a single C# element:

```
[Name("Jeff Ferguson")]
[Name("Jeff Ferguson's Assistant")]
public class MyClass
{
}
```

Multiple-use attributes can also appear in a single set of square brackets, separated by a comma:

```
[Name("Jeff Ferguson"), Name("Jeff Ferguson's Assistant")]
public class MyClass
{
}
```

If you do not specify a value for the AllowMultiple parameter, then multiple use is not allowed.

Setting attribute parameters

Your attribute classes can accept parameters, which appear in parentheses following the attribute name. In the previous example, the Name attribute takes a string naming a code author as a parameter. Some attributes need parameters to associate data with the attribute, such as the name string in the Name attribute shown above. The values of the parameters are passed to the constructor of the attribute class, and the attribute class must implement a constructor that can receive the parameters:

```
[AttributeUsage(AttributeTargets.Class |
AttributeTargets.Struct)]
public class CodeAuthorAttribute : Attribute
{
    public CodeAuthorAttribute (string Name)
    {
    }
}
```

This attribute requires a string parameter to be supplied whenever the attribute is used:

```
[CodeAuthor("Jeff Ferguson")]
```

You must supply parameters specified in the class's constructor when the attribute is used. If you forget to do so, you get an error from the compiler:

```
error CS1501: No overload for method 'CodeAuthorAttribute'
takes '0' arguments
```

The parameters supplied to the constructor of the attribute class are called *positional parameters*. Positional parameters associate parameter data with their parameter name based on the position of the data in the parameter list. For example, the second parameter data item is associated with the second parameter variable specified in the parameter list in the function's declaration. You can also supply named parameters, which are stored by properties implemented in the attribute class. Named parameters are specified with the property name, an equal sign, and the property value. Named parameters associate parameter data with the parameter name based on the parameter name appearing before the value. Named parameters can appear in any order, since the association between a variable name and its value is specified through the parameter name and not through the value's position in the parameter list.

Suppose that you add a named parameter called `Date` to the `CodeAuthorAttribute` attribute. This means that the class can support a property called `Date` whose value can be set in the attribute definition:

```
[AttributeUsage(AttributeTargets.Class |
AttributeTargets.Struct)]
public class CodeAuthorAttribute : Attribute
{
    public CodeAuthorAttribute(string Name)
    {
    }

    public string Date
    {
        set
        {
        }
    }
}
```

After the property is defined, its value can be set by a named parameter when the attribute appears in code:

```
[CodeAuthor("Jeff Ferguson", Date = "Apr 01 2001")]
```

Unlike positional parameters, named parameters are optional and can be omitted from an attribute specification.

Learning about attribute classes by example

In this section, you build a new attribute called ClassAuthor and use it in some C# code. This gives you a feel for how new attributes are defined and used by .NET code. Listing 17-3 adds a new class to the code from Listing 17-2. The new class is called ClassAuthorAttribute and derives from the .NET Attribute class.

Listing 17-3: **Defining New Attribute Classes**

```
using System;
using System.Diagnostics;
using System.Reflection;

[AttributeUsage(AttributeTargets.Class)]
public class ClassAuthorAttribute : Attribute
{
    private string AuthorName;

    public ClassAuthorAttribute(string AuthorName)
    {
        this.AuthorName = AuthorName;
    }

    public string Author
    {
        get
        {
            return AuthorName;
        }
    }
}

[ClassAuthor("Jeff Ferguson")]
public class TestClass
{
    public void Method1()
    {
        Console.WriteLine("Hello from Method1!");
    }

    [Conditional("DEBUG")]
    public void Method2()
    {
        Console.WriteLine("Hello from Method2!");
    }

    public void Method3()
    {
        Console.WriteLine("Hello from Method3!");
```

```
        }

    }

public class MainClass
{
    public static void Main()
    {
        TestClass MyTestClass = new TestClass();

        MyTestClass.Method1();
        MyTestClass.Method2();
        MyTestClass.Method3();

        object [] ClassAttributes;
        MemberInfo TypeInformation;

        TypeInformation = typeof(TestClass);
        ClassAttributes =
TypeInformation.GetCustomAttributes(typeof(ClassAuthorAttribute), false);
        if(ClassAttributes.GetLength(0) != 0)
        {
            ClassAuthorAttribute ClassAttribute;

            ClassAttribute = (ClassAuthorAttribute)(ClassAttributes[0]);
            Console.WriteLine("Class Author: {0}", ClassAttribute.Author);
        }
    }
}
```

The code in Listing 17-3 starts off with a new attribute class called
`CodeAuthorAttribute`. The class serves as an attribute class for an attribute
that can be applied only to other classes. The class takes one string parameter,
which is stored in a private variable and is accessed publicly through a read-only
property called `Author`. The intent of the parameter is to mark a class as having
a specific developer's name attached to it, so that other developers know whom
to contact if they have questions about the class's implementation.

The `TestClass` class uses the `CodeAuthor` attribute and supplies a parameter of
`Jeff Ferguson`.

The interesting feature in Listing 17-3 is the `Main()` method, which gets an attribute
object from the class and prints out the author's name. It does this through a concept called *reflection,* which is implemented by classes in a .NET namespace called
`System.Reflection`. Using *reflection,* code can, at runtime, look into a class's
implementation and discover how it is constructed. Reflection enables code to
examine other pieces of code to derive information such as the methods and properties it supports and the base class it is derived from. Reflection is a very powerful
feature and is fully supported by the .NET Framework.

The code in Listing 17-3 uses reflection to get a list of attributes associated with a particular class. The attribute code starts off by retrieving a `Type` object for the `TestClass` class. The C# operator `typeof()` is used to get the `Type` object. The `typeof()` operator takes as an argument the name of the class whose type information is to be retrieved. The returned `Type` object, which is defined in the .NET Framework `System` namespace, acts as a table of contents, describing everything there is to know about the requested class.

After the `Type` object is retrieved for the class, the `Main()` method calls a method called `GetCustomAttributes()` to get a list of attributes supported by the class described by the `Type` object. This method returns an array of objects and accepts as a parameter the type of attribute that should be retrieved. In Listing 17-3, the `GetCustomAttributes()` method is called with type information for the `CodeAuthorAttribute` class as a parameter. This forces the `GetCustomAttributes()` method to return information only about class attributes that are of type `CodeAuthorAttribute`. If the class had used any other attributes, they would not be returned by the call. The code in Listing 17-3 finishes up by taking the first `CodeAuthorAttribute` attribute in the array and asking it for the value of its `Author` property. The string value is written out to the console.

Running the code in Listing 17-3 writes the following out to the console (assuming that you compile the code without defining the `DEBUG` symbol):

```
Hello from Method1!
Hello from Method3!
Class Author: Jeff Ferguson
```

Summary

The .NET Framework enables attributes to be used in languages that run under the CLR. The concept of an attribute opens the door for expanding the functionality of .NET languages with classes that can add behaviors to code. The C# language enables you to both use attributes built by others in your C# code and write your own attributes, which you can distribute to other .NET developers.

The attribute concept is not unique to C#; rather, it is available to any language running under the CLR. Attributes provide you with the power to extend the language environment and provide new features to developers working with .NET code. The serialization process is a perfect example of this. Serialization is not built into the C# language specification, but its functionality is available through an attribute class written by Microsoft. The attribute class extends the language at runtime to support a feature that was not designed into the language itself.

Like all other constructs in the .NET Framework, attributes are objects. Attributes are defined by classes that derive from the .NET Framework's `System.Attribute` class. You can use C# to develop new attribute classes simply by deriving a new class from the `System.Attribute` base class. The attributes that you develop in C#, as well as the attributes already defined by the .NET Framework, can be used by any language that supports the CLR.

Attributes are used by specifying the attribute's class name in square brackets immediately before the C# construct to which the attribute applies. Attributes can accept data in the form of parameters, which can associate stateful data with the attribute. This data can be retrieved by Reflection code that can query your code and search for attributes.

✦ ✦ ✦

Versioning Your Classes

Much of the code written for today's applications
evolves over time. Software projects start with a set
of requirements, and you design your classes to meet those
requirements. That first code base serves as the source code
to version 1.0 of your application. However, most applications
survive beyond version 1.0. Application upgrades come from
an updated set of requirements, and the version 1.0 code base
must be revised to implement the updated requirements.

The C# language supports constructs that make your classes
robust enough to evolve as the requirements of your application change. In this chapter, you learn how to use the new and
override keywords on C# class methods to ensure that your
classes can continue to be used as your application's requirements change.

Looking at the Versioning Problem

Before you learn about how the new and override keywords
can be used to make your C# classes compatible with a code
base that has to keep up with changing requirements, take a
look at what life would be like without those keywords. If you
remember from Chapter 8, the classes that you are creating
and consuming can be considered base classes. These classes
have core functionality that an application requires. When
you declare an instance of a class, you are deriving from that
class, to use its functionality. The base class libraries in the
.NET Framework are based on this model; everything you
do when developing .NET applications is based on a base
class. The complete framework derives from the base class
System.Object, so even declaring a simple variable means you
are deriving functionality from the base class System.Object.

Listing 18-1 demonstrates base and derived class
characteristics.

Listing 18-1: A Base Class and a Derived Class

```csharp
using System;

public class BaseClass
{
    protected int Value;

    public BaseClass()
    {
        Value = 123;
    }
}

public class DerivedClass : BaseClass
{
    public void PrintValue()
    {
        Console.WriteLine("Value = " + Value);
    }
}

class MainClass
{
    public static void Main()
    {
        DerivedClass DerivedClassObject = new DerivedClass();

        DerivedClassObject.PrintValue();
    }
}
```

The code in Listing 18-1 is relatively straightforward. It contains a base class called BaseClass that holds a protected integer variable. Another class, called DerivedClass, derives from the BaseClass class and implements a method called PrintValue(). The Main() method creates an object of type DerivedClass and calls its PrintValue() method. Running the code in Listing 18-1 writes the following out to the console:

```
Value = 123
```

Now suppose that requirements change and another developer takes over the development of the BaseClass class while you continue work on additions to the DerivedClass class. What happens if that other developer adds a method to the BaseClass class called PrintValue() and provides a slightly different implementation? The code looks like the code in Listing 18-2.

Listing 18-2: **PrintValue() Added to the BaseClass Class**

```
using System;

public class BaseClass
{
    protected int Value;

    public BaseClass()
    {
        Value = 123;
    }

    public virtual void PrintValue()
    {
        Console.WriteLine("Value: " + Value);
    }
}

public class DerivedClass : BaseClass
{
    public void PrintValue()
    {
        Console.WriteLine("Value = " + Value);
    }
}

class MainClass
{
    public static void Main()
    {
        DerivedClass DerivedClassObject = new DerivedClass();

        DerivedClassObject.PrintValue();
    }
}
```

Now, there's a problem. The DerivedClass class derives from the BaseClass class, and they both implement a method called PrintValue(). The BaseClass class has been revised to a new version, while the DerivedClass class has stayed with its original implementation. In Listing 18-2, the relationship between the PrintValue() method in the base class and the PrintValue() method in the derived class is unclear. The compiler must know which method supercedes the base class version. And the complier does not know which implementation should execute when the Main() method calls the PrintValue() method.

As it turns out, this ambiguity is flagged as an warning by the C# compiler:

```
warning CS0114: 'DerivedClass.PrintValue()' hides inherited
member 'BaseClass.PrintValue()'. To make the current member
override that implementation, add the override keyword.
Otherwise add the new keyword.
```

This is a good warning, because the philosophy of the C# language emphasizes clarity, and the C# compiler always warns about code constructs that are unclear.

Solving the Versioning Problem

C# offers two ways to resolve the ambiguity in Listing 18-2:

✦ Use the new modifier to specify that the two methods are actually different.

✦ Use the override modifier to specify that the derived class method should supercede the base class method.

Let's examine both of these approaches.

Using the new modifier

If the two method implementations in Listing 18-2 need to be treated as separate methods that just happen to have the same name, the method in the derived class needs to be prefixed with the new modifier. By using the new modifier, you can explicitly hide members that are inherited from the base class implementation. You simply declare a member in your derived class with the same name, prefix the declaration with the new modifier, and the functionality of the derived class is used, as shown in Listing 18-3.

Listing 18-3: Resolving Ambiguity with the new Keyword

```
using System;

public class BaseClass
{
    protected int Value;

    public BaseClass()
    {
        Value = 123;
    }

    public void PrintValue()
    {
```

```
            Console.WriteLine("Value: " + Value);
        }
    }

public class DerivedClass : BaseClass
    {
        new public void PrintValue()
        {
            Console.WriteLine("Value = " + Value);
        }
    }

class MainClass
    {
        public static void Main()
        {
            DerivedClass DerivedClassObject = new DerivedClass();

            DerivedClassObject.PrintValue();
        }
    }
```

Note The new operator and the new modifier are separate implementations of the new keyword. The new operator is used to create objects, whereas the new modifier is used to hide an inherited member from a base class member.

The code in Listing 18-3 uses the new keyword on the implementation of the PrintValue() method of the DerivedClass class. This instructs the C# compiler to treat this method as one distinct from the base class method, even though the two methods have the same name. Using the new keyword resolves the ambiguity and enables the C# compiler to compile the code without issuing any warnings.

In this case, the Main() method calls the method in the derived class, and Listing 18-3 prints the following to the console:

```
Value = 123
```

You can still execute the base class's method because the new keyword has basically ensured that the two PrintValue() methods in each of the classes can be called separately. You can call the base class method by casting the derived class object to an object of the base class type:

```
BaseClass BaseClassObject = (BaseClass)DerivedClassObject;

BaseClassObject.PrintValue();
```

As you can see, using the new modifier simply enables you to override the functionality in a base class. If you need to use the functionality of the original class, use the fully qualified class name with the class member to ensure that you are using the correct functionality.

Using the override modifier

The other option that you can use to resolve the duplicate method name ambiguity is to use the override modifier to specify that the derived class implementation supercedes the base class implementation. The override modifier does exactly what its name implies: It "overrides" the functionality of the base class member that it is superceding. To override a class member, the signature of the overriding member must be the same as the base class member. For example, if the overriding member has a constructor, the types in the constructor must match those in the base class member. In Listing 18-4, you can see the override modifier in action.

Listing 18-4: **Resolving Ambiguity with the override Modifier**

```csharp
using System;

public class BaseClass
{
    protected int Value;

    public BaseClass()
    {
        Value = 123;
    }

    public virtual void PrintValue()
    {
        Console.WriteLine("Value: " + Value);
    }
}

public class DerivedClass : BaseClass
{
    override public void PrintValue()
    {
        Console.WriteLine("Value = " + Value);
    }
}

class MainClass
{
    public static void Main()
    {
        DerivedClass DerivedClassObject = new DerivedClass();

        DerivedClassObject.PrintValue();
    }
}
```

In Listing 18-4, the override keyword tells the C# compiler that the implementation of PrintValue() in the derived class overrides the implementation of the same method in the base class. The base class implementation is basically hidden from callers. Unlike Listing 18-3, the code in Listing 18-4 contains only one implementation of PrintValue().

The base class implementation of PrintValue() is not accessible to the code in the Main() method, even if the code casts the derived class object to a base class object and calls the method on the base class object. Because the override keyword is used in Listing 18-4, all calls to the method through a casted object are routed to the overridden implementation in the derived class.

Take a look at the code used to call the base class's implementation of PrintValue() when the new operator is used to resolve the ambiguity:

```
BaseClass BaseClassObject = (BaseClass)DerivedClassObject;

BaseClassObject.PrintValue();
```

This code is not enough to force the base class's implementation to be called when the override keyword is used. This is because the object was created as an object of class DerivedClass. You can call the base class's method, but, because the implementation in the base class has been overridden with the code in the derived class, the derived class's implementation will still be called. You must use the C# keyword base to call the base class's implementation, as in the following example:

```
base.PrintValue();
```

This statement calls the implementation of PrintValue() found in the current class's base class. Placing this statement in the DerivedClass class, for example, calls the implementation of PrintValue() found in the BaseClass class. You can equate the base keyword to using the fully qualified namespace.object.method syntax, it simply references the correct base class instance that you are using.

Summary

The examples in this chapter placed all of the listing's classes together in a single source file in the interests of simplicity. However, real-world development may be more complicated. If multiple developers are working on a single project, the project might be made up of more than one source file. The developer working on the base class may place it in one C# source file, and the developer working on the derived class may place it in another C# source file. Matters might be even more complicated if the base class is compiled into an assembly and the derived class is implemented in a project that references the assembly.

The point here is that base classes and derived classes can come from many different sources, and coordinating the design of the classes becomes very important. It is crucial to understand that, over time, base classes and derived classes will add functionality as a project progresses. As a developer, you should keep this in mind: Design your classes so that they can be used in multiple versions of a project and can evolve as project requirements evolve.

Arguably, the other resolution to the versioning problem is even easier: Don't use the same name for methods that have different implementations unless you are actually overriding base class functionality. While this may be the best approach in theory, it isn't always possible in practice. The `new` and `override` keywords in C# help you get around this design problem and enable you to re-use method names if your project calls for it. The main use of the `override` keyword is to announce new implementations of virtual methods found in base classes, but it also serves a versioning role in C# as well.

✦   ✦   ✦

Working with Unsafe Code

When you use the new keyword to create a new instance of a reference type, you are asking the CLR to set aside enough memory to use for the variable. The CLR allocates enough memory for the variable and associates the memory with your variable. Under normal conditions, your code is unaware of the actual location of that memory, as far as a memory address is concerned. After the new operation succeeds, your code is free to use the allocated memory without knowing or caring where the memory is actually located on your system.

In C and C++, developers have direct access to memory. When a piece of C or C++ code requests access to a block of memory, it is given the specific address of the allocated memory, and the code directly reads from and writes to that memory location. The advantage to this approach is that direct access to memory is extremely fast and made for efficient code. There are problems, however, that outweigh the benefits. The problem with this direct memory access is that it is easy to misuse, and misuse of memory causes code to crash. Misbehaving C or C++ code can easily write to memory that has already been deleted, or can write to memory belonging to another variable. These types of memory access problems result in numerous hard-to-find bugs and software crashes.

The architecture of the CLR eliminates all of these problems by handling memory management for you. This means that your C# code can work with variables without needing to know details about how and where the variables are stored in memory. Because the CLR shields your C# code from these memory-related details, your C# code is free from bugs related to direct access to memory.

Occasionally, however, you need to work with a specific memory address in your C# code. Your code may need that extra ounce of performance, or your C# code may need to work with legacy code that requires that you provide the address of a specific piece of memory. The C# language supports a special mode, called *unsafe mode*, that enables you to work directly with memory from within your C# code.

This special C# construct is called unsafe mode because your code is no longer safe from the memory-management protection offered by the CLR. In unsafe mode, your C# code is allowed to access memory directly, and it can suffer from the same class of memory-related bugs found in C and C++ code if you're not extremely careful with the way you manage memory.

In this chapter, you take a look at the unsafe mode of the C# language and how it can be used to enable you to access memory locations directly using C and C++ style pointer constructs.

Understanding Pointer Basics

Memory is accessed in C# using a special data type called a pointer. A *pointer* is a variable whose value points to a specific memory address. A pointer is declared in C# with an asterisk placed between the pointer's type and its identifier, as shown in the following declaration:

```
int * MyIntegerPointer;
```

This statement declares an integer pointer named MyIntegerPointer. The pointer's type signifies the type of variable to which the pointer can point. An integer pointer, for example, can only point to memory used by an integer variable.

Pointers must be assigned to a memory address, and C# makes it easy for you to write an expression that evaluates to the memory address of a variable. Prefixing a unary expression with the C# address-of operator, the ampersand, evaluates to a memory address, as shown in the following code:

```
int   MyInteger = 123;
int * MyIntegerPointer = &MyInteger;
```

The preceding code does two things:

 ✦ It declares an integer variable called MyInteger and assigns a value of 123 to it.

 ✦ It declares an integer pointer called MyIntegerPointer and points it to the address of the MyInteger variable.

Figure 19-1 illustrates how this assignment is interpreted in memory.

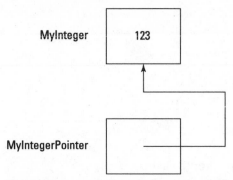

Figure 19-1: A pointer pointing to a variable

Pointers actually have two values:

✦ The value of the pointer's memory address

✦ The value of the variable to which the pointer is pointing

C# enables you to write expressions that evaluate to either value. Prefixing the pointer identifier with an asterisk enables you to obtain the value of the variable to which the pointer is pointing, as demonstrated in the following code:

```
int   MyInteger = 123;
int * MyIntegerPointer = &MyInteger;

Console.WriteLine(*MyIntegerPointer);
```

This code writes 123 to the console.

Understanding pointer types

Pointers can have one of the following types:

✦ sbyte

✦ byte

✦ short

✦ ushort

✦ int

✦ uint

✦ long

✦ `ulong`

✦ `char`

✦ `float`

✦ `double`

✦ `decimal`

✦ `bool`

✦ an enumeration type

✦ `void`, which is used to specify a pointer to an unknown type

You cannot declare a pointer to a reference type, such as an object. The memory for objects is managed by the CLR, and the memory may be deleted whenever the garbage collector needs to free the object's memory. If the C# compiler enabled you to maintain a pointer to an object, your code would run the risk of pointing to an object whose memory may be reclaimed at some point by the CLR's garbage collector.

Suppose that the C# compiler enabled you to write code like the following:

```
MyClass MyObject = new MyClass();
MyClass * MyObjectPointer;

MyObjectPointer = &MyObject;
```

The memory used by `MyObject` is automatically managed by the CLR, and its memory is freed when all references to the object are released and the CLR's garbage collector executes. The problem is that your unsafe code now maintains a pointer to an object whose memory has been freed. There is no way for the CLR to know that you have a pointer to the object, and the result is that you have a pointer that points to nothing after the garbage collector frees the memory. C# gets around this problem by not enabling you to maintain variables to reference types with memory that is managed by the CLR.

Compiling Unsafe Code

By default, the C# compiler compiles only safe C# code. To force the compiler to compile unsafe C# code, you must use the `/unsafe` compiler argument:

```
csc /unsafe file1.cs
```

Unsafe code enables you to write code that accesses memory directly, bypassing the objects that manage memory in managed applications. Unsafe code can perform better in certain types of applications, because memory locations are accessed directly. This command compiles the `file1.cs` source file and allows unsafe C# code to be compiled.

Note   In C#, unsafe code enables you to declare and use pointers as you would in C++.

Specifying pointers in unsafe mode

The C# compiler doesn't enable you to use pointers in your C# code by default. If you try to work with pointers in your code, the C# compiler issues the following error message:

```
error CS0214: Pointers may only be used in an unsafe context
```

Pointers are valid only in C# unsafe mode, and you must explicitly define unsafe code to the compiler. You do so by using the C# keyword `unsafe`. The `unsafe` keyword must be applied to a code block that uses pointers.

You can specify that a block of code executes in the C# unsafe mode by applying the `unsafe` keyword to the declaration of the code body, as shown in Listing 19-1.

Listing 19-1: **Unsafe Methods**

```
using System;

public class MyClass
{
    public unsafe static void Main()
    {
        int MyInteger = 123;
        int * MyIntegerPointer = &MyInteger;

        Console.WriteLine(*MyIntegerPointer);
    }
}
```

The `Main()` method in Listing 19-1 uses the `unsafe` modifier in its declaration. This indicates to the C# compiler that all of the code in the method must be considered unsafe. After this keyword is used, the code in the method can use unsafe pointer constructs.

The `unsafe` keyword applies only to the method in which it appears. If the class in Listing 19-1 were to contain another method, that other method could not use an unsafe pointer constructs unless it, too, is declared with the `unsafe` keyword. The following rules apply to the unsafe modifier:

✦ Classes, structures, and delegates can include the `unsafe` modifier, which indicates that the entire body of the type is considered unsafe.

✦ Fields, methods, properties, events, indexers, operators, constructors, destructors, and static constructors can be defined with the `unsafe` modifier, which indicates that the specific member declaration is unsafe.

✦ A code block can be marked with the `unsafe` modifier, which indicates that the entire block should be considered unsafe.

Accessing members' values through pointers

The unsafe mode of C# enables you to use the `->` operator to access members to structures referenced by a pointer. The operator, which is keyed as a hyphen followed by a greater-than symbol, enables you to access members directly, as shown in Listing 19-2.

Listing 19-2: **Accessing Structure Members with a Pointer**

```csharp
using System;

public struct Point2D
{
    public int X;
    public int Y;
}

public class MyClass
{
    public unsafe static void Main()
    {
        Point2D MyPoint;
        Point2D * PointerToMyPoint;

        MyPoint = new Point2D();
        PointerToMyPoint = &MyPoint;
        PointerToMyPoint->X = 100;
        PointerToMyPoint->Y = 200;
        Console.WriteLine("({0}, {1})", PointerToMyPoint->X,
PointerToMyPoint->Y);
    }
}
```

Listing 19-2 contains a declaration for a structure called `Point2D`. The structure contains two public members. The listing also includes an unsafe `Main()` method that creates a new variable of the structure type and creates a pointer to the new structure. The method then uses the pointer member access operator to assign values to the structure, which is then written to the console.

This differs from member access in the default C# safe mode, which uses the `.` operator. The C# compiler issues an error if you use the wrong operator in the wrong mode. If you use the `.` operator with an unsafe pointer, the C# compiler issues the following error message:

```
error CS0023: Operator '.' cannot be applied to operand of type
'Point2D*'
```

If you use the `->` operator in a safe context, the C# compiler also issues an error message:

```
error CS0193: The * or -> operator must be applied to a pointer
```

Using Pointers to Fix Variables to a Specific Address

When memory for a variable is managed by the CLR, your code works with a variable, and management details about the variable's memory are handled by the CLR. During the CLR's garbage collection process, the runtime may move memory around to consolidate the memory heap available at runtime. This means that during the course of an application, the memory address for a variable may change. The CLR might take your variable's data and move it to a different address.

Under normal conditions, your C# code is oblivious to this relocation strategy. Because your code works with a variable identifier, you usually access the variable's memory through the variable identifier, and you can trust that the CLR works with the correct piece of memory as you work with the variable.

The picture is not as straightforward, however, when you work with pointers. Pointers point to a specific memory address. If you assign a pointer to a memory address used by a variable and the CLR later moves that variable's memory location, your pointer is pointing to memory that is no longer used by your variable.

The unsafe mode of C# enables you to specify a variable as exempt from the memory relocation that the CLR offers. This lets you hold a variable at a specific memory address, enabling you to use a pointer with the variable without worrying that the CLR may move the variable's memory address out from under your pointer. The C# keyword `fixed` is used to specify that a variable's memory address should be fixed. The `fixed` keyword is followed by a parenthetical expression containing a pointer declaration with an assignment to a variable. A block of code follows the fixed expression, and the fixed variable remains at the same memory address throughout the fixed code block, as shown in Listing 19-3.

Listing 19-3: **Fixing Managed Data in Memory**

```
using System;

public class MyClass
{
    public unsafe static void Main()
    {
        int ArrayIndex;
        int [] IntegerArray;

        IntegerArray = new int [5];
        fixed(int * IntegerPointer = IntegerArray)
        {
            for(ArrayIndex = 0; ArrayIndex < 5; ArrayIndex++)
                IntegerPointer[ArrayIndex] = ArrayIndex;
        }
        for(ArrayIndex = 0; ArrayIndex < 5; ArrayIndex++)
            Console.WriteLine(IntegerArray[ArrayIndex]);
    }
}
```

The fixed keyword in Listing 19-3 declares an integer pointer that points to an integer array. It is followed by a block of code that writes values to the array using the pointer. Within this block of code, the address of the IntegerArray array is guaranteed to be fixed, and the CLR does not move its location. This enables the code to use a pointer with the array without worrying that the CLR will move the array's physical memory location. After the fixed code block exits, the pointer can no longer be used and the CLR again considers the IntegerArray variable a candidate for relocation in memory.

Understanding pointer array element syntax

Listing 19-3 also illustrates the array element pointer syntax. The following line of code treats an unsafe mode pointer as if it were an array of bytes:

```
IntegerPointer[ArrayIndex] = ArrayIndex;
```

This line of code treats the pointer as if it were an array. The array element pointer syntax allows your unsafe C# code to view the memory pointed to by the pointer as an array of variables that can be read from or written to.

Comparing pointers

The unsafe mode of C# enables you to compare pointers using the following operators:

✦ Equality (==)

✦ Inequality (!=)

✦ Less-than (<)

✦ Greater-than (>)

✦ Less-than-or-equal-to (<=)

✦ Greater-than-or-equal-to (>=)

As with value types, these operators evaluate to Boolean values of True and False when used with pointer types.

Understanding pointer arithmetic

Pointers can be combined with integer values in mathematical expressions to change the location to which the pointer points. The + operator adds a value to the pointer, and the - operator subtracts a value from the pointer.

The fixed statement in Listing 19-3 could have also been written as follows:

```
fixed(int * IntegerPointer = IntegerArray)
{
for(ArrayIndex = 0; ArrayIndex < 5; ArrayIndex++)
*(IntegerPointer + ArrayIndex) = ArrayIndex;
}
```

In this code block, the pointer is offset by a value, and the sum is used to point to a memory location. The pointer arithmetic is performed in the following statement:

```
*(IntegerPointer + ArrayIndex) = ArrayIndex;
```

This statement reads as follows: "Take the value of IntegerPointer and increment it by the number of positions specified by ArrayIndex. Place the value of ArrayIndex in that location."

Pointer arithmetic increments a pointer position by a specified number of bytes, depending on the size of the type being pointed to. Listing 19-3 declares an integer array and an integer pointer. When pointer arithmetic is used on the integer pointer, the value used to offset the pointer specifies the number of variable sizes to move, not the number of bytes. The following expression uses pointer arithmetic to offset a pointer location by three bytes:

```
IntegerPointer + 3
```

The literal value 3 in this expression specifies that the pointer should be incremented by the space taken up by three integers, not by three bytes. Because the pointer points to an integer, the 3 is interpreted as "space for three integers" and not "space for three bytes." Because an integer takes up four bytes of memory, the pointer's address is incremented by twelve bytes (three integers multiplied by four bytes for each integer), not three bytes.

Using the sizeof operator

You can use the `sizeof` operator in unsafe mode to calculate the number of bytes needed to hold a specific data type. The operator is followed by an unmanaged type name in parentheses, and the expression evaluates to an integer specifying the number of bytes needed to hold a variable of the specified type.

Table 19-1 lists the supported managed types and the values that are returned by a `sizeof` operation.

Table 19-1
Supported sizeof() Types

Expression	Result
sizeof(sbyte)	1
sizeof(byte)	1
sizeof(short)	2
sizeof(ushort)	2
sizeof(int)	4
sizeof(uint)	4
sizeof(long)	8
sizeof(ulong)	8
sizeof(char)	2
sizeof(float)	4
sizeof(double)	8
sizeof(bool)	1

Allocating Memory from the Stack

C# provides a simple memory allocation mechanism in unsafe code. You can request memory in unsafe mode using the C# `stackalloc` keyword, as shown in Listing 19-4.

Listing 19-4: **Allocating Memory from the Stack**

```
using System;

public class MyClass
{
    public unsafe static void Main()
    {
        int * CharacterBuffer = stackalloc int [5];
        int Index;

        for(Index = 0; Index < 5; Index++)
            CharacterBuffer[Index] = Index;
        for(Index = 0; Index < 5; Index++)
            Console.WriteLine(CharacterBuffer[Index]);
    }
}
```

A data type follows the stackalloc keyword. It returns a pointer to the allocated memory block, and you can use the memory just as you would use the memory allocated by the CLR.

There is no explicit operation for freeing the memory allocated by the stackalloc keyword. The memory is freed automatically when the method that allocated the memory exits.

Summary

The unsafe mode in C# enables your code to work directly with memory. Using it can enhance performance because your code accesses memory directly, without having to navigate through the CLR. However, unsafe mode is potentially dangerous and can cause your code to crash if you do not work with the memory properly.

In general, avoid using the C# unsafe mode. If you need that last bit of performance from your code, or if you're working with legacy C or C++ code that requires you to specify a specific memory location, you should stick to the default safe mode and let the CLR handle memory allocation details for you. The minor performance degradation that results is far outweighed by lifting the burden of memory management from your code, and by gaining the freedom to write code that is devoid of bugs related to memory management.

✦   ✦   ✦

Understanding Advanced C# Constructs

In this chapter, you examine some interesting facets of the C# language. You also look at some sample code and learn why the code works the way it does. Understanding programming problems like the ones presented in this chapter will help you understand how to tackle your own tough C# programming questions.

First, you take a look at the implicit conversion feature of C# and see how it applies to objects of derived classes being accessed as objects of the derived class' base class. Remember that you can write implicit operator methods that define how implicit conversions from one type or another are handled; but, as you'll see, things get a bit more complicated when working with compile-time types and runtime types.

Next, you dive into an issue with structure initialization. Structures, as with classes, can contain both fields and properties. Initialization of structures with fields, however, is handled a bit differently than the initialization of structures with properties. In this chapter, you find out why, and you also discover how to resolve the issue.

In the third section of this chapter, you investigate the issue of passing an object of a derived class into a method call where an object of a base class is expected. Since objects of derived classes are inherently objects of the base class, passing a derived class object where a base class object is expected would seem to be straightforward. In this section, you learn why this technique is not as straightforward as it seems.

Finally, you dive into an advanced usage of class indexers. In the vast majority of cases, the indexers that you write serve to make a class behave like an array of elements. Normally, arrays accept integers as the index element specifier. In this section, you take a look at a technique for using data types other than integers for an array index.

Understanding Implicit Operators and Illegal Casts

Recall that your classes can contain implicit operator conversion code. Implicit operators are used to convert one type to another type without any special code. Many implicit conversions are built into the C# language. For example, an integer can be implicitly converted into a long integer without any special code:

```
int MyInt = 123;
long MyLongInt = MyInt;
```

C# does not define implicit conversions for all possible data type combinations. However, as you saw in an earlier chapter, you can write implicit operator conversion code that instructs the Common Language Runtime (CLR) how to behave when a user of your class attempts to implicitly convert between your class and another type. In this section, you explore a facet of the implicit conversion operator dealing with the conversion between two different classes.

Listing 20-1 contains two classes: TestClass and MainClass. The MainClass class contains the application's Main() method. The TestClass class maintains a private variable of type MainClass. It also defines an implicit operator method that converts TestClass objects to MainClass objects. The implicit operator implementation returns a reference to the TestClass object's private MainClass object.

Listing 20-1: **Invalid Cast Exceptions with Implicit Operators**

```
public class TestClass
{
    private MainClass MyMainClassObject;

    public TestClass()
    {
        MyMainClassObject = new MainClass();
    }

    public static implicit operator MainClass(TestClass Source)
    {
        return Source.MyMainClassObject;
    }
}

public class MainClass
{
```

```
public static void Main()
{
    object MyObject;
    MainClass MyMainClassObject;

    MyObject = new TestClass();
    MyMainClassObject = (MainClass)MyObject;
}
}
```

The code in the `Main()` method creates a new `TestClass` object and then casts the object to another object of type `MainClass`. Because an implicit operator is defined in `TestClass`, this cast should succeed. However, if you execute Listing 20-1, you receive the following message on your console:

```
Unhandled Exception: System.InvalidCastException: Exception of
type System.InvalidCastException was thrown.
   at MainClass.Main()
```

Why does the CLR deem the conversion illegal even when an implicit operator is defined? The issue here is that the conversion works between compile-time types, not runtime types.

The `Main()` method creates a new object of type `TestClass` and assigns the new object to a variable of type `object`. This variable is then casted to a type of class `MainClass`. Because the object was created as an object of type `TestClass`, you might expect the cast to convert from an object of type `TestClass` to an object of type `MainClass`.

However, C# does not perform casts based on the type used when the object is created. Instead, it performs casts based on the type of variable used to hold the new object. In Listing 20-1, the new object is assigned to a variable of type `object`. Therefore, the C# compiler generates code that casts an object from type `object` to type `MainClass`. Because a conversion from `object` to `MainClass` is not defined, the cast conversion fails.

Understanding Structure Initialization

As you know, structures can contain language constructs also found in classes, including methods, fields, and properties. You assign values to a structure's methods and fields using a simple assignment statement. However, it's important to remember that the difference between a property and a field is that assigning a value to a property executes code compiled into the structure. This means that extra care must be taken when assigning values to properties of newly created structures. You take a look at this issue in this section.

Initializing structures

Listing 20-2 contains two structures. The first structure is called
`StructWithPublicMembers` and contains two public integer members called X and
Y. The second structure is called `StructWithProperties` and contains public
properties called X and Y, which manage two private integers.

The `Main()` method in Listing 20-2 creates two variables, one having the
`StructWithPublicMembers` structure type and another having the
`StructWithProperties` structure type. The code then assigns values to the X and
Y members of each structure.

Listing 20-2: Accessing Structures with Properties and Public Members

```
public struct StructWithPublicMembers
{
    public int X;
    public int Y;
}

public struct StructWithProperties
{
    private int PrivateX;
    private int PrivateY;

    public int X
    {
        get
        {
            return PrivateX;
        }
        set
        {
            PrivateX = value;
        }
    }

    public int Y
    {
        get
        {
            return PrivateY;
        }
        set
        {
            PrivateY = value;
        }
    }
}
```

```
public class MainClass
{
    public static void Main()
    {
        StructWithPublicMembers MembersStruct;
        StructWithProperties    PropertiesStruct;

        MembersStruct.X = 100;
        MembersStruct.Y = 200;

        PropertiesStruct.X = 100;
        PropertiesStruct.Y = 200;
    }
}
```

Listing 20-2 does not compile. The C# compiler issues the following error:

```
error CS0165: Use of unassigned local variable
'PropertiesStruct'
```

The interesting aspect of this error is that it references the second structure variable defined in the Main() method. The C# compiler does, however, compile the code that works with the first structure variable. In other words, accessing public members in Listing 20-2 is acceptable, but accessing public properties in Listing 20-2 is not. What is the difference?

Resolving initialization problems

The short answer is that the code must use the new operator to create a new structure instance. Listing 20-2 compiles if new structure references are created:

```
StructWithProperties    PropertiesStruct = new
StructWithProperties();
```

The reasoning behind this answer has to do with the fact that properties are implemented by the C# compiler as public functions when it generates the Microsoft Intermediate Language (MSIL) code for the application. You can prove this by looking at the MSIL generated by the C# compiler. The .NET Framework ships with a tool called ILDASM, which stands for ILDisASseMbler. You can use this tool to examine the Intermediate Language (IL) and metadata for any CLR-compatible binary output by a .NET compiler.

Modify Listing 20-2 to include the new operation and compile it to an executable called Listing20-2.exe. After the executable is generated, you can look into the executable's contents with ILDASM. Use the following command line to start the IL disassembler with the executable from Listing 20-2:

```
ildasm Listing20-2.exe
```

Figure 20-1 shows the open ILDASM window with the Listing20-2.exe executable loaded. The executable contains the manifest, which includes identification information for the executable, and also contains metadata describing the code found in the executable.

Figure 20-1: ILDASM loaded with the executable from Listing 20-2

ILDASM displays the executable's classes and structures in a tree view format. The StructWithPublicMembers portion of the tree shows two public variables of type int32 called X and Y. These variables reflect the two properties designed into the structure.

The StructWithProperties portion of the tree shows the two private variables; it also shows four methods that weren't written into the structure:

✦ int32 get_X()

✦ int32 get_Y()

✦ void set_X(int32)

✦ void set_Y(int32)

These methods actually implement the structure's property access. The get_X() method contains the code from the get accessor of the X property, and the get_Y() method contains the code from the get accessor of the Y property. Likewise, the set_X() method contains the code from the set accessor of the X property, and the set_Y() method contains the code from the set accessor of the Y property. This means that when your code accesses a property, you are actually calling a method that implements the functionality of the property.

The problem with Listing 20-2 is that the PropertiesStruct variable is not initialized with a new operator before it is used. This means that the variable is not associated with a structure instance, and methods cannot be called on instances that don't exist. The property statements in the Main() method force the underlying property methods to be called, but there is no instance to use for the call. The C# compiler detects this problem and issues the error message shown after Listing 20-2.

The public member initialization is successful because classes and structures can be initialized directly, without using a constructor, as long as all of the instance's variables have been explicitly given a value.

Understanding Derived Classes

When discussed with regards to C# classes, you saw how classes can be derived from other classes. Derived classes inherit functionality from their parent, or base, class. The relationship between a derived class and a base class is referred to as an "is-a" relationship in object-oriented terms. All classes in C# ultimately derive from the .NET System.Object type, for example, so you can say that your class "is-a" System.Object.

Because all derived classes inherit functionality from their base class, you might assume that objects of a derived class can be used anywhere where an object of the class' base class is expected. The type safety built into the C# language takes precedence, however, and the code in this section explains the issue.

Passing derived classes

Listing 20-3 contains a class called TestClass that contains a public method called Test(). The Test() method accepts a reference to an object as a parameter.

Listing 20-3 also contains a class called MainClass, which creates both an object of the class TestClass and a string. The string is used as the parameter to the call to the TestClass object's Test() method.

Listing 20-3: Passing Strings Where Objects Are Expected

```
public class TestClass
{
    public void Test(ref object ObjectReference)
    {
    }
}

public class MainClass
{
    public static void Main()
    {
        TestClass TestObject = new TestClass();
        string TestString = "Hello from C#!";

        TestObject.Test(ref TestString);
    }
}
```

Listing 20-3 does not compile. The C# compiler issues the following errors:

```
Listing20-3.cs(16,9): error CS1502: The best overloaded method
match for 'TestClass.Test(ref object)' has some invalid
arguments

Listing20-3.cs(16,29): error CS1503: Argument '1': cannot
convert from 'ref string' to 'ref object'
```

At first glance, this doesn't seem reasonable. Because every .NET data type is an object, any data type should ultimately be converted into a variable of type `object`. This should include the `string` object. Why can't the `string` object be implicitly converted into a variable of type `object`?

Resolving issues that arise when passing derived classes

The compiling problem stems from the strict type safety rules built into the C# language. The `Test()` method in Listing 20-3 takes a value of type `object` as a parameter, and the compiler issues an error if anything other than an object is supplied.

Another problem with the approach in Listing 20-3 results from the `ref` parameter modifier used in the `Test()` method. The `ref` modifier enables the method implementation to change the value of the variable, and the change is visible to the caller. This gives the `Test()` method the license to overwrite the

ObjectReference variable with any value that can be casted back to an object. Consider the following alternative implementation of the Test() method:

```
public void Test(ref object ObjectReference)
{
    TestClass TestObject;

    TestObject = new TestClass();
    ObjectReference = (object)TestObject;
}
```

In this implementation, an object of class TestClass is created, the ObjectReference reference variable is assigned to the new object, and the caller sees this assignment.

The problem is that Listing 20-3 passes a string into the Test() method. With this new implementation of the Test() method placed in Listing 20-3, the caller would pass a string in and would get a TestClass object back. The caller might not expect the variable's type to be changed to a different type than what the caller originally supplied, and numerous problems would arise if the caller continued to work with the code under the assumption that the variable is still a string. C# avoids this problem by mandating that only correct parameter types be used when methods are called.

Using Non-Integers as Array Elements

The C# language specifies that only integers can be used as array elements. Sometimes, however, you run into situations in which integers are not the most convenient way to express an array index in your code. Consider a chessboard, for example, where a letter from A through H traditionally references the eight columns of the board, and a number from 1 through 8 traditionally references the eight rows of the board. If you need to represent a chessboard in your C# code, you might choose to use a two-dimensional rectangular array:

```
int [,] Chessboard;

Chessboard = new int [8,8];
```

After the chessboard array is initialized, you might want to reference a cell using the traditional chessboard cell syntax. You might want to reference cell B7, for example, as follows:

```
Chessboard['B',7];
```

You can't do this, however, because C# does not let you use characters, such as the B in this example, as array element references.

Listing 20-4 uses an indexer to solve this problem:

Listing 20-4: Representing a Chessboard with an Indexer

```
using System;

public class Chessboard
{
    private int [,] Board;

    public Chessboard()
    {
        Board = new int[8,8];
    }

    public int this [char Column, int RowIndex]
    {
        get
        {
            int ColumnIndex;

            switch(Column)
            {
                case 'A':
                case 'a':
                    ColumnIndex = 0;
                    break;
                case 'B':
                case 'b':
                    ColumnIndex = 1;
                    break;
                case 'C':
                case 'c':
                    ColumnIndex = 2;
                    break;
                case 'D':
                case 'd':
                    ColumnIndex = 3;
                    break;
                case 'E':
                case 'e':
                    ColumnIndex = 4;
                    break;
                case 'F':
                case 'f':
                    ColumnIndex = 5;
                    break;
                case 'G':
                case 'g':
                    ColumnIndex = 6;
                    break;
```

```
                case 'H':
                case 'h':
                    ColumnIndex = 7;
                    break;
                default:
                    throw new Exception("Illegal column
specifier.");
            }
            Console.WriteLine("(returning cell [{0},{1}]",
ColumnIndex, RowIndex);
            return Board[ColumnIndex, RowIndex];
        }
    }
}

public class MainClass
{
    public static void Main()
    {
        int        CellContents;
        Chessboard MyChessboard = new Chessboard();

        CellContents = MyChessboard ['B', 7];
    }
}
```

The code in Listing 20-4 declares a class called Chessboard to represent a chess-board. The class includes a private, two-dimensional array of integers called Board, which can be used to represent which chess pieces are on which cells in the board. (In the interests of keeping the code listing simple, the array is not actually used.)

The class also implements an indexer with a get accessor. The indexer accepts two parameters: a character and an integer. The indexer assumes that the character specified in the first parameter represents a column identifier, and it translates the character into a column in the private array. A column specifier of A translates to column 0 in the private Board array; a column specifier of B translates to column 1 in the private Board array, and so on. The indexer writes a message specifying the translated index elements to the console and then returns the value of the array element referenced by the indexer parameters.

The Main() method in Listing 20-4 creates a new object of type Chessboard and uses the indexer to reference square B7:

```
CellContents = MyChessboard ['B', 7];
```

When the code in Listing 20-4 is run, the code in the Main() method calls the indexer, which prints the following out to the console:

```
(returning cell [1,7]
```

The indexer translated the first parameter, B, into the integer-based column reference that the C# compiler needs to access an element in the private array. This scheme enables you to design classes that use a syntax that is natural to the application — character-based array element indexes, in this case — while still adhering to the C# requirement of integer-based array element indexes.

Summary

The best way to solve a tough C# programming problem is to try different coding methods with the compiler. Don't be afraid to experiment. The C# compiler tells you if you do something wrong.

You might also consider making use of the ILDASM tool to get under the hood of your assemblies and see how the C# compiler makes executable code from your source code. Understanding the code that the C# compiler generates can help your understanding of why your code works the way it does. In this chapter, you learned that the property accessor code that you write is turned into special methods by the C# compiler. This may be hard to figure out without looking at the code generated by ILDASM. The ILDASM tool works with any assembly produced by a .NET compiler that generates MSIL. Examine some assemblies and .NET applications with ILDASM. Load them into the tool and see how they are built. Looking at other assemblies and their content can give you a better understanding of how .NET code works, and can help make you a better .NET developer.

✦   ✦   ✦

Developing .NET Solutions Using C#

Building WindowsForms Applications

Much of the material written about the .NET Framework has centered on the support given to developers writing Internet applications. The ASP.NET engine and the "software as a service" development models are indeed powerful tools for developing Internet applications. However, the .NET Framework is not just about the Internet.

Microsoft realizes that although many developers are writing Internet-based applications, many other developers are writing desktop-based, Win32-style desktop applications. The .NET Framework has not forgotten these developers. It includes a set of .NET classes that makes it easy to develop Windows desktop applications using a .NET-compatible language. This set of classes and the programming model that it supports is called WindowsForms.

In this chapter, you take a look at the basic structure of a WindowsForms application. You will see how a basic form is created and how controls are added to forms. We'll take a look at the .NET Framework classes available for use in a WindowsForms application, and we'll also take a look at some of the assembly attributes that you can use to add version and copyright information to your applications.

Understanding WindowsForms Architecture

Developing a WindowsForms application requires that you understand how the WindowsForms base classes are used with your .NET applications. This section examines the architecture of the WindowsForms class library.

All the classes that you use to build your WindowsForms applications reside in a .NET Framework namespace called `System.Windows.Forms`. This namespace contains all the classes that you need to build rich Windows desktop applications. These classes enable you to work with forms, buttons, edit controls, check boxes, lists, and many other user-interface elements. All of these classes are at your disposal and ready to use in your WindowsForms applications.

WindowsForms applications make use of two fundamental .NET Framework classes: the `Form` class, which manages the application's forms and the controls placed on the form, and the `Application` class, which manages the application's handling of Windows messages sent to and received from the forms in the application. Both of these classes reside in the .NET Framework's `System.Windows.Forms` namespace and make up the basic anatomy of a WindowsForms application.

The Form class

The `System.Windows.Forms` namespace includes a base class called `Form`. The `Form` class represents a form, or window, in your application. When you create a WindowsForms application in C#, you design a window class and use the `Form` class as the base class for your window class. Your window class inherits all the basic behavior of a window and adds the functionality you need to fit the needs of your application. All the basic window behaviors are built into the base `Form` class, and you inherit all of that behavior automatically if you derive your window classes from the `Form` class.

The Application class

Form classes define the look and feel of a window in your application, but they do not run by themselves. WindowsForms must be run within the context of an application. The `System.Windows.Forms` namespace includes a class called `Application`, which contains methods that help you manage your WindowsForms application.

The `Application` class contains methods that enable you to start, manage, and stop WindowsForms applications. WindowsForms respond to events initiated by the user, such as moving the mouse or pressing a key on the keyboard. Since the very early days of Windows, the Windows desktop application architecture has been designed around the concept of a *message loop*.

In a standard Windows application, the main piece of code sits in a loop and receives messages from the Windows operating system. When the user moves the mouse, presses a key on the keyboard, selects a menu item, or performs any other operation that a window might want to act on, the operating system makes a note of the action and sends a message to the appropriate window, informing the window of the action. It is the responsibility of the window code to handle the message in an appropriate manner.

In the WindowsForms architecture, the basic concepts remain the same. WindowsForms applications have a piece of code that waits for user interaction messages to come from the operating system, which then routes the messages to the appropriate window. In the WindowsForms architecture, the Application class is the main code that manages this message handling, and the Forms class is the class that handles the messages sent to it by the Application class.

The Application class is sealed. You cannot derive classes from it. Its methods are static, which means that you can call its methods without having an object of the Application class available.

Creating Your First WindowsForms Application

Listing 21-1 shows a simple WindowsForms application. It represents a simple WindowsForms application that displays a single form and keeps running until the user closes the form.

Listing 21-1: The Hello, WindowsForms Application

```
using System.Windows.Forms;

public class SimpleHelloWorld : Form
{
    public static void Main()
    {
        Application.Run(new SimpleHelloWorld());
    }

    public SimpleHelloWorld()
    {
        Text = "Hello, WindowsForms!";
    }
}
```

The code in Listing 21-1 declares a class called SimpleHelloWorld. It derives from the .NET Framework Form class, which qualifies the class as a Windows Form class. The class contains a Main() method, which creates a new object of the SimpleHelloWorld class and uses that object as the parameter to a method in the Application class called Run(). The constructor of the SimpleHelloWorld class sets the inherited Text property to Hello, WindowsForms!. This string is displayed as the caption of the form. Figure 21-1 shows what the form looks like when the code in Listing 21-1 is executed.

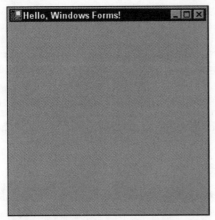

Figure 21-1: Listing 21-1 displays a simple form.

Compiling Your WindowsForms Application

As with console applications designed using C#, WindowsForms applications must be compiled with the C# compiler before you can execute their code. WindowsForms applications compiled with the C# compiler might behave slightly differently when they are launched, depending on how the code was compiled. At a minimum, you can use the following command line when compiling the code in Listing 21-1:

```
csc Listing21-1.cs
```

Like all C# applications, this produces an executable called `Listing21-1.exe`. If you run this executable from a console, the application's window appears. However, something interesting happens when you double-click the executable's icon in Windows Explorer. Launching the executable from Windows Explorer brings up two windows: a console window, which is empty, and the application's WindowsForms window. This behavior differs from most Windows applications. Most Windows applications don't bring up an empty console window when the application is launched. Why does the executable for Listing 21-1 bring up a console window and, more important, how can you get rid of it?

By default, the C# compiler generates console applications. These applications require a console window so that methods, such as `Console.WriteLine()`, have a console to write their messages out to. The .NET runtime interrogates the executable when it is launched, and if the executable is built as a console application, the runtime loader creates a new console window for the application. If you were to build Listing 21-1 using the default C# compiler command line, you would generate a console-based .NET application. This explains the empty console window that appears when the generated executable is run.

WindowsForms work with windows, not with consoles, and the console window is not needed for WindowsForms applications. The C# compiler supports a command-line argument called `target` that you can use to specify the type of application being built. You can use this argument to tell the C# compiler that you want to build a Windows application that does not need a console. The following command line

```
csc /target:winexe Listing21-1.cs
```

instructs the C# compiler to compile the `Listing21-1.cs` file and use its contents to build a Windows executable that does not need a console. If you use this command line to build the code in Listing 21-1, launching the executable from within Windows Explorer brings up the application's form without also bringing up an empty console window.

Note The C# compiler accepts `/t` as shorthand for `/target`. The preceding command line can be shortened to `csc /t:winexe Listing21-1.cs`.

Understanding Assemblies: Adding Version Information to Your WindowsForms Applications

By default, WindowsForms applications do not carry any version information. However, you can use attributes built into the .NET Framework to add version information to your applications. These attributes take effect at the assembly level and are added to the code that the C# compiler outputs. All of these attributes are optional, but using them adds version and copyright information to your .NET binaries. Adding this information enables end users to use the Windows Explorer to right-click the application, select Properties from the context menu, and inspect your embedded attribute values. End users can inspect version and copyright information for your .NET WindowsForms applications just as they can inspect the same information from standard Win32 applications.

The classes that implement these attributes are in a .NET namespace called `System.Reflection`. When using these attributes, you must either reference this namespace with the `using` keyword or prefix the assembly names with the namespace name.

Some of the information specified in these attributes is written into the assembly's manifest, and other pieces of information are stored as a version information resource embedded in the assembly's executable. You can view the assembly's manifest through the ILDASM tool, and you can view the executable's version information resource by right-clicking the file in Windows Explorer and choosing Properties ➪ Version.

Tip You can add these attributes to any .NET code project. The version information is always available in the compiled output of your code.

In this section, you take a look at the following attributes:

✦ `AssemblyTitle`, which assigns a title to the assembly

✦ `AssemblyDescription`, which assigns a description to the assembly

✦ `AssemblyConfiguration`, which describes options used when the assembly was built

✦ `AssemblyCompany`, which assigns a company name to the assembly

✦ `AssemblyProduct`, which assigns product information to the assembly

✦ `AssemblyCopyright`, which assigns copyright information to the assembly

✦ `AssemblyTrademark`, which assigns trademark information to the assembly

✦ `AssemblyCulture`, which assigns locale information to the assembly

✦ `AssemblyVersion`, which assigns a version number to the assembly

AssemblyTitle

The `AssemblyTitle` attribute enables you to give a title to the assembly. The attribute takes a string parameter in its constructor that specifies the title, as shown in the following example:

```
[assembly: AssemblyTitle("Listing 21-2")]
```

The assembly title isn't written to the assembly's manifest, but is available in the `Description` field of the compiled file's version information block.

AssemblyDescription

The `AssemblyDescription` attribute enables you to provide a description for the assembly. The attribute takes a string parameter in its constructor that specifies the description, as shown in the following example:

```
[assembly: AssemblyDescription("This executable was produced by
compiling the code in Listing 21-2.")]
```

The assembly description is written to the assembly's manifest; it is also available in the `Comments` field of the compiled file's version information block.

AssemblyConfiguration

The `AssemblyConfiguration` attribute enables you to specify build configuration information for the assembly. For example, assembly configuration information may specify whether the assembly is built for a retail or debug configuration. The attribute takes a string parameter in its constructor that specifies the configuration information, as shown in the following example:

```
[assembly: AssemblyConfiguration("retail")]
```

The assembly description is written to the assembly's manifest, but isn't available in the compiled file's version information block.

AssemblyCompany

The `AssemblyCompany` attribute enables you to specify a company name to associate with the assembly. The attribute takes a string parameter in its constructor that specifies the company name, as shown in the following example:

```
[assembly: AssemblyCompany("John Wiley, Inc.")]
```

The assembly company name is written to the assembly's manifest; it is also available in the `Company Name` field of the compiled file's version information block.

AssemblyProduct

The `AssemblyProduct` attribute enables you to specify a product name to associate with the assembly. The attribute takes a string parameter in its constructor that specifies the product name, as shown in the following example:

```
[assembly: AssemblyProduct("C# Bible")]
```

The assembly product name is written to the assembly's manifest; it is also available in the `Product Name` field of the compiled file's version information block.

AssemblyCopyright

The `AssemblyCopyright` attribute enables you to specify copyright information for the assembly. The attribute takes a string parameter in its constructor that specifies the copyright information, as shown in the following example:

```
[assembly: AssemblyCopyright("(c) 2002 John Wiley, Inc.")]
```

The assembly product name is written to the assembly's manifest; it is also available in the `Copyright` field of the compiled file's version information block.

AssemblyTrademark

The `AssemblyTrademark` attribute enables you to specify trademark information for the assembly. The attribute takes a string parameter in its constructor that specifies the trademark information, as shown in the following example:

```
[assembly: AssemblyTrademark("Windows is a trademark of
Microsoft Corporation.")]
```

The assembly product name is written to the assembly's manifest; it is also available in the Legal Trademarks field of the compiled file's version information block.

AssemblyCulture

The AssemblyCulture attribute enables you to specify culture information for the assembly. Culture information specifies the language and country information that the assembly uses to do its work. The attribute takes a string parameter in its constructor that specifies the culture information, as shown in the following example:

```
[assembly: AssemblyCulture("us-en")]
```

Culture strings are defined by an Internet standard called RFC1766. The standard is titled Tags for the Identification of Languages and is available on the Internet at www.ietf.org/rfc/rfc1766.txt. The assembly product name is written to the assembly's manifest; it is also available in the Legal Trademarks field of the compiled file's version information block.

Note   Culture information can be added only to libraries and modules. Culture information cannot be added to executables, because executables cannot be localized. Only library-based assemblies can be localized. If you try to add the AssemblyCulture attribute to a code base that is compiled into an executable target, the C# compiler issues the following error message:

```
error CS0647: Error emitting
'System.Reflection.AssemblyCultureAttribute' attribute -
- 'Executables cannot be localized, Culture should
always be empty'
```

The assembly description is written to the assembly's manifest, but isn't available in the compiled file's version information block.

AssemblyVersion

The AssemblyVersion attribute enables you to assign a version number to your assembly. Version numbers in .NET come in four parts:

✦ A major version number

✦ A minor version number

✦ A revision number

✦ A build number

Each of these parts is separated by a period. The attribute takes a string parameter in its constructor that specifies the version number, as shown in the following example:

```
[assembly: AssemblyVersion("1.0.0.0")]
```

You must always specify a version number. If you specify a major and a minor version number, you can let the C# compiler autogenerate the other numbers when the code is built. You may want to do this if you want each build of your code to have a unique version number. By using the asterisk character for a build number, the C# compiler automatically assigns one. The generated build number is equal to the number of days since January 1, 2000, as shown in the following example:

```
[assembly: AssemblyVersion("1.0.0.*")]
```

This example gives the assembly a major version of 1, a minor version of 0, a revision number of 0, and a build number automatically assigned by the C# compiler.

If you use an asterisk for a revision number, the C# compiler automatically assigns a revision number and a build number. The generated revision number is equal to the number of seconds since midnight local time, modulo 2. The generated build number is equal to the number of days since January 1, 2000, as shown in the following example:

```
[assembly: AssemblyVersion("1.0.*")]
```

This example gives the assembly a major version of 1, a minor version of 0, and revision numbers and build numbers automatically assigned by the C# compiler.

The assembly product name is written to the assembly's manifest; it is also available in the `Assembly Version`, `Product Version`, and `File Version` fields of the compiled file's version information block.

Listing 21-2 adds assembly version attributes to the code in Listing 21-1.

Listing 21-2: **Simple Windows Form Application with Version Information**

```
using System.Reflection;
using System.Windows.Forms;

[assembly: AssemblyTitle("Listing 21-2")]
[assembly: AssemblyDescription("This executable was produced by
compiling the code in Listing 21-2.")]
```

Continued

Listing 21-2 *(continued)*

```
[assembly: AssemblyConfiguration("Retail")]
[assembly: AssemblyCompany("John Wiley, Inc.")]
[assembly: AssemblyProduct("C# Bible")]
[assembly: AssemblyCopyright("(c) 2002 John Wiley, Inc.")]
[assembly: AssemblyVersion("1.0.*")]

public class SimpleHelloWorld : Form
{
    public static void Main()
    {
        Application.Run(new SimpleHelloWorld());
    }

    public SimpleHelloWorld()
    {
        Text = "Hello, WindowsForms!";
    }
}
```

Taking a Closer Look at the Application Object

The Application object contains properties, methods, and events that you can use in your WindowsForms code. In this section, you take a look at the class members that you'll use most often.

Understanding Application events

The Application class supports four events that you can handle in your WindowsForms applications:

✦ The ApplicationExit event is fired when the application is about to shut down. Delegates of type EventHandler can be assigned to this event. The EventHandler delegate is defined in the .NET System namespace. The delegate takes two parameters: an object that references the object sending the event and an EventArgs object specifying event arguments. It does not return any value.

✦ The Idle event is fired when the application finishes dispatching messages from the operating system and is about to enter the idle state. The application leaves the idle state when it determines that more messages need to be processed. Delegates of type EventHandler can be assigned to this event. The

EventHandler delegate is defined in the .NET System namespace. The delegate takes two parameters, an object that references the object sending the event, and an EventArgs object specifying event arguments. It does not return any value.

✦ The ThreadException event is fired when an untrapped thread exception is thrown. Delegates of type ThreadExecptionEventHandler can be assigned to this event. The ThreadExecptionEventHandler delegate is defined in the .NET System.Threading namespace. The delegate takes two parameters: an object that references the object sending the event and a ThreadingExceptionEventArgs object specifying event arguments. It does not return any value.

✦ The ThreadExit event fires when a thread is about to shut down. When the main thread for an application is about to be shut down, this event is raised first, followed by an ApplicationExit event. Delegates of type EventHandler can be assigned to this event. The EventHandler delegate is defined in the .NET System namespace. The delegate takes two parameters: an object that references the object sending the event and an EventArgs object specifying event arguments. It does not return any value.

Working with events in code

The code in Listing 21-3 adds to the form code in Listing 21-2 by handling events from the Application object.

Listing 21-3: **Handling Application Events**

```
using System;
using System.Threading;
using System.Reflection;
using System.Windows.Forms;

[assembly: AssemblyTitle("Listing 21-3")]
[assembly: AssemblyDescription("This executable was produced by
compiling the code in Listing 21-3.")]
[assembly: AssemblyCompany("John Wiley, Inc.")]
[assembly: AssemblyProduct("C# Bible")]
[assembly: AssemblyCopyright("(c) 2002 John Wiley, Inc.")]
[assembly: AssemblyVersion("1.0.*")]

public class HelloWorldForm : Form
{
    public HelloWorldForm()
    {
        Text = "Hello, WindowsForms!";
    }
```

Continued

Listing 21-3 *(continued)*

```
}

public class ApplicationEventHandlerClass
{
    public void OnApplicationExit(object sender, EventArgs e)
    {
        try
        {
            Console.WriteLine("The application is shutting
down.");
        }
        catch(NotSupportedException)
        {
        }
    }

    public void OnIdle(object sender, EventArgs e)
    {
        Console.WriteLine("The application is idle.");
    }

    public void OnThreadException(object sender,
ThreadExceptionEventArgs e)
    {
        Console.WriteLine("an exception thrown from an
application thread was caught!");
    }

    public void OnThreadExit(object sender, EventArgs e)
    {
        Console.WriteLine("The application's main thread is
shutting down.");
    }
}

public class MainClass
{
    public static void Main()
    {
        HelloWorldForm FormObject = new HelloWorldForm();
        ApplicationEventHandlerClass AppEvents = new
ApplicationEventHandlerClass();

        Application.ApplicationExit += new
EventHandler(AppEvents.OnApplicationExit);
        Application.Idle += new EventHandler(AppEvents.OnIdle);
        Application.ThreadException += new
ThreadExceptionEventHandler(AppEvents.OnThreadException);
```

```
        Application.ThreadExit += new
EventHandler(AppEvents.OnThreadExit);
        Application.Run(FormObject);
    }
}
```

The new class in Listing 21-3 is called `ApplicationEventHandlerClass` and contains methods that handle the events fired from the `Application` object. The `Main()` method creates an object of the `ApplicationEventHandlerClass` and adds its code to the `Application` class's list of event handlers.

The event handlers in the `ApplicationEventHandlerClass` write to the console. This is perfectly legal, even in a WindowsForms application. If you compile the code in Listing 21-3 using the console executable target (`csc /target:exe Listing21-3.cs`), the event handler messages are written to the console window that is used to start the application. If you compile the code in Listing 21-3 using the Windows executable target (`csc /target:winexe Listing21-3.cs`), no console is associated with the process and the console messages aren't displayed.

Understanding Application properties

The `Application` class supports several properties that you can use in your C# applications. The following sections describe how to use each of these properties.

AllowQuit

The Boolean `AllowQuit` property specifies whether your code can programmatically end the application. The property returns `True` if your code can instruct the application to exit and `False` otherwise. This property is read-only and cannot be set. Ordinarily, users can end applications by closing the application's main form. Some applications are hosted in containers, such as Web browsers, and those applications cannot be programmatically ended. They exit only when their container closes. If the `AllowQuit` property returns `true`, you can call an Application method called `Exit()` to programmatically end the application. You examine the methods of the `Application` object in the section titled "Understanding Application Methods."

CommonAppDataRegistry

The `CommonAppDataRegistry` property returns a reference to an object of class `RegistryKey`. The returned `RegistryKey` object references a key in the Registry that the application can use to store Registry data that should be available to all users of the application. This property is read-only and cannot be set.

The `RegistryKey` class is a part of the .NET Framework and is available in a namespace called `Microsoft.Win32`. It represents a specific key in the Registry and contains methods that enable you to create subkeys, read values, and perform other work related to Registry keys.

CommonAppDataPath

The string `CommonAppDataPath` property references a path on the file system that the application can use to store file-based data that should be available to all users of the application. This property is read-only and cannot be set.

The application data path is stored beneath the Windows documents folder path used for all users, which is usually a path such as `C:\Documents and Settings\All Users\Application Data`. The actual application path points to a folder beneath this "all users" document path having the form `CompanyName\ProductName\ ProductVersion`. The `CompanyName`, `ProductName`, and `ProductVersion` folder names are based on the values of the application properties of the same name. If you do not set these properties, the `Application` class provides reasonable defaults. The code in Listing 21-1, for example, has a common application data path of `C:\Documents and Settings\All Users\Application Data\SimpleHelloWorld\SimpleHelloWorld\V0.0`. If the code in Listing 21-1 were to set the `Application` class's `CompanyName`, `ProductName`, or `ProductVersion` properties, the folder names in the common application data path would change to reflect the values of those properties.

The product version folder path uses only the major and minor version numbers specified in your application, regardless of the number of values you set in your application's `[AssemblyVersion]` attribute. If your application uses an `[AssemblyVersion]` attribute with a value of `1.2.3.4`, for example, the version number portion of the common application data path will be `1.2`. The letter `V` always prefixes your application's major version number in the version number portion of the data path.

CompanyName

The string `CompanyName` property returns the company name associated with the application. This property is read-only and cannot be set. By default, this value is set to the name of the class containing the application's `Main()` method. If your application specifies a company name with the `[AssemblyCompany]` attribute, the value of that attribute is used as the value of the application's `CompanyName` property.

CurrentCulture

The `CurrentCulture` property enables you to work with the culture information for the application. This property can be read from and written to. The property has a class of type `CultureInfo`, which is a class defined by the .NET Framework and found in the `System.Globalization` namespace. The `CultureInfo` class contains methods and properties that enable your code to work with data specific to the cultural environment in which the application is executing. Information, such as the preferred date/time format, calendar settings, and numbering formats, are available from `CultureInfo` objects.

CurrentInputLanguage

The `CurrentInputLanguage` property enables you to work with the application's current input language. The property has a class of type `InputLanguage`, which is a class defined by the .NET Framework and found in the `System.Windows.Forms` namespace. The `InputLanguage` class contains methods and properties that enable your code to work with the application's understanding of the physical keys on a keyboard and how they relate to characters that can be input into an application. Different language-specific versions of Windows map the physical keyboard keys to different language-specific characters, and the `CurrentInputLanguage` class specifies what this mapping looks like.

ExecutablePath

The string `ExecutablePath` property returns the path of the application's executable. This property is read-only and cannot be set.

LocalUserAppDataPath

The string `LocalUserAppDataPath` property references a path on the file system that the application can use to store file-based data that should be available to the user currently logged into the machine. This property is read-only and cannot be set. It is used for local users with operating system profiles on the local machine. Users who have roaming profiles that are used across the network use a separate property, called `UserAppDataPath`, to specify where their application data should be stored.

Like the `CommonAppDataPath` property, the local user data path points to a folder beneath the logged in user's documents path with a folder structure having the form `CompanyName\ ProductName\ ProductVersion`. The `CompanyName`, `ProductName`, and `ProductVersion` folder names are based on the values of the application properties of the same name. If you do not set these properties, the `Application` class provides reasonable defaults. If your code sets the `Application` class's `CompanyName`, `ProductName`, or `ProductVersion` properties, the folder names in the local user application data path change to reflect the values of those properties.

Like the common application data path, the product version folder path uses only the major and minor version numbers specified in your application, regardless of the number of values you set in your application's `[AssemblyVersion]` attribute. If your application uses an `[AssemblyVersion]` attribute with a value of `1.2.3.4`, for example, the version number portion of the local user application data path is `1.2`. The letter `V` always prefixes your application's major version number in the version number portion of the data path.

MessageLoop

The Boolean MessageLoop property returns True if a message loop exists for the application and False otherwise. This property is read-only and cannot be set. Because all WindowsForms applications need a message loop so that Windows messages can be routed to the correct form, WindowsForms applications return True for this property.

ProductName

The string ProductName property returns the product name associated with the application. This property is read-only and cannot be set. By default, this value is set to the name of the class containing the application's Main() method. If your application specifies a product name with the [AssemblyProduct] attribute, the value of that attribute is used as the value of the application's ProductName property.

ProductVersion

The string ProductVersion property returns the version number associated with the application. This property is read-only and cannot be set. By default, this value is set to 0.0.0.0. If your application specifies a version number with the [AssemblyVersion] attribute, the value of that attribute is used as the value of the application's ProductVersion property.

SafeTopLevelCaptionFormat

The string SafeTopLevelCaptionFormat property references a format string that the runtime applies to top-level window captions when the applications execute from an unsafe context.

Security is an integral part of the .NET Framework and the Common Language Runtime (CLR). The CLR honors the different security zones set up in Internet Explorer (Internet, Local Intranet, Trusted Sites, and Restricted Sites), and restricts runtime services to applications that run in untrusted zones. WindowsForms applications that are run from untrusted zones, such as the Internet zone, are adorned with a warning label that describes the application as originating from an untrusted location. The text of this warning label is formatted based on the string format template stored in the SafeTopLevelCaptionFormat property.

StartupPath

The string StartupPath property returns the path to the executable file that launched the application. This property returns only the path. It does not include the executable file's name. This property is read-only and cannot be set.

UserAppDataPath

The string UserAppDataPath property references a path on the file system that the application can use to store file-based data that should be available to the network user currently logged into the machine. This property is read-only and cannot be set. It is used for local users with operating system profiles on the network. Users who have local machine profiles that are not used across the network use a separate property, called `LocalUserAppDataPath`, to specify where their application data should be stored.

Like the `CommonAppDataPath` property, the local user data path points to a folder beneath the logged in user's documents path with a folder structure having the form `CompanyName\ ProductName\ ProductVersion`. The `CompanyName`, `ProductName`, and `ProductVersion` folder names are based on the values of the application properties of the same name. If you do not set these properties, the `Application` class provides reasonable defaults. If your code sets the `Application` class's `CompanyName`, `ProductName`, or `ProductVersion` properties, the folder names in the local user application data path change to reflect the values of those properties.

UserAppDataRegistry

The `UserAppDataRegistry` property returns a reference to an object of class `RegistryKey`. Like the `CommonAppDataRegistry` property, the property returns an object of type `RegistryKey`. The returned `RegistryKey` object references a key in the Registry that the application can use to store Registry data that should be available only to the current user of the application. This property is read-only and cannot be set.

Understanding Application methods

The `Application` class supports eight methods that you can call from your C# applications. These methods are described in the following sections.

AddMessageFilter

The `AddMessageFilter()` method adds a message filter to your application to monitor Windows messages as they are routed to their destinations. The message filter that you install into your application receives the Windows messages before they are sent along to your form. A message filter installed by `AddMessageFilter()` can choose to handle a message that is sent to it, and the filter can choose whether the message should be forwarded to your form.

Listing 21-4 shows how a message filter can be used in a WindowsForms application. The message handler looks for messages that announce when the left mouse button is clicked on the form.

Listing 21-4: Installing a Message Filter

```csharp
using System;
using System.Windows.Forms;

public class BlockLeftMouseButtonMessageFilter : IMessageFilter
{
    const int WM_LBUTTONDOWN = 0x201;
    const int WM_LBUTTONUP = 0x202;

    public bool PreFilterMessage(ref Message m)
    {
        if(m.Msg == WM_LBUTTONDOWN)
        {
            Console.WriteLine("The left mouse button is
down.");
            return true;
        }
        if(m.Msg == WM_LBUTTONUP)
        {
            Console.WriteLine("The left mouse button is up.");
            return true;
        }
        return false;
    }
}

public class MainForm : Form
{
    public static void Main()
    {
        MainForm MyForm = new MainForm();
        BlockLeftMouseButtonMessageFilter MsgFilter = new
BlockLeftMouseButtonMessageFilter();

        Application.AddMessageFilter(MsgFilter);
        Application.Run(MyForm);
    }

    public MainForm()
    {
        Text = "Message Filter Test";
    }
}
```

The AddMessageFilter() method takes one argument: an implementation of an
interface called IMessageFilter. The IMessageFilter interface is defined by the
.NET Framework and is found in the System.Windows.Forms namespace. The
IMessageFilter interface declares one method:

```
public bool PreFilterMessage(ref Message m);
```

The PreFilterMessage() method takes as input a reference to an instance of a structure called Message. The Message structure describes a Windows message and contains the following properties:

✦ HWnd, which describes the handle of the window that should receive the message.

✦ LParam, which describes one piece of integer data that is sent with the message.

✦ Msg, which describes the integer ID number for the message. Each possible Windows message has its own integer ID.

✦ Result, which describes the value that should be returned to Windows in response to handling the message.

✦ WParam, which describes another piece of integer data that is sent with the message.

Listing 21-4 begins by declaring a class called BlockLeftMouseButtonMessage-Filter. This class implements the IMessageFilter interface. The implementation of the class's PreFilterMessage() method checks the message ID of the message passed in to the method. It checks whether the ID states that the left mouse button has been pressed down. If so, a message reading The left mouse button is down. is written to the console. It then checks whether the ID states that the left mouse button has been released. If so, a message reading The left mouse button is up. is written to the console.

Note The BlockLeftMouseButtonMessageFilter class declares constants to give names to the Windows messages that the filter is looking for. The names start with WM, **which stands for** Windows Message, **and match the names defined by Microsoft. All the available Windows messages, as well as their numeric values, are documented in the Microsoft Platform SDK documentation.**

Implementations of the PreFilterMessage() method must return a Boolean value describing whether or not the message should be forwarded to your form after it passes through your filter. If the message does not need to be forwarded to your filter, then the filter should return the True value. If the message needs to be forwarded on to your filter, then the filter should return the False value. The message filter in Listing 21-4 returns True for the two messages that it handles and False for all other messages.

The Main() method in Listing 21-4 creates a new object of the BlockLeftMouse ButtonMessageFilter class and uses it in a call to the Application object's AddMessageFilter() method. After the message filter is installed, the main form is created and executed.

You can see the message filter at work by compiling the code in Listing 21-4. When you run the code, the application's main form appears. When the form appears, move the mouse to point the cursor inside the form and click the left mouse button. The mouse click messages is written to the application's console.

DoEvents

The DoEvents() method processes all messages currently in the application's Windows message queue. The method does not take any arguments and does not return a value. You may want to call this method if you want to make sure that waiting Windows messages are sent along to your form while you are doing other work.

Suppose, for example, that you create a form that performs a lengthy calculation. If another window is moved in front of your form while the calculation is performed, Windows sends your application a Windows message stating that your form needs to be repainted. However, because your code is performing your lengthy calculation, the repaint message will be sitting in your application's message queue; after all, your code is busy performing calculations and is not processing messages. You can call the DoEvents() method at certain points during your processing to ensure that waiting Windows messages are handled when your code is busy with other work.

Exit

The Exit() method forcibly ends the application. The method informs your application's message queue that it should terminate, and your forms are closed after the last Windows messages in the queue are processed. It does not take any arguments and does not return a value.

In simple cases, your code does not need to call the Exit() method. The default Windows form includes a Close box in the upper-right corner of the form, and clicking that box sends a quit message to your Windows message queue. You may want to call Exit(), however, if your form includes a control, such as a button or a menu item, that should exit the application when it is selected.

ExitThread

The ExitThread() method exits the message loop and closes all forms on the current thread. The method does not take any arguments and does not return a value.

If your WindowsForms application contains only one thread (and most do), then calling ExitThread() is the same as calling Exit(). If, however, your application uses multiple threads, then the two methods behave differently. The ExitThread() method shuts down one thread but allows the other threads to continue running. The Exit() method, however, shuts down all threads at once. Like all Windows processes, WindowsForms applications continue running until the last thread ends.

OleRequired

The OleRequired() method initializes OLE on the application's current thread. If your application will be working with a COM-related technology, such as COM, DCOM, ActiveX, or OLE, you must call this application method before you use COM.

The method does not take any arguments, but it returns a value from an enumeration called ApartmentState that describes the type of COM apartment that the thread entered. The ApartmentState enumeration is defined in a .NET Framework namespace called System.Threading, and it can have one of the following values:

✦ STA is returned when the CLR opts to initialize COM for your thread by entering a single-threaded apartment.

✦ MTA is returned when the CLR opts to initialize COM for your thread by entering a multi-threaded apartment.

OnThreadException

The OnThreadException() method raises a ThreadException event. The event can be caught by an OnThreadException() event handler installed into the Application object.

Listing 21-5 shows how a thread exception can be used in a WindowsForms application.

Listing 21-5: **Working with Thread Exceptions**

```
using System;
using System.Threading;
using System.Windows.Forms;

public class BlockLeftMouseButtonMessageFilter : IMessageFilter
{
    const int WM_LBUTTONDOWN = 0x201;

    public bool PreFilterMessage(ref Message m)
  {
        if(m.Msg == WM_LBUTTONDOWN)
        {
            Exception LeftButtonDownException;

            LeftButtonDownException = new Exception("The left
mouse button was pressed.");

Application.OnThreadException(LeftButtonDownException);
            return true;
```

Continued

Listing 21-5 *(continued)*

```csharp
        }
        return false;
    }
}

public class ApplicationEventHandlerClass
{
    public void OnThreadException(object sender,
ThreadExceptionEventArgs e)
    {
        Exception LeftButtonDownException;

        LeftButtonDownException = e.Exception;
        Console.WriteLine(LeftButtonDownException.Message);
    }
}

public class MainForm : Form
{
    public static void Main()
    {
        ApplicationEventHandlerClass AppEvents = new
ApplicationEventHandlerClass();
        MainForm MyForm = new MainForm();
        BlockLeftMouseButtonMessageFilter MsgFilter = new
BlockLeftMouseButtonMessageFilter();

        Application.AddMessageFilter(MsgFilter);
        Application.ThreadException += new
ThreadExceptionEventHandler(AppEvents.OnThreadException);
        Application.Run(MyForm);
    }

    public MainForm()
    {
        Text = "Application Exception Test";
    }
}
```

Listing 21-5 is similar to Listing 21-4, as it includes a message handler that looks for messages announcing when the left mouse button is clicked on the application's form. The difference is that an exception is thrown in Listing 21-5 when the left mouse button down message is received. The message handler constructs a new Exception object and throws it using the Application object method OnThreadException().

The code in Listing 21-5 also includes an application event handler, which is implemented in a class called ApplicationEventHandlerClass. The class handles the OnThreadException() event, and the application's main method installs the event handler using the Application object's ThreadException property.

The thread exception handler installed in the ApplicationEventHandlerClass class extracts the exception from the handler's ThreadExceptionEventArgs object and prints the exception's message to the console. When you run the code in Listing 21-5, the application's main form appears. When the form appears, move the mouse to point the cursor inside the form and click the left mouse button. The message handler throws an exception, and the application's exception handler prints exception messages to the application's console.

RemoveMessageFilter

The RemoveMessageFilter() method removes a message filter installed by the AddMessageFilter() method. It removes the message filter from the message pump of the application. The RemoveMessageFilter() method takes one argument: an implementation of an interface called IMessageFilter. This argument should reference a class that implements IMessageFilter and has already been used in a call to AddMessageFilter(). Listing 21-6 shows how this method works.

Listing 21-6: Removing an Installed Message Filter

```
using System;
using System.Windows.Forms;

public class BlockLeftMouseButtonMessageFilter : IMessageFilter
{
    const int WM_LBUTTONDOWN = 0x201;

    public bool PreFilterMessage(ref Message m)
  {
        if(m.Msg == WM_LBUTTONDOWN)
        {
            Console.WriteLine("The left mouse button is
down.");
            Application.RemoveMessageFilter(this);
            return true;
```

Continued

Listing 21-6 *(continued)*

```
        }
        return false;
    }
}

public class MainForm : Form
{
public static void Main()
    {
        MainForm MyForm = new MainForm();
        BlockLeftMouseButtonMessageFilter MsgFilter = new
BlockLeftMouseButtonMessageFilter();

        Application.AddMessageFilter(MsgFilter);
        Application.Run(MyForm);
    }

    public MainForm()
    {
        Text = "Message Filter Removal Test";
    }
}
```

The code in Listing 21-6 installs a message filter that looks for the left mouse button down message, just as Listing 21-4 does. The difference here is that the implementation of the message filter in Listing 21-6 removes the message filter when the message is received.

When you run the code in Listing 21-6, note that you get only one message written to the console, regardless of the number of times you click the left mouse button while the mouse pointer is over the form. This is because the message filter is removed from the application when the first message is received; and because the message filter is removed, no further messages will be detected. Messages are still sent to your form, but the code in Listing 21-6 removes the object that gets the first shot at detecting the messages after the object is removed from the application's list of event filters.

Tip   Listing 21-6 uses the keyword this as the parameter to the call to the Application object's RemoveMessageFilter() method. Remember that the this keyword is used to reference the object whose code is being executed. You can think of the statement in Listing 21-6 that calls RemoveMessageFilter() as making the statement "remove the reference to this message filter from the Application object."

Run

The Run() method starts the Windows message loop for an application. All the listings in this chapter have used the Run() method, which accepts a reference to a form object as a parameter. You should already be familiar with the way the Run() method works.

Adding Controls to the Form

The default form created by WindowsForms applications isn't very interesting. It contains a caption bar, a default icon, and the Windows standard Minimize, Maximize and Close buttons. Forms found in real-world applications include controls, such as buttons, text boxes, labels, and the like. This section explains how you can add controls to forms in your C# applications.

In this section, you take a look at how controls are supported from within the .NET Framework. The Framework contains .NET class support for the controls built into the Windows operating system, and the examples in this section will illustrate their use in building WindowsForms applications that use controls on the application's forms.

Understanding the control class hierarchy

The .NET Framework includes several classes in the System.Windows.Forms namespace that encapsulate the behavior of a control. User-interface elements, such as buttons, list boxes, check boxes, and the like, are all represented by a control class.

All of these classes inherit from a base class called Control. Figure 21-2 shows the class hierarchy for the control classes. All user interface controls share some functionality: They must all be able to position themselves on their parent container and manage their foreground and background colors. Because all the controls share this behavior, it makes sense to encapsulate it in a base class and derive the control-specific functionality in derived classes. The authors of the control classes found in the .NET Framework took this design approach when building the classes.

Working with controls on a form

Listing 21-7 shows a WindowsForm application that includes a button. The button displays a message in a message box when clicked.

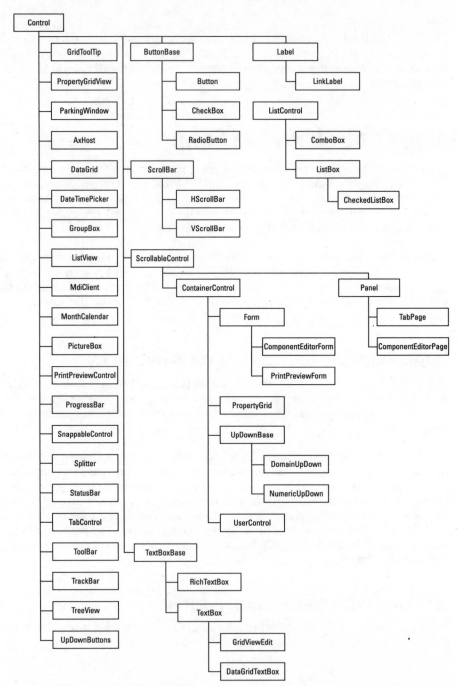

Figure 21-2: Control class hierarchy

Listing 21-7: **Working with a Button on a Form**

```
using System;
using System.Drawing;
using System.Windows.Forms;

public class MainForm : Form
{
    public static void Main()
    {
        MainForm MyForm = new MainForm();

        Application.Run(MyForm);
    }

    public MainForm()
    {
        Button MyButton = new Button();

        Text = "Button Test";
        MyButton.Location = new Point(25, 25);
        MyButton.Text = "Click Me";
        MyButton.Click += new EventHandler(MyButtonClicked);
        Controls.Add(MyButton);
    }

    public void MyButtonClicked(object sender, EventArgs
Arguments)
    {
        MessageBox.Show("The button has been clicked.");
    }
}
```

Listing 21-7 illustrates several important concepts that you need to keep in mind when working with WindowsForms controls. Consider first the form's constructor. It creates a new object of a Button class and sets its position on the form with the button's Location property. This property is inherited from the Control class (which means that the property is available to any control derived from the Control class), and sets the position of the upper-left corner of the button relative to its container. In Listing 21-7, the button's location is set to a position 25 pixels to the right of the form's left edge and 25 pixels below the top of the form. The position is set with a new instance of a structure called Point, which is available in the .NET Framework System.Drawing namespace:

```
MyButton.Location = new Point(25, 25);
```

Tip   Listing 21-7 uses the `Location` property to set the positions of the control. Using this property to programmatically position controls can be tedious for complicated forms with many controls. Visual Studio .NET comes with a forms designer that enables you to visually drag and drop controls onto forms. The designer then generates the equivalent C# forms code for you, freeing you from the burden of having to code all of the positioning logic yourself.

The next important concept in Listing 21-7 has to do with event handling for a control. Control classes support many events that are fired when the user interacts with the control. Many of these events are found in the `Control` base class, although the specific control class handles other events. The most obvious event for a button control would be a `Click` event. Buttons on forms are not useful unless they can respond to a user action of clicking the button.

Controls in the .NET Framework use the standard delegate/event model for supporting their events. Control events are installed using instances of a delegate called `EventHandler`. The `EventHandler` delegate accepts two arguments, an object specifying the sender of the event and an object of a class called `EventArgs` that encapsulates the arguments to the event. The form code in Listing 21-7 includes a method called `MyButtonClicked` that models the `EventHandler` delegate. This method is used as a new event handler and is wired to the button's `Click` event:

```
MyButton.Click += new EventHandler(MyButtonClicked);
```

The `Form` class handles the button's `Click` event by displaying a message box. A class called `MessageBox` supports the display of Windows message boxes. The `MessageBox` class contains a static method called `Show()` that displays a message in a message box.

The last important concept in Listing 21-7 is the statement that adds the control to the form:

```
Controls.Add(MyButton);
```

The `Controls` property is defined in the `Control` base class (remember that the `Form` class is derived from the `Control` class). It is an object of a class called `ControlsCollection` and manages a list of child controls that are managed by the current control. WindowsForms code must add controls to their containing form's `Controls` collection before they can actually be used.

Working with Resources

In Windows, resources are defined as pieces of data that are part of an application but do not affect the execution of the code. These resources may include icons, bitmaps, and strings. The WindowsForms system enables you to store your resources in a separate file during development and include them into an assembly when the application needs to be distributed.

The main advantage to keeping your application's resources in a separate resource repository is to aid in development. If you embed all of your strings inside your C# code, for example, then only someone familiar with C# would know where to look to change the string values. If you write your application using English strings and then need to change your application to display the strings in German, you must read through your source code and change all of the strings. If you keep your strings in a separate string table file, you can hand that separate file off to a translator, who can translate the English strings to the German equivalents without changing your C# source code. In your application, your code will say "read a string from the string table," rather than hardcoding the string in your application.

Working with string resources

String resources are defined in a separate text file, which should have an extension of .txt. The file should contain a set of key/value pairs, separated by an equals sign. The key for each string should be a unique name for the string that you will use in your C# code to reference it. The actual string value follows the equals sign.

You can place comments in your string table files. Comments start with the pound symbol and extend to the end of the line.

Listing 21-8 shows a sample string table file. The file contains one string whose key name is Message and whose value is Hello from the string table!

Listing 21-8: **A Sample String Table Text File**

```
#==============
# String Table
#==============
Message = Hello from the string table!
```

String table files must be compiled into an assembly so that they can be read from your C# applications. The files are compiled into an assembly using a tool called ResGen. The ResGen tool ships with the .NET Framework SDK. It is a console application that reads in the text file and outputs a binary representation of the table with an extension of resources. If the string table in Listing 21-8 were written to a text file called Listing21-8.txt, you could compile the string table using the following command line:

```
resgen Listing21-8.txt
```

This produces a file called Listing21-8.resources. After you build a resources file for your application, you can compile it into your assembly by using the /res argument to the C# compiler, as shown in the following command line:

```
csc /res:string.resources /out:test.exe test.cs
```

This command line instructs the C# compiler to create an executable called test.exe from the C# source file test.cs. It also instructs the C# compiler to embed the resources found in the string.resources file within the test.exe executable. Because the resources are embedded in the executable, you need only ship the executable when you deliver your application. The binary resource file will not be needed at runtime.

After the resources are embedded into your application, you can read the resources from your C# code. Listing 21-9 is a modification of Listing 21-7, in which the message shown in the message box is read from a string resource.

Listing 21-9: **Reading from a String Resource**

```csharp
using System;
using System.Drawing;
using System.Windows.Forms;
using System.Resources;
using System.Reflection;

public class MainForm : Form
{
    public static void Main()
    {
        MainForm MyForm = new MainForm();

        Application.Run(MyForm);
    }

    public MainForm()
    {
        Button MyButton = new Button();

        Text = "Button Test";
        MyButton.Location = new Point(25, 25);
        MyButton.Text = "Click Me";
        MyButton.Click += new EventHandler(MyButtonClicked);
        Controls.Add(MyButton);
    }

    public void MyButtonClicked(object sender, EventArgs Arguments)
    {
        ResourceManager FormResources = new ResourceManager("StringTable",
Assembly.GetExecutingAssembly());
```

```
    string          Message;

    Message = FormResources.GetString("Message");
    MessageBox.Show(Message);
  }
}
```

Listing 21-9 is compiled with a string table resource whose text file contents are as follows:

```
#==============
# String Table
#==============
Message = The button has been clicked.
```

This text file is named `StringTable.txt` and is compiled into a binary resource file called `StringTable.resources` with the following command line:

```
resgen StringTable.txt
```

This command produces a file called `StringTable.resources`. This resource is linked into the application when the main C# code is compiled with the following command line:

```
csc /res:StringTable.resources Listing21-9.cs
```

You can read resources into your C# applications using a .NET Framework class called `ResourceManager`, which is found in a namespace called `System.Resources`. The code in Listing 21-9 creates a new `ResourceManager` object to manage the resources embedded into the executable. The constructor takes two arguments:

✦ The base name of the binary resource file that contains the resource being loaded. You need to specify this name even though you don't need the physical file because your assembly groups the resources into blocks and names the blocks using the base name of the original binary resource file.

✦ A reference to the assembly that contains the resources being loaded. This parameter is a reference to an object of a class called `Assembly`, which is found in the `System.Reflection` namespace. Because the resources being loaded are embedded in the assembly being executed, calling the static method `GetExecutingAssembly()` returns a reference to the current assembly.

After the `ResourceManager` object is initialized, strings can be loaded from the manager using a method called `GetString()`. This method takes one string argument: the key name of the string being retrieved. The method returns the value of the string named by the key.

Working with binary resources

Text-based string tables are not the only resources that you can embed in your assemblies. You can also embed binary resources, such as graphics and icons. Binary resources are encoded using BASE64 encoding into a specially formatted XML document. The XML document has an extension of .resx and is compiled into a resource file using resgen. From there, you can use the methods in the ResourceManager class to work with your binary resources just as you do with your text resources.

Unfortunately, the .NET Framework SDK does not include a tool for generating XML documents with BASE64 encoding, given binary file inputs. However, Visual Studio .NET contains support for embedding binary resources into your assemblies.

Summary

This chapter took a look at the basics of the development process for building WindowsForms applications in C#. It investigated some fundamental classes, such as the Application class, which manages the WindowsForms application as a whole, and the Forms class, which manages a form within the application. You also took a tour through the WindowsForms control class architecture and walked through the assembly attributes that can add version and descriptive information to the assembly.

The .NET Framework contains a rich set of classes for building WindowsForms applications. The WindowsForms subsystem is comprised of several classes; unfortunately, space limitations don't permit a full description of them all in this book. You can examine the documentation for each of the WindowsForms classes. Use the concepts explained in this chapter to start your investigation of all of the classes in the WindowsForms namespace.

✦   ✦   ✦

Creating Web Applications with WebForms

The last decade witnessed unprecedented growth of the Internet as a business platform. Today, the majority of business models are centered around or at least include the concept of the Internet. The focus, therefore, has shifted from desktop applications to Web-based applications. This shift has highlighted the need for technologies that can simplify Web-based application development.

To build Web applications, the .NET Framework includes ASP.NET, which is the next version of ASP 3.0. You can build applications in ASP.NET by using Visual Basic .NET or Visual C# as the server-side scripting language. Visual C# enables programmers to develop powerful Web-based applications. More importantly it helps programmers combat increasingly accelerated cycle times, because it enables them to do more with fewer lines of code and fewer errors, which reduces the cost of a project considerably.

Although all that you need for creating ASP.NET Web applications is a text editor, such as Notepad, you will probably use a development platform, such as Visual Studio .NET. Visual Studio .NET provides an extensive set of tools for designing Web pages. In comparison to earlier Web programming languages, in which you had to do extensive coding, Visual Studio .NET provides the What You See Is What You Get (WYSIWYG) interface. This interface enables you to drag and drop controls onto WebForms, which you can then program in Visual C#. By programming in Visual Studio .NET, you can separate code and HTML content on a WebForm. This makes it very easy to separate programming logic from presentation logic, which enables you to focus on implementing the functionality of the project, rather than the presentation of data.

In this chapter, you learn to create an ASP.NET Web application by using Visual C#. While creating the application, you design a WebForm that uses server controls, such as labels, text boxes, list boxes, hyperlinks, and buttons. Finally, you learn to handle events that are generated by server controls.

Basics of ASP.NET Web Applications

ASP.NET Web applications are applications that are deployed on Web servers. These applications comprise one or more WebForms that are programmed either in Visual C# or Visual Basic .NET.

In this section, you learn about the features and advantages of ASP.NET Web applications and how Visual C# enables you to create ASP.NET applications. You also learn about how ASP.NET applications are different from ASP 3.0 applications.

New features in ASP.NET

ASP.NET includes several new features that were not present in ASP 3.0. These features are briefly described in this section.

Execution in the .NET Framework environment

In comparison to earlier Web-programming languages, applications in Visual C# (and other Visual Studio .NET languages) execute in the .NET framework environment. Thus, these applications are independent of the client browsers, and function in the same manner on all client platforms.

Another advantage that using a different runtime for ASP.NET is that ASP 3.0 applications can coexist with ASP.NET applications. Thus, you can deploy ASP 3.0 and ASP.NET Web sites on the same Web server.

Introduction of WebForms

WebForms are the foundation of a Web-based application. They are used by the Web application to interact with the user. A WebForm can include a number of server controls, such as text boxes, labels, list boxes, radio buttons, check boxes, and buttons, all of which facilitate the interaction of the user with the application.

A WebForm consists of two components: the *user interface (UI)* and the *programming (application) logic*. The user interface is the visual component of a WebForm; it consists of HTML and controls specific to the Web application. The user interface is the container for the text and the controls that need to be displayed on the Web page. It is specified in a file with the .aspx extension.

The programming logic of a Web application in ASP.NET is contained in a separate file that contains the code to handle the user's interaction with the form. This file is known as the *code-behind* file. When a form written in C# executes, the code-behind file dynamically generates the HTML output of the page. The code-behind file in C# has an .aspx.cs extension.

The advantage of separating code from content is that the programmer need not concentrate on the logic that is used to display the output. The Web designer can handle this task.

Integration with Visual Studio .NET

Visual Studio .NET is the rapid application-development tool for ASP.NET. Visual Studio .NET offers complete integration with ASP.NET and enables you to drag and drop server controls and design WebForms as they should appear when a user views them. Some of the other advantages of creating ASP.NET applications in Visual Studio .NET are summarized in the following list:

✦ Visual Studio .NET is a Rapid Application (RAD) tool. Instead of adding each control to the WebForm programmatically, it helps you to add these controls by using the toolbox, saving programming effort.

✦ Visual Studio .NET supports custom and composite controls. You can create custom controls that encapsulate a common functionality you might need to use in a number of applications, just as you use the ASP.NET Web controls provided by Visual Studio .NET.

Introduction of server controls

Apart form the HTML controls that existed in the days of ASP 3.0, ASP.NET introduces server controls that are components of a Web application that are executed at the server end and encapsulate the functionality of the application.

HTML controls refer to the HTML elements that you can use in your WebForms. Normally, when the HTML controls are sent to the server through the browser, the server considers the HTML controls to be opaque. That is, the server does not process them. However, by converting these controls into HTML server controls, they can be exposed to the server for processing. By using attributes, such as ID and RUNAT, you can convert the HTML controls to HTML server controls. You can add these controls to a WebForm by using the HTML tab of the toolbox.

Server controls, on the other hand, are completely transparent to the application and enable a developer to handle events at the server-side to manage the Web application.

Apart from the conventional text box and button controls, this category of controls also includes the validation controls. Validation controls are programmable controls that help you validate user input. For example, you can use these controls to validate the value of a field or the pattern of characters entered by the user. To validate user input, you need to attach these controls to the input controls.

Composite and user controls

If you want to replicate a set of controls on a number of pages, one option is that you draw controls on each form separately. This is not a very useful option. However, another option provided by ASP.NET is by way of user and composite controls.

User controls are ordinary WebForms that have been converted to controls by removing the <HTML> and <FORM> tags of the control. Thus, they represent a unit of code and layout that can be imported into another WebForm.

Another set of controls provided by ASP.NET is composite controls. Composite controls are a set of controls that have been compiled into a library. To use composite controls, you can include a reference to the library as you include references to other libraries.

Controls commonly used in WebForms

The basic task of designing a Web application is to add controls to a WebForm. Some of the most commonly used controls on a WebForm are Label, TextBox, CheckBox, RadioButton, ListBox, DropDownList, HyperLink, Table, Button, and ImageButton. The following sections discuss these controls briefly.

Label control

You use the Label control to display static text in a WebForm. Users cannot edit the text in a Label control. When you add a Label control, the text Label appears as its caption. However, by setting the Text property of the control, you can modify the control's caption.

You can set the properties of the Label control at runtime in the code-behind file (.cs file). For example, you may want to change the text of a label when a user clicks a button. You can do so by using the following code:

```
Label1.Text="Welcome"
```

In the preceding code, Label1 is the ID of the Label control for which you want to change the identification. If you want the Label control to disappear when a user clicks a button, you can use the following code:

```
Label1.Visible=False
```

TextBox control

The TextBox control is used to get information, such as text, numbers, and dates, from users in a WebForm. By default, a TextBox control is a single-line control that enables users to type characters in a single line only. However, you can also set the TextBox control as a multiline control. A multiline text box displays multiple lines and allows text wrapping.

A TextBox control can also be used to accept passwords. A TextBox control that is used to accept passwords masks the characters typed by users, displaying them as asterisks (*).

You can set the appearance of a TextBox control by using its properties, such as BackColor or ForeColor. You can also change the TextMode property of a TextBox control to determine whether a TextBox control functions as a text box to accept a password, a single line of text, or multiple lines of text.

CheckBox and CheckBoxList controls

Check boxes enable users to select one or more options from a given set of options. You can add check boxes to a WebForm by using the CheckBox or CheckBoxList control. The CheckBox control represents a single check box, whereas the CheckBoxList control represents a collection of several check boxes. To add these controls to the form, simply drag them onto the form from the toolbox.

After adding the CheckBoxList control, you need to add a list of items to it. To do so, perform the following steps:

1. In the Properties window, click the ellipsis button for the Items property of the CheckBoxList control. The ListItem Collection Editor dialog box opens.

 Note   If the Properties window is not open, press F4. You can also select View ➪ Properties Window, on the menu bar.

2. In the ListItem Collection Editor dialog box, click Add to create a new item. A new item is created and its properties are displayed at the right side of the dialog box.

3. Verify that the item is selected in the Members list, and then set the item properties. Each item is a separate object and has the following properties:

   • Selected: Represents a Boolean value that indicates whether the item is selected.

   • Text: Represents the text to be displayed for the item in the list.

   • Value: Represents the value associated with the item. The value of a control is not displayed to the user. However, the server uses the value to process information from the control. For example, you might set the

Text property of an item as City Name, and the Value property to the postal code of the city, as a unique identification. When the server processes the information represented by the City Name field, the text supplied by the text box would be ignored, and any processing would be based on the corresponding value used by the field.

4. Specify the text to be displayed to the user.

5. Repeat Steps 2-4 to add the required controls to the CheckBoxList control.

6. Click OK to close the ListItem Collection Editor dialog box.

Tip   The choice between using the CheckBox control and the CheckBoxList control depends on specific needs. The CheckBox control provides more control over the layout of the check boxes on the page. For example, you can set the font and color of the check boxes individually or include text between different check boxes. On the other hand, the CheckBoxList control is a better choice if you need to add a series of check boxes.

RadioButton and RadioButtonList controls

Radio buttons provide a set of options from which a user can select. You can add radio buttons to a WebForm by using either the RadioButton control or the RadioButtonList control. The RadioButton control represents a single radio button to work with. The RadioButtonList control is a collection of radio buttons. Radio buttons are seldom used singly. Instead, they are used in a group. A group of radio buttons provides a set of mutually exclusive options. This means that only one radio button in a group can be selected. A set of radio buttons can be grouped in the following two ways:

✦ You can add a set of RadioButton controls to your page and assign them manually to a group. You can use the GroupName property to do so.

✦ You can add a RadioButtonList control to the page. The radio buttons in the control are automatically grouped, so you don't need to manually group them.

After adding a RadioButtonList control to the WebForm, you need to add the radio buttons. You can do so by using the Items property in the same way as you do for the CheckBoxList control.

ListBox control

The ListBox control represents a collection of list items. The control enables users to select one or more items from the list. You can add the individual list items using the Items property. You can also specify whether a user can select multiple items from a list of just a single item by using the SelectionMode property of the ListBox control.

DropDownList control

The DropDownList control enables users to select an item from a set of predefined items — each item being a separate object with its own properties. You can add items to a DropDownList control by using its Items property. Unlike the ListBox control, you can select only one item at a time, and the list of items remains hidden until a user clicks the drop-down button.

HyperLink control

The HyperLink control enables users to navigate from one WebForm to another in an application. It also enables users to navigate to a URL that might be associated with the control. With the HyperLink control, either text or an image can act as a hyperlink. When a user clicks the control, the target WebForm or the URL opens. The following code snippet illustrates how to set the NavigateUrl property:

```
Hyperlink1.NavigateUrl="http://www.amazon.com";
```

Table, TableRow, and TableCell controls

You use a table to display information in a tabular format. You can add a table to a WebForm by using the Table control. This control can display information statically by setting the rows and columns at design time. However, you can program the Table control to display information dynamically at runtime.

Two other table-related controls that you can use on a WebForm are TableRow and TableCell. Use the TableRow control to declare a row, and use the TableCell control to declare cells in a table.

To understand how the Table, TableRow, and TableCell controls are related to one another, add a Table control to your WebForm (drag it from Solution Explorer) and perform the following steps to add rows and cells to the table:

1. In the Properties window, click the ellipsis button for the Rows property of the Table control. The TableRow Collection Editor dialog box opens.

2. In the TableRow Collection Editor dialog box, which represents the TableRow control, click Add to create a new row. A new row is created and its properties are displayed at the right side of the dialog box.

3. Verify that the row is selected in the Members list, and then click the ellipsis button for the Cells property to add a cell for the row. The TableCell Collection Editor dialog box opens.

4. In the TableCell Collection Editor dialog box, which represents the TableCell control, click Add to create a new cell. A new cell is created and its properties are displayed at the right side of the dialog box.

5. Specify the text to be displayed in the cell and click OK to close the TableCell Collection Editor dialog box.

6. Click OK to close the TableRow Collection Editor dialog box.

Notice that after you perform the preceding steps, a 1 × 1 table is added to your form.

Table 22-1 describes some of the properties of the Table, TableRow, and TableCell controls.

Table 22-1
Properties of the Table, TableRow, and TableCell Controls

Property	Available with	Description
ID	Table	Represents the unique ID of the control.
Rows	Table	Represents a collection of TableRow objects. A TableRow control represents a row in the table.
Cells	TableRow	Represents a collection of TableCell objects. A TableCell control represents a cell in a row in a table.
VerticalAlign	TableCell	Represents the vertical alignment, such as the top and bottom of the cell.
HorizontalAlign	TableCell	Represents the horizontal alignment, such as left align and right align, of the cell.

ImageButton control

The ImageButton control enables programmers to display images in a WebForm and manage these images at design time or runtime. This control represents a graphical button, which enhances the appearance of the WebForm. You can set the ImageUrl property to point to a specific image.

Button and LinkButton controls

The Button control on a WebForm is used to submit the page to the server. Three types of server control buttons can be added to a WebForm:

✦ Button: Represents a standard button.

✦ LinkButton: Represents a button that causes the page to be submitted to the server. In addition, it can also act as a hyperlink to another Web page or WebForm.

✦ ImageButton: This control is covered in the previous section.

Creating and Configuring a Web Application

Visual C# provides the ASP.NET Web Application template to create ASP.NET Web applications. The ASP.NET Web Application template contains the necessary information for building, processing, and deploying ASP applications.

Before you create a Web application project, you need to ensure that the following basic requirements for your Web application are fulfilled on the development platform:

✦ You should have access to a computer running Microsoft IIS Server

✦ You should install the IIS Server on an NTFS partition. An NTFS partition improves the security and performance of the server.

After fulfilling these requirements, you can use Visual Studio .NET to create an ASP.NET Web application. To create a Web application, perform the following steps:

1. Add an ASP.NET Web application project for your application.

2. Create the user interface of the Web application.

3. Code the application logic.

The steps to create a new project are given in the following section.

Creating a new project

You use the ASP.NET Web Application template to create Web application projects. The steps for creating a new Web application by using this template are as follows:

1. Select File ➪ New ➪ Project to open the New Project dialog box, which is shown in Figure 22-1.

 You can also press Ctrl+Shift+N to open the New Project dialog box.

2. Select Visual C# Projects from the Project Types list.

3. Select ASP.NET Web Application from the Templates list of the New Project dialog box.

4. Type the project name in the Name box.

5. Type the name of the IIS Server in the Location box, or accept the default location. The completed New Project dialog box is shown in Figure 22-2.

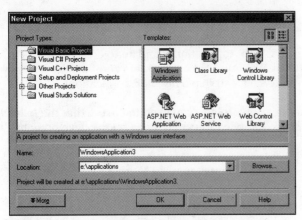

Figure 22-1: You can select one or more enterprise templates from the New Project dialog box.

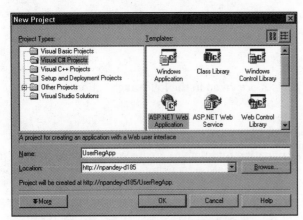

Figure 22-2: Select a template and specify the name of the application in the New Project dialog box.

Tip   If the Web server is installed on your computer, you can also type **http:// localhost** in the Location box.

6. Click OK. A dialog box displays briefly while Visual Studio .NET creates the new ASP.NET Web application. The dialog box is shown in Figure 22-3.

Note You may have to wait for some time while ASP.NET creates the project. You should also ensure that the Web server is turned on, before you create your application. To turn the Web server on, select Start ➪ Run. In the Run dialog box, type **net start iisadmin** and press Enter.

Figure 22-3: Visual Studio .NET creates the new project.

After you create a new Web Application Project, necessary project files — such as AssemblyInfo.cs, Config.Web, and Global.asax — are created automatically by the Web Application Wizard, along with the main page file, WebForm1.aspx. Figure 22-4 shows these files in the Solution Explorer.

Figure 22-4: The Project window shows all the files created by the Web Application Wizard.

A WebForm in Visual Studio .NET has two views — *Design view* and *HTML view*:

✦ **Design view:** You design the user interface of a WebForm in Design view. Design view provides two layouts for the WebForm: grid layout and flow layout:

• **Grid layout:** In grid layout, you can arrange controls on the WebForm based on the coordinates of each control.

• **Flow layout:** In flow layout, a WebForm can be designed linearly, as you design a Microsoft Word document, from top to bottom.

You can switch between different layouts by right-clicking the WebForm and selecting Properties. On the Property pages, you can select the appropriate layout.

✦ **HTML view:** This view represents the corresponding ASP.NET syntax for the WebForm. You need to click the HTML tab to open HTML view. If the HTML tab is not visible, you can right-click and select View HTML Source from the shortcut menu.

Adding controls to the WebForm

You can add controls to a WebForm in two ways:

✦ **Using the toolbox:** You can add controls in Design view of the WebForm (the .aspx file) by using the toolbox included in Visual Studio .NET. Within the toolbox, different types of controls are categorized under separate tabs, such as WebForms, HTML, and Data. For example, you can use the HTML tab to create HTML server controls, and the WebForms tab to create the ASP.NET server controls. All controls discussed previously belong to the Windows Forms tab of the toolbox. When you use the toolbox to add Web controls in Design view, the corresponding C# syntax is automatically generated.

 Tip

When you use HTML controls, you need to convert them to server controls to make them available for coding at the server end. You can do so by right-clicking the required HTML control and selecting the Run As Server Control option from the shortcut menu. This method enables you to create complex WebForms conveniently and quickly.

✦ **Using Visual C# syntax to add the controls programmatically:** You can also add Web controls to a WebForm by using the Visual C# syntax. You can use the C# syntax only in the HTML view of the page (.aspx file). The actual syntax depends on the type of control that you want to add. For example, the syntax used to add an HTML textbox control is as follows:

```
<input id=Text1 Type=text runat="server">
```

 Note

Visual Studio .NET enables you to add ASP.NET server controls by using an Extensible Markup Language (XML) tag. The syntax you use to add an ASP.NET TextBox control is as follows:

```
<asp:TextBox id=TextBox1 runat="server"></asp:TextBox>
```

Every control has an ID property that is used to uniquely identify the control. To set the property of a control at runtime, you need to use the following syntax:

```
Control_ID.Property=Value
```

In the preceding syntax:

✦ `Control_ID` represents the ID property of the control.

✦ `Property` represents the property of the control.

✦ `Value` represents the value assigned to the control's property.

Figure 22-5 displays a WebForm that contains common Web controls, such as labels, text boxes, hyperlinks, radio buttons, check boxes, and buttons. As you can see, the WebForm is a user registration form. The form is designed to accept user input in various controls. After filling out the form, a user can click the Submit button to complete the registration process. The Submit button opens another WebForm displaying a message along with the user name entered in the name `TextBox` control. If the user clicks the Reset button, information filled in by the user is removed from the controls on the form.

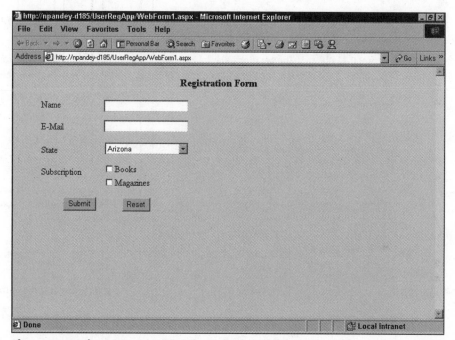

Figure 22-5: The user registration form displays the common controls that can be added to WebForms.

To create the form displayed in Figure 22-5, follow these steps:

1. Select the WebForm1.aspx form, and press F4 to view the Properties window.

2. In the Properties window, click the Ellipsis button for the `bgColor` property, and select Properties. The Color Picker dialog box opens.

3. In the Color Picker dialog box, select a shade of pink and click OK. The color of the WebForm changes to the color that you specified.

4. Add controls to the form and change their properties, as shown in Table 22-2.

Table 22-2
Controls to Add to the WebForm

Control	Properties	Placement
Label	Text=Registration Form Font Bold=True Size=Larger	To be placed on the top, center of the form
Labels for Name, E-Mail, State, Subscription	The text for each label should be the same as the caption desired.	One below the other on the left side of the screen
TextBox	ID=txtName	Next to the Name label
TextBox	ID=txtEmail	Next to the E-Mail label
DropDownList	ID=lstState Items=Arizona, California, Florida	Next to the State label
CheckBoxList	ID=lstOptions Items=Books, Magazines	Next to the Subscription label
Button	ID=BtnSubmit Text=Reset	Below the Subscription label
Button	ID=BtnReset Text=Reset	Next to the Submit button

The interface of your WebForm, shown in Figure 22-6, is ready.

You add the functionality of the Submit and Reset buttons in the next section. However, before proceeding, add another form, which displays details about the registered user when he or she clicks Submit, to the Web application. To add the WebForm, follow these steps:

1. Select Project ⇨ Add WebForm. The Add New Item dialog box opens.

Tip   If you do not find the Add WebForm menu option under the Project menu, click anywhere in the Form window and then select the menu option.

2. Select WebForm from the Templates list, specify a name for the WebForm (or retain the default name), and click Open to create a new WebForm.

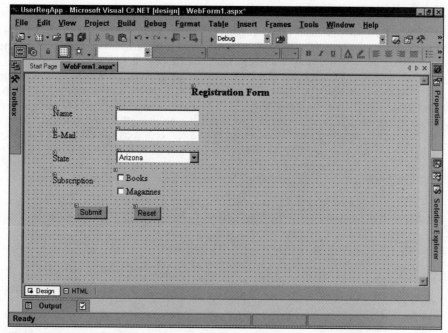

Figure 22-6: Your WebForm should look like this after it is complete.

You can use the newly added WebForm to display a message to the user. Therefore, you need to add a `Label` control to the form. Name the label **lblMessage**.

Having added controls to the form, you need to respond to the events generated by the controls on the form to handle user interaction. For example, if a user clicks a Submit button, the form might need to be processed and the data updated in a database.

The next section describes the procedure to handle events that are generated by controls on a WebForm.

Handling events

When users interact with different Web controls on a page, events are raised. An *event* is an action that can occur on an object or control, which can either be generated by a user action or by the system. For example, when you click a mouse button or press a key, an event is generated.

In traditional client forms or client-based Web applications, events are raised and handled on the client side. In Web applications, events are raised either on the client or on the server. However, the events generated are always handled on the server. ASP.NET server controls support only server-side events, whereas HTML server controls support both server-side and client-side events.

Understanding round-trips

WebForms are processed on the server. For example, consider a user registration form. When a new user specifies a value for the registration name, the server must ensure that the registration name supplied by the user is unique. You can ensure that the registration name is unique by trapping the `Click` event of a button and querying the user name against a data source. Whenever a user interaction requires processing on the server, the WebForm is submitted to the server and processed, and then the output is returned to the client through a browser. This sequence of processing information on the server is called the *round-trip* process, as shown in Figure 22-7.

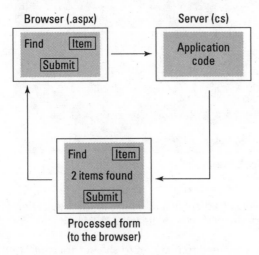

Figure 22-7: The round-trip process

Most user interactions with the server controls result in round-trips. Because a round-trip involves sending the WebForm to the server and then displaying the processed form in the browser, the server control events affect the response time in the WebForm. Therefore, the number of events available in a WebForm's server controls should be as few as possible. Usually, these are limited to the `Click` events.

Note   Events that occur quite often in scripting languages, such as `OnMouseOver`, are not supported by server controls. However, some server controls support events that occur when the value of the control changes.

Table 22-3 describes the commonly occurring events associated with different ASP.NET server controls.

Table 22-3
Events Associated with ASP.NET Server Controls

Control(s)	Event	Description
TextBox	TextChanged	Occurs when the focus moves out of the control.
RadioButton and CheckBox	CheckedChanged	Occurs when you click the control.
RadioButtonList, CheckBoxList, ListBox, and DropDownList	SelectedIndexChanged	Occurs when you change the selection in the list.
Button, LinkButton, and ImageButton	Click	Occurs when you click the button. This event causes the form to be submitted to the server.

In a WebForm, by default, only the Click event of Button, LinkButton, and ImageButton server controls can cause the form to be submitted to the server for processing. In this scenario, the WebForm is *posted back* to the server. When the change events are generated by other controls, they are captured and cached. They do not cause the form to be submitted immediately. It is only when the form is posted back due to a button-click that all cached events are raised and processed. There is no particular sequence for processing these change events on the server. However, the Click event is processed only after all the other change events are processed.

Understanding event handlers

When an event is raised, it needs to be handled for further processing. The procedures that are executed when an event occurs are known as *event handlers*. Event handlers can be created automatically or manually.

When you handle events automatically, double-clicking a control in Design view of the WebForm (.aspx file) creates an event handler. For example, the following code is generated when a button, btnSubmit, is double-clicked. You can then write the code in the event handler in the function that's generated by Visual Studio .NET:

```
Public void btnSubmit_Click(Object sender, System.EventArgs e)
{

}
```

In the preceding code, the procedure btnSubmit_Click is the event handler for the Click event of the button. The procedure takes two arguments. The first argument contains the event sender. An *event sender* is an object, such as a form or a control, that can generate events. The second argument contains additional information associated with an event, such as the *x* and *y* coordinates of the position at which a mouse button is clicked.

To create an event handler manually, you select it from the drop-down list in the Properties window.

You are now ready to implement event handling for the WebForm shown in Figure 22-7.

When you click the Submit button, a new page (WebForm2.aspx, in our case) should be displayed, which shows a welcome message along with the name of the registered user. To implement this functionality, you need to write the following code in the Click event of the Submit button of the WebForm1.aspx WebForm:

```
private void BtnSubmit_Click(object sender, System.EventArgs e)
{
    Response.Redirect("WebForm2.aspx?strName="+ txtName.Text);
}
```

Tip   To code the event for the Submit button, double-click the button in Design view.

In the preceding code, the Redirect method of the HttpResponse class redirects the user to the WebForm2.aspx page and passes the value of the txtName parameter to the destination page.

After passing the value of the text box txtName, you need to initialize WebForm2 to handle the string passed from the registration form. To do so, WebForm2.aspx should have following code in the Load event:

```
private void Page_Load(object sender, System.EventArgs e)
{
    lblMessage.Text="Hi! " + Request.QueryString.Get("strName");
}
```

Tip   To code the Load event for the WebForm2.aspx form, double-click the form in Design view.

In the preceding code, the value stored in the strName variable is set as the caption of the label lblMessage in the WebForm2.aspx file. When the user clicks the Submit button on WebForm1.aspx, he or she is redirected to the WebForm2.aspx page, as shown in Figure 22-8.

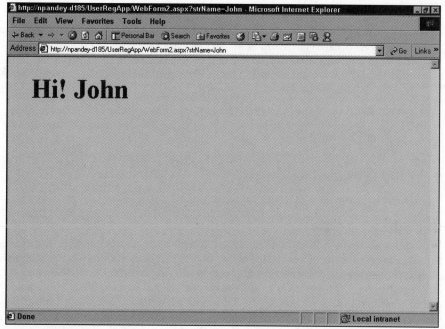

Figure 22-8: When a user is redirected to another page, the name of the user is passed in the query string.

When the user clicks the Reset button, an event must be generated that removes all the controls filled in by the user in WebForm1.aspx. To implement this functionality, you code the Click event of the Reset button as follows:

```
private void BtnReset_Click(object sender, System.EventArgs e)
{
    txtName.Text="";
    txtEmail.Text="";
    lstState.ClearSelection();
    lstOptions.ClearSelection();
}
```

In the preceding code, when the Reset button in the registration form is clicked, the form is reinitialized to its original state.

Handling data postback

As mentioned earlier, a WebForm is posted back to the server only when a Button, LinkButton, or ImageButton control is clicked. After the form is posted to the server, it is processed at the server. You can handle data postback corresponding to the click of a button in one of the following ways:

✦ Write an event handler for the `Click` event of the button.

✦ Write the event handler for the `Load` event of the WebForm. The `Load` event is generated when the form is loaded. You can use the `IsPostBack` property in the `Load` event to determine whether the page has been processed for the first time or by a button click. The following code depicts the event handler for a WebForm's `Load` event:

```
protected void Page_Load(object sender, EventArgs e)
{
    if (!IsPostBack)
        {
        //Evals true first time browser hits the page
        }
}
```

Using the view state

In traditional Web applications, whenever a Web page is processed at the server, the page is created from scratch. The server discards the current page information after it processes the information and sends the page to the client (browser). Because the page information is not preserved on the server, the Web pages are called *stateless*. However, the ASP.NET framework works around this limitation and can save the state information of the form and its controls. To manage state information, Visual Studio .NET provides the following options:

✦ **Save View state:** You can save the view state of server controls to an object. In each round-trip, the state of the server control can be loaded from the saved state, so that the user can view all options that he or she selected previously.

✦ **StateBag:** The `StateBag` class is the storage mechanism for server controls. This class provides properties to store information in key-value pairs. For example, if you want to store data specified by a user for a page, you can use an instance of the `StateBag` class to store this data.

Each server control includes an `EnableViewState` property. When you set this property to true, the state of the control is retained between round trips on the server. Thus, if the user has selected one or more options from a list, the options will be retained through round trips to the server.

Summary

In this chapter, you learned to create a simple Web application by using Visual C# in the ASP.NET framework. You learned the basics of ASP.NET and how you can create Web applications in Visual C#.

ASP.NET includes a separate runtime environment that manages the execution of ASP.NET applications. It also includes new server components, referred to as WebForms, which encapsulate the functionality of a Web page. You can add one or more server controls to a WebForm. Server controls are responsible for displaying data to users and processing user interactions.

You created a Web application project and added a WebForm to it. When creating an application, you used the ASP.NET Web application template to create a solution and add an ASP.NET project to the solution. Next, you designed a Web page by using common Web controls, such as the controls that represent labels, text boxes, list boxes, hyperlinks, buttons, and so on. Finally, you learned to handle events that are generated by controls on the WebForm.

✦   ✦   ✦

Database Programming with ADO.NET

✦ ✦ ✦ ✦

In This Chapter

Introducing
ADO.NET

Understanding
OLEDB and SQL
Server support

Implementing select,
insert, update, and
delete operations

✦ ✦ ✦ ✦

ADO.NET is the newest data access technology and is part of the .NET Framework. ADO.NET builds and improves upon previous data access technologies. Microsoft's foray into universal data access started with open database connectivity (ODBC). The idea behind this ODBC technology — to create a standard way to access databases programmatically — has been used in all subsequent data access technologies coming from Redmond, Washington (where Microsoft's headquarters are located). In the case of ODBC, this standard method is documented as the ODBC API (Application Programmer's Interface). Any database vendor wanting to claim compliance with the ODBC standard is responsible for building the software that translates an ODBC call (made in accordance with the API) into a native database call. Such software is called an *ODBC driver* and is the bridge between a generic client application and a specific database. Through this approach, the application programmers are shielded from having to learn how to use a specific vendor's database API. All an application programmer needs to know is how to write client applications using the ODBC API. This improves productivity, and enables you to write a program that can be used with different databases.

However, the ODBC API was originally designed primarily with C application programmers in mind, and was difficult to use in other languages (such as Visual Basic). This eventually led to the introduction of Active Data Objects (ADO), a data access technology designed for use with any language that supports Microsoft's Common Object Model (COM). ADO introduced a simple object model that made accessing data in MS Windows programs a straightforward task. In addition, ADO introduced the concept of *disconnected recordsets* as a way to transport data between the tiers of a distributed application. The low-level API behind ADO is called OLE DB. This API is designed for C++ programmers and is what database vendors typically use to write OLE DB *providers* (the preferred term for OLE DB drivers, the software that translates ADO calls into native database calls). Microsoft has also written an OLE DB provider for OBDC. This provider enables you to issue ADO calls against any ODBC-compliant database.

As this chapter shows you, ADO.NET keeps an object model that is similar to ADO and improves on the concept of disconnected recordsets by providing a way to bundle more information into an ADO.NET object called a *dataset*. In fact, ADO.NET was designed with the disconnected data in mind, because this stateless approach works best for distributed Internet applications. In this chapter, you learn how to use ADO.NET to manipulate data. If you are familiar with ADO, many of the concepts will look familiar, and even the code will not be completely unfamiliar.

Understanding the Dataset Classes and Their Relatives

This section examines the ADO.NET classes. If you are familiar with ADO, you will recognize many of the concepts presented here. Be aware, however, that some ADO concepts have come a long way in ADO.NET and are considerably expanded from their original forms. Let's start with the new kid on the block: the DataSet class and its relatives.

DataSet expands on the recordset concept found in ADO. As given away by its name, ADO's recordset is an abstraction of a set of records, such as the resulting data retrieved by issuing a SQL Select statement. A recordset can actually contain more than one set of records, but the records are independent of one another and must be processed sequentially by calling NextRecordSet(). ADO.NET's DataSet is an abstraction of an entire database. Not only can a DataSet contain more than one set of records (appropriately called a DataTable), you can define relationships between DataTables. Table 23-1 describes all the DataSet-related classes. Like the ADO classes, the ADO.NET classes make extensive use of collections: the DataSet class contains a collection of DataTables; the DataTable class contains a collection of DataColumns, and so on.

Table 23-1
DataSet and Related Classes

Class	Description
DataSet	An in-memory cache of data, which may consist of several related DataTables. Designed for disconnected use in distributed applications.
DataTable	A container of data, which may consist of several DataColumns. Each row of data is contained in a DataRow.

Class	Description
DataRow	A specific row of data in a DataTable
DataColumn	The definition of a column (name, data type, etc.) in a DataTable
DataRelation	A relationship between two DataTables within a DataSet, typically used to represent foreign-key relationships
Constraint	A restriction on one or more DataColumns, used to represent constraints such as uniqueness
DataColumnMapping	Maps the column names from the table in a database to the column names of the DataTable in the DataSet
DataTableMapping	Maps the table names in a database to the names of the DataTables in the DataSet
DataView	A customized view of a DataTable that can be used for sorting, filtering, and searching

ADO's RecordSet gradually evolved as the standard way to marshal data between tiers of a distributed application. DataSet takes over this role in ADO.NET and provides a number of methods to reconcile the in-memory cache of the data with its source data in the database. These methods include AcceptChanges(), GetChanges(), HasChanges(), HasErrors(), and RejectChanges(). These methods enable you to retrieve any changes in the form of a changed DataSet, inspect the changes for errors, and decide whether to accept or reject the changes. At the end of this process, you can update the source data in the database with a simple call to the Update() method.

Understanding OLE DB and SQL Server Support

ADO.NET contains two sets of similar classes. One set is a generic set of classes that can be used to access all databases that have OLE DB providers. A second set of classes has been fine-tuned for Microsoft's flagship database, SQL Server. The names of the generic classes all start with OleDb. The SQL Server–specific classes all begin with Sql. Each generic class has a corresponding SQL Server–specific class. For example, the class you use to execute SQL statements against SQL Server is called SqlCommand. The generic class is called OleDbCommand.

Note   If you look at any code that was designed with the first public beta of the .NET Framework, you see code with the Ado prefix. This prefix was changed to OleDb starting with beta 2.

This chapter uses the generic classes, even when accessing a SQL Server database. When writing your own applications accessing SQL Server, you need to decide whether to use the speedier SQL Server specific classes or the more generic classes that enable you to switch database vendors simply by changing the connection string. The trade-off is speed versus portability. The SQL Server classes directly call the native database layer. The generic classes use OleDb and go through a COM layer before calling the native database layer. The overhead of an extra layer results in a decrease in performance.

The DataSet classes are used in conjunction with both the OLE DB provider and the SQL Server provider. Table 23-2 lists the provider-specific classes. Many of these look familiar to a trained ADO eye.

<table>
<tr><td colspan="3">Table 23-2
DataSet and Related Classes</td></tr>
<tr><th>SQL Server
Provider Class</th><th>OLE DB
Provider Class</th><th>Description</th></tr>
<tr><td>SqlCommand</td><td>OleDbCommand</td><td>A class wrapper for a SQL statement. The class can manage both direct SQL statements such as a SELECT, UPDATE, DELETE, or INSERT statement and a stored procedure call.</td></tr>
<tr><td>SqlCommandBuilder</td><td>OleDbCommandBuilder</td><td>Used to generate SQL SELECT, UPDATE, DELETE, or INSERT statements</td></tr>
<tr><td>SqlDataConnection</td><td>OleDbConnection</td><td>A connection to a database</td></tr>
<tr><td>SqlDataAdapter</td><td>OleDbDataAdapter</td><td>A set of SELECT, UPDATE, DELETE, or INSERT statements and a connection to a database, which can be used to fill a DataSet and update the underlying database</td></tr>
<tr><td>SqlDataReader</td><td>OleDbDataReader</td><td>A forward-only set of data records</td></tr>
<tr><td>SqlError</td><td>OleDbError</td><td>A warning or error returned by the database, contained in an Errors collection</td></tr>
<tr><td>SqlException</td><td>OleDbException</td><td>The type of exception thrown when database errors occur</td></tr>
<tr><td>SqlParameter</td><td>OleDbParameter</td><td>A parameter to a stored procedure</td></tr>
<tr><td>SqlTransaction</td><td>OleDbTransaction</td><td>A database transaction</td></tr>
</table>

In the next section, you learn how these classes work with the common classes, `DataSet` and its relatives, to perform common database operations.

Understanding Common Database Operations Using ADO.NET

Each of the examples shown in this section omits the `using` declarations for simplicity's sake. The following three namespace declarations are assumed present throughout this chapter:

✦ `using System;`

✦ `using System.Data;`

✦ `using System.Data.OleDb;`

In addition, most functions are taken out of their class context. The functions are supposed to be scoped with the following class definition:

```
namespace ADOdotNET
{
  class ADOdotNET
  {
// NOTE: Function goes here
  }
}
```

With these preliminary remarks out of the way, we can delve into ADO.NET. One by one, this section examines each category of operations that can be performed with ADO.NET:

✦ Operations that do not return rows

✦ Operations that return only one row

✦ Operations that affect only one row

✦ Operations that return multiple rows

✦ Operations that affect multiple rows

✦ Operations that return hierarchical data

Operations that don't return rows

Many SQL operations (for example, `Insert`, `Delete`, and `Update` statements) return only success or failure (or the numbers of rows affected by the operation).

Note The SQL Server programmer controls whether the number of rows affected is returned from a stored procedure through the `SET NOCOUNT [ON | OFF]` statement. SQL Server programmers often turn this feature off with `SET NOCOUNT ON` because of the slight improvement in performance.

Listing 23-3 shows how simple it is to execute a nonrow-returning SQL statement in ADO.NET. You use two objects in this process. You first use an `OleDbConnection` object to establish a connection to a database. Listing 23-1 shows a sample connection string used to access the Northwind database on a locally installed instance of SQL Server.

Listing 23-1: **A Sample Connection String for SQL Server**

```
private static string oleDbConnectionString
{
    get
    {
        // NOTE: Using the sa account in production
        // applications is, of course, a BAD, BAD
        // practice. In addition, leaving the password
        // blank for the sa account is equally
        // inadmissible.
        return "Provider=SQLOLEDB.1;"
            +"User ID=sa;Initial Catalog=Northwind;Data
Source=localhost;";
    }
}
```

Listing 23-2 shows a sample connection string for Access 2000.

Listing 23-2: **A Sample Connection String for Microsoft Access**

```
private static string oleDbConnectionString
{
    get
    {
        // NOTE: This assumes that Microsoft Office Pro
        // was installed in the default location.
        return "Provider=Microsoft.Jet.OLEDB.4.0;"
            +"Data Source=C:\\Program Files\\Microsoft
Office\\Office\\Samples\\Northwind.MDB";
    }
}
```

The second object used to execute a query is the OleDbCommand object. Its constructor takes a string argument (the text of the SQL statement you want to execute) and an OleDbConnection object. The CommandType property lets you specify whether the command being executed is a stored procedure, an Access query, or plain text. The query is executed through the ExecuteNonQuery() method. Errors, such as a primary key violation, are reported through exceptions.

You can also use Command objects to execute SQL commands that do not returns rows of data, such as in the example in Listing 23-3:

Listing 23-3: A Template for Using a Command to Execute a Nonrow-Returning SQL Statement

```
// Declare and set appropriate values for oleDbConnectionString
and strSQLStatement
// Create OleDb objects
OleDbConnection databaseConnection = new
OleDbConnection(oleDbConnectionString);
OleDbCommand databaseCommand = new
OleDbCommand(strSQLStatement, databaseConnection);
// NOTE: Only one of the two following statements should be
used, NOT BOTH.
// If we are dealing with a SQL statement (i.e. NOT a Stored
Proc), use:
  databaseCommand.CommandType = CommandType.Text;
// If we are dealing with a Stored Proc, use:
  databaseCommand.CommandType = CommandType.StoredProcedure;
try
{
    // Establish database connection
    databaseConnection.Open();
    // Execute SQL Command
    int numRows = databaseCommand.ExecuteNonQuery();
    // Do something else, e.g. report numRows
}
catch (Exception e)
{
    // Handle Exception, e.g.:
    Console.WriteLine("****** Caught an exception:\n{0}",
e.Message);
}
finally
{
    databaseConnection.Close();
}
```

Calling a stored procedure with parameters is only slightly more complicated. Listing 23-4 shows the SQL code for a stored procedure that you want to call.

Listing 23-4: A SQL Server Stored Procedure to Insert a Record

```
USE [Northwind]
GO
CREATE PROCEDURE [pc_insCustomers]
    (@CustomerID_1 [nchar](5),
    @CompanyName_2 [nvarchar](40),
    @ContactName_3 [nvarchar](30),
    @ContactTitle_4 [nvarchar](30),
    @Address_5 [nvarchar](60),
    @City_6 [nvarchar](15),
    @Region_7 [nvarchar](15),
    @PostalCode_8 [nvarchar](10),
    @Country_9 [nvarchar](15),
    @Phone_10 [nvarchar](24),
    @Fax_11 [nvarchar](24))
AS
INSERT INTO [Northwind].[dbo].[Customers]
    ( [CustomerID],
      [CompanyName],
      [ContactName],
      [ContactTitle],
      [Address],
      [City],
      [Region],
      [PostalCode],
      [Country],
      [Phone],
      [Fax])
VALUES
    ( @CustomerID_1,
      @CompanyName_2,
      @ContactName_3,
      @ContactTitle_4,
      @Address_5,
      @City_6,
      @Region_7,
      @PostalCode_8,
      @Country_9,
      @Phone_10,
      @Fax_11)
```

The only tricky part is knowing how to define and set the parameters. This is done through the Parameters collection. As with any collection, you create new members with the Add() method. The newly created parameter is returned, and you can set the direction (whether the parameter is used for input only, for output only, or for both) and the value. The parameters of the Add() method are the name of the stored procedure parameter, its name, its data type, and its size. Listing 23-5 shows the code for the whole process.

Listing 23-5: Calling a Parameterized Stored Procedure in ADO.NET

```
static void TestInsertWithSPStatement(string customerID)
{
// Set SQL statement string
string strSQLInsert = "[pc_insCustomers]";

// Create OleDb objects
OleDbConnection databaseConnection = new
OleDbConnection(oleDbConnectionString);
OleDbCommand insertCommand = new OleDbCommand(strSQLInsert,
databaseConnection);

// We are dealing with a Stored Proc (i.e. NOT a SQL statement)
insertCommand.CommandType = CommandType.StoredProcedure;

// Add each parameter (#1 of 11)
OleDbParameter param =
insertCommand.Parameters.Add("@CustomerID_1",
OleDbType.VarChar, 5);
param.Direction = ParameterDirection.Input;
param.Value = customerID;
// Add each parameter (#2 of 11)
param = insertCommand.Parameters.Add("@CompanyName_2",
OleDbType.VarChar, 40);
param.Direction = ParameterDirection.Input;
param.Value = "Hungry Coyote Export Store";
// Add each parameter 3-10
// Etc.
// Add each parameter (#11 of 11)
param = insertCommand.Parameters.Add("@Fax_11",
OleDbType.VarChar, 24);
param.Direction = ParameterDirection.Input;
param.Value = "(503) 555-2376";

try
{
    // Establish database connection
    databaseConnection.Open();

    // Execute SQL Command
    int numRows = insertCommand.ExecuteNonQuery();

    // Report results
    Console.WriteLine("Inserted {0} row(s).",
numRows.ToString());
}
catch (Exception e)
{
```

Continued

Listing 23-5 *(continued)*

```
    Console.WriteLine("****** Caught an exception:\n{0}",
e.Message);
}
finally
{
    databaseConnection.Close();
}
}
```

Data operations that return single-row entities

Some data operations, such as retrieving a record based on a primary key, return
only a single row. ADO.NET provides three ways to retrieve a single row. One way
applies only to single-row entities, while the other two ways are generic and can be
used to retrieve multiple rows (as you learn in the next section).

The most efficient way to retrieve a single-row entity is often through an output
parameter. You can only use this method when you are certain the procedure
returns only a single row, however. Listing 23-6 shows a SQL Server stored procedure that retrieves a single record through output parameters.

Listing 23-6: A SQL Server Stored Procedure to Retrieve a Single Record

```
USE [Northwind]
GO
CREATE PROCEDURE [pc_getContact_ByCustomerID]
    (@CustomerID_1 [nchar](5),
     @ContactName_2 [nvarchar](30) output,
     @ContactTitle_3 [nvarchar](30) output)
AS
SELECT
    @ContactName_2 = [ContactName],
    @ContactTitle_3 = [ContactTitle]
FROM [Northwind].[dbo].[Customers]
WHERE
    [CustomerID] = @CustomerID_1
```

Calling such a stored procedure is similar to the code used to call the stored procedure that inserts a row (refer to Listing 23-3). Of course, the direction for the output
parameters is set to ParameterDirection.Output. After you execute the stored

procedure, you can use the Parameters collection to retrieve the values of the output parameters, as shown in Listing 23-7.

Listing 23-7: **Retrieving a Single Record Through Output Parameters**

```
static void TestSPWithOutParam(string customerID)
{
    // Set SQL statement strings
    string strSQLSelect = "[pc_getContact_ByCustomerID]";

    // Create OleDb objects
    OleDbConnection databaseConnection = new
OleDbConnection(oleDbConnectionString);
    OleDbCommand selectCommand = new OleDbCommand(strSQLSelect,
databaseConnection);

    // We are dealing with a Stored Proc (i.e. NOT a SQL
statement)
    selectCommand.CommandType = CommandType.StoredProcedure;

    // Add each parameter (#1 of 3)
    OleDbParameter param =
selectCommand.Parameters.Add("@CustomerID_1",
OleDbType.VarChar, 5);
    param.Direction = ParameterDirection.Input;
    param.Value = customerID;
    // Add each parameter (#2 of 3)
    param = selectCommand.Parameters.Add("@ContactName_2",
OleDbType.VarChar, 30);
    param.Direction = ParameterDirection.Output;
// Add each parameter (#3 of 3)
    param = selectCommand.Parameters.Add("@ContactTitle_3",
OleDbType.VarChar, 30);
    param.Direction = ParameterDirection.Output;

    try
    {
        // Establish database connection
        databaseConnection.Open();

        // Execute SQL Command
        selectCommand.ExecuteNonQuery();

        // Report results
        string contactName =
selectCommand.Parameters["@ContactName_2"].Value.ToString();
        string contactTitle =
selectCommand.Parameters["@ContactTitle_3"].Value.ToString();
```

Continued

Listing 23-7 *(continued)*

```
        Console.WriteLine("Contact name is {0}, title is {1}.",
contactName, contactTitle);
    }
    catch (Exception e)
    {
        Console.WriteLine("****** Caught an exception:\n{0}",
e.Message);
    }
    finally
    {
        databaseConnection.Close();
    }
        }
```

Now, look at the generic data-reading methods. The first one uses an
OleDbDataReader object. The Command object has an ExecuteReader() method,
which returns an OleDbDataReader object. You can then use the Read() method
to go through the content of the DataReader. Read() returns True when data is
found during the read, and False otherwise. Listing 23-8 shows how this is done.
Note that this example uses a SQL statement to access a stored procedure only to
demonstrate an alternate way of calling a stored procedure. This is done just for
educational purposes, as it is more efficient to call a stored procedure in the way
demonstrated in Listing 23-7.

Listing 23-8: Retrieving a Single Record Through a DataReader

```
static void TestSelectWithDataReader(string customerID)
{
    // Set SQL statement strings, assuming customerID doesn't
contain any embedded quotes
    string strSQLSelect = "EXEC [pc_getCustomer_ByCustomerID]
@CustomerID_1='" + customerID + "'";

    // Create OleDb objects
    OleDbConnection databaseConnection = new
OleDbConnection(oleDbConnectionString);
    OleDbCommand selectCommand = new OleDbCommand(strSQLSelect,
databaseConnection);

    // We are dealing with a SQL statement (i.e. NOT a Stored
Proc)
    selectCommand.CommandType = CommandType.Text;

    try
    {
```

```
        // Establish database connection
        databaseConnection.Open();

        // Execute SQL Command
        OleDbDataReader rowReader =
selectCommand.ExecuteReader();

        // Report results
        if (rowReader.Read())
        {
            string contactName =
rowReader["ContactName"].ToString();
            string contactTitle =
rowReader["ContactTitle"].ToString();
            Console.WriteLine("Contact name is {0}, title is
{1}.", contactName, contactTitle);
        }
        else
        {
            Console.WriteLine("No rows found!");
        }
    }
    catch (Exception e)
    {
        Console.WriteLine("****** Caught an exception:\n{0}",
e.Message);
    }
    finally
    {
        databaseConnection.Close();
    }
}
```

The other generic method of retrieving data is by using the versatile DataSet object. Because the DataSet object was designed to be used independently from its originating data source, there is no OleDbDataSet or SqlDataSet, just a DataSet. A DataSet is used in conjunction with a DataAdapter. A DataAdapter object is data-store specific (that is, you use OleDbDataAdaper) and contains four embedded command objects to perform operations:

✦ InsertCommand

✦ SelectCommand

✦ UpdateCommand

✦ DeleteCommand

After setting the SelectCommand object, you can use the Fill() method to fill a DataSet. The next section shows you how to use the other three commands to alter the data contained in a DataSet. A DataSet contains one or more DataTable objects. Each DataTable contains one or more DataRow objects. These DataRow objects are stored in the Rows collection of the DataSet. A DataRow object contains one or more DataColumn objects. These DataColumn objects are stored in the Columns collection of the DataRow. The Row and the Column collections are indexed both by index and by name. In effect, you can think of the DataSet object as an in-memory database. Listing 23-9 shows a sample program that retrieves a single record using a DataSet object.

Listing 23-9: **Retrieving a Single Record Through a DataSet**

```
static void TestSelectWithDataSet(string customerID)
{
    // Set SQL statement strings
    string strSQLSelect = "EXEC [pc_getCustomer_ByCustomerID]
@CustomerID_1='" + customerID + "'";

    // Create OleDb objects
    OleDbConnection databaseConnection = new
OleDbConnection(oleDbConnectionString);
    OleDbCommand selectCommand = new OleDbCommand(strSQLSelect,
databaseConnection);
    OleDbDataAdapter dsCmd = new OleDbDataAdapter();
    DataSet resultDataSet = new DataSet();

    // We are dealing with a SQL statement (i.e. NOT a Stored
Proc)
    selectCommand.CommandType = CommandType.Text;

    try
    {
        // Establish database connection
        databaseConnection.Open();

        // Execute SQL Command
        dsCmd.SelectCommand = selectCommand;
        int numRows = dsCmd.Fill(resultDataSet, "Customers");

        // Report results
        if (numRows > 0)
        {
                string contactName =
resultDataSet.Tables["Customers"].Rows[0]["ContactName"].ToStri
ng();
                string contactTitle =
resultDataSet.Tables["Customers"].Rows[0]["ContactTitle"].ToStr
ing();

                Console.WriteLine("Contact name is {0},
title is {1}.", contactName, contactTitle);
        }
        else
```

```
            {
                        Console.WriteLine("No rows found!");
            }
        }
    catch (Exception e)
        {
            Console.WriteLine("****** Caught an exception:\n{0}",
    e.Message);
        }
        finally
        {
            databaseConnection.Close();
        }
    }
```

Data operations that affect single-row entities

This section looks at the InsertCommand, UpdateCommand, and DeleteCommand properties of the DataAdapter object. For each of these commands, you can either programmatically set the command or have the command auto-generated. Programmatically setting the command usually results in better performance because there is less overhead.

Insert operations affecting single-row entities

The code in Listing 23-10 uses a common idiom that comes in handy when auto-generating Insert statements. An empty DataSet is fetched through a SelectCommand. The only purpose of this Fill() call is to retrieve the structure of the rows you want to manipulate. This is more flexible than programmatically defining this structure.

The secret to auto-generating DataAdapter commands is creating a CommandBuilder object using the DataAdapter as an argument in the constructor, as shown in the following lines:

```
// The following line is key to auto-generating statements!!!
OleDbCommandBuilder custCB = new OleDbCommandBuilder(dsCmd);
```

Without these lines, the subsequent Update() statement fails because the InsertCommand cannot be auto-generated. The same requirement exists for auto-generated UpdateCommand and DeleteCommand operations.

Listing 23-10 shows the complete procedure in action. After retrieving the structure of the Customers table using a stored procedure (shown in Listing 23-11), a new row is created through a call to the NewRow() method. A value is then set for each column of the new row. Then, the newly filled in row is added to the Rows collection through a call to the AddRow() method. Finally, this change is propagated to the originated data source through a call to the Update() method of the DataAdapter.

Listing 23-10: Adding a Single Record Through an Auto-Generated InsertCommand

```
static void TestAutoInsertWithDataSet(string customerID)
{
    // Set SQL statement strings, we only need the meta-data so
it doesn't matter that
    // no records are matching this CustomerID.
    string strSQLSelect = "EXEC [pc_getCustomer_ByCustomerID]
@CustomerID_1='???'";

    // Create OleDb objects
    OleDbConnection databaseConnection = new
OleDbConnection(oleDbConnectionString);
    OleDbCommand selectCommand = new OleDbCommand(strSQLSelect,
databaseConnection);
    OleDbDataAdapter dsCmd = new OleDbDataAdapter();
    // The following line is key to auto-generating
statements!!!
    OleDbCommandBuilder custCB = new
OleDbCommandBuilder(dsCmd);
    DataSet resultDataSet = new DataSet();

    // We are dealing with a SQL statement (i.e. NOT a Stored
Proc)
    selectCommand.CommandType = CommandType.Text;

    try
    {
        // Establish database connection
        databaseConnection.Open();

        // Execute SQL Command
        dsCmd.SelectCommand = selectCommand;
        // This retrieves the structure of the Customers table
        int numRows = dsCmd.Fill(resultDataSet, "Customers");

        // Create a new Row
        DataRow workRow =
resultDataSet.Tables["Customers"].NewRow();

        // Fill in workrow data
        workRow["CustomerID"] = customerID;               // 1
        workRow["CompanyName"] = "Hungry Coyote Export Store";
// 2
        workRow["ContactName"] = "Yoshi Latimer";          //
3
```

```
            workRow["ContactTitle"] = "Sales Representative";
// 4
            workRow["Address"] = "City Center Plaza 516 Main St.";
// 5
            workRow["City"] = "Elgin";                        // 6
            workRow["Region"] = "OR";                         // 7
            workRow["PostalCode"] = "97827";                   // 8
            workRow["Country"] = "USA";                       // 9
            workRow["Phone"] = "(503) 555-6874";              //
10
            workRow["Fax"] = "(503) 555-2376";                // 11

resultDataSet.Tables["Customers"].Rows.Add(workRow);

            // Reconcile changes with the data source
            dsCmd.Update(resultDataSet, "Customers");

            // Report results
            Console.WriteLine("Inserted 1 row.");
        }
    catch (Exception e)
    {
        Console.WriteLine("****** Caught an exception:\n{0}",
e.Message);
        }
    finally
    {
        databaseConnection.Close();
        }
}
```

Listing 23-11: A Stored Procedure to Retrieve the Structure of the Customers Table

```
USE [Northwind]
  GO
  CREATE PROCEDURE [pc_getCustomer_ByCustomerID]
      (@CustomerID_1 [nchar](5))
AS
  SELECT
    [CustomerID],
    [CompanyName],
    [ContactName],
    [ContactTitle],
    [Address],
    [City],
    [Region],
```

Continued

Listing 23-11 *(continued)*

```
    [PostalCode],
    [Country],
    [Phone],
    [Fax]
FROM [Northwind].[dbo].[Customers]
WHERE
    [CustomerID] = @CustomerID_1
```

You need to programmatically define a command to do the insert. You already learned how to do this with a parameterized stored procedure (one of the most efficient ways to perform data operations, by the way) in Listing 23-5. After you have defined the command and its parameters, all you need to do is set the InsertCommand of the DataAdapter, as shown in Listing 23-12. The remainder of the code (creating a new row, setting the column values, adding the new row, and updating the data source) is identical to the code used when using an auto-generated InsertCommand. Because you use a similar approach to manually create a command for the UpdateCommand and the DeleteCommand, the following section shows only how to use auto-generated commands.

Listing 23-12: **Adding a Single Record Through an InsertCommand**

```
static void TestDataSetInsertCommand(string customerID)
{
    // Set SQL statement strings
    string strSQLSelect = "EXEC [pc_getCustomer_ByCustomerID]
@CustomerID_1='???'";
    string strSQLInsert = "[pc_insCustomers]";

    // Create OleDb objects
    OleDbConnection databaseConnection = new
OleDbConnection(oleDbConnectionString);
    OleDbCommand selectCommand = new OleDbCommand(strSQLSelect,
databaseConnection);
    OleDbDataAdapter dsCmd = new OleDbDataAdapter();
    DataSet resultDataSet = new DataSet();

    // We are dealing with a SQL statement (i.e. NOT a Stored
Proc)
    selectCommand.CommandType = CommandType.Text;

    OleDbCommand insertCommand = new OleDbCommand(strSQLInsert,
databaseConnection);
    insertCommand.CommandType = CommandType.StoredProcedure;
    insertCommand.CommandText = "[pc_insCustomers]";
```

```
    insertCommand.Connection = databaseConnection;

    // Add each parameter (#1 of 11)
    OleDbParameter param =
insertCommand.Parameters.Add("@CustomerID_1",
OleDbType.VarChar, 5);
    param.Direction = ParameterDirection.Input;
    param.SourceColumn = "CustomerID";
    // Add each parameter (#2 of 11)
    param = insertCommand.Parameters.Add("@CompanyName_2",
OleDbType.VarChar, 40);
    param.Direction = ParameterDirection.Input;
    param.SourceColumn = "CompanyName";
    // Add each parameter 3-10
    // Etc.
    // Add each parameter (#11 of 11)
param = insertCommand.Parameters.Add("@Fax_11",
OleDbType.VarChar, 24);
    param.Direction = ParameterDirection.Input;
    param.SourceColumn = "Fax";

    try
    {
        // Establish database connection
        databaseConnection.Open();

        // Execute SQL Command
        dsCmd.SelectCommand = selectCommand;
        dsCmd.InsertCommand = insertCommand;

        int numRows = dsCmd.Fill(resultDataSet, "Customers");

        // Create a new Row
        DataRow workRow =
resultDataSet.Tables["Customers"].NewRow();

        // Fill in workrow data
        workRow["CustomerID"] = customerID;                   // 1
        workRow["CompanyName"] = "Hungry Coyote Export Store";
// 2
        workRow["ContactName"] = "Yoshi Latimer";            //
3
        workRow["ContactTitle"] = "Sales Representative";
// 4
        workRow["Address"] = "City Center Plaza 516 Main St.";
// 5
        workRow["City"] = "Elgin";                         // 6
        workRow["Region"] = "OR";                          // 7
        workRow["PostalCode"] = "97827";                    // 8
        workRow["Country"] = "USA";                        // 9
        workRow["Phone"] = "(503) 555-6874";               //
10
```

Continued

Listing 23-12 *(continued)*

```
        workRow["Fax"] = "(503) 555-2376";                    // 11

        resultDataSet.Tables["Customers"].Rows.Add(workRow);

        // Reconcile changes with the data source
        dsCmd.Update(resultDataSet, "Customers");

        // Report results
        Console.WriteLine("Inserted 1 row.");
    }
    catch (Exception e)
    {
        Console.WriteLine("****** Caught an exception:\n{0}",
e.Message);
    }
    finally
    {
        databaseConnection.Close();
    }
}
```

Update operations affecting single-row entities

For update operations performed through a DataSet, you obviously first need to retrieve the row you want to modify. Therefore, there is no need for the trick shown for the Insert statement. After retrieving a DataSet, you can simply update a column of a specific row. You can then call the Update() method of the DataAdapter to propagate the changes to the data source. By now, the content of Listing 23-13 will look very familiar. As pointed out in the previous section, not using auto-generated statements simply means that you need to manually create a command to handle the Update statement.

Listing 23-13: Updating a Single Record Through an Auto-Generated UpdateCommand

```
static void TestAutoUpdateWithDataSet(string customerID)
{
    // Set SQL statement strings
    string strSQLSelect = "EXEC [pc_getCustomer_ByCustomerID]
@CustomerID_1='" + customerID + "'";

    // Create OleDb objects
    OleDbConnection databaseConnection = new
OleDbConnection(oleDbConnectionString);
```

```
    OleDbCommand selectCommand = new OleDbCommand(strSQLSelect,
databaseConnection);
    OleDbDataAdapter dsCmd = new OleDbDataAdapter();
    // The following line is key to auto-generating
statements!!!
    OleDbCommandBuilder custCB = new
OleDbCommandBuilder(dsCmd);
    DataSet resultDataSet = new DataSet();

    // We are dealing with a SQL statement (i.e. NOT a Stored
Proc)
    selectCommand.CommandType = CommandType.Text;

    try
    {
        // Establish database connection
        databaseConnection.Open();

        // Execute SQL Command
        dsCmd.SelectCommand = selectCommand;
        int numRows = dsCmd.Fill(resultDataSet, "Customers");

        // Report results
        if (numRows > 0)
        {

resultDataSet.Tables["Customers"].Rows[0]["ContactTitle"] =
"Sr. Sales Representative";

            // Reconcile changes with the data source
            dsCmd.Update(resultDataSet, "Customers");

            Console.WriteLine("1 row updated!");
        }
        else
        {
            Console.WriteLine("No rows found!");
        }
    }
    catch (Exception e)
    {
        Console.WriteLine("****** Caught an exception:\n{0}",
e.Message);
    }
    finally
    {
        databaseConnection.Close();
    }
}
```

Delete operations affecting single-row entities

Of course, not all operations affecting single-row entities need to be performed through a DataSet. You can also use a stored procedure or a SQL statement. Listing 23-14 shows how to use a SQL statement to delete a single row in a table.

Listing 23-14: Deleting a Single Record Through a SQL Statement

```
static void TestDeleteStatement(string customerID)
{
    // Set SQL statement strings
    string strSQLDelete = "DELETE FROM Customers WHERE
CustomerID = '" + customerID + "'";

    // Create OleDb objects
    OleDbConnection databaseConnection = new
OleDbConnection(oleDbConnectionString);
    OleDbCommand deleteCommand = new OleDbCommand(strSQLDelete,
databaseConnection);

    // We are dealing with a SQL statement (i.e. NOT a Stored
Proc)
    deleteCommand.CommandType = CommandType.Text;

    try
    {
        // Establish database connection
        databaseConnection.Open();

        // Execute SQL Command
        int numRows = deleteCommand.ExecuteNonQuery();

        // Report results
        Console.WriteLine("Deleted {0} row(s).",
numRows.ToString());
    }
    catch (Exception e)
    {
        Console.WriteLine("****** Caught an exception:\n{0}",
e.Message);
    }
    finally
    {
        databaseConnection.Close();
    }
}
```

Listing 23-15 finishes coverage of auto-generated commands by showing you how to delete a single row using this approach. After filling a DataSet, you can remove a row with a `Delete()` call. As always, an `Update()` call is needed to persist this change to the data source.

Listing 23-15: Deleting a Single Record Through an Auto-Generated DeleteCommand

```
static void TestAutoDeleteWithDataSet(string customerID)
{
    // Set SQL statement strings
    string strSQLSelect = "EXEC [pc_getCustomer_ByCustomerID]
@CustomerID_1='" + customerID + "'";

    // Create OleDb objects
    OleDbConnection databaseConnection = new
OleDbConnection(oleDbConnectionString);
    OleDbCommand selectCommand = new OleDbCommand(strSQLSelect,
databaseConnection);
    OleDbDataAdapter dsCmd = new OleDbDataAdapter();
    // The following line is key to auto-generating
statements!!!
    OleDbCommandBuilder custCB = new
OleDbCommandBuilder(dsCmd);
    DataSet resultDataSet = new DataSet();

    // We are dealing with a SQL statement (i.e. NOT a Stored
Proc)
    selectCommand.CommandType = CommandType.Text;

    try
    {
        // Establish database connection
        databaseConnection.Open();

        // Execute SQL Command
        dsCmd.SelectCommand = selectCommand;
        int numRows = dsCmd.Fill(resultDataSet, "Customers");

        // Report results
        if (numRows > 0)
        {
            resultDataSet.Tables["Customers"].Rows[0].Delete();

            // Reconcile changes with the data source
```

Continued

Listing 23-15 *(continued)*

```
            dsCmd.Update(resultDataSet, "Customers");

            Console.WriteLine("1 row deleted!");
        }
        else
        {
            Console.WriteLine("No rows found!");
        }
    }
    catch (Exception e)
    {
        Console.WriteLine("****** Caught an exception:\n{0}",
e.Message);
    }
    finally
    {
        databaseConnection.Close();
    }
}
```

Data operations returning sets of rows

You already saw two ways of retrieving sets of rows when you examined how to
retrieve a single row. Listing 23-16 uses a stored procedure to illustrate the retrieval
of a set of rows. It uses a TOP 5 statement to keep the number of returned rows to
an acceptable number. The only significant difference between Listing 23-17 and
Listing 23-8 is the use of a while loop (instead of an if statement) to iterate
through all the records.

**Listing 23-16: A SQL Server Stored Procedure to Select a Set
of Records**

```
USE [Northwind]
GO
CREATE PROCEDURE [pc_getCustomers]
AS
SELECT TOP 5
    [CustomerID],
    [CompanyName],
    [ContactName],
    [ContactTitle],
    [Address],
    [City],
    [Region],
```

```
        [PostalCode],
        [Country],
        [Phone],
        [Fax]
FROM [Northwind].[dbo].[Customers]
```

Listing 23-17: **Retrieving a Set of Records with a DataReader**

```
static void TestSelectManyWithDataReader(string customerID)
{
    // Set SQL statement strings
    string strSQLSelect = "[pc_getCustomers]";

    // Create OleDb objects
    OleDbConnection databaseConnection = new
OleDbConnection(oleDbConnectionString);
    OleDbCommand selectCommand = new OleDbCommand(strSQLSelect,
databaseConnection);

    // We are dealing with a Stored Proc (i.e. NOT a SQL
statement)
    selectCommand.CommandType = CommandType.StoredProcedure;

    try
    {
        // Establish database connection
        databaseConnection.Open();

        // Execute SQL Command
        OleDbDataReader rowReader =
selectCommand.ExecuteReader();

        // Report results
        while(rowReader.Read())
        {
            string contactName =
rowReader["ContactName"].ToString();
            string contactTitle =
rowReader["ContactTitle"].ToString();
            Console.WriteLine("Contact name is {0}, title is
{1}.", contactName, contactTitle);
        }
    }
    catch (Exception e)
    {
        Console.WriteLine("****** Caught an exception:\n{0}",
e.Message);
```

Continued

Listing 23-17 *(continued)*

```
    }
    finally
    {
        databaseConnection.Close();
    }
}
```

Using a DataSet object to retrieve a set of records will equally look familiar (refer to Listing 23-9). Again, all that you need to do is add an iteration to catch all the retrieved records. This can be done with a for loop, as shown in Listing 23-18.

Listing 23-18: **Retrieving a Set of Records with a DataSet**

```
static void TestSelectManyWithDataSet(string customerID)
{
    // Set SQL statement strings
    string strSQLSelect = "[pc_getCustomers]";

    // Create OleDb objects
    OleDbConnection databaseConnection = new
OleDbConnection(oleDbConnectionString);
    OleDbCommand selectCommand = new OleDbCommand(strSQLSelect,
databaseConnection);
    OleDbDataAdapter dsCmd = new OleDbDataAdapter();
    DataSet resultDataSet = new DataSet();

    // We are dealing with a Stored Proc (i.e. NOT a SQL
statement)
    selectCommand.CommandType = CommandType.StoredProcedure;

    try
    {
        // Establish database connection
        databaseConnection.Open();

        // Execute SQL Command
        dsCmd.SelectCommand = selectCommand;
        int numRows = dsCmd.Fill(resultDataSet, "Customers");

        // Report results
        if (numRows > 0)
        {
```

```
                // numRows =
resultDataSet.Tables["Customers"].Rows.Count
for (int i=0; i<= numRows - 1; i++)
            {
                string contactName
    =
resultDataSet.Tables["Customers"].Rows[i]["ContactName"].ToStri
ng();
                string contactTitle
    =
resultDataSet.Tables["Customers"].Rows[i]["ContactTitle"].ToStr
ing();

                Console.WriteLine("Contact name is {0}, title
is {1}.", contactName, contactTitle);
            }
        }
        else
        {
            Console.WriteLine("No rows found!");
        }
    }
    catch (Exception e)
    {
        Console.WriteLine("****** Caught an exception:\n{0}",
e.Message);
    }
    finally
    {
        databaseConnection.Close();
    }
}
```

Data operations affecting sets of rows

Data operations affecting a set of rows follow the same structure as operations affecting a single row. Listing 23-19 adds two new rows before calling the Update() command. A comparison with Listing 23-10 reveals no difference apart from the obvious addition of the coding that creates, sets, and adds the second row. Because of the similarities between the code for a single row and the code for multiple rows, this section does not repeat all the examples shown previously for Update and Delete statements affecting multiple rows.

Listing 23-19: Adding Two Records Through an Auto-Generated InsertCommand

```
static void TestAutoInsert2WithDataSet(string customerID1,
string customerID2)
{
    // Set SQL statement strings
    string strSQLSelect = "EXEC [pc_getCustomer_ByCustomerID]
@CustomerID_1='???'";

    // Create OleDb objects
    OleDbConnection databaseConnection = new
OleDbConnection(oleDbConnectionString);
    OleDbCommand selectCommand = new OleDbCommand(strSQLSelect,
databaseConnection);
    OleDbDataAdapter dsCmd = new OleDbDataAdapter();
    // The following line is key to auto-generating
statements!!!
    OleDbCommandBuilder custCB = new
OleDbCommandBuilder(dsCmd);
    DataSet resultDataSet = new DataSet();

    // We are dealing with a SQL statement (i.e. NOT a Stored
Proc)
    selectCommand.CommandType = CommandType.Text;

    try
    {
        // Establish database connection
        databaseConnection.Open();

        // Execute SQL Command
        dsCmd.SelectCommand = selectCommand;
        int numRows = dsCmd.Fill(resultDataSet, "Customers");

        // Create a first new Row
        DataRow workRow =
resultDataSet.Tables["Customers"].NewRow();

        // Fill in workrow data
        workRow["CustomerID"] = customerID1;               //
1
        workRow["CompanyName"] = "Hungry Coyote Export Store";
// 2
        workRow["ContactName"] = "Yoshi Latimer";            //
3
        workRow["ContactTitle"] = "Sales Representative";
// 4
        workRow["Address"] = "City Center Plaza 516 Main St.";
// 5
        workRow["City"] = "Elgin";                           // 6
```

```
        workRow["Region"] = "OR";                        // 7
        workRow["PostalCode"] = "97827";                   // 8
        workRow["Country"] = "USA";                        // 9
        workRow["Phone"] = "(503) 555-6874";                 //
10
        workRow["Fax"] = "(503) 555-2376";                // 11

        resultDataSet.Tables["Customers"].Rows.Add(workRow);

        // Create a second new Row
        workRow = resultDataSet.Tables["Customers"].NewRow();

        // Fill in workrow data
        workRow["CustomerID"] = customerID2;               //
1
        workRow["CompanyName"] = "Hungry Coyote Export Store";
// 2
        workRow["ContactName"] = "Yoshi Latimer";           //
3
        workRow["ContactTitle"] = "Sales Representative";
// 4
        workRow["Address"] = "City Center Plaza 516 Main St.";
// 5
        workRow["City"] = "Elgin";                       // 6
        workRow["Region"] = "OR";                        // 7
        workRow["PostalCode"] = "97827";                   // 8
        workRow["Country"] = "USA";                        // 9
        workRow["Phone"] = "(503) 555-6874";                 //
10
        workRow["Fax"] = "(503) 555-2376";                // 11


        resultDataSet.Tables["Customers"].Rows.Add(workRow);

        // Reconcile changes with the data source
        dsCmd.Update(resultDataSet, "Customers");

        // Report results
        Console.WriteLine("Inserted 2 rows.");
    }
    catch (Exception e)
    {
        Console.WriteLine("****** Caught an exception:\n{0}",
e.Message);
    }
    finally
    {
        databaseConnection.Close();
    }
}
```

Operations that return hierarchical data

A little known feature of ADO is that you can retrieve several sets of data in one pass. ADO.NET also has this feature. In the stored procedure listed in Listing 23-20, notice the two consecutive stored procedures. (Again, the output is limited to five records each for testing purposes.)

Listing 23-20: A SQL Server Stored Procedure with
Two Select Statements

```
USE [Northwind]
GO
CREATE PROCEDURE [pc_getOrdersAndDetails]
AS
SELECT TOP 5
    OrderID,
    CustomerID,
    EmployeeID,
    OrderDate,
    RequiredDate,
    ShippedDate,
    ShipVia,
    Freight,
    ShipName,
    ShipAddress,
    ShipCity,
    ShipRegion,
    ShipPostalCode,
    ShipCountry
FROM Orders

SELECT TOP 5
    OrderID,
    ProductID,
    UnitPrice,
    Quantity,
    Discount
FROM [Order Details]
GO
```

To retrieve this data, you use a DataReader in a similar fashion as you have done to retrieve a set of rows. However, if you compare the code in Listing 23-21 with the code in Listing 23-17, you will notice an extra loop around the row iteration. This extra loops ends when NextResults() is False. That's actually all that is needed to retrieve multiple-row sets.

Listing 23-21: Retrieving Several Sets of Data with a DataReader

```
static void TestSelectHierWithDataReader()
{
    // Set SQL statement strings
    string strSQLSelect = "[pc_getOrdersAndDetails]";

    // Create OleDb objects
    OleDbConnection databaseConnection = new
OleDbConnection(oleDbConnectionString);
    OleDbCommand selectCommand = new OleDbCommand(strSQLSelect,
databaseConnection);

    // We are dealing with a Stored Proc (i.e. NOT a SQL
statement)
    selectCommand.CommandType = CommandType.StoredProcedure;

    try
    {
        // Establish database connection
        databaseConnection.Open();

        // Execute SQL Command
        OleDbDataReader rowReader =
selectCommand.ExecuteReader();

        // Report results
        for (;;)
        {
            while(rowReader.Read())
            {
                string row = "";
                for (int i=0; i<= rowReader.FieldCount - 1;
i++)
                {
                    row = row + rowReader[i] + ", ";
                }
                Console.WriteLine("Row is {0}",
row.Substring(0,row.Length -2));
            }
            if(!rowReader.NextResult())
                break;
            else
                Console.WriteLine("Next Results:");
        }
    }
```

Continued

Listing 23-21 *(continued)*

```
    catch (Exception e)
    {
        Console.WriteLine("****** Caught an exception:\n{0}",
e.Message);
    }
    finally
    {
        databaseConnection.Close();
    }
}
```

In the last code section, you discover one of the strengths of the DataSet object: retrieving related data. Because the DataSet was designed to function as an in-memory database, it has all the functionality you need to deal with parent-child relationships. The next two listings illustrate data retrieval. Listing 23-22 shows how related data is retrieved through a SQL statement, while Listing 23-23 shows how to retrieve related data using a DataSet object. Listing 23-23 demonstrates how you deal with such relationships. Again, it uses a stored procedure that returns data from two Select statements. The Select statements are related and you want to achieve the same result in ADO.NET as if you retrieved the data with a SQL statement similar to the one shown in Listing 23-22.

Listing 23-22: Retrieving Related Data with a SQL Statement

```
SELECT
    Orders.OrderID,
    Orders.CustomerID,
    Orders.EmployeeID,
    Orders.OrderDate,
    Orders.RequiredDate,
    Orders.ShippedDate,
    Orders.ShipVia,
    Orders.Freight,
    Orders.ShipName,
    Orders.ShipAddress,
    Orders.ShipCity,
    Orders.ShipRegion,
    Orders.ShipPostalCode,
    Orders.ShipCountry,
    [Order Details].ProductID,
    [Order Details].UnitPrice,
    [Order Details].Quantity,
    [Order Details].Discount
```

```
FROM Orders
INNER JOIN [Order Details]
    ON Orders.OrderID = [Order Details].OrderID
```

Inside the `try` statement in Listing 23-23, you start by mapping the data tables to the source tables used in the SQL query. The code that follows, filling the DataSet, is the familiar code seen below. Next is the part where you define the relationship between the two tables. You need primary keys when setting up foreign key relationships in a relational database management system (RDBMS), and our in-memory database is no different. The `PrimaryKey` property takes an array of `DataColumn` objects. After you set up the primary keys, you can define a relationship. The first parameter is the name of the relationship, which you use below when retrieving child records. For demonstration purposes, the example retrieves only the first parent row. It then retrieves all associated child rows by using the `GetChildRows()` method using the name of the relationship. You can then loop through the array of `DataRow` objects to display the children.

Listing 23-23: **Retrieving Related Data with a DataSet**

```
static void TestSelectHierWithDataSet()
{
    // Set SQL statement strings
    string strSQLSelect = "[pc_getOrdersAndDetails]";

    // Create OleDb objects
    OleDbConnection databaseConnection = new
OleDbConnection(oleDbConnectionString);
    OleDbCommand selectCommand = new OleDbCommand(strSQLSelect,
databaseConnection);
    OleDbDataAdapter dsCmd = new OleDbDataAdapter();
    DataSet resultDataSet = new DataSet();

    // We are dealing with a Stored Proc (i.e. NOT a SQL
statement)
    selectCommand.CommandType = CommandType.StoredProcedure;

    try
    {
        dsCmd.TableMappings.Add("Orders", "Orders");
        dsCmd.TableMappings.Add("Orders1", "Order Details");

        // Establish database connection
```

Continued

Listing 23-23 *(continued)*

```
        databaseConnection.Open();

        // Execute SQL Command
        dsCmd.SelectCommand = selectCommand;
        // Since there were no tables within the DataSet prior
to invoking the Fill method,
        // the OleDbDataAdapter will automatically create the
tables for the DataSet
        // and populate them with the returned data. If you
build the tables prior to executing
        // the FillDataSet method, the OleDbDataAdapter will
simply fill the existing tables.
        int numRows = dsCmd.Fill(resultDataSet, "Orders");

        // Reduce the number of dots by saving the references
to the tables
        DataTable orderTable = resultDataSet.Tables["Orders"];
        DataTable detailsTable = resultDataSet.Tables["Order
Details"];

        // Set the Primary Key for the Tables
        orderTable.PrimaryKey =
            new DataColumn[] {
orderTable.Columns["OrderID"]
                };
        detailsTable.PrimaryKey =
new DataColumn[] {
detailsTable.Columns["OrderID"],
detailsTable.Columns["ProductID"]
};
// Establish the Foreign Key relationship between the tables
        resultDataSet.Relations.Add(new
DataRelation("Order_Detail",
                        new DataColumn[] {
orderTable.Columns["OrderID"]
                            },
                        new DataColumn[] {
                        detailsTable.Columns["OrderID"]
                            }));
        // Report results
        // Display an order
        DataRow orderRow = orderTable.Rows[0];
        Console.WriteLine("Order ID is {0}, date is {1}, Ship
To is {2}.",
orderRow["OrderID"],
orderRow["OrderDate"],
orderRow["ShipName"]);
        // Retrieve child rows for the order using the Name of
the Relation
```

```
        DataRow[] detailRows =
orderRow.GetChildRows("Order_Detail");
        // Do something with the child rows collection
        DataRow detailRow;
        for (int i=0; i <= detailRows.Length - 1; i++)
        {
            // Do something with the detail row
            detailRow = detailRows[i];
            Console.WriteLine("Product ID is {0}, Quantity is
{1}.",
detailRow["ProductID"],
detailRow["Quantity"]);
        }
    }
    catch (Exception e)
    {
        Console.WriteLine("****** Caught an exception:\n{0}",
e.Message);
    }
    finally
    {
        databaseConnection.Close();
    }
}
```

Summary

This chapter describes all the types of operations you may want to perform with ADO.NET. You see how easy and versatile the objects in the System.Data namespace are, including the powerful DataSet object, which acts as an in-memory database. It also describes how to return rows with single entities and how to delete and update operations.

Keep in mind that the ADO.NET provider architecture is reflected in the .NET Framework classes that support ADO.NET. You can use the Sql classes to make use of the ADO.NET SQL Server provider or the OleDb classes to make use of the ADO.NET OLE DB provider. If your application is going to support only SQL Server, then you should use the Sql classes, since the SQL Server provider for ADO.NET is more efficient and a better performer than the OLE DB provider when targeting SQL Server. If your application may need to support databases other than SQL Server, then using the OleDb classes will be a better choice.

✦　　✦　　✦

Working with Files and the Windows Registry

File operations are something every programmer has to deal with at one point or another. The System.IO class contains a plethora of methods for reading and writing to and from files. This class makes file IO and manipulation simple yet enables you a great deal of control when accessing files. Much like file IO in the past, accessing the Windows Registry was always a tedious task. Accessing the Windows Registry involved many API calls that degraded application performance and typically forced programmers to write their own wrapper classes for these operations. With .NET all of this changes.

In this chapter you learn to read and write data to and from files. The chapter covers IO operations that deal with standard text as well as binary data. It then covers some useful file operations, such as moving, renaming, and deleting files. Finally, you learn to monitor the file system for changes to specific files and then move on to navigating the Windows Registry.

Accessing Files

File access in .NET is generally handled with stream objects. A few classes, however, rely on the stream object for access to files. In this chapter, you examine two of these classes to build on your knowledge of file IO.

Binary access

The `BinaryReader` and `BinaryWriter` classes support binary file access. These classes permit binary operations to and from streams. Because streams are used, the classes can be very flexible, and they don't have to deal with details, such as stream position or access. The following section examines the `BinaryWriter` access class.

BinaryWriter

The `BinaryWriter` class allows primitive data types to be written to streams; and with the use of subclassing, you can override the methods of this class and fulfill your own unique character encoding requirements. Because this class uses an underlying stream, you have very few methods and properties to deal with. Table 24-1 contains the five basic properties and methods that you would typically use when dealing with the `BinaryWriter` class.

Table 24-1
Basic BinaryWriter Class Members

Name	Type	Purpose
BaseStream	Property	Allows access to the BinaryWriter's underlying stream
Close	Method	Closes the `BinaryWriter` class and the underlying stream, flushing out all pending write operations
Flush	Method	Flushes out all data to the underlying stream and then clears the buffers
Seek	Method	Sets the current position within the current stream
Write	Method	This overloaded method writes a value out to the current stream. Write currently supports 18 data type variations.

To write binary data to a file, first you must create a file stream. You can then instantiate a new `BinaryWriter` class, passing it your stream. After you create the `BinaryWriter` class, simply call its `Write()` method and pass it the data to be written, as shown in Listing 24-1.

Listing 24-1: **Write String Data to a File Stream Using the BinaryWriter Class**

```
static void Main(string[] args)
{
   FileStream myFStream = new  FileStream ("c:\\TestFile.dat",
FileMode.OpenOrCreate, FileAccess.ReadWrite);
   BinaryWriter binWrit = new BinaryWriter(myFStream);
   string testString = "This is a test string.";
   binWrit.Write(testString);
   binWrit.Close();
   myFStream.Close();
}
```

Ensure that when you finish with the BinaryWriter class, you close it and the stream. Failure to close the BinaryWriter or FileStream class can result in a loss of data.

BinaryReader

The BinaryReader class, much like the BinaryWriter class, relies on a FileStream object for accessing files.

To demonstrate the BinaryReader class, examine the application in Listing 24-2, which reads the binary header information from a bitmap file. From this header information, you can determine both the horizontal and vertical size of the image file as well as the color depth in bits.

Listing 24-2: **BitmapSize Application**

```
using System;
using System.IO;

namespace BitmapSize
{
  class Class1
  {
    static void Main(string[] args)
    {
      long bmpWidth    = 0;
      long bmpHeight   = 0;
      int bmpPlanes    = 0;
      int bmpBitCount  = 0;
```

Continued

Listing 24-2 *(continued)*

```
        string [] cma    = Environment.GetCommandLineArgs();

        if (cma.GetUpperBound(0) >= 1)
        {
          FileStream myFStream = new
FileStream(cma[1],FileMode.Open,FileAccess.Read);
          BinaryReader binRead = new BinaryReader(myFStream);
          binRead.BaseStream.Position=0x12;
          bmpWidth = binRead.ReadInt32();
          bmpHeight= binRead.ReadInt32();
          bmpPlanes= binRead.ReadInt16();
          bmpBitCount = binRead.ReadInt16();

          Console.WriteLine("[{0}]  {1}x{2} {3}-
bit",cma[1],bmpWidth,bmpHeight,bmpBitCount);
          binRead.Close();
          myFStream.Close();
        }
      }
    }
}
```

The first thing you must do in this application is declare some variables to hold the information you read from the bitmap file, and then you store all the command-line arguments within a string array. In the preceding example, you store the command-line arguments within an array, because one of these arguments determines which file to process.

Element one of the string array should contain the name of the file to process. After you determine whether there is a command-line argument, you can create a FileStream object by passing the filename and the mode you want to use to open the file, as shown here:

```
FileStream myFStream = new FileStream( cma[1], FileMode.Open, FileAccess.Read);
```

As with the BinaryWriter class, you create your BinaryReader object and pass it the FileStream object that you want to use. At this point, you are ready to read a file using binary mode. After examining the layout of a bitmap file, you know that the information you want to obtain begins at position 18 (hex position 12) within the file. By using the BaseStream object of your BinaryReader class, you can directly access the FileStream object. From here, you set the Position property of the object to 0x12, which seeks into the file, to the position from which you want to read.

When your file pointer is in position, you need to read two long values from the file, followed by two integer values. A long value consumes four bytes, so you use the ReadInt32 method twice to retrieve the values. Following this, you use the ReadInt16 method to retrieve the two integer files from the file. See Table 24-2 for a list of the most commonly used methods within the BinaryReader class.

Table 24-2 Commonly Used Methods Within the BinaryReader Class	
Method	**Description**
Close	Closes the BinaryReader object and the base stream
PeekChar	Reads the next available byte from the stream but does not advance the byte or character position within the file
ReadBoolean	Reads a Boolean (True/False) value from the stream
ReadByte	Reads a single byte from the stream. There is also a ReadBytes method for specifying the number of bytes to read.
ReadChar	Reads a single Char value from the stream. There is also a ReadChars method for specifying the number of Chars to read.
ReadInt16	Reads an integer value (2 bytes)
ReadIn32	Reads a long value (4 bytes)
ReadInt64	Reads an eight-byte signed integer

After the information has been retrieved from the file, you simply out put your stored values to the console. After you compile this application, go to a console window and test it with a bitmap image, as shown in Figure 24-1.

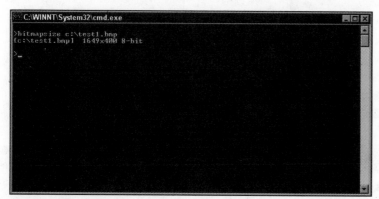

Figure 24-1: Using BinaryReader, you can view the image size of a bitmap file.

Monitoring file changes

Monitoring file changes with C# has become increasingly easier with the use of the FileSystemWatcher object. This object enables you to watch a particular file, a group of files, a directory, or the entire drive for a variety of events, including file changes, file deletions, file creations, and file renaming.

You can begin to use the FileSystemWatcher object in one of two ways. You can create a FileSystemWatcher object using code and then build methods to handle the various events, or you can take the easier approach. The toolbox in the Visual Studio.NET IDE also contains a FileSystemWatcher object that you can insert into your project by double-clicking.

Applications, such as Microsoft Word and Microsoft Excel, both monitor the files you are currently using in case external changes are made to the files. You are then presented with an option to reload the file so you can view all changes made to it. To explore the features of the FileSystemWatcher object, you build an application that monitors all text files on the root of the C: drive and displays relevant information in the application window.

Using File monitor

To begin this sample application, you need to start a new C# Windows application. When the new project window opens up, add two buttons and a list box. After you add the components to Form1, change the names of the buttons to btnStart and btnStop. Change the Text properties of these buttons to Start and Stop, respectively. Now that the controls are in place, arrange them in a fashion similar to Figure 24-2.

Figure 24-2: Drag and drop controls onto the File monitor interface as shown here.

You need to add one additional object to the project: the FileSystemWatcher. Select the Components tab within the toolbox, as shown in Figure 24-3. Double-click the FileSystemWatcher to add an instance of this object to the project.

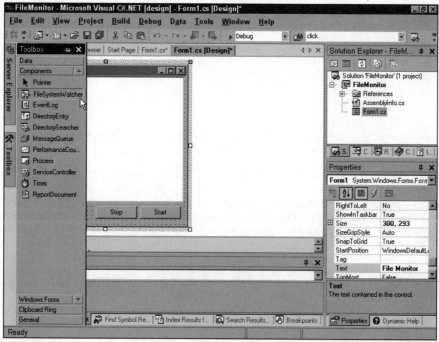

Figure 24-3: The Components tab within the toolbox contains the FileSystemWatcher object.

Select the fileSystemWatcher1 component just below Form1 in the Form Designer. The EnableRaisingEvents property activates the object and allows it to begin watching for file system events. Because you have a Start and Stop button to accomplish this, you need to ensure that the object doesn't activate when the application runs. Change the EnableRaisingEvents property to False. The Filter property enables you to set a file mask of files to watch. You want to watch all text files, so set the Filter property to *.txt. Finally, you need to define the folder in which you want to monitor files. Set the Path property to C:\. to ensure that you are watching only files in the root of the C: drive. It is possible to monitor the entire drive by setting the IncludeSubdirectories property to True, but this is likely to degrade system performance.

Double-click the Start button on Form1, and add the code in Listing 24-3 to the Click event handler.

Listing 24-3: **Start Button Click Event**

```
private void btnStart_Click(object sender, System.EventArgs e)
{
    fileSystemWatcher1.EnableRaisingEvents = true;
    btnStop.Enabled = true;
   btnStart.Enabled = false;
}
```

The preceding code sets the EnableRaisingEvents property to True, which activates the FileSystemWatcher object. You then disable the Start button, so it cannot be clicked again, and enable the Stop button. Now you must add some code to your Stop button to disable the FileSystemWatcher. Add the code in Listing 24-4 to the Click event of the Stop button.

Listing 24-4: **Stop Button Click Event**

```
private void btnStop_Click(object sender, System.EventArgs e)
{
  fileSystemWatcher1.EnableRaisingEvents = false;
  btnStop.Enabled = false;
  btnStart.Enabled = true;
}
```

The FileSystemWatcher is now functional, but you need to add the event handlers to capture all file events. Return to the Form Editor by double-clicking Form1 in the Solution Explorer, and then click the fileSystemWatcher1 object. In the Properties window, click the Events icon on the toolbar. When you click the events listed in the window, you are taken to the code editor to modify those event handlers. Listing 24-5 contains the code that you should enter into the four events.

Listing 24-5: **FileSystemWatcher Event Handlers**

```
private void fileSystemWatcher1_Deleted(object sender,
System.IO.FileSystemEventArgs e)
{
  listBox1.Items.Add( "[" + e.Name + "] Deleted" );
}
private void fileSystemWatcher1_Renamed(object sender,
System.IO.RenamedEventArgs e)
{
  listBox1.Items.Add( "[" + e.OldName + "] Renamed to " + e.Name );
}
```

```
private void fileSystemWatcher1_Changed(object sender,
System.IO.FileSystemEventArgs e)
{
  listBox1.Items.Add( "[" + e.Name + "] Changed" );
}
private void fileSystemWatcher1_Created(object sender,
System.IO.FileSystemEventArgs e)
{
  listBox1.Items.Add( "[" + e.Name + "] Created");
}
```

These event handlers are simplistic; they merely display a message within the list box when a file operation has occurred. Before you test this application, it's important to realize a few things. As you can see by each of these functions, the Changed, Created, and Deleted events all expose the same data; therefore, they have the same signature. The odd one here is the Renamed event. Because three of the four events pass the same data into the event procedure, you could use one event handler to handle all three of these, but you still need a separate handler to take care of the Renamed event.

Press F5 to run the program so you can begin testing it as follows:

1. When the program opens, click the Start button. The application is monitoring the root of the C: drive for changes to text files.

2. Open Windows Explorer; right-click in the Explorer window, and choose New ➪ Text Document to open a new document.

3. In the new document, you note an entry in the list box of your File Monitor application, indicating that a file has been created. Open this new text file; add some text to it, and save it. Again, you see entries in the log window of your application.

4. Now try renaming the file and then deleting it. The results should resemble those shown in Figure 24-4.

Figure 24-4: Your File monitor in action displays file activity in real time.

Understand that the Changed event might fire several times, because the FileSystemWatcher is watching several characteristics of the file. If the file size changes, the Changed event fires. If the modification date and time stamp of the file change, the Changed event fires again, and so on. Don't be discouraged if an event fires more than once. It's generally not an application problem, but insurance that the correct NotifyFilters are set.

Coding the FileSystemWatcher

You can add a FileSystemWatcher to your C# project without using the Visual Studio toolbox. To accomplish this, add a declaration for the object just below your class declaration, as shown in Listing 24-6.

Listing 24-6: Add a FileSystemWatcher Instance to Your Class Declarations

```
public class Form1 : System.Windows.Forms.Form
{
  private FileSystemWatcher MyFileWatcher = new FileSystemWatcher();
```

Because you are creating the control at runtime, you can't go to the Properties window and set the various properties as needed. Instead, you handle these tasks within the Click event of the Start button. After you set the properties as you did in the previous example in Listing 24-6, you need to create event handlers and point them to the proper functions. Listing 24-7 shows the updated listing for your Start button's Click event.

Listing 24-7: Create the Event Handler Declarations in Your Start Button's Click Event

```
private void btnStart_Click(object sender, System.EventArgs e)
{
  MyFileWatcher.Path = "c:\\";
  MyFileWatcher.Filter = "*.txt";
  MyFileWatcher.IncludeSubdirectories = false;
  MyFileWatcher.EnableRaisingEvents = true;

  this.MyFileWatcher.Renamed += new System.IO.RenamedEventHandler(
this.MyFileWatcher_Renamed );
  this.MyFileWatcher.Changed += new System.IO.FileSystemEventHandler(
this.MyFileWatcher_Changed );
  btnStart.Enabled = false;
  btnStop.Enabled = true;
}
```

You can continue by adding some code for the Stop button and then creating your event handlers for the FileSystemWatcher. The function names for these event handlers must match the declaration you placed in the Start buttons click event. Listing 24-8 contains the Stop Click event and the event handlers for your Changed and Renamed events.

> ### Listing 24-8: **Create the Event Handlers for the FileSystemWatcher Object**

```
private void btnStop_Click(object sender, System.EventArgs e)
{
  MyFileWatcher.EnableRaisingEvents = false;
  btnStop.Enabled = false;
  btnStart.Enabled = true;
}

private void MyFileWatcher_Changed(object sender, System.IO.FileSystemEventArgs e)
{
  listBox1.Items.Add ("[" + e.FullPath + "]  Changed");
}

private void MyFileWatcher_Renamed(object sender, System.IO.RenamedEventArgs e)
{
  listBox1.Items.Add("[" + e.OldName + "]  renamed to " + e.Name);
}
```

Manipulating files

File manipulation is file access that manipulates only the file and not the contents. Manipulating the file might include copying the file, deleting the file, or moving it. .NET provides a class called FileInfo within the System.IO namespace for just such actions. This section describes some of the manipulation methods and how to use them properly.

Copying files

The FileInfo class contains, among other things, a method for copying files. This method, CopyTo, is overloaded and has two variations. Variation one simply takes the destination filename. If a file already exists with that name, the method dies. Variation two accepts a destination filename and a Boolean value indicating whether files should be over written.

To demonstrate the CopyTo method, this section shows you how to build a console application for copying files. Because Windows already comes equipped with a Copy command, you name this cp, which is the copy command for the UNIX world.

Listing 24-9 shows the C# implementation of the Copy command in its entirety. Create a new C# console application named cp, and enter the following code.

Listing 24-9: **C# Implementation of the File Copy Command**

```
using System;
using System.IO;
namespace cp
{
  class Class1
  {
    static void Main(string[] args)
    {
      string [] cla  = Environment.GetCommandLineArgs();
      if (cla.GetUpperBound(0) == 2)
      {
        FileInfo fi = new FileInfo(cla[1]);
        fi.CopyTo(cla[2],true);
        Console.WriteLine("Copied " + fi.Length + " bytes.");
      }
      else
        Console.WriteLine ("Usage: cp <input file> <output file>");
    }
  }
}
```

This code uses the GetCommandLineArgs method of the Environment class to retrieve the command-line arguments that are passed to the application. If the number of arguments is not equal to 2, you simply display a usage message, as shown in the bottom of Listing 24-9, and exit. Otherwise, the command-line arguments are stored within your cla string array for later use.

When using the FileInfo class, you must first create a FileInfo object and pass it the name of the file you are dealing with. When using this application, the first command-line argument is the name of the source file. Because this is stored in element 1 of the string array, simply pass this to your FileInfo object.

To copy a file using this class, simply call its CopyTo method along with the destination filename (which is in element 2 of the string array), and a Boolean value indicating whether a file with the same name should be overwritten. Go to a command prompt to test this program after compiling, as shown in Figure 24-5.

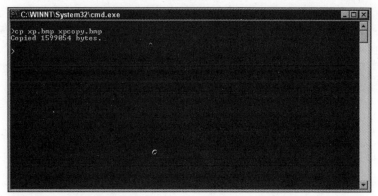

Figure 24-5: Using CopyTo, you can copy a file and display additional information.

You added a bit of a twist on this program, as you can see. After the CopyTo method has completed, you display a message on the console indicating that the operation has completed; and you display the number of bytes that you copied, thanks to the Length property of the FileInfo class.

Deleting files

Deleting files with the FileInfo class is as simple as calling the Delete() method. If the file you want to delete has its Read-Only attribute set, you receive an exception. The example shown in Listing 24-10 creates a C# implementation of the file's Delete command. After the file is deleted, the utility displays the name of the file that was deleted, as well as its attributes.

Create a new C# console application project named rm and enter in the code contained in Listing 24-10.

Listing 24-10: **Use the FileInfo Class to Delete Files with Ease**

```
using System;
using System.IO;
namespace rm
{
  class Class1
  {
    static void Main(string[] args)
    {
      string [] cla  = Environment.GetCommandLineArgs();
      if (cla.GetUpperBound(0) == 1)
      {
```

Continued

Listing 24-10 *(continued)*

```
        FileInfo fi = new FileInfo(cla[1]);
        fi.Delete();
        Console.WriteLine("File       : " + cla[1]);
        Console.WriteLine("Attributes: " + fi.Attributes.ToString());
        Console.WriteLine("File Deleted...");
      }
    else
        Console.WriteLine ("Usage: rm <filename>");
  }
 }
}
```

As with the previous examples, you are storing the command-line arguments within a string array. If that array does not contain the correct number of elements, you simply display a usage message and exit.

Tip

> By using the Delete() method of the FileSystemInfo class, you can delete directories as well as files.

After calling the Delete() method of the FileInfo class, you can display the filename and its attributes to the user, indicating that it was deleted. Using the Attributes property, you can safely determine, before the file is deleted, if it has a Read-Only attribute set. If so, you can prompt the user and/or remove the Read-Only attribute using the Attributes property along with the FileAttributes enumerator.

After your program is compiled, go to a command prompt and test it. Simply type **rm** followed by the filename to delete. The results should resemble those in Figure 24-6.

Moving files

The MoveTo() method of the FileInfo class actually encapsulates two different methods: CopyTo() and Delete(). After a file is copied to the appropriate filename or directory, MoveTo() simply deletes the file much as the Delete() method does.

The following sample application accepts two command-line arguments: Source Filename and Destination Filename. After the file is moved, the program displays when the file was actually created and where the file was moved to. Neither of these outputs has a practical use except to demonstrate how the certain attributes can be obtained, such as the creation time using the CreationTime property.

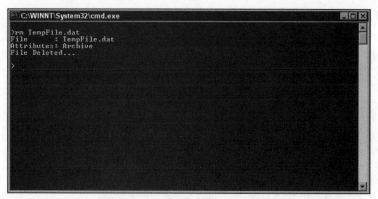

Figure 24-6: The Delete( ) method of the FileInfo class shows the attributes of the deleted file.

Start a new C# console application and name this project **mv**, after the UNIX-based command of the same name. Listing 24-11 shows the application in its entirety.

Listing 24-11: File Move Implementation

```
using System;
using System.IO;
namespace mv
{
  class Class1
  {
    static void Main(string[] args)
    {
      string [] cla  = Environment.GetCommandLineArgs();
      if (cla.GetUpperBound(0) == 2)
      {
        FileInfo fi = new FileInfo(cla[1]);
        fi.MoveTo(cla[2]);
        Console.WriteLine("File Created : " + fi.CreationTime.ToString());
        Console.WriteLine("Moved to     : " + cla[2]);
      }
      else
        Console.WriteLine ("Usage: mv <source file> <destination file>");
    }
  }
}
```

Figure 24-7 shows the output from your File Move utility.

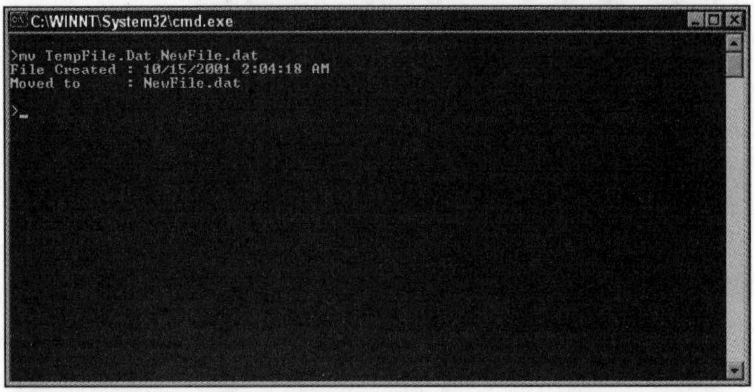

Figure 24-7: Move files with the MoveTo method of the FileInfo class.

Note that in this example, the destination filename can be either a filename or a directory name. If a directory name is specified, the file is moved. If a filename is present, the file is renamed and/or moved. The `MoveTo()` method essentially incorporates copy and rename functions in one method.

Accessing the Registry

Registry access was rather burdensome with the Windows API. C# provides you with some class objects that enable you to read and write to and from the Registry with ease. Using the Registry provides several benefits over older methods, such as text-based INI files. Because the Registry is indexed, searching for keys is fast. The Registry is a structured "document," which allows for structured information, such as a database, just to name one type.

Reading Registry keys

Registry access functionality is contained within the `Microsoft.Win32` namespace, so you need to include this namespace in all your projects by entering the following line at the top of your source code file:

```
using Microsoft.Win32;
```

To read a Registry key, you must use the `RegistryKey` object. To begin exploring this object, examine Listing 24-12, an application that retrieves two pieces of information from the Registry.

Listing 24-12: Retrieve the CPU Type and Speed from the Registry

```
using System;
using Microsoft.Win32;

namespace CPUInfo
{
  class Class1
  {
    static void Main(string[] args)
    {
      RegistryKey RegKey = Registry.LocalMachine;
      RegKey = RegKey.OpenSubKey(
"HARDWARE\\DESCRIPTION\\System\\CentralProcessor\\0");
      Object cpuSpeed = RegKey.GetValue("~MHz");
      Object cpuType  = RegKey.GetValue("VendorIdentifier");
      Console.WriteLine("You have a {0} running at {1}
MHz.",cpuType,cpuSpeed);
    }
  }
}
```

When instantiating an instance of the `RegistryKey`, you set it equal to a member of the `Registry` class. The preceding example sets the `RegistryKey` object equal to the `Registry.LocalMachine` field, which enables you access to the `HKEY_LOCAL_MACHINE` base key. Table 24-3 contains a list of all public fields within the Registry class.

After you establish your `RegistryKey` object, you call its `OpenSubKey()` method and provide the key that you want to open. In this particular case, you want to navigate to the `HKEY_LOCAL_MACHINE\HARDWARE\DESCRIPTION\System\` `Central\Processor\0\` key and read two values from that key. Keep in mind that you must include double backslash characters in the string, so that they are not interpreted as an escape character.

After you open the subkey, issue the following two lines of code to retrieve the `"~MHz"` and `"VendorIdentifier"` values within that subkey:

```
Object cpuSpeed = RegKey.GetValue("~MHz");
Object cpuType  = RegKey.GetValue("VendorIdentifier");
```

Now you have the values stored within the appropriate variables, so you can display the information on the screen. Test the program from a console window, as shown in Figure 24-8.

Table 24-3
Public Fields Within the Registry Class

Field	Description
ClassesRoot	ClassesRoot defines the types of documents and the properties associated with those types. This field starts in the Windows Registry from the key HKEY_CLASSES_ROOT.
CurrentConfig	CurrentConfig contains information pertaining to your computer's hardware. This field starts in the Windows Registry from the key HKEY_CURRENT_CONFIG.
CurrentUser	All preferences for the current user are stored here. This field starts in the Windows Registry from the key HKEY_CURRENT_USER.
DynData	DynData.
LocalMachine	LocalMachine contains configuration information for the computer. This field starts in the Windows Registry from the key HKEY_LOCAL_MACHINE.
PerformanceData	The base key stores performance-related information about the different software components. This field starts in the Windows Registry from the key HKEY_PERFORMANCE_DATA.
Users	This base key contains information that will be applied to a default user's configuration. This field starts in the Windows Registry from the key HKEY_USERS.

Figure 24-8: The RegistryKey class simplifies the reading of important information from the Registry.

Those of you running on multiple processor machines can obtain a list of all processors by enumerating the CentralProcessor key. You find a subkey within CentralProcessor for each CPU contained within your machine.

Writing Registry keys

Creating and writing Registry keys is also accomplished using the RegistryKey object. Several methods in the RegistryKey class are useful when writing keys. Table 24-4 describes the purpose of some of the more prevalent members.

Table 24-4
Common RegistryKey Members

Name	Type	Description
SubKeyCount	Property	This property retrieves a count of the subkeys for the current key.
ValueCount	Property	This property retrieves a count of the number of values for the current key.
Close	Method	This method closes the current key. If changes have been made to the key, changes are flushed to disk.
CreateSubKey	Method	This method creates a new subkey if one doesn't exist, or opens the subkey if it does exist.
DeleteSubKey	Method	This method deletes a subkey. This method is overloaded and contains a Boolean parameter that allows an exception to be thrown if the key cannot be found.
DeleteSubKeyTree	Method	This method deletes a subkey and all child subkeys recursively.
DeleteValue	Method	This method deletes a value from a key. This method is overloaded and contains a Boolean parameter that allows an exception to be thrown if the value is missing.
GetSubKeyNames	Method	This method returns a string array containing all subkey names.
GetValue	Method	This method retrieves a value for a specific key. This method is overloaded and contains a parameter that permits a default value. If the value for a key is not found, the default value you specify will be returned.

Continued

Table 24-4 *(continued)*

Name	Type	Description
GetValueNames	Method	This method returns a string array containing all values for the specified key.
OpenSubKey	Method	This method opens a subkey for processing (read/write access).
SetValue	Method	This method sets a value for a key. To set the default value for a key, set the `subKey` parameter to an empty string.

Caution   Writing values can be dangerous and can cause your system to become unresponsive if care is not taken. Double-check all code before testing any application that writes values to the Registry.

Listing 24-13 shows a simple application that writes two values to the Registry and then reads those values back in to display them.

Listing 24-13: **Write a Text and DWord Value to the Registry**

```csharp
using System;
using Microsoft.Win32;

namespace WriteRegValues
{
  class Class1
  {
    static void Main(string[] args)
    {
      RegistryKey RegKeyWrite = Registry.CurrentUser;
      RegKeyWrite = RegKeyWrite.CreateSubKey
("Software\\CSHARP\\WriteRegistryValue");
      RegKeyWrite.SetValue("Success","TRUE");
      RegKeyWrite.SetValue("AttemptNumber",1);
      RegKeyWrite.Close();

      RegistryKey RegKeyRead = Registry.CurrentUser;
      RegKeyRead = RegKeyRead.OpenSubKey
("Software\\CSHARP\\WriteRegistryValue");
      Object regSuccessful = RegKeyRead.GetValue("Success");
      Object regAttemptNumber = RegKeyRead.GetValue("AttemptNumber");
      RegKeyRead.Close();

      if ((string)regSuccessful == "TRUE")
```

```
        Console.WriteLine("Succeeded on attempt # {0}",regAttemptNumber);
      else
        Console.WriteLine("Failed!");
    }
  }
}
```

After you create a `RegistryKey` object, you can create a new subkey with the `CreateSubKey()` method. Ensure that when using this method, you use double backslash characters, so the compiler doesn't interpret the characters as an escape sequence. In this example, you are creating a new key under HKEY_CURRENT_USER. Store your values in the \Software\CSHARP\WriteRegistryValue subkey.

With the new key in place, use the `SetValue()` method to specify the name of the value and the actual value. This example, stores text in the Success value and a DWord in the AttemptNumber value. After the values are set, it's best to close the key in case of a power outage or similar failure. At this point, the changes have been committed to the Registry. If you open RegEdit and navigate to the proper key, you should see the values shown in Figure 24-9.

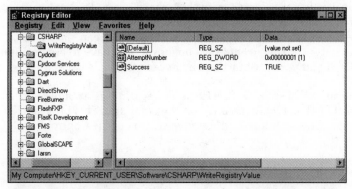

Figure 24-9: RegEdit reveals that your values have been saved.

As with the previous example, you now create a new RegistryKey object and read the values back in. If the Success value is in fact True, you display the information on the screen, as shown in Figure 24-10.

This application demonstrates a simple technique for writing values to the Registry. This method would prove useful for keeping track of program settings, recording the last position and size of your applications interface, and so on. The possibilities are endless.

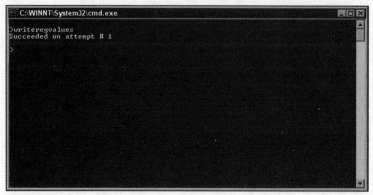

Figure 24-10: Keys read from the Registry are displayed on the console.

Enumerating Registry keys

Enumerating Registry keys is a lot like the Find Files feature in Windows. It enables you to scan from any point in the Registry and retrieve all subkeys and values below that starting point.

No methods are currently incorporated into .NET to enumerate Registry keys; it is up to you to build functions to support your needs. Knowing the structure of the keys you want to enumerate makes things much easier, as you can simply use a loop. If the structure of the Registry entries is unknown, you have to create a function that can call itself and pass the starting key in each time it is called.

Listing 24-14 is an example of enumerating Registry keys. In this example, you scan the Registry for a list of all software installed on the computer. This program lists any application that shows up in the Add/Remove section of the Control Panel.

Listing 24-14: **Enumerating Registry Keys**

```
using System;
using Microsoft.Win32;

namespace Installed
{
  class Class1
  {
    static void Main(string[] args)
    {
      RegistryKey myRegKey=Registry.LocalMachine;
      myRegKey=myRegKey.OpenSubKey
("SOFTWARE\\Microsoft\\Windows\\CurrentVersion\\Uninstall");
```

```
      String [] subkeyNames = myRegKey.GetSubKeyNames();
      foreach (String s in subkeyNames)
      {
        RegistryKey UninstallKey=Registry.LocalMachine;
        UninstallKey=UninstallKey.OpenSubKey
("SOFTWARE\\Microsoft\\Windows\\CurrentVersion\\Uninstall\\" + s);
        try
        {
          Object oValue=UninstallKey.GetValue("DisplayName");
          Console.WriteLine(oValue.ToString());
        }
        catch (NullReferenceException)
        {
        }
      }
    }
  }
}
```

After you have created a `RegistryKey` object, you open the `Uninstall` subkey, which contains a list of all programs installed. From here, you use `GetSubKeyNames`, which returns a string array of all subkeys. Now that you have your list of subkeys, you use the `foreach` operator to iterate through all elements in your subkey string array.

When you iterate through each key, you search for a value called `DisplayName`. This `DisplayName` value is the name that is shown in the Add/Remove Programs section of the Control Panel. Remember that not all keys will have this value. Therefore, you must encapsulate your `GetValue` method with a `try..catch` statement to catch any exceptions that may occur. After a `DisplayName` value is found, you retrieve the value and display it on the screen. The `foreach` statement then moves on to the next Registry key contained in the string array.

Press F5 to try the application. You'll probably see a long list of applications scroll by as the program scans the Registry (see Figure 24-11).

One thing that you did not tackle in this program is arranging the applications alphabetically. The items in the Registry are not stored in this manner, but to overcome this, you could simply store the results within a string array and call the `Sort` method to arrange the output in any manner allowed.

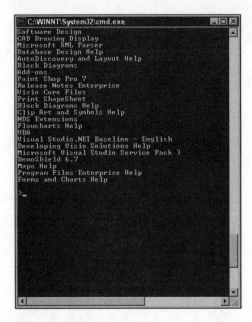

Figure 24-11: Scan all installed applications with a Registry enumerator.

Summary

The .NET Framework has greatly reduced the amount of code and time it takes to effectively deal with files and the Windows Registry. Among the many benefits that the .NET Framework, you now have access to components such as the `FileSystemWatcher` which enables you to watch a file system for changes made to any file. You must take care, however, when writing applications that deal with the Windows Registry because accidentally removing Registry keys can cause your system to become unstable or even inoperable.

✦   ✦   ✦

Accessing Data Streams

The .NET Framework ships with classes that provide a high level of support for reading and writing data. Traditionally, languages have provided built-in support for reading and writing to disk-based files, and have relied on operating system programming interfaces to provide support for reading and writing to other types of data streams, such as network sockets or memory-based files. The .NET Framework unifies data I/O by providing a common set of classes that support data reads and writes regardless of the underlying storage mechanism used to provide the data access. All of these classes can be used from C# code.

In this chapter, you learn to use streams. You learn how to use readers and writers to read data from and write data to a stream and how to perform file operations in the background.

Understanding the Data I/O Class Hierarchy

Figure 25-1 illustrates the class hierarchy for the basic .NET Framework classes used in data I/O work. The classes are grouped into one of three categories: streams, writers, and readers.

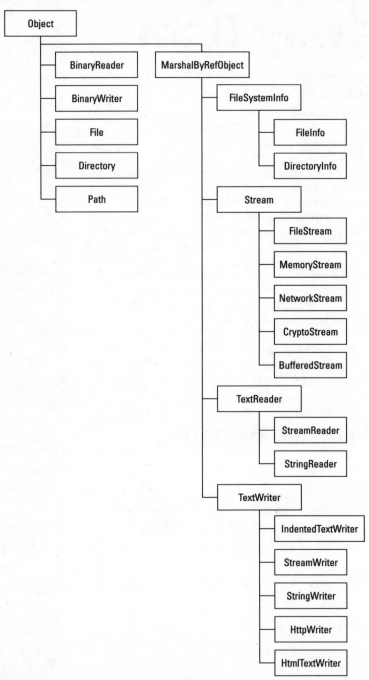

Figure 25-1: Data I/O class hierarchy

Using streams

Stream classes provide a mechanism for referring to a data container. Stream classes share a common base class called Stream, which is defined in a .NET Framework namespace called System.IO. The Stream base class contains properties and methods that enable callers to work with the data stream.

The .NET Framework ships with several classes that derive from the base Stream class. Each class provides a specific implementation of a data stream used for a particular environment. The FileStream class, for example, provides an implementation that enables callers to work with streams of data tied to a disk-based file. Similarly, the NetworkStream class provides an implementation that enables callers to work with streams of data accessed over a network.

Using writers

Streams support data access at the byte level. They include methods called Read() and Write(), which work with an array of bytes that are processed during the call. However, working at the byte level might not be ideal for your application. Suppose, for example, that your application needs to write a series of integers to a stream. Because integers in the 32-bit implementation are four bytes wide, your C# code would need to translate each integer into a string of four bytes that could be used in a call to the stream's implementation of Write(). The .NET Framework includes writer classes that support writing various higher-level data types to a stream. A writer might support many overloads of a Write() method. For example, a write can accept such data types as int, long, or double. The writer class implementations translate the data type into a series of bytes and pass that translated byte stream to a Stream object. This class design frees your code from having to deal with streams at the byte level. Your C# application code can simply state, "write this unsigned long into the stream," for example, and enable the writer class to do the work needed to get the value stored into the stream as a series of bytes.

Using readers

Reader classes complement the writer classes. Like the writer classes, reader classes provide support for reading data types that transcend the simple byte array support offered by stream classes. A matching reader class complements each writer class in the .NET Framework. Reader classes provide several overloads of a Read() method that enables your application code to read several types of data, such as strings, integers, longs, and so on.

Working with Streams

Streams support two methods of I/O:

✦ Synchronous I/O, in which method calls that perform stream I/O do not return to the caller until the requested I/O operation is complete

✦ Asynchronous I/O, in which method calls that perform stream I/O return before the requested operation is complete and notify the caller about the operation's completion at a later time

Understanding synchronous I/O

Listing 25-1 illustrates synchronous stream I/O. It creates a file and writes 256 bytes of binary data into the file. It then reads the 256 bytes back from the file and ensures that the data read matches the data written.

Listing 25-1: **Synchronous File I/O**

```
using System;
using System.IO;

class FileTestClass
{
    private FileStream BinaryFile;
    private byte []    ByteArray;

    public FileTestClass()
    {
        BinaryFile = new FileStream("test.dat", FileMode.Create,
FileAccess.ReadWrite);
        ByteArray = new byte [256];
    }

    public void WriteBytes()
    {
        int ArrayIndex;

        for(ArrayIndex = 0; ArrayIndex < 256; ArrayIndex++)
            ByteArray[ArrayIndex] = (byte)ArrayIndex;
        BinaryFile.Write(ByteArray, 0, 256);
    }

    public bool ReadBytes()
    {
```

```
        int ArrayIndex;

        BinaryFile.Seek(0, SeekOrigin.Begin);
        BinaryFile.Read(ByteArray, 0, 256);
        for(ArrayIndex = 0; ArrayIndex < 256; ArrayIndex++)
        {
            if(ByteArray[ArrayIndex] != (byte)ArrayIndex)
                return false;
        }
        return true;
    }
}

class MainClass
{
    static public void Main()
    {
        FileTestClass FileTest = new FileTestClass();
        bool          ReadTest;

        FileTest.WriteBytes();
        ReadTest = FileTest.ReadBytes();
        if(ReadTest == true)
            Console.WriteLine("The readback test was successful.");
        else
            Console.WriteLine("The readback test failed.");
    }
}
```

Listing 25-1 implements two C# classes: `FileTestClass`, which contains the stream I/O code, and `MainClass`, which contains the application's `Main()` method. The `Main()` method creates an object of the `FileTestClass` class and asks the object to write and read data.

The `FileTestClass` class contains a private member representing a `FileStream` object. The class's constructor creates a new `FileStream` object using a constructor that accepts three arguments:

✦ The pathname of the file stream to be operated on

✦ A file operation mode specification

✦ A file access mode specification

The file operation mode specification is represented by an enumeration named `FileMode`. The `FileMode` enumeration is found in the .NET `System.IO` namespace and supports the following enumeration members:

✦ Append, which instructs the file stream class to open the named file if it exists. If the named file exists, the file stream class initializes itself to write data to the end of the existing file. If the named file does not exist, the class creates a new file with the specified name.

✦ Create, which instructs the file stream to create the named file. If the file already exists, it is overwritten.

✦ CreateNew, which, like Create, instructs the file stream to create the named file. The difference between CreateNew and Create is how existing files are handled. If the file already exists when CreateNew is specified as the file mode, the file stream class throws an exception of class IOException.

✦ Open, which instructs the file stream to open the named file.

✦ OpenOrCreate, which instructs the file stream to create the named file. If the named file already exists, the FileStream object opens the named file.

✦ Truncate, which instructs the file stream to open the named file and then immediately truncate it so that its size is zero bytes.

The file access mode specification is represented by an enumeration named FileAccess. The FileAccess enumeration is also found in the .NET System.IO namespace and supports the following enumeration members:

✦ Read, which specifies that the FileStream class should allow read access to the named file. Data can be read from the file, but not written to the file.

✦ ReadWrite, which specifies that the FileStream class should allow both read and write access to the named file.

✦ Write, which specifies that the FileStream class should allow write access to the named file. Data can be written to the file, but not read back.

The FileTestClass constructor shown in Listing 25-1 creates a new file stream that manages a file named test.dat. The file is opened in creation mode for read/write access.

The WriteBytes() method of the FileTestClass populates a 256-byte buffer, which is created by the class's constructor. It populates the buffer with 256 bytes with values from hex 00 to hex FF. The buffer is then written to the stream with the file stream method Write(). The Write() method accepts three arguments:

✦ A reference to the byte buffer containing the data to be written

✦ An integer specifying the array element of the first byte in the buffer to be written

✦ An integer specifying the number of bytes to be written

The Write() method is synchronous, and the method does not return until the data has actually been written to the stream.

The ReadBytes() method of the FileTestClass reads the 256 bytes written by
WriteBytes() and compares the bytes with the byte pattern implemented by
WriteBytes().

The first operation that the ReadBytes() method performs involves moving the
stream pointer back to the beginning of the file. Stream positioning is an important
concept and deserves special mention. Streams support the concept of file positioning. A stream position refers to a position in the stream where the next I/O operation will take place. Usually, a stream position is set to the beginning of a stream
when the stream is initialized. As data is read from or written to the stream, the
stream position is advanced to the position just beyond the last operation.

Figure 25-2 illustrates this concept. It shows a stream with six bytes of data.

FileStream state at object initialization

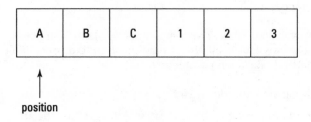

FileStream state after three bytes are read

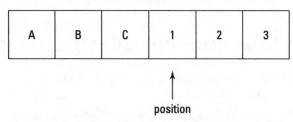

Figure 25-2: Stream I/O advances the stream position.

When the stream is initially opened, the stream position points to the first byte in
the stream. This is illustrated in the top diagram in Figure 25-2. Suppose that the
code that manages the stream reads three bytes from the file. The three bytes are
read, and the stream position will point to the byte just beyond the last read position. Using this example, the stream position points to the fourth byte in the
stream. This is illustrated in the bottom diagram in Figure 25-2.

The issue with the code in Listing 25-1 has to do with the fact that a file is created and 256 bytes are written to the file. After the bytes are written, they are read back. However, it is important to remember two stream positioning concepts:

✦ The file position is updated after every read or write operation to point to a position just beyond the last operation.

✦ Read and write operations start at the byte referenced by the stream position.

When the code in Listing 25-1 creates the new file stream, the file position is set to the beginning of the (empty) file. After the 256 bytes are written, the file position is updated to reference the position just after the 256 bytes. If the code were to read the 256 bytes just after the write operation, the read operation would fail because the stream position points to the end of the file after the write operation, and a read operation would attempt to read 256 bytes starting at that position, and there are no bytes available for reading at that position. The code needs to say, "before the read operation begins, adjust the file pointer back to the beginning of the stream so that the read operation is successful."

A method in the Stream class called Seek() accomplishes this task. The Seek() method enables your code to move, or seek, the stream position to any available in . the stream. The Seek() method takes two parameters:

✦ A long integer, specifying a positioning offset in bytes

✦ A value from an enumeration called SeekOrigin, which specifies the stream position that should be used as the starting point for the seek operation

The SeekOrigin enumeration is declared in the System.IO namespace and supports the following values:

✦ Begin, which indicates that the seek operation should be performed relative to the beginning of the stream

✦ Current, which indicates that the seek operation should be performed relative to the current stream position

✦ End, which indicates that the seek operation should be performed relative to the end of the stream

The Seek() method adjusts the stream position so that it points to the stream position referenced by the SeekOrigin enumeration, which is then offset by the specified number of bytes. The byte offset used in the Seek() method can be positive or negative. The following example uses a positive offset value:

```
File.Seek(4, SeekOrigin.Begin);
```

The preceding line adjusts the stream pointer to point to four bytes beyond the beginning of the stream. Positive offset values move the stream pointer toward the end of the stream. The following example uses a negative offset value:

```
File.Seek(-2, SeekOrigin.End);
```

This example adjusts the stream pointer to point to two bytes before the end of the stream. Negative offset values move the stream pointer toward the beginning of the stream.

The code in Listing 25-1 uses the following seek code before the 256 bytes are read:

```
BinaryFile.Seek(0, SeekOrigin.Begin);
```

This call adjusts the stream pointer back to the beginning of the stream. When the read operation begins, it starts reading from the beginning of the stream.

The ReadBytes() method uses the FileStream method called Read() to perform synchronous read I/O on the stream. The Read() method accepts three arguments:

✦ A reference to the byte buffer to be used to contain the bytes read from the stream

✦ An integer specifying the array element of the first byte in the buffer to contain data read from the stream

✦ An integer specifying the number of bytes to be read

The Read() method is synchronous and does not return until the data has actually been read from the stream. When the read operation is complete, the code checks the byte pattern found in the array to ensure that it matches the byte pattern that was written.

Understanding asynchronous I/O

Listing 25-2 is a modification of Listing 25-1 that illustrates asynchronous I/O. Unlike synchronous I/O, in which calls to read and write operations do not return until the operation is complete, calls to asynchronous I/O operations return soon after they are called. The actual I/O operation is performed behind the scenes, on a separate thread created by the implementation of the asynchronous I/O methods in the .NET Framework, and your code is notified when the operation is complete through a delegate. The advantage to asynchronous I/O is that your main code need not be tied up waiting for an I/O operation to complete. Performing lengthy I/O operations in the background frees your application to perform other tasks, such as processing Windows messages in Windows Forms applications.

Reading asynchronously

Listing 25-2 builds on the example shown in Listing 25-1 by performing the read operation asynchronously. The write operation is still performed synchronously. The stream is initialized in the same manner regardless of the way I/O is performed. Streams can be operated on in a synchronous manner for all I/O operations, in an asynchronous manner for all I/O operations, or in a combination of synchronous and asynchronous manners.

Listing 25-2: **Synchronous Writing, Asynchronous Reading**

```
using System;
using System.IO;
using System.Threading;

class FileTestClass
{
    private FileStream     BinaryFile;
    private byte []        ByteArray;
    private IAsyncResult   AsyncResultImplementation;
    private AsyncCallback  ReadBytesCompleteCallback;

    public FileTestClass()
    {
        AsyncResultImplementation = null;
        BinaryFile = new FileStream("test.dat", FileMode.Create,
FileAccess.ReadWrite);
        ByteArray = new byte [256];
        ReadBytesCompleteCallback = new AsyncCallback(OnReadBytesComplete);
    }

    public void WriteBytes()
    {
        int ArrayIndex;

        for(ArrayIndex = 0; ArrayIndex < 256; ArrayIndex++)
            ByteArray[ArrayIndex] = (byte)ArrayIndex;
        BinaryFile.Write(ByteArray, 0, 256);
    }

    public void ReadBytes()
    {
        BinaryFile.Seek(0, SeekOrigin.Begin);
        AsyncResultImplementation = BinaryFile.BeginRead(ByteArray, 0, 256,
ReadBytesCompleteCallback, null);
    }

    public void OnReadBytesComplete(IAsyncResult AsyncResult)
    {
```

```
        int ArrayIndex;
        int BytesRead;
        int Failures;

        BytesRead = BinaryFile.EndRead(AsyncResult);
        Console.WriteLine("Bytes read........: {0}", BytesRead);
        Failures = 0;
        for(ArrayIndex = 0; ArrayIndex < 256; ArrayIndex++)
        {
            if(ByteArray[ArrayIndex] != (byte)ArrayIndex)
            {
                Console.WriteLine("Read test failed for byte at offset {0}.",
ArrayIndex);
                Failures++;
            }
        }
        Console.WriteLine("Read test failures: {0}", Failures);
    }

    public void WaitForReadOperationToFinish()
    {
        WaitHandle WaitOnReadIO;

        WaitOnReadIO = AsyncResultImplementation.AsyncWaitHandle;
        WaitOnReadIO.WaitOne();
    }
}

class MainClass
{
    static public void Main()
    {
        FileTestClass FileTest = new FileTestClass();

        FileTest.WriteBytes();
        FileTest.ReadBytes();
        FileTest.WaitForReadOperationToFinish();
    }
}
```

The write operations code in Listing 25-2 is handled synchronously, and its code is identical to the write operations code in Listing 25-1. The read operation, however, is quite different.

The read operations code in Listing 25-2 starts not with a call to the stream's synchronous Read() method but with a call to the stream's asynchronous BeginRead() method. This call accepts five parameters. The first three parameters match the parameters accepted by the synchronous Read() method, but the last two parameters are new:

✦ A reference to the byte buffer to be used to contain the bytes read from the stream

✦ An integer specifying the array element of the first byte in the buffer to contain data read from the stream

✦ An integer specifying the number of bytes to be read

✦ Call-specific data

The callback delegate must be an object of a class called AsyncCallback. The AsyncCallback class is declared in the .NET Framework System namespace and manages a method that returns nothing and accepts a reference to an interface called IAsyncResult. Listing 25-2 creates an instance of this delegate in the constructor of the FileTestClass class:

```
ReadBytesCompleteCallback = new AsyncCallback(OnReadBytesComplete);
```

The FileTestClass class in Listing 25-2 includes a new method called OnReadBytesComplete(), which is used as the delegate method. The Stream object invokes this delegate when the read operation is complete.

The IAsyncResult interface, which is used as the parameter to the AsyncCallback delegate, is defined in the .NET Framework System namespace. It supports four properties that can be used to obtain more information about the nature of the asynchronous operation:

✦ AsyncState, which is a reference to the object that was provided as the last parameter of the BeginRead() method. The asynchronous I/O methods enable you to associate data with a specific operation in the last parameter to the I/O method. A copy of that data is available in the AsyncState property. Listing 25-2 has no need for data to be associated with the call, so it passes null as the last parameter to BeginRead(). As a result, the AsyncState property also has a value of null. You might want to use this data, for example, to distinguish one I/O call from another. It is legal for you to use the same delegate reference in multiple asynchronous I/O calls, for instance, and you might want to pass along data that distinguishes one call from another.

✦ AsyncWaitHandle, which is a reference to an object of class WaitHandle. The WaitHandle class is declared in the .NET Framework System.Threading namespace. This object encapsulates a synchronization primitive and serves as a base class for specific primitives, such as mutexes and semaphores. Your code can wait on this handle to determine when the read operation actually completes. The code in Listing 25-2 does just that.

✦ `CompletedSynchronously`, which is a Boolean that is set to `True` if the `BeginRead()` call completed synchronously, and `False` otherwise. Most stream implementations return `False` for this property when the interface references an asynchronous I/O operation.

✦ `IsCompleted`, which is a Boolean that is set to `True` when the `Stream` object has completed the asynchronous operation. The property is set to `False` until then. Your code can destroy any stream-related resources after the `IsCompleted` property returns `True`.

An implementation of the `IAsyncCallback` interface is also returned from the call to `BeginRead()`. The code in Listing 25-2 caches the interface reference for later use.

The `AsyncCallback` method, which, in Listing 25-2, is the `OnReadBytesComplete()` method, is called by the `Stream` object when the asynchronous operation completes. The implementation shown in Listing 25-2 begins with a call to `EndRead()`, which returns the number of bytes actually read from the operation. This number should match the number of bytes that were requested to be read by `BeginRead()`.

Tip

The call to `EndRead()` in Listing 25-2 is shown so that the number of bytes affected by the asynchronous operation can be found. If your code does not need this value, you do not need to call `EndRead()` at all.

The remainder of the implementation of the `OnReadBytesComplete()` method checks the byte pattern read in from the I/O operation and reports its findings to the console.

The `Main()` method in Listing 25-2 adds a new method call to the code from Listing 25-1, which is to a private method in the `FileTestClass` object called `WaitForReadOperationToFinish()`. Because the asynchronous read operation is the last operation in the code, the application could exit before the read operation can complete. Remember that the processing of the asynchronous I/O operation is performed on a separate thread. If the main thread exits before the I/O thread has a chance to finish, the code in `OnReadBytesComplete()` may not get a chance to finish. The `WaitForReadOperationToFinish()` method ensures that the operation completes before it returns to the caller.

The `WaitForReadOperationToFinish()` method uses the wait handle in the `IAsyncCallback` interface implementation to do its work. The method calls the `WaitHandle` method `WaitOne()` to wait until the wait handle is signaled. The call to `WaitOne()` does not return until the wait handle is signaled. The `Stream` object signals the wait handle only after the I/O operation completes. After the call to `WaitOne()` returns, you can be sure that the entire operation has completed.

Writing asynchronously

Asynchronous write I/O operations are similar to asynchronous read I/O operations. The only difference is that the `BeginWrite()` method is used instead of `BeginRead()`. Listing 25-3 improves on Listing 25-2 by implementing an asynchronous write operation.

Listing 25-3: Asynchronous Writing, Asynchronous Reading

```
using System;
using System.IO;
using System.Threading;

class FileTestClass
{
    private FileStream    BinaryFile;
    private byte []       ByteArray;
    private IAsyncResult  AsyncReadResultImplementation;
    private IAsyncResult  AsyncWriteResultImplementation;
    private AsyncCallback ReadBytesCompleteCallback;
    private AsyncCallback WriteBytesCompleteCallback;

    public FileTestClass()
    {
        AsyncReadResultImplementation = null;
        BinaryFile = new FileStream("test.dat", FileMode.Create,
FileAccess.ReadWrite);
        ByteArray = new byte [256];
        ReadBytesCompleteCallback = new AsyncCallback(OnReadBytesComplete);
        WriteBytesCompleteCallback = new AsyncCallback(OnWriteBytesComplete);
    }

    public void WriteBytes()
    {
        int ArrayIndex;

        for(ArrayIndex = 0; ArrayIndex < 256; ArrayIndex++)
            ByteArray[ArrayIndex] = (byte)ArrayIndex;
        AsyncWriteResultImplementation = BinaryFile.BeginWrite(ByteArray, 0,
256, WriteBytesCompleteCallback, null);
    }

    public void ReadBytes()
    {
        WaitForWriteOperationToFinish();
        BinaryFile.Seek(0, SeekOrigin.Begin);
        AsyncReadResultImplementation = BinaryFile.BeginRead(ByteArray, 0, 256,
ReadBytesCompleteCallback, null);
    }

    public void OnReadBytesComplete(IAsyncResult AsyncResult)
    {
```

```
        int ArrayIndex;
        int BytesRead;
        int Failures;

        BytesRead = BinaryFile.EndRead(AsyncResult);
        Console.WriteLine("Bytes read........: {0}", BytesRead);
        Failures = 0;
        for(ArrayIndex = 0; ArrayIndex < 256; ArrayIndex++)
        {
            if(ByteArray[ArrayIndex] != (byte)ArrayIndex)
            {
                Console.WriteLine("Read test failed for byte at offset {0}.",
ArrayIndex);
                Failures++;
            }
        }
        Console.WriteLine("Read test failures: {0}", Failures);
    }

    public void WaitForReadOperationToFinish()
    {
        WaitHandle WaitOnReadIO;

        WaitOnReadIO = AsyncReadResultImplementation.AsyncWaitHandle;
        WaitOnReadIO.WaitOne();
    }

    public void OnWriteBytesComplete(IAsyncResult AsyncResult)
    {
        BinaryFile.EndWrite(AsyncResult);
    }

    private void WaitForWriteOperationToFinish()
    {
        WaitHandle WaitOnWriteIO;

        WaitOnWriteIO = AsyncWriteResultImplementation.AsyncWaitHandle;
        WaitOnWriteIO.WaitOne();
    }
}

class MainClass
{
    static public void Main()
    {
        FileTestClass FileTest = new FileTestClass();

        FileTest.WriteBytes();
        FileTest.ReadBytes();
        FileTest.WaitForReadOperationToFinish();
    }
}
```

The `EndWrite()` method does not return a value, unlike the `EndRead()` method. The two methods are alike, however, in that they both block until the I/O operation is complete.

Understanding Writers and Readers

The .NET Framework ships with a variety of reader and writer classes that help you work with data more complicated than simple byte streams. Readers and writers encapsulate a stream and provide a translation layer that turns values into their byte stream equivalents (for writers) and vice versa (for readers).

Reader and writer classes in .NET are typically named to reflect the type of formatting that they perform. For example, the `HtmlTextWriter` class writes values destined for HTTP response information sent by ASP.NET, while the `StringReader` class reads values written using their string representation.

The writer and reader classes also handle varying encoding schemes, which is not possible using lower-level stream objects. The classes derived from the abstract `TextWriter` class, for example, enable your C# code to write text and have it encoded in the stream using ASCII, Unicode, UTF7, or UTF8 encoding algorithms.

Writing to streams with BinaryWriter

Listing 25-4 shows the `BinaryWriter` class in action. The job of the `BinaryWriter` class is to translate C# data types to a series of bytes that can be written to an underlying stream.

Listing 25-4: **Working with the BinaryWriter Class**

```
using System;
using System.IO;

class FileTestClass
{
    private BinaryWriter   Writer;
    private FileStream      BinaryFile;

    public FileTestClass()
    {
        BinaryFile = new FileStream("test.dat", FileMode.Create,
FileAccess.ReadWrite);
        Writer = new BinaryWriter(BinaryFile);
    }

    public void WriteBinaryData()
```

```
    {
        Writer.Write('a');
        Writer.Write(123);
        Writer.Write(456.789);
        Writer.Write("test string");
    }
}

class MainClass
{
    static public void Main()
    {
        FileTestClass FileTest = new FileTestClass();

        FileTest.WriteBinaryData();
    }
}
```

The code in Listing 25-4 is structured with a class design similar to the design in Listing 25-3. The code contains a `MainClass` and a `FileTestClass`. The constructor of the `FileTestClass` class in Listing 25-4 creates a file stream and then creates a `BinaryWriter` object. A reference to the file stream is passed to the constructor of the `BinaryWriter` object, which sets up the relationship between the binary writer and the stream to which it writes its data. In Listing 25-4, all data written to the binary writer eventually makes its way to the file stream set up in the constructor.

The `WriteBinaryData()` method writes a character, an integer, a double, and a string to the underlying stream. The `BinaryWriter` class implements several overloads of a method named `Write()`. The `Write()` method overloads support the writing of the following data types to the writer class:

✦ Booleans

✦ Bytes

✦ Arrays of bytes

✦ Characters

✦ Arrays of characters

✦ Decimal values

✦ Double values

✦ Signed and unsigned short integer values

✦ Signed and unsigned integer values

✦ Signed and unsigned long integer values

    ✦ Sbytes

    ✦ Floating-point values

    ✦ Strings

If you compile and execute the code in Listing 25-4, a file called `test.dat` is created. You can examine the contents of the new file in a hex editor to verify that binary representations of values were written to the file.

Reading from streams with BinaryReader

Listing 25-5 adds the `BinaryReader` class to the code in Listing 25-5. This class reassembles stream bytes back into their constituent data types and returns the values to the caller.

Listing 25-5: **Working with the BinaryReader Class**

```
using System;
using System.IO;

class FileTestClass
{
    private BinaryReader  Reader;
    private BinaryWriter  Writer;
    private FileStream    BinaryFile;

    public FileTestClass()
    {
        BinaryFile = new FileStream("test.dat", FileMode.Create,
FileAccess.ReadWrite);
        Writer = new BinaryWriter(BinaryFile);
        Reader = new BinaryReader(BinaryFile);
    }

    public void ReadBinaryData()
    {
        char   ReadCharacter;
        double ReadDouble;
        int    ReadInteger;
        string ReadString;

        BinaryFile.Seek(0, SeekOrigin.Begin);
        ReadCharacter = Reader.ReadChar();
        ReadInteger = Reader.ReadInt32();
        ReadDouble = Reader.ReadDouble();
        ReadString = Reader.ReadString();

        Console.WriteLine("Character: {0}", ReadCharacter);
```

```
            Console.WriteLine("Integer: {0}", ReadInteger);
            Console.WriteLine("Double: {0}", ReadDouble);
            Console.WriteLine("String: {0}", ReadString);
        }

    public void WriteBinaryData()
    {
        Writer.Write('a');
        Writer.Write(123);
        Writer.Write(456.789);
        Writer.Write("test string");
    }
}

class MainClass
{
    static public void Main()
    {
        FileTestClass FileTest = new FileTestClass();

        FileTest.WriteBinaryData();
        FileTest.ReadBinaryData();
    }
}
```

Unlike the `BinaryWriter` class, which contained one overloaded method for all operations, the `BinaryReader` class contains separate read methods for each data type. The code in Listing 25-5 uses some of these read methods, such as `ReadChar()` and `ReadInt32()`, to read values from the stream written in the `WriteBinaryData()` method. The values read from the stream are sent to the console. Executing Listing 25-5 should produce the following output on the console:

```
Character: a
Integer: 123
Double: 456.789
String: test string
```

Writing Well-Formed XML Using the XmlWriter Stream

Streams can do more than simply read from and write to various data streams. They can also add value to the data being sent through the stream. A good example of this technology is the `XmlWriter` class, which encapsulates data sent to a stream within well-formed XML elements. The result is a well-formed XML document that can be processed by any XML document processor, as shown in Listing 25-6.

Listing 25-6: **Writing XML with the XmlWriter Class**

```
using System;
using System.IO;
using System.Xml;

class XMLStreamWriterClass
{
    private XmlTextWriter XmlWriter;

    public void WriteXML()
    {
        XmlWriter = new XmlTextWriter(Console.Out);

        XmlWriter.WriteStartDocument();
        XmlWriter.WriteComment("This XML document was automatically generated by
C# code.");
        XmlWriter.WriteStartElement("BOOK");
        XmlWriter.WriteElementString("TITLE", "C# Bible");
        XmlWriter.WriteElementString("AUTHOR", "Jeff Ferguson");
        XmlWriter.WriteElementString("PUBLISHER", "Wiley");
        XmlWriter.WriteEndElement();
        XmlWriter.WriteEndDocument();
    }
}

class MainClass
{
    static public void Main()
    {
        XMLStreamWriterClass XMLStreamWriter = new XMLStreamWriterClass();

        XMLStreamWriter.WriteXML();
    }
}
```

The code in Listing 25-6 creates a new instance of the XmlWriter class and associates it with the console's output stream, which sends the stream's output to the application console. The code simply calls various methods in the XmlWriter class to output data, and the methods surround the data with XML elements names that are specified when the method is called. Take a look at the following line from Listing 25-6:

```
XmlWriter.WriteElementString("AUTHOR", "Jeff Ferguson");
```

This call instructs the XmlWriter class to write an XML element called <AUTHOR>, which has a value of Brian Patterson, to the stream output device. The method's implementation supplies the XML end tag automatically.

Compiling and executing the code in Listing 25-6 sends the following well-formed XML document to the application console:

```
<?xml version="1.0" encoding="IBM437"?>
<!--This XML document was automatically generated by C# code.-->
<BOOK>
<TITLE>C# Bible</TITLE>
<AUTHOR>Jeff Ferguson</AUTHOR>
<PUBLISHER>Wiley</PUBLISHER>
</BOOK>
```

Summary

Streams provide powerful support for both synchronous and asynchronous I/O for your C# applications. Streams operate at the byte level and require you to read and write blocks of bytes. Readers and writers encapsulate streams and provide access to data at a higher level. You can use readers and writers to work with standard C# data types, enabling the readers and writers to translate between the data type values and their byte representations.

Your C# code will most likely work with readers and writers, as they provide support for working with the standard data types without forcing you to be concerned about translating between a data type value and its binary representation. Streams are available, however, should you feel the need to work with them directly. You might also want to work with streams if the data that you are reading is in a proprietary format that is not supported by the standard reader and writer classes shipped with the .NET Framework. You might also consider developing your own reader class, derived from the base TextReader or StreamReader classes, and use your class to read from the proprietary format stream.

✦　　✦　　✦

Drawing with GDI+

In Windows, programmatic access to the graphics subsystem was first accomplished using the GDI APIs available since Windows 3.1. GDI offered developers the capability to control any type of user interface element, and this capability has been reworked from the ground up in the .NET Framework. GDI+ has replaced GDI as the API that is used to access the graphics subsystems of Windows. With GDI+, you can access fonts, manipulate any type of image, and work with shapes in your C# applications. To get a complete picture of how to use GDI+ in your applications, you need to understand how to use the `Graphics`, `Pen`, `Brush`, and `Color` objects. With these four objects, you can accomplish nearly anything you need to do with the GUI and images in .NET. This chapter explores these objects, and familiarizes you with using GDI+ in C#. The available classes in GDI+ could cover their own thousand-page book, so you should still use the SDK as a reference to the more complex and less frequently used graphics functionality not covered in this chapter.

Working with Graphics

When working with GDI+ in .NET, the main object that you need to work with is the `Graphics` object. The `Graphics` object is the actual surface that you use to paint shapes, work with images, or display text. Visual Basic 6 and earlier offered limited built-in support for working with graphics, making it difficult for VB developers to write custom graphics applications. The one thing that VB did do was keep track of how forms and the objects on forms were painted on the screen. The `AutoRedraw` property enabled your forms to let Windows keep track of what was on top of other windows and, if necessary, automatically repaint a form if another form was on top of it for any period of time. You were hidden from having to deal with the actual painting process of the form. In .NET, the exact opposite is true. The `Graphics` object has no memory of when it was painted or what was painted with it. Therefore, you need to redraw objects as necessary if other windows end up on top of your window. This may seem like a pain, but the PaintEventArgs variable in the Paint event of a form can handle this nicely. If your painting code is kept there, then each time Windows paints the actual form, your objects will be painted correctly.

The following code snippet receives a reference to a Graphics object through the PaintEventArgs variable in the Paint event of a form:

```
private void Form1_Paint(object sender,
  System.Windows.Forms.PaintEventArgs p)
{
  Graphics g = p.Graphics;
}
```

You can also create a Graphics object using the CreateGraphics method of a control or form. The following code demonstrates the CreateGraphics method:

```
private void createManually()
{
  Graphics g;
  g = this.CreateGraphics;
}
```

The third and final method of creating a Graphics object is to pass an image file directly to the object when you instantiate it, as the following code demonstrates by grabbing a bitmap image from the file system:

```
private void createFromFile()
{
  Graphics g;
  Bitmap b;
  b = new Bitmap(@"C:\Enterprise.bmp");
  g = Graphics.FromImage(b);
}
```

If you have been adding these snippets to a WindowsForm, it is clear that nothing happens when any of the code executes. To actually implement some functionality, you need to use members of the Graphics class to make things happen.

 Note   If you create a Graphics object using the CreateGraphics method, you should call Dispose on that object after you finish using it. This ensures that the Graphics object is released from memory.

Table 26-1 lists the properties of the Graphics class, and Table 26-2 lists the available methods of the Graphics class. The Graphics class is located in the System.Drawing namespace, which is added as the default reference when you create a new Windows Forms application. This does not mean that you cannot use Graphics objects in ASP .NET; in fact, you can write extremely optimized image processing applications in ASP .NET using Graphics objects.

Table 26-1
Graphics Class Properties

Property	Description
Clip	Gets or sets a `Region` object that limits the drawing region of this `Graphics` object
ClipBounds	Gets the `RectangleF` structure that bounds the clipping region of this `Graphics` object
CompositingMode	Gets a value that specifies how composited images are drawn to this `Graphics` object
CompositingQuality	Gets or sets the rendering quality of composited images drawn to this `Graphics` object
DpiX	Gets the horizontal resolution of this `Graphics` object
DpiY	Gets the vertical resolution of this `Graphics` object
InterpolationMode	Gets or sets the interpolation mode associated with this `Graphics` object
IsClipEmpty	Gets a value indicating whether the clipping region of this `Graphics` object is empty
IsVisibleClipEmpty	Gets a value indicating whether the visible clipping region of this `Graphics` object is empty
PageScale	Gets or sets the scaling between world units and page units for this `Graphics` object
PageUnit	Gets or sets the unit of measure used for page coordinates in this `Graphics` object
PixelOffsetMode	Gets or sets a value specifying how pixels are offset during rendering of this `Graphics` object
RenderingOrigin	Gets or sets the rendering origin of this `Graphics` object for dithering and for hatch brushes
SmoothingMode	Gets or sets the rendering quality for this `Graphics` object
TextContrast	Gets or sets the gamma correction value for rendering text
TextRenderingHint	Gets or sets the rendering mode for text associated with this `Graphics` object
Transform	Gets or sets the world transformation for this `Graphics` object
VisibleClipBounds	Gets or sets the bounding rectangle of the visible clipping region of this `Graphics` object

Table 26-2
Graphics Class Methods

Method	Description
AddMetafileComment	Adds a comment to the current `Metafile` object
BeginContainer	Saves a Graphics container with the current state of this `Graphics` object and opens and uses a new graphics container
Clear	Clears the entire drawing surface and fills it with the specified background color
DrawArc	Draws an arc representing a portion of an ellipse specified by a pair of coordinates, a width, and a height
DrawBezier	Draws a Bézier spline defined by four Point structures
DrawBeziers	Draws a series of Bézier splines from an array of Point structures
DrawClosedCurve	Draws a closed cardinal spline defined by an array of Point structures
DrawCurve	Draws a cardinal spline through a specified array of Point structures
DrawEllipse	Draws an ellipse defined by a bounding rectangle specified by a pair of coordinates, a height, and a width
DrawIcon	Draws the image represented by the specified `Icon` object at the specified coordinates
DrawIconUnstretched	Draws the image represented by the specified `Icon` object without scaling the image
DrawImage	Draws the specified `Image` object at the specified location and with the original size
DrawImageUnscaled	Draws the specified `Image` object with its original size at the location specified by a coordinate pair
DrawLine	Draws a line connecting the two points specified by coordinate pairs
DrawLines	Draws a series of line segments that connect an array of Point structures
DrawPath	Draws a `GraphicsPath` object
DrawPie	Draws a pie shape defined by an ellipse specified by a coordinate pair, a width, and a height and two radial lines
DrawPolygon	Draws a polygon defined by an array of Point structures

Method	Description
DrawRectangle	Draws a rectangle specified by a coordinate pair, a width, and a height
DrawRectangles	Draws a series of rectangles specified by Rectangle structures
DrawString	Draws the specified text string at the specified location with the specified `Brush` and `Font` objects
EndContainer	Closes the current graphics container and restores the state of this `Graphics` object to the state saved by a call to the `BeginContainer` method
EnumerateMetafile	Sends the records in the specified `Metafile` object, one at a time, to a callback method for display at a specified point
ExcludeClip	Updates the clip region of this `Graphics` object to exclude the area specified by a Rectangle structure
FillClosedCurve	Fills the interior of a closed cardinal spline curve defined by an array of Point structures
FillEllipse	Fills the interior of an ellipse defined by a bounding rectangle specified by a pair of coordinates, a width, and a height
FillPath	Fills the interior of a `GraphicsPath` object
FillPie	Fills the interior of a pie section defined by an ellipse specified by a pair of coordinates, a width, and a height and two radial lines
FillPolygon	Fills the interior of a polygon defined by an array of points specified by Point structures
FillRectangle	Fills the interior of a rectangle specified by a pair of coordinates, a width, and a height
FillRectangles	Fills the interiors of a series of rectangles specified by Rectangle structures
FillRegion	Fills the interior of a `Region` object
Flush	Forces execution of all pending graphics operations and returns immediately without waiting for the operations to finish
FromHdc	Creates a new `Graphics` object from the specified handle to a device context
FromHwnd	Creates a new `Graphics` object from the specified handle to a window
FromImage	Creates a new `Graphics` object from the specified `Image` object

Continued

Table 26-2 *(continued)*

Method	Description
GetHalftonePalette	Gets a handle to the current Windows halftone palette
GetHdc	Gets the handle to the device context associated with this Graphics object
GetNearestColor	Gets the nearest color to the specified Color structure
IntersectClip	Updates the clip region of this Graphics object to the intersection of the current clip region and the specified Rectangle structure
IsVisible	Indicates whether the point specified by a pair of coordinates is contained within the visible clip region of this Graphics object
MeasureCharacterRanges	Gets an array of Region objects, each of which bounds a range of character positions within the specified string
MeasureString	Measures the specified string when drawn with the specified Font object
MultiplyTransform	Multiplies the world transformation of this Graphics object and specified the Matrix object parameters
ReleaseHdc	Releases a device context handle obtained by a previous call to the GetHdc method of this Graphics object
ResetClip	Resets the clip region of this Graphics object to an infinite region
ResetTransform	Resets the world transformation matrix of this Graphics object to the identity matrix
Restore	Restores the state of this Graphics object to the state represented by a GraphicsState object
RotateTransform	Applies the specified rotation to the transformation matrix of this Graphics object
Save	Saves the current state of this Graphics object and identifies the saved state with a GraphicsState object
ScaleTransform	Applies the specified scaling operation to the transformation matrix of this Graphics object by prepending it to the object's transformation matrix

Method	Description
SetClip	Sets the clipping region of this Graphics object to the Clip property of the specified Graphics object
TransformPoints	Transforms an array of points from one coordinate space to another using the current world and page transformations of this Graphics object
TranslateClip	Translates the clipping region of this Graphics object by specified amounts in the horizontal and vertical directions
TranslateTransform	Prepends the specified translation to the transformation matrix of this Graphics object

As you can see, the Graphics class provides every possible method that you would ever want to use to work with any type of GUI element. Listing 26-1 uses several of the methods in the Graphics class to produce the output displayed in Figure 26-1.

Note As there is no AutoRedraw property, you still need a way to redraw a form if it is resized. Using the SetStyles method and passing the ControlStyles. ResizeRedraw stylecorrectly calls the Paint method of a form. After the call the InitializeComponent; in your form, you should type SetStyle-(ControlStyles.ResizeRedraw, true) to guarantee that the Paint event will be called when your form is resized. Look up SetStyle in the .NET Framework SDK to learn more about what you can do with the SetStyle method.

Listing 26-1: Using Methods from the Graphics Class

```
private void drawLine()
{
    /* create a Graphics object that can be resued
     * for each of the samples */

    Graphics g;
    g = this.CreateGraphics();

    // Use the Pen object to create a line

    Pen p;
    p = new Pen(Color.Red, 50);

    /* DrawLine is an overloaded method,
```

Continued

Listing 26-1 *(continued)*

```
 * pass the x1, y1, x2, y2 coordinates */

g.DrawLine(p, 100F, 100F, 500F, 100F);

// draw an icon from the file system

Icon i;
i = new Icon(@"C:\Desktop.ico");

// call DrawIcon passing the x and y coordinates

g.DrawIcon(i, 150, 15);

// draw a Rectangle

Pen p2;
p2 = new Pen(Color.PapayaWhip, 7);

/* draw the Rectangle passing the x, y,
 *   height and width */

g.DrawRectangle(p2, 50, 50, 100, 100);
}
```

If you call this method from a Windows Forms application, your results will look something like what is shown in Figure 26-1.

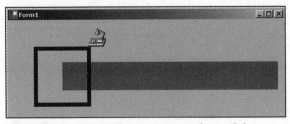

Figure 26-1: Output from using members of the Graphics class

Alone, the Graphics class does nothing. To create lines, rectangles, images, and fonts, you use other objects along with the Graphics object. Listing 26-1 created a Pen object to use in conjunction with the Graphics object to draw a red line on the form. It also created an Icon object, which the Graphics object used to draw the desktop icon on the form. As mentioned earlier, you can perform numerous tasks with GDI+; draw shapes and lines, manipulate images, and work with fonts. The following sections delve more deeply into these topics, describing how you can use objects such as the Pen, Brush, and Image in conjunction with members of the Graphics class to take full advantage of the vast array of GDI+ capabilities in .NET.

Working with Images in GDI+

If you need to render images that exist in the file system, the Image class gives you the capability to render images on surfaces created with the Graphics object. Contained in the System.Drawing namespace, the Image class is an abstract class that provides you with all of the functionality you need to use bitmaps, icons, and metafiles with a Graphics object to render predefined Image objects on a form. The rendered images can come directly from the file system, or they can come from a memory stream; either way, you are still dealing with some sort of image source. Images can be of type JPG, ICO, or BMP.

In Listing 26-2, you load a JPG file from the local drive to display on a form. This example is slightly different from what you have done earlier. Here, you are going to override the OnPaint event of the form so that the image will not be destroyed if another window happens to sit on top of your window. This example also shows you how to implement calling Dispose method in the Graphics object that is used to paint the JPG image when the form is destroyed.

Listing 26-2: **Using Images with GDI+**

```
namespace RenderJPG
{
  public class Form1 : System.Windows.Forms.Form
  {
    private System.ComponentModel.Container
          components = null;

    // declare image variable
    private Image img;

    public Form1()
  {
  InitializeComponent();

  // load the image
  img = new Bitmap(@"C:\money.jpg");
  //
```

Continued

Listing 26-2 *(continued)*

```
    }

protected override void Dispose( bool disposing )
  {
   if( disposing )
     {
        // Call DISPOSE on the Img object
        img.Dispose();
        //
        if (components != null)
          {
              components.Dispose();
          }
     }
    base.Dispose( disposing );
  }
static void Main()
  {
   Application.Run(new Form1());
  }

  // override the OnPaint event
  protected override void OnPaint(PaintEventArgs p)
    {
       Graphics g = p.Graphics;
       g.DrawImage(img, 0,0);
    }
  }
}
```

Running this application should produce output similar to that shown in Figure 26-2.

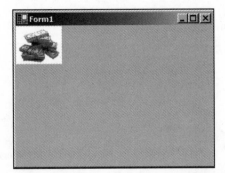

Figure 26-2: Output from Listing 26-2 using a JPG with GDI+

The DrawImage method used to paint the image on the form has about 20 overloaded constructors. Basically, each one directs the method how to paint the image, such as coordinates or height and width. By making a simple change to the DrawImage method, you can fill the entire form with the bitmap. If you pass the constant ClientRectangle to DrawImage, as the next snippet demonstrates, your output will look like Figure 26-3, with the entire bitmap filling the screen:

```
// override the OnPaint event
protected override void OnPaint(PaintEventArgs p)
  {
    Graphics g = p.Graphics;
    g.DrawImage(img, ClientRectangle);
  }
```

Figure 26-3: Image filling the entire form

You can also return properties on an image without displaying it. In the following Load event, you examine several of the available properties of the money.jpg image that you loaded earlier:

```
private void Form1_Load(object sender, System.EventArgs e)
{
  MessageBox.Show
          (img.PhysicalDimension.ToString() );
  MessageBox.Show
          (img.Height.ToString() );
  MessageBox.Show
          (img.Width.ToString() );
  MessageBox.Show
          (img.RawFormat.ToString() );
  MessageBox.Show
          (img.Size.ToString() );
}
```

Table 26-3 describes each of the properties that are available for images through the Image class.

Table 26-3
Image Class Properties

Property	Description
Flags	Gets attribute flags for this Image object
FrameDimensionsList	Gets an array of GUIDs that represent the dimensions of frames within this Image object
Height	Gets the height of this Image object
HorizontalResolution	Gets the horizontal resolution, in pixels-per-inch, of this Image object
Palette	Gets or sets the color palette used for this Image object
PhysicalDimension	Gets the width and height of this Image object
PixelFormat	Gets the pixel format for this Image object
PropertyIdList	Gets an array of the property IDs stored in this Image object
PropertyItems	Gets an array of PropertyItem objects that describe this Image object
RawFormat	Gets the format of this Image object
Size	Gets the width and height of this Image object
VerticalResolution	Gets the vertical resolution, in pixels-per-inch, of this Image object
Width	Gets the width of this Image object

You can also use several methods in the Image class, which enable you to manipulate your images in virtually unlimited ways. The following code flips the image 90 degrees:

```
img.RotateFlip(RotateFlipType.Rotate90FlipY);
```

The RotateFlipType enumeration enables you to specify how you want to flip or rotate an image on the graphics surface.

Table 26-4 lists the remaining methods in the Image class that you can use to manipulate an image.

Table 26-4
Image Class Methods

Method	Description
Clone	Creates an exact copy of this Image object
FromFile	Creates an Image object from the specified file
FromHbitmap	Creates a Bitmap object from a Windows handle
FromStream	Creates an Image object from the specified data stream
GetBounds	Gets a bounding rectangle in the specified units for this Image object
GetEncoderParameterList	Returns information about the parameters supported by the specified image encoder
GetFrameCount	Returns the number of frames of the specified dimension
GetPixelFormatSize	Returns the color depth (number of bits per pixel) of the specified pixel format
GetPropertyItem	Gets the specified property item from this Image object
GetThumbnailImage	Returns the thumbnail for this Image object
IsAlphaPixelFormat	Returns a value that indicates whether the pixel format for this Image object contains alpha information
IsCanonicalPixelFormat	Returns a value that indicates whether the pixel format is canonical
IsExtendedPixelFormat	Returns a value that indicates whether the pixel format is extended
RemovePropertyItem	Removes the specified property item from this Image object
RotateFlip	This method either rotates, flips, or rotates and flips the Image object
Save	Saves this Image object to the specified Stream object in the specified format
SaveAdd	Adds the information in the specified Image object to this Image object. The specified EncoderParameters object determines how the new information is incorporated into the existing image
SelectActiveFrame	Selects the frame specified by the dimension and index
SetPropertyItem	Sets the specified property item to the specified value

As this section has demonstrated, the `Image` class offers very robust capabilities when used with a `Graphics` object. In the next section, you learn how to use pens and brushes to work with images and draw shapes and lines.

Working with Pens and Brushes

As you have seen with the `Image` class, the `System.Drawing` namespace gives you everything you need to work with images that come from a stream or the file system. The .NET Framework also offers built-in support for working with shapes, lines, and images through the `Pen` and `Brush` classes. This section describes how to work with the `Pen` and `Brush` classes to manipulate shapes, lines, and images to achieve the effects you want.

Using the Pen class

The `Pen` class enables you to draw lines and curves on a graphics surface. The namespace that contains the features used by the `Pen` and `Brush` classes is the `System.Drawing.Drawing2D` namespace, so be sure to add this with the `using` statement in your class files. By setting various properties on an instance of a `Pen`, you can alter the outcome of the pen display. By calling methods in the `Graphics` class, you can dictate the type of shape you want to output.

The following code sets the `Color` and `DashStyle` properties to create an ellipse resembling the one shown in Figure 26-4:

```
private void Form1_Load(object sender,
     System.EventArgs e)
{
  Pen p = new Pen(Color.Blue, 10);
  p.DashStyle = DashStyle.DashDot ;
  Graphics g = this.CreateGraphics();
  g.DrawEllipse(p, 10, 15, 105, 250);
}
```

Table 26-5 lists the possible values of the `DashStyle` enumeration used to set the style of the dashed line in the ellipse.

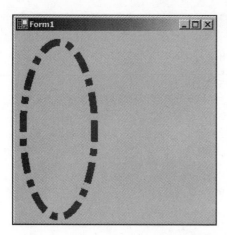

Figure 26-4: Drawing an ellipse using the Color and DashStyle properties

Table 26-5
DashStyle Enumeration

Value	Description
Custom	Specifies a user-defined custom dash style
Dash	Specifies a line consisting of dashes
DashDot	Specifies a line consisting of a repeating pattern of dash-dot
DashDotDot	Specifies a line consisting of a repeating pattern of dash-dot-dot
Dot	Specifies a line consisting of dots
Solid	Specifies a solid line

You can also customize lines with the StartCap and EndCap properties using the LineCap enumeration, which is also located in the System.Drawing.Drawing2D namespace. Listing 26-3 illustrates several variations using the LineCap enumeration to draw different types of lines, which results you can see in Figure 26-5.

Listing 26-3: **Using the LineCap Enumeration**

```
protected override void OnPaint(PaintEventArgs e)
{
 Graphics g = e.Graphics;
 Pen p = new Pen(Color.Brown, 15);

 // set the Arrow
```

Continued

Listing 26-3 *(continued)*

```
p.StartCap = LineCap.ArrowAnchor ;
p.EndCap = LineCap.ArrowAnchor ;
g.DrawLine(p,30, 30, Width-50, 30);

// round ends
p.StartCap = LineCap.Round  ;
p.EndCap = LineCap.Round ;
g.DrawLine(p,30, 80, Width-50, 80);

// round Anchor
p.StartCap = LineCap.RoundAnchor ;
p.EndCap = LineCap.RoundAnchor ;
g.DrawLine(p,30, 120, Width-50, 120);

// triangle
p.StartCap = LineCap.Triangle  ;
p.EndCap = LineCap.Triangle  ;
g.DrawLine(p,30, 150, Width-50, 150);

// square Anchor
p.StartCap = LineCap.SquareAnchor;
p.EndCap = LineCap.SquareAnchor ;
g.DrawLine(p,30, 190, Width-50, 190);

}
```

Figure 26-5 shows the results of running the preceding code using the `LineCap` enumeration.

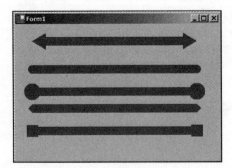

Figure 26-5: Using the LineCap enumeration

Using the Brush class

Using the Brush class in conjunction with a Graphics object gives you the capability to render images and solid objects on a drawing surface. The following code demonstrates how to create a solid filled ellipse:

```
protected override void OnPaint(PaintEventArgs e)
{
 Graphics g = e.Graphics;
 SolidBrush sb = new SolidBrush(Color.Black);
 g.FillEllipse(sb, ClientRectangle);
}
```

Running the preceding code produces an image like the one shown in Figure 26-6.

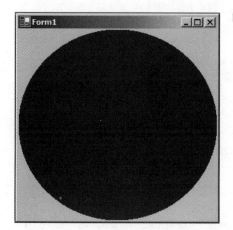

Figure 26-6: A solid ellipse using a brush

The types of brush that you can create come in several flavors. A SolidBrush, which was used in the preceding example, fills a shape with a solid color. Using a HatchBrush enables you to get a little crazy with the way your graphics appear. The HatchBrush uses the HatchStyle enumeration and the HatchFill enumeration to display different pattern types. Listing 26-4 prints several of the HatchBrush variations using the HatchStyle enumeration. The HatchStyle enumeration has over 40 members, so it is worth looking up in the .NET Framework SDK. If you ever need to do any type of pattern drawing, you can find substantial support.

Listing 26-4: **Using the HatchBrush Class with HatchStyles**

```
protected override void OnPaint(PaintEventArgs e)
{
    Graphics g = e.Graphics;

    HatchBrush hb =
                new HatchBrush
                (HatchStyle.Plaid,
                Color.AntiqueWhite ,Color.Black);
        g.FillEllipse(hb,30, 30, Width-50, 30);

    HatchBrush hb2 = new HatchBrush
                (HatchStyle.LargeCheckerBoard,
                Color.AntiqueWhite ,Color.Black);
            g.FillEllipse(hb2, 30, 80, Width-50, 30);

    HatchBrush hb3 =
                new HatchBrush
                (HatchStyle.DashedHorizontal,
                Color.AntiqueWhite ,Color.Black);
            g.FillEllipse(hb3, 30, 130, Width-50, 30);

        HatchBrush hb4 =
                new HatchBrush
                (HatchStyle.ZigZag,
                Color.AntiqueWhite ,Color.Black);
            g.FillEllipse(hb4, 30, 180, Width-50, 30);
```

Running the preceding code produces something similar to what is shown in Figure 26-7.

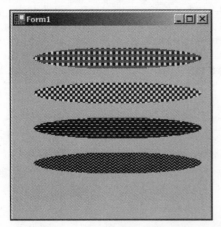

Figure 26-7: HatchBrush with different HatchStyles

Table 26-6 describes each of the pen types available in the PenType enumeration that you can use with the Brush class, You have already seen HatchFill and SolidColor in action. Based on their descriptions, you can probably imagine the other brush types without seeing them in action.

	Table 26-6	
	PenType Enumeration	
Member	**Description**	
HatchFill	Specifies a hatch fill	
LinearGradient	Specifies a linear gradient fill	
PathGradient	Specifies a path gradient fill	
SolidColor	Specifies a solid fill	
TextureFill	Specifies a bitmap texture fill	

Working with text and fonts also requires using a Brush object along with a Graphics object. To use text, you create an instance of the Font class, which resides in the System.Drawing namespace, and set the face, style, and text size properties, and then call the DrawString method from the Graphics object that will hold the brush. Listing 26-5 prints the phrase C# is cool onto the current form and outputs something similar to what is shown in Figure 26-8.

Listing 26-5: **Using the DrawString Method**

```
protected override void OnPaint(PaintEventArgs e)
{
  Graphics g = e.Graphics;
  e.Graphics.FillRectangle(
          new SolidBrush(Color.White),
          ClientRectangle);

  g.DrawString("C# is cool", this.Font,
          new SolidBrush(Color.Black), 15, 15);
}
```

Note In .NET, fonts used on a Form object are inherited from the form itself. In this example, the font property in the form is set to 24, so when the this.Font value is passed to the DrawString method, it uses the current font size of the form.

Figure 26-8: Using the DrawString method and the Font class to output text

Table 26-7 lists the available properties of the Font class. By setting or retrieving these properties on Font objects that you create, you can completely control the output of the text on the screen.

Table 26-7 Font Class Properties	
Property	**Description**
Bold	Gets a value that indicates whether this Font object is bold
FontFamily	Gets the FontFamily object associated with this Font object
GdiCharSet	Gets a byte value that specifies the GDI character set that this Font object uses
GdiVerticalFont	Gets a Boolean value that indicates whether this Font object is derived from a GDI vertical font
Height	Gets the height of this Font object
Italic	Gets a value that indicates whether this Font object is italic
Name	Gets the face name of this Font object
Size	Gets the em size of this Font object in design units
SizeInPoints	Gets the size, in points, of this Font object
Strikeout	Gets a value that indicates whether this Font object specifies a horizontal line through the font
Style	Gets style information for this Font object
Underline	Gets a value that indicates whether this Font object is underlined
Unit	Gets the unit of measure for this Font object

Summary

GDI+ offers a robust array of classes that enable you to write any type of graphics support into your applications. This chapter presented an overview of the capabilities of GDI+, but you can do much more with the `System.Drawing` and `System.Drawing.Drawing2D` namespaces than can be covered in a single chapter.

To manipulate or create graphics using GDI+, you first need to create a `Graphics` object which gives you the surface with which you paint objects on. After your `Graphics` object is created, you then use pens, brushes, bitmaps, or fonts to render the type of image you are looking for.

✦   ✦   ✦

Building Web Services

Web services are arguably the most exciting and innovative feature of Microsoft's .NET initiative, and they are likely to profoundly affect the way businesses interact using computer applications. So, what exactly is a Web service? From 10,000 feet, a Web service is simply a server-side component that can be invoked over the Internet. Such a server-side component would typically perform a core business service, such as user authentication, credit card validation, pricing a derivatives security, placing a purchase order for a stock, or pricing a same-day shipment. Obviously, the list of possible Web services is as varied as the list of possible business opportunities. Web services enable applications to invoke business services using a standards-based mechanism (using XML and HTTP), and as you will learn in this chapter, how this is realized represents a significant breakthrough in application interoperability. XML is the basic building block for many of the standards used when creating Web Services. If you are not familiar with XML, you can find a brief primer on it in this book's appendix.

In this chapter, you learn which XML-based standards govern defining and using of Web services, Then you create a Web service using Visual Studio .NET. Finally, you use this newly created Web service in a second Visual Studio .NET project.

Understanding How Web Services Work

Two optional technologies are involved in defining Web services: the *discovery mechanism* and the *service description*. These two technologies can be bypassed by using other means of communications; for example, if there is a dialogue (e.g., phone calls) between the developers of the Web service and the developers of the client that will be accessing the Web service. The discovery mechanism uses an XML document on the server to enable client applications to detect that a Web service exists and to find the detailed description of that service. Initially, Microsoft was proposing to use DISCO (discovery of Web services) for this discovery mechanism, but UDDI (Universal Description, Discovery and Integration) has since become the de facto standard for discovery. You can find out more about UDDI at http://www.uddi.org. The service description describes the inputs and outputs of the Web service. Service descriptions use the Web Service Description Language (WSDL) standard, described later in this chapter. UDDI (or DISCO, its now deprecated predecessor) and WSDL are essential building blocks that can be used to create precise documentation about how to invoke the Web service. And because these technologies are standardized, the descriptions are also readable by applications. However, after a client has been implemented, there may be no need to use the discovery mechanism or to refer to the service description. The use of these technologies is not essential to create or use Web services that are geared to a specific application.

Three technologies are involved during the actual invocation of a Web service: the *wire protocol*, the *message format* and the *invocation mechanism*. Only the former two are specified in the Web service standards. The wire protocol is the transport mechanism used to communicate between the client and the server. Typically, this is HTTP, the TCP/IP-based Internet protocol. The message format is the format used to invoke a Web service. A Web service can be invoked by using raw HTTP or by using an XML message in a specific format called Simple Object Access Protocol (SOAP). The third technology, which governs the way in which the server-side components gets invoked, is not specified by the Web service standards. That is an implementation detail left to the discretion of the implementer of the Web service. In other words, the programmer building the Web service chooses the technology used to call the business code on the server: a Visual Basic developer may use COM+ to invoke a COM object, a Java developer may use RMI to invoke a Java object, and so on.

The two sides of a Web service can be described as the creator (client) and the consumer (server). The creator develops the server-side component and exposes this service to the appropriate audience. For example, a financial institution develops a credit card validation system and exposes this to online vendors. Exposing a Web service means publishing the URL that users need to invoke the Web service. The consumer can use the exposed service by sending a SOAP request message to the published URL. Upon receiving the SOAP request message written in XML, the server-side component behind the Web service is invoked on the creator's server. The results from this invocation are formatted into a SOAP response message and are sent back to the service consumer. Figure 27-1 shows the parties involved in a Web service.

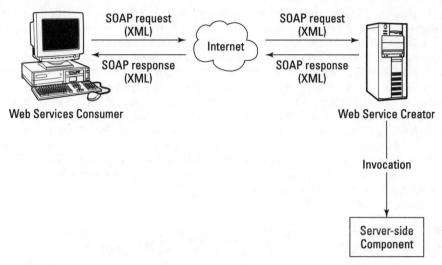

Figure 27-1: Web services have two sides: za consumer and a creator.

Web services use a set of standards to define how the interaction between client and server is realized. These standards define the transport mechanism to be used and both the format and content of the interaction. At the Transport level, the ubiquitous HTTP Internet protocol is used. The server and client communicate with each other using XML messages. The content of these messages is also standardized and must conform to the rules of SOAP (more about these rules follows later in this chapter). The nature of the services available in a Web service can be described in an XML file whose content conforms to the rules of the Web Service Description Language (WSDL). Finally, a client can dynamically discover which Web Services are exposed on a site by retrieving the XML file whose content conforms to the rules of DISCO.

Note that no mention has been made yet about any company-specific technologies. Nowhere has there been any assumption about the operating system running on the client or the server, the programming language used to write the server-side component, or the mechanism used to invoke the server-side component. These choices are irrelevant to a Web service. A client written in C# running on Windows XP, for example, can invoke a Web service written in Java running on Sun Solaris. In fact, a client has no way of knowing what technologies are used to expose the Web service.

The implications of Web services are far-reaching. Microsoft jump-started component-based programming with the introduction of OLE controls (OCXs), a refinement of the groundbreaking concepts introduced by Visual Basic Controls (VBXs). OCXs are based on Microsoft's Component Object Model (COM), and work well. However, COM and its distributed counterpart, Distributed Component Object Model (DCOM), are limited in their reach. Aside from the Windows family of operating systems, there is limited support for COM/DCOM. In addition, although on the desktop the Windows family is widely used, on the server-side a greater variety of operating systems are in use. For example, several varieties of the UNIX operating system, such as Solaris and Linux, have a significant presence. Web services eliminate the need to choose which operating system runs on the server when integrating two Web-based applications. Using Web services, you can now assemble a Web-based application using components from other sites. For example, you could use a Web service from a credit card company to validate the credit card, a Web service from a shipping company to determine the shipping charge, and so on. This is the both the essence and the promise of Web services: the next generation of component-based programming for the next generation of distributed applications.

Web Services and Visual Studio .NET

If Web services are platform-independent, what does Microsoft hope to gain from them? The answer is simple: Microsoft has publicly stated that it will strive to make Windows the best operating system to host Web services, and Visual Studio .NET the best development environment to create Web services. Because this programming book is about C#, the focus of this discussion about Web services is on C# and its integrated development environment. In the hands-on section later in this chapter, you will be able to judge for yourself how flexible and easy to use the Visual Studio .NET development environment is.

Visual Studio .NET does a wonderful job of simplifying the creation and consumption of Web services. Much of the programmer-unfriendly stuff (creating all the XML-based documents, for example) happens automatically, without much effort on the programmer's side. All you have to do when programming is declare your intention to expose a piece of code as a Web service, and the tool does most of the work. In fact, the tool does such a fantastic job that you may never see any XML at all when building a Web service and a Web service consumer. In fact, this is exactly what you do in this chapter. Before you begin, however, take a quick look at the concept that makes all this automation possible. It's called attribute-based programming.

Attribute-based programming is a powerful concept that enables Visual Studio .NET to automate a lot of programmer-unfriendly tasks (such as creating a WSDL document for a Web service). You simply mark a piece of code, such as a class or method, in a special way to denote what you intend to do with it. As a result of this, Visual Studio .NET generates the necessary files to implement your intention. A short example shows how this works in the context of transforming a class into a Web service.

Listing 27-1 illustrates how you might implement a simple game. Granted, this game isn't very fair (the player always loses), but this chapter is concerned with Web service programming, not game programming. Take a quick look at what's involved in turning this piece of code into a Web service and what Visual Studio .NET generates for you during this process. The main point of this exercise is to give you an idea of the amount of work involved when turning a piece of finished code into a Web service using Visual Studio .NET.

Listing 27-1: **A Simple Game**

```
namespace MyFirstWebService
{
    public class GameWS
    {
        // SIMPLE GAME EXAMPLE
        // The example game returns the string "Sorry, you
lose!"
        // To test this game, press F5
        public string Play(string opponentName)
        {
            return "Sorry " + opponentName + ", you lose!";
        }
    }
}
```

Your first step to turn this piece of code into a Web service is to save the code in a new file called GameWS.asmx. Then, perform the following four steps:

1. Add a header indicating three things: that the file contains a Web service, the language used, and the class that contains the implementation:

   ```
   <%@ WebService Language="c#" Class="MyFirstWebService.GameWS"
   %>
   ```

2. Add a System.Web.Service directive just below the Web service header:

   ```
   using System.Web.Services;
   ```

3. Mark the class as a Web service and choose the XML namespace associated with the Web service:

   ```
   [WebService(Namespace="http://www.boutquin.com/GameWS/")]
       public class GameWS : System.Web.Services.WebService
   ```

4. Mark the methods within the class as being accessible from the Web:

   ```
           [WebMethod]
           public string Play(string opponentName)
   ```

Listing 27-2 shows the final result. The comments have also been changed to reflect the changes made to the original code.

Listing 27-2: **A Simple Game Exposed as a Web Service**

```
<%@ WebService Language="c#" Class="MyFirstWebService.GameWS"
%>

using System.Web.Services;

namespace MyFirstWebService
{
    [WebService(Namespace="http://www.boutquin.com/GameWS/")]
    public class GameWS : System.Web.Services.WebService
    {
        // WEB SERVICE EXAMPLE
        // The Play() method returns the string "Sorry, you
lose!"
        // To test this web service, press F5
         [WebMethod]
        public string Play(string opponentName)
        {
            return "Sorry " + opponentName + ", you lose!";
        }


    }
}
```

When you build a Web services project in Visual Studio, a service description file that describes the Web service is automatically created. This file is an XML dialect called Web Service Description Language (WSDL). A WSDL file looks like the following:

```
<?xml version="1.0" encoding="UTF-8"?>
<methods
href='http://www22.brinkster.com/boutquin/GameWS.asmx'>
    <method name='Play' href='Play'>
        <request>
            <param dt='string'>opponentName</param>
        </request>
    <response dt='string'/>
    </method>
</methods>
```

The WSDL describes the functions that are exposed (the format shown is actually a simplification of the actual format, but the concept remains the same). You can call

the service through a URL (www22.brinkster.com/boutquin/GameWS.asmx/
Play?opponentName=Pierre, in this case) or send a properly formatted XML
message to the URL (via an HTTP post or get statement). Such an XML message
would be a SOAP message like the following:

```
<?xml version="1.0" encoding="utf-8"?>
<soap:Envelope
  xmlns:xsi="http://www.w3.org/2001/XMLSchema-instance"
  xmlns:xsd="http://www.w3.org/2001/XMLSchema"
  xmlns:soap="http://schemas.xmlsoap.org/soap/envelope/">
    <soap:Body>
    <Play xmlns="http://www.boutquin.com/GameWS/">
            <opponentName>Pierre</opponentName>
        </Play>
      </soap:Body>
</soap:Envelope>
```

Invoking the service, either through the URL or by posting a SOAP message, results
in an XML response such as the following:

```
<?xml version="1.0" encoding="UTF-8"?>
 <string xmlns="http://www.boutquin.com/GameWS/">Sorry Pierre,
you lose!</string>
```

The following sections examine the essentials of SOAP and WSDL, after which you
dive into the details of Web service creation and invocation.

Understanding the Web Service Description Language (WSDL)

WSDL is the XML vocabulary used to describe Web services. This description
includes information about how to access them. The .NET Framework takes care of
generating these Web services for you, so you do not need to know much about
WSDL to use Web services. To see what the WSDL for a service looks like, you can
add ?wsdl to its URL and see the result in a XML-capable browser; for example,
www22.brinkster.com/boutquin/GameWS.asmx?wsdl.

This section briefly describes this XML vocabulary.

WSDL uses a default namespace, xmlns="http://schemas.xmlsoap.org/wsdl/".
It uses a root element called definitions and contains several sections. One of
these sections is the service section, where—you guessed it!—services are
described. The following snippet is a skeleton of a WSDL file. An actual WSDL file
uses several namespace declarations, which are omitted here for simplicity's sake:

```
<?xml version="1.0" encoding="UTF-8"?>
<definitions xmlns='http://schemas.xmlsoap.org/wsdl/'>

        <service name="GameWS" >

   <!-- Service is described here -->

   </service>

</definitions>
```

The first attribute in a service description defines the location from which you can call the service. This is described in the address element inside a port element. (Element and attribute are XML terms, as you can learn in the appendix.) The following example illustrates the binding attribute:

```
<?xml version="1.0" encoding="UTF-8"?>
<definitions xmlns='http://schemas.xmlsoap.org/wsdl/'>

        <service name="GameWS" >

        <port name="GameWSSoap" binding="s0:GameWSSoap">
          <soap:address

location="http://www22.brinkster.com/boutquin/GameWS.asmx" />
        </port>

   </service>

</definitions>
```

If a Web service is exposed through an HTTP post or get statement, its location is stored in an http:address element:

```
        <port name="GameWSHttpPost"
binding="s0:GameWSHttpPost">
                <http:address
location="http://www22.brinkster.com/boutquin/GameWS.asmx" />
   </port>
```

Next, you need to define the input and output parameters. You accomplish this action through message elements. In such an element, you give each message a name; and within a message, you describe each parameter (name and data type):

```
<message name ="PlayInput" >

<part name="opponentName" element='xsd:string'/>

</message>
```

```
<message name ="PlayOutput" >

  <part name='Result' type=''xsd:string"/>

</message>
```

You can then associate the messages with the port using a `portType` element. In the `portType`, you use the name you assigned to this port in the `port` element; and for each of the Web services, you create an `operation` tag containing an `input` and `output` element that use the message as the attribute:

```
<portType name="GameWSSoap">
  <operation name="Play">
          <input message="PlayInput" />
          <output message="PlayOutput" />
  </operation>
</portType>
```

Finally, the `binding` element describes the specifics relevant to the transport mechanism used. A SOAP binding, for example, needs to specify the SOAP action:

```
<binding name="GameWSSoap" type="s0:GameWSSoap">
  <soap:binding
  transport="http://schemas.xmlsoap.org/soap/http"
style="document" />
  <operation name="Play">
          <soap:operation
soapAction="http://www.boutquin.com/GameWS/Play"
style="document" />
          <input>
                  <soap:body use="literal" />
          </input>
          <output>
                  <soap:body use="literal" />
          </output>
  </operation>
</binding>
```

Using Simple Object Access Protocol (SOAP)

SOAP is the XML dialect used by Web services. It specifies which server-side action you want to invoke to pass the information (that is, the parameters) to the Web service. SOAP also specifies how the information is returned from the Web service (both return values and exceptions).

SOAP messages follow a standard format: an outer envelope that identifies the message as being a SOAP message, a body section that contains the main payload, and an optional header section for additional information about the message. You can use the header section to pass information that is not per se part of the server-side invocation. You can, for example, pass the date and time of the request, or user authentication in this header. The body contains an element whose name matches the name of the server-side method being called. The children of this element are elements whose names match the names of the parameters:

```
<?xml version="1.0" encoding="utf-8"?>
<soap:Envelope
  xmlns:xsi="http://www.w3.org/2001/XMLSchema-instance"
  xmlns:xsd="http://www.w3.org/2001/XMLSchema"
  xmlns:soap="http://schemas.xmlsoap.org/soap/envelope/">
  <soap:Header>

    <!-- Optional information goes here -->

  </soap:Header>
  <soap:Body>

    <MethodName>
      <Param1Name>value1</Param1Name>
      <Param2Name>value2</Param2Name>
      <!-- etc. -->
    </MethodName>

  </soap:Body>
</soap:Envelope>
```

The same format is used to send back a response. The parameter names (here `Param1Name` and `Param2Name`) in the response are, of course, the output parameters; or "return" when the method only returns one value (e.g., `<return>value</return>`).

When errors occur, the error information is sent back in a fault section. The fault section is found in the SOAP body:

```
<soap:Fault>

  <faultcode>x00</faultcode>
  <faultstring>description<faultstring>
  <runcode>Yes<runcode>

</soap:Fault>
```

Creating Web Services Using Visual Studio .NET

Creating (and, in the following section, accessing) a Web service using Visual Studio .NET is deceptively simple. You don't even need to be aware that XML is used.

The Web service you will build in this section will simply retrieve and display a list of books. This simulates the catalog function of a Web-based commerce site, although in reality you probably would want to introduce categories to avoid returning a huge list of books. Since the focus in this chapter is on what's required to build a Web service, the business aspect is being simplified.

The sample you build here uses one table and one stored procedure. The code to create this is shown in the following example (you may also want to put some sample data in the Books table):

```
CREATE TABLE [Books] (
  [ISBN] [char] (14) NOT NULL ,
  [Title] [varchar] (150) NOT NULL ,
  [Price] [money] NOT NULL
)
GO

ALTER TABLE [dbo].[Books] WITH NOCHECK ADD
  CONSTRAINT [PK_Books] PRIMARY KEY  CLUSTERED
  (
          [ISBN]
  )  ON [PRIMARY]
GO
CREATE PROCEDURE [pc_getBooks]
AS
SELECT
   [ISBN],
   [Title],
   [Price]
FROM [Books]
GO
```

Now you are ready to build a simple Web service that returns a list of books using the stored procedure:

1. Open Visual Studio .NET and select File ⇨ New Project.

2. Select ASP.NET Web Service as the project type in the New Project dialog box.

3. Name the project **BookSeller** (see Figure 27-2).

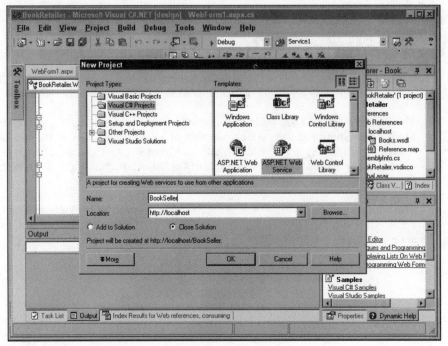

Figure 27-2: A Web service is a separate project type.

4. Rename the Web service from Service1.asmx to **Books.asmx**.

5. Switch to Code view, by clicking the Books.asmx.cs tab, and change all occurrences of Service1 to **Books** (see Figure 27-3).

6. Change the using section to contain the following:

```
using System;
using System.Web.Services;
using System.Data;
using System.Data.OleDb;
```

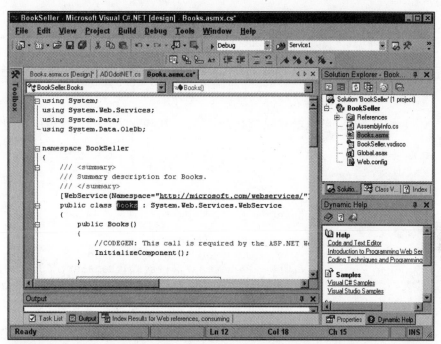

Figure 27-3: You can change the default service name to something more descriptive.

7. Add the following methods and property to the Books class:

```
private static string oleDbConnectionString
{
get
    {
        // NOTE: Using the sa account in production
applications
        // is, of course, a BAD, BAD practice. In addition,
leaving the
        // password blank for the sa account is equally
inadmissible.
            return "Provider=SQLOLEDB.1;"
                +"User ID=sa;Initial
Catalog=WebService_1_0_0;Data Source=localhost;";

    }
}

// WEB SERVICE EXAMPLE
 [WebMethod]
public DataSet getList()
{
// Set SQL statement strings
    string strSQLSelect = "[pc_getBooks]";
```

```
    // Create OleDb objects
    OleDbConnection databaseConnection = new
OleDbConnection(oleDbConnectionString);
    OleDbCommand selectCommand = new
OleDbCommand(strSQLSelect, databaseConnection);
    OleDbDataAdapter dsCmd = new OleDbDataAdapter();
    DataSet resultDataSet = new DataSet();

    // We are dealing with a Stored Proc (i.e. NOT a SQL
statement)
    selectCommand.CommandType = CommandType.StoredProcedure;

    try
    {
        // Establish database connection
        databaseConnection.Open();

        // Execute SQL Command
        dsCmd.SelectCommand = selectCommand;
        int numRows = dsCmd.Fill(resultDataSet, "Books");

    }
    catch (Exception e)
    {
        Console.WriteLine("****** Caught an exception:\n{0}",
e.Message);
    }
    finally
    {
        databaseConnection.Close();
    }

    return resultDataSet;
}
```

The `oleDbConnectionString` property contains the connection string to the SQL Server database. In production code, you would use an account with proper security rights (and a password) instead of the almighty "sa" account. The `getList()` method opens a connection to the SQL Server database, and retrieves a DataSet containing the list of books by invoking the `pc_getBooks` command. You can see how straightforward it is to use ADO.NET.

You also find more details on ADO.NET in Chapter 23.

8. That's it! You can also add a namespace declaration to the class, as shown in the following example:

```
[WebService(Namespace="http://microsoft. com/webservices/")]
```

```
public class Books : System.Web.Services.WebService
```

Namespaces are a way to avoid duplication of names. A unique prefix is used to distinguish similarly named Web services. Typically, URLs are used as the basis for these unique names. This is in accordance on how URLs are used in XML namespaces as described in the appendix.

9. Save the project, then press F5 to test the Web service.

Now that you have created a Web service, try creating a client application that uses this Web service.

Using Visual Studio .NET to Access a Web Service

The following example shows the steps required to create a Web service application in C#:

1. Open Visual Studio .NET and select File ➪ New Project.

2. Select ASP.NET Web Application as the project type.

3. Name the project **BookRetailer**.

4. Choose Project ➪ Add Web Reference.

5. Click Web References on Local Server to have Visual Studio .NET automatically detect the available Web services on localhost.

6. Select `http://localhost/BookSeller/BookSeller.vsdisco` and then click Add Reference.

You have imported the information needed to call this Web service.

7. In Design mode, add a `Label` control to the top of the page and a `DataGrid` control below the label, and then switch to Code view.

8. Add a `using` declaration to the ASP.NET page: This tells the compiler that you will be using the code from the Web service.

```
using BookRetailer.localhost;
```

9. Add the following code to the `Page_Init` method. In this example, you set the text for the label and then populate the DataGrid in a quick and easy way (this page will not win any awards for aesthetics):

```
private void Page_Init(object sender, EventArgs e)
{
//
        // CODEGEN: This call is required by the ASP.NET
Windows Form Designer.
```

```
                        //
                        InitializeComponent();

                        // Added by PGB
                        Label1.Text = "Available Books";

                        Books books = new BookRetailer.localhost.Books();
                        DataSet bookList = books.getList();
                        DataGrid1.DataSource =
                  bookList.Tables["Books"].DefaultView;
                        DataGrid1.DataBind();
                        // End PGB Addition
                  }
```

10. Save and run the project (using the F5 shortcut). A screen similar to the one shown in Figure 27-4 appears.

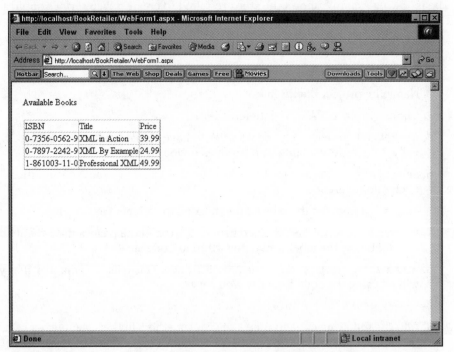

Figure 27-4: A Web service in action, having retrieved a list of books from the Web service provider

Let's reflect on what we have accomplished. You created a Web service (that would run on a server connected to the Internet). In this section, you built a Web page (that would run on a different server) that uses this Web service to retrieve a list of books from the first server.

Summary

In this chapter, you have examined the XML-based standards behind Web services. You looked at the two optional technologies involved in defining Web services: UDDI for the discovery mechanism and WSDL for the service description. You also looked at the message format used during the actual invocation of a Web service: SOAP. You built a simple Web service using Visual Studio. Then, you built a second project that was using the Web service you previously built.

✦   ✦   ✦

Using C# in ASP.NET

The advent of Internet and corporate intranets has led to the development of distributed applications. A distributed application can access information from different data sources that might be spread across multiple geographical locations. Visual Studio .NET takes distributed applications to new heights by enabling you to utilize Web services and Web service clients.

ASP.NET Web services are XML-based services that are exposed on the Internet that can be accessed by other Web services and Web service clients. A Web service exposes Web methods that can be accessed by Web service clients, which implement the functionality of the Web service.

Before Visual Studio .NET, ASP programming was done using VBScript. However, with the advent of Visual Studio .NET, you can use two languages for ASP programming: Visual C# and Visual Basic .NET. Visual C# enables you to write ASP.NET code for Web services and Web applications. Finally, you can learn how to deploy the Web application by using Visual Studio .NET.

In this chapter, you learn to use C# for creating ASP.NET applications. You begin by creating a Web service in Visual C#. After creating the Web service, you create a Web service client in C#, which is actually a Web application that uses the Web service.

Creating a Web Service

In Visual Studio .NET, Web services are used for integrating remote applications with your present line-of-business solutions. Broadly speaking, Web services offer two advantages:

✦ You can utilize a Web service offered by another organization to build a customized application for your organization. For example, you can use the Microsoft Passport authentication service to enable Microsoft Passport authentication on your Web site. You can benefit from such a venture because you need not establish the necessary infrastructure to implement custom authentication on your Web site. In addition, your site can cater to a larger audience because all users registered with the Passport service (which includes all Hotmail and MSN users) can log on to your Web site.

✦ You can also utilize Web services to communicate with your business partners. To cite a simple example, consider a bookseller who houses the books of numerous publishers. If each publisher can host a Web service that provides information about the latest books that are released by them, the bookseller can develop a Web service client that connects to these Web services and retrieves details about these books.

For more information on Web services, refer to Chapter 27.

Now you create a Web service that utilizes a database. Therefore, in the first step, you learn how to create the database for the Web service. Next, you learn how to use the database and create the Web service.

While creating the Web service in this example, you concentrate only on the tasks involved in its creation. Refer to Chapter 27 to learn about the concepts involved in implementing Web services.

Creating a database for a Web service

Web services or Web applications often employ a database to store data that pertains to the application. In an enterprise environment, databases, such as Microsoft SQL Server and Oracle, are well suited for managing data.

In the Web service that you create in this chapter, you use an SQL Server database. Before you create the SQL Server database and tables for the Web service, quickly review important Relational Database Management Systems (RDBMS) concepts.

Relational Database Management Systems concepts

A Relational Database Management System (RDBMS) is best suited for enterprise business solutions. An RDBMS, such as Microsoft SQL Server, Oracle, and DB2, enables the creation, updating, and administration of relational databases. A *relational database* is a collection of data organized in the form of tables. Applications can access data in tables using the Structured Query Language (SQL) statements. In an RDBMS, you can access data and reorganize data without reorganizing the entire database. This improves the performance of the database considerably. In addition, you can easily apply business rules, validations, and constraints to the data in the tables of an RDBMS. Business rules and validations ensure data integrity. For example, when you book a passenger on a flight in an airway reservation system, the flight number should exist. You can determine the flight number by establishing a business rule and using it while booking a ticket.

SQL Server data types

Data in a database is stored in tables, as rows and columns. The columns of a table store categorized information, such as product identification number, product name, and quantity available. The rows of a table store specific records. Each column in a table has a specific data type. Table 28-1 describes some of the common SQL Server data types.

Table 28-1 SQL Data Types	
Data type	**Description**
Integer	Used to store whole numbers.
Float	Used to store decimal numbers.
char(n)	Used to store character data that can be alphabetical, numerical, special characters, such as #, %, or $, or a combination of letters and characters. A char data type stores a single character. To store more than one character, you use char(n), where n refers to the number of characters that you want to store.
varchar(n)	Used to store character data, where n refers to the number of characters you want to store. A varchar data type is different from a char data type because the memory allotted to a varchar data type depends upon the size of data, unlike the char data type, in which allocated memory is predefined.
Datetime	Used to store date and time data.
Money	Used to store currency-related data values that demand high precision.

Tip Each table must have at least one column that uniquely identifies a row (referred to as a *record*) in the table. Such a column is the primary key of the table. For example, the ProductID column in a Products table identifies each row uniquely and is therefore a primary key. No two values in a primary key can be identical.

Creating databases and tables

In Microsoft SQL Server, you can create databases, tables, stored procedures, and queries by using Transact-SQL (T-SQL).

Tip You can also use SQL Server Enterprise Manager to create a database and tables. SQL Server Enterprise Manager provides a graphical interface to perform the same steps that are performed by using T-SQL statements.

To create a database or a table using T-SQL, you use the `Create` statement. For example, to create a database Sales, you write the following code in the query analyzer window:

```
Create Database Sales
```

After creating the database, you can add tables to it. Add the Products table to the Sales database by using the following syntax:

```
Create Table Products
(
ProductID VarChar (4) Primary Key,
ProductName VarChar (20),
UnitPrice Integer,
QtyAvailable Integer
)
```

Retrieving data

You can retrieve information stored in tables by using the `Select` statement. For example, to retrieve all the records from the Products table of the Sales database, you use the following statements:

```
Use Sales
Select * From Products
```

Inserting, updating, and deleting data

You can add, update, and delete data from an SQL Server database by using the steps outlined in the following list:

✦ **Add a record:** To add a new row to an SQL Server table, you use the `Insert` statement. For example, to add a new record to the Products table, you use the following statement:

```
Insert Into Products (ProductID, ProductName, UnitPrice,
QtyAvailable)
Values ('P001', 'Baby Food', 2.5, 12000)
```

Caution

In order for the insert operation to be successful, the column values must be supplied in the same order as the columns in the table. In addition, if the data type of a column is `char`, `varchar`, or `datetime`, you need to specify values in quotes.

✦ **Modify a record:** To modify a record in an SQL Server table, you use the `Update` statement:

```
Update Products
Set UnitPrice=75
Where ProductID="P010"
```

The preceding code updates the unit price of the record whose product ID is P010 to 75.

✦ **Delete a record:** To delete a record from a table, you use the `Delete` statement. For example, to delete a record from the Products table with the Product ID of P011, you specify the following statement:

```
Delete From Products where ProductID="P011"
```

Using stored procedures

A *stored procedure* is a set of SQL statements used to perform specific tasks. A stored procedure resides on the SQL Server and can be executed by any user who has the appropriate permissions. You can create a stored procedure by using the `Create Procedure` statement. Create a stored procedure that accepts the `ProductID` as a parameter and returns the unit price of the record matching the ProductID by using the following code:

```
Create Procedure ProductPrice (@id char (4))
As
Select UnitPrice
From Products Where ProductID=@id
Return
```

The preceding procedure requires a parameter, `@id`, at the time of execution.

Stored procedures are particularly useful when you need to perform a number of tasks on a database one after the other. For example, when you want to cancel the reservation of a passenger, you might need to calculate the fare that needs to be refunded to the customer and delete the reservation of the customer from a reservations table. At the same time, you might also need to update the status of other passengers who might be overbooked on the flight. Instead of specifying SQL queries each time you want to cancel a reservation, you can use a stored procedure to cancel the reservation of a passenger.

Caution   Each stored procedure must end with a `Return` statement.

To execute the preceding procedure to display the price of the product with the ID P010, use the following code:

```
Execute ProductPrice "P010"
```

Creating the database structure

In this chapter, you need to create a Sales database for your Web service. After creating the Sales database, you add a Products table to the database. To create the Sales database and add the Products table to it, follow these steps:

1. Select Start ➪ Programs ➪ Microsoft SQL Server ➪ Query Analyzer to open Query Analyzer. The Connect to SQL Server dialog box opens.

2. In the Connect to SQL Server dialog box, type the name of the SQL Server in the SQL Server text box, specify a login name in the Login Name text box, and specify the password for the login name in the Password text box.

3. Click OK to connect to the SQL Server and open the query editor.

4. In the query editor, enter the following statements to create the Sales database and add the Products table to the database:

```
Create database Sales
GO
Use Sales
Create Table Products
(
ProductID VarChar (4) Primary Key,
ProductName VarChar (20),
UnitPrice Integer,
QtyAvailable Integer
)
GO
```

5. Select Query ➪ Execute to execute the query.

After you execute the query, the database structure is in place. You are now ready to create the Web service—the first of the ASP.NET applications that you create in this chapter. The Web service that is created in this chapter adds records to the Products table of the Sales database that you created in this section.

Using the ASP.NET Web service template

You need to use the ASP.NET Web Service project template to create a Web service. This project serves as a Web-based template for creating the Web service components. To create a Web service, perform the following steps:

1. Select File ➪ New ➪ Project to open the New Project dialog box.

Tip   You can also press Ctrl+Shift+N simultaneously to open the New Project dialog box.

2. From the Project Types list, select Visual C# Projects.

3. From the Templates pane on the right side of the dialog box, select ASP.NET Web Service.

4. In the Name box, type **OrdersWebService**. In the Location box, and enter the name of your Web server as **http://<servername>**. Click OK.

Tip   You can also type **localhost** in the Location box if the Web server is installed on the computer on which you are creating the Web service.

Note   You may have to wait for some time while Visual Studio .NET creates the Web service.

After Visual Studio .NET creates the Web service, you can configure the Web service to manage data in SQL Server. You do that in the next section.

Adding data controls to the Web service

You need to add data controls to your Web service to enable communication with the Sales database that you created in the previous section. To communicate with the party database, you need to add the following controls to your Web service:

✦ `SqlDataAdapter`: You use the `SqlDataAdapter` control to transfer data between data sources.

✦ `SqlConnection` and `SqlDataAdapter`: You use the `SqlDataAdapter` and `SqlConnection` controls to connect to the data source.

✦ `SqlCommand`: After connecting to the data source, you use the `OleDbCommand` control to access data.

✦ `DataSet`: You store data in a `DataSet` control.

The steps to add the `SqlDataAdapter` control are as follows:

1. Select View ➪ Toolbox to open the toolbox.

2. In the toolbox, click Data to activate the Data tab.

3. Drag the `SqlDataAdapter` control from the toolbox to the Component Designer.

4. When you drag the `SqlDataAdapter` control from the toolbox, the Data Adapter Configuration wizard launches. On the Welcome screen of the wizard, click Next.

5. The Choose Your Data Connection dialog box of the wizard, shown in Figure 28-1 appears. Click New Connection to create a new connection by using the `OleDbDataAdapter` control.

6. The Data Link Properties dialog box opens. By default, the Connection tab of this dialog box is selected. Specify the name of the SQL Server on the Select or Enter a Server Name dialog box.

7. Select the user name and password to connect to the SQL Server, and select the Sales database from the Select the Database on the Server drop-down list. The completed Data Link Properties screen is shown in Figure 28-2. Click OK.

8. The data adapter that you configured appears in the Choose Your Data Connection dialog box. Click Next to continue.

Figure 28-1: The Choose Your Data Connection dialog box

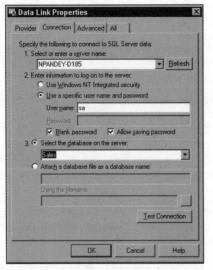

Figure 28-2: Connect to the data source by using the Data Link Properties dialog box.

9. The Choose a Query Type dialog box opens. To use an SQL query for retrieving data from the database, retain the default option, Use SQL Statements, and click Next.

10. The Generate the SQL Statements dialog box opens. In this dialog box, type the query **Select * from Products** and click Next.

11. The View Wizard Results dialog box opens. This dialog box summarizes the options that you selected in the preceding dialog boxes of the wizard. Click Finish to complete the Data Adapter Configuration Wizard.

After you complete the Data Adapter Configuration Wizard, the `SqlDataAdapter` control is configured for your application. As shown in Figure 28-3, the `sqlDataAdapter1` and `sqlConnection1` controls are added to your application.

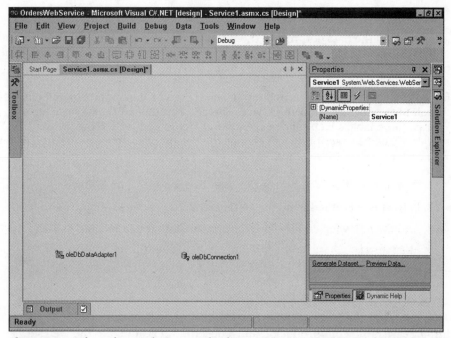

Figure 28-3: The sqlDataAdapter1 and sqlConnection1 controls are added to your application.

Next, add the `SqlCommand` control to the Web service. The `SqlCommand` control is used to specify commands that need to be executed on the data source. Follow these steps to add an `SqlCommand` control to your application:

1. Drag the `SqlCommand` control from the toolbox to the Component Designer.

2. Open the Properties window and select `sqlConnection1` for the Connection property of the `SqlCommand` control.

Next, you need to generate a dataset for storing data that is retrieved by the data controls:

1. To generate the dataset, select the `SqlCommand1` control that you added in the preceding steps, and select the Data ⇨ Generate Dataset menu option.

2. The Generate Dataset dialog box opens. In this dialog box, the Products table of the Sales database is already selected. Select the Add This Dataset to the Designer check box, and click OK to generate the dataset and add it to the Component Designer.

The four controls that you added to the Web service are now visible in the Component Designer. You now need to code the methods of the Web service, which you do in the next section.

Coding the Web service

After you add the data controls to the Web service, you need to code the methods of the Web service. This chapter demonstrates how you can code a method to add products to the Products database by using the Web service.

Before you code the methods of the Web service, add a description to and change the default namespace of the Web service. The description and the namespace of the Web service enable a Web service client developer to understand the usage of the Web service. To add a description and change the default namespace associated with the Web service, follow these steps:

1. Double-click the Component Designer to open the Code Editor.

2. In the Code Editor, locate the statement `public class Service1`.

3. Add the following code before the statement that you located in Step 2:

```
[WebService(Namespace="http://ServiceURL.com/products/",
    Description="Use the Web service to add products to the
Sales
    database.")]
```

After you enter the preceding line of code, the namespace of the Web service is http://ServiceURL.com/products/, and a description is added to the Web service.

Next, write the code for adding products to the Products table. This code needs to be written immediately below the declaration of the Web service. The code for the AddProduct method, which adds product details to the Products table, is as follows:

```
[WebMethod(Description="Specify the product ID, product name,
unit price, and quantity to add it to the Sales catalog")]
public string AddProduct(string PID, string ProductName, int
Price, int Qty)
{
    try
    {
        ProductName=ProductName.Trim();
        if (Price<0)
            return "Please specify a valid value for price";
        if (Qty<0)
            return "Please specify a valid value for quantity";
        sqlConnection1.Open();
```

```
        sqlCommand1.CommandText="INSERT INTO Products(ProductID,
            ProductName, UnitPrice, QtyAvailable) VALUES ('" +
PID +
            "', '" + ProductName + "', '" + Price + "', '" + Qty
+
            "')";
        sqlCommand1.ExecuteNonQuery();
        sqlConnection1.Close();
        return "Record updated successfully";
    }
    catch(Exception e)
    {
        return e.Message;
    }
}
```

The preceding code uses the `sqlConnection1` control to add a record to the Products table. When you add records to the Web service, you use the values that are supplied to the `AddProduct` function as parameters.

As you code the `AddProduct` method of the Web service, you can code other methods to retrieve product details in the Products database or perform other custom actions. To test the Web service after you add the methods to it, follow these steps:

1. Select Build ➪ Build Solution to build the Web service.

2. To start debugging the Web service, select the Debug ➪ Start menu option.

The Web service opens in Internet Explorer. The first dialog box displays the methods that you coded for your Web service. To test the `AddProduct` method, follow these steps:

1. Click AddProduct on the Service1 Web Service dialog box.

2. The AddProduct dialog box opens, as shown in Figure 28-4. In this dialog box, you can invoke the `AddProduct` function after supplying the required parameters to test its output.

3. Type the parameters for PID, ProductName, Price, and Qty as **P002**, **PDA**, **100**, **200**, respectively, and click Invoke to test its output.

4. When the record is added successfully to the Web service, you see the output displayed in Figure 28-5.

After you successfully test your Web service, you can create a Web service client to access the Web service.

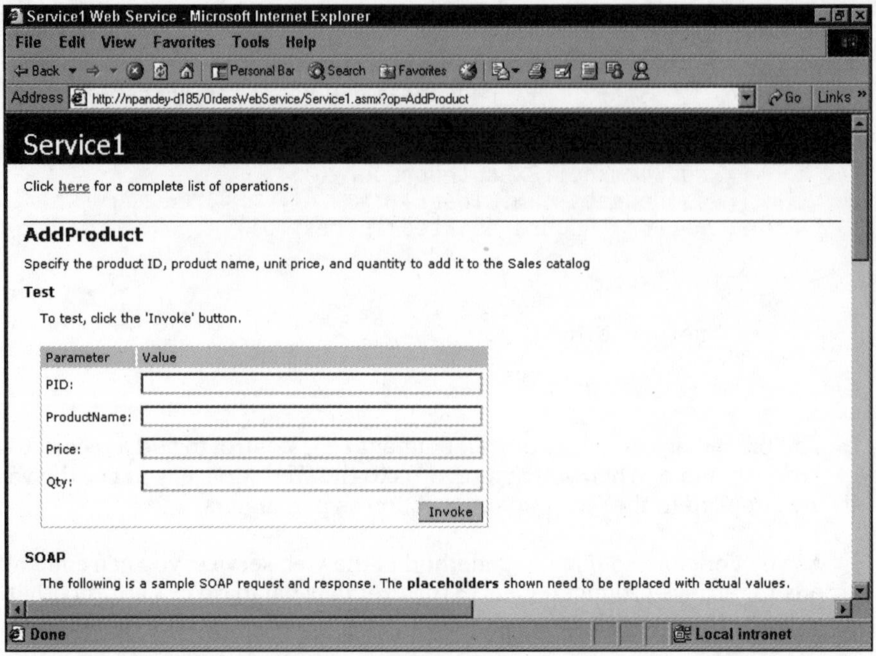

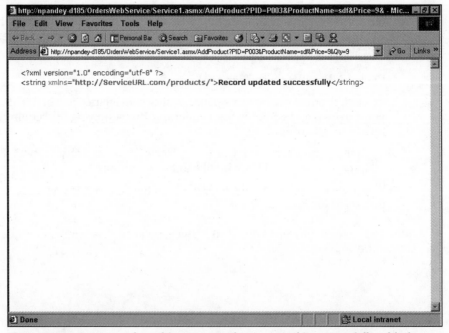

Figure 28-4: Specify the parameters for the AddProduct function in order to test it.

Figure 28-5: Output such as this appears when a record is successfully added to the Web service.

Creating a Web Service Client

A Web service client in ASP.NET is a Web application that comprises one or more WebForms. In this section, you create an ASP.NET Web application that accesses the Web service you created in the previous section.

 Cross-Reference   For more information on WebForms, see Chapter 22, "Creating Web Applications with WebForms."

To create a Web service client, you need to follow these steps:

1. Create a new ASP.NET Web Application project.

2. Add a Web reference to the Web application.

3. Implement the methods of the Web service in the Web application.

The following section examines each of these steps in detail.

Creating a new ASP.NET Web application project

To create a Web application project, follow these steps:

1. Select the File ➪ New ➪ Project menu option. The New Project dialog box opens.

2. In the New Project dialog box, select the ASP.NET Web Application project template from the Visual C# Projects list.

3. Enter **OrdersWebApplication** as the name of the project and click OK to create the Web application.

Adding a Web reference

After you create the Web service, you need to add a Web reference to the Web service that you created in the preceding section. When you add a Web reference, the Web service client downloads the description of the Web service and creates a proxy class for the Web service. A proxy class includes proxy functions for methods of the Web service. To add a Web reference to the Web service, follow these steps:

1. Select the WebForm1.aspx Web form and then Select the Project ➪ Add Web Reference menu option. The Add Web Reference menu option opens.

2. In the Add Web Reference dialog box, click the Web References on Local Web Server link. The Web services available on the local Web server appear in the Available references list, as shown in Figure 28-6.

3. In the Add Web Reference dialog box, select the link to the OrdersWebService Web service, and click Add Reference to add a reference to the Web service.

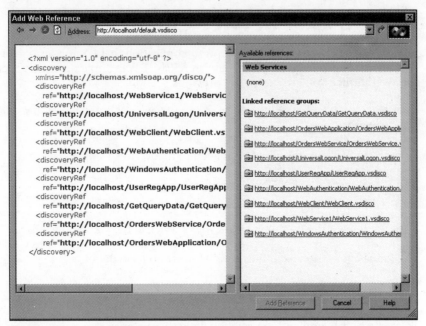

Figure 28-6: Available Web services are displayed in the Add Web Reference dialog box.

The reference to the Web service that you add appears in the Solution Explorer. By default, it is named `localhost`. You can change the name of the Web service to a name of your choice. In Figure 28-7, it is named OS1.

Figure 28-7: References to Web services appear in the Solution Explorer.

Implementing the methods of the Web service

To implement the methods of the Web service, you need to design a WebForm. The WebForm accepts information that needs to be added to the Sales database. The WebForm designed for the Web application is shown in Figure 28-8.

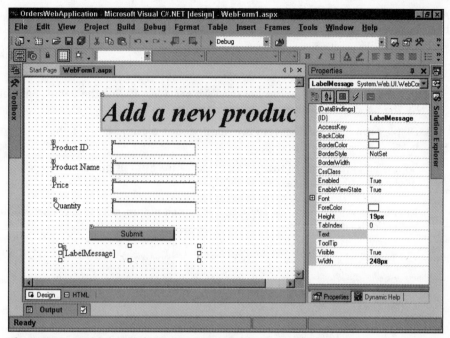

Figure 28-8: Design a WebForm to accept information from users.

To design the form, you can add the controls listed in Table 28-2.

	Table 28-2
	Web Form Controls

Control Type	*Properties Changed*
Label	Six labels were added: the main caption of the page, Product ID, Product Name, Price, Quantity, and Message, respectively. The ID of the last label was changed to LabelMessage and its text cleared.
TextBox	ID=PID
TextBox	ID=ProductName
TextBox	ID=Price
TextBox	ID=Quantity
Button	ID=Submit
	Text=Submit

After you design the WebForm, write the code for the `Click` event of the Submit button. When the user clicks the Submit button, the code of the `Click` event should do the following:

1. Create an instance of the Web service.

2. Call the `AddProduct` method of the Web service, passing the values entered by the user on the WebForm as parameters.

3. Display the return value from the `AddProduct` method in the `LabelMessage` label.

Following is the code of the `Click` event of the Submit button that accomplishes the preceding tasks:

Tip

To enter code for the `Click` event of the Submit button, double-click the Submit button in the design view.

```
private void Submit_Click(object sender, System.EventArgs e)
{
    OS1.Service1 Web1=new OS1.Service1();
    LabelMessage.Text=Web1.AddProduct(PID.Text,
ProductName.Text,
        Convert.ToInt32(Price.Text), Convert.ToInt32
        (Quantity.Text));
}
```

4. Select Debug ➪ Start to run the Web service. The output of the Web application is shown in Figure 28-9.

Specify values in the Product ID, Product Name, Price, and Quantity text boxes and click Submit. The Web application adds the required information to the Sales database, and a message appears in the `LabelMessage` label, as shown in Figure 28-10.

Deploying the Application

The last step in integrating various Visual Studio .NET applications is to deploy the application that you have built. To deploy your application, you can use one or more deployment projects provided by Visual Studio .NET. The following sections examine the deployment projects provided by Visual Studio .NET and then describe the steps you take to deploy an ASP.NET application.

Deployment projects in Visual Studio .NET

Visual Studio .NET provides four types of setup projects: Cab projects, Merge Module projects, Setup projects, and Web Setup projects. The following list describes these project types:

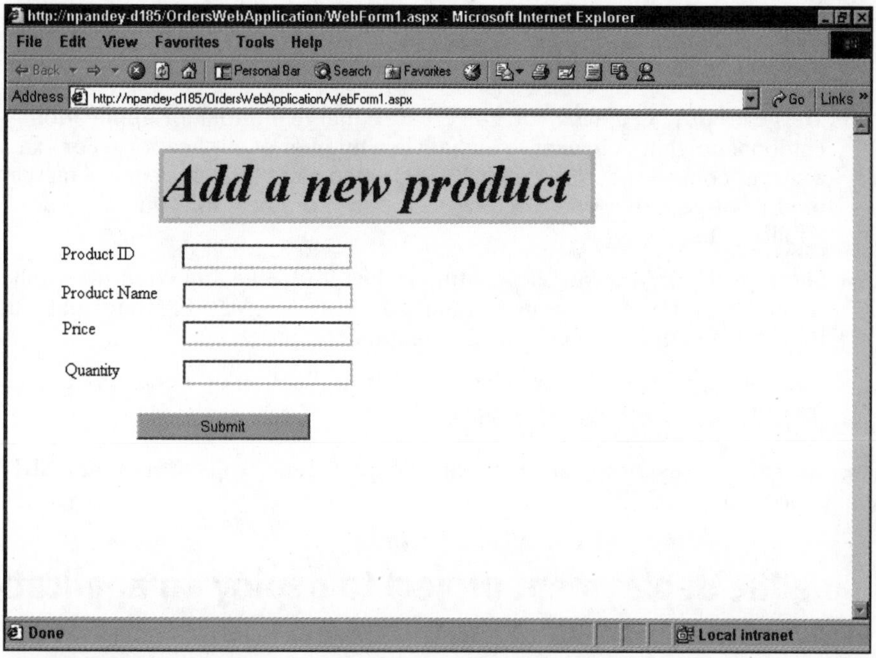

Figure 28-9: This WebForm represents the output of the Web application.

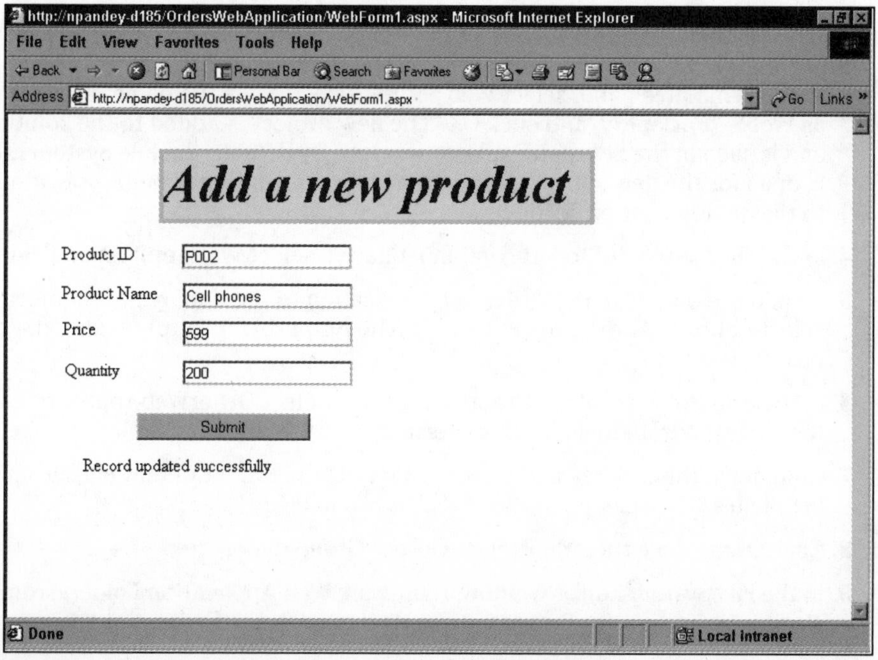

Figure 28-10: You can add a record to the Sales database through the Web application.

✦ **Cab projects:** You can create a cabinet (CAB) file for packaging ActiveX controls. When you package an ActiveX control in a CAB file, the control can be downloaded from the Internet.

✦ **Merge Module projects:** You can create a merge module for application components that you want to include in a number of applications. For example, a server control that you might have created can be packaged as a merge module project that you can include in Setup projects for your Windows applications.

✦ **Setup projects:** You can use a Setup project for packaging Windows applications. A Setup project creates a Microsoft Installer (MSI) file that can be used to install an application on the destination computer.

✦ **Web Setup projects:** For an ASP.NET Web application or Web service, you can use the Web Setup project template.

The next section describes how to create a deployment project for an ASP.NET Web application.

Using the deployment project to deploy an application

The steps for deploying an ASP.NET application are as follows:

1. In the Solution Explorer window, right-click the solution, OrdersWebApplication. From the shortcut menu that appears, select Add ➪ New Project.

2. In the Add New Project dialog box that opens, select Setup and Deployment Projects from the Project Types pane.

3. In the Templates pane, select Web Setup Project. Type the name of the project as **WebSetupDeploy**, and click OK. The new project is added to the solution and is seen in the Solution Explorer window. By default, the File System Editor is open for the deployment project. The File System Editor helps you add files to the deployment project.

4. In the File System Editor (the left-most pane), select WebApplication Folder.

5. To add the output of the OrderWebApplication to the deployment project, select Action ➪ Add ➪ Project Output. The Add Project Output Group dialog box opens.

6. In the Add Project Output Group dialog box, select OrderWebApplication from the Projects drop-down list, if necessary.

7. Hold down the Ctrl key and select Primary Output and Content Files from the list of files. The selected options are shown in Figure 28-11.

8. Click OK to close the Add Project Output Group dialog box.

9. In the File System Editor window, right-click Web Application Folder. From the shortcut menu, select Properties Window to open the Properties window.

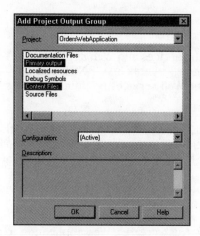

Figure 28-11: The Add Project Output Group dialog box shows the options you selected.

10. Type OrderWebApplication as the name of the virtual directory in the VirtualDirectory property and close the Properties window.

11. Select the Build ⇨ Build Solution menu option.

A Microsoft Installer (MSI) file for your project is created. You can double-click the file to install your application on a computer.

Deploying a project by using the Copy Project option

If you do not want to take the trouble of creating a deployment project for your application and using the project to deploy your application, you can also use the Copy Project option in Visual Studio .NET to copy all files of your application to the destination folder.

The Copy Project option is useful when you need to deploy a project over a network. However, this option does not work when you need to deploy your application on a remote computer that is not accessible on a network.

To use the Copy Project option, follow these steps:

1. Open the project that you want to copy.

2. Select the Project ⇨ Copy Project menu option. The Copy Project dialog box opens.

3. Specify the destination path where you want to copy the project in the Destination project folder dialog box.

4. Select the files of the project that you want to copy, and click OK. Your project is copied to the destination that you specified in Step 3. After you copy the project, you can run the project from the new location.

Summary

The role of C# in ASP.NET pertains to Web services and Web applications. You can create a Web service by using the C# language syntax in ASP.NET. You can also create a Web application that accesses the Web service and builds upon its functionality.

When you create an application in ASP.NET, you first design the database that needs to be used in the application. Next, you create a new project in ASP.NET by using the ASP.NET Web Application or ASP.NET Web Service project templates.

After creating a project in ASP.NET, you use the data controls that are provided by Visual Studio .NET to connect to a data source and utilize it.

If you have created a Web service, you can also create a Web application to utilize the Web methods that are provided by the Web service.

✦   ✦   ✦

Building Custom Controls

In this chapter you learn to build custom controls. These controls may take the form of a visible component that can be added to a form or may simply be a class object encapsulated within a DLL. In each instance, these controls build upon your knowledge of code reuse when you begin to package and distribute functionality as a control that can be used time and again.

Understanding the Windows Control Library

A Windows Control Library is a project that enables you to build components similar to those displayed within the toolbox of the Visual Studio IDE. In the past, these controls have always been COM objects or ActiveX controls. You can now add COM components to the toolbox, or you can create a control that presents itself in the form of a dynamic link library (DLL).

Previous versions of Visual Studio provided wizards to help with the creation of controls, and Visual Studio.NET is no different. The tasks associated with creating properties, methods, and fields are simplified because of the included wizards.

Properties

You use properties primarily for setting and retrieving control parameters. When properties are granted both Read and Read-Write access at design time, they consist of two functions called `get` and `set`. Since a property must call a method when values are assigned or retrieved from it, it can perform calculations or other useful functions at the drop of a hat. In this respect, they are much different from fields. An example of a property would be the `BackColor` property. By using this property, you can either specify the color to be used as the background color of a control or check to see what the current background color is.

Properties are easily implemented in your project by using the Visual Studio.NET IDE a very simple wizard. Within the Class View window, right-click your control's class, and then choose Add ➪ Add Property. The wizard, shown in Figure 29-1, enables you to set the type of access, the property type (int, bool, and so on), the property name, accessors, and modifiers.

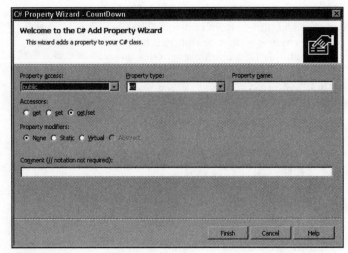

Figure 29-1: The Add Property Wizard enables you to add a property to your project.

After you complete the wizard, you are greeted with a skeleton code for your property:

```
public int TestProperty
{
  get
  {
    return 0;
  }
  set
  {
  }
}
```

Some basic elements are missing in this code. When setting the property to a value, the information is not being stored. You must first create a private class variable that this property can use to store and retrieve the value. In this case, you simply include the following declaration at the top of your class declaration:

```
private int m_TestProperty;
```

From within the set method of your property, you can assign the data to your private variable using the value keyword:

```
set
{
  m_TestProperty = value;
}
```

Now that the value of the property has been stored in the private class variable, you have to ensure that the Get method returns the correct value when used. The following code accomplishes this; simply return the value of the private variable within the get block, as shown in the following snippet:

```
get
{
  return m_TestProperty
}
```

It is also useful to map properties from existing components in your control. For example, assume you have created a control that contains a label. Your control should contain a Font property that gets and sets the font of the label component within your control. To enable the container to manipulate the font of your label, simply create a property as follows:

```
public Font CurrentFont
{
  get
  {
      return label1.Font;
  }
  set
  {
      label1.Font = value;
  }
}
```

This code creates a property called CurrentFont, which returns the current font of the label control when requested. When the container wishes to change the font, you simply set the current font of the label control to that of value.

Methods

A method is defined as a function that is part of a class. Methods are implemented in the same manner as many other languages, such as C++, C, VB, and so on. Methods are most commonly used for initiating an action within a control. An example of this would be the Start method within the Timer control.

You can add a method to a control in one of two ways. You can use the C# Method Wizard, accessible through the Solution Explorer while in Class view, or you can simply add a public function to your project.

The C# Method Wizard, shown in Figure 29-2 enables you to specify the method name, return type, access method, and parameter information in a very straightforward manner.

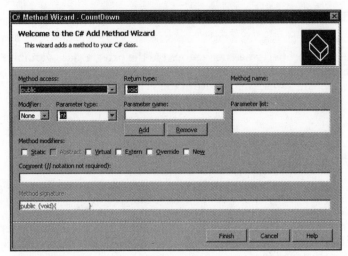

Figure 29-2: The C# Method Wizard creates the skeleton code needed for a method.

The drawback to the Method Wizard is that it provides you with only simple return types. For example, suppose you want a method that returns a value of type Font. The Font type is not an option in the Return Type combo box. When you experiment with the wizard, you learn that you can enter your own types in these boxes; you are not limited to the options they contain. The options presented are merely the most commonly used types so as not to confuse the new programmer. After all, if every option were presented in this wizard, it would take a considerable amount of time to scroll through the list in search of the type you require.

The .NET Framework also brings some much-needed functionality to methods. Methods can now be overloaded. That is, they can have the same name just as long as their parameter lists are different.

Fields

Fields are simply public variables defined within a control. The container application can set the field to a particular value and retrieve the value. Because these are merely variables, they have no functions associated with them; fields cannot perform calculations or call other methods when a value is set or retrieved from them.

There are two types of fields: instance and static. A field is defined as an instance field by default. An instance field can contain its own data within each object that contains it. When a field is declared as static, the field contains the same data across all instances of the object. A static field is normally not a good idea because other instances of an object can change the value while the remaining instances are unaware of it.

Fields provide low coding overhead but are also limited in terms of functionality. You can set and retrieve a field's values, but doing so cannot trigger other actions within the control itself. Fields are useful when you need to assign operating parameters to a control.

Events

To define an event, you must first make a public class declaration, such as the following:

```
Public event EventHandler Expired;
```

You can use events in one of two ways with Windows controls: You can either click the Event icon within the Properties window and double-click the event to automatically add the handler, or you can create an event handler yourself.

A basic event is declared as type `EventHandler`, but you have many more event types to choose from, and each one has a unique signature. The parameter of every event contains a `System.EventArgs` structure. This structure enables the control to pass information into the event, defining many things, such as what fired the event, which control caused the event to fire, and so on. Before picking an event type for your control, be sure to explore the different types, as well as the parameters they pass.

Knowledge by Example

Let's begin by building a countdown timer control. This exercise enables you to examine the ins and outs of building controls.

Creating a countdown timer

Before you begin building the countdown timer control, you need to identify what this control should and should not do. This mapping simplifies the process of building the control. It's always a good idea to have everything mapped out well in advance of beginning a control project, more so than with any typical programming project. This particular control should have the following features:

✦ The control should be a visible component that you can place on a form. This control should have typical properties, such as `BackColor`, `Anchor`, and so on.

✦ The control should accept a value indicating the number of seconds to count down.

✦ The control should have a `Start()` and `Stop()` method to begin and end the countdown.

✦ Finally, the control should fire an event when the countdown has reached zero.

With the requirements defined, you can begin building your control.

Open Visual Studio.NET and create a new Windows Control Library project. Name this project **CountDown**, as shown in Figure 29-3.

Figure 29-3: Create a new Windows Control Library project.

1. When Visual Studio has created your skeleton control, you are presented with a `UserControl`. This will be the visual interface to your `CountDown` control. It is here that you place any visual elements that you want the user to view and/or interact with.

2. The first thing you must do is place a `Label` control on the `UserControl`, as shown in Figure 29-4.

3. Change the `Anchor` property of this `Label` control to `Top,Left,Bottom,Right`. This ensures that when the control is resized, the label is resized along with it. You should exercise much care when adding existing components to a control because many elements can change visually when the user places a control on the form.

4. Now you must add a `Timer` control to the project (from the toolbox). The `Timer` control enables you to count one second at a time until you have determined that the time has expired. The visual aspect of your control is now complete. You must now add the code to support this control.

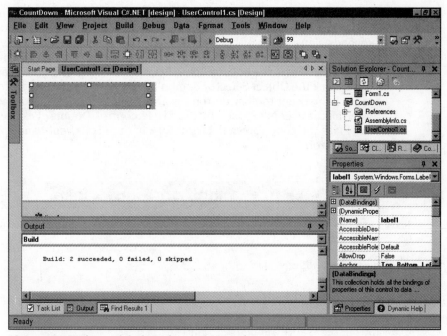

Figure 29-4: Place a label on the UserControl.

5. In Listing 29-1, you declare a member variable to hold the number of seconds the countdown timer counts down from. You must also declare an EventHandler to fire when the control reaches the end of the countdown. Place the following code just below the class declaration within UserControl:

Listing 29-1: **Public Members**

```
private int m_Seconds;
public event EventHandler Expired;
```

6. The m_Seconds variable doesn't need to be exposed to the controls container, but only to control itself, so you make the variable private. By declaring a public EventHandler, Expired shows up within the Event window. You can then program this event by simply double-clicking it.

7. In the `Tick` event of the `Timer` object, you must subtract a second from your total number of seconds. You can then check to see whether the total number of seconds elapsed has reached zero. If so, you have to stop the timer and then fire off `Expired` event. After this, you can update the `Label` control to reflect the current value of your `CountDown Timer` control. In the Properties window, click the Object Selector combo box, and select the `Timer` control. Next click the Event toolbar button toward the top of the Properties window. You see all the events exposed by the `Timer` control. Double-click the `Tick` event. Place the code shown in Listing 29-2 in the `Tick` event handler of the `Timer` control.

Listing 29-2: **The Tick Event Updates Your Control**

```
private void timer1_Tick(object sender, System.EventArgs e)
{
  m_Seconds -= 1;
  if (m_Seconds <= 0)
  {
    timer1.Stop();
    Expired(this,e);
  }
  label1.Text = m_Seconds.ToString();
}
```

8. Your control also needs a `public()` method that enables the container to start the control on its journey to counting seconds. Listing 29-3 defines the interval of the `Timer` control (in milliseconds) and then starts the `Timer` control. After the timer has been started, you must update the `Label` control because it won't be get updated until 1 second later when the timer fires the `Tick` event for the first time.

9. To add a method to the control, switch the Solution Explorer to Class view by clicking the Class View tab. Expand the Class view, until you come to the controls class. Right-click; select Add, and then select Add Method. The C# Method Wizard opens, as shown in Figure 29-5.

10. Name this new method **Start** and ensure that it is a public method. You can leave all the other settings at their default. After you create the new method, add the code shown in Listing 29-3 to the method's code listing.

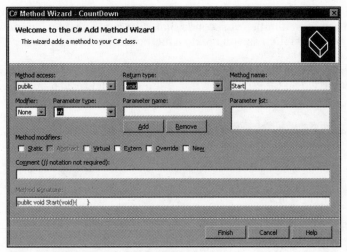

Figure 29-5: The C# Method Wizard

Listing 29-3: **Start Method**

```
public void Start()
{
  timer1.Interval = 1000;
  timer1.Start();
  label1.Text=m_Seconds.ToString();
}
```

11. A Stop() method complements your Start() method. The Stop() method should first stop the Timer control so that the Tick event no longer fires. You must also assign the value of the Seconds property to your m_Seconds member variable. This ensures that if the control is started again, it starts from the beginning and not from where it left off when it was stopped. Create a new method called Stop(), just as you created the Start() method. Add the code from Listing 29-4 to this new method.

Listing 29-4: **Stop Method**

```
public void Stop()
{
  timer1.Stop();
  m_Seconds = this.Seconds;
}
```

You have not yet created the Seconds property. The Seconds property enables you to get and set the total number of seconds that your control will count down from. You create a property much as you create a method.

1. From Class view in the Solution Explorer, right-click and choose Add and then Add Property. The C# Property Wizard, shown in Figure 29-6 opens.

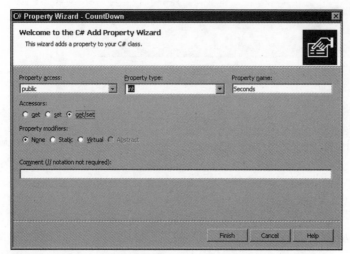

Figure 29-6: In the C# Property Wizard, name this property Seconds. Ensure that this property has public access and that the property type is set to Int.

2. You want the controls container application to be able to assign a value to this property or read the value from this property. Therefore, you want the accessor set to get/set. Add the code in Listing 29-5 to the code created by the C# Property Wizard.

Listing 29-5: **Seconds Property**

```
public int Seconds
{
  get
  {
    return m_Seconds;
  }
  set
  {
    m_Seconds = value;
  }
}
```

Pay special attention to the `value` keyword. When a value is passed in to a property (e.g., `set`), it can be retrieved with the `value` keyword.

Thus far, your control isn't very advanced, nor does it look good, but it is functional. At this point, you can build the new control by selecting Build Solution from the Build menu.

Now you build a test harness that uses this control and enables you to test all methods, properties, and events of the control.

Creating a CountDown test harness

One of Visual Studio's strengths is that it enables you to add a project to an existing project, which plays an important role when it comes to testing controls. This capability enables you to create a test harness application that uses a control you just created. When errors are encountered, not only does your application break, but it breaks in the code where your control malfunctioned. This saves you countless hours of debugging code when you start to build complex controls. Perform the following steps to create a test harness:

1. From within your CountDown control project, click the File menu and select New ➪ Project. The New Project window opens.

2. Select Windows Application and name this application **CDHarness**. At the bottom of this window, ensure that the Add To Solution radio button is clicked. Click OK.

3. The Solution Explorer displays both projects. Right-click the CDHarness application in the Solution Explorer and select Set As Startup Project. When you run the application now, your test harness will be the main application to run, and it can use any other projects currently loaded in the "group."

4. Ensure that you are within the CDHarness project by clicking it on the Solution Explorer. Right-click the toolbox and choose Customize Toolbox.

5. When the Customize Toolbox window opens, click the .NET Framework Components tab. It is here that you add your new control to the project.

6. Click the Browse button and browse for the CountDown timer control. When you find it, select it and highlight it. Click OK.

7. In the list of controls, you see this control; check the box next to it. Now you can click OK on this form. From within the control toolbox, you see the CountDown timer control listed.

8. Double-click the control to add it to your project. While you are in the toolbox, add two buttons to your form as well. The first button is used to start the countdown timer; and the second button is used to stop the `Countdown` control. Arrange and set the text properties as shown in Figure 29-7.

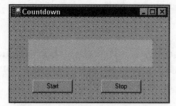

Figure 29-7: The main
interface for your CountDown
harness application

9. Double-click the Start button within your application so you can begin coding.
Add the code in Listing 29-6 to the Click event of the Start button.

Listing 29-6: **Start Your Control**

```
private void button1_Click(object sender, System.EventArgs e)
{
    cdTimer1.Seconds=60;
    cdTimer1.Start();
}
```

10. The Start button serves one purpose and one purpose only: to prepare and
start your CountDown control. To begin, you set the number of seconds to **60**,
and then you call the Start method of the control.

11. You also need to be able to stop your control. Double-click the Stop button so
you can place code in the Click event of this button. Place the following code
from Listing 29-7 in the Click event of the Stop button.

Listing 29-7: **Stop Your Control**

```
private void button2_Click(object sender, System.EventArgs e)
{
    cdTimer1.Stop();
}
```

12. The Expired event of the CountDown control needs to perform some action
so you know that your countdown has reached zero. In the Properties window, click the Events button on the toolbar. Now double-click the Expired
event. It is within this code that you want to code this special action. You
won't attempt anything extravagant here; you are simply going to change the

caption of your form to Done. Place the code shown in Listing 29-8 into the Expired **event of the** CountDown **control.**

Listing 29-8: Expired Event Code

```
private void cdTimer1_Expired(object sender, System.EventArgs e)
{
    this.Text="Done!";
}
```

Your control and test application are now ready to roll. Press F5 to run the application. When the applications opens, click the Start button to begin the countdown. Your test application should begin to count down. When the countdown has reached zero, the caption of the form should change, thanks to your Expired **event.**

Using a Class Library

A class library is an efficient means to re-use and distribute re-usable code. Class libraries are stored in DLLs, but there is no need to wrap the code with export statements and declarations as required in languages, such as C++.

As with any re-usable component, class libraries provide class constructs and destructors for initialization and cleanup, but these items are not actually required.

To begin your journey into class libraries, you build a simple DLL with a few public methods for demonstration purposes; and then you build upon the control with some additional bells and whistles.

Building the windchill calculations class

Not only will your windchill calculation class library provide a function to calculate the windchill, it will also provide functions to ascertain Celsius from Fahrenheit and Fahrenheit from Celsius.

Because the operations you are going to perform in this class library fall under two distinct categories, Conversion and Calculation, you are going to include two separate classes. Create a new class library project and name it **Temperature**. Visual Studio creates the skeleton code shown in Listing 29-9.

Listing 29-9: **Code Created for a Class Library by Visual Studio**

```
using System;

namespace TmpTure
{
    /// <summary>
    /// Summary description for Class1.
    /// </summary>
    public class Class1
    {
        public Class1()
        {
            //
            // TODO: Add constructor logic here
            //
        }
    }
}
```

Visual Studio has created a namespace, a class, and a class constructor. Both the class and class constructor are public. This isn't coincidental. Any application that uses this library needs access to both the class and specific members within the class.

1. To begin your sample, you remove the class and class constructor and replace it with the code shown in Listing 29-10.

Listing 29-10: **The Calc Class and Constructor**

```
public class Calc
{
    public Calc()
    {
    }
}
```

2. The Calc class is where you place your windchill calculation method. This ensures that your windchill calculation is separated from the conversion methods that you will soon add. Paste the code shown in Listing 29-11 into the Calc class.

Listing 29-11: **Calculate the Current Windchill**

```
public double WindChill(double DegreesF, double WindSpeedMPH)
{
    double WindRaised;
    WindRaised = System.Math.Pow(WindSpeedMPH,.16);
    return 35.74 + (.6215 * DegreesF) - (35.75 * WindRaised) + (.4275 * DegreesF
* WindRaised);
}
}
```

3. You will also be adding a few methods that aren't calculations, but rather conversions. Therefore, you need to add a new class. This new class will be called Conversion, as shown in Listing 29-12. Add the new class and class constructor to the project.

Listing 29-12: **Add a Second Class to the Class Library**

```
public class Conversion
{
    public Conversion()
    {
    }
}
```

4. Begin your new class with a function that calculates the temperature in Fahrenheit, given the Celsius temperature. Both the return value and parameter are unlikely to be integer values, so it's important to make both double values. Listing 29-13 contains the function listing in its entirety. Add this code to the Conversion class.

Listing 29-13: **Celsius to Fahrenheit Conversion**

```
public double CelcToFahr(double Celsius)
{
    return (9/5) * (Celsius + 32);
}
```

5. Because you have included a Celsius to Fahrenheit conversion function, it is only logical to include a conversion in the opposite direction. Add the method shown in Listing 29-14 to the Conversion class.

Listing 29-14: **Fahrenheit to Celsius Conversion**

```
public double FahrToCelc(double Fahrenheit)
{
    return (5/9) * (Fahrenheit - 32);
}
```

That concludes the functionality you want to include in the Class Library object, so you can create the DLL by selecting Build Solution from the Build menu. Now that everything is in place, take a look at how to go about utilizing the public methods contained therein.

1. Create a new console application project and name it **DLLTest**. From the Project menu, choose Add Reference, and then click the Browse button. Locate the DLL that you just created and double-click it. You can then click OK to exit the Add Reference window.

2. After you add a reference, you can simply create a new variable of the appropriate type, and reference the method of your choice. Listing 29-15 contains the entire code listing for the DLLTest application.

Listing 29-15: **DLLTest Application Source Code**

```
using System;

namespace DLLTest
{
  /// <summary>
  /// Summary description for Class1.
  /// </summary>
  class Class1
  {
    static void Main(string[] args)
    {
      Temperature.Calc WCMethod = new Temperature.Calc();
      Temperature.Conversion ConvMethod = new Temperature.Conversion();

      Console.WriteLine("Wind chill at 50 degrees with 35 MPH : {0}
Degrees",WCMethod.WindChill(50,35));
      Console.WriteLine("32 Degrees Fahrenheit to Celsius : {0}
Degrees",ConvMethod.FahrToCelc(32));
      Console.WriteLine("0 Degrees Celsius to Fahrenheit : {0}
Degrees",ConvMethod.CelcToFahr(0));
    }
  }
}
```

Accessing the methods is a very simple task: create new variables of type `Temperature.Conversion` and `Temperature.Calc` and then access their public methods. This sample application calculates the current windchill given a temperature of 50 degrees with a 35-mile-per-hour wind speed; and then it calculates temperatures in both Celsius and Fahrenheit. The output from this application is shown in Figure 29-8.

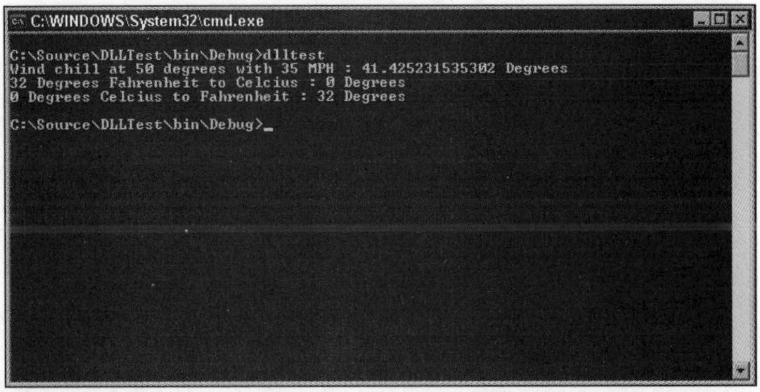

Figure 29-8: DLLTest shows you how to use a Class Library control.

Summary

.NET introduces some extremely important advances in the way that you build controls. As you build controls for your own projects or to deploy to the Web, advances in programming, such as the `State` object, poke their heads out and save you an enormous amount of time.

✦　　✦　　✦

Building Mobile Applications

Mobile Web applications are a group of emerging technologies that enable you to deploy Web content to an even larger audience than the Internet currently provides. You can make corporate intranet applications available to employees who travel through company buildings or to employees a continent away as they travel on business. This chapter describes several areas of mobile Web applications.

Understanding the Wireless Web

The concept of accessing the Internet with mobile devices has been around for a while now but it has been slow to catch on. The proper tools for creating mobile Web content have been quite sparse. The .NET Framework, along with the Microsoft Mobile Internet Toolkit, enables you to create exciting Web applications for use on many different types of mobile devices.

These mobile devices can include Windows CE devices, Pocket PC–powered devices, and many mobile phones. Clearly, most mobile devices are extremely limited in comparison to the Web browsers we are accustomed to using. Not only do mobile devices provide less actual screen space for content, many of these devices are devoid of color, or otherwise lack the capability to display graphics.

This chapter begins by looking at the software you need, along with suitable emulators that you can use for testing purposes, in the event that you don't have access to an Internet-capable mobile device.

Introducing the Mobile Internet Toolkit

The Microsoft Mobile Internet Toolkit enables Visual Studio to create mobile Web applications by selecting it as a project from the New Project menu. This toolkit isn't currently packaged with Visual Studio .NET and thus must be downloaded separately from Microsoft's Web site.

The Mobile Internet Toolkit is currently in version 1.0 and can be download from `http://msdn.microsoft.com/download`. When you arrive on this page, you must select Software Development Kits in the left frame of your Web browser, and then select Microsoft Mobile Internet Toolkit.

The current Software Development Kit (SDK) is just over 4MB and contains many ASP.NET controls for generating Wireless Markup Language (WML) and several flavors of HTML, as well as the actual Visual Studio .NET add-in, documentation, and sample applications. Ensure that when you install the SDK, any instances of Visual Studio are shut down.

Understanding emulators

Emulators enable you to write applications for devices and test the application without actually having to purchase one of the devices. There are emulators for cellular phones, PDAs, desktops sets, and everything in between. The following sections talk about some of the more popular emulators you can download and begin writing applications for.

Nokia

At the Nokia Web site (`http://www.nokia.com`), you can download a Nokia phone emulator for testing out your mobile Web applications. This download is around 22MB and requires the Java runtime environment, which adds another 5MB to your download time. The current Nokia emulator currently lets you select from one of three different Nokia models for testing purposes. This application proves to be a valuable asset when testing your applications.

Pocket PC

The Pocket PC emulator is included with the Microsoft Embedded Devices Toolkit. This is an excellent emulator to have if you don't actually own a Pocket PC because the Pocket Internet Explorer supports a far larger array of functionality than many other mobile devices on the market today. Be aware that the current size of this toolkit is upwards of 300MB. If you don't have a high-speed Internet connection, you should stick with the Microsoft Mobile Explorer, discussed in the following section.

Microsoft Mobile Explorer

The Microsoft Mobile Explorer is only a 3MB download and is primarily used for integration into Visual Studio. You set the MME as your default browser when testing your applications.

Building an Age Calculator

After you install the Microsoft Mobile Internet Toolkit, create a new C# project. You see a new option titled Mobile Web Application, as shown in Figure 30-1.

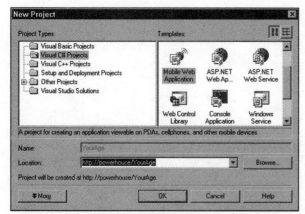

Figure 30-1: The new Mobile Web Application option was added when the Mobile Internet Toolkit was installed.

This example application accepts the year in which you were born and then calculates what your current age is (or will be).

1. Name the project YourAge, and when Visual Studio creates your skeleton application, you see a blank Mobile Web form titled Form1.

2. Right-click this form and select Copy. Now right-click below the form and select Paste. This application requires two forms: one for acquiring the information from the user and one for displaying the results.

3. Now that you have both forms, place a `Button`, a `Label`, and a `TextBox` control on Form1. Place a `Label` and a `Link Label` control on Form2. Arrange these controls as shown in Figure 30-2.

Now that the controls have been arranged, you need to assign all their appropriate properties. Table 30-1 contains the properties for each control. Set them accordingly before moving on.

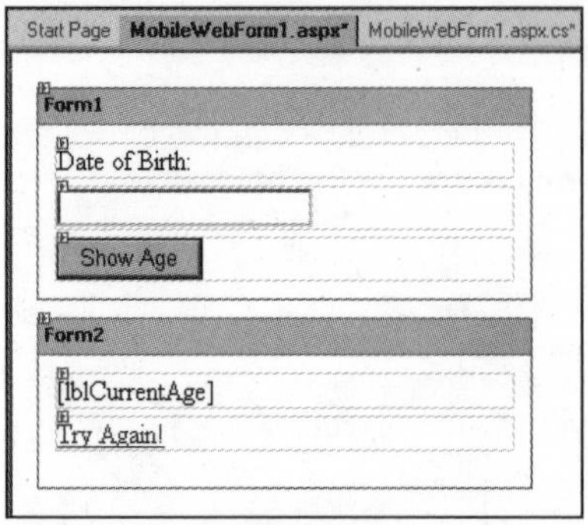

Figure 30-2: These forms are needed for your YourAge application.

Table 30-1
YourAge Control Properties

Form	Control	Name Property	Text Property
Form1	Label	Label1	Year of Birth
Form1	Text Box	txtDOB	<Empty>
Form1	Button	Command1	Show Age
Form2	Label	lblCurrentAge	<Empty>
Form2	Link Label	Link1	Try Again

You need to set one other property before you can begin coding. Select the Link Label control and set the NavigateUrl property to Form1. This ensures that when the link is clicked, the user is returned to Form1 of the project.

Before you begin with the code necessary to power your program, examine the code behind these Mobile Web Forms. At the bottom of the Form Designer are two buttons labeled Design and HTML. Click the HTML button to display the HTML code behind these forms, which should be similar to the code in Listing 30-1.

Listing 30-1: **HTML Code Behind the YourAge Web Forms**

```
<%@ Register TagPrefix="mobile" Namespace="System.Web.UI.MobileControls"
Assembly="System.Web.Mobile, Version=1.0.3300.0, Culture=neutral,
PublicKeyToken=b03f5f7f11d50a3a" %>
<%@ Page language="c#" Codebehind="MobileWebForm1.aspx.cs"
Inherits="YourAge.MobileWebForm1" AutoEventWireup="false" %>
<meta name="GENERATOR" content="Microsoft Visual Studio 7.0">
```

```
<meta name="CODE_LANGUAGE" content="C#">
<meta name="vs_targetSchema" content="http://schemas.microsoft.com/Mobile/Page">
<body Xmlns:mobile="http://schemas.microsoft.com/Mobile/WebForm">
    <mobile:Form id="Form1" runat="server">
        <mobile:Label id="Label1" runat="server">Year of Birth:</mobile:Label>
         <mobile:TextBox id="txtDOB" runat="server"></mobile:TextBox>
        <mobile:Command id="Command1" runat="server">Show Age</mobile:Command>
    </mobile:Form>
    <mobile:Form id="Form2" runat="server">
        <mobile:Label id="lblCurrentAge" runat="server"></mobile:Label>
        <mobile:Link id="Link1" runat="server" NavigateUrl="#Form1">Try
Again!</mobile:Link>
    </mobile:Form>
</body>
```

This code is standard HTML combined with some elements that are defined by
the `MobileControls` namespace. This linking of the HTML page and the .NET
`MobileControls` class can be seen in the line following `Namespace`. When you
begin coding, note that several namespaces will have already been added to the
project for just this reason.

You are now ready to begin coding your mobile Web application. This project
requires code in one place. Double-click the button you previously placed on
Form1. Listing 30-2 contains the code you should place behind the `click` event
of this button.

Listing 30-2: **Calculating the Age in the Click Event**

```
private void Command1_Click(object sender, System.EventArgs e)
{
  int iDOB = System.Convert.ToInt16(txtDOB.Text);
  int YearsOld;

  if (iDOB > 1000)
    YearsOld = 2002 - iDOB;
  else
    YearsOld = 100 - iDOB + 2;

  lblCurrentAge.Text = YearsOld.ToString() + " years old.";

  ActiveForm = Form2;
}
```

In this section of code, you need to accomplish only a few tasks. First, you convert
the year that is entered into an Integer value using the `Convert` class. Then,

depending on the size of that year (either two-digit or four-digit), you calculate the age accordingly, using a current year of 2002.

After the age has been calculated you assign the age and a string to your current age label. Your application is now functional, but although you have assigned your output to the appropriate label, you still haven't shown the page that contains the information. In the last line of Listing 30-2, you set the `ActiveForm` to Form2. This loads Form2 into the user's browser to display the results.

You can run this application by pressing F5; and if all the coding was done correctly, your default Web browser opens. To view this application on a mobile device, run your favorite emulator and enter the URL accordingly. Figure 30-3 shows the application running in a Pocket PC emulator.

Figure 30-3: Running YourAge on a Pocket PC emulator

After you enter your birth year, click the Show Age button and you are presented with Form2, as shown in Figure 30-4.

Congratulations on your first mobile Web application. For those of you who used either Internet Explorer or the Pocket PC emulator for testing purposes, you may be wondering just how the Web application presents itself on a mobile phone. Figure 30-5 shows the same application running in the Nokia cellular phone emulator.

Figure 30-4: YourAge
results on the Pocket PC

Figure 30-5: The Nokia 7110
with the YourAge application
running

As you can see, the page looks much the same as with the previous emulator with
the exception of some navigation details. Because Pocket PCs are point-and-click

devices, the navigation is handled much more smoothly. The cellular phone, on the other hand, handles all navigation using the 20 or so buttons it contains. Therefore, you can't simply click a button or link to proceed—you must use the buttons provided to scroll up and down and select links before you can follow them.

Understanding Mobile Device Capabilities

The `System.Web.Mobile.MobileCapabilities` class contains several dozen properties that are used to detect the capabilities of a mobile device. For example, you can check the screen resolution of a device, see whether it displays in color or black and white, and check whether the device is capable of sending mail, just to name a few.

When building mobile Web applications, it is important to take into account the various types of devices that might be accessing your application. Unlike conventional browsers, which vary only slightly in functionality, you can see dramatic differences when viewing a page from a cellular phone as compared to a Windows CE–powered PDA, for example. You need to ensure that your pages are rendered appropriately for each device.

Begin by using the `Device` class to check your mobile devices for the maximum characters allowed horizontally and vertically across the screen. Open the YourAge application you developed in Listing 30-2 and add two `Label` controls to Form2. Change the `Name` properties for these labels to `lblHeight` and `lblWidth`.

Now you must modify your original source code to populate these labels after Form2 is displayed. Listing 30-3 contains the code you must add (in bold) in order for this new functionality to take effect.

Listing 30-3: Displaying Device Capabilities

```
private void Command1_Click(object sender, System.EventArgs e)
{
  int iDOB = System.Convert.ToInt16(txtDOB.Text);
  int YearsOld;

  if (iDOB > 1000)
    YearsOld = 2002 - iDOB;
      else
    YearsOld = 100 - iDOB + 2;

  lblCurrentAge.Text = YearsOld.ToString() + " years old." ;
    lblHeight.Text = "Height: " + Device.ScreenCharactersHeight;
  lblWidth.Text = "Width: " + Device.ScreenCharactersWidth;
  ActiveForm = Form2;
}
```

On a Pocket PC, you can achieve 17×34 characters, whereas you can achieve only 4×22 on a Nokia 7110 cellular phone, as shown in Figure 30-6.

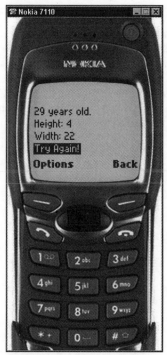

Figure 30-6: Screen height and width on the Nokia emulator

Not all the properties contained within this class work across all devices. The help file for the Microsoft Mobile Internet Toolkit contains a Device Capabilities Table that defines what properties will generally work with HTML, cHTML, and with WML.

The Visual Studio .NET toolbox also contains a control called `DeviceSpecific` that you can place upon your form to perform certain tasks (depending on what device it is communicating with). This is done with filters and greatly reduces the amount of effort it would take to code all the possible scenarios.

Understanding How Mobile Controls Work

The mobile Web controls must be very adaptable when it comes to displaying visual interfaces. Some of the controls require more space than is available on most mobile devices. When this happens, it is up to the control to determine how to handle the situation. The following sections cover two of these controls — `Calendar` and `Image` — and how they change their visual interfaces when the need arises.

Using the Calendar control

The `Calendar` control enables you to display a full-fledged calendar within a mobile Web page. To examine just how versatile this control is, create a new Mobile Web Application and place a `Calendar` control on Form1 of the project.

When you run this new application using your default browser or the Pocket PC emulator, you see a full monthly calendar that enables you to click any day of the week. Shown in Figure 30-7 is this application running on a Pocket PC.

Figure 30-7: Calendar test application running on the Pocket PC emulator

How could this calendar possibly be displayed on a much smaller device, such as a cellular phone? The `Calendar` control knows what type of device it is to be displayed on and changes its user interface accordingly. Figure 30-8 shows this same Web application running in the cellular phone emulator.

You no longer see the calendar, but instead see the current date followed by two options. These options enable you to type in a date directly or browse by one week at a time and then by each day of the week.

This type of behavior is accomplished with no programming required, which takes a great deal of burden off of the programmer.

Figure 30-8: Calendar test application running on the Nokia emulator

Using the Image control

The Image control is another unique control much like the Calendar control. It enables you to display an image on many types of mobile devices with little or no programming. Create a new C# mobile Web application and place an Image control on Form1. Set the ImageUrl of this Image control to the path of the image you wish to display. This image can bit a bitmap (bmp), JPEG image (jpg), or one of several others. For demonstration purposes, select a color jpg image.

Running this application on a Pocket PC results in the picture being displayed correctly, as shown in Figure 30-9.

Figure 30-9: The Pocket PC displays your image with no apparent problems

If you attempt to view this same page with the Nokia cellular phone emulator, you receive an error message saying that the page cannot be loaded. This is obviously because the image isn't of a type that can be viewed on a black-and-white screen of such small size.

You can overcome this problem, however. You can convert your JPG image to a two-color (black and white) bitmap — otherwise known as a *wireless bitmap* (WBMP), which the mobile device can then handle. On the Page Load event of Form1, you can then check the Device.PreferredRenderingType property to see what image should be loaded. If this property returns wm111, you should set the Image control's ImageUrl property to WBMP picture; otherwise, you can show the original.

Paging on Mobile Devices

Also referred to as *pagination,* paging is the mobile device's capability to break large amounts of content into several pages of information. This occurs, for example, when you display a long list of contacts on the mobile Web form and the particular device cannot display that much on its small screen.

You'll be happy to know that you can program this type of behavior to be handled automatically by the mobile Web form by changing just two properties. The Paginate property, when set to True, automatically breaks up all content into several pages of information, depending on the capabilities of the remote device. You must also set the ItemsPerPage property for a particular control — the List control, for example — to force pagination to a certain number of items. Generally, this is not needed, however, as the default of seven typically works well.

You can test this out by creating a new mobile Web application called Contacts. Set the Paginate property of Form1 to True, and then add a List control to the page. Set the ItemsPerPage property of the List control to 7.

Now you need to add several items to this List control, as shown in the following code:

```
List1.Items.Add("Kim Pack");
List1.Items.Add("Timothy Hyde");
List1.Items.Add("Donna Malone");
List1.Items.Add("Joshua Trueblood");
List1.Items.Add("Staci Springer");
List1.Items.Add("Chris Stephens");
List1.Items.Add("Amy Sherman");
List1.Items.Add("Steve Million");
List1.Items.Add("Jim Mattingly");
List1.Items.Add("Ryan Boyles");
List1.Items.Add("Scott Leathers");
```

These 11 items are added to your list. Therefore, you should see seven items on the first page, along with a Next link to a second page containing four items.

Run the application in the mobile device of your choice. As expected, your first seven items show up on the first page, along with a link to the next page, as shown in Figure 30-10.

Figure 30-10: First seven items of the list

The user can click the Next button to view the second page. On the second page, you don't have four items as expected but a full seven items, because your List control wrapped the contents from the first page onto the second page, as shown in Figure 30-11.

Figure 30-11: The remaining list items are shown on the second page.

When pagination is enabled as demonstrated here, several properties can now be taken advantage of, such as `Page`, which enables you to specify an index number of the page to view.

Summary

In this chapter, you looked at the different features of the Mobile Internet Toolkit, which enables you to deploy Web content to mobile devices. You built several applications that demonstrate how mobile Web controls dynamically change their presentation at runtime depending on the mobile device on which they are used. You also explored ways to detect device capabilities to exploit the features of various mobile devices.

Though the chapter only touched on some of these features, you now have an excellent starting point for building very dynamic Web content for mobile deployment.

✦   ✦   ✦

C# and the .NET Framework

Working with Assemblies

Code that is designed to take advantage of the .NET
Framework is built into a packaging unit called an
assembly. Assemblies are at the heart of the code deployment
and security strategy for the .NET Framework, so it is important to understand them and how they work.

In this chapter, you take a look at assemblies and how you can
write C# code to work with the information in assemblies. The
.NET Framework contains a class called Assembly that makes
working with assemblies simple, and this chapter will introduce
you to the inner workings of the Assembly class.

Understanding Assemblies

Assemblies can contain code, resources, or a combination of
both. Code contained in an assembly must contain the actual
Microsoft Intermediate Language (MSIL) instructions that can
be executed by the Common Language Runtime (CLR), as well
as a *manifest* that describes the contents of the code. *Manifests*
contain type and other descriptive information that describes
the code to the CLR. Assemblies also form boundaries around
the code that they enclose. Assemblies form type boundaries,
in that any type that can be used in any .NET code comes
from a single assembly, and similarly named types from
different assemblies are, in fact, different types. Assemblies
also form a security boundary, whereby all of the code in the
assembly holds the same set of security information, restric-
tions, and allowances.

Assemblies are packaged using the Win32 Portable Execution
file format, and can be packaged as DLLs or EXEs. Any code
produced by a CLR-aware compiler and build into a console
executable, a Windows executable, or a library is packaged
into an assembly. This packaging forms a unit of deployment
for a set of types in an assembly. Do not assume that only
DLL-based .NET code can be considered an assembly. Any

packaging of .NET code, resources, and metadata that targets an executable or a library is an assembly, even if the packaging takes the form of an executable. WinForms applications, for example, are valid .NET assemblies, just as DLL-based class libraries are valid assemblies.

Keep in mind that the C# compiler can also produce modules, but that modules are not assemblies. Modules are compiled pieces of code (and possibly resources) that are merged into an assembly at a later date. Modules contain MSIL, and they contain metadata describing the types found in the module, but do not contain a manifest. Modules cannot be loaded and executed by the CLR, and thus cannot be considered to be assemblies.

Finding loaded assemblies

You begin exploring the assembly concept by writing a small console application that lists a bit of information about assemblies loaded into a process. If type information comes from assemblies, the CLR must load assembly information into the process space of an executing piece of .NET code. For every type referenced in an application, the CLR must retrieve information from the assembly that contains the type, so that the CLR can use the type properly. These assemblies are called *referenced assemblies*, because they are referenced by another .NET assembly.

Discovering the list of referenced assemblies is a simple process. Consider the simple console application in Listing 31-1.

Listing 31-1: Retrieving a List of Referenced Assemblies

```
using System;
using System.Reflection;

public class MainClass
{
    static void Main()
    {
        Assembly EntryAssembly;

        EntryAssembly = Assembly.GetEntryAssembly();
        foreach(AssemblyName Name in
EntryAssembly.GetReferencedAssemblies())
            Console.WriteLine("Name: {0}", Name.ToString());
    }
}
```

Listing 31-1 introduces many important concepts. First, it introduces a .NET class called Assembly, which is found in the .NET System.Reflection namespace. The Assembly class is the class through which any .NET code can examine and work with the contents of a .NET assembly. If you need to do any work with a .NET assembly, you need to use the `Assembly` class to examine the assembly's contents.

The second important concept reflected by Listing 31-1 is that of an *entry assembly*. The entry assembly is the first assembly to begin executing in the current process. For executables, such as the console executable produced by Listing 31-1, the entry assembly is the assembly containing the entry point function. Normally, the entry point function is named `Main()` for executable-based assemblies, although that can be changed through C# by using the `/main` argument and specifying another entry point for the assembly. Accessing the entry assembly is performed through a static method on the `Assembly` class called `GetEntryAssembly()`. This method returns an instance of an `Assembly` object that references the entry assembly.

The third important concept reflected by Listing 31-1 is that an assembly may contain referenced assemblies. Information on referenced assemblies is obtained through a call to an assembly method called `GetReferencedAssemblies()`. This method returns an array of objects of a class called `AssemblyName`. `AssemblyName` objects fully describe the name of an assembly and can be easily turned into a simple string using the familiar `ToString()` method. Obtaining a string-based representation of an assembly name makes it easy for applications to display assembly name information in user interfaces.

Given this information, digesting the operation of Listing 31-1 is simple. The code obtains a reference to the entry assembly and sends the names of referenced assemblies to the console. Compiling and executing the code in Listing 31-1 results in the following information being sent to the console:

```
Name: mscorlib, Version=1.0.3300.0, Culture=neutral,
PublicKeyToken=b77a5c561934e089
```

How does the .NET Framework know that Listing 31-1 references the `mscorlib` assembly? That information is stored in the manifest for the Listing 31-1 assembly. To see this information, launch the ILDASM tool that ships with the .NET Framework and load the Listing 31-1 assembly into it. Double-click the manifest entry in the tree that appears, and the manifest for the assembly is shown in a separate window, as shown in Figure 31-1.

```
MANIFEST
.assembly extern mscorlib
{
  .publickeytoken = (B7 7A 5C 56 19 34 E0 89 )              // .z\U.4..
  .ver 1:0:3300:0
}
.assembly 'Listing31-1'
{
  .custom instance void [mscorlib]System.Reflection.AssemblyKeyNameAttribute::.ctor(st
  .custom instance void [mscorlib]System.Reflection.AssemblyKeyFileAttribute::.ctor(st
  .custom instance void [mscorlib]System.Reflection.AssemblyDelaySignAttribute::.ctor(
  .custom instance void [mscorlib]System.Reflection.AssemblyTrademarkAttribute::.ctor(
  .custom instance void [mscorlib]System.Reflection.AssemblyCopyrightAttribute::.ctor(
  .custom instance void [mscorlib]System.Reflection.AssemblyProductAttribute::.ctor(st
  .custom instance void [mscorlib]System.Reflection.AssemblyCompanyAttribute::.ctor(st
```

Figure 31-1: External assembly references in a manifest

The manifest contains an entry labeled `.assembly extern`. This manifest entry describes an external assembly on which the assembly containing the manifest depends. This entry notes that the assembly containing this manifest depends on version 1.0.3300.0 of an external assembly called `mscorlib`. It is the task of the .NET Framework to read this manifest and load dependent assemblies into the currently executing process space.

> **Note** The `mscorlib` assembly contains core type information for classes such as `System.Object`, and is always referenced without any special compiler arguments. Other assemblies can be referenced using the `/r` option to the C# command-line compiler, or with the Add References menu item in Visual Studio .NET.

Understanding strong assembly names

The output of Listing 31-1 may seem a bit confusing at first, as it lists more than just the assembly name, which in this case is named `mscorlib`. This output actually defines four pieces of information for the assembly name:

- ✦ The name itself (`mscorlib`)
- ✦ A version number (`1.0.3300.0`)
- ✦ Culture information (`neutral`)
- ✦ A public key token (`b77a5c561934e089`)

At a minimum, all assemblies contain a name, a version, and a culture. However, assemblies can contain a public key. An assembly containing all four pieces of information is said to be *strongly named*.

Only assemblies that contain strong names can be stored in the global assembly cache. The global assembly cache (GAC) is a disk-based collection of .NET assemblies that can be accessed by any piece of .NET code on the machine containing the GAC. The .NET Framework looks for an assembly in the entry assembly directory when an assembly needs to be loaded. This deployment scheme is simple; however, it can create several copies of an assembly on a disk volume for heavily used assemblies, as each assembly needs to be copied to each entry assembly that needs the referenced assembly. The .NET Framework includes the GAC to simplify things, so that heavily used assemblies, such as the assemblies that ship with the .NET Framework, can be placed on a machine once and referenced many times. The .NET Framework checks the GAC when searching for an assembly.

When the .NET Framework is installed on a machine, the setup process installs a Windows Explorer shell extension that makes the GAC appear as a standard Windows folder. The base Windows directory, which is `C:\WINDOWS` on most machines, contains a folder called assembly on machines with the .NET Framework installed. This folder shows the contents of the GAC, with strong name information in columns, as shown in Figure 31-2.

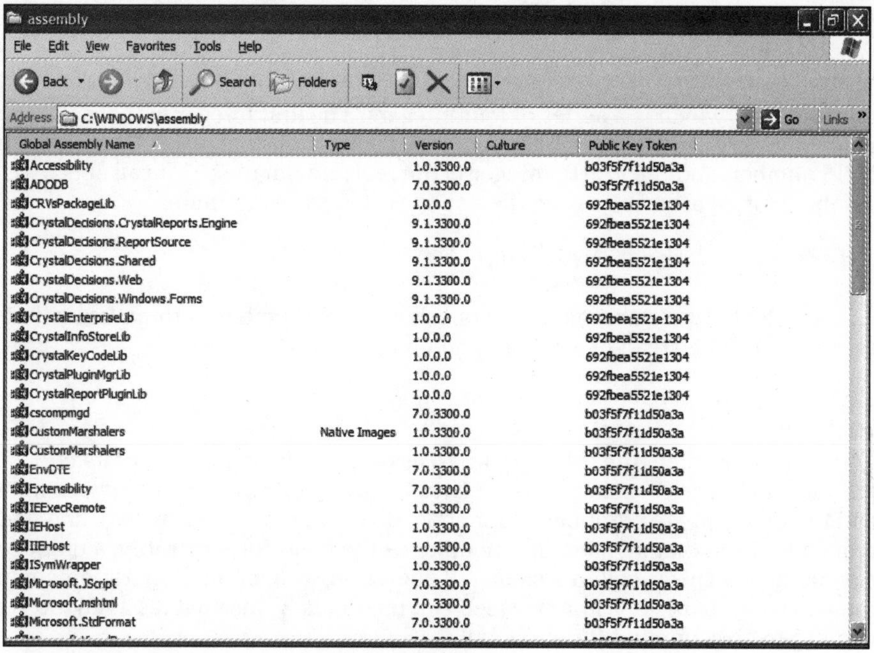

Figure 31-2: Viewing the GAC as a Windows folder

You can place assemblies with different strong names side by side in the global assembly cache, even if the segment names match. For example, version 1.0.0.0 of an assembly named `assembly.dll` can be installed in the global assembly cache along with version 2.0.0.0 of an assembly also named `assembly.dll`. Code that references a strongly named assembly has the assembly's strong name listed in the manifest and always binds to the assembly with that strong name, even if other assemblies with some components of the strong name are the same. If an entry assembly references version 1.0.0.0 of `assembly.dll`, for example, the .NET Framework always loads version 1.0.0.0 of `assembly.dll` into the process space of the entry assembly, even if other versions of `assembly.dll` exist in the GAC.

Setting the information that comprises a strong name for an assembly is as easy as adding some attributes to one of the source code files for a project. These attributes can be added to a source file containing C# code or can be added to a separate file containing only the attributes themselves.

Note Visual Studio .NET adds a source file called `AssemblyInfo.cs` to new C# projects and places attributes needed for strongly named assemblies into that source file. The filename can be changed once it is created and will still work, as long as the renamed file remains a part of the project build.

Setting version information

You can set assembly version information using an attribute called `AssemblyVersion`. The `AssemblyVersion` attribute takes a string describing the version number for the assembly, which is a series of four integers. The first integer is the major version number; the second integer is the minor version number; the third integer is the build number; and the fourth integer is the revision number. You can specify all four numbers for an assembly using the `AssemblyVersion` attribute:

```
[assembly: AssemblyVersion("1.0.0.0")]
```

As a shortcut, the C# compiler generates a revision number automatically if an asterisk is used instead of a revision number:

```
[assembly: AssemblyVersion("1.0.0.*")]
```

This syntax instructs the C# compiler to assign a revision number of its choosing to the assembly. The C# compiler calculates the number of seconds between midnight and the time you are compiling your code, divides the number by two, and uses the remainder from that division that number as the basis for generating a unique revision number. (This is called a *modulo 2* operation, as a modulo operation computes the remainder of the division between two operands.) This enables a unique version number to be generated for every build.

As a further shortcut, the C# compiler generates a build number and a revision number automatically if an asterisk is used as the build number:

```
[assembly: AssemblyVersion("1.0.*")]
```

This syntax instructs the C# compiler to assign a build number and a revision number of its choosing to the assembly. In addition to the automatic revision number calculation already described, the C# compiler also calculates a build number using the number of days between January 1, 2000 and the day the code is compiled.

Setting culture information

Culture information specifies the culture for which the assembly is designed. Culture information is specified using an attribute called `AssemblyCulture`. The culture attribute accepts a string describing the culture for which the assembly is designed. The string can be specified with an empty string, which informs the .NET Framework that the assembly is culture-neutral and does not contain any culture-specific code or resources:

```
[assembly: AssemblyCulture("")]
```

The string can also specify a language and country for which the assembly was designed. The string that specifies the language and country information must be in a format documented in Internet RFC 1766, which takes the form of language–country:

```
[assembly: AssemblyCulture("en-US")]
```

Tip The RFC 1766 standard is titled "Tags for the Identification of Languages," and is available on the Internet at `http://www.ietf.org/rfc/rfc1766.txt`.

Only DLL-based assemblies should specify culture information. EXE-based assemblies should use an empty string for culture information. Specifying culture information for an EXE-based assembly results in an error from the C# compiler.

Setting key information

The .NET Framework ships with a command-line utility called the strong name utility, or `sn` for short, which helps build strong names for .NET assemblies. One of its most frequently used features enables the generation of a new set of digital signature keys that can be installed into an assembly and used as a part of the strong name for an assembly. The keys are written into a binary file, whose name is specified with the `-k` argument to the `sn` utility, as shown in the following command line:

```
sn -k KeyPair.snk
```

This command line instructs the `sn` utility to generate a new pair of digital signature keys and output the keys to a binary file named `KeyPair.snk`. This file is named as an argument to an attribute called `AssemblyKeyFile`:

```
[assembly: AssemblyKeyFile("KeyPair.snk")]
```

The `.snk` extension is not required. Any extension can be used for the key file generated by the strong name utility.

Working with the Assembly class

Now that you have been introduced to the `Assembly` class, you can take a closer look at it. The following sections describe how you can use its properties and methods.

Finding assembly location information

The `Assembly` class contains properties that describe the location of an assembly. A `Location` property specifies the location of the file that contains the manifest for the assembly. A `CodeBase` property specifies the location of the assembly as a Uniform Resource Identifier (URI). The related `EscapedCodeBase` property specifies the URI for the assembly, with special characters replaced with the equivalent escape codes (spaces in `CodeBase` values, for instance, are replaced with the escape sequence %20 in the `EscapedCodeBase` property). The `GlobalAssemblyCache` property is a Boolean that evaluates to `True` if the assembly is loaded from the GAC, and `False` otherwise.

Listing 31-2 shows a simple console application that gets a reference to the application's entry assembly and sends its location information to the console.

Listing 31-2: **Examining Location Information**

```
using System;
using System.Reflection;

public class MainClass
{
    static void Main()
    {
        Assembly EntryAssembly;

        EntryAssembly = Assembly.GetEntryAssembly();
        Console.WriteLine("Location: {0}", EntryAssembly.Location);
        Console.WriteLine("Code Base: {0}", EntryAssembly.CodeBase);
        Console.WriteLine("Escaped Code Base: {0}",
EntryAssembly.EscapedCodeBase);
        Console.WriteLine("Loaded from GAC: {0}",
EntryAssembly.GlobalAssemblyCache);
    }
}
```

Compiling and executing the code in Listing 31-2 sends the following information to the console:

✦ **Location:** `C:\Documents and Settings\User\My Documents\ Listing31-2\bin\Debug\Listing31-2.exe`

✦ **Code Base:** `file:///C:/Documents and Settings/User/My Documents/ Listing31-2/bin/Debug/Listing31-2.exe`

✦ **Escaped Code Base:** `file:///C:/Documents%20and%20Settings/User /My%20Documents/Listing31-2/bin/Debug/Listing31-2.exe`

✦ **Loaded from GAC:** `False`

The path information varies depending on the actual location of the code when it is executed, but the results are basically the same: The `Location` property references a location on disk, and the `CodeBase` and `EscapedCodeBase` properties reference the assembly location as URIs.

Finding assembly entry points

Some assemblies contain *entry points*. Think of entry points as the "starting method" for an assembly. The most obvious example of an entry point for an assembly is the `Main()` method found in C#-based executables. The CLR loads an executable, searches for the entry point for the assembly, and begins executing with that entry point method.

DLL-based assemblies, by contrast, do not typically have entry points. These assemblies generally hold resources or types that are used by other pieces of code, and they are passive in that they wait to be called before any of the code in the assembly is executed.

The `Assembly` class contains a property called `EntryPoint`. The `EntryPoint` property is a value of a type called `MethodInfo`, which is found in the .NET `System.Reflection` namespace. The `MethodInfo` class describes the specifics of a method, and calling `ToString()` on an object of type `MethodInfo` returns a string that describes the method's return type, name, and parameters. The `EntryPoint` property is null if the assembly reference does not have an entry point, or a valid `MethodInfo` object if the assembly reference does have an entry point, as shown in Listing 31-3.

Listing 31-3: **Working with an Assembly Entry Point**

```
using System;
using System.Reflection;

public class MainClass
{
    static void Main(string[] args)
    {
        Assembly EntryAssembly;

        EntryAssembly = Assembly.GetEntryAssembly();
        if(EntryAssembly.EntryPoint == null)
            Console.WriteLine("The assembly has no entry point.");
        else
            Console.WriteLine(EntryAssembly.EntryPoint.ToString());
    }
}
```

Compiling and executing Listing 31-3 sends the following information to the console:

```
Void Main(System.String[])
```

In the simple example of Listing 31-3, the `EntryPoint` property is never null, but it is always good practice to check for the possibility of a null value, especially with more complicated pieces of code.

Loading assemblies

In many applications, assemblies that contain types needed by an application are referenced when the application is built. It is also possible, however, to load assemblies programmatically. There are several ways to load an assembly dynamically, and each of these loading techniques returns an `Assembly` object that references the loaded assembly.

The first assembly loading technique uses a static assembly method called `Load()`. The `Load()` method takes a string naming the assembly to be loaded. If the named assembly cannot be found, the `Load()` method throws an exception. By contrast, the `LoadWithPartialName()` method searches both the application directory and the GAC for the specified assembly, using as much naming information as available from the caller. Listing 31-4 illustrates the difference between these two methods.

Listing 31-4: Loading Assemblies Dynamically with Load() and LoadWithPartialName()

```csharp
using System;
using System.Reflection;
using System.IO;

public class AssemblyLoader
{
    private Assembly LoadedAssembly;

    public AssemblyLoader(string LoadedAssemblyName, bool
PartialName)
    {
        try
        {
            Console.WriteLine("+--------------------");
            Console.WriteLine("| Loading Assembly {0}",
LoadedAssemblyName);
            Console.WriteLine("+--------------------");
            if(PartialName == true)
                LoadedAssembly =
Assembly.LoadWithPartialName(LoadedAssemblyName);
            else
                LoadedAssembly =
Assembly.Load(LoadedAssemblyName);
            WritePropertiesToConsole();
        }
        catch(FileNotFoundException)
        {
            Console.WriteLine("EXCEPTION: Cannot load
assembly.");
        }
    }

    private void WritePropertiesToConsole()
    {
        Console.WriteLine("Full Name: {0}",
LoadedAssembly.FullName);
        Console.WriteLine("Location: {0}",
LoadedAssembly.Location);
        Console.WriteLine("Code Base: {0}",
LoadedAssembly.CodeBase);
```

```
        Console.WriteLine("Escaped Code Base: {0}",
LoadedAssembly.EscapedCodeBase);
        Console.WriteLine("Loaded from GAC: {0}",
LoadedAssembly.GlobalAssemblyCache);
    }
}

public class MainClass
{
    static void Main(string[] args)
    {
        AssemblyLoader Loader;

        Loader = new AssemblyLoader("System.Xml,
Version=1.0.3300.0, Culture=neutral,
PublicKeyToken=b77a5c561934e089", false);
        Loader = new AssemblyLoader("System.Xml", false);
        Loader = new AssemblyLoader("System.Xml", true);
    }
}
```

Listing 31-4 illustrates a class called AssemblyLoader, whose constructor accepts an assembly name and a Boolean flag specifying whether the named assembly should be loaded using a partial name. The constructor loads the assembly and then calls a private method to print some of the base-naming and location properties of the loaded assembly to the console.

The Main() method in Listing 31-4 creates new objects of the AssemblyLoader class and attempts to load the .NET Framework System.XML assembly, found in the GAC, in various ways.

Executing Listing 31-4 results in the following information being written out to the console:

```
+---------------------

| Loading Assembly System.Xml, Version=1.0.3300.0,
Culture=neutral, PublicKeyTok
en=b77a5c561934e089
+----------------------
Full Name: System.Xml, Version=1.0.3300.0, Culture=neutral,
PublicKeyToken=b77a5
c561934e089
Location:
c:\windows\assembly\gac\system.xml\1.0.3300.0__b77a5c561934e089
\system
.xml.dll
Code Base:
file:///c:/windows/assembly/gac/system.xml/1.0.3300.0__b77a5c56
1934e0
```

```
89/system.xml.dll
Escaped Code Base:
file:///c:/windows/assembly/gac/system.xml/1.0.3300.0__b77a5c
561934e089/system.xml.dll
Loaded from GAC: True
+--------------------
| Loading Assembly System.Xml
+--------------------
EXCEPTION: Cannot load assembly.
+--------------------
| Loading Assembly System.Xml
+--------------------
Full Name: System.Xml, Version=1.0.3300.0, Culture=neutral,
PublicKeyToken=b77a5
c561934e089
Location:
c:\windows\assembly\gac\system.xml\1.0.3300.0__b77a5c561934e089
\system
.xml.dll
Code Base:
file:///c:/windows/assembly/gac/system.xml/1.0.3300.0__b77a5c56
1934e0
89/system.xml.dll
Escaped Code Base:
file:///c:/windows/assembly/gac/system.xml/1.0.3300.0__b77a5c
561934e089/system.xml.dll
Loaded from GAC: True
```

Look closely at what is happening here. In the first case, the `Main()` method specifies the strong name for the `System.Xml` assembly, including its name, public key, version information and culture specifics. Because the `System.Xml` assembly is in the GAC, it is not stored in the application's directory, and the `Load()` method is unable to find the assembly in the directory containing the executable for Listing 31-4. However, because the strong name for the assembly was specified, the `Load()` method has enough information to search for the assembly in the GAC. The `Load()` method can find the assembly in the GAC and the loading operation succeeds.

In the second case, the `Main()` method specifies only the base name of the `System.Xml` assembly. Because the `System.Xml` assembly is in the GAC, it is not stored in the application's directory, and the `Load()` method is unable to find the assembly in the directory containing the executable for Listing 31-4. In addition, the `Load()` method does not have enough information to locate the assembly in the GAC, as multiple instances of `System.Xml` might exist in the GAC with different version numbers or public keys, and the load fails.

In the third and final case, the `Main()` method specifies only the base name of the `System.Xml` assembly and instructs the loader to find an assembly using only a partial name. Again, because the `System.Xml` assembly is in the GAC, it is not stored in the application's directory and the `LoadWithPartialName()` method is unable to find the assembly in the directory containing the executable for Listing 31-4. However, the `LoadWithPartialName()` method takes the partially supplied name and attempts to match the name to an assembly in the GAC. Because a partial name of System.Xml is supplied, and because there is an assembly with the name System.Xml in the GAC, the load operation succeeds.

Caution Using the LoadWithPartialName() method is not recommended. If the partially named assembly has multiple copies in the GAC — perhaps with different version numbers, cultures, or public keys — the actual instance loaded may not be the expected version. In addition, the loaded instance may be a different version than the one you were expecting to load once newer versions of the assembly are loaded into the GAC. Use Load() instead of LoadWithPartialName() wherever possible.

Working with assembly type information

Assemblies can contain types, resources, or a combination of both. After an assembly is loaded, information about the types found in the assembly can be obtained. In addition, instances of the types can be created programmatically. Listing 31-5 illustrates these concepts.

Listing 31-5: **Finding and Creating Assembly Types**

```
using System;
using System.Reflection;

public class MainClass
{
    static void Main(string[] args)
    {
        Assembly XMLAssembly;
        Type[] XMLTypes;

        XMLAssembly = Assembly.Load("System.Xml, Version=1.0.3300.0,
Culture=neutral, PublicKeyToken=b77a5c561934e089");
        XMLTypes = XMLAssembly.GetExportedTypes();
        foreach(Type XMLType in XMLTypes)
        {
            object NewObject;

            try
            {
                Console.Write(XMLType.ToString());
                NewObject = XMLAssembly.CreateInstance(XMLType.ToString());
                if(NewObject != null)
                    Console.WriteLine(" - Creation successful");
                else
                    Console.WriteLine(" - CREATION ERROR");
            }
            catch(Exception e)
            {
                Console.WriteLine(" - EXCEPTION: {0}", e.Message);
```

Continued

Listing 31-5 *(continued)*

```
}
      }
    }
}
```

The code in Listing 31-5 loads the `System.Xml` assembly from the GAC and calls a method on the `Assembly` class called `GetExportedTypes()` to obtain an array of type objects representing types that are found in the assembly and can be used or exported outside of the assembly. The code visits each type in the returned array and calls another assembly method called `CreateInstance()` to create an object instance of the named type. If the creation is successful, the `CreateInstance()` method returns a valid object reference. If the creation is not successful, `CreateInstance()` either returns a null object reference or throws an exception, depending upon the nature of the error.

Following are the first several lines of output from Listing 31-5:

```
System.Xml.XPath.XPathNavigator - EXCEPTION: Constructor on
type System.Xml.XPath.XPathNavigator not found.
System.Xml.IHasXmlNode - EXCEPTION: Constructor on type
System.Xml.IHasXmlNode not found.
System.Xml.XPath.XPathNodeIterator - EXCEPTION: Constructor on
type System.Xml.XPath.XPathNodeIterator not found.
System.Xml.EntityHandling - Creation successful
System.Xml.IXmlLineInfo - EXCEPTION: Constructor on type
System.Xml.IXmlLineInfo not found.
System.Xml.XmlNameTable - EXCEPTION: Constructor on type
System.Xml.XmlNameTable not found.
System.Xml.NameTable - Creation successful
System.Xml.ReadState - Creation successful
System.Xml.ValidationType - Creation successful
System.Xml.WhitespaceHandling - Creation successful
```

The exceptions result because not all of the exported types have constructors, and only reference types with suitable constructors can be created with `CreateInstance()`.

Tip   After a reference to a `Type` object is obtained, a reference to the assembly containing the type can be found in the `Assembly` property of the `Type` object. This lets code discover the assembly that references a type.

Generating Native Code for Assemblies

When the CLR needs to execute code in an assembly, it passes the code through a just-in-time (JIT) compiler and turns the MSIL to native code that can be executed by the machine's CPU. The advantage to this JIT design is that you can ship MSIL code without having to worry about optimizing your code for the target processor. The .NET Framework will most likely be ported to a variety of CPU architectures found in a variety of devices from computers to handheld systems, and attempting to write optimal code for each of those processors would be a daunting task. This work is unnecessary, because each implementation of the .NET Framework ships with a JIT compiler that turns MSIL instructions into instructions optimal for the target CPU.

If performance is of the utmost concern in your application, you can turn your MSIL code into CPU-specific machine code through a process known as *native image generation*. During this process, MSIL instructions found in an assembly are translated into native CPU-specific instructions, which can then be written to disk. After this native image generation has completed, the CLR can make use of that code and can skip the JIT step normally employed for assemblies.

The .NET Framework ships with a tool called the Native Image Generator, which generates a native image for an assembly. This command-line tool is found in an executable called `ngen.exe` and takes an assembly name as input:

```
ngen assembly
```

The native image is placed in a cache of native images for assemblies.

Keep in mind that `ngen` must be run on the device that executes the generated code. You cannot, for example, build assemblies as part of your build process, run `ngen` on the assemblies, and ship the native images to your customers. Your build machine might very well have a different CPU than your customer's machines, and `ngen` generates code for the CPU on which `ngen` is executing. If it is important for your customers to have native images for your assemblies, you must run `ngen` on the customer's machines as a part of the installation process.

It is also important to note that the original .NET assemblies must be available at all times, even if native code is available in the native image cache. The native images are standard Win32 Portable Executable (PE) files and lack all of the metadata available in a .NET assembly. If code loads your native image assembly and executes code that forces the .NET Framework to examine metadata (using Reflection, for example, to obtain type information for the assembly), then the original .NET assembly must be available so that the CLR can query its metadata. The metadata will not be carried with the native image.

Summary

In this chapter, you examined the concept of a .NET assembly from the perspective of C# applications that access assembly information. Access to assembly information is performed through the Assembly class. The Assembly class exposes naming information for the assembly and enables assemblies to be loaded dynamically. Types managed by the assembly can be created on the fly.

You can apply the concepts illustrated in this chapter to build some very powerful .NET applications. Some of the tools that ship with the .NET Framework, such as the ILDASM tool, use a combination of Assembly class methods and other classes in the System.Reflection namespace to provide a fully detailed view of already compiled assemblies. You can obtain a great deal of information from assemblies, even if the source code used to build the assembly is not available, using the methods in the Assembly class and other reflection classes.

✦   ✦   ✦

Reflection

An important characteristic of the .NET Framework is its ability to discover type information at runtime. Specifically, you can use the `reflection` namespace to view type information contained within assemblies which you can later bind to objects and you can even use this namespace to generate code at runtime. This technology extends the COM Automation technology with which many of you may be familiar.

As a programmer, you might often need to use an object without quite understanding what the object does. Using Reflection, you can take an object and examine its properties, methods, events, fields, and constructors. Because Reflection revolves around `System.Type`, you can examine an assembly and use methods, such as `GetMethods()` and `GetProperties()`, to return member information from the assembly. With this information, you can dig in deeper using the `MethodInfo()` method to return parameter lists and even call methods within the assembly with a method called `Invoke`.

In this chapter, you learn to use the `Reflection` namespace for examining objects at runtime. You also learn to late bind to objects and use methods and properties within these late bound objects.

Understanding the Type Class

The `Type` class acts as a window into the Reflection API, enabling access to metadata. The abstract class, `System.Type`, represents a type in the Common Type System (CTS). This Common Type System is what enables you to examine objects across all languages in the .NET family. Because each object uses the same framework, runtime, and type system, object and type information is easily obtainable.

One of the `Type` classes greatest assets is the capability to create objects dynamically and use them at runtime.

Retrieving type Information

Type information can be retrieved from objects using several methods. The following sections describe how to do this in three different ways: by using a type name, by using a process name, or by specifying an assembly name to retrieve the information. Although all of these implementations perform essentially the same task, each is useful in its own right. Depending on the requirements of your application, you might only need to use one form of the type-gathering abilities.

Retrieving types by name

By simply specifying the name of a type, you can query almost all aspects of the object. You can determine whether the object is a class, what its base system type is, and many other properties.

To test this, you can build a simple application to view some properties of the System.String class, as shown in Listing 32-1.

Listing 32-1: Querying Type Information by Name

```
using System;
using System.Reflection;

class NameType
{
   public static void Main()
   {
        Type t = Type.GetType("System.String");
      Console.WriteLine("Name : {0}",t.Name);
      Console.WriteLine("Underlying System Type :
{0}",t.UnderlyingSystemType);
      Console.WriteLine("Is Class : {0}",t.IsClass);
   }
}
```

Figure 32-1 shows that System.String is the base system type, and that the object is indeed a class.

You may be wondering why this information is useful. Suppose you are building an application that needs to generate insert statements to put information into SQL Server. Typing a large amount of information takes an extremely long time. Using Reflection and the Type class, you can examine the underlying type of each piece of information you want to insert into SQL Server and map those types to a valid SQL Server data type. This greatly eases the process of programmatically generating the insert statements that you require.

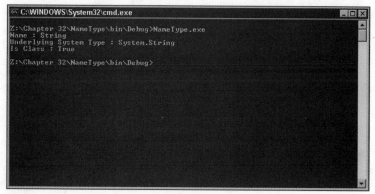

Figure 32-1: Query type information by object name.

Retrieving types by instance

Rather than use the name of a type, you may simply use an instance of an object that you want to examine. Listing 32-2 represents an example similar to the preceding one.

Listing 32-2: Querying Type Information Using the Instance of an Object

```
using System;
using System.Reflection;

class InstanceType
{
  public static void Main()
  {
      String myVar = "Brian Patterson";
      Type t = myVar.GetType();
      Console.WriteLine("Name : {0}",t.Name);
      Console.WriteLine("Underlying System Type :
{0}",t.UnderlyingSystemType);
      Console.WriteLine("Is Class : {0}",t.IsClass);
  }
}
```

In this example, rather than specify that you want to view type information of System.String, you create an instance of a string variable on which you then call the GetType() method. The information obtained here is the same as that obtained in the preceding example, the difference being that you don't have to know the type before the fact. You simply call the GetType() method and assign it to a Type object, which you can the query for the name, underlying system type, and so on.

Retrieving types in an assembly

Many times, you will want to examine types contained within an assembly. This assembly could be an executable or even a dynamic link library contained on the system.

Listing 32-3 contains the code necessary to examine the type information of the executable itself.

Listing 32-3: Examining a Currently Running Process for Type Information

```
using System;
using System.Reflection;
using System.Diagnostics;

class AssemType
{

  public static void Main(string[] args)
  {
      Process p = Process.GetCurrentProcess();
      string assemblyName = p.ProcessName + ".exe";
      Console.WriteLine("Examining : {0}", assemblyName);
      Assembly a = Assembly.LoadFrom(assemblyName);

      Type[] types = a.GetTypes();
      foreach(Type t in types)
      {
          Console.WriteLine("\nType : {0}",t.FullName);
          Console.WriteLine("\tBase class :
{0}",t.BaseType.FullName);
      }
  }
}
```

The preceding code introduces a few new items. The process type is used to examine running processes. In this context, you use it to get the name of your program, and then append .exe to the end of the name so you can examine the assembly. You can just as easily hard code in the name of your application, but this method ensures that it will work no matter what you name the application.

Figure 32-2 shows the output for this application. Not a very dramatic result, as your program contains only one class.

Figure 32-2: Process information obtained with the Reflection API

As you can see in Figure 32-2, you have examined the current running process and the actual application itself and displayed all internal classes and their types. For the sake of experimentation, trying adding a few more dummy classes to this project and then rerun the application. You should see a list of all the classes contained therein, as well as their types.

Interrogating objects

Listing 32-4 contains the source listing for the ReflectionTest application, which examines a class and provides the details about that class. This application is a good conglomerate of everything you learned about Reflection up to this point.

Listing 32-4: Class Objects Are Easily Transversed for Member Information

```
namespace ReflectionTest
{
  using System ;
  using System.Reflection ;

  public class Class1
  {

    public static int Main (  )
    {
      Type t = typeof( aUsefulClass ) ;
      Console.WriteLine ( "Type of class: " + t ) ;
      Console.WriteLine ( "Namespace: " + t.Namespace ) ;
      ConstructorInfo[] ci = t.GetConstructors( );
        Console.WriteLine("---------------------------------------------------");
      Console.WriteLine( "Constructors are:" ) ;
```

Continued

Listing 32-4 *(continued)*

```
foreach( ConstructorInfo i in ci )
    {
      Console.WriteLine( i ) ;
    }

    PropertyInfo[] pi = t.GetProperties( );
    Console.WriteLine("------------------------------------------------");
    Console.WriteLine( "Properties are:" ) ;

    foreach( PropertyInfo i in pi )
    {
      Console.WriteLine( i ) ;
    }
    MethodInfo[] mi = t.GetMethods( ) ;
    Console.WriteLine("------------------------------------------------");
    Console.WriteLine( "Methods are:" ) ;

    foreach( MethodInfo i in mi )
    {
      Console.WriteLine( "Name: " + i.Name ) ;
      ParameterInfo[] pif = i.GetParameters () ;
      foreach ( ParameterInfo p in pif )
      {
        Console.WriteLine("Type: " + p.ParameterType + " parameter name: " +
p.Name ) ;
      }
    }
    return 0 ;
  }


  public class aUsefulClass
  {
    public int pubInteger ;
    private int _privValue;

    public aUsefulClass()
    {
    }

    public aUsefulClass ( int IntegerValueIn )
    {
      pubInteger = IntegerValueIn ;
    }

    public int Add10 ( int IntegerValueIn )
    {
      Console.WriteLine ( IntegerValueIn ) ;
      return IntegerValueIn + 10 ;
    }
```

```
public int TestProperty
{
  get
  {
    return _privValue ;
  }

  set
  {
    _privValue = value ;
  }

}

  }
  }
}
```

Here you have created two classes, Class1 and aUsefulClass. Class1 contains the main entry point into our application (void Main), while the other class is there for examination purposes only.

To examine the aUsefulClass, perform the following steps within the main procedure: First, declare a Type object and, using the typeof keyword, point it to the aUsefulClass. You then display the class Type and the namespace. You then use the GetConstructors to retrieve a list of the class constructs. Next, loop through this of constructors and display them on the screen. As with the constructors, use GetProperties to retrieve a list of all the properties so that you can iterate through the list and the properties out the console window.

GetMethods retrieves all the method names, as well as the methods that make up the get and set accessors of your properties. This information is then iterated and displayed at the console. You also call GetParameters to retrieve a list of the parameters for each method and display that information as well.

As you can see in Figure 32-3, your application has revealed a wealth of information about the class object.

Obviously, this application isn't particularly useful, as you have the source code for the class in question and don't need Reflection to give you the details. The important thing to remember here is that Reflection works in the exact same manner even if you are dealing with an assembly for which you do not have the source code.

```
C:\WINDOWS\System32\cmd.exe                              _ □ ×
Z:\Chapter 32\Reflect\bin\Debug>ReflectionTest.exe
Type of class: ReflectionTest.Class1+aUsefulClass
Namespace: ReflectionTest
─────────────────────────────────────────────────
Constructors are:
Void .ctor()
Void .ctor(Int32)
─────────────────────────────────────────────────
Properties are:
Int32 TestProperty
─────────────────────────────────────────────────
Methods are:
Name: GetHashCode
Name: Equals
Type: System.Object parameter name: obj
Name: ToString
Name: Add10
Type: System.Int32 parameter name: IntegerValueIn
Name: get_TestProperty
Name: set_TestProperty
Type: System.Int32 parameter name: value
Name: GetType
─────────────────────────────────────────────────
Z:\Chapter 32\Reflect\bin\Debug>
```

Figure 32-3: The Reflection and Type classes reveal a great deal of information regarding the class object.

Generating dynamic code through Reflection

You can create code at runtime using the `System.Reflection.Emit` namespace. Using the classes in this namespace, an assembly can be defined in the memory, a module can be created for that assembly, new types can be defined for a module (including its members), and MSIL *opcodes* for the application's logic can be emitted.

> **Note** "Opcodes" is short for operation codes. This is the actual code that is generated by the .NET compiler.

Listing 32-5 contains the code that can be used to generate code at runtime.

Listing 32-5: **Generating Code Dynamically at Runtime**

```csharp
using System;
using System.Reflection;
using System.Reflection.Emit;

namespace DynamicCode
{
    class CodeGenerator
    {
        Type t;
        AppDomain currentDomain;
        AssemblyName assemName;
        AssemblyBuilder assemBuilder;
        ModuleBuilder moduleBuilder;
        TypeBuilder typeBuilder;
        MethodBuilder methodBuilder;
        ILGenerator msilG;
```

```
public static void Main()
{
        CodeGenerator codeGen = new CodeGenerator();
        Type t = codeGen.T;

        if (t != null)
        {
                            object o = Activator.CreateInstance(t);
                            MethodInfo helloWorld =
t.GetMethod("HelloWorld");

                            if (helloWorld != null)
                            {
                            // Run the HelloWorld Method
                            helloWorld.Invoke(o, null);
                            }

else

                            {
                            Console.WriteLine("Could not retrieve
MethodInfo");

                            }
                }
                else
                {
                            Console.WriteLine("Could not access the
Type");
                }


        public CodeGenerator()
        {
                // Get the current Application Domain.
                // This is needed when building code.
                currentDomain = AppDomain.CurrentDomain;

                // Create a new Assembly
for our Methods
                assemName = new AssemblyName();
                assemName.Name = "BibleAssembly";

                assemBuilder =
currentDomain.DefineDynamicAssembly(assemName, AssemblyBuilderAccess.Run);

                // Create a new module within this assembly
                moduleBuilder =
                    assemBuilder.DefineDynamicModule("BibleModule");

                // Create a new type within the module
                typeBuilder =
moduleBuilder.DefineType("BibleClass",TypeAttributes.Public);
```

Continued

Listing 32-5 *(continued)*

```
                    // Now we can add the
                    // HelloWorld method to the class that was just created.
                    methodBuilder =
typeBuilder.DefineMethod("HelloWorld", MethodAttributes.Public,null,null);

                       // Now we can generate some Microsoft Intermediate
                    // Language Code that simply writes a line of text out
                    // to the console.
                    msilG = methodBuilder.GetILGenerator();
                    msilG.EmitWriteLine("Hello from C# Bible");
                    msilG.Emit(OpCodes.Ret);
                    // Create a type.
                    t = typeBuilder.CreateType();
            }

        public Type T
        {
            get
            {
                    return this.t;
            }
        }
    }
}
```

As expected, this application simply prints a message out to the console, as shown in Figure 32-4.

Figure 32-4: The results of the dynamically generated code

This capability of Reflection to generate objects and code at runtime is truly impressive and provides the backbone for generating fuzzy logic applications that adapt and learn as they see fit.

Note   Fuzzy logic is defined as a form of algebra that uses the values of true and false to make decisions based on imprecise data. Fuzzy logic is generally attributed to artificial intelligence systems.

Summary

The `Reflection` and `Type` classes go hand in hand when you need to discover type information at runtime. These classes enable you to examine objects, load the objects dynamically at runtime, and even generate code as needed.

✦   ✦   ✦

C# Threading

The multithreading power of the .NET Framework enables you to write very robust multithreaded applications in any .NET language. In this chapter, you learn the ins and outs of threading. The chapter starts with an overview of the different types of threading and how they work in the .NET Framework, and then you learn what you can do with multithreading in your own applications. As you read this chapter, carefully consider the dangers of adding multiple threads to your applications before implementing them, because multithreading is not a trivial concept.

Understanding Threading

Before you start writing multithreaded applications, you should understand what happens when threads are created, and how the operating system handles threads.

When an application executes, a primary thread is created, and the application's scope is based on this thread. An application can create additional threads to perform additional tasks. An example of creating a primary thread would be firing up Microsoft Word. The application execution starts the main thread. Within the Word application, the background printing of a document would be an example of an additional thread being created to handle another task. While you are still interacting with the main thread (the Word document), the system is carrying out your printing request. After the main application thread is killed, all other threads created as a result of that thread are also killed.

Consider these two definitions from the Microsoft Foundation Classes Software Development Kit (MFCSDK):

+ **Process:** An executing instance of an application
+ **Thread:** A path of execution within a process

C++ and the MFC have long supported the concept of developing multithreaded applications. Because the core of the Windows operating system is written using these tools, it is important that they support the capability to create threads in which tasks can be assigned and executed. In the early days of Windows 3.1, multi-tasking did not exist; this concept became a reality in Windows NT 3.5, and NT 4.0, and then Windows 95, 98, 98SE, ME, 2000, and XP. To take advantage of the operating system's features, multithreaded applications became more important. Now, performing more than one task at a time is a necessary feature of an application. Visual Basic 6.0 and earlier compiled down to single-threaded applications, which meant that no matter what was going on, the VB application could only do one thing at a time.

In reality, on a single-processor system, it doesn't matter what tool you use to write your application; everything is still happening in a linear process. If you are a C++ developer, you can create new threads and perform a task while something else is going on, but it is really just sharing the same time with everything else that is running on the system. If there is only one processor, only one thing can happen at a time. This concept is called *preemptive multitasking*.

Understanding preemptive multitasking

Preemptive multitasking splits the processor time between running tasks, or threads. When a task is running, it is using a *time slice*. When the time slice has expired for the running task, somewhere around 20 milliseconds, depending on the operating system you are using, it is preempted and another task is given a time slice. The system saves the current context of the preempted task, and when the task is allocated another time slice, the context is restored and the process continues. This loop for a task continues repeatedly until the thread is aborted or the task ends. Preemptive multitasking gives the user the impression that more than one thing is happening at a time. Why do some tasks finish before others, even if you started the one that finished last first?

Understanding threading priorities and locking

When threads are created, they are assigned a priority either by the programmer or by the operating system. If an application seems to be locking up your system, it has the highest priority, and it is blocking other threads from getting any time slices. Priorities determine what happens, and in what order. Your application might be 90 percent complete with a certain process when suddenly a brand-new thread starts and races ahead of the thread that your application is currently executing, causing that thread to be reassigned to a lower priority. This frequently happens in Windows. Certain tasks take priority over others. Consider the new Windows Media Player. Starting up this process basically causes anything that is running to stop responding until it is completely loaded, including the Media Guide page.

One of the biggest dangers facing programmers writing applications that are using multiple threads are *locking* situations, in which two or more threads attempt to use the same resource. A thread lock occurs when a shared resource is being access by a thread and another thread with the same priority attempts to access that resource. If both threads have the same priority, and the lock is not coded correctly, the system slowly dies, because it cannot release either of the high-priority threads that are running. This can easily happen with multithreaded applications. When you assign thread priorities and are sharing global data, you must lock the context correctly in order for the operating system to handle the time slicing correctly.

Understanding symmetrical multiprocessing

On a *multiprocessor* system, more than one task can truly occur at the same time. Because each processor can assign time slices to tasks that are requesting work, you can perform more than one task at a time. When you need to run a processor-intensive long-running thread, such as sorting 10 million records by first name, address, Zip code, middle name, and country, using multiple processors gets the job done faster than a single processor. If you could delegate that job to another processor, then the currently running application would not be affected at all. Having more than one processor on a system enables this kind of *symmetrical multiprocessing* (*SMP*). Figure 33-1 shows the processor options for SQL Server 2000.

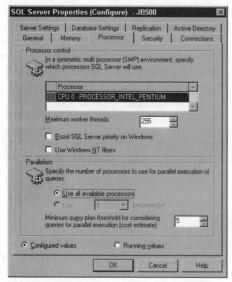

Figure 33-1: SQL Server 2000 Processor options dialog box

If you are running SQL Server on a multiprocessor machine, you can define the number of processors it should use for labor-intensive, long-running tasks of the sort just mentioned. SQL takes this a step further, performing queries across different processors, bringing the data together after the last thread is completed, and outputting the data to the user. This is known as *thread synchronization*. The main thread, which creates multiple threads, must wait for all of the threads to complete before it can continue the process.

When using an SMP system, note that a single thread still only runs on a single processor. Your single-threaded VB6 application does not perform one iota better if you throw another processor at it. Your 16-bit Access 2.0 application does not run any better either, because 16 bits still equals a single process. You need to actually create processes on the other processors in order to take advantage of them. This means that you do not design a multiprocessor GUI. You create a GUI that creates other processes and can react when those processes are completed or interrupted, while still enabling the user to use the GUI for other tasks.

Using resources: the more the merrier

Threads consume resources. When too many resources are being used, your computer is painstakingly slow. If you attempt to open 80 instances of Visual Studio .NET while installing Exchange 2000 on a computer with 96MB of RAM, you will notice that the screen does not paint correctly, the mouse doesn't move very fast, and the music you were listening to in Windows Media Player is not playing anymore. These performance problems are caused by too many threads running at the same time on an operating system with hardware that cannot handle this amount of work. If you attempt the same action on your new server, the 32-processor Unisys box with 1 terabyte of RAM, you do not see any performance degradation at all. The more memory you have, the more physical address space there is the running applications to create more threads. When you write applications that create threads, be sure you take this into consideration. The more threads you create, the more resources your application consumes. This could actually cause poorer performance than a single-threaded application, depending on the OS. The more the merrier does not include threads. Therefore, use caution when creating threads in that new version of multithreaded Tetris you are writing in C#.

Understanding application domains

Earlier, you learned that the MFC SDK defines a process as an executing instance of an application. Each application that is executing creates a new main thread, which lasts the lifetime of that application instance. Because each application is a process, each instance of an application must have process isolation. Two separate instances of Microsoft Word act independently of each other. When you click Spell Check, InstanceA of Word does not spell-check the document running in InstanceB of Word. Even if InstanceA of Word attempts to pass a memory pointer to InstanceB of Word, InstanceB would not know what to do with it, or even know where to look for it, as memory pointers are only relative to the process in which they are running.

In the .NET Framework, application domains are used to provide security and application isolation for managed code. Several application domains can run on a single process, or thread, with the same protection that would exist if the applications were running on multiple processes. Overhead is reduced with this concept, as calls do not need to be marshaled across process boundaries if the applications need to share data. Conversely, a single application domain can run across multiple threads.

This is possible because of the way the CLR executes code. Once code is ready to execute, it has already gone through the process of verification by the JIT compiler. By passing this verification process, the code is guaranteed not to do invalid things, such as access memory it is not supposed to, causing a page fault. This concept of *type-safe* code ensures that your code does not violate any rules after the verifier has approved it passing from MSIL to PE code. In typical Win32 applications, there were no safeguards against one piece of code supplanting another piece of code, so each application needed process isolation. In .NET, because type safety is guaranteed, it is safe to run multiple applications from multiple providers within the same application domain.

Understanding the benefits of multithreaded applications

Several types of applications can take advantage of multithreading.

✦ Applications with long processes

✦ Polling and listener applications

✦ Applications with a Cancel button in the GUI

The following sections state the case for each of these reasons.

Applications with long processes

Applications that involve long processes with which the user does not need to interact can benefit from multithreading because the long-running process can be created on a worker thread that processes information in the background until a notification that the thread has completed is made to the process that called the thread. In the meantime, the user is not kept waiting, staring at an hourglass cursor, to move on to the next task.

Polling and listener applications

Polling applications and listener applications can benefit from multithreading. Suppose you have an application that has created threads that are listening or polling. When something happens, a thread can consume that particular event, and the other threads can continue to poll or listen for events to occur. An example of this is a service that listens for requests on a network port, or a polling application that checks the state of Microsoft Message Queue (MSMQ) for messages. An example of an off-the-shelf polling applications is Microsoft Biztalk Server. Biztalk is constantly polling for things like files in a directory, or files on an SMTP server. It cannot accomplish all of this on a single thread, so multiple threads poll different resources. Microsoft Message Queue has an add-on for Windows 2000 and a feature in Windows XP called Message Queue Triggers. With MSMQ Triggers, you can set properties that cause a trigger to fire an event. This is a multithreaded service that can handle thousands of simultaneous requests.

Cancel buttons

Any application that has a Cancel button on a form should follow this process:

1. Load and show the form modally.

2. Start the process that is occurring on a new thread.

3. Wait for the thread to complete.

4. Unload the form.

By following these steps, the `click` event of your Cancel button occurs if the user clicks the button while another thread is executing. If the user does click the Cancel button, it actually clicks, as the process is running on a thread other than the currently running thread handling the click event, your code should then stop the process on the other running thread. This is a GUI feature that turns a good application into a great application.

Creating Multithreaded Applications

Now it's time to begin creating multithreaded applications. Threading is handled through the `System.Threading` namespace. The common members of the Thread class that you use are listed in Table 33-1.

Table 33-1
Common Thread Class Members

Member	Description
CurrentContext	Returns the current context on which the thread is executing
CurrentThread	Returns a reference to the currently running thread
ResetAbort	Resets an abort request
Sleep	Suspends the current thread for a specified length of time
ApartmentState	Gets or sets the apartment state of the thread
IsAlive	Gets a value that indicates whether the thread has been started and is not dead
IsBackground	Gets or sets a value indicating whether the thread is a background thread
Name	Gets or sets the name of the thread
Priority	Gets or sets the thread priority
Threadstate	Gets the state of the thread
Abort	Raises the `ThreadAbortException`, which can end the thread
Interrupt	Interrupts a thread that is in the `WaitSleepJoin` thread state
Join	Waits for a thread
Resume	Resumes a thread that has been suspended
Start	Begins the thread execution
Suspend	Suspends the thread

Creating new threads

Creating a variable of the `System.Threading.Thread` type enables you to create a new thread to start working with. Because the concept of threading involves the independent execution of another task, the `Thread` constructor requires the address of a procedure that will do the work for the thread you are creating. The `ThreadStart` delegate is the only parameter the constructor needs to begin using the thread.

To test this code, create a new project with the Console application template. The code in Listing 33-1 creates two new threads and calls the `Start` method of the `Thread` class to get the thread running.

Listing 33-1: Creating New Threads

```csharp
using System;
using System.Threading;

public class Threads
{
  public void Threader1()
  {

  }

  public void Threader2()
  {

  }

}

public class ThreadTest
{

  public static int Main(String[] args)
  {

    Threads testThreading = new Threads();

    Thread t1 = new
      Thread(new ThreadStart(testThreading.Threader1));
    t1.Start();

    Thread t2 = new
      Thread(new ThreadStart(testThreading.Threader2));
    t2.Start();

    Console.ReadLine();
    return 0;
  }
}
```

When you create a variable of type thread, the procedure that handles the thread must exist for the ThreadStart delegate. If it does not, an error occurs and your application does not compile.

The Name property sets or retrieves the name of a thread. This enables you to use a meaningful name instead of an address or hash code to reference the running threads. This is useful when using the debugging features of Visual Studio .NET. In the debugging toolbar, a drop-down list of the names of the running threads is available. Although you cannot "step out" of a thread and jump into another thread with the debugger, it is useful to know on which thread an error may have occurred.

Now that the thread variables are declared, named, and started, you need to do something on the threads you have created. The procedure names that were passed to the thread constructor were called Threader1 and Threader2. You can now add some code to these methods to see how they act. Your code should now look something like Listing 33-2.

Listing 33-2: Retreiving Information on Runnnig Threads

```csharp
using System;
using System.Threading;

public class Threads
{
  public void Threader1()
  {
    Console.WriteLine  (" *** Threader1 Information ***");
    Console.WriteLine
      ("Name: " + Thread.CurrentThread.Name);
    Console.WriteLine
      (Thread.CurrentThread);
    Console.WriteLine
      ("State: " + Thread.CurrentThread.ThreadState);
    Console.WriteLine
      ("Priority: " + Thread.CurrentThread.Priority);
    Console.WriteLine(" *** End Threader1 Information ***");
  }

  public void Threader2()
  {
    Console.WriteLine  (" *** Threader2 Information ***");
    Console.WriteLine
      ("Name: " + Thread.CurrentThread.Name);
    Console.WriteLine
      (Thread.CurrentThread);
    Console.WriteLine
      ("State: " + Thread.CurrentThread.ThreadState);
    Console.WriteLine
      ("Priority: " + Thread.CurrentThread.Priority);
    Console.WriteLine(" *** End Threader2 Information ***");
  }

}

public class ThreadTest
```

Continued

Listing 33-2 *(continued)*

```
{

   public static int Main(String[] args)
   {
      Threads testThreading = new Threads();

      Thread t1 = new
         Thread(new ThreadStart(testThreading.Threader1));
      t1.Name = "Threader1";
      t1.Start();

      Thread t2 = new
         Thread(new ThreadStart(testThreading.Threader2));
      t2.Name = "Threader2";
      t2.Start();

      Console.ReadLine();
      return 0;
   }
}
```

When you run the application, your console output should look something like that shown in Figure 33-2.

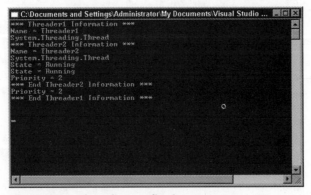

Figure 33-2: Threading application output

The output displayed in Figure 33-2 is not very pretty. If you recall, you are working with threads. Without setting a property or two, your Threader1 procedure never completes before Threader2 starts.

When the following code executes

```
t1.Start();
```

it begins the execution of the `Threader1` code. Because it is a thread, it has roughly 20 milliseconds of the time slice. In that time period, it reached the second line of code in the function, passed control back to the operating system, and executed the following line of code:

```
t2.start();
```

The `Threader2` procedure then executes for its slice of time and is preempted by the `t1` thread. This back-and-forth process continues until both procedures can finish.

Understanding thread priority

For the `Threader1` procedure to finish before the `Threader2` procedure begins, you need to set the `Priority` property to the correct `ThreadPriority` enumeration to ensure that the `t1` thread has priority over any other thread. Before the `t1.Start` method call, add the following code:

```
t1.Priority   = ThreadPriority.Highest;
```

When you set the priority to highest, `t1` finishes before `t2`. If you run the application again, your output should look similar to that shown in Figure 33-3.

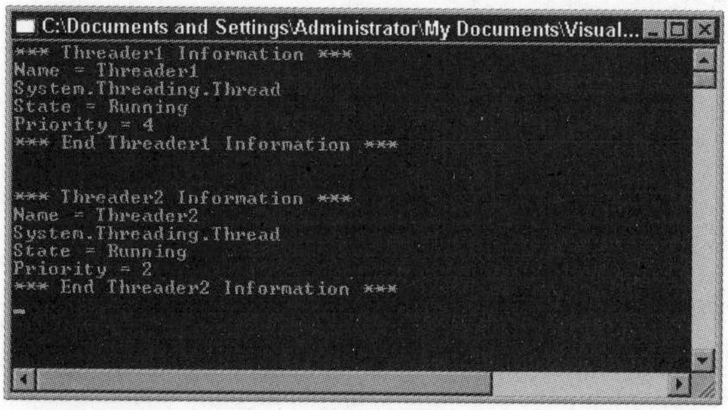

Figure 33-3: Output after setting the thread priority

The `ThreadPriority` enumeration dictates how a given thread is scheduled based on other running threads. `ThreadPriority` can be any one of the following: AboveNormal, BelowNormal, Highest, Lowest, or Normal. The algorithm that determines thread scheduling varies depending on the operating system on which the threads are running. By default, when a new thread is created, it is given a priority of 2, which is Normal in the enumeration.

Understanding thread state

When you create a new thread, you call the `Start()` method. At this point, the operating system allocates time slices to the address of the procedure passed in the thread constructor. Though the thread might live for a very long time, it still passes in between different states while other threads are being processed by the operating system. This state might be useful to you in your application. Based on the state of a thread, you could determine that something else might need to be processed. Besides `Start`, the most common thread states you will use are `Sleep` and `Abort`. By passing a number of milliseconds to the `Sleep` constructor, you are instructing the thread to give up the remainder of its time slice. Calling the `Abort` method stops the execution of the thread. Listing 33-3 shows some code that uses both `Sleep` and `Abort`.

Listing 33-3: **Using the Thread.Sleep Method**

```
using System;
using System.Threading;

public class Threads
{
  public void Threader1()
  {
    for(int intX = 0; intX < 50;intX ++)
    {
      if(intX == 5){
        Thread.Sleep(500);
        Console.WriteLine("Thread1 Sleeping");}
    }
  }

  public void Threader2()
  {
    for(int intX = 0; intX < 50;intX ++)
    {
      if(intX == 5){
        Thread.Sleep(500);
        Console.WriteLine("Thread2 Sleeping");}
    }
  }

}

public class ThreadTest
{

  public static int Main(String[] args)
  {

    Threads testThreading = new Threads();
```

```
Thread t1 = new
    Thread(new ThreadStart(testThreading.Threader1));
t1.Priority = ThreadPriority.Highest;
t1.Start();

Thread t2 = new
    Thread(new ThreadStart(testThreading.Threader2));
t2.Start();

Console.ReadLine();
return 0;
    }
}
```

If you notice, the Priority property is set to highest for the t1 thread. This means that no matter what, it executes before t2 starts. However, in the Threader1 procedure, you have the following if block:

```
for(int intX = 0; intX < 50;intX ++)
{
  if(intX == 5){
     Thread.Sleep(500);
     Console.WriteLine("Thread2 Sleeping");}
}
```

This tells the t1 thread to sleep for 500 milliseconds, giving up its current time slice and allowing the t2 thread to begin. After both threads are complete, the Abort method is called, and the threads are killed.

The Thread.Suspend method calls suspend a thread, indefinitely, until another thread wakes it back up. If you ever noticed the processor meter in the task manager spike at 100 percent when you aren't losing any memory, you can understand what happens when a thread is suspended. To get the thread back on track, you need to call the Resume method from another thread so it can restart itself. The following code demonstrates Suspend and Resume methods:

```
Thread.CurrentThread.Suspend;
Console.WriteLine("Thread1 Suspended");
Thread.CurrentThread.Resume;
Console.WriteLine("Thread1 Resumed");
```

A big caution is in order here: Suspending threads can cause undesirable results. You must ensure that the thread is resumed by another thread. Figure 33-4 demonstrates the issues described in the preceding paragraph. Notice in the figure that the console window is at the T1 Suspended line of code. This example reflects a test case, so you can get rid of the Resume method. The task manager results speak for the state of the system.

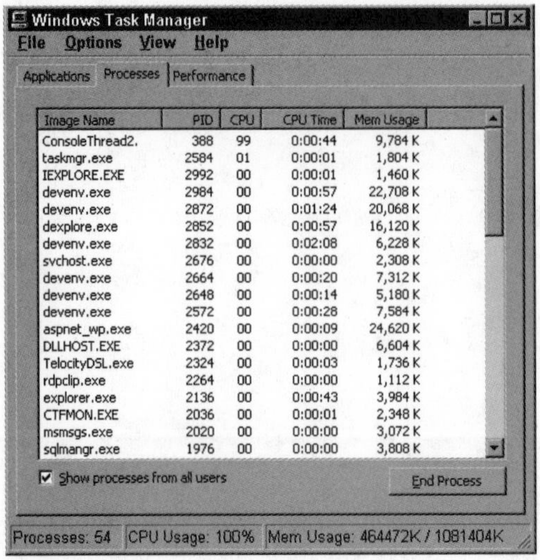

Figure 33-4: Spiked processor from a
suspended thread

ThreadState is a bitwise combination of the FlagsAttribute enumeration. At any
given time, a thread can be in more than one state. For example, if a thread is a background thread, and it is currently running, then the state would be both Running
and Background. Table 33-2 describes the possible states a thread can be in.

Table 33-2	
ThreadState Members	
Member	**Description**
Aborted	The thread has aborted.
AbortRequested	A request has been made to abort a thread.
Background	The thread is executing as a backgroung thread.
Running	The thread is being executed.
Suspended	The thread has been suspended.
SuspendRequested	The thread is being requested to suspend.
Unstarted	The thread has not been started.
WatSleepJoin	The thread is blocked on a call to Wait, Sleep, or Join.

Joining threads

The `Thread.Join` method waits for a thread to finish before continuing processing. This is useful if you create several threads that are supposed to accomplish a certain task, but before you want the foreground application to continue, you need to ensure that all of the threads you created were completed. In the following code, switch

```
T2.Join();
```

with

```
Console.Writeline("Writing");
```

You get two sets of results, the second time you run the code. The console output of `Writing` does not show up until both threads have finished.

Listing 33-4: **Joining Threads**

```
using System;
using System.Threading;

public class Threads
{
  public void Threader1()
  {
    for(int intX = 0; intX < 50;intX ++)
    {
      if(intX == 5)
      {
        Thread.Sleep(500);
        Console.WriteLine("Thread1 Sleeping");
      }
    }
  }

  public void Threader2()
  {
    for(int intX = 0; intX < 50;intX ++)
    {
      if(intX == 5)
      {
        Thread.Sleep(500);
        Console.WriteLine("Thread2 Sleeping");
      }
    }
  }
}
```

Continued

Listing 33-4 *(continued)*

```
}

public class ThreadTest
{

   public static int Main(String[] args)
   {

     Threads testThreading = new Threads();

     Thread t2 = new
        Thread(new ThreadStart(testThreading.Threader2));
     t2.Start();

     Thread t1 = new
        Thread(new ThreadStart(testThreading.Threader1));
     t1.Priority = ThreadPriority.Highest;
     t1.Start();

     /* Call Join to wait for all threads to complete */

     t2.Join();

      Console.WriteLine("Writing");


     Console.ReadLine();
     return 0;
   }
}
```

As you can see, setting various properties on threads makes it very simple to control them. Keep in mind that after you suspend a thread, you need to resume it, or your system consumes unnecessary resources.

Synchronizing threads

Data synchronization is a critical aspect of using threads. Although it is not a complex programming task, your data risks corruption if you fail to address it.

When threads are running, they are sharing time with other running threads. This is evident in the sample you have run in this chapter. If you have a method that is running on multiple threads, each thread has only several milliseconds of processor time before the operating system preempts the thread to give another thread time in the same method. If you are in the middle of a math statement, or in the middle on concatenating a name, your thread could very well be stopped for several milliseconds, and another running thread overwrite data that another thread was using. This is not the end of the world, however, because several methods enable you to stop this from occurring. Consider the following code:

```
{
   int Y;
   int V;
   for(int Z = 0; Z < 20; Z++){
     return Y * V;}
}
```

It is highly likely that during the loop, a running thread will stop to allow another thread a chance at this method. Remember that this only occurs if you are allowing multiple threads to access this code block. When you write multithreaded applications, this happens frequently, so you need to know how to address the situation. The following code solves this problem:

```
lock(this){
   int Y;
   int V;
   for(int Z = 0; Z < 20; Z++){
   return Y * V;}
   }
```

The Lock statement is one way to force the joining of threads. Its implementation is a little different from the Join method. With Lock, you are evaluating an expression passed to the Lock block. When a thread reaches the Lock block, it waits until it can get an exclusive lock on the expression being evaluated before it attempts any further processing. This ensures that multiple threads cannot corrupt shared data.

The Monitor class enables synchronization using the Monitor.Enter, Monitor.TryEnter, and Monitor.Exit methods. After you have a lock on a code region, you can use the Monitor.Wait, Monitor.Pulse, and Monitor.PulseAll methods to determine if a thread should continue a lock, or if any previously locked methods are now available. Wait releases the lock if it is held and waits to be notified. When Wait is called, the lock is freed and it returns and obtains the lock again.

Polling and Listening

Polling and listening are two more instances that represent the usefulness of multithreading. Class libraries, such as System.Net.Sockets, include a full range of multithreaded classes that can aid you in creating TCP listeners, UDP listeners, and a bevy of other network-related tasks that require multithreading.

Take note of the `TimerCallBack` class of the `System.Threading` namespace. This class is very similar to others you have been using so far, except that a timer period is part of the constructor, which enables you to poll for something to happen at certain intervals.

You can accomplish the same result by adding a timer control to your form, but by using the `TimerCallBack` class, the timing and the callback to the addressed procedure are automatic.

Listing 33-5 uses a timer callback to poll for files in a directory. If a file is found, it is promptly deleted. You should only run this code against a test directory, because it deletes files. The following sample code expects a C:\Poll directory. The constructor for the `TimerCallBack` class expects an address for the thread to execute on; an object data type representing the state of the timer; a due time, which represents a period of time to poll until; and a period, which is a millisecond variable indicating when the polling interval occurs.

Listing 33-5: **Using the TimerCallBack Delegate**

```
using System;

using System.IO;
using System.Threading;

namespace cSharpTimerCallBack
{
    class Class1
{
    public static void Main()
  {
Console.WriteLine
    ("Checking direcotry updates every 2 seconds.");
Console.WriteLine
    ("    (Hit Enter to terminate the sample)");
Timer timer = new
    Timer(new TimerCallback(CheckStatus), null, 0, 2000);
Console.ReadLine();
timer.Dispose();
    }
      static void CheckStatus(Object state)
    {
string[] str = Directory.GetFiles("C:\\Poll");
if(str.Length>0)
{
    for(int i = 0; i < str.Length;i++)
      {
Console.WriteLine(str[i]);
```

```
File.Delete(str[i]);
      }
}
Console.WriteLine("Directory Empty");
    }
}
```

After running this for a while and periodically copying a few files into the C:\Poll directory, the console output should look similar to that shown in Figure 33-5.

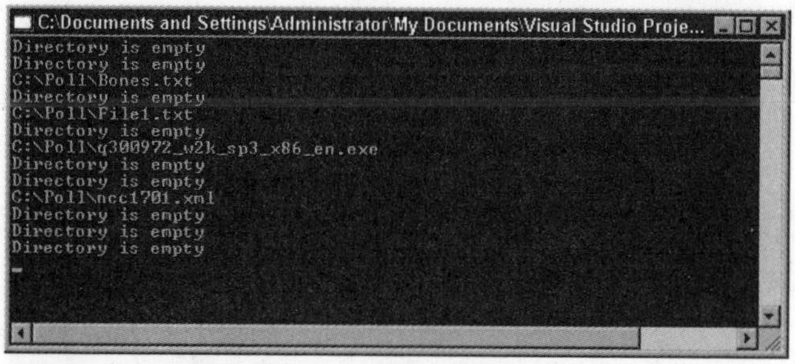

Figure 33-5: Output from Listing 33-2

Summary

In this chapter, you learned how to implement multithreading in C# with the `System.Thread` namespace.

The basic idea behind multithreading is simple: By creating more than one thread, you can accomplish more than one task at a time. The number of threads you create has to be determined by solid testing. Too many threads can cause resource problems. Not creating enough threads can result in your application not performing to its full potential.

With the examples you created here, you should be well equipped to implement threading in your own applications. Just avoid running with scissors, because before you know it, your multithreaded applications can turn into a multithreaded headache.

As with anything else, carefully consider your applications beforehand, and decide whether multithreading is appropriate as part of this planning process.

✦   ✦   ✦

Working with COM

As a Windows developer, you have most likely created many COM components, either as standalone DLLs or DLLs that run inside of COM+ services. With the advent of .NET, you might wonder whether you need to rewrite everything with this new language. The good news is that you do not have to rewrite any of your components. Microsoft was kind enough to provide you with the tools that you need to use your existing components from .NET. Moreover, those components can be safely invoked from the Common Language Runtime environment. In this chapter, you learn how easy it is to leverage your existing code and use it from a .NET-managed client. The client could be anything—a Web application, another .NET component, or even a Service-based application. It doesn't matter; the core functionality works across all types of applications.

Although you always have the option to rewrite your code, you do not have to. You will most likely want to start using .NET for all of your development, especially the GUI development, as it is so much easier to use than previous versions. At the same time, you do not want to rewrite all of the core business logic that your applications use. With .NET, this is all possible; you can port your applications to .NET while still using the thousands of lines of existing code that you have already written in components.

In this chapter, you learn how to consume your existing COM components from a .NET client using the tools that are provided with .NET, and you see how it all happens under the hood.

 Chapter 35 covers working with COM+ Services, such as transactions and object pooling within your C# applictions. This chapter covers the basics of interoperating with COM objects.

Introducing the Runtime-Callable Wrapper

.NET code can access unmanaged code through a proxy called the Runtime-Callable Wrapper, or RCW. The RCW enables a .NET application to see the unmanaged component as a managed component. It does this by marshalling method calls, events, and properties through a wrapper created by your application or created manually using tools (such as the Type Library Importer) provided in the Framework. Using information from the COM type library, the RCW handles the interoperability between the managed and unmanaged code. When your application runs, it is unaware that the code being executed is from an unmanaged, or COM, DLL. The consumers of the components do not need any special knowledge of how the code was written, what language it was written in, or if it is a .NET component. All of the features of the managed environment, such as garbage collection and exception handling, are available to the .NET client as if it were consuming managed code. This makes it extremely simple to port modules in your pre-.NET applications to .NET, without having to reinvent the wheel or fully understand the intricacies of whatever .NET language you are using, be it C#, J#, or VB .NET, or whatever. You can rework the client code and leave your existing business and data logic in place by using COM Interop. Figure 34-1 shows the relationship between the COM DLL, the RCW and the managed .NET application.

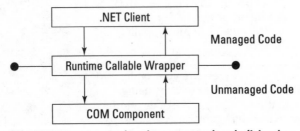

Figure 34-1: Managed and unmanaged code living in peace together

Creating .NET Assemblies from COM Components

To use your COM component in your .NET application, you need to create the Interop Assembly, or RCW, that marshals the method calls from your .NET client to the COM server. There are several ways to do this in .NET. The two most common ways are as follows:

✦ The Type Library Importer utility, or Tlbimp.exe, supplied with the .NET Framework

✦ Directly reference the COM from your VS .NET C# application

Both of these are covered in detail within this chapter.

The proxy that is created for Interop is based on the metadata exposed in the type library of the COM component you are attempting to access. COM type libraries can be made available in one of two forms:

✦ Type libraries can be found as standalone files. Standalone type libraries usually have an extension of TLB. Older standalone type libraries may ship with an extension of OLB. If you are creating a Visual Basic ActiveX DLL, you can create a standalone type library for your component by selecting the Remote Server Files option in the project's Property dialog box.

✦ Type libraries can also be found embedded in a COM server as a binary resource. In-process COM servers, packaged as DLLs, as well as out-of-process COM servers, packaged as EXEs, can include the type library as a resource in the COM server itself. COM components built with Visual Basic have the type library compiled inside of the DLL.

In the following section, you learn how to create the Interop assembly from a COM DLL using the two methods described in the beginning of this section: using the Tlbimp utility and directly referencing the DLL from Visual Studio .NET.

Using the Tlbimp utility

The Tlbimp utility is a standalone console application that creates the .NET Interop assembly based on the COM DLL that you specify. It is located in the Framework SDK directory in Program Files. The following code snippet demonstrates the syntax of Tlbimp:

```
tlbimp [COMDllFilename] /[options]
```

The command-line options for tlbimp.exe are described in Table 34-1.

<table>
<tr><td colspan="2" align="center">Table 34-1
Tlbimp.exe Options</td></tr>
<tr><td>*Option*</td><td>*Description*</td></tr>
<tr><td>/asmversion:versionnumber</td><td>Specifies the version of the assembly to create</td></tr>
<tr><td>/delaysign</td><td>Tells Tlbimp to sign the assembly using delayed signing</td></tr>
<tr><td>/help</td><td>Displays help options for tlbimp.exe</td></tr>
<tr><td>/keycontainer:containername</td><td>Signs the assembly with a strong name using the public/private key pair found in the key container specified in the *containername* parameter</td></tr>
</table>

Continued

	Table 34-1 *(continued)*	
Option	*Description*
/nologo	Suppresses the Microsoft startup banner display
/out:*filename*	Specifies the name of the output file to be created. By default, the output file has the same name as the COM DLL, but you are warned if you attempt to overwrite the file if it exists in the same path.
/primary	Produces a primary Interop assembly for the type library
/publickey:*filename*	Specifies the file containing the public key to use to sign the resulting assembly
/reference:*filename*	Specifies the assembly file to use to resolve references to types defined outside of the current type library
/silent	Suppresses the display of success messages
/strictref	Does not import a type library if the tool cannot resolve all references defined within the current assembly or assemblies specified with the /reference option
/sysarray	Imports any COM-style SafeArray as a managed System.Array Class type
/unsafe	Produces interfaces without .NET Framework security checks. You should not use this option unless you are aware of the risks of exposing code as unsafe.
/verbose	Displays additional information about the imported type library when tlbimp.exe is run
/?	Displays help about the syntax for tlbimp.exe

This command produces a .NET assembly with a DLL extension whose base name is set to the name of the library embedded in the type library file (which may be different from the filename of the type library itself). The tlbimp command can accept the name of a type library file as input:

```
tlbimp server.tlb
```

It can also accept the name of a COM server that holds an embedded type library:

```
tlbimp server.dll
```

By using the /out option, you can specify an alternate name for the .NET assembly created:

```
tlbimp server.dll /out:dotNetServer.dll
```

The assembly that is output by the Tlbimp.exe tool is a standard .NET assembly that you can view with Ildasm.exe. The assembly does not contain the COM server's code; instead, it contains references that help the CLR find the COM objects housed in the server, such as the COM object's GUIDs. Think of the assembly generated by `tlbimp` as a bridge that connects your .NET code to your COM server. Because the COM code still resides in the COM server, you need to remember to install and register any COM servers you plan to use with your .NET applications. This actually works to your advantage. Because the COM server is still registered with Windows, standard COM applications that are not .NET-aware can continue to use the same COM server without moving any of the code to a .NET-specific platform.

Creating a COM component

Before using the Tlbimp utility, you need a COM component to work with. Listing 34-1 shows the code for a simple VB6 ActiveX DLL with several common class functions, such as setting and retrieving a property, firing an event, and returning a value from a method that has input parameters.

Listing 34-1: **Visual Basic 6.0 COM Server Code**

```
Option Explicit

Private strMessage As String

Public Event COMEvent(Message As String)

Private Sub Class_Initialize()
    strMessage = "Default Message"
End Sub

Public Property Get Message() As String
    Message = strMessage
End Property

Public Property Let Message(ByVal vNewValue As String)
    strMessage = vNewValue
End Property

Public Function SquareIt(int1 As Integer, int2 As Integer) As Integer
    SquareIt = int1 * int2
End Function

Public Sub FireCOMEvent()
    RaiseEvent COMEvent(strMessage)
End Sub
```

This code is placed into a class module named COMObject. The class module is enclosed in a project named VB6COMServer. Visual Basic 6.0 compiles this code into an in-process COM server and embeds a type library into the server. The readable representation of the type library, written in COM's Interface Description Language (IDL), is shown in Listing 34-2.

Listing 34-2: IDL Source for the COM Server In Listing 34-1

```
// Generated .IDL file (by the OLE/COM Object Viewer)
//
// typelib filename: VB6COMServer.dll

[
  uuid(B4096C50-ACA4-4E1F-8D36-F36F1EE5F03B),
  version(1.0)
]
library VB6COMServer
{
    // TLib :        // TLib : OLE Automation :
{00020430-0000-0000-C000-000000000046}
    importlib("stdole2.tlb");

    // Forward declare all types defined in this typelib
    interface _COMObject;
    dispinterface __COMObject;

    [
      odl,
      uuid(5960D780-FEA2-4383-B2CB-9F78E4677142),
      version(1.0),
      hidden,
      dual,
      nonextensible,
      oleautomation
    ]
    interface _COMObject : IDispatch {
        [id(0x68030000), propget]
        HRESULT Message([out, retval] BSTR* );
        [id(0x68030000), propput]
        HRESULT Message([in] BSTR );
        [id(0x60030002)]
        HRESULT SquareIt(
                        [in, out] short* int1,
                        [in, out] short* int2,
                        [out, retval] short* );
        [id(0x60030003)]
        HRESULT FireCOMEvent();
    };
```

```
[
  uuid(50730C97-09EB-495C-9873-BEC6399AA63A),
  version(1.0)
]
coclass COMObject {
    [default] interface _COMObject;
    [default, source] dispinterface __COMObject;
};


[
  uuid(A4D4C3D8-DFFF-45DB-9A14-791E4F82EF35),
  version(1.0),
  hidden,
  nonextensible
]
dispinterface __COMObject {
    properties:
    methods:
        [id(0x00000001)]
        void COMEvent([in, out] BSTR* Message);
};
};
```

To create the Interop assembly that enables your C# application to consume the unmanaged DLL, you need to run the Tlbimp utility described in the preceding section. In Figure 34-2, you can see that the /out: parameter is used to give the Interop assembly the name compinterop.dll. The name of the output assembly can be anything that you choose—it can even be the same name as the original COM component.

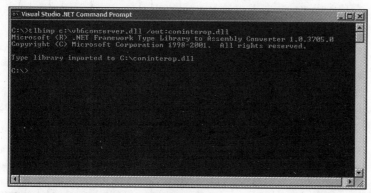

Figure 34-2: The Tlbimp utility in action

The VB6COMServer.dll that was created using VB6 can now be consumed from any .NET client — as long as the `cominterop.dll` assembly is referenced by the application, and the VB6 component is registered on the machine that is attempting to consume the code. Because the output from Tlbimp is now a .NET assembly, you can use the ILDASM utility to view details about the metadata that was created from the ActiveX DLL that the CLR actually uses. Figure 34-3 shows the ILDSM utility when run against the new `cominterop.dll` just created.

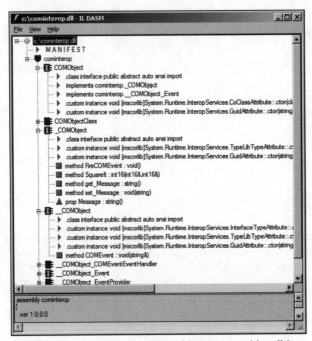

Figure 34-3: ILDASM with assembly generated by Tlbimp

The assembly generated by importing the type library whose source code is shown in Listing 34-3 includes a namespace called `cominterop`, which is the name of the assembly that was passed to the `/out` parameter from the Tlbimp utility. This namespace must be treated just like a namespace defined by your code or the .NET Framework: Your code must reference the namespace when using any of the classes in the namespace.

Figure 34-3 illustrates the classes inserted into the assembly generated by `tlbimp`. The class that you use in your C# code to work with the COM object has the same name as the name given to the COM object in the IDL source's `coclass` statement. In Listing 34-3, the COM object is given a coclass name of `COMObject`. The assembly generated by `tlbimp` includes a .NET class of the same name, and this is the class that you use in your code to work with the Visual Basic COM object.

Using the Interop assembly from C#

Consuming the COM component from C# is very straightforward now that you have created the Interop assembly. To use your Interop assembly, perform the following steps:

1. Create a test client application. For simplicity, create a new Windows Forms application and call it Interop.

2. Once the application is created, you put your code in the `click` event of a button, so go ahead and add a button to the default Form1.cs. Next, right-click References in the Solution Explorer, and select Add. The Add Reference dialog box opens. This is similar to the Add Reference dialog box in VB6. Basically, you need to make a reference to the assembly that you need to use, just as any other .NET assembly is not added by default to a new project.

3. To add a reference to the Cominterop DLL that you created earlier, click the Browse button and locate the assembly on your hard drive. Once you have done this, your Add Reference dialog box should look something like Figure 34-4.

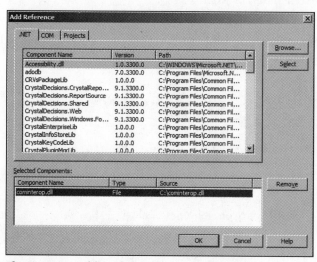

Figure 34-4: Adding the Cominterop reference

After the assembly is referenced by your application, you can use it just as you would any other .NET assembly. Because Visual Studio .NET has such great features — such as auto-complete and auto-list members — once the reference is added, your methods, events, and properties are available to you through the IDE. Figure 34-5 shows the auto-list members in action once the instance of the `Cominterop` object is created and the assembly is reference with the `using` statement.

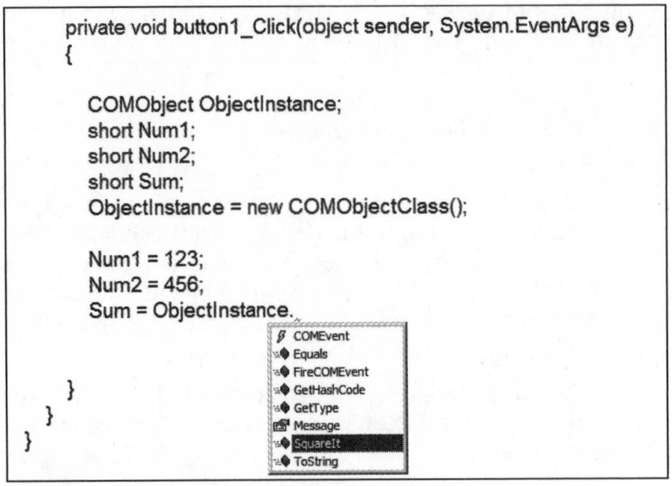
private void button1_Click(object sender, System.EventArgs e)
{
COMObject ObjectInstance;
short Num1;
short Num2;
short Sum;
ObjectInstance = new COMObjectClass();
Num1 = 123;
Num2 = 456;
Sum = ObjectInstance.
COMEvent
Equals
FireCOMEvent
GetHashCode
GetType
Message
SquareIt
ToString
}
}
}

Figure 34-5: Auto-List members in action

To test all of the methods, properties, and events that you wrote in the ActiveX DLL, duplicate Listing 34-3 in your WindowsForms application.

Listing 34-3: **COM Client Code Written in C#**

```
        /// <summary>
        /// The main entry point for the application.
        /// </summary>
        [STAThread]
        static void Main()
        {
                Application.Run(new Form1());
        }

        // Create a handler for the event
        private __COMObject_COMEventEventHandler
COMEventHandlerInstance;

        private void button1_Click(object sender,
System.EventArgs e)
        {

                // create new instance of the COMObject class
                COMObject ObjectInstance;
                short Num1;
```

```
                short Num2;
                short Sum;
                ObjectInstance = new COMObjectClass();

                Num1 = 5;
                Num2 = 6;
                // Call the SquareIt method
                Sum = ObjectInstance.SquareIt(ref Num1, ref
Num2);

                listBox1.Items.Add  (Sum.ToString());
                listBox1.Items.Add (ObjectInstance.Message);

                // Set the value of message different than the
default
                ObjectInstance.Message = "C# Rocks";

                COMEventHandlerInstance = new
__COMObject_COMEventEventHandler(COMEventHandler);
                ObjectInstance.COMEvent +=
COMEventHandlerInstance;
                ObjectInstance.FireCOMEvent();
        }

        void COMEventHandler(ref string Message)
        {
                listBox1.Items.Add(Message);
        }


        }
    }
```

The output from this application looks similar to what is shown in Figure 34-6.

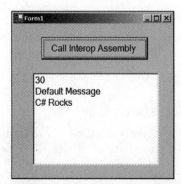

Figure 34-6: Output from the
C# client using the COM component

Like any other object in .NET, you use the `new` operator to create a new instance of the `COMObject` class, as the following snippet demonstrates:

```
ObjectInstance = new COMObject();
```

Once the variable name `ObjectInstance` is instantiated, you use the object just as you would any other .NET object; nothing special needs to be done. The RCW handles all of the Interop, type conversions and object marshalling for the types, so you are completely hidden from any of the COM marshalling internals that are occurring.

If you have used COM Interop from VB .NET, you will notice something different about the way the parameters are passed to the methods in C#. If you look at the C# code for the `SquareIt` method, note the addition of the `Ref` keyword:

```
Num1 = 5;
Num2 = 6;
//  Call the SquareIt method
Sum = ObjectInstance.SquareIt(ref Num1, ref Num2);
```

Visual Basic COM servers may pass values by value or by reference. Your C# code needs to use the appropriate keywords when passing parameters into COM method calls. You can use ILDASM to help you determine whether a parameter should be passed by value or by reference.

Open the assembly generated by Tlbimp using the ILDASM tool and look at the definition of the method that you want to call. In this case, you need to call the `SquareIt()` method. The `SquareIt()` method is listed in the assembly with the following signature:

```
SquareIt : int16(int16&,int16&)
```

The type of the return value returned by the method follows the colon. The signature of the `SquareIt()` method lists a return type of `int16`, which, in Intermediate Language parlance, denotes a 16-bit integer. The ampersands that follow the parameter types signify that the parameter must be passed by reference. Parameters that need to be passed by reference must be adorned with the `ref` keyword in the C# client. Parameters that need to be passed by value are not shown with the ampersand in the assembly. The C# client doesn't need to use the `ref` keyword on the parameters in this case.

Directly referencing the COM DLL from C#

In the previous section, you learned how to use the Interop assembly created from Tlbimp.exe in a C# Windows Forms application. The main reason to use Tlbimp.exe to create the Interop assembly is because it can be given a strong name with the SN.exe utility, and then installed in the Global Application Cache using the GACUTIL utility. Once in the GAC, the assembly can be shared among many other .NET assemblies or projects. If you are writing an application that uses COM Interop and the assembly does not need to be shared, you can simply reference the COM DLL directly through Visual Studio .NET, which will create the RCW for you.

To add a reference to a COM DLL directly to your C# project, follow these steps:

1. Right-click the References folder in the Solution Explorer. The Add Reference dialog box, shown in Figure 34-7, opens. The second tab, COM, lists all of the COM objects registered on the local machine.

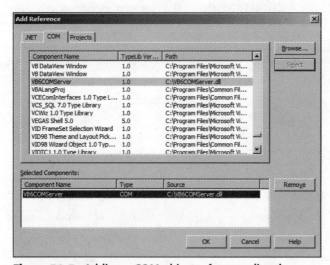

Figure 34-7: Adding a COM object reference directly

2. After you have selected the COM component that you need to consume, you can use the same code that you used to write the Windows Forms application, the only difference being the assembly that you are referencing, which in this case would be VB6ComServer, and not Cominterop.

```
using VB6COMServer;
ObjectInstance = new COMObjectClass();
```

As you can see, referencing a COM component directly from the IDE is even easier than using the Tlbimp utility, though you lose some flexibility in terms of what you can actually do with the component.

Handling Interop Errors

In the .NET Framework, the CLR reports errors by throwing exceptions when things go wrong. In COM, HRESULTs are the avenue in which errors are reported, so the RCW needs to be able the map the HRESULT for a given error to the equivalent .NET exception.

Table 34-2 maps the standard HRESULTs in COM to their counterparts as .NET exceptions.

Table 34-2	
HRESULTs to .NET Exceptions	
HRESULT	**.NET Exception**
MSEE_E_APPDOMAINUNLOADED	AppDomainUnloadedException
COR_E_APPLICATION	ApplicationException
COR_E_ARGUMENT or E_INVALIDARG	ArgumentException
COR_E_ARGUMENTOUTOFRANGE	ArgumentOutOfRangeException
COR_E_ARITHMETIC or ERROR_ARITHMETIC_OVERFLOW	ArithmeticException
COR_E_ARRAYTYPEMISMATCH	ArrayTypeMismatchException
COR_E_BADIMAGEFORMAT or ERROR_BAD_FORMAT	BadImageFormatException
COR_E_COMEMULATE_ERROR	COMEmulateException
COR_E_CONTEXTMARSHAL	ContextMarshalException
COR_E_CORE	CoreException
NTE_FAIL	CryptographicException
COR_E_DIRECTORYNOTFOUND or ERROR_PATH_NOT_FOUND	DirectoryNotFoundException
COR_E_DIVIDEBYZERO	DivideByZeroException
COR_E_DUPLICATEWAITOBJECT	DuplicateWaitObjectException
COR_E_ENDOFSTREAM	EndOfStreamException
COR_E_TYPELOAD	EntryPointNotFoundException
COR_E_EXCEPTION	Exception
COR_E_EXECUTIONENGINE	ExecutionEngineException
COR_E_FIELDACCESS	FieldAccessException

HRESULT	.NET Exception
COR_E_FILENOTFOUND or ERROR_FILE_NOT_FOUND	FileNotFoundException
COR_E_FORMAT	FormatException
COR_E_INDEXOUTOFRANGE	IndexOutOfRangeException
COR_E_INVALIDCAST or E_NOINTERFACE	InvalidCastException
COR_E_INVALIDCOMOBJECT	InvalidComObjectException
COR_E_INVALIDFILTERCRITERIA	InvalidFilterCriteriaException
COR_E_INVALIDOLEVARIANTTYPE	InvalidOleVariantTypeException
COR_E_INVALIDOPERATION	InvalidOperationException
COR_E_IO	IOException
COR_E_MEMBERACCESS	AccessException
COR_E_METHODACCESS	MethodAccessException
COR_E_MISSINGFIELD	MissingFieldException
COR_E_MISSINGMANIFESTRESOURCE	MissingManifestResourceException
COR_E_MISSINGMEMBER	MissingMemberException
COR_E_MISSINGMETHOD	MissingMethodException
COR_E_MULTICASTNOTSUPPORTED	MulticastNotSupportedException
COR_E_NOTFINITENUMBER	NotFiniteNumberException
E_NOTIMPL	NotImplementedException
COR_E_NOTSUPPORTED	NotSupportedException
COR_E_NULLREFERENCE or E_POINTER	NullReferenceException
COR_E_OUTOFMEMORY or E_OUTOFMEMORY	OutOfMemoryException
COR_E_OVERFLOW	OverflowException
COR_E_PATHTOOLONG or ERROR_FILENAME_EXCED_RANGE	PathTooLongException
COR_E_RANK	RankException
COR_E_REFLECTIONTYPELOAD	ReflectionTypeLoadException
COR_E_REMOTING	RemotingException
COR_E_SAFEARRAYTYPEMISMATCH	SafeArrayTypeMismatchException

Continued

Table 34-2 (continued)	
HRESULT	**.NET Exception**
COR_E_SECURITY	SecurityException
COR_E_SERIALIZATION	SerializationException
COR_E_STACKOVERFLOW or ERROR_STACK_OVERFLOW	StackOverflowException
COR_E_SYNCHRONIZATIONLOCK	SynchronizationLockException
COR_E_SYSTEM	SystemException
COR_E_TARGET	TargetException
COR_E_TARGETINVOCATION	TargetInvocationException
COR_E_TARGETPARAMCOUNT	TargetParameterCountException
COR_E_THREADABORTED	ThreadAbortException
COR_E_THREADINTERRUPTED	ThreadInterruptedException
COR_E_THREADSTATE	ThreadStateException
COR_E_THREADSTOP	ThreadStopException
COR_E_TYPELOAD	TypeLoadException
COR_E_TYPEINITIALIZATION	TypeInitializationException
COR_E_VERIFICATION	VerificationException
COR_E_WEAKREFERENCE	WeakReferenceException
COR_E_VTABLECALLSNOTSUPPORTED	VTableCallsNotSupportedException
All other HRESULTs	COMException

If your application needs to get extended error information and the COM object supports the IErrorInfo interface, you can use the IErrorInfo object to get further information about the exception. Table 34-3 describes the additional error information.

Table 34-3 COM Interop Extended Error Information	
Exception Field	**COM Source Information**
ErrorCode	HRESULT returned from the method call

Exception Field	COM Source Information
HelpLink	If `IErrorInfo->HelpContext` is nonzero, the string is formed by concatenating `IErrorInfo->GetHelpFile` and `"#"` and `IErrorInfo->GetHelpContext`. Otherwise, the string is returned from `IErrorInfo->GetHelpFile`.
InnerException	Always null
Message	String returned from `IErrorInfo->GetDescription`
Source	String returned from `IErrorInfo->GetSource`
StackTrace	The .NET generated stack trace for this exception
TargetSite	The method name that caused the `HRESULT` to be passed back to .NET

Obviously, you need to include error handling in your applications, even if you are using COM Interop. There is essentially no difference in the way that you code the COM components versus .NET assemblies, so the structured exception handling in .NET should be used whenever you are writing code that has the possibility of causing an exception.

Using Platform Invoke

If you are a Visual Basic 6 developer, the Win32 API has been the way to harness the true power of Windows development. In .NET, you can still access the Win32 API from C#, although most or all of the functionality that you will likely be using is already present in the .NET Framework. Calling exported functions from C DLL's is accomplished by using the Platform Invoke service. *Platform invoke* is a service that enables managed code to call unmanaged functions COM DLL's. Using the `DLLImportAttribute` class, you can specify the name of the DLL and the DLL function that you need to use in your C# application. Just like accessing the Win32 API in VB6, you need to know the name of the DLL and the function in the DLL that you need to execute. Once you have accomplished this, you can simply call the function using the `DLLImport` attribute in a method marked with `static` and `extern` modifiers, as the following code demonstrates:

```
using System.Runtime.InteropServices;
[DllImport("user32.dll")]
public static extern int MessageBox(int hWnd, String text,
            String caption, uint type);
```

When using platform invoke, you may need to alter the default behavior of the interoperability between the managed and unmanaged code. You can do this by modify the fields of the `DLLImportAttribute` class. Table 34-4 describes the fields that can be customized for the `DLLImportAttribute` class.

Table 34-4
DLLImportAttribute Fields

Object Field	Description
EntryPoint	Specifies the DLL entry point to be called
CharSet	Controls the way that string arguments should be marshaled to the function. The default is `CharSet.Ansi`.
ExactSpelling	Prevents an entry point from being modified to correspond to the character set. The default value varies by programming language.
CallingConvention	Specifies the calling-convention values used in passing method arguments. The default is `WinAPI`, which corresponds to `__stdcall` for the 32-bit Intel-based platforms.
PreserveSig	Indicates that the managed method signature should not be transformed into an unmanaged signature that returns an `HRESULT`, and might have an additional `[out, retval]` argument for the return value. The default is `True` (the signature should not be transformed).
SetLastError	Enables the caller to use the `Marshal.GetLastWin32Error` API function to determine whether an error occurred while executing the method. In Visual Basic, the default is `True`; in C# and C++, the default is `False`.

Calling DLL functions from C# is similar to calling them from Visual Basic 6. With the `DLLImport` attribute, however, you are simply passing the DLL's name and the method that you need to call.

Note   It is recommended that your DLL function calls be grouped in separate classes. This simplifies coding, isolates the external function calls, and reduces overhead.

Summary

This chapter described how to use COM objects in .NET code and how to use the Tlbimp utility to generate .NET assemblies. You also took a brief look at how to interpret generated assemblies. In addition, you learned how to write COM client code in C#, including calling COM methods and working with COM properties. As you can see, the .NET Framework enables you to easily integrate existing COM code into your .NET applications. This easy integration gives you the opportunity to slowly move portions of an application to .NET, without having to rewrite all of the COM component logic in C#.

✦   ✦   ✦

Working with COM+ Services

Microsoft has steadily enhanced the functionality of
the COM subsystem since it was first released in
1993. One of the most significant enhancements to the COM
programming model was introduced in 1997 with the release
of Microsoft Transaction Server (MTS). MTS, first released as
an add-on to Windows NT 4.0, enabled developers to develop
components using an object broker that provided transaction,
role-based security, and resource pooling services.

With the release of Windows 2000, Microsoft elevated the
programming model offered by MTS to a first-class subsystem. COM+ is, in large part, a merging of the traditional COM
programming model and the MTS programming model. For
the first time, Windows provided support for both traditional
COM (or unconfigured) components with attributed (or configured) MTS-style components directly from the operating
system.

The .NET Framework offers both styles of components to
developers writing component-based software. This chapter
examines how to develop C# classes that you can use as configured components with COM+.

Caution Although the .NET Framework is available on a variety of
operating system platforms, COM+ is not available on the
same set of platforms. Components written in C# that take
advantage of COM+ services can only be used on platforms that support COM+. The COM+ class code built into
the .NET Framework throws an exception of class
`PlatformNotSupported` if your code attempts to access
a feature that does not exist on the runtime platform.

Understanding the System.EnterpriseServices Namespace

Any C# class can be used by COM clients as a COM component, regardless of the class's inheritance tree. C# classes can be derived from nothing more than `System.Object` and still be used as COM components. Taking advantage of COM+ services within your C# classes, however, requires a more stringent inheritance policy.

The `System.EnterpriseServices` namespace provides the classes, enumerations, structures, delegates, and interfaces that you need to write applications that take advantage of COM+ and its enterprise-level services. If you have written components in C++ or Visual Basic 6 that ended up running inside of the COM+ Services Runtime, most of this chapter will seem familiar to you. From the standpoint of an experienced COM+ developer, the `System.EnterpriseServices` namespace wraps the functionality to which you previously had programmatic access. If you have written components in VB6, then you will be happy to see that previously unavailable features, such as object pooling, are now fully available to you through the Framework. Services, such as just-in-time (JIT) activation, object pooling, transaction processing, and shared property management, are all available as classes or attributes in the `System.EnterpriseServices` namespace.

Table 35-1 describes each of the classes available in the `System.EnterpriseServices` namespace.

Table 35-1	
System.EnterpriseServices Classes	
Class	*Description*
ApplicationAccessControlAttribute	Enables security configuration for the library or server application housing the application. This class cannot be inherited.
ApplicationActivationAttribute	Specifies whether components in the assembly run in the creator's process or in a system process.
ApplicationIDAttribute	Specifies the application ID (as a GUID) for this assembly. This class cannot be inherited.
ApplicationNameAttribute	Specifies the name of the COM+ application to be used for the install of the components in the assembly. This class cannot be inherited.
ApplicationQueuingAttribute	Enables queuing support for the marked assembly and enables the application to read method calls from Message Queuing queues. This class cannot be inherited.

Class	Description
AutoCompleteAttribute	Marks the attributed method as an `AutoComplete` object. This class cannot be inherited.
BYOT	Wraps the COM+ `ByotServerEx` class and the COM+ DTC interfaces `ICreateWithTransactionEx` and `ICreateWithTipTransactionEx`. This class cannot be inherited.
ComponentAccessControlAttribute	Enables security checking on calls to a component. This class cannot be inherited.
COMTIIntrinsicsAttribute	Enables you to pass context properties from the COM Transaction Integrator (COMTI) into the COM+ context.
ConstructionEnabledAttribute	Enables COM+ object construction support. This class cannot be inherited.
ContextUtil	Obtains information about the COM+ object context. This class cannot be inherited.
DescriptionAttribute	Sets the description on an assembly (application), component, method, or interface. This class cannot be inherited.
EventClassAttribute	Marks the attributed class as an event class. This class cannot be inherited.
EventTrackingEnabledAttribute	Enables event tracking for a component. This class cannot be inherited.
ExceptionClassAttribute	Sets the queuing exception class for the queued class. This class cannot be inherited.
IISIntrinsicsAttribute	Enables access to ASP intrinsic values from `ContextUtil.GetNamedProperty`. This class cannot be inherited.
InterfaceQueuingAttribute	Enables queuing support for the marked interface. This class cannot be inherited.
JustInTimeActivationAttribute	Turns just-in-time (JIT) activation on or off. This class cannot be inherited.
LoadBalancingSupportedAttribute	Determines whether the component participates in load balancing, if the component load balancing service is installed and enabled on the server.

Continued

Table 35-1 *(continued)*

Class	Description
MustRunInClientContextAttribute	Forces the attributed object to be created in the context of the creator, if possible. This class cannot be inherited.
ObjectPoolingAttribute	Enables and configures object pooling for a component. This class cannot be inherited.
PrivateComponentAttribute	Identifies a component as a private component that is only seen and activated by components in the same application. This class cannot be inherited.
RegistrationErrorInfo	Retrieves extended error information about methods related to multiple COM+ objects. This also includes methods that install, import, and export COM+ applications and components. This class cannot be inherited.
RegistrationException	The exception that is thrown when a registration error is detected.
RegistrationHelper	Installs and configures assemblies in the COM+ catalog. This class cannot be inherited.
ResourcePool	Stores objects in the current transaction. This class cannot be inherited.
SecureMethodAttribute	Ensures that the infrastructure calls through an interface for a method or for each method in a class when using the security service. Classes need to use interfaces to use security services. This class cannot be inherited.
SecurityCallContext	Describes the chain of callers leading up to the current method call.
SecurityCallers	Provides an ordered collection of identities in the current call chain.
SecurityIdentity	Contains information regarding an identity in a COM+ call chain.
SecurityRoleAttribute	Configures a role for an application or component. This class cannot be inherited.
ServicedComponent	Represents the base class of all classes using COM+ services.

Class	Description
ServicedComponentException	The exception that is thrown when an error is detected in a serviced component.
SharedProperty	Accesses a shared property. This class cannot be inherited.
SharedPropertyGroup	Represents a collection of shared properties. This class cannot be inherited.
SharedPropertyGroupManager	Controls access to shared property groups. This class cannot be inherited.
SynchronizationAttribute	Sets the synchronization value of the component. This class cannot be inherited.
TransactionAttribute	Specifies the type of transaction that is available to the attributed object. Permissible values are members of the `TransactionOption` enumeration.

If you plan to write classes that run inside of COM+ services, you will be writing what is known as *serviced components*. Serviced components take advantage of the features in the `System.EnterpriseServices` namespace, and enable you to use the available enterprise features of COM+.

Understanding the ServicedComponent Class

Any class designed to take advantage of COM+ services must be derived directly from `ServicedComponent` or from a class that has `ServicedComponent` somewhere in its inheritance tree. All of the COM+ services that you use are available through setting attributes on classes that are derived from the `ServicedComponent` class.

The `ServicedComponent` class does not support any properties; however, it does support a series of public methods that can be called by class clients. Most of these methods, including `Activate()`, `Deactivate()`, and `CanBePooled()`, map to methods defined by COM+ interfaces. such as `IObjectControl`. These methods are virtual and can be overridden by derived classes to provide specific functionality.

Listing 35-1 shows a simple COM+ class written in C#. This object participates in COM+ object pooling.

Listing 35-1: **Poolable COM+ Component in C#**

```csharp
using System.EnterpriseServices;

[ObjectPooling(5, 10)]
public class PooledClass : ServicedComponent
{
    public PooledClass()
    {
    }

    ~PooledClass()
    {
    }

    public override bool CanBePooled()
    {
        return  true;
    }

    public override void Activate()
    {
    }

    public override void Deactivate()
    {
    }
}
```

The class in Listing 35-1 uses a .NET Framework attribute called ObjectPooling to mark the PooledClass class as one that should be poolable in COM+. The ObjectPooling attribute supports several constructors. Listing 35-1 uses the constructor that accepts two integers representing the minimum and maximum pool size. The code uses values of 5 and 10, which instructs COM+ to support a minimum of five and a maximum of ten objects of this class in the COM+ object pool.

COM+ components written in C# that want to participate in COM+ object pooling must override the virtual CanBePooled() method found in the ServicedComponent base class, and must return True. A return value of False signifies that the component does not want to participate in object pooling.

Your poolable COM+ components can also override virtual ServicedComponent methods called Activate() and Deactivate(). The Activate() method is called when the object is removed from the object pool and assigned to a client, and the Deactivate() method is called when the object is released by a client and returned to the pool. You should follow the guidelines set forth by standard COM+

development and place all significant object state construction and destruction code in the `Activate()` and `Deactivate()` methods. The constructor and destructor for your class are called, but they are called only once. The constructor is called only when COM+ creates instances of your object for placement into the COM+ object pool, and the destructor is called only when COM+ destroys your object after removing it from the pool. The `Activate()` method differs from your constructor in that it is called every time the instance is assigned to a COM+ client. The `Deactivate()` method differs from your destructor in that it is called every time the instance is released from a COM+ client and returned to the COM+ object pool. If you have any code that needs to perform any initialization whenever a new client is assigned use of the object, place the code in `Activate()`, rather than in your class constructor. Likewise, if you have any code that needs to perform any uninitialization whenever a new client releases the object, place the code in `Deactivate()`, rather than in your class destructor.

Registering Classes with COM+

Your C# classes that are designed for use in a COM+ application must follow the same basic rules as C# classes that are designed for use by classic COM clients. Chapter 34 describes how C# is used to build COM components. Like COM components written in C#, COM+ components written in C# must be compiled into a DLL-based assembly, and must have a strong name (which requires that the assembly have a public-key pair and version information). Like COM components, this information can be specified for COM+ components through attributes specified in your C# source code.

You can install your classes into a COM+ application using a command-line tool called regsvcs that ships with the .NET Framework. This command-line tool registers all public classes found in a DLL-based assembly with COM+, and performs all the registration necessary to make the classes visible as COM+ classes.

Listing 35-2 is a slight modification to Listing 35-1. It contains the attributes necessary to prepare the generated assembly to support a strong name.

Listing 35-2: **Poolable COM+ Object with Strong Name Attributes**

```
using System.Reflection;
using System.EnterpriseServices;

[assembly:AssemblyKeyFile("keyfile.snk")]
[assembly:AssemblyVersion("1.0.*")]
```

Continued

Listing 35-2 *(continued)*

```
[ObjectPooling(5, 10)]
public class PooledClass : ServicedComponent
{
    public PooledClass()
    {
    }

    ~PooledClass()
    {
    }

    public override bool CanBePooled()
    {
        return  true;
    }

    public override void Activate()
    {
    }

    public override void Deactivate()
    {
    }
}
```

You can expose this class as a COM+ class with just a few command-line tools. First, generate a new key pair for the strong name of the assembly with the standard sn command-line tool:

```
sn -k keyfile.snk
```

Then compile the code into a DLL-based assembly:

```
csc /target:library Listing35-2.cs
```

After the assembly is generated, you can use the regsvcs tool to register the assembly with COM+:

```
regsvcs /appname:Listing28-2App Listing35-2.dll
```

Tip   The .NET/COM+ interop infrastructure supports COM+ applications based on assemblies in the global assembly cache. If multiple clients use your code, you might want to install your assembly in the global assembly cache before registering it with COM+.

The /appname argument to the regsvcs tool specifies the COM+ application name created to house the public classes found in the assembly. If a COM+ application already exists with the given name when regsvcs runs, the classes are added to the preexisting application.

Figure 35-1 shows the COM+ Explorer running with the assembly generated from the code in Listing 35-2 registered with COM+. The PooledClass is automatically detected by the registration process and added to the COM+ application.

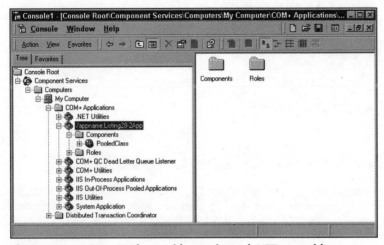

Figure 35-1: COM+ Explorer with a registered .NET assembly

Launch the COM+ Explorer by performing the following steps:

1. Click the Windows Explorer Start button. The Start menu appears.

2. Choose Programs ⇨ Administrative Tools. The icons for applications in the Administrative Tools program group appear.

3. Select Component Services. The COM+ Explorer appears.

Figure 35-2 shows the COM+ property sheet for the PooledClass class. Note that the object pooling information specified in the attributes in Listing 35-2 are automatically detected by the registration process and added to the COM+ application.

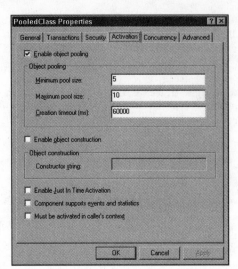

Figure 35-2: COM+ class property page with object pooling information

Using Attributes for COM+ Classes

The object pooling attribute used in Listing 35-2 is but one of many .NET attributes you can use in your C# classes. The .NET Framework supports several attributes that you can use to configure COM+ settings for your C# classes. All COM+-related .NET attributes are found in the `System.EnterpriseServices` namespace. The following sections describe some of the other interesting COM+ service attributes.

Note For COM+ attributes in the `System.EnterpriseServices` namespace, an unconfigured default value refers to the value that COM+ assigns to the attribute when the attribute is omitted from your code. A configured default value refers to the value assigned to the attribute if you assign the attribute but omit a value for it.

ApplicationAccessControl

The `ApplicationAccessControl` attribute specifies whether security can be configured for an assembly. This attribute accepts a Boolean argument and must be `True` if security configuration is allowed, and `False` otherwise. The unconfigured default value is `False`, whereas the configured default value is `True`.

ApplicationActivation

The ApplicationActivation attribute is an assembly-level attribute that specifies whether the class should be added to a library or a server COM+ application. The attribute takes a parameter of a type of enumeration called ActivationOption. The ActivationOption enumeration supports the following values:

✦ Library, which specifies a COM+ library application

✦ Server, which specifies a COM+ server application

The unconfigured default value is Library.

ApplicationID

The ApplicationID attribute can be used to specify the GUID to be assigned to the COM+ application created to hold the COM+ class. The GUID is specified using its string representation, which is supplied to the attribute's constructor.

The ApplicationID attribute must be applied at the assembly level, as in the following code snippet:

```
[assembly:ApplicationID("{E3868E19-486E-9F13-FC8443113731}")]
public class MyClass
{
}
```

The attribute takes a string as a parameter that describes the application's GUID.

ApplicationName

You use the ApplicationName attribute to specify the name to be assigned to the COM+ application created to hold the COM+ class. You supply the name to the attribute's constructor. If you specify this attribute in your code, you will not need the /appname argument to the regsvcs command-line tool.

The ApplicationName attribute must be applied at the assembly level, as in the following code snippet:

```
[assembly:ApplicationName("MyName")]
public class MyClass
{
}
```

The attribute takes a string as a parameter that describes the application name, and the default value is the assembly name for an unconfigured default value.

ApplicationQueuing

You use the ApplicationQueuing attribute to specify that the class should be configured as a COM+ queued component. The attribute does not accept any parameters.

The ApplicationQueuing attribute must be applied at the assembly level, as in the following code snippet:

```
[assembly:ApplicationQueuing]
public class MyClass
{
}
```

The attribute does not accept any parameters.

AutoComplete

The AutoComplete attribute can be applied to methods in a COM+ class. Calls to methods marked as AutoComplete methods are automatically followed by a call to SetComplete() by the .NET Framework if the method call is made within the scope of a transaction and the method call completes normally. You do not need to make an explicit call to SetComplete() for AutoComplete methods. If an AutoComplete() method throws an exception, SetAbort() is called and the transaction is rolled back.

The AutoComplete attribute must be applied at the method level, as in the following code snippet:

```
public class MyClass
{
    [AutoComplete]
    public MyMethod()
    {
    }
}
```

The AutoComplete attribute does not accept any parameters. False is the default for the unconfigured default value, and True is the configured default value.

ComponentAccessControl

The ComponentAccessControl attribute enables or disables security checking on calls to class instances. The attribute accepts a Boolean as a parameter, which should be True if call-level security checking should be enabled, or False otherwise.

The `ComponentAccessControl` attribute must be applied at the class level, as in the following code snippet:

```
[ComponentAccessControl]
public class MyClass
{
}
```

The `ComponentAccessControl` attribute does not accept any parameters. `False` is the default for the unconfigured default value, and `True` is the configured default value.

ConstructionEnabled

The `ConstructionEnabled` attribute enables COM+ object construction. The COM+ object construction mechanism enables a string to be passed as a constructor string to instantiated object instances. The attribute does not specify the string; instead, it merely enables the COM+ object construction support. The attribute accepts a Boolean as a parameter, which should be `True` if COM+ object construction should be enabled for the class, and `False` otherwise. C# classes that support object construction must implement the `IObjectConstruct` interface. The interface's `Construct()` method is called by COM+ to pass the constructor string to the object.

The `ConstructionEnabled` attribute must be applied at the class level, as in the following code snippet:

```
[ConstructionEnabled]
public class MyClass
{
}
```

The `ConstructionEnabled` attribute does not accept any parameters. `False` is the default for the unconfigured default value, and `True` is the configured default value.

JustInTimeActivation

The `JustInTimeActivation` attribute enables or disables just-in-time (JIT) activation for a class. The attribute accepts a Boolean as a parameter, which should be `True` if JIT activation should be enabled for the class, and `False` otherwise. JIT activation must always be enabled for objects that participate in transactions.

The `JustInTimeActivation` attribute must be applied at the class level, as in the following code snippet:

```
[JustInTimeActivation]
public class MyClass
{
}
```

The `JustInTimeActivation` attribute does not accept any parameters. `False` is the default for the unconfigured default value, and `True` is the configured default value.

LoadBalancingSupported

The `LoadBalancingSupported` attribute enables or disables load-balancing support for a class. The attribute accepts a Boolean as a parameter, which should be `True` if load-balancing support should be enabled for the class, and `False` otherwise.

The `LoadBalancingSupported` attribute must be applied at the class level, as in the following code snippet:

```
[LoadBalancingSupported]
public class MyClass
{
}
```

The `LoadBalancingSupported` attribute does not accept any parameters. `False` is the default for the unconfigured default value, and `True` is the configured default value.

SecurityRole

The `SecurityRole` attribute specifies a security role. This attribute can be applied to a class, a method, or an entire assembly. The constructor takes a string as an argument, and the string must specify the name of the role that callers should be a member of, as shown in the following code snippet:

```
[assembly:SecurityRole("MySecurityRole")]
public class MyClass
{
}
```

Processing Transactions

Transaction support in COM+ was one of the biggest driving forces that led to its popularity. With transaction support, you can write code that performs more that one task, but the application sees it as a single unit of work, such as updating a table in one database and deleting a record in another table in a completely different database. With transactions, you can guarantee that an all-or-nothing model applies to such scenarios. If the delete fails in the second database, the update in the first database is rolled back also.

Without transactions, data would be mismatched, and you could not write enterprise-level applications. One of the first sample applications using transaction support that Microsoft published was called ExAir. ExAir is a fictional airline company. The basic concept behind the application is a ticket agent taking reservations for flights. When a customer requests a flight, he or she must also request a type of meal, such as meat, vegetarian, or pasta. The food portion of the application attempts to insert the data into a database other than the airline seating chart database. The different database represents a distributed transaction to another company, the food supplier. If the first method contains code that inserts the ticket request into the airline's database, and a second method contains code that attempts to insert data into the food supplier's database, what would happen if the food supplier's database were down? The original information containing the flight details would be inserted into the airline's database, but when the customers showed up for the flight, they would not have a meal, because the second part of the transaction did not succeed. Clearly, this is not a desirable scenario for an enterprise application. If the food supplier is down, the ticket should not be inserted into the airline's database. This dilemma can easily be handled by wrapping the two method calls into a transaction.

Note   In the ExAir example, it is not in the airline's best interests to not book a ticket just because the link to the food supplier database is down. In this situation, the solution would be to use something like Queued Components or Microsoft Message Queue. With Message Queue services, which are located in the `System.Messaging` namespace, you can guarantee eventual delivery of the food request by sending it to a message queue instead of attempting to immediately write the data to the remote database. With this type of architecture, the application can always accept the orders for tickets, and the food supplier can simply pull messages out of the message queue when they are ready to process the food orders.

Understanding ACID properties

For transactions to work, they must conform to the ACID properties. ACID is an acronym for atomicity, consistency, isolation and durability. Table 35-2 describes the definitions for the ACID properties.

Table 35-2 ACID Properties	
Property	**Description**
Atomicity	All work is atomic, or occurs as a single unit of work.
Consistency	All data that is used in the transaction is left in a consistent state.
Isolation	Each transaction is isolated from other transactions, enabling transactions to overwrite the data in other processes, preserving consistency.
Durability	After the transaction has committed, all data must be in a durable store, such as a database. If the transaction fails, all data used in the transaction must be rolled back. Durability guarantees that the data survives unnatural events, such as power outages or hurricanes.

Writing transactional components

The `Transaction` attribute specifies a transaction support level that should be available for this object. The attribute accepts as a parameter a value from an enumeration in the `System.EnterpriseServices` namespace called `TransactionOption`, which supports any of the following values:

✦ `Disabled`, which specifies that the object should ignore any transaction in the current context

✦ `NotSupported`, which specifies that the object should create the component in a context with no governing transaction

✦ `Required`, which specifies that the object should share a transaction if one exists, or create a new transaction if necessary

✦ `RequiresNew`, which specifies that the object should create the component with a new transaction, regardless of the state of the current context

✦ `Supported`, which specifies that the object should share a transaction if one exists

The `Transaction` attribute must be applied at the class level, as in the following code snippet:

```
[Transaction(TransactionOption.Supported)]
public class MyClass
{
}
```

The attribute accepts a single parameter naming a value from the `Transaction-Option` enumeration and describing the transaction level that the class design supports. The attribute can also be used without parameters, as in the following code snippet:

```
[Transaction]
public class MyClass
{
}
```

Specifying the `Transaction` attribute without specifying a parameter sets the class's transaction support level to `Required`.

Listing 35-3 shows the complete code for the ExAir scenario. There are two methods, each accessing different resources; and because they are wrapped in a transaction, you are guaranteed the following: the processing of the order occurs as a single unit of work; the process is isolated from other orders that may be occurring; the order data is left in a consistent state; and once the order commits, it is in a durable data store.

Listing 35-3: **Transactional Database Example**

```
namespace TransactionSupport
{

using System;
using System.Data.SqlClient;
using System.EnterpriseServices;

    [Transaction(TransactionOption.Required)]
    public class ExAirMain : ServicedComponent
    {
public void Process()
{
    /* call methods to add Food info and Ticket info */

    AddFood process1 = new AddFood();
    AddAirline process2 = new AddAirline();
    process1.Add();
    process2.Add();

}
    }

    [Transaction(TransactionOption.Supported)]
    [AutoComplete]
    public class AddFood : ServicedComponent
    {
public void Add()
{
SQLConnection cnn = new
              SQLConnection("FoodSupplierConnection");
    SQLCommand cmd = new SQLCommand();
    cnn.Open();
    cmd.ActiveConnection = cnn;
    cmd.CommandText = ""; // Insert statement to DB
    cmd.ExecuteNonQuery();
    cnn.Close();
}
    }

    [Transaction(TransactionOption.Supported)]
    [AutoComplete]
    public class AddAirline : ServicedComponent
    {
public void Add()
    {
SQLConnection cnn = new
SQLConnection("AirlineConnection");
```

Continued

Listing 35-3 *(continued)*

```
SQLCommand cmd = new SQLCommand();
cnn.Open();
cmd.ActiveConnection = cnn;
cmd.CommandText = "" // Insert statement to DB
cmd.ExecuteNonQuery();
cnn.Close();
    }
        }
}
```

Accessing Object Context

The `System.EnterpriseServices` namespace includes a class called `ContextUtil`, which can be used by C# classes to access an object's COM+ runtime context. In Visual Basic 6, you accessed the object context of the current component through the `ObjectContext` object, as the following code demonstrates:

```
Dim ctx as ObjectContext
ctx = GetObjectContext
```

The `ContextUtil` class contains several properties and methods that give callers access to COM+ context state information. All of the methods and properties in the class are static, which means that you can access the members directly from the `ContextUtil` class without creating an object of the class. Table 35-3 describes the properties of the `ContextUtil` class, and Table 35-4 describes the methods of the `ContextUtil` class.

The code in Listing 35-4 implements a transactional COM+ component that implements a public method called `DoWork()`. The `DoWork()` method checks the `IsCallerInRole()` property to determine the caller's COM+ role. If the caller's role is the `ClientRole` role, then the object's transaction is committed with a call to `SetComplete()`. If the caller's role is a role other than the `ClientRole` role, then the object's transaction is rolled back with a call to `SetAbort()`.

Table 35-3
ContextUtil Class Properties

Property	Description
ActivityId	Gets a GUID representing the activity containing the component
ApplicationId	Gets a GUID for the current application
ApplicationInstanceId	Gets a GUID for the current application instance
ContextId	Gets a GUID for the current context
DeactivateOnReturn	Gets or sets the done bit in the COM+ context
IsInTransaction	Gets a value indicating whether the current context is transactional
IsSecurityEnabled	Gets a value indicating whether role-based security is active in the current context
MyTransactionVote	Gets or sets the consistent bit in the COM+ context
PartitionId	Gets a GUID for the current partition
Transaction	Gets an object describing the current COM+ DTC transaction
TransactionId	Gets the GUID of the current COM+ DTC transaction

Table 35-4
ContextUtil Class Properties

Property	Description
DisableCommit	Sets both the consistent bit and the done bit to `False` in the COM+ context
EnableCommit	Sets the consistent bit to `True` and the done bit to `False` in the COM+ context
GetNamedProperty	Returns a named property from the COM+ context
IsCallerInRole	Determines whether the caller is in the specified role
SetAbort	Sets the consistent bit to `False` and the done bit to `True` in the COM+ context
SetComplete	Sets the consistent bit and the done bit to `True` in the COM+ context

Listing 35-4: Accessing COM+ Context Through the ContextUtil Class

```
using System.Reflection;
using System.EnterpriseServices;

[assembly:AssemblyKeyFile("keyfile.snk")]
[assembly:AssemblyVersion("1.0.*")]

[ObjectPooling(5, 10)]
[Transaction(TransactionOption.Required)]
[SecurityRole("ClientRole")]

public class PooledClass : ServicedComponent
{
    public PooledClass()
    {
    }

    ~PooledClass()
    {
    }

    public override bool CanBePooled()
    {
        return  true;
    }

    public override void Activate()
    {
    }

    public override void Deactivate()
    {
    }

    public void DoWork()
    {
        bool IsInRole;

        IsInRole = ContextUtil.IsCallerInRole("ClientRole");
        if(IsInRole ==  true)
            ContextUtil.SetComplete();
        else
            ContextUtil.SetAbort();
    }
}
```

Summary

Exposing your C# class as a COM+ application takes very little effort and is certainly easier than implementing the same functionality using earlier versions of Visual Studio 6.0. COM+ applications written using Visual C++ 6.0 needed much more code to complete the same tasks, and some COM+ features (such as object pooling) were not even available to COM+ components written in Visual Basic 6.0.

Developing COM+ components using C# involves only four simple concepts:

✦ Derive your class from `ServicedComponent`

✦ Add attributes to describe your application's settings

✦ Use the `regsvcs` tool to build a COM+ application for your public classes

✦ Call methods and properties on the `ContextUtil` class to access the COM+ context at runtime.

Microsoft dropped hints about this COM+ programming model as far back as 1997. Back then, they described a model based on attributed programming, in which COM components could be described with attributes and the runtime would take over details such as class factories and `IUnknown`-style reference counting. It is now clear that the .NET model of COM+ component development is the fulfillment of that original vision.

✦   ✦   ✦

Working with .NET Remoting

The .NET Framework provides several mechanisms that enable you to write applications that do not exist in the same application domain, server process, or machine. Based on the requirements of your application, such as the capability of non-.NET servers to access your data, you can choose any of the different types of object communication methods. In this chapter, you learn about .NET remoting. Using remoting, you can marshal objects and method calls across process boundaries and effectively pass data between applications.

In earlier chapters, you learned that ASP.NET and XML Web services were also excellent ways to pass objects and data between process boundaries, but depending on your application infrastructure, those services may not be the best option available. Remoting fills in any of the gaps that were left open by these services. In this chapter, you learn how to implement remoting, how to create the client and server objects in a remoting framework, and how to effectively pass data using remoting across process boundaries.

Introducing Remoting

.NET remoting enables applications to communicate between objects that reside on different servers, different processes, or different application domains. Before the .NET Framework was introduced, you could pass objects across process boundaries by using distributed COM, or DCOM. DCOM worked well, but it had limitations, such as the types of data that could be passed, and security context passed between the client caller and server activation. Moreover, it was based on COM, which meant that although you could communicate across machine boundaries, all machines had to be running a Microsoft operating system. This isn't a critical limitation, but it limited your options regarding what you could do with your existing infrastructure. In .NET, remoting takes care of these issues, and expands upon what DCOM offered as a viable method to remotely communicate between objects.

With remoting, you implement a server, or host application, and a client application. On the host or client, the application can be any of the .NET application templates that are available, including console applications, Windows services applications, ASP.NET applications, WindowsForms applications, and IIS applications. On the host, you programmatically configure — or use a configuration file to specify — the type of activation that will be allowed by clients. Clients can use one of several types of activation methods, including `Singleton` and `SingleCall`, which is covered in the section "Activating the Remote Object," later in this chapter. It is at this point that you specify the channel and the port over which the object communicates, and the format the data will have when it is passed between host and client. You learn how channels and ports are implemented a little bit later. The format of the data is important, based on the system design; you can use binary data, SOAP, or a custom format to marshal the data. After you specify the channel, port, and format, based on the type of remoting host you are exposing, you need to determine how to expose the metadata to the clients. You can do this in several ways, such as by allowing the caller to download the assembly, or by making the source available to the caller. Either way, the client needs to know what object it is creating, so the metadata in some form needs to be made available to the caller. After the host is properly built and configured, you then write the client. On the client, all you need to do is create an instance of the object on the specified channel and port that is expecting requests on the server. You accomplish this programmatically or through a configuration file. At this point, the method calls are no different from any other object that you consume from a .NET application. After you create objects, you call methods, set and retrieve properties, and fire off events just as you would with an object that is not using the remoting framework.

This may seem like a lot of steps, but it is actually very simple after you have done it once. You can break down the overall process into the following broader tasks, which are illustrated in Figure 36-1.

1. Specify the channels and ports that marshal objects between the host and the client.

2. Use formatters (which you will learn about later in the chapter) to specify the format in which the data is serialized and deserialized in between the host and the client.

3. Determine how the host objects are activated and how long the activation lasts.

In the following sections, you learn how to create the host application in a remoting scenario, including the specifics of formatters, channels, and ports, and how the host will be activated. After the host is built, you learn how to consume the remote object from a client application.

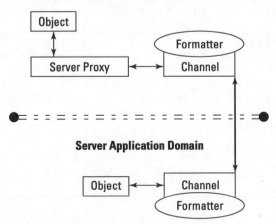

Client Application Domain

Server Application Domain

Figure 36-1: .NET remoting overview

Creating a Remoting Host Assembly

To begin your remoting application, you need to create an assembly containing the actual method calls that the host application will use. Once you have created the assembly, you then create the host application that accepts client requests for the methods in the assembly. In the following steps, you build the assembly that implements the methods to be called:

1. Create a new C# Class Library application and call it HostObject. For simplicity, I have created a directory on my C drive called cSharpRemoting, and have added three subfolders named Host, HostObject, and Client. You might see where we are going with this. The HostObject Class Library application should be created in the cSharpRemoting\HostObject directory. This makes is easier for you to run the console applications you create later.

2. After you create the HostObject class library application, you add a public method that accepts a parameter, called customerID, and returns the name of the customer from the Northwind database from SQL Server based on the customerID passed in. Your completed class for the HostObject application should look something like the one shown in Listing 36-1.

Listing 36-1: **Creating the Host Object Application**

```csharp
using System;
using System.Data;
using System.Data.SqlClient;

namespace HostObject
{
  public class Class1: MarshalByRefObject
  {
      public string thisCustomer;

      public Class1()
      {
       Console.WriteLine("HostObject has been activated");
      }

      public string  ReturnName(string customerID)
      {
        // Create connection, command object to SQL

        string cnStr = "Initial Catalog=Northwind;Data" +
          "Source=localhost;Integrated Security=SSPI;";

          SqlConnection cn = new SqlConnection(cnStr);

          string strSQL =
        ("Select CompanyName from Customers " +
        " where CustomerID = '" + customerID + "'");

        SqlCommand cmd = cn.CreateCommand();

        cmd.CommandText = strSQL;

        cn.Open();

        SqlDataReader rdr = cmd.ExecuteReader
          (CommandBehavior.CloseConnection);

    while (rdr.Read())
    {
       thisCustomer =  rdr.GetString(0);
    }

    Console.WriteLine(thisCustomer +
  " was returned to the client");

        return thisCustomer;
      }
    }
}
```

The preceding code performs a simple query to SQL Server to grab the CompanyName field in the Customers database based on the parameter customerID, which is passed into the method. As you can see, this code is no different from any other class library that you would create in C#. The next step is to create the host application that services the client requests for this class library.

Creating the Remoting Server

To create the application that will host the HostObject assembly, which is where you actually start to use some of the remoting features created in Listing 36-1, you need to create a console application called Host in the C:\cSharpRemoting\Host directory. This host application is the actual remoting server that uses the features of the System.Runtime.Remoting namespace.

Before you start any coding, several key features of remoting need to be described. The namespace that contains the remoting functionality is the System.Runtime. Remoting namespace, whose classes are described in Table 36-1. Although you do not use all of these classes when writing remoting applications, several of the classes are extremely important to inplementing a remoting infrastrucure; namely, the ObjRef class, RemotingConfiguration class, the RemotingServices class, and the WellKnownObjectMode enumeration. You learn more about each of these in detail later in this section as you write the code for your host application.

Table 36-1
System.Runtime.Remoting Classes

Class	Description
ActivatedClientTypeEntry	Holds values for an object type registered on the client end as a type that can be activated on the server
ActivatedServiceTypeEntry	Holds values for an object type registered on the service end as one that can be activated on request from a client
ObjectHandle	Wraps marshal by value object references, enabling them to be returned through an indirection
ObjRef	Stores all relevant information required to generate a proxy to communicate with a remote object
RemotingConfiguration	Provides various static methods for configuring the remoting infrastructure
RemotingException	The exception that is thrown when something has gone wrong during remoting

Continued

	Table 36-1 *(continued)*	
Class	*Description*	
RemotingServices	Provides several methods for using and publishing remoted objects and proxies. This class cannot be inherited	
RemotingTimeoutException	The exception that is thrown when the server or the client cannot be reached for a previously specified period of time	
ServerException	The exception that is thrown to communicate errors to the client when the client connects to non-.NET Framework applications that cannot throw exceptions	
SoapServices	Provides several methods for using and publishing remoted objects in SOAP format	
TypeEntry	Implements a base class that holds the configuration information used to activate an instance of a remote type	
WellKnownClientTypeEntry	Holds values for an object type registered on the client as a well-known type object (single call or singleton)	
WellKnownServiceTypeEntry	Holds values for an object type registered on the service end as a well-known type object (single call or singleton)	

To begin writing the host application, you need to understand what the remoting infrastructure needs to operate. To refresh your memory regarding the steps you need to take to create the host application, review the following three steps outlined earlier in the chapter:

1. Specify the channels and ports that marshal objects between the host and the client.

2. Use formatters to specify the format in which the data is serialized and deserialized in between the host and the client.

3. Determine how the host objects are activated, and how long the activation lasts.

The following sections examine each one of these steps.

Specifying channels and ports

In the remoting infrastructure, channels handle the transporting of messages, or data, between the client and the server objects. Recall what is actually happening when you are remoting objects: You are crossing a boundary, such as an application domain, a server process, or a physical machine. The specific channel that you provide handles all of the underlying details of getting the data to and from the remote objects; you simply specify a channel type and all of the dirty work is done for you. The System.Runtime.Remoting.Channels class provides the implementations for creating the channels that are used in your remoting host. When you register a channel in your application, you must make sure that it is registered before you attempt to access the remote objects. Failing to correctly register your channels causes an error. If another application is listening on a channel that you are attempting to listen on, an error occurs and your host application fails to load. You need to know which channels are being used, and which channel your application needs to use, based on what the client is calling on. After you declare an instance of the channel type that you are going to use, you call the RegisterChannel() method of the ChannelServices class, which registers the channel for use. Table 36-2 describes the methods of the ChannelServices class that are available to you.

Table 36-2
ChannelServices Class Methods

Method	Description
AsyncDispatchMessage	Asynchronously dispatches the given message to the server-side chain(s) based on the URI embedded in the message
CreateServerChannelSinkChain	Creates a channel sink chain for the specified channel
DispatchMessage	Dispatches incoming remote calls
GetChannel	Returns a registered channel with the specified name
GetChannelSinkProperties	Returns an IDictionary of properties for a given proxy
GetUrlsForObject	Returns an array of all the URLs that can be used to reach the specified object
RegisterChannel	Registers a channel with the channel services
SyncDispatchMessage	Synchronously dispatches the incoming message to the server-side chain(s) based on the URI embedded in the message
UnregisterChannel	Unregisters a particular channel from the registered channels list

Not listed in this table is a property in the ChannelServices class called RegisteredChannels, which sets or gets the registered channels in the current object instance.

The following code snippet creates and registers a TCP and HTTP channel on specific ports using the RegisterChannel method of the ChannelServices class:

```
TcpChannel chan1 = new TcpChannel(8085);
ChannelServices.RegisterChannel(chan1);

HttpChannel chan2 = new HttpChannel(8086);
ChannelServices.RegisterChannel(chan2);
```

When you create a channel, you also specify a type of formatter for the channel. The following sections describe the formatter types available.

Specifying a channel format

At the same time that you create a channel, you also specify a format for the type of channel that you have picked. Two default formatter types are available in the System.Runtime.Remoting.Channels namespace: the TCP channel and the HTTP channel.

System.Runtime.Remoting.Channels.Tcp Namespace

The System.Runtime.Remoting.Channels.Tcp namespace contains channels that use the TCP protocol to transport data between remote objects. The default encoding for the TCP is binary encoding, which makes this an efficient way to pass data between remote objects. Binary data always has a smaller footprint than the equivalent XML data passed through SOAP on an HTTP channel. The downside to using the TCP protocol is that it is a proprietary format, so it only works on systems that understand this formatting type. To make your remote object more accessible, you should use the HTTP channel for encoding, as it will be passing data down the wire in the SOAP protocol. Table 36-3 summarizes the available classes in the System.Runtime.Remoting.Channels.Tcp namespace.

Table 36-3
System.Runtime.Remoting.Channels.Tcp Namespace

Class	Description
TcpChannel	Provides an implementation for a sender-receiver channel that uses the TCP protocol to transmit messages. This class is a combination of the TcpClientChannel class and the TcpServerChannel class, which enables automatic two-way communication over TCP.
TcpClientChannel	Provides an implementation for a client channel that uses the TCP protocol to transmit messages.
TcpServerChannel	Provides an implementation for a server channel that uses the TCP protocol to transmit messages.

System.Runtime.Remoting.Channels.Http Namespace

The `System.Runtime.Remoting.Channels.Http` namespace contains channels that use the HTTP protocol to transport data between remote objects. The default encoding for the HTTP protocol is SOAP, which makes this a flexible way to pass data between remote objects. Table 36-4 summarizes the available classes in the `System.Runtime.Remoting.Channels.Http` namespace.

Table 36-4 System.Runtime.Remoting.Channels.Http Namespace	
Class	**Description**
HttpChannel	Provides an implementation for a sender-receiver channel that uses the HTTP protocol to transmit messages. This class is a combination of the `Http-ClientChannel` class and the `HttpServerChannel` class, which enables automatic two-way communication over HTTP.
HttpClientChannel	Provides an implementation for a client channel that uses the HTTP protocol to transmit messages.
HttpRemotingHandler	Implements an ASP.NET handler that forwards requests to the remoting HTTP channel.
HttpRemotingHandlerFactory	Initializes new instances of the `HttpRemotingHandler` class.
HttpServerChannel	Provides an implementation for a server channel that uses the HTTP protocol to transmit messages.

Up to this point, you can add the correct namespaces and code to register an HTTP channel and a TCP channel for the host application. Listing 36-2 shows how the host application should look after the channels are registered.

Listing 36-2: **Registering Channels**

```
using System;
using System.Runtime.Remoting;
using System.Runtime.Remoting.Channels;
using System.Runtime.Remoting.Channels.Tcp;
using System.Runtime.Remoting.Channels.Http;

namespace Client
{
```

Continued

Listing 36-2 *(continued)*

```
/// <summary>
/// Summary description for Class1.
/// </summary>
class RemotingClient
{

    [STAThread]
    static void Main(string[] args)
    {
    TcpChannel chan1 = new TcpChannel(8085);
    ChannelServices.RegisterChannel(chan1);

    HttpChannel chan2 = new HttpChannel(8086);
    ChannelServices.RegisterChannel(chan2);


    }
  }
}
```

Note   You do not need to use an HTTP channel and a TCP channel in the host application. If you are enabling clients to call on both channel types, you can register both
channel types; normally, however, you use one formatter, TCP or HTTP, based on
the type of clients that are accessing your remote object.

Activating the remote object

The last task to perform to host the remote object is to register the assembly
with the remoting framework. In your host application, before you can activate
the assembly that contains your methods, you first need to add a reference to the
assembly. Right-click the `References` object in the Solution Explorer, which brings
up the Add Reference dialog box. In the application you are writing here, you need
to browse to the `C:\cSharpRemoting\HostObject` directory and add the
`HostObject.dll` assembly to your application. After you add this, you can add
the `HostObject` namespace to your class file using the `using` statement, as the
following snippet shows:

```
using System;
using System.Runtime.Remoting;
using System.Runtime.Remoting.Channels;
using System.Runtime.Remoting.Channels.Http;
using System.Runtime.Remoting.Channels.Tcp;
using HostObject;
```

Now that you have added a reference to your remoting assembly created earlier, you can add the code that registers the object with the remoting framework. You can do this in one of two ways:

✦ Use the `RegisterWellKnownServiceType()` method of the `Remoting-Configuration` class to pass the type of the object that you are creating, the URI of the object, and the activation mode of the object.

✦ Use the `Configure()` method of the `RemotingConfiguration` class to pass a configuration file with the object activation details.

Each activation method works the same way, but storing your activation details in a configuration file gives you more flexibility if any of the activation details change, such as the port number of the channel you are using. You will consider both types of activation, but first examine the available methods and properties of the `RemotingConfiguration` class described in Table 36-5 and Table 36-6, respectively. Besides the activation methods described previously, you can use many helpful methods and properties in this class to discover information at runtime about your running objects.

Table 36-5
RemotingConfiguration class Methods

Method	Description
Configure	Reads the configuration file and configures the remoting infrastructure.
GetRegisteredActivatedClientTypes	Retrieves an array of object types registered on the client as types that will be activated remotely.
GetRegisteredActivatedServiceTypes	Retrieves an array of object types registered on the service end as types that can be activated on request from a client.
GetRegisteredWellKnownClientTypes	Retrieves an array of object types registered on the client end as well-known types.
GetRegisteredWellKnownServiceTypes	Retrieves an array of object types registered on the service end as well-known types.
GetType (inherited from Object)	Gets the type of the current instance.
IsActivationAllowed	Returns a Boolean value indicating whether the specified type is allowed to be client activated.
IsRemotelyActivatedClientType	Overloaded. Checks whether the specified object type is registered as a remotely activated client type.

Continued

Table 36-5 *(continued)*

Method	Description
IsWellKnownClientType	Overloaded. Checks whether the specified object type is registered as a well-known client type.
RegisterActivatedClientType	Overloaded. Registers an object type on the client end as a type that can be activated on the server.
RegisterActivatedServiceType	Overloaded. Registers an object type on the service end as one that can be activated on request from a client.
RegisterWellKnownClientType	Overloaded. Registers an object type on the client end as a well-known type (single call or singleton).
RegisterWellKnownServiceType	Overloaded. Registers an object Type on the service end as a well-known type (single call or singleton).

Table 36-6
RemotingConfiguration Class Properties

Property	Description
ApplicationId	Gets the ID of the currently executing application
ApplicationName	Gets or sets the name of a remoting application
ProcessId	Gets the ID of the currently executing process

Registering objects with RegisterWellKnownServiceType

To register an object with the `RegisterWellKnownServiceType()` method of the `RemotingConfiguration` class, you simply pass the name of the class, which is `HostObject.Class1`; the URI of the remote object, which is `ReturnName`; and the type of mode in which the object will be created, which in this case is `SingleCall`. You look at the `WellKnownObjectMode` enumeration later in this section. Listing 36-3 completes the host application using the `RegisterWellKnownServiceType` method.

Listing 36-3: **Using RegisterWellKnownServiceType**

```
using System;
using System.Runtime.Remoting;
using System.Runtime.Remoting.Channels;
```

```
using System.Runtime.Remoting.Channels.Http;
using System.Runtime.Remoting.Channels.Tcp;
using HostObject;

namespace Host
{
  /// <summary>
  /// Summary description for Class1.
  /// </summary>

  class Class1

  {
        /// <summary>
        /// The main entry point for the application.
        /// </summary>

        [STAThread]

        static void Main(string[] args)
        {

         TcpChannel chan1 = new TcpChannel(8085);

         ChannelServices.RegisterChannel(chan1);

         RemotingConfiguration.RegisterWellKnownServiceType(
             typeof(HostObject.Class1), "ReturnName",
             WellKnownObjectMode.SingleCall);

         Console.WriteLine("Press any key to exit");
         Console.ReadLine();

        }
   }
}
```

Because the host application is a console application, you add the `Console.ReadLine` statement at the end so that the console window stays open while clients are using the remote object. The lifetime of the channel is the length of time that window happens to be open. After you close the console window, the channel is destroyed and the lease on that particular channel is expired in the remoting framework.

The `WellKnownObjectMode` enumeration contains two members that define how objects are created. If the `WellKnownObjectMode` is `SingleCall`, then each request from a client is serviced by a new object instance. This would be represented by the following pseudo-code:

```
Create Object X
Call Method of Object X
Return data back to caller
Destroy Object X
Garbage Collect
```

If the `WellKnownObjectMode` is `Singleton`, then each request from a client is serviced by the same object instance. This can be described in the following pseudo-code:

```
Create Object X
Call Method of Object X
Return data back to caller
Call Method of Object X
Return data back to caller
... continue until channel destroyed
```

This loop continues until the channel with which this object is registered in the remoting framework is destroyed.

Depending on the type of application you are writing, you determine which activation mode to use by considering the following factors:

✦ **Overhead:** If creating the remote object consumes resources and takes time, then using the `SingleCall` mode may not be the most efficient way to create your object, as the object is destroyed after each client is done using it.

✦ **State Information:** If you are storing state data in your remote object, such as properties, you use `Singleton` objects, which are capable of maintaining state data.

Registering objects with the Configure method

If you need a more flexible way of maintaining the configuration data that the remoting framework needs to register your object, you can use the `Configure()` method of the `RemotingConfiguration` class. The configuration information that is stored in the file is the same information that you can use in the `RegisterWellKnown-ServiceType()` method. The benefit of using a configuration file is that if any of the settings for the object change, you can alter the configuration file, and not change any of your code. The schema for the configuration is shown in Listing 36-4, with the explanation of each element in Table 36-7.

Listing 36-4: **Remoting Configuration File**

```
<configuration>
   <system.runtime.remoting>
      <application>
         <lifetime>
         <channels> (Instance)
```

```
        <channel> (Instance)
            <serverProviders> (Instance)
                <provider> (Instance)
                <formatter> (Instance)
            <clientProviders> (Instance)
                <provider> (Instance)
                <formatter> (Instance)
    <client>
        <wellknown> (Client Instance)
        <activated> (Client Instance)
    <service>
        <wellknown> (Service Instance)
        <activated> (Service Instance)
    <soapInterop>
        <interopXmlType>
        <interopXmlElement>
        <preLoad>
<channels> (Template)
    <channel> (Template)
        <serverProviders> (Instance)
            <provider> (Instance)
            <formatter> (Instance)
        <clientProviders> (Instance)
            <provider> (Instance)
            <formatter> (Instance)
<channelSinkProviders>
        <serverProviders> (Template)
            <provider> (Template)
            <formatter> (Template)
        <clientProviders> (Template)
            <provider> (Template)
            <formatter> (Template)
<debug>
```

Although there are many options in the configuration file, you only need to use what your application requires. For example, the snippet of code in Listing 36-5 represents a configuration file for an HTTP-activated object that is a `SingleCall` mode object.

Listing 36-5: **Configuration File Example**

```
<configuration>
  <system.runtime.remoting>
    <application>

      <client url="http://localhost/HostObject">
```

Continued

Listing 36-5 *(continued)*

```
            <wellknown type="HostObject.Class1,
               ReturnName"
            url="http://localhost/HostObject/Class1.soap" />
        </client>

        <channels>
          <channel ref="http" />
        </channels>

      </application>
    </system.runtime.remoting>
</configuration>
```

After you create the configuration file, creating the host object is dramatically simpler than it is when registering an object with the `RegisterWellKnown-ServiceType()` method of the `RemotingConfiguration` class. The code in Listing 36-6 demonstrates how to register the object using the `Configure()` method.

Listing 36-6: **Using a Remoting Configuration File in the Host Class**

```
namespace Host
{
  /// <summary>
  /// Summary description for Class1.
  /// </summary>
  class Class1
  {
    /// <summary>
    /// The main entry point for the application.
    /// </summary>
    [STAThread]
    static void Main(string[] args)
     {

       RemotingConfiguration.Configure("Host.Exe.Config");

       Console.WriteLine("Press any key to exit");
       Console.ReadLine();

     }
   }
 }
```

As you can see, your code is reduced from about 15 lines to 1 line.

Note The name of the configuration file should be the name of the executable, including the exe extension, with an additional config extension added. In the case of the host application, the configuration file would be named host.exe.config, and the file would be located in the Bin directory where the executable file for the host application resides.

Table 36-7 lists all of the available elements and their uses for the remoting configuration file schema.

Table 36-7
Schema for Remoting Settings Configuration File

Element	Description
<system.runtime.remoting>	Contains information about remote objects and channels
<application>	Contains information about remote objects that the application consumes and exposes
<lifetime>	Contains information about the lifetime of all client-activated objects serviced by this application
<channels> (Instance)	Contains channels that the application uses to communicate with remote objects
<channel> (Instance)	Configures the channel that the application uses to communicate with remote objects
<serverProviders> (Instance)	Contains providers for channel sinks that are to become part of the default server-side channel sink call chain for this channel template when the template is referenced elsewhere in the configuration file
<provider> (Instance)	Contains the channel sink provider for a channel sink that is to be inserted into the channel sink chain
<formatter> (Instance)	Contains the channel sink provider for a formatter sink that is to be inserted into the channel sink chain
<clientProviders> (Instance)	Contains providers for channel sinks that are to become part of the default client-side channel sink call chain for this channel template when the template is referenced elsewhere in the configuration file

Continued

Table 36-7 *(continued)*

Element	Description
<client>	Contains objects that the application consumes
<wellknown> (Client Instance)	Contains information about server-activated (well-known) objects the application wants to consume
<activated> (Client Instance)	Contains information about client-activated objects the application wants to consume
<service>	Contains objects that the application exposes to other application domains or contexts
<wellknown> (Service Instance)	Contains information about server-activated (well-known) objects the application wants to publish
<activated> (Service Instance)	Contains information about client-activated objects the application wants to publish
<soapInterop>	Contains type mappings used with SOAP
<interopXmlType>	Creates a bidirectional map between a common language runtime type and an XML type and XML namespace
<interopXmlElement>	Creates a bidirectional map between a common language runtime type and an XML element and XML namespace
<preLoad>	Specifies the type to load the mappings from classes that extend SoapAttribute
<channels> (Template)	Contains channel templates that the application uses to communicate with remote objects
<channel> (Template)	Contains the channel template that specifies how to communicate with or listen to requests for remote objects
<channelSinkProviders>	Contains templates for client and server channel sink providers. Any channel sink providers specified underneath this element can be referenced anywhere a channel sink provider might be registered
<serverProviders> (Template)	Contains channel sink templates that can be inserted into a server channel call chain
<provider> (Template)	Contains the channel sink provider template for a channel sink that is to be inserted into the server or client channel sink chain

Element	Description
<formatter> (Template)	Contains the channel sink provider for a formatter sink that is to be inserted into the client or server channel sink chain
<clientProviders> (Template)	Contains channel sink templates that can be inserted into a client channel call chain
<debug>	Specifies whether types should be loaded in the configuration file when the application starts

Until this point, this chapter has explained the intricacies of creating the host application that registers the remote object with the remoting framework. Now you need to write the client application that makes the requests to the remote object, which is the subject of the next section.

Writing the Remoting Client

So far, you have created the host object and the host server application that manages the client requests for the host object through the remoting framework. The final step in writing this remoting application is to write the client application that makes requests to the remote object. In this case, the client calls the ReturnName method of the HostObject assembly and passes a customerID parameter that is used by the ReturnName() method to look up the customer's company name in the Northwind database.

To begin, create a new console application called Client in the C:\cSharpRemoting\Client directory. You can call the remote object with any type of application, but for simplicity, you create a console application.

Calling the remote object from the client can be accomplished in one of three ways:

✦ Call the GetObject() method of the Activator class, which is server-activated.

✦ Call the CreateInstance() method of the Activator class, which is client-activated.

✦ Use the new keyword, which can be server- or client-activated.

The difference between client activation and server activation is *when* the object is actually created. Each type of activation can be accomplished programmatically or through a configuration file (using the same format as described in Table 36-7), but for client activation, a round-trip is made to the server to create the object when the CreateInstance() method is called. Conversely, when an object is server-activated, the server object is not created until a call is made to the method from the client. Server-activated objects create a proxy that the client uses to discover the properties and methods available on the server object. The major disadvantage to server activation is that only default constructors are allowed, so if you need to pass multiple parameters to a method's constructor, you need to use client-side activation through the CreateInstance() method of the Activator class. All of the methods of the Activator class are listed in Table 36-8.

Table 36-8
Activator Class Methods

Method	Description
CreateComInstanceFrom	Creates an instance of the COM object whose name is specified, using the named assembly file and the constructor that best matches the specified parameters.
CreateInstance	Overloaded. Creates an instance of the specified type using the constructor that best matches the specified parameters.
CreateInstanceFrom	Overloaded. Creates an instance of the type whose name is specified, using the named assembly file and the constructor that best matches the specified parameters.
GetObject	Overloaded. Creates a proxy for a currently running remote object, a server-activated well-known object, or an XML Web service.

After you decide what type of activation your application requires, you can write the client code. Listing 36-7 shows the full client application code. Like the host code, you register a channel first. When registering a channel from the client, you do not specify the channel number. The call to the URI's endpoint point the client to the correct channel, because it is included in the GetObject() method call; you specify the object that you are attempting to create and the location of the object. After the object is created, you can call methods and set properties as you would with any other class.

Listing 36-7: **The remoting client application**

```
using System;
using System.Runtime.Remoting;
using System.Runtime.Remoting.Channels;
using System.Runtime.Remoting.Channels.Tcp;
```

```
using HostObject;

namespace Client
{
  /// <summary>
  /// Summary description for Class1.
  /// </summary>
  class RemotingClient
  {

        [STAThread]
        static void Main(string[] args)
        {

        ChannelServices.RegisterChannel(new TcpChannel());

        HostObject.Class1 x = (Class1)Activator.GetObject(
          typeof(Class1),
          "tcp://localhost:8085/ReturnName",null);

        Console.WriteLine(x.ReturnName("ALFKI"));
        Console.ReadLine();

        }

  }
}
```

After you write the client, you can run the Host.exe application and then run the client application; and you should see results similar to those shown in Figure 36-2. The host application stays open forever, or until you close it, while each client application call to the host application returns the company name for the customerID **ALFKI**, which is the customer ID passed in the client application.

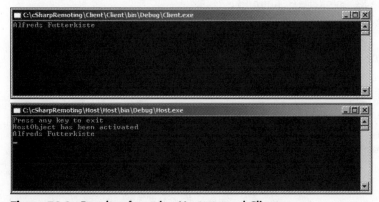

Figure 36-2: Results of running Host.exe and Client.exe

If you leave the original host application's code in `SingleCall` mode, then each time you run the client application, the server object is destroyed and re-created. By changing the `WellKnownObjectMode` to `Singleton`, you notice the difference between `SingleCall` and `Singleton` mode. The following snippet shows the host application code that creates the object in `Singleton` mode:

```
RemotingConfiguration.RegisterWellKnownServiceType(
        typeof(HostObject.Class1), "ReturnName",
    WellKnownObjectMode.SingleCall);
```

Figure 36-3 demonstrates the difference between the host application outputs after running the client application several times.

Figure 36-3: Host application running in SingleCall vs. Singleton mode

As you can see, the `Singleton` mode does not destroy the object after the method goes out of scope, whereas the `SingleCall` mode needs to re-create the object each time the `ReturnName()` method is called.

Summary

This chapter has given you a solid understanding of the remoting framework in .NET. Using remoting, you can activate objects across process boundaries, application domains, and machine boundaries. If you are going to implement remoting, there are a few more advanced topics in the SDK that would be worth looking at before you begin:

✦ **Creating customer formatters:** You can create customer formatters if the TCP and HTTP formatters do not satisfy your data marshaling needs. Search for Sinks and Sink Chains in the Framework SDK.

✦ **Asynchronous remoting:** Remoting is another .NET technology with built-in asynchronous capabilities. Search for Asynchronous Remoting in the Framework SDK to learn how to use delegates and events with remoting.

There are many good reasons to investigate remoting, but before you dive in, make sure you look at the capabilities of XML Web services and ASP.NET to accomplish cross-process communication. You may save yourself some time and effort creating the host applications and modifying the way your clients instantiate objects.

✦   ✦   ✦

C# and .NET Security

One of the most important things to remember when moving to C# and the .NET Framework is security. You must ensure that when building n-tiered applications, security is a top priority because the chances for a security breech in a distributed application are much greater than in a standalone application. It is for this reason that the .NET Framework was built with security in mind, which is reflected in every aspect of the framework. The .NET Framework is capable of remote execution, dynamic downloading of new components, and even dynamic execution. With this type of environment, if a programmer has the task of creating the security model, it could easily take longer to code than the actual program itself.

When building applications, the security model used is typically based on the user level or the group level. The application will either perform certain functions or it will not. The .NET Framework provides developers with a means to define *role-based security*, which operates in a similar fashion to user-level and group-level security. Role-based security is abstracted into principals and identities, while also providing code-level security, which is generally referred to as *code-access security* or *evidence-based security*.

When a user launches an application that employs code-access security, he or she may indeed have access to a resource (a network drive for example), but if the code contained within the application is not trusted, the program is not be able to access that network drive. This type of security is based on mobile code. You may not want to use a mobile application and let that application access all of the resources you have entrusted to you. Role-based security prevents malicious programmers from writing applications that can run as you and perform any number of actions on your local computer or across your corporate network.

The security contained within the .NET Framework sits on top of the security already contained within your operating system (OS). This second level of security is much more extensible than OS security. Both types of security, OS and .NET Framework, can complement each other.

This chapter touches on several security-related issues, such as using Windows roles to determine permissions. You then learn to demand and deny permissions within code while performing Registry operations. Finally you learn to use attribute-based permissions to define the rights your code has at runtime.

Understanding Code Security

Code-access security determines whether an assembly is allowed to run based on several pieces of evidence, such as the URL from which the assembly came and who authored the control. When you install the .NET Framework, default permissions are configured, which greatly reduces the chances that an untrustworthy control from the Internet or a local intranet can run on your machine. You may have encountered this if you have attempted to run any applications or use any controls from a network drive that require special security privileges. These special security privileges include writing to a disk file, reading or writing to and from the Registry, as well as network-related operations. You generally receive a security exception similar to the following when you attempt to do this if you don't change the security policy to allow this type of behavior:

```
Unhandled Exception: System.Security.SecurityException: Request for the permissi
on of type System.Security.Permissions.FileIOPermission
...
The state of the failed permission was:
<IPermission class="System.Security.Permissions.FileIOPermission, mscorlib, Vers
ion=1.0.3300.0, Culture=neutral, PublicKeyToken=b77a5c561934e089"
          version="1"
          Read="Z:\test.dat"
          Write="Z:\test.dat"/>
```

Code-access security works only on verifiable code. During the just-in-time (JIT) compilation, the Microsoft Interpreted Language (MSIL) is examined to ensure type safety. Type-safe code has access to only those memory locations to which it has rights. Actions, such as pointer operations, are prohibited, so functions can only be entered and exited from predefined entry and exit points. This isn't a foolproof method; bugs can still occur. However, it does ensure that a malicious piece of code cannot forcefully generate an error in your application and then exploit some bug in the operating system, thus gaining access to the stack. Under these types of circumstances, when a piece of malicious code has forcefully generated an error, the code that generated an error can only access the memory locations that JIT has determined it has access to.

Understanding code security policy

Code-access security enables a platform to assign a level of security to an application or assembly. Because this is accomplished with evidence collected from the component in question, code-access security is also referred to as evidence-based security. The evidence collected from the code could be the location on the Internet from which the code was downloaded, a digital signature located within the code, or code the author actually wrote.

Code security policies define several code groups, each of which has a set of permissions. When an application has been executed, it is then analyzed for evidence. Given the evidence within the code, the code is placed into a code group, thus inheriting the permissions of that group. These security policies can be set at the enterprise, machine, user, or application domain level, thus providing a strong degree of control over what runs and with what access. You may have enabled your code to have unrestricted rights, but your network administrator can define some enterprise security policies that supercede yours.

Understanding code permissions

The CLR, when granting security permissions, grants only permissions to code on the operations it is allowed to perform. The CLR uses objects called *permissions* to implement this type of security on managed code. The main uses for permissions are as follows:

✦ Code may request the permissions it is intending to use or might possibly need. The .NET Framework has the task of determining whether these requests are valid. Security requests are honored only if evidence collected from the code allows it to do so. Code never receives more permissions than the current security allows. Code can, on the other hand, receive less permission than that specified upon request.

✦ The CLR grants permissions to the code based on several factors: the code's identity (such as the URL it was obtained from, who wrote the code, and so on); the permissions that you request; and the amount the code can be trusted, as defined by the various security policies.

✦ Code can make a demand to have a certain permission. If a demand is made with the code, all code that runs within the scope of the application must also have access to the permission for the permission to be granted.

Code can be granted three kinds of permissions, each of which has a specific purpose:

✦ **Code access permissions** represent access to a protected resource or the authority to perform a protected operation.

✦ **Identity permissions** indicate that the code has credentials that support a particular kind of identity, such as code can have an "Administrator" identity and therefore run with all the permissions that an administrator would have.

✦ **Role-based security permissions** provide a mechanism for discovering whether a user (or the agent acting on the user's behalf) has a particular identity or is a member of a specified role. PrincipalPermission is the only role-based security permission.

The runtime provides built-in permission classes in several namespaces and supplies support for designing and implementing custom permission classes.

Understanding User Security

Many security systems in use today implement something called *user security*. These types of security systems require information from users seeking access. For example, they need to know who he person is, and what the user has access to. User security plays an important role in computer systems because when you run an application on your computer, the application generally takes on the identity of the person running it. Therefore, if you run an application, that application has all the rights and permissions on your local machine and across the enterprise network that you would have.

Unlike Windows services, which enables you to configure who the application runs as, a typical Windows-driven application has never really given us this type of control before. This fact has fueled many viruses and Trojan horses that computer users and businesses have to deal with on a day-to-day basis. By enabling you to determine what kind of permissions applications have on your machine, you greatly reduce the chance of an attack by a malicious piece of code. Operations, such as reading the Registry, overwriting system files, or looping through your personal address book, would not be possible. You can quickly test the whether the applications you execute run as the user who ran them by trying the program shown in Listing 37-1.

Listing 37-1: Environment Variables for Simple Security Tasks

```
using System;
namespace SimpleSecurity
{
  class Class1
  {
    [STAThread]
    static void Main(string[] args)
    {
```

```
        Console.WriteLine("I am currently running as:");
        Console.WriteLine("User    : {0}",Environment.UserName);
        Console.WriteLine("Domain : {0}",Environment.UserDomainName);
    }
  }
}
```

When you run this program, you should see the name you used to log onto Windows, as well as the name of your domain, as shown in Figure 37-1.

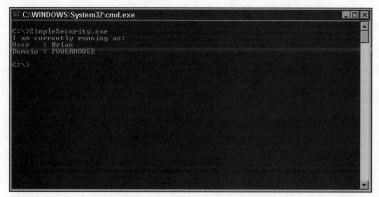

Figure 37-1: The Environment class can be used for simple security tasks.

If you aren't logged into a network domain, you simply see the name of your computer system as the domain name. The simplest type of security you could probably implement at that point would be to have your code compare the username and domain name to something valid, and if all is well, continue on with your program. That's adequate until you move your application to another machine, and then it quits working because you have strongly typed names in your code. The following section reviews this type of security along with other simplistic types.

Understanding .NET and Role-Based Security

Role-based security is based on the `PrincipalPermission` class. You can use `PrincipalPermission` to determine whether the current user has a certain name (such as John Doe) or whether that user belongs to a particular group. This class is the only role-based security permission supplied by the .NET Framework class library.

After you define `Identity` and `Principal` objects, you can perform security checks against them in one of the following ways:

✦ Using imperative security checks

✦ Using declarative security checks

✦ Directly accessing the `Principal` object

When using managed code, you can use imperative or declarative security checks to determine whether a particular principal object is a member of a known role, has a known identity, or represents a known identity acting in a role. To perform the security check using imperative or declarative security, a demand for the `PrincipalPermission` object must be made. During the security check, the common language runtime examines the caller's principal object to determine whether its identity and role match those represented by the `PrincipalPermission` being demanded. If the principal object does not match, a `SecurityException` is thrown. When this happens, only the principal object of the current thread is checked. The `PrincipalPermission` class does not walk the stack as it does with code access permissions, as this would cause serious security concerns.

Additionally, you can access the values of the principal object directly and perform checks without a `PrincipalPermission` object. In this case, you simply read the values of the current thread's `Principal` or use the `IsInRole` method to perform authorization.

Assigning Windows roles

Generally, when you need to assign multiple users to specific roles or groups, it is best to use the group functionality built right into Windows NT 4.0, Windows 2000, and Windows XP. Rather than add privileges on a per-user basis, you can create a new group with certain access rights and then add users to the particular group. These roles save an appreciable amount of time and enable server administrators to control a large number of users.

Let's begin by adding a new group within Windows 2000/Windows XP:

1. Right-click My Computer and select Manage. When the Microsoft Management console opens, expand the tree view in the left pane to expose User Groups by clicking Local Users and Groups, and then click Groups.

2. When you click Groups, you see a list of approximately seven groups that are built into the Windows operating system, as shown in Figure 37-2.

3. Right-click in the right pane and select Add Group. Name this group **Developers,** as shown in Figure 37-3.

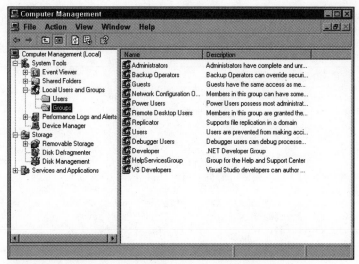

Figure 37-2: Group management is accomplished with the Microsoft Management console.

Figure 37-3: Add a Developers group to Windows.

4. After you create this group, click the Add button and add your user account to the group. For this example, ensure that you are not in the Administrator group. If you are an administrator, you may want to test the following application with an alternate Windows account.

Now that you have your new group in place, you are going to delve into the WindowsPrincipal and WindowsIdentity class. When used together, these two classes can determine whether the current Windows user belongs to specific groups. Examine the sample application shown in Listing 37-2.

Listing 37-2: WindowsPrincipal Enables You to Check for Role Membership

```
using System;
using System.Security.Principal;

class Class1
{
    static void Main()
  {
    WindowsIdentity wi = WindowsIdentity.GetCurrent();
    WindowsPrincipal wp = new WindowsPrincipal(wi);

        // This checks for local administrator rights if you in a Domain
        if (wp.IsInRole(WindowsBuiltInRole.Administrator))
        Console.WriteLine("Your are an Administrator!");
      else
        Console.WriteLine("You are not an Administrator.");

      if (wp.IsInRole("POWERHOUSE\\Developer"))
        Console.WriteLine("You are in the Developer group!");
      else
        Console.WriteLine("You are not in the Developer group.");
  }
}
```

This code creates a new WindowsIdentity object (based on the identity of the current user) with the GetCurrent method. The WindowsPrincipal object uses this identity object as a parameter in its constructor so that you can retrieve certain information about the person or object. It then calls the IsInRole method of the WindowsPrincipal class to determine whether the user belongs to the Administrator group. The IsInRole method has three overloaded variations of which you use two. The first one takes a WindowsBuiltInRole enumeration. When checking for any groups that are built into Windows, you should use this enumeration. Depending on whether you are an administrator, you see one of two messages.

The code then checks to see whether the current user belongs to your new Developer group, using variation number two of the IsInRole method. This variation simply takes a string parameter specifying the computer or domain name followed by the group name.

In the preceding code, substitute the word POWERHOUSE with the name of your domain or computer. Those of you who belong to both the Administrator group and the Developer group might notice that this sample application shows you present in only the Administrator group, as shown in Figure 37-4.

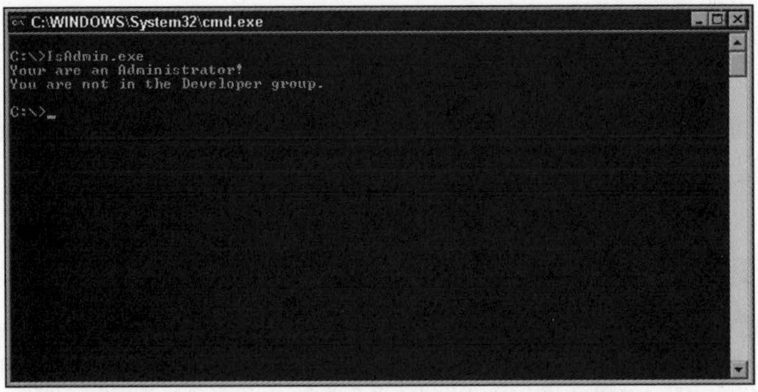

Figure 37-4: Belonging to the Administrator group can confuse IsInRole.

This mix-up occurs because if you are an administrator, you are inherently part of all groups and have access to everything. Therefore, when checking for roles in your own applications, it is wise to check for both the specific group and all other groups that have more power than the group you are checking (for example, Administrator, Power Users, and so on).

Understanding principals

Each thread in a .NET application is associated with a CLR principal. The principal contains an identity representing the user ID that is running that thread. By using a static property called `Thread.CurrentPrincipal`, you can return the current principal associated with the thread.

Principal objects implement the `IPrincipal` interface. The `IPrincipal` interface contains only one method and one property. The `Identity` property returns the current identity object, and the `IsInRole` method is used to determine whether a user belongs to a specific role/security group.

Currently, two principal classes are contained with the .NET framework: `Windows-Principal` and `GenericPrincipal`. The `GenericPrincipal` class is used when you need to implement your own principal. The `WindowsPrincipal` class represents a Windows user and his or her associated roles/groups.

An `Identity` object implements the `IIdentity` interface. The `IIdentity` interface has just three properties:

✦ `Name` is the string associated with the current identity. This is given to the Common Language Runtime by the operating system of the authentication provider. NTLM (Windows NT Challenge/Response), which authenticates Windows NT logins, is an example of an authentication provider.

✦ IsAuthenticated is a Boolean value indicating whether the user was authenticated or not.

✦ AuthenticationType is a string that indicates which type of authentication was used. Some of the possible authentication types include Basic, Forms, Kerberos, NTLM, and Passport.

Understanding Code Access Permissions

Before any .NET application is executed, it must pass a series of security checks that result in the application being granted access to perform certain operations. The permissions that are granted to your code can also be requested in code, or denied by code. All of these permissions are determined by a security policy that the .NET Framework relies on very heavily. These security policies contain permissions to resources, as shown in Table 37-1.

| Table 37-1 | | |
| **Common Code Access Permissions** | | |
Resource	**Permission**	**Description**
DNS	DNSPermission	Access to the Domain Name Service.
Environment Variables	EnvironmentPermission	Access to environment variables within the system.
Event Log	EventLogPermission	Access to the event log. This includes existing event logs and the creating of new event logs.
File Operations	FileIOPermission	Access to perform file operations such as reading from or writing to a file.
Registry	RegistryPermission	Access to the Windows Registry.
User Interface	UIPermission	Access to user interface functionality.
Web	WebPermission	Access to make or accept connection on a Web address.

When you run an application, the right to any of the aforementioned permissions is based solely on whether the code has the right to the permission. It has nothing to do with which user is running the actual code. Therefore, these permissions are referred to as code-access security.

Creating a simple permission code request

In this section, you examine just how easy it is to request permission, with code, to perform a specific action. In this example, you attempt to read a key from the Registry, which indicates to whom the current operating system is registered.

When using the RegistryPermission class, you need to specify just which kind of access to the Registry you require (read, write, and so on) and what specific key you want to access. Generally, if you only need read access to a particular key in the Registry, you should only request read permission. This ensures that you don't accidentally overwrite any Registry information and that subsequent, possibly malicious, code cannot change the information. In addition, you should always wrap your permissions requests with some sort of structured error handler. If the request for permission is denied by the Common Language Runtime, a SecurityException is thrown. If you attempt this request within a try/catch block, you won't have any issues because your error is gracefully handled. Although you may know you have this type of permission on your development machine, you can't foresee security policies that might block this access on other machines or networks.

After you create a permission request, you simply call the Demand() method of the RegistryPermission class. If Demand() executes without generating an exception, your permission request was granted. Listing 37-3 contains the sample application.

Listing 37-3: Demand Permission with a Structured Error Handler

```
using System;
using Microsoft.Win32;
using System.Security.Permissions;

class Class1
{
  static void Main(string[] args)
  {
    try
    {
      RegistryPermission regPermission = new
RegistryPermission(RegistryPermissionAccess.AllAccess,"HKEY_LOCAL_MACHINE\\SOFTW
ARE\\Microsoft\\Windows NT\\CurrentVersion");
      regPermission.Demand();
    }
    catch (Exception e)
    {
      Console.WriteLine(e.Message);
      return;
```

Continued

Listing 37-3 *(continued)*

```
    }

    RegistryKey myRegKey=Registry.LocalMachine;
    myRegKey=myRegKey.OpenSubKey ("SOFTWARE\\Microsoft\\Windows
NT\\CurrentVersion");
    try
    {
      Object oValue=myRegKey.GetValue("RegisteredOwner");
      Console.WriteLine("OS Registered Owner: {0}",oValue.ToString());
    }
    catch (NullReferenceException)
    {
    }
  }
}
```

Keep in mind that even if the .NET security policy allows this code to execute, the security policy of the underlying operating system must also allow it to execute.

After you have demanded permissions to the appropriate Registry key, you simply read the RegisteredOwner key and display the information in your console window.

Denying permissions

As with the Demand method covered earlier, you can also call the Deny() method, which removes permissions for an operation. Typically, it's a good idea to remove any permission that you know you will not need before the fact. You can request the permissions as the code requires. You use the Deny() method in circumstances when you have completed an operation and know that no further operations are required.

Denying permissions serves several purposes. For example, if you are using third-party libraries, you want to ensure that after you manipulate the Registry, no other code is allowed to do so. Denying a permission is a way of accomplishing this.

The code in Listing 37-4 uses a modified version of the preceding example to first deny a Registry permission. After the permission is denied, it attempts to read the Registry key, which results in a SecurityException. If you want to undo a Deny operation within code, simply use the RevertDeny() method to remove the permission denial; and any further attempt to read the requested Registry key completes successfully.

Listing 37-4: Deny Permissions You Don't Want to Access

```
using System;
using Microsoft.Win32;
using System.Security.Permissions;

class Class1
{
  static void Main(string[] args)
  {
    try
    {
      RegistryPermission regPermission = new
RegistryPermission(RegistryPermissionAccess.AllAccess,"HKEY_LOCAL_MACHINE\\SOFTW
ARE\\Microsoft\\Windows NT\\CurrentVersion");
      regPermission.Deny();
    }
    catch (Exception e)
    {
      Console.WriteLine(e.Message);
      return;
    }

    RegistryKey myRegKey=Registry.LocalMachine;
    myRegKey=myRegKey.OpenSubKey ("SOFTWARE\\Microsoft\\Windows
NT\\CurrentVersion");
    try
    {
      Object oValue=myRegKey.GetValue("RegisteredOwner");
      Console.WriteLine("OS Registered Owner: {0}",oValue.ToString());
    }
    catch (NullReferenceException)
    {
    }
  }
}
```

If you are running this example within Visual Studio, the application should break
on your Registry manipulation lines. Running this application from the console
results in a long list of exception errors detailing what the problem is.

Using attribute-based permissions

Attribute permission requests are a way to ensure that you have sufficient
permissions to various resources before the application actually runs. The JIT
and CLR parse the attributes when the application is compiled.

In Listing 37-5, you use the `RegistryPermissionAttribute` and `Demand` on the `SecurityAction`. If this permission is granted at compile time, the application fails to execute. This isn't always the best way to go when coding an application; you generally have more efficient ways to handle errors of this type. For example, when creating a network chat program, it wouldn't be a good idea to prevent the program from running when it doesn't have file IO rights, as you could always prompt the user for operating parameters. It would make sense, however, to disallow the application to run if it doesn't have access to network operations. This type of security request is crucial to the operation of the said application.

Listing 37-5: Using Attribute Permissions

```csharp
using System;
using Microsoft.Win32;
using System.Security.Permissions;

[RegistryPermissionAttribute(SecurityAction.Demand)]
class Class1
{
  static void Main(string[] args)
  {

    RegistryKey myRegKey=Registry.LocalMachine;
    myRegKey=myRegKey.OpenSubKey ("SOFTWARE\\Microsoft\\Windows
NT\\CurrentVersion");
    try
    {
      Object oValue=myRegKey.GetValue("RegisteredOwner");
      Console.WriteLine("OS Registered Owner:
{0}",oValue.ToString());
    }
    catch (NullReferenceException)
    {
    }
  }
}
```

Understanding the Security Policy

The security policy is the heart and soul of evidence-based security. After evidence is retrieved from an assembly, that code is then assigned to a code group. That code group in turn has a permission set, defining what the code can and cannot do. Not only can you modify the security policy to fit your needs, you can modify it at several levels; and you create custom code groups to go with the security policies that you have defined.

Understanding security policy levels

There are four security policy levels: enterprise, machine, application domain, and user. All these levels have to agree to a security permission or the permission is denied, as shown in Figure 37-5.

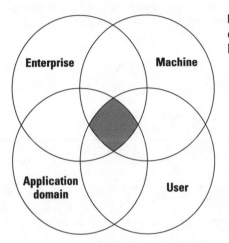

Figure 37-5: Security policy levels are overlapped to determine a final security level.

If you change your machine policy to allow certain types of operations from code downloaded from the Internet, for example, your network administrator can apply an enterprise security policy to disallow the operations.

Understanding code groups

All of the security policy levels contain code groups, which in turn contain zones for each code group. This result is a very detailed adjustment of security settings across all of the policy levels, and allows different types of security at each policy level depending on the zone of the code in question.

Immediately under the code group is an All_Code node. As the name implies, these permissions sets apply to all code. In addition to this All_Code node, you can add more nodes to fit your needs. For example, you can create nodes for code that you receive from consultants or any source you'd like.

When evaluating security levels, keep in the mind the way in which that code policy is actually evaluated. For each level in the security policy, the permissions for an assembly are joined together. By joining all of these permissions, you wind up with one very large permission set. Each of these permissions sets are then overlapped so that a comparison can be performed, and the most restrictive value for each permission is then used for the final permission set.

Understanding named permission sets

A named permission set is a set of permissions that administrators or developers can associate with a code group. A named permission set consists of at least one permission and a name and description for that particular permission set. Administrators can use named permission sets to establish or modify the security policy for code groups, much like Windows NT groups are used to manage groups of users. You can associate more than one code group with the same named permission set.

Table 37-2 describes the built-in named permission sets provided by the common language runtime.

Table 37-2
Built-in Named Permission Sets

Permission Set	Description
Nothing	No permissions (code cannot run)
Execute	Permission to run (execute), but no permissions to use protected resources
Internet	The default policy permission set suitable for content from unknown origin
LocalIntranet	The default policy permission set within an enterprise
Everything	All standard (built-in) permissions, except permission to skip verification
FullTrust	Full access to all resources

Altering security policies

Before actually experimenting with coding techniques to demand and refuse security permissions, you should first familiarize yourself with the tools available for altering security settings. The security settings discussed so far are kept in XML files. The machine security policy is kept in the security.config file located in the \WINNT\Microsoft.NET\Framework\vx.x.xxxx\CONFIG directory. The user security settings can be found in security.config, located in the \Documents and Settings\<UserName>\Application Data\Microsoft\CLR Security Config\vx.x.xxxx directory. You can navigate to the Control Panel, select Administrative Tools, and then select Microsoft .NET Framework Configuration for all of your configuration needs. This tool not only has several built-in wizards that ease the configuration process, it is much easier to use than an XML editor.

After you open the configuration tool, expand the Runtime Security Policy node, as shown in Figure 37-6.

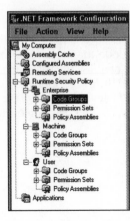

Figure 37-6: The Microsoft .NET Framework configuration tool

It is here that you can actually see the different security levels, code groups for each level, permissions sets, and policy assemblies.

Adding new codes groups is remarkably simple. Right-click within the left-hand pane and select New. A wizard opens, asking for the name of this new code group and whether it should be modeled after an existing group or have custom permissions (see Figure 37-7). This wizard walks you through all of the available permissions, and you even have the option to package the security policy to distribute to the enterprise.

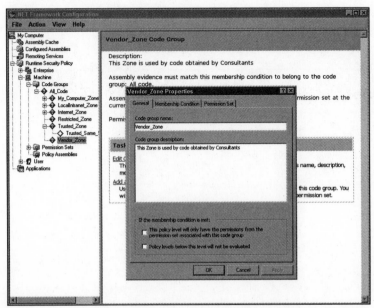

Figure 37-7: A wizard aids you in creating custom security policies.

Summary

The .NET Framework sits atop a vast amount of security code that monitors every aspect of an application or user. This security framework enables the developer and enterprise administrator to control how much or how little an application can do. You learned about both user-identity security and code-access security. By using both of these in conjunction with the underlying operating system security, you can make applications more secure than ever before.

✦   ✦   ✦

XML Primer

Unless you have lived in a cave for the past few years, you've already heard about XML. Indeed, XML has received a lot of good press, most of which it deserves. However, in spite of what you may have read in some glossy marketing brochure, XML is unlikely to solve world hunger, bring world peace, or cure all known diseases. After reading this section, you will master the essentials of XML and its associated standards, such as schemas and namespaces.

Simply put, XML is a simplified SGML dialect designed for interoperability, and has been nominated as the ASCII of the future. For the last decade, ASCII has been the traditional standard for text-based data interchange, but it is rapidly being displaced by XML as the new standard. Throughout this section, you learn to appreciate the sheer elegance of XML: its unique combination of pure simplicity and raw power. You also learn what other standards complement XML. The XML family of complementing standard has grown tremendously over the last few years, so for brevity's sake only those standards that are relevant to this book are discussed.

XML's Design Goals

XML is a mark-up language that is extensible. Of course, this is not much of a revelation given what the abbreviation stands for (eXtensible Mark-up Language), but it is worth pointing out this obvious fact because it really captures the essence of XML. *Extensible* means that you can add new words to the language to suit your specific purpose. A mark-up language embeds special symbols in a document for some specific purpose. This purpose varies from one mark-up language to another. One of XML's strengths is that its purpose is broad: it serves as a universal text-based language for structured data.

HyperText Mark-up Language (HTML), Standard Generalized Mark-up Language (SGML), and Rich Text Format (RTF) are other examples of mark-up languages you may have heard of.

Note   Because XML is a universal computer language, some have coined the term "Esperanto of the Computers" as a term to designate XML. This is a good simile, except that Esperanto is not generally considered a success story.

Before diving into the syntax and grammar of XML, it is worthwhile to examine the ten design goals of XML as set out by its creators. These goals are listed here and each one is explained in more detail below. Some of these goals are rather technical in nature and will not become entirely clear until later in this appendix, when some of the terms they mention (for example, document type definition) are explained. However, most goals immediately give valuable insight to the intent of XML.

1. XML shall be straightforwardly usable over the Internet.

2. XML shall support a wide variety of applications.

3. XML shall be compatible with SGML.

4. It shall be easy to write programs that process XML documents.

5. The number of optional features in XML is to be kept to the absolute minimum, ideally zero.

6. XML documents should be human-legible and reasonably clear.

7. The XML design should be prepared quickly.

8. The design of XML shall be formal and concise.

9. XML documents shall be easy to create.

10. Terseness in XML markup is of minimal importance.

Goal 1: XML shall be straightforwardly usable over the Internet

This goal does *not* mean that XML documents should be readable using the current breed of browsers. Instead, this goal refers to the bigger picture: taking into account the needs of distributed applications running in a large-scale networked environment, such as the Internet. Web Service makes this goal a reality. As for which browsers support XML, Internet Explorer 5.*x* and later as well as Netscape Navigator 6.*x* support XML.

Goal 2: XML shall support a wide variety of applications

This second goal can be seen as counter-balancing the first goal. XML is designed to work well on the Internet, but it is not limited to the Internet. Testimony that this goal has been reached is the large number of application domains outside the Net where XML is used, such as publishing, data interchange, and database applications. Moreover, rapid adoption of XML has been facilitated by a proliferation of tools: authoring tools, simple filters, display engines, formatting engines, and translators.

Goal 3: XML shall be compatible with SGML

This goal was established so that SGML tools could process (that is, parse) XML documents. This goal has 4 sub-goals:

1. Existing SGML tools will be able to read and write XML data.

2. XML instances are SGML documents as they are, without changes to the instance.

3. For any XML document, a document type definition (DTD) can be generated such that SGML will produce "the same parse" as would an XML processor.

4. XML should have essentially the same expressive power as SGML.

While this goal (and its sub-goals) ensures that an XML document is also an SGML document, the reverse is not true: an SGML document is NOT an XML document. This is because XML leaves out many of the complex features of SGML.

Goal 4: It shall be easy to write programs that process XML documents

This goal was originally quantified by the benchmark that someone with a computer science degree should be able to write a basic XML processor in a week or two. In hindsight, this quantitative goal may have been a bit too ambitious, but the large number of available (many of them freely) XML processors is a clear indication that this goal has been reached qualitatively. However, on the flip side, the recent proliferation of XML-related standard (XML Schema, X-Path, X-Link, etc.) has caused some to declare that XML has failed to reach this specific goal.

Goal 5: The number of optional features in XML is to be kept to the absolute minimum, ideally zero

This goal was put in place to ensure to ensure a consistent feature set among all XML processors because there is no choice as to what features to implement. Therefore, every XML processor in the world should be able to read every XML document in the world (assuming that it can decode the characters — more about this later). SGML, on the other hand, has many optional features in the specification. In practice, this means that interchanging a SGML document created with one SGML processor to another depends on what optional features are implemented in each processor.

Goal 6: XML documents should be human-legible and reasonably clear

This goal speaks for itself and has the advantage that you can use a text editor, even a basic one such as Notepad, to do useful XML work.

Goal 7: The XML design should be prepared quickly

This goal was stipulated to win the race to publish a standard. The creators of XML realized that if they waited too long, another organization might come up with another standard.

Goal 8: The design of XML shall be formal and concise

This goal is closely related to the ease of programming goal (#4). A data format is programmer-friendly only if a programmer can easily make sense out of the specification. To accomplish this, the XML specification makes use of a notation used by computer scientists when describing computer languages: Extended Backus-Naur Form (EBNF).

✦ EBNF is a set of rules, called productions

✦ Every rule describes a specific fragment of syntax

✦ A document is valid if it can be reduced to a single, specific rule, with no input left, by repeated application of the rules.

Goal 9: XML documents shall be easy to create

This goal extends both Goal 4 and Goal 6. While a text editor is fine for small XML documents, large documents are more easily created using dedicated tools. This goal expresses the intent to design XML so that it would be straightforward to design and build XML authoring systems.

Goal 10: Terseness in XML markup is of minimal importance

This goal indicates that when a choice had to be made between clarity and conciseness, that clarity was selected as a rule.

A Brief Lesson in HTML

Because HTML bears a lot of resemblance to XML, a brief synopsis of this language follows. If you know HTML, this lessens the learning curve of XML. (If you don't know HTML, don't worry—we explain everything step by step.) To simplify the presentation, our coverage of HTML omits some details (for example, it may imply something is required when it is actually optional) and is limited to what is has in common with XML. Of course, you are already aware of the main distinction between the two languages: XML is extensible while HTML is not (more about this a little later).

HTML is the language used to describe Web pages. A *Web page* is a document that contains special markers, called *tags*, that define how the content is to be presented in a web browser. A starting marker and an ending marker (we'll go ahead and call them tags from now on) surrounds the content, for example: <tag>content</tag>.

The starting tag, content, and ending tag together are called an *element*. Angled brackets (< and >) surround both the starting tag and the ending tag. The end tag uses the same word contained in the starting tag preceded by a forward slash (/). So if the starting tag is ⟨font⟩, the ending tag has to be ⟨/font⟩. In XML, tags are case-sensitive, so the words used in the starting and end tag have to match case. Therefore, in XML, you cannot use ⟨font⟩ (with a lowercase *f*) for the starting tag and ⟨/Font⟩ (with a uppercase *F*) for the ending tag. In HTML, tags are not case-sensitive, so the tags with different capitalization would be accepted.

In HTML, the tags you may use are predefined. Examples of HTML tags are h1 (⟨h1⟩ and ⟨/h1⟩) for Header 1 and b (⟨b⟩ and ⟨/b⟩) for bold. Knowing HTML means knowing when to use each predefined tag. For example, to have the word "Abbreviation" show up in bold face in the browser, you would write ⟨b⟩Abbreviation⟨/b⟩. When the browser reads this combination of tag and content, it strips out the tags and display the content in bold face.

An arbitrary combination of HTML tags and content does not usually produce a valid HTML document. An HTML page must follow a certain structure. The content of the document must be enclosed between ⟨html⟩ and ⟨/html⟩ and consists of a head and a body. Each of these sections is delimited by tags (not surprisingly called *head* and *body*) and contains content, optionally surrounded by presentation tags. Listing A-1 shows the structure of an HTML document. Incidentally, this listing also demonstrates how comments are embedded in an HTML page: ⟨!-- COMMENT GOES HERE --⟩

Note Comments are ignored and have no effect on how the page is displayed in the browser. They are merely used to convey information to the human reader of the HTML source code. Some comments contain special codes that specific programs (for example the Web server) understand, but this is outside the scope of this brief discussion of HTML.

Listing A-1: **The Structure of an HTML Document**

```
<html>

<head>
<!-- HEAD CONTENT GOES HERE -->
</head>

<body>
<!-- BODY CONTENT GOES HERE -->
</body>

</html>
```

HTML also has a mechanism to add further information to a tag, called attributes. An attribute specifies a property that belongs to a tag, such as the size of a font. For example to have the word "Meaning" appear in a font with size 4, you would write

```
<font size="4">Meaning</font>
```

As you can see from the example above, attributes are written in the starting tag and a space separates the tag name from the attribute name. They take the form

```
attribute_name=value_string
```

or, showing the element in its entirety:

```
<tag attribute_name=value_string>content</tag>
```

In HTML, the attributes you can use with each tag are predefined, just like the tags. The font tag, for example, has a size attribute. Attribute values must be enclosed in a pair of double or single quotes (it does not matter which ones you use as long as the opening and closing quote are of the same type).

A tag may contain more than one attribute. Each attribute is separated by a space. For example, you may want to specify the border, width and height of a table, for example

```
<table border="1" width="359" height="110"></table>
```

Actually, HTML also accepts attribute values that are not enclosed in quotes. XML, on the other hand, requires the quotes. You may have recognized a trend here: XML has a stricter set of rules than HTML.

Listing A-2 shows a simple HTML document, mixing tags (some with one or more attributes) with content. Just in case you are trying to decipher the HTML tags in this document, here is how an HTML table is created (an HTML table looks like a table in a word processor). The table is enclosed in a `<table>` tag. Each row is enclosed in a `<tr>` (table row) tag. Within each row a cell is created using the `<td>` (table divisor) tag. The rest of the HTML document is pretty self-explanatory. (Don't worry if there is a detail you don't understand when reading this HTML document. This is a section about XML, so the HTML coverage is superficial.)

Listing A-2: **A Simple HTML Document**

```
<html>

<head>
<title>A Glossary in HTML</title>
</head>

<body>
```

```
<h1>Glossary</h1>
<div align="left">
  <table border="1" width="359" height="110">
    <tr>
      <td width="125" height="22">
        <b><font size="4">Abbreviation</font></b>
      </td>
      <td width="234" height="22">
        <b><font size="4">Meaning</font></b>
      </td>
    </tr>
    <tr>
      <td width="125" height="22">
        ADO
      </td>
      <td width="234" height="22">
        <b>A</b>ctive <b>D</b>ata <b>O</b>bjects
      </td>
    </tr>
    <tr>
      <td width="125" height="22">
        SOAP
      </td>
      <td width="234" height="22">
        <b>S</b>imple <b>O</b>bject <b>A</b>ccess
<b>P</b>rotocol
      </td>
    </tr>
    <tr>
      <td width="125" height="22">
        UDA
      </td>
      <td width="234" height="22">
        <b>U</b>niversal <b>D</b>ata <b>A</b>ccess
      </td>
    </tr>
    <tr>
      <td width="125" height="22">
        XML
      </td>
      <td width="234" height="22">
        e<b>X</b>tensible <b>M</b>arkup <b>L</b>anguage
      </td>
    </tr>
  </table>
</div>

</body>

</html>
```

XML = HTML with User-Defined Tags

Now let us discuss XML and fill out the missing details so you can create your first XML document. An XML document consists of three parts: prologue, body, and epilogue. Only the body of the document is required. The prologue and epilogue may be omitted.

Here is the basic structure of an XML document:

Prologue:

```
XML Declaration (optional)
<!-- Comments may go here -->
Document Type Declaration (optional)
<!-- Comments may go here -->
```

Body:

```
Document Element
<Document>
<!-- Document goes here -->
</Document>
```

Epilogue:

```
<!-- Comments may go here -->
```

An XML starts with a prologue. If you exclude the optional comments, the prologue contains two main elements (which are each optional as well). The XML declaration has one required attribute used to specify the version of the XML specification to which the document conforms. The XML declaration also has two optional attributes: one to specify the character encoding used and one to specify whether the document relies on an external document type definition (DTD). Following is an example of a complete XML declaration, using all three attributes.

```
<?xml version="1.0" encoding="UTF-8" standalone="yes"?>
```

The attributes in the XML declaration must be used in the order shown in the example. The version attribute is mandatory and must have the value of "1.0". The character encoding of XML documents and document type definitions are discussed below.

A root tag must enclose the document element. In the example above, this root tag is the `<Document>` tag, but you are free to use any tag to enclose the document element. Finally, all tags in an XML document must nest properly. If an element is contained in another element, then the contained element is called a *child*, while the containing element is called the *parent*. Here is an example:

```
<Book Category="Chess">
<Title>My System</Title>
<Author>Aron Nimzowitsch</Author>
</Book>
```

In the example above the `<Book>` tag is a parent to two children, the `<Author>` and `<Title>` elements. Proper nesting requires that children be always completely contained within their parent. In other words, the end tag of a child cannot appear after the end tag of the parent, as in the following:

```
<Book>
<Title>Improper Nesting in XML Explained
</Book>
</Title>
```

The epilogue, which can contain only comments (as well as white space and processing instructions), is frequently omitted.

You are now ready for a first look at an XML document, shown in Listing A-3. The line numbers are not part of the document and are only there to make the line-by-line explanation below easier to follow.

Listing A-3: **A Simple XML Document**

```
 1:    <?xml version="1.0" encoding="UTF-8" standalone="yes"?>
 2:    <!-- A list of recommended books on XML -->
 3:    <!-- Compiled on March 17, 2000 by PGB -->
 4:    <XMLBooks>
 5:        <Book ISBN="0-7897-2242-9">
 6:             <Title>XML By Example</Title>
 7:             <Category>Web Development</Category>
 8:             <Author>Benoit Marchal</Author>
 9:        </Book>
10:        <Book ISBN="1-861003-11-0">
11:             <Title>Professional XML </Title>
12:             <Category>Internet</Category>
13:             <Category>Internet Programming</Category>
14:             <Category>XML</Category>
15:             <Author>Richard Anderson</Author>
16:             <Author>Mark Birbeck</Author>
17:             <Author>Michael Kay</Author>
18:             <Author>Steven Livingstone</Author>
19:             <Author>Brian Loesgen</Author>
20:             <Author>Didier Martin</Author>
21:             <Author>Stephen Mohr</Author>
22:             <Author>Nikola Ozu</Author>
23:             <Author>Bruce Peat</Author>
24:             <Author>Jonathan Pinnock</Author>
25:             <Author>Peter Stark</Author>
```

Continued

Listing A-3 *(continued)*

```
26:            <Author>Kevin Williams</Author>
27:       </Book>
28:       <Book ISBN="0-7356-0562-9">
29:            <Title>XML in Action</Title>
30:            <Category>Internet</Category>
31:            <Category>XML</Category>
32:            <Author>William J. Pardy</Author>
33:       </Book>
34: </XMLBooks>
```

Line 1 in Listing A-3 contains a complete XML declaration, containing all three attributes. Lines 2 and 3 are comments used here to indicate the purpose of the document. The body of the XML document follows, starting at line 4 and ending with line 34. This document does not contain an epilogue, as is usually the case. The document element is enclosed by the <XMLBooks> tag (the starting tag is on line 4, the ending tag on line 34). The document element contains three children, each enclosed by a <Book> tag. Child 1 starts from line 5 and ends on line 9. Child 2 starts from line 10 and ends on line 27. Child 3 starts from line 28 and ends on line 33. Each <Book> element has an ISBN attribute and a number of children: one <Title>, one or more <Category> and one or more <Author>. Here you see a significant advantage of XML over traditional text files: XML is well equipped to deal with parent/child structures.

It is worth pointing out that as the document creator I invented the tags and attributes used in this document (XMLBooks, Book, ISBN, Title, Category, Author). Another author may for example have preferred <ShelvingCategory> instead of <Category>. You can also judge by yourself how well the current XML specification does on reaching goal #6 (XML documents should be human-legible and reasonably clear).

Document Type Definitions

The XML document shown in Listing A-3 above has a more defined structure than the structure mandated by XML. A document type definition (DTD) provides a way to specify this structure, the data model corresponding to the data model. The comparison can be made with a database schema that defines the data model of a database. This comparison works well because both a database and an XML document contain structured data. The DTD is the schema corresponding to the XML document. Listing A-4 shows the DTD that corresponds to Listing A-3.

Listing A-4: **DTD Schema Corresponding to XML Document**

```
<?xml version="1.0"?>
<!--     The top-level element,
XMLBooks, is a list of books -->
<!ELEMENT XMLBooks    (Book+)>

<!--     A Book element
contains 1 Title, 1 or more Category,
and 1 or more Author -->
<!ELEMENT Book          (Title,Category*,Author+)>

<!--     A Book has 1 required attribute -->
<!ATTLIST Book ISBN ID #REQUIRED>

<!--     The Title, Category, and Author
   elements contain text -->
<!ELEMENT Title          (#PCDATA)>
<!ELEMENT Category       (#PCDATA)>
<!ELEMENT Author         (#PCDATA)>
```

The structure of the DTD is pretty close to the Extended Backus-Naur Form mentioned above. The DTD is a set of successive rules describing how to assemble the data into the XML document model. Every rule describes a specific element or attribute that the model can contain. An XML document is valid if it can be reduced to a single, specific rule in the DTD, with no input left, by repeated application of the rules.

Following is a description of the syntax used in this DTD. Note that DTDs use a different syntax than XML documents.

Each element is described using an element description line.

```
<!ELEMENT element_name (element_content)>
```

The element_name uses the tag to identify each element. In element_content, you either put other elements or #PCDATA to indicate that the element contains text. Leafs elements are elements that have no children. These elements are often specified as containing #PCDATA.

Special characters after an element name indicate the cardinality of the contained elements. The cardinality indicates how many of these elements can occur, and whether the element is optional or required. There are four ways to indicate cardinality.

✦ A contained element without any special symbol — such as Title in Listing A-4 — must appear exactly once in the element being defined (cardinality: 1).

✦ A contained element followed by a question mark (?) is optional and can appear only once in the element (cardinality: 0..1).

The next two ways define repeating elements, one for required and one for optional.

✦ A contained element followed by a plus sign (+) — such as `Book` and `Author` in Listing A-4 — is required and can repeat (cardinality: 1..N).

✦ A contained element followed by an asterisk (*) — such as `Category` in Listing A-4 — is optional and can repeat (cardinality: 0..N).

```
<!ATTLIST element_name attribute_name attribute_content
optionality>
```

Attribute lists are defined in a separate line. The `element_name` is again the tag to which the attribute belongs. The `attribute_name` is the name of the attribute (for example, ISBN in Listing A-4). The attribute content is defined using a series of key-words. The most common is CDATA indicating that the attribute takes character data. The optionality is indicated by the keyword #REQUIRED for required attributes and #IMPLIED for optional attributes.

XML Schemas

On May 2, 2001, the standards body governing over the XML standard announced that an important member of the XML family has reached standard status (a proposed recommendation, as `www.w3.org` calls it). This standard is called XML Schemas and is poised to replace DTDs as the preferred way to validate XML documents.

XML Schemas offer two distinct advantages over DTDs:

✦ An XML Schema is an XML document

✦ XML Schemas allow you to specify data characteristics (such as type, size and precision) of elements and attributes

A schema documents looks as follows:

```
<?xml version="1.0" encoding="UTF-8"?>
 <xsd:schema xmlns:xsd="http://www.w3.org/2001/XMLSchema">

<!-- schema content goes here -->

</xsd:schema>
```

The `xmlns:xsd` attribute of the schema element is a namespace declaration, which is covered in the next section. Note that the value of this attribute has changed over time, so if you encounter a schema with a different value for this attribute (for example, `www.w3.org/2000/10/XMLSchema`), then this schema was properly created according to a draft version of the XML Schema standard.

The schema content consist of definitions for the elements and attributes that this schema can contain. An element is defined as follows

```
<xsd:element name="theElementName">

<!--element specifics goes here -->

</xsd:element>
```

while an attribute is defined as follows

```
<xsd:attribute name="theAttributeName">

<!--attribute specifics goes here -->

</xsd: attribute >
```

You can add documentation with comments or stick an annotation element inside the element or attribute definition. The annotation element contains a documentation element where you can document the specifics of the element or attribute.

```
<xsd:annotation>
<xsd:documentation>Some explanation here...</xsd:documentation>
</xsd:annotation>
```

You can group elements and attributes by sticking them inside a complexType tag.

```
<xsd:complexType>
</xsd:complexType>
```

This type of grouping is required each time you see an element definition such as this:

```
<!ELEMENT Book        (Title,Category*,Author+)>
```

Elements grouped within a sequence need to be presented in the order they are defined.

```
<xsd:sequence>
</xsd:sequence>
```

So, if you define a Book element as follows, then a Book element needs to contain a Title, Category and Author element in this exact order (Title, Author and Category would for example not be valid).

```
<xsd:element name="Book">
xsd:complexType>
<xsd:sequence>
<xsd:element name="Title">
</xsd:element>
<xsd:element name="Category"/>
```

```
<xsd:element name="Author"/>
</xsd:sequence>
</xsd:complexType>
</xsd:element>
```

The cardinality of elements is assumed one. If you want to create a repeating element, you may do so by adding a maxOccurs="unbounded" attribute to the element definition. If you want to create an optional element, you may do so by adding a minOccurs="0" attribute to the element definition. You may of course combine these attributes to create an optional repeating element.

Finally, you can specify the data type of an element with a type="xsd:*datatype*" attribute. In our example, we use only the string data type. The XML Schema allows for a wide range of data types, such as integer, long, date, time, double, float, and so on.

Listing A-5 lists the XML Schema that corresponds to the DTD discussed above. XML Schemas have a .xsd file extension and are therefore sometimes called XSDs.

Listing A-5: XML Schema Corresponding to DTD

```
<?xml version="1.0" encoding="UTF-8"?>
<!-- W3C Schema for a List of Books -->
<xsd:schema xmlns:xsd="http://www.w3.org/2001/XMLSchema">
  <xsd:element name="XMLBooks">
        <xsd:annotation>
                <xsd:documentation>The top-level element,
XMLBooks, is a list of books.</xsd:documentation>
        </xsd:annotation>
        <xsd:complexType>
                <xsd:sequence>
                        <xsd:element name="Book"
maxOccurs="unbounded">
                                <xsd:annotation>
                                        <xsd:documentation>A Book
element contains 1 Title, 1 or more Category, and 1 or more
Author.</xsd:documentation>
                                </xsd:annotation>
                                <xsd:complexType>
                                        <xsd:sequence>
                                                <xsd:element
name="Title" type="xsd:string">

<xsd:annotation>

<xsd:documentation>The Title, Category, and Author elements
contain text.</xsd:documentation>

</xsd:annotation>
                                                </xsd:element>
```

```
                                                <xsd:element
name="Category" type="xsd:string" minOccurs="0"
maxOccurs="unbounded"/>
                                                <xsd:element
name="Author" type="xsd:string" maxOccurs="unbounded"/>
                                    </xsd:sequence>
                                    <xsd:attribute name="ISBN"
type="xsd:string" use="required" id="isbn">
                                        <xsd:annotation>

<xsd:documentation>A Book has 1 required
attribute.</xsd:documentation>
                                        </xsd:annotation>
                                    </xsd:attribute>
                        </xsd:complexType>
                    </xsd:element>
                </xsd:sequence>
        </xsd:complexType>
    </xsd:element>
</xsd:schema>
```

Listing A-6 shows how an XML document can refer to its associated XML Schema.

Listing A-6: XML Document That Refers to Its Associated XML Schema

```
<?xml version="1.0" encoding="UTF-8"?>
<XMLBooks xmlns:xsi="http://www.w3.org/2001/XMLSchema-instance"
xsi:noNamespaceSchemaLocation="./Books.xsd">
    <Book ISBN="0-7897-2242-9">
        <Title>XML By Example</Title>
        <Category>Web Development</Category>
        <Author>Benoit Marchal</Author>
    </Book>
    <Book ISBN="0-7356-0562-9">
        <Title>XML in Action</Title>
        <Category>Internet</Category>
        <Category>XML</Category>
        <Author>William J. Pardy</Author>
    </Book>
</XMLBooks>
```

XML Namespaces

The extensibility of XML is both a blessing and a curse. Allowing anyone to create his or her own tags runs the risk of creating a Babylonian confusion. Luckily, the designers of the XML standards recognized the danger and came up with a solution, namely Namespaces. You are already familiar with the idea of namespaces through your study of C# (the same idea is present in C++, Java and the other .NET languages). The implementation varies a little from case to case, but the basic idea is always the same.

You associate a unique name with a prefix and use this prefix to qualify the names that might have collided without the prefix. Because XML is Web-based, the designers chose to use URL as the unique names.

You specify the namespace used in a XML Schema by adding a `targetNamespace=` `"www.myurl.com"` attribute to the schema. You define this namespace by adding a special `xmlns` attribute to the schema element. You may append the namespace prefix to this attribute by using a colon to separate the `xmlns` attribute and the prefix. It is the responsibility of the Schema designer to ensure that the value of this attribute is unique. This is often achieved by using the company's URL.

```
xmlns:prefix="http://www.myurl.com"
```

After you have defined a namespace prefix, you need to append it to all elements contained in the namespace.

```
<?xml version="1.0" encoding="UTF-8"?>
<!-- W3C Schema for a List of Books -->
<xsd:schema
   targetNamespace="www.myurl.com"
   xmlns:xsd="http://www.w3.org/2001/XMLSchema"
   xmlns:book="www.myurl.com">
   <xsd:element name="XMLBooks">
        <xsd:annotation>
                <xsd:documentation>The top-level element,
XMLBooks, is a list of books.</xsd:documentation>
        </xsd:annotation>
        <xsd:complexType>
                <xsd:sequence>
                        <xsd:element name="Book"
maxOccurs="unbounded">
                                <xsd:annotation>
                                        <xsd:documentation>A Book
element contains 1 Title, 1 or more Category, and 1 or more
Author.</xsd:documentation>
                                </xsd:annotation>
                                <xsd:complexType>
                                        <xsd:sequence>
```

```
                                                       <xsd:element
name="Title" type="xsd:string">

<xsd:annotation>

<xsd:documentation>The Title, Category, and Author elements
contain text.</xsd:documentation>

</xsd:annotation>
                                                   </xsd:element>
                                              <xsd:element
name="Category" type="xsd:string" minOccurs="0"
maxOccurs="unbounded"/>
                                              <xsd:element
name="Author" type="xsd:string" maxOccurs="unbounded"/>
                                          </xsd:sequence>
                                      <xsd:attribute name="ISBN"
type="xsd:string" use="required" id="isbn">
                                          <xsd:annotation>

<xsd:documentation>A Book has 1 required
attribute.</xsd:documentation>
                                          </xsd:annotation>
                                      </xsd:attribute>
                                  </xsd:complexType>
                          </xsd:element>
                    </xsd:sequence>
              </xsd:complexType>
      </xsd:element>
</xsd:schema>
```

The following XML document shows how to create an XML document that refers to a schema using name spaces. This is done by adding three attributes to the root element. The first attribute defines the prefix used by the namespace and the unique string associated with this namespace. The second attribute specifies which version of the XML Schemas you are using. Finally, the third attribute tells you which namespace the XML Schema is using and where the XML Schema is located.

```
<?xml version="1.0" encoding="UTF-8"?>
<book:XMLBooks
   xmlns:book="www.myurl.com"
   xmlns:xsi="http://www.w3.org/2001/XMLSchema-instance"
   xsi:schemaLocation="www.myurl.com .\Books.xsd">
   <Book ISBN="0-7897-2242-9">
        <Title>XML By Example</Title>
        <Category>Web Development</Category>
        <Author>Benoit Marchal</Author>
   </Book>
   <Book ISBN="0-7356-0562-9">
        <Title>XML in Action</Title>
```

```
            <Category>Internet</Category>
            <Category>XML</Category>
            <Author>William J. Pardy</Author>
       </Book>
   </book:XMLBooks>
```

Because most elements in an XML document belong to the same namespace, it is possible to create a default namespace and omit the namespace prefix, for example, `xmlns ="www.myurl.com"`.

Lastly, it is possible to have several namespace declarations in the same XML document. This is done by adding all the namespace attributes to the root element. Note that a document can only point to 1 XML Schema though.

✦   ✦   ✦

Index

Continued